Law and Ethics in the Business Environment

Terry Halbert, Elaine Ingulli

Australia • Brazil • Japan • Korea • Mexico • Singapore • Spain • United Kingdom • United States

CENGAGE
Learning™

Law and Ethics in the Business Environment

Terry Halbert, Elaine Ingulli

Executive Editor:
Maureen Staudt
Michael Stranz

Senior Project Development Manager:
Linda de Stefano

Marketing Specialist:
Sara Mercurio
Lindsay Shapiro

Production/Manufacturing Manager:
Donna M. Brown

PreMedia Supervisor:
Joel Brennecke

Rights & Permissions Specialist:
Kalina Hintz
Todd Osborne

Cover Image:
Getty Images*

For product information and technology assistance, contact us at
Cengage Learning Customer & Sales Support, 1-800-354-9706

For permission to use material from this text or product,
submit all requests online at **cengage.com/permissions**
Further permissions questions can be emailed to
permissionrequest@cengage.com

Source: Law & Ethics in the Business Environment, 6e, Terry Halbert, Elaine Ingulli, 2009, 2006 South Western Cengage Learning, ISBN#0324657323

ISBN-13: 978-1-111-21958-1

ISBN-10: 1-111-21958-3

Cengage Learning
5191 Natorp Boulevard
Mason, Ohio 45040
USA

Cengage Learning is a leading provider of customized learning solutions with office locations around the globe, including Singapore, the United Kingdom, Australia, Mexico, Brazil, and Japan. Locate your local office at:
international.cengage.com/region

Cengage Learning products are represented in Canada by Nelson Education, Ltd.

For your lifelong learning solutions, visit **www.cengage.com/custom**

Visit our corporate website at **www.cengage.com**

Printed in the United States of America
3 4 5 6 7 12 11 10

To Bill
—T. H.

In memory of Anne Marie Phillips
—E. I.

BRIEF TABLE OF CONTENTS

TABLE OF CONTENTS

6 Sustainable Economies: Global Environmental Protection 192

7 Marketing and Technology: Choice and Manipulation 230

8 Risk Allocation: Products Liability 274

9 Ownership and Creativity: Intellectual Property 314

Appendices 356

Glossary 371

Index 377

This book presents a set of flashpoints where global business imperatives, legal rules, and ethical concepts collide. Our goal has been to make these complex situations come alive and to give students the tools to wrestle with them. It is, in a sense, a simulated minefield, where they can practice confronting some of the toughest decisions they will make as managers. It is a set of scenarios that tend to disturb and destabilize pat response, creating spaces for students to begin to develop critical habits of mind.

Focus on Teaching & Learning

We cannot effectively teach everything about the legal system—even everything about business law—in just one semester. The material itself is fluid; the vast "seamless web" is always in flux, as legislatures and courts channel the cultural, economic, and political forces that impact upon it. We know that the law is, in fact, a kind of moving target, and we believe in studying why and how it changes. We have selected readings that allow us to teach the process of the law as it evolves—at the pressure points where controversy is brewing and where ethical issues tend to surface.

People learn best when they are grappling with problems that they feel are important, when they are discussing and debating questions that they find compelling. Assuming that every student can be motivated to chase down a good question, we have conceived our job as a matter of laying out good questions, of equipping students with enough information to sustain their curiosity without giving them so much that they feel there is nothing left to discover.

Our students know a good story when they see one, and this is what can hold their attention. So we have taken advantage of what the law offers us. A case is a stylized, rich form of a story, with protagonist, antagonist, dispute, resolution. Every one of our chapters starts with a lightly-edited case, selected not just because it is current, or landmark, but because it is "sexy"— likely to provoke reaction and to effectively problematize the theme of the chapter.

We follow that lead case with a mix of readings from scholarly and media sources, from different areas of expertise, and from different cultural perspectives, offering a variety of prisms through which students can view the chapter theme.

Overall, this book is designed to develop in our students the ability to make their own informed judgments, and to become engaged citizens of a globalized world.

Continuity and Change: The Sixth Edition

For this edition we have added an exploration of Corporate Social Responsibility to Chapter 1, with a 2006 *Harvard Business Review* article by Michael Porter and Mark Kramer, a shareholders derivative lawsuit, and a chapter project that guides students through a CSR audit. We continue to use offshoring of jobs to India as a way to introduce ethical theory; although this issue is less prominent in the media of late, Indian outsourcing companies experienced an expansion rate of 47 percent in the first six months of 2007. Here and throughout this revision, we emphasize material related to globalization. We cover the debate on immigration

(Chapters 4 and 5), food safety in the global marketplace (Chapter 8), and global warming (Chapter 6). We have threaded global human rights through Chapters 2, 4, 5, and 9.

We include Supreme Court cases decided since our last edition, launching Chapter 6 on environmental issues with a 2007 landmark case about climate change, and placing the Court's 2006 public employee speech rights decision in Chapter 2 on whistleblowing. Chapter 9 on intellectual property now begins with *MGM v. Grokster.* Other important new cases involve the marketing of pharmaceuticals (Chapter 3), toxic exposure to workers following the collapse of the World Trade Center (Chapter 5), and toxic exposure of children to lead paint (Chapter 8). New, too, in this edition is expanded coverage of corporate governance (Chapters 1, 2, and 6) and material on the marketing of junk food to children.

In response to a reviewer's suggestion, we have written a new appendix, "How to Read and Brief a Case."

While we have updated the entire book, we have also included the clearest, most *teachable* cases from prior editions.

Thanks

We want to thank our students and colleagues. Their response to our work gives us the incentive to treat each revision with attention and care.

We also want to thank our reviewers for their thoughtful input:

Dr. G. Howard Doty,	*Nashville State Tech Community College, Nashville, TN*
Dr. Paul Fiorelli,	*Xavier University, Cincinnati, OH*
Dr. Ronnie Cohen,	*Christopher Newport University, Newport News, VA*
Dr. Lucy Katz,	*Fairfield University, Fairfield, CT*
Dr. James M. Lammendola,	*Temple University, Philadelphia, PA*

We are grateful to the staff at Cengage Learning: Acquisitions editor Steve Silverstein and developmental editor Jennifer King listened to us with care through a hectic set of deadlines and managed to tweak the system, allowing for several changes that were important to us. Project managers Malvine Litten and Diane Bowdler, with copyeditor Juli Cook, put our text through a pain-free, but fine-toothed review. Michelle Kunkler, Patti Hudepohl, and Joe Pagliaro produced a fresh, handsome layout design. It was a genuine pleasure to work with this team.

We thank our husbands, Brian Ackerman and Bill Coleman. Bill was especially important this time as a reader, editor, researcher, and writer.

Finally, we continue to enjoy and be grateful for our enduring and productive friendship.

LAW, ETHICS, BUSINESS

An Introduction

Law must be stable, and yet it cannot stand still.

— ROSCOE POUND

Neither fire nor wind, birth nor death, can erase our good deeds.

— BUDDHA

Business has become, in the last half century, the most powerful institution on the planet. The dominant institution in any society needs to take responsibility for the whole.... Every decision that is made, every action that is taken, must be viewed in light of that kind of responsibility.

— DAVID KORTEN

•

Law is not a static phenomenon, yet in certain ways it appears bounded and clear cut. Where it holds jurisdictional authority, law provides a set of rules for behavior. When these rules are broken, behavior is punishable. If you have been driving carelessly and hit another car, you might pay money damages. If you are caught stealing, you might go to jail. If you are caught polluting, you may be forced to stop. The creation of law and the delivery of sanctions for rule breaking are contested processes. How law is made, how it is enforced, and how it is interpreted are always in dispute, constantly changing, and responsive to the power relations that surround it. Still, we can identify its purposes: law both sets behavioral standards and sets up a system for compliance with them. Within the reach of a legal system, we are on notice that we must meet its standards or risk penalty. Chances are we were not directly involved in the making of the rules—we may even disagree strongly with them—but we understand that the legal system shadows us anyway. It may be the closest we can get to a shared reality.

Ethics, on the other hand, presents a menu of options, often disconnected from official sanctions.[1] While law concerns what we *must* do, ethics concerns what we *should* do. Suppose you work for an advertising agency and have just been offered a chance to work on a new ad campaign for a certain fast-food chain. Burgers, fries, and sodas are legal products. Under the First Amendment of the U.S. Constitution, fast-food companies have the legal right to get their messages out to consumers. But you may believe that their ads are particularly attractive to children, who are at risk of becoming accustomed and even addicted to the empty calories

---

1 We distinguish ethics from "professional ethics," which are binding on those with professional licenses for the practice of law or accounting, for example. Indeed, licensing authorities have enforcement powers not unlike those of legal authorities to sanction those who violate their professional codes of ethics.

that make them fat and unhealthy. Although no law requires it, you may feel you should decline to participate in the campaign. Or suppose a company manufactures a pesticide that can no longer be sold in the United States because the Environmental Protection Agency has banned its primary ingredient, but that *can* be sold in places like India or Africa, where environmental regulations are far less stringent. Legally, the company is free to sell its pesticide overseas; but should it?

Ethical preferences are not preselected for us by legislators or by judges; they involve critical consciousness, engaging each of us in a process of bringing reason and emotion to bear on a particular situation. The right way to behave is not necessarily a matter of aligning our actions with the norm—a community or religious norm, for instance—although it may be. Yet we struggle to carve out some form of consensus on ethics, especially in areas where law does not seem to cover the significant bases. In the above examples, where the law allows people to profit in the marketplace by selling highly dangerous products, we may want to say that certain "shoulds" are universally compelling.

The question of what should be done in a given situation, of the right way to live our lives, is complicated by divergent and overlapping cultural inputs. Within the borders of the United States, and in the global marketplace, we are confronted with a kaleidoscopic array of ethical traditions. Does this mean that there can be no such thing as consensus, no agreement about what is good behavior?

Then there is the "business environment." Ever since Dutch and English explorers proved that private, entrepreneurial settlements across the oceans could be more robust than the projects of mere kings and queens, private investment has been setting the pace of economic expansion on the planet. European hegemony around the world was largely spear-headed in the seventeenth century by profit-seeking joint stock companies. In the mid-nineteenth century, the Union victory in the American Civil War showed that Northern capitalism could produce more guns, bullets, and blankets than the slave economy of the agrarian South. The defeat of fascism and the dissolution of the USSR in the twentieth century demonstrated the resources that the market economy could muster against competing systems.

Today, almost half of the 100 largest economies in the world are multinational corporations. Comparing corporate revenues to the gross domestic product of nations, Wal-Mart, BP, Exxon Mobil, and Royal Dutch/Shell all generated more income than Saudi Arabia, Norway, Denmark, Poland, South Africa, and Greece in 2005.[2] The largest 200 companies in the world account for more than one-fourth of the world's economic activity. By 2002, they had twice the economic clout of the poorest four-fifths of humanity. Business has powerful effects on our natural environment. It strongly affects what we eat, how we transport ourselves, what our communities look like, and how we take care of ourselves when we are sick. In many ways, the impact of global business has been beneficial. Multinationals provide new jobs, pay higher taxes, and produce new or less expensive goods and services. They introduce technology, capital, and skills to their host countries and raise the standard of living. On the other hand, multinationals have been blamed for hastening the collapse of traditional ways of life; for taking advantage of weak and/or corrupt governments in some of the countries where they do business; for questionable safety, environmental, and financial practices; for addicting the world to unsustainable technologies while blocking technologies antithetical to their interests; and for intensifying the disparities between rich and poor.

As bearers of a diverse set of cultural achievements, we need to find points of agreement, both in legal and ethical terms, as to how human societies can best flourish. And as participants in the global economy, we need to discover ways of tempering the tremendous power of the market, of shaping it to allow the planet and its inhabitants to thrive.

---

2 http://news.mongabay.com/2005/0718-worlds_largest.html

In this chapter we introduce values—and a tension between values—that will thread throughout this book. On the one hand, the value of maximizing individual freedom of choice, our right to believe and to act as autonomous beings; on the other hand, the value of building community, our duty as interdependent social beings to care about and for one another. We start with a case about the law of rescue. We then present a basic toolkit for ethical analysis, as we move from individual decision making to decision making in the corporate organizational setting.

Freedom versus Responsibility: A Duty to Rescue?

In this first case, a man is sued for failing to do anything to rescue his drowning friend. While we only know the story as told by the widow—the case is dismissed before the facts can be fully investigated by both sides in a trial setting—we can see how, in this kind of scenario, the law views the conflict between freedom and responsibility.

YANIA v. BIGAN

Supreme Court of Pennsylvania, 1959

155 A.2d 343

JONES, Benjamin R., Justice. ☀

… On September 25, 1957 John E. Bigan was engaged in a coal strip-mining operation in Shade Township, Somerset County. On the property being stripped were large cuts or trenches created by Bigan when he removed the earthen overburden for the purpose of removing the coal underneath. One cut contained water 8 to 10 feet in depth with side walls or embankments 16 to 18 feet in height; at this cut Bigan had installed a pump to remove the water.

At approximately 4 p.m. on that date, Joseph F. Yania, the operator of another coal strip-mining operation, and one Boyd M. Ross went upon Bigan's property for the purpose of discussing a business matter with Bigan, and, while there, [were] asked by Bigan to aid him in starting the pump. Bigan entered the cut and stood at the point where the pump was located. Yania stood at the top of one of the cut's side walls and then jumped from the side wall—a height of 16 to 18 feet—into the water and was drowned.

Yania's widow [sued], contending Bigan was responsible for Yania's death.

She contends that Yania's descent from the high embankment into the water and the resulting death were caused "entirely" by the spoken words … of Bigan delivered at a distance from Yania. The complaint does not allege that Yania slipped or that he was pushed or that Bigan made any physical impact upon Yania. On the contrary, the only inference deducible from the … complaint is that Bigan … caused such a mental impact on Yania that the latter was deprived of his … freedom of choice and placed under a compulsion to jump into the water. Had Yania been a child of tender years or a person mentally deficient then it is conceivable that taunting and enticement could constitute actionable negligence if it resulted in harm. However, to contend that such conduct directed to an adult in full possession of all his mental faculties constitutes actionable negligence is … completely without merit.

[The widow then claims] that Bigan … violated a duty owed to Yania in that his land contained a dangerous condition, i.e. the water-filled cut or trench, and he failed to warn Yania of such condition.… Of this condition there was neither concealment nor failure to warn, but, on the contrary, the complaint specifically avers that Bigan not only requested Yania and Boyd to assist him in starting the pump to remove the water from the cut but "led" them to the cut itself. If this cut possessed any potentiality of danger, such a condition was as obvious and apparent to Yania as to Bigan, both coal strip-mine operators. Under the circumstances herein depicted Bigan could not be held liable in this respect.

Lastly, [the widow claims] that Bigan failed to take the necessary steps to rescue Yania from the water. The mere fact that Bigan saw Yania in a position of peril in the water imposed upon him no legal, although a moral, obligation or duty to go to his rescue unless Bigan was legally responsible, in whole or in part, for placing Yania in the perilous position. "[The deceased] voluntarily placed himself in the way of danger, and his death was the result of his own act.... That his undertaking was an exceedingly reckless and dangerous one, the event proves, but there was no one to blame for it but himself. He had the right to try the experiment, obviously dangerous as it was, but then also upon him rested the consequences of that experiment, and upon no one else; he may have been, and probably was, ignorant of the risk which he was taking upon himself, or knowing it, and trusting to his own skill, he may have regarded it as easily superable. But in either case, the result of his ignorance, or of his mistake, must rest with himself and cannot be charged to the defendants." The law imposes on Bigan no duty of rescue.

Order [dismissing the complaint] affirmed.

QUESTIONS

1. What happened in this case? If Yania couldn't swim, why did he jump?

2. Identify each of the arguments made by Yania's widow. For each, explain how the judge dealt with it.

3. According to the judge, Bigan would have been liable in this case under certain circumstances that did not apply here. What are those circumstances?

4. Suppose you could revise the law of rescue. Would you hold people responsible for doing something to help others in an emergency? If so, what circumstances would trigger a duty to rescue? How much would be required of a rescuer?

Justifying the "No Duty to Rescue" Rule

The men who wrote the Bill of Rights were not concerned that government might do too little for the people, but that it might do too much to them.

— RICHARD POSNER[3]

The ruling in *Yania v. Bigan* is still valid. While there are some exceptions, in general, in the U.S. legal system, we do not have a duty or responsibility to rescue those who are endangered.

There are both philosophical and practical reasons against imposing a duty to rescue. Traditionally, our society has tended to grant maximum leeway to individual freedom of choice. Requiring that people help one another in emergencies would infringe on that freedom by forcing people to act when they might choose not to. Further, imposing an affirmative duty to rescue presupposes that there is agreement that rendering assistance is always the right thing to do. Is there really such consensus? Opinions, beliefs, and concepts of the right way to

---

3 *Jackson v. City of Joliet*, 715 F. 2d 1200, 1203 (7th Cir. 1983), in which Judge Richard Posner explains why someone in need of emergency assistance has no constitutional right to it.

behave in a given situation might vary radically between individuals and between cultures, particularly as they mix and clash in our diverse society. If we are to grant genuine respect to each person's freedom of conscience, shouldn't we insist on legal enforcement of "right" behavior only when it is unavoidable? Shouldn't we reserve punishment or liability for the times when people actively injure others, and allow rescue to be a matter of personal choice? In a sense, those who do not choose to rescue are not behaving badly; rather, they are merely doing nothing. As U.S. Supreme Court Justice Oliver Wendell Holmes once said, "While there is properly in law a duty not to harm, there is not … a negative duty not to allow harm to happen."

In the next excerpt, nineteenth-century philosopher John Stuart Mill describes the connection between individual freedom of choice and the law of the liberal democratic state.

ON LIBERTY

JOHN STUART MILL

Over himself, over his own body and mind, the individual is sovereign….

This, then, is the appropriate region of human liberty. It comprises, first, the inward domain of consciousness; demanding liberty of conscience, in the most comprehensive sense; liberty of thought and feeling; absolute freedom of opinion and sentiment on all subjects, practical or speculative, scientific, moral, or theological. … Secondly, the principle requires liberty of tastes and pursuits; of framing the plan of our life to suit our own character; of doing as we like, subject to such consequences as may follow; without impediment from our fellow-creatures, so long as what we do does not harm them, even though they should think our conduct foolish, perverse, or wrong. Thirdly, from this liberty of each individual, follows the liberty, within the same limits, of combination among individuals; freedom to unite, for any purpose not involving harm to others: the persons combining being supposed to be of full age, and not forced or deceived.

No society in which these liberties are not, on the whole, respected, is free, whatever may be its form of government; and none is completely free in which they do not exist absolute and unqualified. The only freedom which deserves the name, is that of pursuing our own good in our own way, so long as we do not attempt to deprive others of theirs, or impede their effort to obtain it. Each is the proper guardian of his own health, whether bodily, or mental and spiritual. Mankind are greater gainers by suffering each other to live as seems good to themselves, than by compelling each to live as seems good to the rest.

Creating a legal duty to rescue would not only run into resistance on philosophical grounds. There would also be practical objections. How would we enforce such a rule? Where would we draw the line? Must a person attempt to rescue even if it would be terribly dangerous? Should a rescuer be compensated by the victim for any injuries suffered? Who, in a crowd, are the potential rescuers: The closest witnesses? Anyone at the scene? Anyone aware of the incident?

Radical Change?

> Lawgivers make the citizens good by training them in habits of
> right … this is the aim of all legislation, and if it fails to do this it is a
> failure; this distinguishes a good form of constitution from a bad one.
>
> — ARISTOTLE, NICHOMACHEAN ETHICS

While the Anglo-American tradition emphasizing individual freedom of choice is a major reason our legal system demands no duty to rescue, law professor Steven Heyman argues that recognition of a duty to rescue is in line with that very tradition. His article appeared in a communitarian journal. Communitarians are concerned with reviving the notion of shared responsibility and interconnectedness at a time when, they believe, too many people view social change solely in terms of defining and enforcing an ever-growing number of personal rights.

He begins his essay by mentioning two famous examples in which bystanders chose to ignore those who desperately needed help. The first incident happened one night in March 1964. Twenty-eight-year-old Kitty Genovese was returning home to her apartment complex in a quiet, respectable neighborhood in Queens, New York. Manager of a bar in another part of Queens, she was arriving late; it was 3:00 a.m. As she left her red Fiat and began walking to her apartment, she saw a man walking towards her. He chased her, caught up with her, and attacked her with a knife. She screamed, "Oh my God, he stabbed me! Please help me! Please help me!" People opened windows, someone called out, "Let that girl alone," and several lights went on. But as more than a half hour passed, none of the witnesses did anything more. The killer had time to drive away, leaving Ms. Genovese collapsed on the sidewalk, and then to drive back to stab her again. Thirty-eight people later admitted they had heard Ms. Genovese's screams, but no one even called the police until after she was dead.[4]

The second incident happened many years later. In 1983, in New Bedford, Massachusetts, a young woman went into a bar to buy a pack of cigarettes. She was gang-raped on the pool table while customers watched and even cheered.[5]

THE DUTY TO RESCUE:
A LIBERAL-COMMUNITARIAN APPROACH

Steven J. Heyman[6]

Rescue and the Common-Law Tradition

Consider two notorious incidents: the 1964 slaying of Kitty Genovese and the 1983 New Bedford tavern rape. In both cases, neighbors or bystanders watched as a young woman was brutally and repeatedly assaulted, yet they made no effort to intervene or call for help. Under current doctrine, their inaction breached no legal duty, however reprehensible it may have been morally.

Suppose, however, that a police officer had been present at the time. Surely we would not say that the officer was free to stand by and do nothing while the attack took place. The state has a responsibility to protect its citizens against criminal violence. It performs this function largely through its police force. An officer who unjustifiably failed to prevent a violent crime would be guilty of a serious dereliction of duty, which might result in dismissal from the force or even criminal prosecution. Thus the officer would have a legal duty to act. But what if there is no officer on the scene? In that situation, the state can fulfill its responsibility to prevent violence only by relying on the assistance of those persons who *are* present.

Contrary to the conventional view, there is strong evidence that, for centuries, the common law of England and America did recognize an individual duty to act in precisely such cases. According to traditional legal doctrine, every person was entitled to protection by the government against violence and injury. In return for this protection,

4 A. M. Rosenthal, *Thirty-Eight Witnesses: The Kitty Genovese Case* (Berkeley, CA: University of California Press, 1999).

5 This incident became the basis of a film, *The Accused*, with Kelly McGinnis and Jody Foster.

6 *The Responsive Community*, Vol. 7, No. 3, Summer 1997, pp. 44–49.

individuals had an obligation not merely to obey the law, but also, when necessary, to actively help enforce it.... Thus, individuals at the scene of a violent crime had a duty to intervene if they could do so without danger to themselves. If they could not, they were required to notify the authorities.

With the development of modern police forces in the 19th century, this tradition of active citizen participation in law enforcement gradually declined. In recent decades, however, it has become increasingly clear that effective crime prevention requires the efforts of the whole community—a recognition that is reflected, for example, in neighborhood crime watch and community policing programs....

Rescue and the Liberal Tradition

A duty to prevent violence finds support not only in the Anglo-American common-law tradition but also in liberal political theory. According to Locke and other natural rights theorists, individuals enter into society to preserve their lives, liberties, and properties. Under the social contract, citizens obtain a right to protection by the community against criminal violence. In return, they promise not only to comply with the laws, but also to assist the authorities in enforcing those laws. In this way, Locke writes, the rights of individuals come to be defended by "the united strength of the whole Society." In *On Liberty*, John Stuart Mill recognizes a similar duty on the part of individuals.... Mill agrees "that every one who receives the protection of society owes a return for the benefit," including an obligation to bear one's fair share of "the labours and sacrifices incurred for defending the society or its members from injury."

In addition to endorsing a duty to prevent violence, liberal thought suggests a way to expand that duty into a general duty to rescue. According to liberal writers, the community has a responsibility to preserve the lives of its members, not only against violence but also against other forms of harm. For example, Locke, Blackstone, and Kant all maintain that the state has an obligation to relieve poverty and support those who are unable to provide for their own needs. In Locke's words, both natural right and "common charity" teach "that those should be most taken care of by the law, who are least capable of taking care of themselves." Of course, this is also a major theme in contemporary liberal political thought....

Rescue and Communitarian Theory

Communitarian theory supports and deepens the argument for a duty to rescue. On this view, community is valuable not merely as a means to the protection of individual rights, but also as a positive human good. Human nature has an irreducible social dimension that can be fulfilled only through relationships with others. The community has a responsibility to promote the good of its members. But this can be fully achieved only within a society whose members recognize a reciprocal obligation to act for the welfare of the community and their fellow citizens. A core instance is the duty to rescue.

Of course, some might doubt whether contemporary society is characterized by the kind of community required for a duty to rescue. Community is not simply given, however; it must be created. Common action, and action on behalf of others, plays a crucial role in creating relationships between people. Thus the adoption of a duty to rescue might not merely reflect, but also promote, a greater sense of community in modern society.

The Contours of a Duty to Rescue

Advocates of a duty to rescue usually propose that it be restricted to cases in which one can act with little or no inconvenience to oneself. But this does not go far enough. Because its purpose is to safeguard the most vital human interests, the duty should not be limited to easy rescues, but should require an individual to do anything reasonably necessary to prevent criminal violence or to preserve others from death or serious bodily harm. Rescue should not require self-sacrifice, however. Thus the duty should not apply if it would involve a substantial risk of death or serious bodily injury to the rescuer or to other innocent people.

This responsibility falls on individuals only in emergency situations when no officer is present. Moreover, the duty would often be satisfied by calling the police, fire department, or rescue services....

In performing the duty to rescue, one acts on behalf of the community as a whole. For this reason, one should receive compensation from the community for any expense reasonably incurred or any injury suffered in the course of the rescue. Any other rule would mean that some people would be required to bear a cost that should properly be borne by the community at large, simply because they happened to be at a place where rescue was required....

Far from diminishing liberty, the recognition of a duty to rescue would enhance it by strengthening protection for the most basic right of all—freedom from criminal violence and other serious forms of harm. And by requiring action for the sake of others, a duty to rescue also has the potential to promote a greater sense of community, civic responsibility, and commitment to the common good.

QUESTIONS

1. According to the writer, a change in our law—a new duty to rescue—might change the way people think, heightening their awareness of one another as members of a community, and leading them to be more responsive to one another. Do you think law can have such power? Can you think of any examples where a change in the law seemed to improve the moral climate of our society?

2. Do you think law should be used as a tool for shaping a shared moral climate? Why or why not?

When Rescue Is Required

The law recognizes a number of exceptions to the "no duty to rescue" rule. Many states impose criminal penalties, for example, for failing to report child abuse or an accident in which someone is killed. Only a few states—Rhode Island, Vermont, Wisconsin, Hawaii, and Minnesota—impose a more general duty to rescue by statute. In theory, violators would be fined. In fact, however, the statutes are rarely, if ever, invoked.

One means of finding a legal duty to rescue is through contract law. Certain persons assume contractual responsibilities to help others or to prevent them from being harmed. A lifeguard, for instance, cannot ignore a drowning swimmer, nor can a firefighter let a building burn. While a person could be disciplined or fired for refusing to attempt rescue under such circumstances,[7] to commit to a dangerous job such as policing or firefighting is itself a statement of willingness to risk one's life to save lives—to risk rescue as a part of an ordinary day's work. In fact, of the 343 firefighters killed on September 11, 2001, 60 were not on duty that day, but responded to the alarm as if they were.

continued

---

7 For reasons of public policy, however, civil lawsuits against police, fire, or other government workers are rarely permitted.

When people—trained or not—volunteer to rescue, they become legally bound to take reasonable care in finishing what they have started. In one case, an 80-year-old woman had a stroke while she was shopping at a department store. A salesclerk led her to the store infirmary and left her unattended for six hours. By the time help arrived, her condition was irreparably aggravated, and the store was held liable for failing to carry through on the rescue attempt.[8] Liability is imposed in this kind of case for making a bad situation worse: The person in trouble may be lulled into a false sense of security, believing they will be helped, and other would-be rescuers may not realize assistance is needed.

Another exception to the "no duty to rescue" rule applies when a person has endangered another, even indirectly, or has participated in creating a dangerous situation. When professionals in a mental institution release a violent psychotic without taking measures to make certain he will be properly medicated, they may be putting members of the public in danger. When organizers of a rock concert sell general admission tickets to a performance of a wildly popular group and do not provide lane control, they may be held responsible for the fatal result as fans are suffocated in the crush to gain entry.

Finally, a set of exceptions is triggered when there is a "special relationship" between the person who needs help and the person who must take responsible action. Special relationships may be based on their custodial, rather intimate nature, such as that between a parent and child or between a teacher and young pupils. Or such relationships may exist because of an economic connection, such as that between an employer and employees or between a provider of public transportation and its passengers. In either type, the relationship involves a degree of dependency. The law allows those who are dependent to expect reasonable protection from harm and requires the more powerful to provide it. A father must make some effort to save his drowning infant, and a city transportation system must take reasonable steps to protect its subway riders from criminal attacks.

Ethical Decision Making: A Toolkit

We have been looking at the way U.S. law addresses the question of balancing two important values, that of freedom—the freedom of individuals like Mr. Bigan to choose not to help in an emergency—and that of responsibility—the responsibility we might have to respond to one another in certain circumstances.

We now alter the scenario: Suppose a business strategy, although legal, happens to have harmful effects on certain people. Again, there is an interplay between freedom and responsibility, but here the focus will be more on ethics than on law. We'll begin with a business news story.

The Ethics of Offshoring: Outsourcing IBM Jobs to India

In late 2003 the *Wall Street Journal* reported that IBM planned to move nearly 5,000 jobs overseas to save expenses, the latest twist in the "offshoring" phenomenon that had become pronounced in the U.S. high-tech industry. Employees at IBM facilities in Texas, North Carolina, New York, Colorado, and Connecticut would be affected; IBM had already hired hundreds of engineers in India to begin taking on their work. According to the *Journal*, IBM workers slated for replacement throughout 2004 would be expected to train their foreign replacements.

8 *Zelenko v. Gimbel Bros. Inc.*, 287 N.Y.S. 134 (1935).

For years U.S. firms had been shifting manufacturing and other blue-collar jobs to Asia where labor costs are much lower, but IBM's plans made headlines because they were depicted as part of a disturbing new trend: Job losses would now affect well-educated, white-collar employees. Having begun with call centers and information technology positions, offshoring had mushroomed to include accountants, production control specialists, industrial engineers, medical transcriptionists, and others. By late 2003 the U.S. Bureau of Labor Statistics estimated that half a million high-tech professionals had lost their jobs since 2001, a figure that was expected to double by the end of 2004. Although many IT jobs had been eliminated due to the bursting of the dot-com bubble, U.S. corporate foreign outsourcing was predicted to be the main driver of future losses.

Late in 2003, Sam Palmisano, chairman of IBM's board of directors and its chief executive officer, justified the company's decision to move to India for skilled labor in a speech to the Council on Competitiveness in Washington, D.C. He stated that the nations of Asia not only provide low-cost labor, but also have heavily invested in their educational and communication infrastructure. It would only be fair to respond to what they offer:

> China, India, South Korea, and other rapidly developing nations are replicating the structural advantages that historically have made the U.S. the center of innovation. We can't—shouldn't—regret improvements in other nations' competitiveness. Their people deserve to participate fully in the benefits of innovations.

Was Sam Palmisano's decision ethical?

There are many different ways to answer this question. Ethical analysis, unlike much quantitative analysis, can be a messy, complex business, without a clear and definitive outcome. However, we do have tools at our disposal to help us make these complicated assessments.

First, let's turn to an approach that will be familiar to you. It amounts to the bedrock principle of strategic management; it underlies the entire free market system. This value system is so embedded in both business theory and business reality that we might fail to recognize it as not only an economic perspective, but also as an ethical one.

Free Market Ethics

A basic assumption of classic microeconomic theory is that the overriding goal of any business is to be profitable. As trustees (**fiduciaries**) of the shareholders, managers have a primary responsibility to try to improve the value of shareholder investment. In fact, under the law of corporations, managers are answerable to the owners of a company—its stockholders—if they fail to take reasonable care in running it.

Milton Friedman, a well-known free market economist and a proponent of this view, has written:

> In a free enterprise, private property system, a corporate executive is the employee of the owners of the business. He has a direct responsibility to his employers. That responsibility is to conduct the business in accordance with their desires, which generally will be to make as much money as possible while conforming to the basic rules of society, both those embodied in law and those embodied in ethical custom.... In a free society, there is one and only one social responsibility of business—to use its resources and engage in activities designed to increase its profits so long as it stays within the rules of the game, which is to say, engages in open and free competition without deception or fraud.[9]

Friedman argues it is wrong for managers to use corporate resources to deal with problems in society at large. Decisions regarding what might be best for society should be made in the political arena, and implementation of policies agreed upon there should be funded by tax dollars. For managers to make those kinds of decisions themselves, and to use corporate monies to pay for them, is the equivalent of theft—theft of stockholders' resources.

9 "The Social Responsibility of Business Is to Increase Its Profits," *New York Times*, September 13, 1970.

Let's apply Friedman's thinking and free market ethical theory to Sam Palmisano's decision to move several thousand IBM jobs to India. First we must ask: Will this choice be profitable for the company? The answer is yes. In India, chemists with doctoral degrees and employees in high-tech jobs earn one-fifth of the salaries of their American counterparts; a software programmer in Bangalore will earn about one-third of what someone with comparable skills in the United States would earn. Even with extra communication costs, IBM would save at least 50 percent by hiring overseas. There are other profit factors. Offshoring yields capacity increases, providing service more rapidly while taking advantage of time zone variations. Offshoring allows companies like IBM to concentrate on what they do best. Highly innovative work may still be done domestically, while maintenance chores, minor enhancements, and bug-fixing that make up most of what programmers do in a large software firm can be handled overseas.

Looking ahead, the flexibility offered by offshoring would seem to be the best way for IBM to remain competitive. In 2003, offshore outsourcing increased by 60 percent. Because other high-tech companies were participating in this trend[10]—it would seem to be in IBM's best interests to position itself ahead of the curve.[11]

Using Friedman's analysis we would also need to know whether the process of moving jobs to India was legal. At this writing, there are no legal impediments to outsourcing, other than a federal rule passed in January 2004 stating that any private contracting done for a federal agency "may not be performed by the contractor at a location outside the United States" unless the work had been done outside the country previously. According to an IBM spokesperson, its federal government contracts generally do not involve offshore work.[12]

In microeconomic terms then, the decision to move jobs to India should focus on shareholder interests and not be swayed by the interests of other stakeholders—except to the extent that these would impact profits. Sam Palmisano's choice should not be made out of concern for the families dependent on jobs at IBM, for example, or out of concern for possible degrading of educational systems dependent on local property taxes in those places—Dallas, Poughkeepsie, Boulder, and Raleigh—where the job losses will take place. Palmisano should not be troubled by the political storm that might be brewing as his company outsources to India. (Campaigning for president in 2004, John Kerry called executives who participated in offshoring "Benedict Arnolds," unpatriotic in the extreme.) He should not worry about controversy unless it reaches such a pitch that there is real public outrage. Only if offshoring becomes a focal point for consumer activism, and only if profits are likely to be significantly affected, would Friedman urge IBM to put the brakes on its plans.

The decision to move jobs to India could—in the long run—turn out better for all concerned. It allows IBM to react to market forces with minimal losses, to be flexible as it faces domestic and global competition, and may put the company in a better position to expand and create new jobs in the future. Since 2005, profits at IBM have risen steadily.[13] In other words,

---

10 Cisco, Dell, General Electric, Accenture, EDS, Microsoft, and SAP are a few of these companies.

11 As of July 2007, IBM employed 53,000 people in India. The company continues to tap the global labor pool, and to automate wherever possible. As Sam Palmisano puts it, "We couldn't keep building out labor. The long-term strategic answer was not to have a half a million people working for IBM." IBM and other multinationals are making use of a network of employees around the world, globalizing services, much as they have already globalized manufacturing.

12 A politically hot topic in the election year of 2004, offshore outsourcing was the target of several proposed state laws banning or restricting such moves on the part of those contracting with government. At this writing, none of them had been enacted.

13 As of July 2007, it appeared that Sam Palmisano's "huge reinvention" of the company was the right thing to do, at least for shareholders. As Steve Lohr of the New York Times put it: IBM has been reorganized from a classic multinational company with country-by-country operations, working in isolation, to a more seamless global enterprise with centers of expertise in industries and technical skills, scattered around the world, each a hub in a global network for delivering services. Its experience offers a textbook case of a company successfully navigating the twin challenges of globalization and rapid technological change....So far, it seems to be working ."IBM Showing that Giants Can be Nimble," New York Times, July 18, 2007.

what works for IBM may have long-term benefits for many other stakeholders, but cost-benefit shareholder analysis of offshoring would not take such possibilities into account.

Notice that this analysis aligns with a belief in maximum freedom of choice for individuals—and minimal power of government to obstruct that freedom. This strand of thought, which we saw supporting the "no duty to rescue" rule, has been key in the development of both our market economy and our legal system. It would support both IBM's freedom to invest where it can best make a profit and the freedom of IBM's employees to leave their jobs and seek work elsewhere. The idea is that we can best progress as a society if we grant as much leeway as possible to private preference, allowing people (and private associations of people, like corporations) the right to do what they think is best with their property and their personal lives. This ethical perspective is deeply imprinted upon the economic and cultural lives of most people in the developed world.

Utilitarianism: Assessing Consequences

Through much of our history, the most influential ethical reference point was religious; the rules to be followed were "written in the heavens" and were guidelines for achieving immortality of the soul. It was a radical break with tradition, then, for eighteenth-century philosopher and social thinker Jeremy Bentham to suggest an entirely new frame of reference. Ethical behavior, he argued, was not a matter of pleasing God, but of bringing about as much happiness as possible for the greatest number of people. According to Bentham, the definitive moral standard is that of "utility," requiring us to consider the consequences of an act (or a social policy) for all those affected by it. One of Bentham's followers, nineteenth-century philosopher John Stuart Mill (discussed earlier), would become the best-known proponent of this ethical approach, known as **utilitarianism**.

According to the principle of utilitarianism, the right way to behave in a given situation is to choose the alternative that is likely to produce the greatest overall good. Cost-benefit analysis, the sort of efficiency calculation that is common to business decision making—what IBM CEO Sam Palmisano probably used as he chose to outsource thousands of jobs to India—is based on notions of utility. As an ethical theory, however, utilitarianism asks us to compare the harms and benefits of an action not just for the decider, but for *all persons who will be affected by the decision.* In the IBM scenario, this would mean, at the least, not only weighing the effects of offshoring upon IBM shareholders, but also looking at the consequences to IBM employees whose jobs were lost (and their families) and at those in India who were hired to replace them (and their families). Since local communities in both the United States and India are affected, consequences to people in that wider circumference must also be assessed.

Hardest hit would have to be IT employees who are laid off. While job retraining programs exist for manufacturing workers when their jobs move overseas, there is no such safety net for workers in IT or in other white-collar fields. According to the December 8, 2003 issue of *Business Week*, only about one-third of those Americans displaced by offshoring found jobs at the same or higher pay. The utilitarian calculation asks us to consider not only the immediate and direct consequences, but also those that are indirect, and those that are foreseeable into the future. Suppose the offshoring job exodus continued—and most experts forecasted that it would, estimating that by 2005 some 600,000 IT jobs for American-based companies would be performed elsewhere. What would happen to a local community as many of its citizens lose well-paying jobs? As the tax base diminished, would its libraries, schools, police and fire forces experience cutbacks? There was concern too about another major ripple effect: Offshoring, and the threat of offshoring, could become leverage, putting downward pressure on the salaries and benefits of all U.S. workers.

Yet some analysts saw a silver lining. As the *Washington Post* reported in September 2003, offshoring could be a "healthy trend":

> Some IT workers here may be forced to leave the "computer industry" and move into non-offshorable jobs, but this may not mean they give up doing computer work, because as our economy continues to shift away from manufacturing and toward services, we may see ... many non-portable

IT "support" jobs created.... The upshot: Even though hundreds of thousands of programming and other IT jobs are likely to leave the U.S. over the next few decades, the vast majority of U.S. IT workers will survive, and possibly even prosper in the end, although they may have new employers and work in new fields.

Quoting an editorial in the Silicon Valley's *San Jose Mercury News*, the *Post* article highlighted how tricky it might be to track the consequences of offshoring for U.S. workers:

It is impossible to make a direct link between a job lost here and a job gained elsewhere. The economics of labor are more complex. First, the savings incurred by U.S. companies when they hire low-paid workers overseas help generate profits used to hire workers, or make new investments, here. Second, Valley companies sell nearly two-thirds of their products overseas, so the rise in overseas markets helps boost their fortunes.

The extent of the threat to U.S. service jobs remained in dispute. There was a high tide of anxiety throughout 2004, the year after IBM made its announcement; more than 1,000 references to outsourcing appeared in the media that year. Then concern appeared to subside. In 2006, the director of the McKinsey Global Institute was stating that, by 2008, outsourcing would have affected less than 2 percent of all U.S. service jobs.[14] Offshoring might end up boosting the American economy overall. According to McKinsey, "at least two-thirds of the economic benefit from sending jobs offshore will flow back to the U.S. economy in the form of lower prices, expanding overseas markets for U.S. products, and fatter profits that U.S. companies can plow back into even more innovative businesses."[15] By 2007, most economists viewed the impact of offshoring as minimal or even positive in the long run, with savings to companies and increased productivity resulting in better cheaper services, and from there to more competition, more innovation, and more growth.[16]

Then there are the benefits of offshoring, both short and long range, overseas. In India, revenue from U.S. outsourcing shot up 50 percent through 2003 to $3.6 billion, and was predicted to do the same in 2004. Consider the positive effects as thousands of competent individuals begin to earn decent salaries in a country where half of the population lives on pennies a day. A critical mass of new wage earners materializes, each one in a position to produce significant benefits for themselves and their loved ones. As they rise into the middle class, they create markets for refrigerators, cars, computers, and so on—to the benefit of producers in India and elsewhere. And as this happens, there are cultural side effects. In her July 2004 *New Yorker* article, "The Best Job in Town," Katherine Boo wrote about Office Tiger, a firm where college-educated Indians perform various types of data entry for U.S. companies:

[I]t was the possibility that one could rise up from a lowly position that had made Office Tiger one of the city's status employers, a firm whose workers were so pleased by their affiliation that they put

---

14 Daniel Gross, "Why 'Outsourcing' May Lose Its Power as a Scare Word," *New York Times*, August 13, 2006. Gross quotes Princeton economist Alan Binder, who disagrees with the McKinsey estimates, arguing that as technology improves and offshore workers gain experience, the capacity to deliver services electronically will rise. He believes far more than 2 percent of jobs will migrate overseas.

15 Even within management ranks there is no consensus that offshoring makes sense long term, however. William J. Holstein, editor of *Chief Executive Magazine*, recently noted that direct labor costs represent a shrinking percentage of the overall costs of production for many businesses, making the savings from offshoring less significant. He also pointed to less tangible negative effects: "I don't think of many things as more intrinsic to the long-range thrust of a company, to the development of a company as a place of innovation and creativity … than the ability to design your own products and build your own products. You have to lovingly make them and care about their quality. It's difficult to wrap numbers around that and prove it, but I think it's central." "Does Outsourcing Cost More Than It Saves, "*New York Times*, June 6, 2004. Links to articles with similar import can be found at http://www.yourjobisgoingtoindia.com, where a posted article included survey results of 100 executives representing New York's largest companies who were not finding offshoring to be as cost efficient as they had expected it would be. Linda Prospero, "New York Survey Finds Outsourcing Not a Panacea," *Reuters*, July 19, 2004.

16 "Offshoring has faded, like Y2K, Red Menace," *Philadelphia Inquirer*, February 18, 2007.

it on their wedding invitations, just below their fathers' names. A foreign notion—that jobs should be distributed on the basis of merit—was amending the rules of society where employment had for millennia been allotted by caste, and great possibilities abounded.[17]

The utilitarian weighing of pluses and minuses becomes complex, especially because it is not simply a matter of numerical quantifying. How to assess the harm—the emotional hurt and anxiety—that a person feels when they lose a well-paid job in a "jobless recovery"? How much weight to give the loss of a job in Dallas, Texas? Might that be a city with plenty of other options for IT professionals? Of the thousands of jobless in the United States, how can we know how each employee (and each family of each employee) will be affected? One person whose job has gone to Bangalore may be married to someone earning more than enough to comfortably support the family; another may be a single parent with no real backup. All of these immeasurables play havoc with neat measurement.

Although it is difficult to meaningfully assess comparative harms and benefits, our analysis does seem to suggest that IBM's decision was ethical, given all the actual and potential benefits of offshoring, and given that relatively few people would be harmed by it. This outcome points to one of the problems with utilitarian theory. Consider another situation: The federal government requires that new drugs be tested on humans after they have been tested on animals. Drug companies must advertise widely and offer to pay as much as $250 a day to attract test subjects. But one company, Eli Lilly, does not have to advertise and pays only $85 per day, because most of its subjects are homeless alcoholics recruited through word-of-mouth from soup kitchens, shelters, and prisons across the country.[18] What happens when we run this arrangement through the utilitarian analysis? Where is the harm? New drugs are brought to market, benefiting the public—Lilly developed Prozac, for example. Cost savings may not be passed on to consumers, but they enhance corporate profits, benefiting the employees and stockholders. Alcoholism in volunteers does not skew the company's data, since those with severe liver disease will fail the initial screening process and be excluded in the first place. Even the test subjects are comfortable: Those who have participated in Lilly's program describe themselves as happy with the "easy money" they can earn—as much as $4,500 when the testing continues over months. Is this an ethical outcome? Arguably it is, on utilitarian grounds. We might wonder if the homeless alcoholics are capable of making decisions that are truly voluntary. We may wonder if it is fair to use a small number of relatively desperate people in this way, even if the results benefit many more people.

Deontology: Rights and Duties

In contrast to the utilitarian concern with maximizing social welfare, **deontological**[19] ethics is marked by steadfastness to universal principles—for example, respect for life, fairness, telling the truth, keeping promises—no matter what the consequences. At the core of this approach to making ethical choices is the understanding that moral action should be guided by certain overriding rights and duties.

The most famous deontological thinker, eighteenth-century German philosopher Immanuel Kant, believed that human beings could reason their way to a set of absolute rules for right behavior. A person should never lie, according to Kant, even when lying seems to produce a good result. Suppose someone running away from a murderer tells you where he is going to hide, and then the murderer rushes up to ask you where the first person went. Wouldn't this be a good time to lie? Kant would say there is never a good time, even in this example.

---

17 More on the plus side: Some Indian companies have found that offshoring is creating a positive synergy, enabling them to do more hiring of their own—even in the United States. By 2007, Indian high tech firms were recruiting Americans to work in India.

18 Laurie P. Cohen, "Stuck for Money," *Wall Street Journal*, November 14, 1996, pp. 1, 10.

19 From the Greek *deon*, or duty.

Moral behavior, then, is a matter of holding, without exception, to certain principles. Kant believed that each person has the right to be treated with respect as the equal of every other, and that each person has the corresponding duty to treat everyone else with respect as an equal.

He arrived at this by means of his **categorical imperatives**. The first of these states that a people should be willing to have the reasons for their actions become universal principles. That is, people should be willing to live in a world where an action they chose to take would be repeated for the same reasons whenever the same situation arose, even if they wound up on the receiving end of such actions.

Think of IBM and offshoring. If we apply Kant's first categorical imperative, the decision maker should ask: Would I want to live in a world where multinational corporations cut labor costs by replacing skilled white-collar U.S. employees with equally competent employees in other countries? Perhaps Mr. Palmisano would be comfortable with a universe of such behavior until it was his job that was eliminated. So, in Kantian terms, his action might not be an ethical one.

In another formulation of the categorical imperative, Kant states that we should have respect for the intrinsic value of other people and not just use them as means to achieve our own purposes. By this Kant did not mean that people should *never* use other people at all. People "use" one another in mutually beneficial ways all the time. For example, in a typical contractual transaction, each party to the agreement gives something up to get what it wants. Each party "uses" the other to get what it wants; if you purchase gasoline, you "use" the oil company's product and it "uses" you to pay for it. Kant would have no objection here. Rather, he believed it was unethical for people to use others *only* as a means to accomplishing their own purposes, with no mutual benefit attached. So, if the oil company uses slave labor to build an oil pipeline in Southeast Asia, it would be violating this Kantian categorical. Here one party—the more powerful one—is able effectively to remove the free will of the other, to make it do what it wants the way a puppeteer would pulls a marionette's strings. What is lost—of great ethical value in deontology—is the right to autonomy, the right to make fully informed decisions for oneself about how to live one's life. Consider IBM and offshoring. Was IBM manipulating its U.S. engineers? Think of the way the company expected them to spend several weeks training their own replacements. This does appear to involve some manipulation. Were the engineers really in any position to make decisions for themselves?

In late 2003 the *Wall Street Journal* obtained IBM documents which indicated that IBM was also trying to conceal information as it offered pointers to its managers on how to "sanitize" the offshoring process. "The words 'offshore' or 'on-shore' should never be used," the company warned. "Do not be transparent regarding the purpose/intent" of offshore outsourcing. Assuming the *WSJ* report is accurate, if IBM was attempting to cover up what was really happening, we could say it was violating Kant's categorical imperative.

So far the deontological approach appears to be leaning against the decision to go ahead with the offshoring. There can be real murkiness within this moral framework, though, when it comes to interpreting those universal rights and duties that Kant considered "absolute"—beyond compromise. In the offshoring scenario, for example, how should we interpret the duty to be "fair"? Sam Palmisano, we might say, is caught in a latticework of different versions of fairness. On the one hand, moving white-collar jobs away from well-educated American employees is unfair to them and to their families. But not to go through with the offshoring plan is arguably unfair to IBM's shareholders, who deserve the best possible return on investment, and to the well-qualified employees in India and their families. Recall how Palmisano himself used the concept of fairness when explaining offshoring:

> China, India, South Korea, and other rapidly developing nations are replicating the structural advantages that historically have made the U.S. the center of innovation. We can't—shouldn't—regret improvements in other nations' competitiveness. Their people deserve to participate fully in the benefits of innovations.

Another difficulty with deontology is the confusion created when different universal rights and duties crop up in the same ethical problem, and seem to conflict with one another. How does one decide which absolute value should prevail? These situations can get ugly. Consider the intensity of conflicting beliefs on the question of abortion. Both the right-to-life and the pro-choice factions are convinced that their points of view derive from natural rights; both embrace referents that each of them consider beyond debate, beyond compromise. How do we resolve competing claims of this type? The "war on terror" presents us with other examples of clashing rights and duties, such as lengthy detentions under the USA PATRIOT Act of suspects not charged with any crime, proposals to allow the Pentagon to randomly monitor personal e-mail, and problems with prisoner abuse in Afghanistan and Iraq. Conflicting views here pit the right to life and safety against the right to privacy, the duty to be fair, and the categorical imperative to respect others—including those of Middle Eastern origin or beliefs—as equals.

Virtue Ethics: Habits of Goodness

For some critics, both the utilitarian and deontological frameworks are inadequate in a fundamental sense; while both set forth logical bases for deciding what might be called moral minima—the floor beneath which no one should drop in terms of ethical choices—they are silent on the concept of moral excellence. They also focus on the moral acceptability of *actions*. Virtue ethics, on the other hand, directs our attention to what human beings are capable of *being*, on how they can cultivate the habits of good character that will naturally lead them to their fullest potential.

This strand of thinking derives from Aristotle, who argued that people develop their moral abilities, called **virtues**, through training, by being repeatedly exposed to demonstrations of decent behavior within families and communities. We learn to become courageous, generous, just, honest, cooperative, and cheerful gradually, as we become habituated to living in social settings where these qualities are exhibited and valued. Ethics, then, is not a matter of teasing out the correct choice given a series of knotty dilemmas; it is instead a lifelong conditioning process. In harmonious relationship with their communities, people thrive, reaching the fullest unfolding of their potential, learning the habits that allow them to excel at everything they are capable of doing.

Virtue ethics does raise its own set of questions, however. What does it mean to define moral character in term of one's community? What community? As the new millennium unfolds, too many Americans are living in family environments in which relatedness endures in spite of severe economic and psychological stresses. Half the population of the world lives in poverty. If children grow up in hardship, where the natural environment is harshly degraded and the social fabric is weakened, does the transmittal of virtuous habit become a luxury? If families cannot effectively teach virtue to their young, what are the alternatives? Schools? Religious communities? And when these are in such diverse forms—sometimes in sharp opposition—how do we judge which moral community is best? We call the men who flew into the World Trade Center terrorists, but at some schools in the deserts of the Middle East, boys memorize the Koran and learn the heroic significance of being a suicide bomber. Which system can claim moral hegemony?

And what do we mean by community in the business context? Where is the community touchstone in the IBM scenario? To answer this question about a large company like IBM, we must examine what is called "corporate culture." Here one scholar describes what that is meant by the culture of an organization:

> *The pattern of basic assumptions that a given group has invented, discovered, or developed in learning to cope with its problems of external adaptation and internal integration, and that have worked well enough to be considered valid, and, therefore, to be taught to new members as the correct way to perceive, think, and feel in relation to those problems.*[20]

More colloquially, a company might describe its culture as "the way we do things around here." In studies by Harvard corporate management guru John Kotter, as of 1987–1991, IBM was ranked at

---

20 Edgar H. Schein's definition. Professor Schein is a management expert at MIT.

number 8 (out of the more than 2,300 firms studied) in terms of the strength of its corporate culture. We can see how it got that way by looking at its ascendancy under Thomas Watson, Sr., called "the greatest capitalist in history" by *Fortune Magazine*. It was Watson who named the company International Business Machines in 1924. Originally a manufacturer of tabulating machines, IBM would move into electric punch-card accounting and then into early computers. Throughout its growth in the 1920s and 1930s, Watson posted the motto "T-H-I-N-K" in all offices and required all his salesmen to wear blue suits and white shirts. An intense focus on sales and on a "buttoned-down" image would stay with the company throughout the twentieth century. Extremely charismatic, vain, and proud of his company, Watson built a corporate culture designed to instill loyalty and enthusiasm. IBM had company sports teams, family events, and was one of the first firms to offer workers paid vacations, life insurance, and survivor benefits. During the Depression, even as sales weakened, IBM managed to avoid mass layoffs. By mid-century the company had an unparalleled reputation as a fair employer. IBM continued to pay salaries to employees serving in WWII, while the company used weapons manufacturing profits to help widows and orphans of IBM employees killed in the conflict.[21] The firm covered moving expenses for transferees, guaranteed minimum resale prices on their homes, and paid for retraining. Most impressively, during this time IBM guaranteed lifetime employment for all employees. For years Watson told his people: "The IBM is not merely an organization of men; it is an institution that will go on forever."

A powerhouse of the computer mainframe market, the company would continue to grow through the 1950s, 1960s, and 1970s. "Big Blue" was ranked the most admired company in the United States year after year. By 1984 it was the most valuable company in the world, famous for consistent stock and dividend growth. It stood for the best of American big business—for its stockholders, its consumers, and its workforce.

Then—a crisis. As technology advanced, the computer market changed. Personal computers came to the fore, innovative upstarts such as Apple entered the field, and by the 1990s, IBM had suffered serious losses. As its stock lost half of its value, tens of thousands of workers were laid off. The very strength of IBM's culture was blamed, in part, for this catastrophe. As one commentator put it:

> *The company, it seemed, had become the epitome of an overgrown, anonymous, monopolistic, bureaucratic monster—outmatched in marketing and technology by swifter, nimbler competitors; too big to change, it appeared destined to collapse under its own ungainly weight.*[22]

Although it recovered profitability by the late 1990s, IBM would never recover its former image as a benevolent giant, with a strong, paternalistic and compassionate corporate environment.

Returning to our question: If virtue ethics is a matter of moral characteristics ingrained within a community, and if CEO Sam Palmisano attends to the culture of his corporate community, he would be guided by this ethical code, touted today by IBM.

The IBM Principles

1. The marketplace is the driving force behind everything we do.
2. At our core, we are a technology company with an overriding commitment to quality.

---

21 There were less salutary aspects to IBM's activities during this period. Thomas Watson accepted a medal from the Nazi regime in 1937, an event featured in Edwin Black's recent book, *IBM and the Holocaust*. Although IBM was not alone in its willingness to do business with Hitler, Black tells how crucial its role was. IBM's German subsidiary, acting "with the knowledge of its New York headquarters," supplied the Nazis with a punch card system that organized, tabulated, and analyzed population data, making possible mass deportations and executions. From Black's introduction: [D]azzled by its own swirling universe of technical possibilities, IBM was self-gripped by a special amoral corporate mantra: If it can be done, it should be done. To the blind technocrat, the means were more important than the ends. The destruction of the Jewish people became even less important because the invigorating nature of IBM's technical achievement was only heightened by the fantastical profits to be made at a time when bread lines stretched across the world.

22 Steven Kotok, *St. James Encyclopedia of Popular Culture*, 2002 Gale Group. See http://articles.findarticles.com/p/articles/ mi_g1epc/is_tov/ai_2419100611

3. Our primary measures of success are customer satisfaction and shareholder value.

4. We operate as an entrepreneurial organization with a minimum of bureaucracy and a never-ending focus on productivity.

5. We never lose sight of our strategic vision.

6. We think and act with a sense of urgency.

7. Outstanding, dedicated people make it all happen, particularly when they work together as a team.

8. We are sensitive to the needs of all employees and to the communities in which we operate.

As you review these guidelines, and Sam Palmisano's speech to the Council on Competitiveness, can you sense whether the culture of IBM supports offshoring?

What forces inside a company determine the type of culture that develops inside it? What forces outside a company might influence that process? Are there *business* virtues?[23] What might they be?

Ethic of Care

> *The elusive mystery of women's development lies in its recognition of the continuing importance of attachment in the human life-cycle ... while masculine development litany intones the celebration of separation, autonomy, individuation and natural rights.*
>
> — CAROL GILLIGAN

> *I hope I would have the guts to betray my country before I would betray my friend.*
> — E.M. FORSTER, "WHAT I BELIEVE," 1938

The ethical theories we have looked at so far assume that a decision about the right thing to do is ultimately a private decision, made by an individual in isolation. Whether using their intellectual powers or responding to trained habit, people act as autonomous beings, as free agents in this process. A different approach to ethics assumes that people are deeply connected to one another in webs of relationships, and that ethical decisions cannot be made outside the context of those relationships. This alternative view holds that ethics is essentially a matter of nurturing and reinforcing the ties we have with one another. This has become known as the "ethic of care," as it is based on caring for others.

The notion of an ethic of care was developed by feminist theorists such as Carol Gilligan, a psychologist who studied moral development. Her research led her to believe that men and women approach moral issues from different perspectives. While most men have an individualistic focus on abstract rights and justice, women tend to focus on caring, on supporting human interconnectedness—an approach that Gilligan saw as undervalued, and which she characterized as "a different voice." Over time this understanding has shifted: Rather than a split between male versus female ethics, it is thought that there are two different approaches to moral problem solving that can be accessed by either men or women.

In the following reading Leslie Bender, professor of law at Syracuse University, suggests a feminist reframing of negligence law and the "no duty to rescue" rule. She begins by referencing Gilligan's work.

---

23 Robert C. Solomon thinks so. He has written extensively about Aristotle and business. Included in his list of business virtues are friendliness, charisma, fairness, heroism, style, toughness, and wittiness. See his book, *A Better Way To Think About Business* (New York: Oxford University Press, 1999).

A PRIMER OF FEMINIST THEORY AND TORT

Leslie Bender[24]

A Feminist Ethic of Caring and Interconnectedness

Gilligan recognized that there are two thematic approaches to problem solving that generally correlate with gender, although she makes no claims about the origin of the difference.... When she asked what characterizes the different methods for resolving and analyzing moral dilemmas, Gilligan found that the "right" answers (according to the traditionally formulated stages of moral development) involve abstract, objective, rule-based decisions supported by notions of individual autonomy, individual rights, the separation of self from others, equality, and fairness. Often the answers provided by women focus on the particular contexts of the problems, relationships, caring (compassion and need), equity, and responsibility. For this different voice "responsibility" means "response to" rather than "obligation for." The first voice understands relationships in terms of hierarchies or "ladders," whereas the "feminine" voice communicates about relationships as "webs of interconnectedness...."

While an ethic of justice proceeds from the premise of equality—that everyone should be treated the same—an ethic of care rests on the premise of nonviolence—that no one should be hurt.

Negligence Law: A Feminist Ethic of Care and Concern
as a Basis for the Standard of Care

Our traditional negligence analysis asks whether the defendant met the requisite standard of care to avoid liability.

In tort law we generally use the phrase "standard of care" to mean "level of caution." How careful should the person have been? What precautions do we expect people to take to avoid accidents? We look to the carefulness a reasonable person would exercise to avoid impairing another's rights or interest. If a defendant did not act carefully, reasonably, or prudently by guarding against foreseeable harm, she would be liable. The idea of care and prudence in this context is translated into reasonableness, which is frequently measured instrumentally in terms of utility or economic efficiency.

When the standard of care is equated with economic efficiency or levels of caution, decisions that assign dollar values to harms to human life and health and then balance those dollars against profit dollars and other evidences of benefit become commonplace.... The risk of their pain and loss becomes a potential debit to be weighed against the benefits or profits to others. The result has little to do with care or even with caution, if caution is understood as concern for safety.

What would happen if we understood the "reasonableness" of the standard of care to mean "responsibility" and the "standard of care" to mean the "standard of caring" or "consideration of another's safety and interests?" What if, instead of measuring carefulness or caution, we measured concern and responsibility for the well-being of others and their protection from harm? Negligence law could begin with Gilligan's articulation of the feminine voice's ethic of care—a premise that no one should be hurt...

"No Duty" Cases

One of the most difficult areas in which questions of duty and the standard of care arise is the "no duty to rescue" case. The problem is traditionally illustrated by the drowning-stranger hypothetical and the infamous case of *Yania v. Bigan.*

24 38 *J. Leg. Educ.* 3 (1988), pp. 63–68.

How would this drowning-stranger hypothetical look from a new legal perspective informed by a feminist ethic based upon notions of caring, responsibility, interconnectedness, and cooperation?

If we put abstract reasoning and autonomy aside momentarily, we can see what else matters. In defining duty, what matters is that someone, a human being, a part of us, is drowning and will die without some affirmative action. That seems more urgent, more imperative, more important than any possible infringement of individual autonomy by the imposition of an affirmative duty.

If we think about the stranger as a human being for a moment, we may realize that much more is involved than balancing one person's interest in having his life saved and another's interest in not having affirmative duties imposed upon him in the absence of a special relationship....

The drowning stranger is not the only person affected by the lack of care. He is not detached from everyone else. He no doubt has people who care about him—parents, spouse, children, friends, colleagues; groups he participates in—religious, social, athletic, artistic, political, educational, work-related; he may even have people who depend upon him for emotional or financial support. He is interconnected with others. If the stranger drowns, many will be harmed. It is not an isolated event with one person's interests balanced against another's. When our legal system trains us to understand the drowning-stranger story as a limited event between two people, both of whom have interests at least equally worth protecting, and when the social ramifications we credit most are the impositions on personal liberty of action, we take a human situation and translate it into a cold, dehumanized algebraic equation. We forget that we are talking about human death or grave physical harms and their reverberating consequences when we equate the consequences with such things as one person's momentary freedom not to act....

Bender goes on to write:

The duty to act with care for another's safety, which under appropriate circumstances would include an affirmative duty to act to protect or prevent harm to another, would be shaped by the particular context.

This is one of the hallmarks of the ethic of care, a willingness to be concerned with the particulars of a situation, and from there an interest in discovering compromise—creative ways to find a solution that might work for all the stakeholders.

How might the IBM offshoring decision look through the lens of the ethic of care? The strongest relational connection in the scenario must be between IBM and its employees. Some of them may have survived the deep job cuts of the 1990s, but even if not, they were probably well aware of the effort the company had recently made to turn itself around and become profitable again. What happens, though, when market pressures interfere with established relationships? How can we reconcile these apparently opposite forces, the urge to do the right thing for the people you know best, and the imperatives of business? The ethic of care suggests that the specific context of offshoring at IBM receive attention. Who are these people about to lose their positions? How can IBM ease their transition? From what we know of the facts—that many employees will be told to train their replacements for weeks, and that most cannot expect to be rehired anytime soon—these are a harsh set of particulars.

The ethic of care might lead Sam Palmisano to investigate *how* the offshoring process will be managed at IBM. If the process itself cannot be reversed, then the way it is to be implemented might be changed. What can IBM do to soften the blow? Are there any resources to retrain and/or rehire workers, to assist them in job searches? Open communication can be very important, both for laid-off employees and for local communities. The ethic of care suggests that creative efforts be made, not just for the sake of "damage control," but because there is value in relationships that have been nourished over time.

Ironically, putting relationships first can end up positively affecting the bottom line. When his large textile mill burned to the ground just before Christmas 1995, owner Aaron Feuerstein perceived the tragedy as one for a network of stakeholders, his family, his employees, and the surrounding community. As he responded by including all of those affected in his plans for rebuilding, the network responded in turn. Donations came in from local businesses; customers such as Patagonia and Lands' End pledged support and promised to wait for their Polartec; citizens from neighboring New Hampshire donated Christmas trees and toys for idled workers. Once the rebuilt factory was in operation, productivity rose 25 percent.

Problems arise with the ethic of care, though, as with the other theories. Sometimes there are several relationships at stake, and it becomes difficult to rank and care for them. The ethic of care can be troubling in another way. Suppose you have the responsibility of recommending someone from your work team for promotion. One of the team members is your friend. She's a single parent and could really use the extra income. But she isn't the most deserving person in your group. If you are fair, you'll recommend the best person for the job—but the ethic of care might push you to recommend your friend, as care deteriorates into favoritism.

Why Ethical Theory?

Having explored several approaches to ethics, we have seen potential flaws in each. We may feel unsettled by the journey, uncertain how useful it has been. Yet this unresolved aftertaste may be exactly appropriate. There are no easy answers at the intersection of law, ethics, and business. The best we can hope for may be a reflective approach, combining one or more frameworks to reach several possible solutions, and then comparing the solutions to see if they "agree."

Ideally, familiarity with these theories will support you in at least two ways as you face business dilemmas in the future. First, the models for analysis can spark creative thinking, as you brainstorm ways of handling the dilemmas. Second, they offer you a means of explaining your decisions to others. Explanations can be useful. Suppose you are working for the pesticide manufacturer that cannot sell certain of its products in the United States because they are hazardous by U.S. standards, yet the company plans to sell them overseas. Knowing the theoretical basis for ethical decision making could help you understand your own position, and help you articulate it to your superiors, your co-workers, and those who report to you in the organization. There is a familiar "language" in the business world for most decision making: cost-benefit analysis. Ethical theory offers you another language, making you "bilingual" in complex situations.

Corporate Governance

Corporate Roles, Rights, and Responsibilities

Shareholders

Shareholders are, collectively, the owners of a corporation. As their holdings rise in value, they profit; when their shares lose value, shareholders lose. They may be private shareholders—individual investors, both large and small—or they may be institutional shareholders, such as pension funds, mutual funds, insurance companies. The

continued

legal liability of shareholders is limited by law to the amount of investment they make in the company. Their rights include:

Receipt of true and accurate financial reports
Dividends whenever dividends declared
Attendance at shareholder meetings
Vote (by proxy or in person) on

Membership of board of directors
Significant mergers and acquisitions
Changes in charter or by-laws
Proposals by management or shareholders

Shareholders can also hold managers and directors accountable by bringing shareholder derivative suits (see below).

Board of Directors

Board members are elected by shareholders from a slate provided by management. They can be "inside directors" with ongoing or previous contractual relationships with the company, or "outside" or "independent directors" with no financial relationship with the company other than as a member of its board. Directors are held by law to a **duty of loyalty**. They cannot interfere with corporate opportunities, compete with the corporation, take secret profits or engage in other forms of self-dealing at the company's expense. They are also required to abide by a **duty of care**—to act in good faith and as reasonably prudent persons in their role as directors. These two duties are known as **fiduciary duties**, to be carried out by those who are entrusted with responsibility for other peoples' investments.

The board may create committees and delegate certain powers to them; since the Sarbanes-Oxley Act of 2002, all public companies must have audit committees made up of independent directors, which hire independent public accountants to supervise the audit of company financial records.

In a broad oversight function, the board sets company policy and goals. In addition, it:

Presents financial data to shareholders
Hires and fires management
Slates membership of the board and of its committees
Is authorized to file lawsuits on behalf of corporation to recover damages

Officers and Management

The chief executive officer (CEO or President) of a company and other officers are appointed by the board of directors, and must report to the board about the ongoing operations of the corporation. Like the directors, management is held to both a duty of loyalty and a duty of care, and must.

Run the company on a day-to-day basis
Implement decisions made by the board of directors
Prepare reports for the board of directors and shareholders

Although the structure outlined above appears to confer a degree of representative democracy to the corporate form, with investors having the ability to vote on proposals and to sue for misconduct of managers and board members, the shareholders of a corporation have limited power to influence or control the decisions of corporate officers and directors. In Chapter 7 you will read about the hurdles shareholders face when they attempt to make proposals and bring them to a vote; their right to sue will meet resistance based on the way in which state corporate law is structured to protect the ability of officers and directors to run a company as they see fit.

A **shareholders derivative lawsuit** can be initiated by individual shareholders on behalf of the corporation as a whole against persons or entities that have harmed the company—most often one or more of its own directors or officers for breach of fiduciary duty. (In other words, shareholders attempt to bring a suit that they believe the board of directors should have brought.) First, however, they must give the board a chance to act by making a "demand" that the board pursue the suit. To a large degree the board has the power to refuse to do so. A board's decision to reject the demand is seldom overturned by a court—the **business judgment rule** gives wide latitude to the board to make such a call. Under certain circumstances, however, shareholders are excused from first making this demand. They can argue that doing so would be futile, because board members themselves are very much "part of the problem" that the shareholders derivative suit seeks to redress. But shareholders must allege specific facts that prove so-called **demand futility**. In most states, that means demonstrating why the board members who decided not to launch the suit were not "disinterested, informed and rational." (A "disinterested" board member would be someone without any competing personal stake in the situation.)

The next case is an example of a shareholders derivative suit that survived a motion to dismiss. Note the interplay among shareholders, management and board, both in terms of what allegedly happened, and in how the law structures their relationships.

Career Education Corporation (CEC) provides private, for-profit post-secondary education on dozens of campuses throughout the United States, Canada, France, United Kingdom, and United Arab Emirate, and an online university. According to shareholder Scott McSparran, the board of directors artificially inflated CEC's stock price by enrolling students without complete financial aid, enrolling students who did not actually attend classes, and claiming inflated job-placement rates for CEC graduates. Much of the information that should have alerted directors to this fraud—newspaper articles, court papers, and stock analyst reports—was available to the public.

MCSPARRAN v. LARSON

United States District Court, Illinois, 2006
2006 WL 250698

ANDERSEN, J. ☀

… According to the plaintiffs, defendants' scheme enabled them to dispose of 2.8 million shares of CEC stock for proceeds of over $136 million.

The Complaint posits that the defendants knew exactly what was happening at CEC and lied about the extent of the problems CEC faced even after the accounting irregularities came to light, all so that they could continue to sell stock at high prices.…

Also detailed in the Complaint are the ties between CEC's CEO and Chairman of the Board, and each and every other member of CEC's Board of Directors. While CEC's CEO and Chairman of the Board unquestionably had some degree of control over the compensation of officers of CEC, the Complaint does not allege other business relationships that would allow him to control the compensation of outside directors. Instead, the

Complaint refers to general social and business ties and mentions fees paid to the directors for their services. . . .

The Supreme Court of Delaware created a two-part test for demand futility in *Aronson v. Lewis*. Under this test, we ask whether "a reasonable doubt is created that: (1) the directors are disinterested and independent and (2) the challenged transaction was otherwise the product of a valid exercise of business judgment." Plaintiffs assert two main grounds for demand futility: (i) the Board of Directors is dominated and controlled by CEC's CEO and Chairman of the Board; and (ii) a majority of the Board of Directors are interested in the outcome of this litigation because they face a substantial likelihood of liability for claims predicated on the fact their decisions were not protected by the business judgment rule. As such, the two-part test laid out in *Aronson* is distilled in the present case into questions of independence and interest.

Delaware courts have noted that "[a]t bottom, the question of independence turns on whether a director is, *for any substantial reason*, incapable of making a decision with only the best interests of the corporation in mind. That is, . . . cases ultimately focus on impartiality and objectivity." However, "neither mere personal friendships alone, nor mere outside business relationships alone, are sufficient to raise a reasonable doubt regarding a director's independence."

Nor does the fact that directors receive directorial fees destroy their independence. ("[T]he fact that each [director] is paid an annual retainer of $30,000 plus a fee of $1000 for each meeting attended and annual grants of stock options does not make them beholden to [the company's CEO].")

There is no substantial reason to question the independence of a majority of CEC's Board of Directors. Plaintiff has not put forth any allegations outside directors have their salary set by any board member, or are otherwise financially dependent upon other directors. If mere social acquaintances and prior business relationships with other board members coupled with the receipt of directorial fees destroyed a board member's independence, few boards would have any independent members. . . .

. . . A reasonable doubt regarding a director's interest is raised when a corporate decision "will have a materially detrimental impact on a director, but not on the corporation or the stockholders." . . . As such, if plaintiffs' Complaint pleads facts that indicate a majority of CEC's Board of Directors face a "substantial likelihood" of personal liability, a demand upon the Board of Directors is futile.

Generally, board members are protected from individual liability by the business judgment rule, which provides a "presumption that in making a business decision the directors of a corporation acted on an informed basis, in good faith and in the honest belief that the action taken was in the best interests of the company. Absent an abuse of discretion, that judgment will be respected by the courts." . . . [As the Delaware Supreme Court determined in 1996, however,] individual liability for directors can result from two possible contexts: (i) . . . a board decision that results in a loss because that decision was ill advised , negligent, or intentionally adverse to the best interests of the company and (ii) . . . "from an unconsidered failure of the board to act in circumstances in which due attention would, arguably, have prevented the loss."

. . . [A] board's extreme indifference or failure to act may create individual liability for board members. "[A] director's obligation includes a duty to attempt in good faith to assure that a corporate information and reporting system, which the board concludes is adequate, exists, and that failure to do so under some circumstances may, in theory at least, render a director liable for losses caused by noncompliance with applicable legal standards." Moreover, it is beyond dispute that a director who profits from confidential corporate information and takes actions adverse to the corporation's best interest is personally liable to the corporation. [As Delaware courts held in 1949,] "a person in a confidential or fiduciary position, in breach of his duty, uses that knowledge to make a profit from himself, he is accountable for such profit."…

Plaintiffs' Complaint contains two alternative allegations. Defendants were allegedly either active participants in a scheme to report false accounting of revenues and enrollment figures so that they could sell their holdings of CEC stock at inflated prices, or they failed to act in the face of evidence that should have prompted remedial measures. Either of these two scenarios could result in personal liability for the defendants. In support of these allegations, the Complaint details company policy that should have brought CEC's false accounting to the attention of the defendants, quotes from news articles, court filings, and analyst reports that discussed allegations of false accounting, and names of two defendants who supposedly received comparisons of accurate information versus the inaccurate information that was provided to the public and the federal government. Additionally, the Complaint alleges that all defendants except for one sold sizable stock holdings while they knew, or should have known, of significant, non-public, problems with CEC's reported financial and enrollment figures. In fact, the plaintiffs contend that the reason CEC was engaged in the reporting of false figures was primarily to allow defendants to profit from selling their holdings of CEC stock. The Complaint also explains that the reporting of false figures to the federal government was extremely adverse to the interests of CEC due to the dire consequences a revocation of HEA loan eligibility would visit upon the company.…

At this stage in the litigation plaintiffs have met their burden of pleading with particularly their reasons for demand futility. The plaintiffs have told us the "who, what, when, where, and how" of a story that a raises a reasonable doubt about the defendants' personal liability. Since the defendants may have personal liability, they are interested parties to any demand upon the Board of Directors to institute litigation. As such, plaintiffs are excused from making a demand upon the Board of Directors based on the doctrine of demand futility.…

[Held: Defendants' motion to dismiss is denied.]

QUESTIONS

1. What is a shareholder derivative suit? On what grounds was such a suit brought against CEC?

2. What is the business judgment rule? In what ways were defendants alleged to have violated that rule?

3. The judge explains that the fact that members of the board have personal relationships with management, or receive considerable fees for serving does not destroy their status as "independent." For about two weeks work a year, independent directors at Enron averaged $87,000 from cash and stock options.[25] What effect might treating directors this well have on corporate governance? What ethical issues arise here?

4. Defendants argued that there were no damages to CEC, despite allegedly high legal fees and diminished business reputations. How would you articulate the shareholders' claims that the behavior of its officers and directors amounted to harm to the corporation?

---

25 Robert Bryce, *Pipe Dreams: Greed, Ego, and the Death of Enron* (New York: Public Affairs, 2002).

Corporate Social Responsibility as Creation of Shared Value

The notion that corporations have a responsibility to their stakeholders—not only their stockholders—is not new. Waves of scandal—defense contracting in the 1970s, insider trading in the 1980s, and most recently and spectacularly, the financial fraud that bankrupted companies like Enron and WorldCom at the turn of the twenty-first century—have been accompanied by public relations problems for corporations, a certain amount of public soul-searching on their part, and calls, sometimes heeded, for a ratcheting up of government regulation. The drama is a predictable one, with business leaders cast first as villains, then as penitents, demonstrating each time fresh concern for those stakeholders who are not shareholders—employees, regulators, local community members, the American investing public, and so on. What appears to have remained constant through all of these cycles is that most businesses will strive to be ethical in order to stay out of crisis management mode—until and unless the profit imperative simply becomes too strong. Even an organizational culture that supports ethical decision making can be put at risk when the pressures of market competition overwhelm it.

This final article raises the hopeful possibility that companies might build ethics into their value chain, becoming responsive to stakeholder networks in a way that is sustainable. Michael E. Porter, professor at Harvard Business School, and Mark R. Kramer, senior fellow at Harvard's Kennedy School of Government, co-founded FSG Social Impact Advisors, an international nonprofit consulting firm. In this article they urge businesses to take a proactive or "strategic" approach to Corporate Social Responsibility (CSR), in which companies can zero in on what they do best to benefit both themselves and the larger society. Strategic CSR, they write, goes beyond philanthropy, and beyond mitigating any harmful impacts a firm might have on its surroundings, to take advantage of an important reality: the mutual dependence of business and society.

STRATEGY & SOCIETY: THE LINK BETWEEN COMPETITIVE ADVANTAGE AND CORPORATE SOCIAL RESPONSIBILITY

Michael Porter, Mark R. Kramer[26]

Integrating Business and Society

Successful corporations need a healthy society. Education, health care, and equal opportunity are essential to a productive workforce. Safe products and working conditions not only attract customers but lower the internal costs of accidents. Efficient utilization of land, water, energy, and other natural resources makes business more productive. Good government, the rule of law, and property rights are essential for efficiency and innovation. Strong regulatory standards protect both consumers and competitive companies from exploitation. Ultimately, a healthy society creates expanding demand for business, as more human needs are met and aspirations grow. Any business that pursues its ends at the expense of the society in which it operates will find its success to be illusory and ultimately temporary.

At the same time, a healthy society needs successful companies. No social program can rival the business sector when it comes to creating the jobs, wealth, and innovation that improve standards of living and social conditions over time. If governments, NGOs, and other participants in civil society weaken the ability of business to operate productively, they may win battles but will lose the war, as corporate and regional competitiveness fade, wages stagnate, jobs disappear, and the wealth that pays taxes and supports nonprofit contributions evaporates.

Leaders in both business and civil society have focused too much on the friction between them and not enough on the points of intersection. The mutual dependence of corporations and society implies that both business decisions and social policies must follow the principle of shared value. That is, choices must benefit both sides …

[Porter and Kramer identify "inside-out linkages," or points at which businesses can impact society—from waste disposal to hiring practices. Inside-out linkages can exist all along a company's "value chain," the series of operations it performs to produce goods or services. The authors also note "outside-in linkages," or ways in which the external environment impinges on business operations—from the quality of the labor pool, to the nature of consumer demand, to the way government creates and enforces rules and offers incentives. Outside-in linkages, according to Porter and Kramer, provide the "competitive context" for any business.]

Choosing Which Social Issues to Address

No business can solve all of society's problems or bear the cost of doing so. Instead, each company must select issues that intersect with its particular business. Other social agendas are best left to those companies in other industries, NGOs, or government institutions that are better positioned to address them. The essential test that should guide CSR is not whether a cause is worthy but whether it presents an opportunity to create shared value—that is, a meaningful benefit for society that is also valuable to the business.

Our framework suggests that the social issues affecting a company fall into three categories that distinguish between the many worthy causes and the narrower set of social issues that are both important and strategic for the business.

Generic social issues may be important to society but are neither significantly affected by the company's operations nor influence the company's long-term competitiveness. **Value chain social impacts** are those that are significantly affected by the company's activities in the ordinary course of business. **Social dimensions of competitive context** are factors in the external environment that significantly affect the underlying drivers of competitiveness in those places where the company operates.

Every company will need to sort social issues into these three categories for each of its business units and primary locations, and then rank them in terms of potential impact. Into which category a given social issue falls will vary from business unit to business unit, industry to industry, and place to place.

Supporting a dance company may be a generic social issue for a utility like Southern California Edison but an important part of the competitive context for a corporation like American Express, which depends on the high-end entertainment, hospitality, and tourism cluster. Carbon emissions may be a generic social issue for a financial services firm like Bank of America, a negative value chain impact for a transportation-based company like UPS, or both a value chain impact and a competitive context issue for a car manufacturer like Toyota. The AIDS pandemic in Africa may be a generic social issue for a U.S. retailer like Home Depot, a value chain impact for a pharmaceutical company like GlaxoSmithKline, and a competitive context issue for a mining company like Anglo American that depends on local labor in Africa for its operations.…

Creating a Corporate Social Agenda

[Porter and Kramer argue that companies can and should engage in "responsive CSR," acting as good corporate citizens with philanthropic activity and taking care to address any harmful impacts they might have caused. Such CSR is fittingly "responsive to stake-holders" they write, but "it cannot stop there."]

Strategic CSR

For any company, strategy must go beyond best practices. It is about choosing a unique position—doing things differently from competitors in a way that lowers costs or better serves a particular set of customer needs....

Strategic CSR moves beyond good corporate citizenship and mitigating harmful value chain impacts to mount a small number of initiatives whose social and business benefits are large and distinctive. Strategic CSR involves both inside-out and outside-in dimensions working in tandem. It is here that the opportunities for shared value truly lie.

Many opportunities to pioneer innovations to benefit both society and a company's own competitiveness can arise in the product offering and the value chain. Toyota's response to concerns over automobile emissions is an example. Toyota's Prius, the hybrid electric/gasoline vehicle, is the first in a series of innovative car models that have produced competitive advantage and environmental benefits. Hybrid engines emit as little as 10 percent of the harmful pollutants conventional vehicles produce while consuming only half as much gas. Voted 2004 Car of the Year by Motor Trend magazine, Prius has given Toyota a lead so substantial that Ford and other car companies are licensing the technology. Toyota has created a unique position with customers and is well on its way to establishing its technology as the world standard.

Urbi, a Mexican construction company, has prospered by building housing for disadvantaged buyers using novel financing vehicles such as flexible mortgage payments made through payroll deductions. Crédit Agricole, France's largest bank, has differentiated itself by offering specialized financial products related to the environment, such as financing packages for energy-saving home improvements and for audits to certify farms as organic.

Strategic CSR also unlocks shared value by investing in social aspects of context that strengthen company competitiveness. A symbiotic relationship develops: The success of the company and the success of the community become mutually reinforcing. Typically, the more closely tied a social issue is to the company's business, the greater the opportunity to leverage the firm's resources and capabilities, and benefit society.

Microsoft's Working Connections partnership with the American Association of Community Colleges (AACC) is a good example of a shared-value opportunity arising from investments in context. The shortage of information technology workers is a significant constraint on Microsoft's growth; currently, there are more than 450,000 unfilled IT positions in the United States alone. Community colleges, with an enrollment of 11.6 million students, representing 45 percent of all U.S. undergraduates, could be a major solution. Microsoft recognizes, however, that community colleges face special challenges: IT curricula are not standardized, technology used in classrooms is often outdated, and there are no systematic professional development programs to keep faculty up to date.

Microsoft's $50 million five-year initiative was aimed at all three problems. In addition to contributing money and products, Microsoft sent employee volunteers to colleges to assess needs, contribute to curriculum development, and create faculty development institutes. Note that in this case, volunteers and assigned staff were able to use their core professional skills to address a social need, a far cry from typical volunteer programs. Microsoft has achieved results that have benefited many communities while having a direct—and potentially significant—impact on the company.

Integrating Inside-out and Outside-in Practices

... Activities in the value chain can be performed in ways that reinforce improvements in the social dimensions of context. At the same time, investments in competitive context have the potential to reduce constraints on a company's value chain activities. Marriott, for example, provides 180 hours of paid classroom and on-the-job training to chronically unemployed job candidates. The company has combined this with support for local community service organizations, which identify, screen, and refer the candidates to Marriott. The net result is both a major benefit to communities and a reduction in Marriott's cost of recruiting entry-level employees. Ninety percent of those in the training program take jobs with Marriott. One year later, more than 65 percent are still in their jobs, a substantially higher retention rate than the norm.

Creating a Social Dimension to the Value Proposition

At the heart of any strategy is a unique value proposition: a set of needs a company can meet for its chosen customers that others cannot. The most strategic CSR occurs when a company adds a social dimension to its value proposition, making social impact integral to the overall strategy.

Consider Whole Foods Market, whose value proposition is to sell organic, natural, and healthy food products to customers who are passionate about food and the environment. Social issues are fundamental to what makes Whole Foods unique in food retailing and to its ability to command premium prices. The company's sourcing emphasizes purchases from local farmers through each store's procurement process. Buyers screen out foods containing any of nearly 100 common ingredients that the company considers unhealthy or environmentally damaging. The same standards apply to products made internally. Whole Foods' baked goods, for example, use only unbleached and unbromated flour.

Whole Foods' commitment to natural and environmentally friendly operating practices extends well beyond sourcing. Stores are constructed using a minimum of virgin raw materials. Recently, the company purchased renewable wind energy credits equal to 100 percent of its electricity use in all of its stores and facilities, the only Fortune 500 company to offset its electricity consumption entirely. Spoiled produce and biodegradable waste are trucked to regional centers for composting. Whole Foods' vehicles are being converted to run on biofuels. Even the cleaning products used in its stores are environmentally friendly. And through its philanthropy, the company has created the Animal Compassion Foundation to develop more natural and humane ways of raising farm animals. In short, nearly every aspect of the company's value chain reinforces the social dimensions of its value proposition, distinguishing Whole Foods from its competitors.

Not every company can build its entire value proposition around social issues as Whole Foods does, but adding a social dimension to the value proposition offers a new frontier in competitive positioning....

The Moral Purpose of Business

...Corporations are not responsible for all the world's problems, nor do they have the resources to solve them all. Each company can identify the particular set of societal problems that it is best equipped to help resolve and from which it can gain the greatest competitive benefit. Addressing social issues by creating shared value will lead to self-sustaining solutions that do not depend on private or government subsidies. When a well-run business applies its vast resources, expertise, and management talent to problems that it understands and in which it has a stake, it can have a greater impact on social good than any other institution or philanthropic organization.

QUESTIONS

1. How do Porter and Kramer support the claim that business and society are interdependent?

2. According to the writers, how should a business begin to position itself in terms of strategic CSR?

3. Porter and Kramer write: "For any company, strategy must go beyond best practices. It is about choosing a unique position—doing things differently from competitors in a way that lowers costs or better serves a particular set of customer needs." What does this mean with regard to strategy for CSR?

4. Reconsider IBM's decision to offshore jobs to India in light of Porter and Kramer's arguments. Has IBM acted in a socially responsible way? How might IBM alter its strategic plan for social responsibility?

5. When immigration reform re-appeared on the nation's legislative agenda in 2007, Bill Gates and other leaders in the high tech field entered the debate, advocating changes in the law to make it easier for highly skilled software engineers to gain legal entry to the United States. How would Porter and Kramer characterize their lobbying for changes in the law?

6. Whole Foods Company is touted in this article as a prime example of integrated strategic CSR. John Mackey, CEO of Whole Foods, was in the news in July 2007 for very different reasons: He was accused of an ethical breach as a blogger, using the name Rahodeb.

Internet Assignment: Find out what Mackey was doing. Is the firm's CSR reputation intact?

CHAPTER **PROBLEMS**

1. Analyze this scenario from the standpoint of law, and of ethics: For years, Dr. Eddingfield, a licensed physician, had been the Hurley family doctor. When Hurley became dangerously ill, he sent a messenger to Dr. Eddingfield, who told him of Hurley's violent sickness, explained that no other doctor was available, and offered to pay Eddingfield's fee for services. At the time, none of his other patients needed attention, so Dr. Eddingfield was free to help the sick man, but he chose not to do so. Mr. Hurley died.

2. Internet Assignment:

   a. Although in the United States there is no general "duty to rescue," other countries do have such requirements. In France, Germany, and Russia, for example, bystanders may not legally ignore a fellow citizen who needs help in an emergency. What can you find about laws that require rescue in other parts of the world?

   b. Several states in the United States, including Wisconsin, Vermont, and Minnesota, also have such legislation. Many states require certain persons to report specific kinds of crimes, most often child abuse. Find and compare two state statutes.

   c. While rescue is not required in the United States, it is encouraged by the existence in every state of "Good Samaritan" laws, protecting people who assist in an emergency from liability in most circumstances. Locate the Good Samaritan law in your home state. Describe it in your own words. Does it protect those who do not have medical training?

3. In late 2004, after some ten years of taking tax breaks and union concessions, Maytag closed its refrigerator manufacturing plant in Galesburg, Illinois (population 33,000) and relocated it to Mexico. The company had received more than $10 million from the town and the state. Galesburg District Attorney Paul Mangieri wanted to sue the firm to reclaim tax money that the town would have spent on its schools: "We gave Maytag these incentives and they accepted them. We did it on faith and trust." Yet other locals believed such a strategy would backfire, driving away other potential business interests. "Maytag's leaving town

has devastated our community," car dealer Jeff Klinck pointed out, "But I don't think any good comes from revenge. We want to move forward, not back."

Internet Assignment: A final decision as to whether to sue Maytag was made in November 2004. What happened? Find out if any other communities in the United States went to court to catch up with corporations which had benefited from tax abatements but ended up closing down operations for more cost-efficient locations. See: *Township of Ypsilanti v. General Motors*, 1993 Wl 132385 (Michigan Cir. Ct.) and *Ypsilanti v. GM*, 506 N.W.2d 556 (Michigan Court of Appeals, 1993).

4. In mid-2004, a carpenter from Durham, North Carolina, found out that his potentially fatal heart condition required surgery that would cost $200,000. As one of the 45 million uninsured American citizens, he could not afford it. So he outsourced the job to India, flying to Delhi for a heart valve replacement that would cost only $10,000, including airfare and a side trip to the Taj Mahal! Approximately 150,000 so called "medical tourists" traveled to India for similar reasons in 2004, a growing number from the United States. They are taking advantage of lower costs and quality services—everything from airport pickups to private hospital rooms to treatments that include yoga and other traditional forms of healing. Overall, India's health care system is poor, but there is an increasing number of private medical facilities there that provide services as good as or better than those in the developed world. For example, while the death rate for heart bypass at Escorts Heart Institute and Research Centre in Delhi was just 0.8 percent, the 1999 death rate for the same procedure at the New York hospital where former president Bill Clinton had bypass surgery was 2.35 percent.[27]

Internet Assignment: What can you find out about the trend to outsource high-end services like these? Is it on the up tick? Is it expanding to include other services which require advanced professional training?

5. As companies increasingly do business around the world, they often must decide how to behave in developing countries where the legal system may be more lax than that of their home base. Some believe in the principle, "When in Rome, do as the Romans do," justifying activities abroad that are illegal and unacceptable at home. Others argue that transnational companies must use their influence to nudge other businesses and nations towards higher standards, even attempting to make a difference in the way foreign governments handle human rights. In the 1980s many companies stopped doing business in South Africa, in an effort to pressure that government to end apartheid. In 1992 Levi Strauss withdrew operations from Burma, claiming, "It is not possible to do business [there] without directly supporting the military government and its pervasive violations of human rights." In 1994 Reebok and Liz Claiborne pulled out of Burma; in 1995 Eddie Bauer and Amoco also withdrew, citing growing opposition in the United States to company involvement there. Wal Mart, IKEA, Crate and Barrel, Jones New York, and (under pressure from activists) Ames Department Stores have promised to stop sourcing products from Myanmar (formerly Burma). In 1998, after many strikes and negative press reports, Nike announced plans to improve conditions in Indonesia. It offered education and business loans to workers' families, promised to improve air quality in its plants, bringing them in line with U.S. OSHA standards, agreed to open its plants to inspections, and raised wages by 40 percent. Rejected at a 1998 shareholders' meeting was a proposal that Nike spend about 2 percent of its yearly advertising budget to double the wages of its workers in Indonesia, which would have provided them with what critics claim is a living wage.

27 John Lancaster, "Surgeries, Side Trips for Medical Tourists," *Washington Post Foreign Service*, October 21, 2004.

Where should companies draw the line in their activities abroad? If they decide to go in the direction of challenging the moral climate, is that a form of "cultural imperialism"? How wide should they spread their net of rescue in these settings? Is it enough to raise their own employees' wages, or should they also be concerned with the behavior of their suppliers? Should they try to improve infrastructure (education, environment)? Should they try to influence government policies? What about boycotting products from an "outlaw" state?

6. Plato believed that the rulers of the ideal society should be paid no more than four times what the lowliest member of that society was paid. In the United States today, executives commonly earn many times more than ordinary employees do. In 1980, CEO compensation was estimated to be 42 times that of average employees; by 2005, it was 411 times. In 2006, the average CEO of a Standard and Poors 500 Company earned $14.78 million.

   And corporate leaders are often recompensed heftily even after leading their companies into disaster. In 2006, Henry McKinnell of Pfizer and Robert Nardelli of Home Depot departed from their respective companies with exit packages valued at more than $200 million. Under McKinnell's tenure as CEO, Pfizer stock dropped nearly 40 percent, while McKinnell earned $60 million in salary and other compensation. Nardelli received more than $240 million in compensation over the six years he headed Home Depot, while company stock fell 8 percent.

   Business reporter Cassidy traces the use of stock options as a form of executive compensation back to the "stockholder value credo," the notion that CEOs should act as agents for shareholders, and that a smart way to make them keep shareholders' best interests in focus would be to tie their financial rewards to their firm's stock performance. Stock options, granting the right to buy stock in the company at a certain price at a certain future date, became increasingly popular between 1980, when they were given to fewer than one-third of the CEOs of publicly traded companies, and 1997, when 92 of the top 200 CEOs received options with an average value of $31 million.[28] Suddenly these executives had very big incentives to drive stock prices up—at least temporarily, so they could realize enormous profits. The cascade of corporate scandals that included Enron was, experts now agree, at least in part caused by greedy senior executives who wanted to get the numbers up by any means necessary.

   Analyze stock options and executive compensation with the ethical toolkit. How would Milton Friedman want to recompense corporate executives? How would a utilitarian? A deontological thinker? What would a virtue ethicist have to say about executive compensation? What would be the response of the ethic of care?

7. In 2004, M.J. Furman, owner of 1,600 shares of Wal-Mart stock, demanded that Wal-Mart's board of directors sue certain members of the board and senior officers for breaching their fiduciary duty, recklessly mismanaging the company by authorizing and encouraging labor practices that systematically violated federal civil rights, employment, and labor laws. As a result, she claimed, Wal-Mart suffered lawsuits, market losses, loss of goodwill, and a deteriorating public image, causing its stock to underperform compared to competitors. When the board declined to bring suit—holding a final decision until the outcome of a pending discrimination suit (the largest in U.S. history)—Furman filed a shareholder derivative suit.

   Internet Assignment: The case was decided in California in 2007. Find out what happened.

8. Commerce Bank was founded in New Jersey with a single location in 1971. Its founder, chairman and CEO, Vernon W. Hill II was a real estate developer, whose wife owned an interior decorating business. By 2007, it had 450 branches from New York City to

28 www.aflcio.org/corporatewatch/paywatch/pay/index.cfm. John Cassidy, "The Greed Cycle," *The New Yorker*, 64, September 23, 2002.

Washington D.C., open 7 days a week. With branches springing up like Burger Kings, Commerce Bank became the fastest growing bank in America. Mr. Hill was in all things entrepreneurial. He persuaded his board of directors to pay millions in rent for buildings owned by his family and over $50 million to Mrs. Hill for her decorating services. In June 2007, in the face of numerous federal investigations, and at the insistence of his board of directors, Mr. Hill resigned all of his posts at Commerce Bank. His severance package has been estimated at $17 million, however, and his Commerce Bankcorp shares, when he stepped down, were worth $225 million. What corporate responsibilities were violated in this scenario? Who are the stakeholders? What can any of them do?

9. As practices surrounding the timing of options grants for public companies came under increased scrutiny in early 2006, Merrill Lynch analyzed the timing of stock option grants from 1997 to 2002 for the semiconductor and semiconductor equipment companies that comprise the Philadelphia Semiconductor Index. It revealed that backdated options—a common practice before Sarbanes-Oxley was implemented in 2002—often yielded higher returns, a result that spawned numbers of shareholder derivative suits. By 2007, the Securities and Exchange Commission (SEC) was investigating more than 160 companies involved in stock options backdating.

   Internet Assignment: Read any one of those suits and find out if the shareholders won. If not, why not?

10. In a part of the reading not included in this chapter, Porter and Kramer offer this example of strategic CSR so well integrated with business operations it is not possible to distinguish day-to-day operations from social impact:

   Nestlé…works directly with small farmers in developing countries to source the basic commodities, such as milk, coffee, and cocoa, on which much of its global business depends. The company's investment in local infrastructure and its transfer of world-class knowledge and technology over decades has produced enormous social benefits through improved health care, better education, and economic development, while giving Nestlé direct and reliable access to the commodities it needs to maintain a profitable global business.

   Internet Assignment: Find another company—not mentioned in the article above—that has accomplished this degree of CSR integration. What are its inside-out and outside-in linkages?

CHAPTER **PROJECT**

The Social Responsibility Report[29]

The objective of this project is to expand your understanding of social responsibility for corporations. This is a topic that continues to generate considerable controversy—from free market theorists who believe that corporations violate their duty to shareholders when they engage in

---

29 This project was developed by Professor Ronnie Cohen of Christopher-Newport University and is reprinted with her permission.

activities that are not directly related to increasing shareholder wealth, to reformers who believe that the enormity of corporate power comes with a corresponding responsibility to use that power in ways that benefit society as a whole, in addition to serving the interests of shareholders. Is corporate social responsibility a desirable and/or an attainable goal?

Two important and very readable books on the subject of corporate social responsibility are Paul Hawken's, *The Ecology of Commerce*, and Ray Anderson's, *Midcourse Correction*. The first book sets out a vision of sustainable commerce, giving many examples—some practical, some theoretical; in the second the CEO of the world's largest carpet manufacturer describes his company's effort to build sustainable practices into every aspect of the value chain. If there is another book on the subject that interests you, your instructor may want to consider it as a possible additional choice.

The assignment requires you to read one of the two books to gain an understanding of what a socially responsible corporation might do that is different from how the majority of corporations currently operate. You are also required to look at a publicly held company's performance on specific social responsibility criteria. Finally, you need to reach a conclusion about how the current legal environment could accommodate a social responsibility requirement for publicly held corporations and give your opinion about whether you believe this is a goal worth seeking.

Specific components of the assignment are:

Section One: Read one of the two books. Explain what social responsibility means to the author. How does he believe it relates to the current model of corporate accountability as structured through the legal system? Use the material in this chapter and additional readings at the end of this assignment to give you some background for this analysis. This section should be two to three pages long.

Section Two: Once you have read your chosen book, go to http://www.vhcoaudit.com/ SRAarticles/responsibilityaudits.htm. This is the Web site for Vasin, Heyn & Co, Accountants, a company that performs social responsibility audits. Choose any two of the audit programs listed (community development, diversity, employee relations, environmental, international relationships, marketplace practices, fiscal responsibility, or accountability). Select a publicly traded company and obtain a copy of their most recent annual report. Using the report and other publicly available information, evaluate the company's performance in light of the standards for those two audit programs. Depending on the complexity of your company's activities, this section should be from three to five pages long. Be specific with examples of how the company does or does not meet the criteria. Don't just rely on company-generated information. Look at other sources that are likely to be more objective in their assessments. Try to verify all company claims by doing an Internet search. At a minimum, your examples should be based on at least two outside sources in addition to whatever company generated information you use. If you choose a local company, you may be able to interview key corporate officials for additional sources. Following the samples provided, give your opinion—qualified or unqualified—regarding the audit.

Section Three: Considering the perspective of the author of the book you read, and the practical observations about the company you audited, what changes would have to be made in corporation law in the areas of governance, fiduciary duty, organizational structure, and liability of officers and directors, in order to legally enforce a social responsibility requirement on publicly held corporations? Some ideas about corporate governance are included in the suggested readings on the next page. This section should be one to two pages long.

Section Four: Finally, give your opinion about whether you think imposing such a requirement is warranted, productive, and/or desirable. This section should be between one to two pages long.

Additional Readings

Andrew Savitz and Karl Weber. *The Triple Bottom Line: How Today's Best-Run Companies Are Achieving Economic, Social, and Environmental Success—and How You Can Too* (Jossey-Bass, 2006).

From the Corporate Governance Web Site

Browse these sites for other relevant info:

    http://www.corpgov.net/library/definitions.html
    http://www.corpgov.net/forums/commentary/entine1.html
    http://www.corpgov.net/forums/commentary/Four%20Ideas.html

2 THE DUTY OF LOYALTY
Whistleblowing

The woods were filled with smart people at Enron, but there were really no wise people, or people who could say "this is enough."

— JOHN OLSON, ENERGY INDUSTRY ANALYST

What matters ... is not what a person is, but how closely his many personae mesh with the organizational ideal; not his willingness to stand by his actions, but his agility in avoiding blame; not what he stands for, but whom he stands with in the labyrinths of his organization.

— ROBERT JACKALL, MORAL MAZES: BUREAUCRACY AND MANAGERIAL WORK

●

This chapter is about people who feel morally driven to call attention to problems they see at work, at the risk of disturbing the status quo, alienating others, and bringing damaging repercussions upon themselves and their families. It is about being caught between conflicting loyalties—to one's employer, and to one's conscience—the dilemma faced by a person who must decide whether to become a "whistleblower."

Whistleblowers are people who decide to report unethical or illegal activities under the control of their employers. They may be working for private companies, nonprofit organizations, or for the government. They may disclose information inside or outside their organizations—to supervisors, regulators, or to the media. What unites all whistleblowing is the urge to bring a disturbing situation to light, the urge to bring about some corrective change. The motivating issues range from airline, nuclear, and environmental safety to the kinds of improper accounting practices that brought down Enron and WorldCom.

This chapter explains the legal doctrine known as **employment-at-will**, which gives employers broad discretion to fire employees "for a good reason, a bad reason, or no reason at all." Although twentieth-century exceptions to this rule have blunted its harshness, the cases demonstrate that whistleblowers often experience retaliation and have little recourse under the common law. Statutes passed in all 50 states provide some protection for employees, but wide variation exists among them; we will look at one of them. We turn to the Sarbanes-Oxley Act, passed in 2002 in the wake of financial and accounting scandals, to assess the degree to which it protects corporate whistleblowers. And we consider how First Amendment freedom of speech has been interpreted by the Supreme Court to give public employees limited rights to blow the whistle.

Finally, widening our enquiry to a global perspective, we ask whether multinational corporations with clear and appropriate reporting procedures might positively impact the societies in which they do business abroad.

Whistleblowing can wreak havoc. Those who insist that bad news must be heard may damage the reputations of their employers; they risk having their own careers destroyed. In this chapter we see that in spite of the costs, we may yet appreciate the role of the dissenters in serving the public interest when the checkpoints of our systems fail us.

*****

In 1993, Dr. Donn Milton was hired by a nonprofit scientific research organization, IIT Research Institute (IITRI), to oversee a contract with the federal government. By 1995, his responsibilities widened as he was promoted to vice president of IITRI's Advanced Technology Group. Like other nonprofits, IITRI had been established with a public mission and was classified as tax exempt. As Dr. Milton discovered, however, the organization was "abusing its tax-exempt status by failing to report … taxable income generated by the substantial portion of … business that did not constitute scientific research in the public interest."

DONN MILTON, DR., v. IIT RESEARCH INSTITUTE
Fourth Circuit Court of Appeals, 1998
138 F.3d 519

WILKINSON, Chief Judge. ☀

Milton voiced his concerns to IITRI management, to no avail. In 1995, after similar allegations by a competitor, IITRI initiated an internal examination of the issue. In connection with this inquiry, IITRI received an outside opinion letter concluding that the IRS could well deem some of IITRI's projects unrelated business activities and that the income from these activities was likely taxable. Milton urged the President of IITRI, John Scott, to take action in response to the letter, but Scott refused. Milton raised the issue with IITRI's Treasurer, who agreed that IITRI was improperly claiming unrelated business income as exempt income and promised to remedy the problem after Scott's then-imminent retirement. However, this retirement did not come to pass. Finally, in November 1996, when Scott falsely indicated to IITRI's board of governors that IITRI had no problem with unrelated business income, Milton reported the falsity of these statements to Lew Collens, Chairman of the Board of IITRI, and informed Collens of the opinion letter.

On January 1, 1997, Scott called Milton at home and informed him that he had been relieved of his Group Vice President title and demoted to his previous position as supervisor of TSMI. On February 12, 1997, Milton's attorney contacted IITRI about the demotion, alleging that it was unlawful retaliation for informing management of IITRI's unlawful practices. Two days later … Milton received a letter from Collens terminating his employment with IITRI.

[The general legal rule is that employees can be fired with or without cause, but there is an exception: Under the tort of "wrongful discharge," an employee can argue that the firing clearly conflicts with "public policy."]

Milton filed suit against IITRI … for wrongful discharge….

Maryland has recognized a "narrow exception" to the general rule of at-will employment: "discharge may not contravene a clear mandate of public policy." Maryland courts have found such a mandate only in limited circumstances: (1) "where an employee has been fired for refusing to violate the law …"and (2) "where [an] employee has been terminated for exercising a specific legal right or duty…."

Milton makes no claim that he was asked to break the law. He had no role in preparing IITRI's submissions to the IRS and no responsibility for their content. Instead, Milton claims he was fired for fulfilling his fiduciary duty as a corporate officer to inform IITRI's Board of activities injurious to the corporation's long-term interests….

Maryland law does provide a wrongful discharge cause of action for employees who are terminated because they perform their "statutorily prescribed duty." However, this exception to the norm of at-will employment has been construed narrowly by the Maryland courts and is not available in Milton's case…. [I]n *Thompson v. Memorial Hospital*, the … court … held that, because a hospital employee was not chargeable with the hospital's regulatory duty to report misadministration of radiation, he did not state a claim for wrongful discharge when he was fired for making such a report. By contrast, in *Bleich v. Florence Crittenden Services* (1993), the court recognized that an educator terminated for filing a report of child abuse and neglect, as she was explicitly required to do by Maryland law, did state a claim for wrongful discharge. These cases indicate that, for Milton to recover, it is not enough that *someone* at IITRI was responsible for correcting its tax filings or that the corporation may have been liable for tax fraud. This responsibility was never Milton's, nor did he face any potential liability for failing to discharge it, so his claim fails.

Milton argues that his fiduciary obligations as an officer of IITRI supply the legal duty that was missing in *Thompson* and that supported the cause of action in *Bleich*. But in fact Milton labored under no "specific legal duty," to report IITRI's tax fraud to the Board. He points to no statute or other legal source that imposes on him a specific duty to report, and the broad fiduciary obligations of "care and loyalty" he alleges are simply too general to qualify as a specific legal duty that will support the claim that his discharge violates a "clear mandate of public policy." Recognizing whistle-blower protection for every corporate officer fired in the wake of a disagreement over an employer's business practices would transform this "narrow exception" into a broad one indeed.

This search for a specific legal duty is no mere formality. Rather it limits judicial forays into the wilderness of discerning "public policy" without clear direction from a legislative or regulatory source.

[Judgment of dismissal affirmed.]

QUESTIONS

1. In legal terms, why did Milton lose?

2. The court here expresses concern that, if Dr. Milton were permitted to win, it would open a "Pandora's box," with "every corporate officer fired in the wake of a disagreement over an employer's business practices" a potential successful plaintiff. Reframe this argument. What is at stake here for employers?

3. This case is about conflicting loyalties. Make a list of the stakeholders (those primarily affected by the situation). Now describe the various links of loyalty—who felt responsible to whom? Analyze the situation using the ethical theories and the information about corporate governance in Chapter 1. Did Milton do the right thing?

4. Should it make any difference how the whistle is blown—internally or externally? Dr. Milton tried to discuss his concerns inside his organization with the president, the treasurer, and eventually with the board of directors. Former Enron executive Maureen Casteneda gave an interview to ABC News in late January 2002, in which she described ongoing, large-scale document shredding at the company. When might it be ethically appropriate to blow the whistle (a) internally; (b) to the enforcing authorities, such as SEC regulators; and (c) to the media?

Employment-at-Will

The right of an employee to quit the services of the employer, for whatever reason, is the same as the right of the employer, for whatever reason, to dispense with the services of such employee.

— JUSTICE HARLAN IN *ADAIR V. U.S.*, 208 U.S. 161 (1908).

The Law, in its majestic equality, forbids the rich, as well as the poor, to sleep under the bridges, to beg in the streets, and to steal bread.

— ANATOLE FRANCE

Employment-at-will is a legal rule that developed in the nineteenth century, giving employers unfettered power to "dismiss their employees at will for good cause, for no cause, or even for cause morally wrong, without being thereby guilty of a legal wrong."[1] The economic philosophy of laissez-faire provided theoretical support for employment-at-will. Its legal underpinnings consisted mainly of "freedom of contract," the idea that individuals are free to choose how to dispose of what they own, including their labor, as they see fit, and that the voluntary contractual promises they make are legitimately enforceable.

Exceptions to the Rule

The earliest adjustments to the doctrine of employment-at-will were made as workers fought for the right to organize and form unions. In 1935, they were guaranteed these rights, and not long after, the U.S. Supreme Court announced that an employer could not use employment-at-will as a means of "intimidat[ing] or coerc[ing] its employees with respect to their self organization."[2] In other words, employees could not be fired as punishment for attempting to organize themselves into unions. Although at this writing only a fairly narrow slice of the U.S. workforce is unionized,[3] collective bargaining agreements typically cut against employment-at-will, protecting workers from being fired except for "good cause."

Beginning in the 1960s, federal civil rights laws created remedies against employers who fire workers because of their race, national origin, color, religion, sex, age, or disability.[4] In the 1970s and 1980s, federal and state statutes included protection from retaliation for employees who report violations of environmental or workplace safety laws, for example.[5] And in 2002 Congress passed corporate fraud reform legislation with whistleblower provisions protecting those who report financial misconduct in publicly traded companies. This law is known as Sarbanes-Oxley, or SOX.

1 *Payne v. Webster & Atlantic R.R. Co.*, 81 Tenn. 507, 519–20 (1884).
2 *NLRB v. Jones & Laughlin Steel Corp.*, 301 U.S. 1, 45–46 (1937).
3 According to the Bureau of Labor Statistics, for the past 20 years, union membership in the United States has been declining steadily. In 2006, only 12 percent of the U.S. workforce was unionized. http://www.bls.gov/news.release/union2.nr0.htm
4 For example, *Civil Rights Act of 1964*, 42 U.S.C. Sec. 2000e-2a (1976); *Age Discrimination in Employment Act of 1967*, 29 U.S.C. Sec. 623(a) (1976); *Americans with Disabilities Act*, 42 U.S.C. Sec. 12112(b)(5)(A). Civil rights laws are discussed more fully in Chapter 4. Most states have similar laws, and some of these go further than the federal statutes, protecting employees against discrimination on the basis of family status or sexual orientation, for example.
5 Federal laws include the *Toxic Substances Control Act*, 15 U.S.C. Sec. 2622(a) (1988); *Occupational Safety and Health Act*, Sec. 660(c)(1) (1988); *Water Pollution Control Act*, 33 U.S.C. Sec. 1367(a) (1988); *Safe Drinking Water Act*, 42 U.S.C.A. Sec. 300j-9(i)(1); *Energy Reorganization Act*, 42 U.S.C. Sec. 5851(a)(3) (1982); *Solid Waste Disposal Act*, 42 U.S.C. Sec. 6971(a) (1982); *Comprehensive Environmental Response, Compensation, and Liability Act*, Sec. 9961O(a); *Clean Air Act* Sec. 7622(a).

The common law, too, has evolved to create exceptions to the employment-at-will rule. In some states, courts have set limits by means of contract law. There are two main approaches: (1) to imply a promise of "good faith and fair dealing" in the contract of employment, or (2) to imply contractual terms (not to dismiss except for good cause, for instance) from an employer's handbook, policy statement, or behavior. However, fewer than a dozen states use the first approach. And, although the second approach has been recognized by most states, employers are on notice, and unlikely to make any express or implied promises that might be interpreted to cut against employment-at-will. In fact, they are more likely to promise the reverse, as in the following paragraph, recommended for inclusion in employment handbooks for law firms:

> *Your employment with the Firm is voluntarily entered into and you are free to resign at any time. Similarly, the Firm is free to conclude an employment relationship with you where it believes it is in the Firm's best interest at any time. It should be recognized that neither you, nor we, have entered into any contract of employment, express or implied. Our relationship is and will be always one of voluntary employment "at will."* [6]

Tort law has also made inroads into employment-at-will, offering a plaintiff the chance to convince a jury to award substantial money damages. For almost four decades, most U.S. state courts have been shaping the tort of "wrongful discharge," a firing that contradicts "public policy"—in other words, a dismissal that undermines what is beneficial to society in general.

The problem has been how to define public policy.[7] As with contract law, this exception to employment-at-will developed simultaneously in different states, producing a crazy quilt of different rules. Most state courts are comfortable looking to the legislature—to laws that have already been passed—for guidance. For instance, they will protect from retaliation employees who have simply exercised their legal rights to file a worker's compensation or a sexual harassment claim,[8] or who have merely performed their legal duty to serve on a jury.[9] And, if employers put their employees "between a rock and a hard place," expecting them to participate in breaking the law or be fired, most courts would again see a violation of public policy, triggering the tort of wrongful discharge.[10] For example, suppose you were an employee of Arthur Andersen, and your supervisor told you to delete computer files related to the government investigation of Enron. Once the SEC subpoenas were issued, destroying those files would amount to obstruction of justice. So, if you refused to destroy them and were fired for that, you would succeed in a suit for wrongful discharge.

But some states still do not recognize the tort at all. In New York, for instance, while an employer could be fined for refusing to allow an employee time for jury service, the employee could not then sue for wrongful discharge.[11] As we have seen, other jurisdictions, such as Maryland, are conservative in identifying violations of public policy.

Inconsistencies like these complicate the risk for whistleblowers. They have noticed a situation at work that troubles them. It may be illegal; it may be "merely" unethical; it may be one they are expected to participate in; it may be one they are expected to ignore; it may involve a

---

6 Victor Schachter, "The Promise of Partnership," *National Law Journal*, October 8, 1984, p. 15.

7 Public policy is generally understood to mean that which benefits society as a whole. But this is a fuzzy concept indeed and very likely to mirror the personal and political beliefs of individual judges. As one commentator put it, "Public policy is the unruly horse of the law."

8 *Frampton v. Central Indiana Gas Co.*, 297 N.E.2d 425 (Indiana 1973). Plaintiff fired for filing a worker's compensation claim.

9 *Reuther v. Fowler & Williams*, 386 A.2d 119 (Pa. 1978). Plaintiff fired for jury service.

10 For example, in *Petermann v. Int'l. Brotherhood of Teamsters*, 344 P.2d 25 (1969), plaintiff was instructed by his employer to lie when testifying before a legislative investigatory committee. He refused and was fired. The court allowed his suit for wrongful discharge, describing public policy as "that principle of law which holds that no citizen can lawfully do that which has a tendency to be injurious to the public or against the public good." *Id.* at 27.

11 *Di Blasi v. Traffax Traffic Network*, 681 N.Y.S.2d 147 (N.Y. App. Div 1998).

2005 Ethics Resource Center Survey

ERC's survey of more than 3,000 employees shows that, although more employers have implemented ethics training, the rate of observed misconduct is rising, whereas the rate at which employees are reporting misconduct is dropping.

The Ethics Resource Center found that more than half of American employees have observed at least one kind of ethical wrongdoing at work, a slight increase from 2003.

Types of misconduct	Employees observing it
Abusive or intimidating behavior toward employees	21%
Lying to employees, customers, vendors, or the public	19%
Putting employee interests over organizational interests	18%
Violations of safety regulations	16%
Misreporting of actual time worked	16%
Discrimination	12%
Stealing	11%
Sexual harassment	9%

But employee reporting of observed misconduct decreased since the last time the ERC did this survey in 2003—by 10 percent.

Across the board, survey results showed increases in almost every factor considered key for effective formal ethics programs: written codes, training, ethics advice mechanisms, anonymous reporting mechanisms, and disciplining of employees who violate standards. (The only factor not on the increase: tying performance evaluation to ethical conduct.)

Most significantly, the ERC survey results showed that corporate culture has a much greater effect on rates of both wrongdoing and reporting of wrongdoing than formal ethics training. Workers in organizations with a weak ethical culture reported much greater levels of observed misconduct (70%) than workers in organizations where a strong ethical cultures existed (34%). And reporting rates also were very different: Weak ethical cultures produced a reporting rate of 48 percent while people working within strong ethical cultures reported misconduct 79 percent of the time.

statute that carries protection for whistleblowers; it may not. Whistleblowers react first and must worry about the reach of "public policy" later. Characteristically unable to remain passive in the face of what they believe is wrong, they speak out. Research reveals that whistleblowers are typically long-term, highly loyal employees who feel strongly that their companies should do the right thing, and who tend to disclose to outsiders only after trying to make headway internally.[12] The whistleblower profile is such that, if nothing is done to respond to their internal complaints, they often feel compelled to disclose to authorities outside the company—even to the media. In any case, they are taking the chance that they will not be covered under the wrongful discharge exception to employment-at-will. As one commentator put it,

---

12 Marlene Winfield, "Whistleblowers as Corporate Safety Net," in *Whistleblowing: Subversion or Corporate Citizenship?* 21, 22 (New York: St. Martin's Press: 1994).

effectively, those who blow the whistle "very often must choose between silence and driving over a cliff."[13]

Conflicting Loyalties: Whistleblowing and Professional Ethics

> THE MAYOR: *We shall expect you, on further investigation, to come to the conclusion that the situation is not nearly as pressing or as dangerous as you had at first imagined.*
>
> DR. STOCKMANN: *Oh! You expect that of me, do you?*
>
> THE MAYOR: *Furthermore we will expect you to make a public statement expressing your faith in the management's integrity and in their intention to take thorough and conscientious steps to remedy any possible defects.*
>
> DR. STOCKMANN: *But that's out of the question, Peter. No amount of patching or tinkering can put this matter right; I tell you I* know! *It is my firm and unalterable conviction—*
>
> THE MAYOR: *As a member of the staff you have no right to personal convictions.*
>
> DR. STOCKMANN: *(With a start) No right to—?*
>
> THE MAYOR: *Not as a member of the staff—no! As a private individual—that's of course another matter. But as a subordinate in the employ of the Baths you have no right to openly express convictions opposed to those of your superiors.*
>
> DR. STOCKMANN: *This is too much! Do you mean to tell me that as a doctor—a scientific man—I have no right to—!*
>
> THE MAYOR: *But this is not purely a scientific matter; there are other questions involved—technical and economic questions.*
>
> DR. STOCKMANN: *To hell with all that! I insist that I am free to speak my mind on any and all questions!*[14]

In the next case, the plaintiff is a doctor caught in a conflict between what her employer expects her to do, and what she feels is in line with her professional ethical responsibilities.

PIERCE v. ORTHO PHARMACEUTICAL CORP.

Supreme Court of New Jersey, 1980

417 A.2d 505

POLLOCK, J. ✳

This case presents the question whether an employee-at-will has a cause of action against her employer to recover damages for the termination of her employment following her refusal to continue a project she viewed as medically unethical....

Ortho specializes in the development and manufacture of therapeutic and reproductive drugs. Dr. Pierce is a medical doctor who was first employed by Ortho in 1971 as an Associate Director of Medical Research. She signed no contract except a secrecy agreement, and her employment was not for a fixed term. She was an employee-at-will. In 1973, she became the

---

13 Joseph Henkert, "Management's Hat Trick: Misuse of 'Engineering Judgment' in the Challenger Incident," 10 *J. Bus. Ethics* 617, 619 (1991).

14 Henrik Ibsen, *An Enemy of the People.*

Director of Medical Research/Therapeutics, one of three major sections of the Medical Research Department. Her primary responsibilities were to oversee development of therapeutic drugs and to establish procedures for testing those drugs for safety, effectiveness, and marketability. Her immediate supervisor was Dr. Samuel Pasquale, Executive Medical Director.

In the spring of 1975, Dr. Pierce was the only medical doctor on a project team developing loperamide, a liquid drug for treatment of diarrhea in infants, children, and elderly persons. The proposed formulation contained saccharin. Although the concentration was consistent with the formula for loperamide marketed in Europe, the project team agreed that the formula was unsuitable for use in the United States.[15] An alternative formulation containing less saccharin might have been developed within approximately three months.

By March 28, however, the project team, except for Dr. Pierce, decided to continue with the development of loperamide. That decision was made apparently in response to a directive from the Marketing Division of Ortho. This decision meant that Ortho would file an investigational new drug application (IND) with the Federal Food and Drug Administration (FDA), continuing laboratory studies on loperamide, and begin work on a formulation....

Dr. Pierce ... continued to oppose the work being done on loperamide at Ortho. On April 21, 1975, she sent a memorandum to the project team expressing her disagreement with its decision to proceed.... In her opinion, there was no justification for seeking FDA permission to use the drug in light of medical controversy over the safety of saccharin.

Dr. Pierce met with Dr. Pasquale on May 9 and informed him that she disagreed with the decision to file an IND with the FDA.... She concluded that the risk that saccharin might be harmful should preclude testing the formula on children or elderly persons, especially when an alternative formulation might soon be available....

After their meeting on May 9, Dr. Pasquale informed Dr. Pierce that she would no longer be assigned to the loperamide project. On May 14, Dr. Pasquale asked Dr. Pierce to choose other projects.... She felt she was being demoted, even though her salary would not be decreased. Dr. Pierce [submitted a] letter of resignation.... [This is called "constructive discharge," the legal equivalent of being fired.]

Dr. Pierce claimed damages for the termination of her employment. Her complaint alleged: "The Defendant, its agents, servants and employees requested and demanded Plaintiff follow a course of action and behavior which was impossible for Plaintiff to follow because of the Hippocratic oath she had taken, because of the ethical standards by which she was governed as a physician, and because of the regulatory schemes, both federal and state, statutory and case law, for the protection of the public in the field of health and human well-being, which schemes Plaintiff believed she should honor...."

Under the common law, in the absence of an employment contract, employers or employees have been free to terminate the employment relationship with or without cause....

Commentators have questioned the compatibility of the traditional at-will doctrine with the realities of modern economics and employment practices.... The common law rule has been modified by the enactment of labor relations legislation [prohibiting employers from firing workers because they organize or join a union]....

Recently [many] states have recognized a common law cause of action for employees-at-will who were discharged for reasons that were in some way "wrongful." The courts in those jurisdictions have taken varied approaches, some recognizing the action in tort, some in contract. Nearly all jurisdictions link the success of the wrongful discharged employee's action to proof that the discharge violated public policy....

15 The group's toxicologist, for instance, noted that saccharin was a "slow carcinogen"; it had produced benign and malignant tumors in test animals after 17 years. The harm it might cause would be obvious only after a long period of time, and "any intentional exposure of any segment of the human population to a potential carcinogen is not in the best interest of public health of the Ortho Pharmaceutical Corporation."

In recognizing a cause of action to provide a remedy for employees who are wrongfully discharged, we must balance the interests of the employee, the employer, and the public. Employees have an interest in knowing they will not be discharged for exercising their legal rights. Employers have an interest in knowing they can run their businesses as they see fit as long as their conduct is consistent with public policy. The public has an interest in employment stability and in discouraging frivolous lawsuits by dissatisfied employees.

Although the contours of an exception are important to all employees-at-will, this case focuses on the special considerations arising out of the right to fire an employee-at-will who is a member of a recognized profession. One writer has described the predicament that may confront a professional employed by a large corporation: Consider, for example, the plight of an engineer who is told that he will lose his job unless he falsifies his data or conclusions, or unless he approves a product which does not conform to specifications or meet minimum standards … and the predicament of an accountant who is told to falsify his employer's profit and loss statement in order to enable the employer to obtain credit.

Employees who are professionals owe a special duty to abide not only by federal and state law, but also by the recognized codes of ethics of their professions. That duty may oblige them to decline to perform acts required by their employers. However, an employee should not have the right to prevent his or her employer from pursuing its business because the employee perceives that a particular business decision violates the employee's personal morals, as distinguished from the recognized code of ethics of the employee's profession.

We hold that an employee has a cause of action for wrongful discharge when the discharge is contrary to a clear mandate of public policy. The sources of public policy include legislation; administrative rules, regulations or decisions; and judicial decisions. In certain instances, a professional code of ethics may contain an expression of public policy. However, not all such sources express a clear mandate of public policy. For example, a code of ethics designed to serve only the interests of a profession or an administrative regulation concerned with technical matters probably would not be sufficient. Absent legislation, the judiciary must define the cause of action in case-by-case determinations.… [U]nless an employee-at-will identifies a specific expression of public policy, he may be discharged with or without cause.

[B]efore loperamide could be tested on humans, an IND had to be submitted to the FDA to obtain approval for such testing. The IND must contain complete manufacturing specifications, details of pre-clinical studies [testing on animals] which demonstrate the safe use of the drug, and a description of proposed clinical studies. The FDA then has 30 days to withhold approval of testing. Since no IND had been filed here, and even giving Dr. Pierce the benefit of all doubt regarding her allegations, it is clear that clinical testing of loperamide on humans was not imminent.

Dr. Pierce argues that by continuing to perform research on loperamide she would have been forced to violate professional medical ethics expressed in the Hippocratic oath. She cites the part of the oath that reads: "I will prescribe regimen for the good of my patients according to my ability and my judgment and never do harm to anyone." Clearly, the general language of the oath does not prohibit specifically research that does not involve tests on humans and that cannot lead to such tests without governmental approval.

We note that Dr. Pierce did not rely on or allege violation of any other standards, including the "codes of professional ethics" advanced by the dissent. Similarly, she did not allege that continuing her research would constitute an act of medical malpractice or violate any statute.…

The case would be far different if Ortho had filed the IND, the FDA had disapproved it, and Ortho insisted on testing the drug on humans.…

[I]mplicit in Dr. Pierce's position is the contention that Dr. Pasquale and Ortho were obliged to accept her opinion. Dr. Pierce contends, in effect, that Ortho should have stopped research on loperamide because of her opinion about the controversial nature of the drug.

Dr. Pierce espouses a doctrine that would lead to disorder in drug research.... Chaos would result if a single doctor engaged in research were allowed to determine, according to his or her individual conscience, whether a project should continue. An employee does not have a right to continued employment when he or she refuses to conduct research simply because it would contravene his or her personal morals. An employee-at-will who refuses to work for an employer in answer to a call of conscience should recognize that other employees and their employer might heed a different call. However, nothing in this opinion should be construed to restrict the right of an employee-at-will to refuse to work on a project that he or she believes is unethical....

Under these circumstances, we conclude that the Hippocratic oath does not contain a clear mandate of public policy that prevented Dr. Pierce from continuing her research on loperamide. To hold otherwise would seriously impair the ability of drug manufacturers to develop new drugs according to their best judgment.

The legislative and regulatory framework pertaining to drug development reflects a public policy that research involving testing on humans may proceed with FDA approval. The public has an interest in the development of drugs, subject to the approval of a responsible management and the FDA, to protect and promote the health of mankind....

[Appellate division judgment for the plaintiff is reversed and the case is remanded.]

PASHMAN, J. , dissenting. ✹

The majority's analysis recognizes that the ethical goals of professional conduct are of inestimable social value. By maintaining informed standards of conduct, licensed professions bring to the problems of their public responsibilities the same expertise that marks their calling. The integrity of codes of professional conduct that result from this regulation deserves judicial protection from undue economic pressure. Employers are a potential source of this pressure, for they can provide or withhold until today, at their whim, job security and the means of enhancing a professional's reputation. Thus, I completely agree with the majority's ruling that "an employee has a cause of action for wrongful discharge when the discharge is contrary to a clear mandate of public policy" as expressed in a "professional code of ethics."

The Court pronounces this rule for the first time today. One would think that it would therefore afford plaintiff an opportunity to seek relief within the confines of this newly announced cause of action. By ordering the grant of summary judgment for defendant, however, the majority apparently believes that such an opportunity would be an exercise in futility. I fail to see how the majority reaches this conclusion. There are a number of detailed, recognized codes of medical ethics that proscribe participation in clinical experimentation when a doctor perceives an unreasonable threat to human health. Any one of these codes could provide the "clear mandate of public policy" that the majority requires.

Three other points made by the majority require discussion.... The first is the majority's characterization of the effect of plaintiff's ethical position. It appears to believe that Dr. Pierce had the power to determine whether defendant's proposed development program would continue at all. This is not the case, nor is plaintiff claiming the right to halt defendant's developmental efforts. [P]laintiff claims only the right to her professional autonomy. She contends that she may not be discharged for expressing her view that the clinical program is unethical or for refusing to continue her participation in the project. She has done nothing else to impede continued development of defendant's proposal; moreover, it is undisputed that defendant was able to continue its program by reassigning personnel. Thus, the majority's view that granting doctors a right to be free from abusive discharges would confer on any one of them complete veto power over desirable drug development, is ill-conceived.

The second point concerns the role of governmental approval of the proposed experimental program. In apparent ignorance of the past failures of official regulation to safeguard against pharmaceutical horrors, the majority implies that the necessity for administrative approval for human testing eliminates the need for active, ethical professionals within the drug industry. But we do not know whether the United States Food and Drug Administration (FDA) would be aware of the safer alternative to the proposed drug when it would pass upon defendant's application for the more hazardous formula. The majority professes no such knowledge. We must therefore assume the FDA would have been left in ignorance. This highlights the need for ethically autonomous professionals within the pharmaceutical industry....

The final point to which I must respond is the majority's observation that plaintiff expressed her opposition prematurely, before the FDA had approved clinical experimentation. Essentially, the majority holds that a professional employee may not express a refusal to engage in illegal or clearly unethical conduct until his actual participation and the resulting harm is imminent. This principle grants little protection to the ethical autonomy of professionals that the majority proclaims. Would the majority have Dr. Pierce wait until the first infant was placed before her, ready to receive the first dose of a drug containing 44 times the concentration of saccharin permitted in 12 ounces of soda?

I respectfully dissent.

QUESTIONS

1. The *Pierce* majority announces a new "cause of action in New Jersey for wrongful discharge when the discharge is contrary to a clear mandate of public policy." Such a mandate, it goes on to say, could be found in a professional code of ethics, yet Dr. Pierce had failed to identify one in her complaint with enough specificity. How does the dissenting judge respond to this point?

2. What is the procedure for obtaining FDA approval of a new drug? Do you agree with the majority that when Dr. Pierce stopped working on the loperamide project, the risk to human test subjects was not "imminent"?

3. Surveying the interests at stake in the case, the *Pierce* majority states:

   [W]e must balance the interests of the employee, the employer, and the public. Employees have an interest in knowing they will not be discharged for exercising their legal rights. Employers have an interest in knowing they can run their businesses as they see fit as long as their conduct is consistent with public policy. The public has an interest in employment stability and in discouraging frivolous lawsuits by dissatisfied employees.

   Are there any important stakeholder interests not mentioned here?

4. The dissent mentions "past failures of official regulation to safeguard against pharmaceutical horrors." There have been more recent failures. Since 2000, the cholesterol-lowering Baycol caused muscle tissue breakdown, the diet drug Fen-Phen led to lung and heart disorders, antidepressants like Zoloft and Prozac caused some children to commit suicide, and the painkiller Vioxx was found to double the risk of heart attack. In each instance, there was evidence that the pharmaceutical firms had evidence suggesting serious problems with drugs that were in development or had already been brought to market. By the time Merck recalled Vioxx in late 2004, there were congressional hearings underway. A doctor in the FDA's Office of Drug Safety, David Graham, told Congress that Vioxx may have caused as many as 55,000 deaths. Graham charged his agency with being "incapable of protecting America" against dangerous drugs. A study led by Dr. Graham that looked at the cardiovascular risks of taking Vioxx was supposed to be published in a prestigious medical journal but was pulled at the last minute after Dr. Graham received a warning from his supervisor. FDA management then began a smear campaign, with anonymous claims that his study could reflect scientific misconduct, and that Graham "bullied" his staff.

Internet Assignment: Fearing his job was at risk, Graham sought help from the whistleblower support organization, the Government Accountability Project. Find out what happened.

5. The regulatory apparatus of our government depends on ethical behavior on the part of corporations. It depends on corporations to generate accurate data for agencies such as the FDA, the FAA, and the EPA to use in analyzing safety risks. The government's resources are limited; it cannot perform all the necessary tests itself, but must rely on companies to do their own tests, and to share all relevant results—particularly when those results point to safety problems. Business decisions to hold back adverse information from regulators can be both fatal and expensive. Consider the Bridgestone/Ford debacle of 2000. In the 1970s, the National Highway Traffic Safety Administration (NHTSA) collected safety data directly from a network of repair shops, but after the budget cuts of the 1980s, this agency began relying on data generated by industry. NHTSA also made reports of foreign car recalls voluntary. In 1999, both Bridgestone and Ford knew the Wilderness tire/Ford Explorer combo was dangerous; there had been dozens of tread separations and SUV rollover deaths abroad, particularly in hot climates. The two companies planned a recall in Saudi Arabia but then made a joint decision not to alert NHTSA, fearing this would lead to a recall in the United States. By late 2000, after SUV rollovers caused more than 100 fatalities in the United States, Bridgestone was forced to recall more than 6 million tires, and both companies faced countless lawsuits.

The dissent in *Pierce* mentions the need to protect "professional autonomy." What does this phrase mean? What connection might professional autonomy have with the U.S. safety regulatory scheme?

6. In 1986, responding to the *Pierce* decision of its supreme court, the New Jersey legislature adopted *The Conscientious Employee Protection Act*,[16] shielding from retaliation employees who object to, or refuse to participate in, "any activity, policy or practice which the employee reasonably believes to be incompatible with a clear mandate of public policy concerning the public health, safety or welfare." What would have been the likely outcome had Dr. Pierce sued under this new law?

Internet Assignment: By 2000, every state in the United States had adopted whistleblower protection statutes of some type. Locate one such law from your home state. Under what circumstances are whistleblowers protected? Are private sector as well as government employees covered? Does coverage under the statute exclude the possibility of suing in tort?

Whistleblowers: Who Are They?

> Physical courage is remarkably widespread in [the U.S.] population.... Moral and intellectual courage are not in nearly so flourishing a state, even though the risks they entail—financial or professional disadvantage, ridicule, ostracism—are comparatively minor.... These forms of courage suffer from the disadvantage of requiring new definitions continually, which must be generated out of individual perception and judgment. They threaten or violate loyalty, group identity.... They are, intrinsically, outside the range of consensus.
>
> — MARILYNNE ROBINSON

Who are these people who blow the whistle? Are they informers, troublemakers, tattletales, or are they, as one sociologist has described them, "ethical resisters,"[17] brave dissenters, the watchdogs of the general good? Do they deserve to be ostracized or treated like heroes?

The next reading describes a survey of whistleblowers.

16 N.J.S.A. 34:19-1 et. seq.
17 Myron Peretz and Penina Migdal Glazer, *The Whistleblowers* (New York: Basic Books, 1989).

SURVEY OF WHISTLEBLOWERS FINDS RETALIATION BUT FEW REGRETS

C. H. FARNSWORTH[18]

Workers who reveal waste, fraud, and abuse can expect retaliation, financial loss and high emotional and physical stress, according to a survey by two Maryland researchers.

Donald R. Soeken, a psychiatric social worker, and his wife, Karen L. Soeken, a statistician, found that whistleblowers win little more than increased self-respect. But they also found, in the first systematic effort to determine what actually happens to whistleblowers, that most of them would do it again.

A whistleblower who worked in a nuclear power plant wrote: "This has turned out to be the most frightening thing I have ever done. But it has been the most satisfying. I think I did the right thing, and I have caused some changes to be made in the plant."

Their study shatters a perception of whistleblowers as misfits. The average whistleblower in the survey was a 47-year-old family man who was employed seven years before exposing wrongdoing. Most were driven by conscience.

As a group, the whistleblowers were moderately religious. They tended to assume that the best could be achieved by following universal moral codes, which guided their judgments.

After exposing misdeeds, all those in the private sector reported they were dismissed. Because of Civil Service administrative appeals, it is more difficult to dismiss government workers, but 51 percent of these whistleblowers reported they were no longer with the same agency.

One out of every five of those in the survey reported they were without a job, and 25 percent mentioned increased financial burdens on the family as the most negative result of their action. Seventeen percent lost their homes.

Fifty-four percent of the whistleblowers said they were harassed by peers at work. Mrs. Soeken said, "We got replies like 'People made fun of me,' or 'People who I thought were my best friends stopped associating with me….'"

A government worker said, "don't do it unless you're willing to spend many years, ruin your career and sacrifice your personal life." Fifteen percent view their subsequent divorce a result of their whistleblowing activity. Ten percent report having attempted suicide. Others admit having considered it.

But an engineer in private industry replied more positively: "Do what is right. Lost income can be replaced. Lost self-esteem is more difficult to retrieve."

Another federal employee confided, "Finding honesty within myself was more powerful than I expected."

The whistleblowing experience took a high toll in physical and emotional health, the survey showed. Eighty percent reported physical deterioration, with loss of sleep and added weight as the most common symptoms. Eighty-six percent reported negative emotional consequences, including feelings of depression, powerlessness, isolation, anxiety, and anger.

Montana's Statute on Wrongful Discharge

In 1987, Montana passed the following law, the first in the nation to override employment-at-will.

MONTANA: WRONGFUL DISCHARGE FROM EMPLOYMENT ACT[19]

Purpose

This part sets forth certain rights and remedies with respect to wrongful discharge. Except as limited in this part, employment having no specified term may be terminated at the will of either the employer or the employee on notice to the other for any reason considered sufficient by the terminating party.

Definitions

In this part, the following definitions apply:

(2) "Discharge" includes a constructive discharge ... and any other termination of employment, including resignation, elimination of the job, layoff for lack of work, failure to recall or rehire, and any other cutback in the number of employees for a legitimate business reason.

(3) "Employee" means a person who works for another for hire. The term does not include a person who is an independent contractor....

(5) "Good cause" means reasonable job-related grounds for dismissal based on a failure to satisfactorily perform job duties, disruption of the employer's operation, or other legitimate business reason. The legal use of a lawful product by an individual off the employer's premises during nonworking hours is not a legitimate business reason....

(7) "Public policy" means a policy in effect at the time of the discharge concerning the public health, safety, or welfare established by constitutional provision, statute, or administrative rule.

Elements of Wrongful Discharge

A discharge is wrongful only if:

1. it was in retaliation for the employee's refusal to violate public policy or for reporting a violation of public policy;
2. the discharge was not for good cause and the employee had completed the employer's probationary period of employment; or
3. the employer violated the express provisions of its own written personnel policy.

Remedies

1. If an employer has committed a wrongful discharge, the employee may be awarded lost wages and fringe benefits for a period not to exceed 4 years from the date of discharge, together with interest thereon....
2. The employee may recover punitive damages otherwise allowed by law if it is established by clear and convincing evidence that the employer engaged in actual fraud or actual malice in the discharge of the employee [for refusing to violate public policy or for reporting a violation of public policy].

Exemptions

This part does not apply to a discharge:

1. that is subject to any other state or federal statute that provides a procedure or remedy for contesting the dispute. Such statutes include those that prohibit discharge for filing complaints, charges, or claims with administrative bodies or that prohibit unlawful discrimination based on race, national origin, sex, age, handicap, creed, religion, political belief, color, marital status, and other similar grounds.

---

19 39 *Montana Code Annotated* Chapter 2, Part 9. Puerto Rico has been the only other U.S. jurisdiction that has passed equivalent legislation.

2. of an employee covered by a written collective bargaining agreement or a written contract of employment for a specific term.

Preemption of Common-Law Remedies

Except as provided in this part, no claim for discharge may arise from tort or express or implied contract.

QUESTIONS

1. How would the *Milton* case have been decided had this law been in effect in Maryland? How would Dr. Pierce have fared under it?

2. What parts of this law seem to benefit employees? Employers?

3. The state laws protecting whistleblowers vary enormously, but none of them protect whistleblowers who turn to the media first. Why do you think that is so? Does that seem like sound policy to you? Does it encourage or discourage ethical behavior?

Sarbanes-Oxley and the Corporate Whistleblower

> *Ms. Watkins is no whistleblower in the conventional sense. She was and is a loyal employee.*
>
> — JAMES GREENWOOD (R., PA.) CHAIRMAN OF CONGRESSIONAL COMMITTEE
> INVESTIGATING THE COLLAPSE OF ENRON

At the crux of the whistleblower's decision is the question of loyalty, and of divided loyalties. An employee such as Dr. Pierce who blows the whistle experiences opposite pulls—allegiance to the employer and allegiance to a professional code of values. The same might be said of Sherron Watkins, the most well-known whistleblower associated with Enron Corporation.

Although Ms. Watkins was not the first or the only person inside Enron who raised concerns about shady accounting practices employed by the firm's CFO, she was the one in the spotlight at the time Enron collapsed. In the following article, law professor Leonard Baynes takes up the example of Sherron Watkins as a means of discussing the difficult position of the corporate insider who chooses to blow the whistle. He goes on to ask whether the Sarbanes-Oxley Act, the new federal law designed to prevent future Enrons, adequately addresses the quandary of the corporate whistleblower.

JUST PUCKER AND BLOW: AN ANALYSIS OF CORPORATE WHISTLEBLOWERS

LEONARD M. BAYNES[20]

You know how to whistle, don't you, Steve? You just put your lips together—and blow.

— LAUREN BACALL TO HUMPHREY BOGART IN *TO HAVE AND TO HAVE NOT*

Ms. Watkins was a Vice-President at Enron Corp. She earned a master's degree in professional accounting from the University of Texas at Austin. In 1982, she began her

---

20 Source: Leonard M. Baynes, "Just Pucker Corporate Whistleblowers," 76 St. John's L. Rev. 875, Fall 2002.

career as an auditor with the accounting firm Arthur Andersen, spending eight years at its Houston and New York offices. In 1983, she became a certified public accountant. Enron Vice-President Andrew Fastow hired Ms. Watkins to manage Enron's partnership with the California Public Employee Retirement System. From June to August 2001, Ms. Watkins worked directly for Mr. Fastow. During this time, Ms. Watkins learned that Enron was engaging in accounting improprieties with certain affiliated entities. She believed that Enron was using its own stock to generate gains and losses on its income statement. [She] … failed to receive satisfactory explanations regarding these accounting transactions from Enron executives.… [S]he was troubled by the accounting practices but was uncomfortable reporting them to either Mr. Fastow or former Enron President Jeff Skilling, fearing termination.… On August 15, 2001, Ms. Watkins sent to Kenneth Lay, the CEO of Enron, a seven-page anonymous letter. In the letter, Ms. Watkins asked, "Has Enron become a risky place to work?" She also more specifically described the accounting improprieties and stated that "to the layman on the street [it will look like] we are hiding losses in a related company and will compensate that company with Enron stock in the future." She shared her prescient fears that Enron might "implode in a wave of accounting scandals." On August 22, 2001, Ms. Watkins met with Mr. Lay and outlined her concerns about the accounting improprieties, and requested a transfer from working for Mr. Fastow. In late August she was reassigned to the human resources group. Ms. Watkins reported that Mr. Lay assured her that he would investigate the irregularities. Ms. Watkins never reported her concerns to the SEC, the Department of Treasury, or any other governmental official.…

Ms. Watkins is the prototypical whistleblower because she had knowledge of damaging information and she disclosed it to her supervisor's supervisor. At the same time, she is very atypical for several reasons. First, as an accountant, she had the expertise to know that her corporation was possibly breaking the law and defrauding the public. Second, her disclosure in and of itself to the president of the corporation did not lead to the type of investigation that was necessary to stop any wrongdoing. Her actions did not cause the immediate collapse of the Enron financial giant. Third, even though she "ratted" out her boss … her disclosure did not compromise her job security. In fact, Ms. Watkins has received a lot of positive press from her actions.… Ms. Watkins was even named Time magazine's "Person of the Week.…" A movie deal also is reportedly in the works that will paint Ms. Watkins as a "feminist icon," like Erin Brockovich.…

[Baynes next points to the dangerous tight rope a corporate whistleblower typically walks, who may be "damned if she does 'just pucker and blow,' and damned if she does not." He explains that corporate executives must be responsive to two common law obligations. First, they are under a "duty of loyalty."]

They must act in good faith and in a manner that they reasonably believe will be in the best interests of the corporation, including safeguarding corporate information.… The nature of the corporation requires it to rely on the officers and managers to run the day-to-day business. These employees have access to a very precious commodity, that is, vital and privileged corporate information. In the more mundane duty of loyalty cases, the senior executive has access to important corporate information dealing with customer lists, customer preferences, customer pricing, new opportunities, and secret formulas.

[T]hese principles still apply in the whistleblowing context. For example, the whistleblower may convert corporate proprietary information by taking corporate records and sharing them with the authorities. The whistleblower could disclose information that, at worst, could lead to civil or criminal liabilities for the corporation and its other senior officers and directors. At best, certain disclosures could lead to significant embarrassment or humiliation. In either case, deciding how to make such disclosures would usually be a decision of the board of directors and senior managers of the corporation. For example, if the disclosure might give rise to criminal or civil liability, the corporation under the best of circumstances would want to vest its decision with its attorneys in an effort to minimize its potential liability and maximize profits. If the whistleblower discloses the information, she may make it impossible for the corporation and other senior executives to obtain a good deal from prosecutors. If the information disclosed is not rooted in civil or criminal misconduct, but nevertheless is scandalous, the corporation may want to refrain from disclosing such information. The whistleblower may cause a great deal of public relations harm by disclosing such information.... [S]enior executives know where the corporation may be most vulnerable ... [and] are in a position to inflict harm on the corporation in a way that strangers cannot.

[Baynes then outlines the other pole of responsibility for corporate executives.]

Corporate officers and senior executives have a duty of care to the corporation. They have an obligation to perform their duties with the care that a person in a like position would reasonably exercise under similar circumstances. This duty has been analogized to the diligence, care, and skill that ordinarily prudent individuals would exercise in the management of their affairs....

In the case of whistleblowing, tension between the duty of loyalty and duty of care exists. The senior executive is required to disclose her objections to certain actions that she believes are illegal. But how is she supposed to do that? As a non-director officer, she could disclose her objections to her supervisor or her supervisor's supervisor like Sherron Watkins did at Enron. This objection may take the form of a "cover your ass" memo. But will this really stop wrongdoing? In some cases, such a memo may be insufficient to stop the wrongdoing, and the senior executive may have an obligation to report the matter to the authorities. She may, however, be in a bind because her contractual obligations and her duty of loyalty responsibilities may limit the type of information that she could give to the authorities. In addition, unless someone has real inside information allowing them to actually observe the wrongdoing and has the expertise to know that the wrongdoing is illegal, what safe harbor exists to protect the senior executive from mistakenly reporting wrongdoing?

[In 2002 the Sarbanes-Oxley Act was passed in response to the wave of corporate scandals that began with Enron. As Baynes explains, it "was designed to promote investor confidence by ensuring that the public receives more information about possible corporate fraud. Such disclosures would ensure that the markets have perfect information so that investors could make informed investment choices."]

The Sarbanes-Oxley Act prohibits any public company from discriminating against any employee who lawfully provides information or otherwise assists in an investigation of conduct that the employee "reasonably believes" constitutes a violation of the federal securities laws. This provision was designed from the lessons learned from Sherron Watkins's testimony. As Senator Patrick Leahy stated, "'We learned from Sherron Watkins of Enron that these corporate insiders are the key witnesses that need to be encouraged to report fraud and help prove it in court.'" The legislation protects an employee from retaliation by an employer for testifying before Congress or a federal regulatory agency, or giving evidence to law enforcement of possible securities fraud violations....

[Baynes now asks whether the anti-retaliation provision of the new law adequately addresses the dilemma of the corporate whistleblower, caught in the "vortex" of the duty of loyalty and the duty of care.]

Undoubtedly, the Sarbanes-Oxley Act provides an extra level of protection for employees. Despite this ... we must be cognizant that federal whistleblowers have low success rates in their suits before government agencies. The Whistleblowers Survival Guide reports that "the rate of success for winning a reprisal lawsuit ... for federal whistleblower laws has risen to between 25 and 33 percent in recent years." Under the Act, the corporate senior executive or employee is likely ... also [to] have a low rate of success under its whistleblowing provisions. First, the statute only affords protection against retaliations based on securities fraud. Whistleblowing of other kinds of wrongdoing remain unprotected under this Act. In these cases, the whistleblower then must rely on the vagaries of state law, which generally give preference to those allegations dealing with public safety. For example, a senior executive may overhear a high-ranking executive make disparaging remarks about a particular racial group and state that he would never hire or promote members of that group. The corporation employs very few members of this particular group and has none in senior management. The senior executive believes that the corporation is engaged in race discrimination. The senior executive has a fiduciary obligation to hold certain corporate information like employee demographics in confidence but has an obligation to resign or object from his position when confronting corporate wrongdoing. The Act provides protection only for those matters that involve security fraud. If this senior manager discloses, she would have to rely on the protections of the state laws.

Second, low-level employees are also relatively unprotected. They probably are unaware of these new protections. They may feel particularly oppressed by the many layers of management that may exist in some corporations. Some may be unsophisticated and may not know whether certain actions violate the law. Many of the wrongful or illegal activities that they observe may not rise to the level of securities fraud. For example, an employee at McDonald's may notice that large numbers of pre-packaged hamburgers disappear shortly after delivery. The disappearance may be the result of conversion by the store manager. The McDonald's employee might be in the best position to ascertain whether this wrongdoing is occurring, but she is unprotected by the Sarbanes-Oxley Act because this conversion does not involve securities fraud.... In addition, many of these employees rely very heavily on their paychecks; a high turnover rate exists in these jobs. Students and those re-entering the workforce hold many of these jobs. These individuals may be particularly reluctant to "rock the boat" and report wrongdoing unless they are guaranteed that their job is protected. The Act does nothing to address this population of whistleblowers.

Third, for both senior executives and low-level employees, the Sarbanes-Oxley Act gives little guidance as to the circumstances under which an employee is to disclose allegations of wrongdoing to her supervisor as opposed to law enforcement authorities. Senior executives also have an obligation to use "reasonable efforts" to disclose to the principal information which is "relevant to affairs entrusted to [the agent]" and which the principal would desire to have.... In some instances, however, the whistleblowing employee who reports wrongdoing to her supervisor might not be doing enough to stem the wrongdoing behavior. For instance, once she has made the report, the wrongdoing supervisor might exclude the employee from access to information that would allow her to continue to observe the wrongful behavior. In those cases, the reporting employee may have breached her duty of care to the corporation by using insufficient actions to stop the wrongdoing.... Conversely, if the whistleblowing employee reports the evidence of wrongdoing immediately to law enforcement authorities, she may be violating her duty of loyalty to the corporation.... She has an obligation to protect certain proprietary and confidential corporate information. Also by going to the law enforcement authorities right away, she may be depriving the corporation of the opportunity to resolve the matter or, in the case of wrongdoing, get the best deal for the corporation. In addition, the employee who jumps the gun and goes to law enforcement authorities may be putting herself in a difficult political situation at her corporation. Even though the terms of her position and employment may remain the same, she will always, to her detriment, be remembered for making that report.

Fourth, the Sarbanes-Oxley Act gives no guidance concerning whether the whistleblowing employee should disclose the information to her direct supervisor or her supervisor's supervisor. Who is the principal of senior executives? Is it the corporation? Is it the board of directors? Is it the senior executive's boss?

[Baynes writes that the same kinds of problems raised above arise here. If the report goes to a direct supervisor, the employee may not be doing enough to stop the behavior. But by going over his head, she prevents her direct supervisor from fixing the problem himself, and risks being "perceived as a 'rat fink,'" something Baynes euphemistically notes "may be a career-limiting move."]

Fifth, the legislative history of the Sarbanes-Oxley Act states that the employee's actions have to be reasonable in making reports.... Most cases may not be as clear-cut as the one involving Sherron Watkins. Because she was an accountant, she had a very good idea that Enron's accounting policies were illegal. For most other whistleblowers, they may have only a slight inkling that something might be amiss. In those circumstances, what are they supposed to do?...

Sixth, the Sarbanes-Oxley Act prohibits a corporation from "discharg[ing], demot-[ing], suspend[ing], threaten[ing], harass[ing], or in any other manner discriminat[ing] against an employee in the terms and conditions of employment" because she blew the whistle. Senator Leahy conceded, however, that "most corporate employers, with help from their lawyers, know exactly what they can do to a whistleblowing employee under the law." The types of retaliation that can occur include: (1) "attacking the [whistleblower's] motives, credibility, [or] professional competence"; (2) "build[ing] a damaging record against [the whistleblower]"; (3) threatening the employee with "reprisals for whistleblowing"; (4) "reassign[ing]" the employee to an isolated work location; (5) "publicly humiliat[ing]" the employee; (6) "set [ting] … up [the whistleblower] for failure" by putting them in impossible assignments; (7) "prosecut[ing the employee] for unauthorized disclosures [of information]"; (8) "reorganiz[ing]" the company so that the whistleblower's job is eliminated"; and (9) "blacklist[ing]" the whistleblower so she will be unable to work in the industry. Of course some methods on this list would clearly violate the Act. A deft supervisor, however, could "set up" the whistleblowing employee for failure. For instance, the employer may place the whistleblower in a job unsuitable to her skill level to ensure her failure. The employer could then document the employee's poor performance. The Act provides protections for whistleblowing employees except in cases where valid business reasons exist for their termination like inferior work performance. In addition, even if the employer refrains from discriminating against the whistleblowing employee in the terms and conditions of her employment, the employer is unlikely to give that employee any opportunities for advancement. By blowing the whistle, she may have "tapped out" her career trajectory....

QUESTIONS

1. Describe the conflict faced by corporate insiders who discover unethical or illegal activities within their organizations.

2. Would the SOX law have protected Dr. Donn Milton? Dr. Grace Pierce? What kinds of corporate wrongdoing might a senior executive discover that would not be covered by SOX?

3. Suppose Sherron Watkins had been fired by Enron before SOX went into effect. How would she have fared under Maryland law? New Jersey? Montana? After SOX, would she have any basis for a lawsuit?

4. Baynes identifies these weaknesses in the SOX law:

   (1) "non-securities fraud matters are not covered;

   (2) low-level employees may not be aware of the protections;

   (3) no guidance is given as to when to report wrongdoing to outside authorities or to a supervisor;

(4) no guidance is given as to when the whistleblower should go over his or her supervisor's head to senior management; and

(5) no protection is given to undercover retaliations that do not quite manifest themselves as a 'discharge, demotion, suspension, threat, or other manner of discrimination.'"

Working with a group of classmates, tackle each of these issues. How would you amend the law to respond to them? Might some of these concerns be more effectively addressed by changes in corporate policy or culture? If so, what changes would your group recommend?

Group Think

Seven months after the Columbia shuttle crashed, in August 2003, a report on the causes of the disaster was released. It had been a gargantuan effort. Some 25,000 workers had gathered more than 84,000 pieces of debris by walking slowly across eastern Texas and western Louisiana, collecting evidence. According to the final report, the "broken safety culture" inside NASA was at least as much to blame for the crash as the chunk of foam tile that blew a hole in the wing of Columbia just after liftoff. Engineers, hoping a high-risk rescue might be possible, had asked management for outside assistance in getting photos of the damage, but these requests were rejected:

> As much as the foam, what helped to doom the shuttle and its crew, even after liftoff, was not a lack of technology or ability … but missed opportunities and a lack of leadership and open-mindedness in management. The accident "was probably not an anomalous, random event, but rather likely rooted to some degree in NASA's history and the human spaceflight program's culture."[21]

Similar problems appear to have affected the CIA in the months leading up to the U.S. invasion of Iraq. According to a scathing congressional report released in July 2004, key assessments used to justify the war were not supported by the government's own evidence:

> Among the central findings, endorsed by all nine Republicans and eight Democrats on the committee, were that a culture of "group think" in intelligence agencies left unchallenged an institutional belief that Iraq had illicit weapons; … and that intelligence agencies too often failed to acknowledge the limited, ambiguous and even contradictory nature of their information about Iraq and illicit arms.[22]

Studies have shown that, within large organizations, there is a tendency to go along with the majority. Most people are not likely to challenge the worthiness of the task at hand, or the way in which the task at hand is being accomplished. This reality, combined with the pressures that affect an organization from the outside—time and money pressures in the case of NASA's Columbia shuttle, political pressures in the case of the United States in Iraq—can obscure good judgment.

---

21 John Schwartz and Matthew Wald, "Report on Loss of Shuttle Focuses on NASA Blunders," *New York Times*, August 27, 2003.

22 Douglas Jehl, "Senators Assail C.I.A. Judgments on Iraq's Arms as Deeply Flawed, *New York Times*, July 10, 2004.

Public Employees and Freedom of Speech

> *What I was surprised at was the silence, the collective silence by so many people that had to be involved, that had to have seen something or heard something.*
>
> — SGT. SAMUEL PROVANCE, KEY WITNESS IN GOVERNMENT INVESTIGATION OF ABU GHRAIB PRISON ABUSE

People who work for the government or for any of its branches—such as police, air traffic controllers, and those employed by government-supported institutions such as hospitals or schools—are called public employees. For almost 200 years, public employees were thought to have no greater speech rights than those who worked in the private sector. The leading case, which dates back to the nineteenth century, involved a policeman who was fired for publicly criticizing the management of his department. He sued to get his job back, relying on his free speech rights. Judge Oliver Wendell Holmes refused his claim, stating, "The petitioner may have a constitutional right to talk politics, but he has no constitutional right to be a policeman."[23]

Then, in 1968, the Supreme Court re-interpreted the First Amendment of the U.S. Constitution to give public employees limited speech protections. Marvin Pickering, a public school teacher, was fired for publishing a letter in the local paper critical of the Board of Education's allocation of funds to its athletic program. He sued, losing in the lower courts. On appeal, however, the Court ruled in his favor. In *Pickering v. Board of Education*,[24] the Court weighed "the interests of the teacher, as a citizen, in commenting upon matters of public concern" against the "interest of the State, as an employer, in promoting the efficiency of the public services it performs through its employees." On balance, Pickering's free speech interests were greater. In 1983, the Supreme Court re-affirmed and clarified the *Pickering* test as it decided *Connick v. Myers*.[25] Sheila Myers had distributed a questionnaire at her place of employment. The circular inquired not only about internal matters, such as an office transfer policy, but also about matters of legitimate public concern, including pressure put on employees to work on certain political campaigns. Based on its content, form, and context, the *Connick* Court determined that the questionnaire was tinged with just enough public interest to be examined under the *Pickering* test, although a statement limited to internal matters would not be. Myers lost her case, however, since the government demonstrated that her questionnaire interfered with working relationships by causing a "mini-insurrection" that could have disrupted the office. Had her speech been of greater importance to the public, the Court explained, the government may have had a harder case.

In 2006, the Supreme Court revisited the *Pickering* rule. The facts of the case were as follows: Richard Ceballos began working as a deputy district attorney in Los Angeles County in 1989. By 2000, he was a "calendar" attorney, supervising other lawyers in the DA's office. In February of that year, a defense attorney contacted Ceballos to tell him he would be challenging a search warrant because it was based on "inaccuracies" in the supporting affidavit. Ceballos agreed to investigate. When he went to the location described in the warrant as a "long driveway," he found a separate road. The affidavit described tire tracks that led from a stripped-down truck to the premises to be searched. But Ceballos found a road surface that would make it difficult or impossible to leave visible tire tracks.

---

23 *McAuliffe v. Mayor of New Bedford*, 29 N.E. 517 (1892).
24 391 U.S. 563 (1968).
25 *Connick v. Myers*, 461 U.S. 138 (1983).

After a telephone conversation with the affiant—a deputy sheriff—Ceballos told his supervisors that the case should be dismissed because there were serious misrepresentations in the affidavit supporting the search warrant. He repeated the same concerns in a memorandum. Then, at heated meeting with Ceballos, his supervisors, and the sheriff who had made the statements in the warrant, Ceballos was sharply reprimanded. Later, he claims, he experienced a series of retaliations, including being reassigned, transferred, and denied promotion.

He sued, claiming those actions violated his First Amendment rights.

GARCETTI v. CEBALLOS

U.S. Supreme Court, 2006
126 S.Ct. 1951

Justice KENNEDY delivered the opinion of the Court. ※

Pickering and the cases decided in its wake identify two inquiries to guide interpretation of the constitutional protections accorded to public employee speech. The first requires determining whether the employee spoke as a citizen on a matter of public concern. If the answer is no, the employee has no First Amendment cause of action....If the answer is yes, then the possibility of a First Amendment claim arises. The question becomes whether the relevant government entity had an adequate justification for treating the employee differently from any other member of the general public....

When a citizen enters government service, the citizen by necessity must accept certain limitations on his or her freedom....Government employers, like private employers, need a significant degree of control over their employees' words and actions; without it, there would be little chance for the efficient provision of public services....

At the same time, the Court has recognized that a citizen who works for the government is nonetheless a citizen. The First Amendment limits the ability of a public employer to leverage the employment relationship to restrict, incidentally or intentionally, the liberties employees enjoy in their capacities as private citizens. So long as employees are speaking as citizens about matters of public concern, they must face only those speech restrictions that are necessary for their employers to operate efficiently and effectively....

[T]he First Amendment interests at stake extend beyond the individual speaker... [to include] the public's interest in receiving the well-informed views of government employees engaging in civic discussion... [and] the necessity for informed, vibrant dialogue in a democratic society....

With these principles in mind we turn to the instant case....

Ceballos wrote his ... memo because that is part of what he, as a calendar deputy, was employed to do.... The significant point is that the memo was written pursuant to Ceballos' official duties.... Contrast, for example, the expressions made by the speaker in *Pickering*, whose letter to the newspaper had no official significance and bore similarities to letters submitted by numerous citizens every day.

Ceballos did not act as a citizen when he went about conducting his daily professional activities, such as supervising attorneys, investigating charges, and preparing filings. In the same way he did not speak as a citizen by writing a memo that addressed the proper disposition of a pending criminal case. When he went to work and performed the tasks he was paid to perform, Ceballos acted as a government employee. The fact that his duties sometimes required him to speak or write does not mean his supervisors were prohibited from evaluating his performance.

... Supervisors must ensure that their employees' official communications are accurate, demonstrate sound judgment, and promote the employer's mission. Ceballos' memo is illustrative. It demanded the attention of his supervisors and led to a heated meeting with employees from the sheriff's department. If Ceballos' superiors thought his memo was inflammatory or misguided, they had the authority to take proper corrective action....

Proper application of our precedents thus leads to the conclusion that the First Amendment does not prohibit managerial discipline based on an employee's expressions made pursuant to official responsibilities. Because Ceballos' memo falls into this category, his allegation of unconstitutional retaliation must fail....

Justice STEVENS, dissenting. ✳

The proper answer to the question "whether the First Amendment protects a government employee from discipline based on speech made pursuant to the employee's official duties," is "Sometimes," not "Never." Of course a supervisor may take corrective action when such speech is "inflammatory or misguided," But what if it is just unwelcome speech because it reveals facts that the supervisor would rather not have anyone else discover?

... [P]ublic employees are still citizens while they are in the office. The notion that there is a categorical difference between speaking as a citizen and speaking in the course of one's employment is quite wrong. Over a quarter of a century has passed since then-Justice Rehnquist, writing for a unanimous Court, rejected "the conclusion that a public employee forfeits his protection against governmental abridgment of freedom of speech if he decides to express his views privately rather than publicly." ... [It] is senseless to let constitutional protection...hinge on whether [words] fall within a job description. Moreover, it seems perverse to fashion a new rule that provides employees with an incentive to voice their concerns publicly before talking frankly to their superiors.

Justice SOUTER, with whom Justice STEVENS and Justice GINSBURG join, dissenting. ✳

...Open speech by a private citizen on a matter of public importance lies at the heart of expression subject to protection by the First Amendment.... At the other extreme, a statement by a government employee complaining about nothing beyond treatment under personnel rules raises no greater claim to constitutional protection against retaliatory response than the remarks of a private employee.... In between these points lies a public employee's speech unwelcome to the government but on a significant public issue. Such an employee speaking as a citizen, that is, with a citizen's interest, is protected from reprisal unless the statements are too damaging to the government's capacity to conduct public business to be justified by any individual or public benefit thought to flow from the statements. *Pickering v. Board of Ed. of Township High School Dist.* (1968)....

This significant, albeit qualified, protection of public employees who irritate the government is understood to flow from the First Amendment, in part, because a government paycheck does nothing to eliminate the value to an individual of speaking on public matters, and there is no good reason for categorically discounting a speaker's interest in commenting on a matter of public concern just because the government employs him.... [in part on] the value to the public of receiving the opinions and information that a public employee may disclose. "Government employees are often in the best position to know what ails the agencies for which they work." *Waters v. Churchill*, (U.S. 1994).

The reason that protection of employee speech is qualified is that it can distract coworkers and supervisors from their tasks at hand and thwart the implementation of legitimate policy, the risks of which grow greater the closer the employee's speech gets to commenting on his own workplace and responsibilities. It is one thing for an office clerk to say there is waste in government and quite another to charge that his own department pays full-time salaries to part-time workers....

... [I]t stands to reason that a citizen may well place a very high value on a right to speak on the public issues he decides to make the subject of his work day after day. Would anyone doubt that a school principal evaluating the performance of teachers for promotion or pay adjustment retains a citizen's interest in addressing the quality of teaching in the schools?...Would anyone deny that a prosecutor like Richard Ceballos may claim the interest of any citizen in speaking out against a rogue law enforcement officer, simply because his job requires him to express a judgment about the officer's performance? (But the majority says the First Amendment gives Ceballos no protection, even if his judgment in this case was sound and appropriately expressed.)

Indeed, the very idea of categorically separating the citizen's interest from the employee's interest ignores the fact that the ranks of public service include those who share the poet's "object ... to unite [m]y avocation and my vocation." These citizen servants are the ones whose civic interest rises highest when they speak pursuant to their duties, and these are exactly the ones government employers most want to attract....

...Were they not able to speak on these matters, the community would be deprived of informed opinions on important public issues. The interest at stake is as much the public's interest in receiving informed opinion as it is the employee's own right to disseminate it. This is...true when an employee's job duties require him to speak about such things: when, for example, a public auditor speaks on his discovery of embezzlement of public funds, when a building inspector makes an obligatory report of an attempt to bribe him, or when a law enforcement officer expressly balks at a superior's order to violate constitutional rights he is sworn to protect. (The majority, however, places all these speakers beyond the reach of First Amendment protection against retaliation.)...

[T]he lesson of *Pickering* (and the object of most constitutional adjudication) is still to the point: when constitutionally significant interests clash, resist the demand for winner-take-all; try to make adjustments that serve all of the values at stake....

Justice BREYER, dissenting. ☀

...The facts present two special circumstances that together justify First Amendment review.

First, the speech at issue is professional speech—the speech of a lawyer. Such speech is subject to independent regulation by canons of the profession. Those canons provide an obligation to speak in certain instances....

Second, the Constitution itself here imposes speech obligations upon the government's professional employee. A prosecutor has a constitutional obligation to learn of, to preserve, and to communicate with the defense about exculpatory and impeachment evidence in the government's possession. [Exculpatory evidence is evidence that proves innocence. Ceballos believed that what he learned about the affidavit was exculpatory.]

Where professional and special constitutional obligations are both present, the need to protect the employee's speech is augmented, the need for broad government authority to control that speech is likely diminished....

Thus I would apply the *Pickering* balancing test here.

With respect, I dissent.

QUESTIONS

1. Dissenting Justices Souter, Stevens, and Ginsburg write: "When constitutionally significant interests clash, resist the demand for winner-take-all; try to make adjustments that serve all of the values at stake." Think about the values that underlie each portion of this opinion. Which ones are most prominent for Justice Kennedy with the majority? For Justice Stevens in dissent? Which are framed in the dissent led by Souter? What value does Breyer mention?

2. The majority adds a preliminary requirement to the analysis of First Amendment claims for public employees. Before the *Pickering* balancing test is triggered, the majority would first ask "whether the employee spoke as a citizen on a matter of public concern." How does the majority go about making that threshold determination? How would the dissenters want the Court to analyze this case?

3. In a part of this case not included in this text, Justice Kennedy writes that he expects public employers, in their exercise of good judgment, to be "receptive to constructive criticism offered by their employees."

   Internet Assignment: Find a recent case involving whistleblowing by a public employee. Did the employer exercise good judgment? Was the employee protected by whistleblowing laws?

4. Consider the following scenarios. Try to apply these legal standards to the following news events. If these whistleblowers sued, would they succeed in their free speech claims?

   • Richard H. Carmona served as surgeon general during the Bush administration from 2002–2006. In 2007, he testified to a congressional committee investigating the extent to which scientific information was being distorted by political considerations. Dr. Carmona told lawmakers that, while he was surgeon general, top Bush administration officials had repeatedly attempted to dilute or suppress important public health reports for political reasons. For example, although he was not permitted to mention stem cells, contraception, sex education, or global health issues in his speeches, he was required to mention President Bush three times on each page of every speech he gave. Suppose Dr. Carmona had complained to officials in the Department of Health and Human Services before his tenure ended—and was removed from his position in retaliation.

   • On February 1, 2003, as it was making its re-entry to land, the Columbia space shuttle burst into flame and broke apart over Texas. All 11 astronauts were killed. Two weeks later, scientists learned that foam tiles had broken away from the spacecraft, striking its left wing. A few NASA engineers strongly believed that images of the resultant damage should be created and analyzed. They met with institutional resistance, a "bureaucratic dead end," and the pictures were never taken. Suppose they had persisted in their requests, pressed their superiors, and then been fired.[26]

   • For 20 years Russell Tice worked at the National Security Agency on mass surveillance, known as "black world" operations. In January 2006 he decided to go to ABC News, claiming some of the government's secret operations since 9/11 were illegal, with millions of phone calls tapped. This contradicted President Bush's comments that he had authorized the NSA to intercept only the communications of people with known links to terror organizations: "We're not trolling through the personal lives of millions of innocent Americans." But Tice told ABC: "The mentality was, 'We need to get these guys, and we're going to do whatever it takes to get them.'" Suppose the Bush administration had retaliated against Tice.

   • Carlos Blackman worked for the New York Transit Authority as a car inspector at the 240th Street maintenance shop. A union member and outspoken on many issues, including employee heath and safety, he was elected local Union Chairman in 2003. Some months later, a disgruntled employee, who had been fired from his position as a car cleaner, shot and killed two of his former supervisors. In a conversation the first day at work after the murders, Blackman remarked, "I hate to say this, but those two guys deserve what they got for getting the [employee-turned-murderer] fired." At this point,

---

26 James Glanz and John Schwartz, "Dogged Engineer's Effort to Assess Shuttle Damage," *New York Times*, 2003.

one of Blackman's co-workers turned to him and asked, "If you lost your livelihood, what would you do?" Blackman essentially repeated himself: "[T]hose two scumbags deserved what they got." The Transit Authority filed a disciplinary action against him.

Global Norms and Internal Corporate Communication

In the next reading, Terry Morehead Dworkin, a leading authority on employment-at-will, makes intriguing connections among whistleblowing, multinational corporations (MNCs), and world peace. She argues that whistleblowing protections developed by MNCs in response to legal pressures in the United States can become valuable tools when implemented in other countries. Dworkin writes: "Whistleblowing is a procedural way to reinforce the transparency necessary to free trapped capital, encourage foreign investment and move economies, especially transitional ones, away from reliance on personal relationships and bribes." Noting that countries rife with cronyism tend also to be plagued by violence, Dworkin argues that by protecting whistleblowing worldwide, MNCs support democratic institutions and "help deliver on the promise of peace through commerce."

WHISTLEBLOWING, MNCS, AND PEACE

TERRY MOREHEAD DWORKIN [27]

… Work organizations, both governmental and civil, are growing in size and complexity, and individuals are often little more than "cogs" in the organization in which they work. Individual jobs have also grown in complexity, and as a result have become more specialized and expertise-based. This, in turn, makes the detection of wrongful conduct more difficult due to both lack of knowledge and access to information. At the same time, the information and technology revolutions have increased the opportunities for significant fraud and other harmful and illegal activities. Whistleblowing is one way to obtain—or regain—societal control over the large organizations that increasingly dominate society.

The premise behind recent governmental promotion of whistleblowing is that people of conscience work within these large, complex organizations, and would normally take action against wrongdoing except for fear of losing their jobs or other forms of retaliation. Thus, if adequately protected from retaliation, they will come forward with evidence of wrongdoing before external detection is possible. Harms from the wrongdoing could be reduced, wrongful behavior stopped, and the expense of public oversight and investigation would be reduced if such reporting occurs. Also, if whistleblowing proved a relatively common occurrence, wrongdoing would decrease because potential wrongdoers would be aware that their activities were not truly secret.

[Dworkin describes the evolution of the law related to whistleblowing in the United States, noting how catastrophes such as the 1981 Challenger explosion spurred protective measures across all three branches of both state and federal government. Importantly, she points to "a shift toward encouraging internal whistleblowing and away from the almost exclusive legislative emphasis on reporting outside the organization." An organization can save litigation costs and avoid reputational damage by adopting effective internal mechanisms for reporting wrongdoing. And, unlike punishment that is meted out

27 35 Vand. J. Transnat'l L. 457 (March 2002).

after public exposure, internal reporting can prevent losses—of resources and even lives. Laws like the 1991 U.S. Sentencing Guidelines that allow reduced fines for wrongdoing if a company has an appropriate deterrence program in place—an ethical code supported by "a meaningful reporting system, and protection of whistleblowers from reprisals"—have driven this trend to set up internal reporting systems.

The question now becomes: Is whistleblowing protection exportable?]

The Cultural Dimension

… [M]odern, non-political whistleblowing is a Western phenomenon. The countries that have adopted it have common law-based legal systems and societies that prize individualism. While "snitching" is not generally condoned, the idea of citizen law enforcement has long roots in the United Kingdom and the United States, and whistleblowing has been advocated as a way to control large organizations for over thirty years. In some Western countries such as France, Greece, and Luxembourg, however, whistleblowing is seen as little different from informing the government about a neighbor's dissident views. This, in turn, is frowned on at least in part because it is considered an attribute of totalitarian or Communist states.…

The idea of reporting the wrongdoing of one's group is alien to many other cultures in which group membership, rather than individualism is the norm. In Japan, for example, the traditions of consensus, company mentality, and lifetime employment make whistleblowing almost unheard of and highly risky. One employee who defied this tradition, an ex-Honda engineer who allegedly quit in a dispute over safety issues, is now a plaintiff's expert witness in the United States in suits against Honda. His testimony provides an income that he could no longer earn in Japan because of his dissent.

An explanation for these differences can be drawn from [one of] several studies that show basic differences in value systems between national cultures.[28]… [It] identifies five dimensions on which cultures vary: power distance, individualism, uncertainty avoidance, masculinity, and Confucian dynamism.… Of these five, power distance, individualism, and Confucian dynamism are most relevant to examining whistleblowing among cultures. Cultures with a high power distance are more willing to accept that power is unequally distributed among individuals and are therefore more willing to accept inequality, autocratic leadership, and centralization of authority. Cultures high in individualism have a loosely knit social framework in which people believe they are responsible for themselves and their immediate family instead of believing that they are members of an in-group which will look out for them. A society which scores high in Confucian dynamism is a dynamic, future-oriented society, while a society low in this dimension tends to be tradition bound and static.

These classifications are, of course, only tools of analysis, and countries may vary along a continuum in each dimension. Nonetheless, they may help explain why the United States, Australia, and the United Kingdom are some of the first countries with whistleblower legislation, and other countries are more reluctant to accept the idea. Japan is a low-scoring country on individualism, relatively low-scoring on dynamism, and high-scoring on power distance. People living in a low individualistic, high power distance country are less likely to challenge authority, and those in authority are less likely to tolerate challenges. Additionally, loyalty to the group will be stronger in this climate, thus making reporting on someone within the group less likely. Finally, going against societal norms to blow the whistle is less likely in a low-dynamic society.

The United States, Australia, and the United Kingdom, by contrast, are countries which score at the high end on the individualism and dynamism dimensions, and low

---

28 Gert Hofstede, *Culture's Consequences: International Differences in Work-Related Values* (abridged ed. 1984).

on power distance. Thus, people in these societies are more likely to challenge authority, and doing so is more likely to be socially acceptable....

This analysis does not imply that whistleblowing procedures cannot be successfully implemented in countries like Japan. It does indicate that it will be more difficult, and MNCs will have to carefully consider and structure what they ask their employees to do if internal reporting is to be used as an ethical control mechanism. This may be easier now than it would have been even a decade ago for two reasons. First, the societies studied are dynamic. Japan, for example, is slowly moving away from life-time employment … and independent thinking and challenges to authority are becoming more common. Second, whistleblowing is increasingly being discussed and considered on an international scale, so it is not as radical an idea as it once may have appeared....

[Given these cultural differences, Dworkin next suggests how standards and reporting mechanisms might work.]

Reporting Procedures

A large number of studies have been conducted on whistleblowers, particularly on what distinguishes observers of wrongdoing who blow the whistle from those who do not. The most important predictor is whether there is a clear reporting procedure that is seen as effective....

… In situations where great emphasis is placed on organizational conformity and loyalty to co-workers and the organization, the organization must convince employees that whistleblowing is normative and desired.... Reporting requirements, if implemented and seriously followed, will help achieve this "normative" behavior.

To have an effective compliance program an organization should:

- Establish a written compliance program. Written compliance programs should be clearly written, easily understood, relatively brief, and lack legal verbiage. To the extent feasible, employees from all sectors of the organization should participate in the formation of the requirements....

- Train employees regarding compliance.... Policies should stress that employees can be held personally liable for failure to comply and that the organization may be legally liable for compliance failure. Corporations should stress that non-retaliation is an integral part of the policy.

- Establish a simple reporting procedure.... Establishing a special person [to receive reports] sends the message that the organization takes the issues seriously and is open to dissent. Having someone like an ombudsperson, independent of management, reinforces this message.

- Investigate and respond quickly. To the extent possible, the privacy of the parties involved should be maintained during the investigation. The response should include a report back to the whistleblower to demonstrate that the company has listened and taken action....

Appropriate Ethical Norms and Cultural Adaptability

… To foster participation, the code should concern relatively few issues that can garner wide acceptance or understanding....

The easiest norm for employees to understand is compliance with the law. Other norms on which a company could get broad agreement are fair treatment of employees, protection of the environment, and rules against bribery.

[Using the example of sexual harassment, Dworkin discusses the problem of culturally divergent attitudes. Pointing to Wharton professors Donaldson and Dunfee's notion of "hypernorms,"[29] she argues that there are ways of identifying globally shared values.]

---

29 Thomas Donaldson and Thomas W. Dunfee, *Ties that Bind: A Social Contracts Approach to Business Ethics*, 49–81 (1999).

A hypernorm is a [principle] "so fundamental to human existence that [it serves] as a guide in evaluating lower level moral norms." Because of its importance, the hypernorm is likely to be reflected in global principles that are generally recognized....

An examination of numerous global and regional declarations and other documents, such as the 1948 Universal Declaration of Human Rights, the UN Convention on the Elimination of All Forms of Discrimination Against Women, OECD Guidelines for Multinational Enterprises, the Council of Europe's 1996 Social Charter, EC Directives and Codes of Practice, as well as the laws and philosophies of particular countries, suggest there are three hypernorms relevant to harassment: personal security, respect for human dignity, and nondiscrimination. At a minimum, these hypernorms support global rules against ... [b]eing forced to trade sexual favors for the right to employment [because this] threatens personal security, undermines human dignity, and is generally acknowledged to be discriminatory....

MNC implementation of global equal treatment standards that are reinforced by reporting procedures is not only feasible, but can help reduce conflict. Some studies indicate there is a positive correlation between gender equality and nonviolence. Creating an atmosphere where inter-group interactions are fostered under conditions of equal treatment helps reduce conflict. It can help defuse resentment and limit disruptive behavior by contributing to a feeling of psychological security and increased physical security....

[Dworkin next looks at another example, bribery.]

Despite the lack of uniformity, it is feasible for an MNC to ban bribery. Every country in the world prohibits bribery of its officials. This would be the starting point of such a code, along with compliance with local laws. However, allowance for legitimate gift-giving can be made on a [local] basis with appropriate discussion and training.

... [B]ribery can cause conflict. One important reason is that it undermines free trade, and free trade helps foster peace. Corporations that adopt bribery bans and enforce them through reporting procedures potentially contribute to peace by allowing better utilization of resources. This, in turn, frees up more resources for those at the bottom of the economic rungs, and will have an increased impact in the emerging economies that are most harmed by bribery.

Contributions of Open Reporting to the Corporation and to Peace

... Internal whistleblowing procedures and codes of ethics will operate more effectively when organizations operate as mediating institutions. Mediating institutions are relatively small organizations where moral identity and behavior are formed. Studies indicate that as the size of an organization increases, individual ethical decision-making behavior decreases. Thus, for large multinational corporations, the need for training in relatively small groups at the local level is heightened....

There are benefits to the organization that adopts these policies and procedures. Global strategic alliances represent a type of competitive weapon. In order to take the best advantage of the alliance, organizations must listen to multicultural perspectives. Additionally, firm-specific fairness norms promote efficiency.

Organizations that foster internal reporting and open discussion are likely to find that external reporting will be virtually nonexistent. Problems can be raised and resolved earlier if employees feel free to engage in discussion and dissent....

Conclusion

MNCs can help in the evolution of a normative global village. They can create conditions that socialize and empower individuals and give them the tools to interact more successfully in their society. To the extent that ideas such as fairness and responsibility for compliance are learned within the company and are then taken externally, organizations have the ability to have an impact far beyond their individual realm. At the same time, exporting the idea of whistleblowing helps promote transparency and good government in larger society. Organizational norms matter most when law is the weakest.

QUESTIONS

1. According to Dworkin, how might an MNC's compliance and reporting procedures affect the society in which it operates? How might the cultural setting where an MNC operates in turn affect those procedures?

2. Cultural imperialism, according to Wikipedia, is a pejorative phrase for "the practice of promoting, distinguishing, separating, or artificially injecting the culture or language of one nation into another. It is usually the case that the former is a large, economically or militarily powerful nation and the latter is a smaller, less affluent one." Do Dworkin's recommendations amount to cultural imperialism? Why/why not?

3. In line with Dworkin's remarks about Japan, as a "low-scoring country on individualism," is the Japanese aphorism: "The nail that sticks up gets hammered." Yet Dworkin also notes that Japan is becoming more "dynamic," and suggests change is on the way.

   Internet Assignment: What can you find out about this? Has any whistleblowing legislation been passed? Any cases won? Any other signs that a cultural shift is underway around workplace norms? Look into the activities of MNCs in Japan. Is there any indication that they have been instrumental in driving change?

4. One of the legal pressures on U.S. corporations identified by Dworkin elsewhere in this article is the revised False Claims Act (FCA), a law that rewards employees for reporting fraud against the government. As she explains:

   While the Act itself encourages external reporting through filing lawsuits in the government's name, the extraordinarily large whistleblowers' awards, fines, and recoveries paid to the federal government, and the dramatic increase in FCA whistleblowing, have led many organizations, especially those in the defense and healthcare industries, to self-police. Under the FCA, whistleblowers who successfully prosecute FCA claims against those who have fraudulently claimed federal funds receive up to thirty percent of recovered monies. Because of the amount of fraud, treble damages, and fines as high as ten thousand dollars per false claim, the average recovery for a successful FCA whistleblower is over one million dollars. The government recovered over three billion dollars between 1986, when the law was revised, and 1999. FCA suits increased from an average of six per year to approximately two per day in 1999.

   A plaintiff under this law is called *qui tam*, an abbreviation of a Latin phrase that may be translated as "who sues on behalf of a king as well as for himself." As of 2007, the FCA has been pivotal in returning some $20 billion to the U.S. government.

   (a) Is the False Claims Act a sensible response to the problem it seeks to address? Or does it turn employees into bounty hunters, too eager to turn against their employers? To help you think about this, check http://www.quitam.com or http://www.taf.org.

   (b) **Internet Assignment:** Update Dworkin's statistics. Find out if the FCA cases are still on the rise. Locate a recent case. How much was the award to the whistleblower?

5. Dworkin writes: "Rules reinforced by whistleblowing can help to deliver transparency."

   Internet Assignment: What is meant by "transparency" in the context of global business? Check the Web site of Transparency International. Compare corruption indices across countries. Do the countries with lower transparency rates also have weaker whistleblowing protections, reinforcing Dworkin's analysis?

CHAPTER **PROBLEMS**

1. What should be the result when an employee-at-will is fired for being a Good Samaritan? Kevin Gardner had a job driving an armored car. At a scheduled stop at a certain bank in Spokane, Washington, he waited in the vehicle while his co-worker was in the bank. Suddenly he spotted a woman, whom he recognized as the manager, running out of the bank screaming, "Help me!" Chasing her was a man with a knife.

   Gardner described the expression on her face: "It was more than fear. There was a real—it was like a horrified kind of a look, like you—I can't describe it other than that, I mean she—she was horrified, not just afraid." Gardner looked around the parking lot and saw nobody coming to help the manager. After the manager and the suspect ran past the front of the truck, Gardner got out, locking the door behind him. As he got out of the truck, he temporarily lost sight of the manager and the suspect, who were both on the passenger side of the truck. While out of Gardner's view, the manager reached a drive-in teller booth across the parking lot, where she found refuge. It is unclear whether the manager was safe before Gardner left the truck, but by the time Gardner walked forward to a point where he could see the suspect, the suspect had already grabbed another woman who was walking into the bank. Gardner recognized the second woman as Kathy Martin, an employee of Plant World, who watered plants at the bank. The suspect put the knife to Ms. Martin's throat and dragged her back into the bank. Gardner followed them into the bank where he observed his partner with his gun drawn and aimed at the suspect. When his partner distracted the suspect, Gardner and a bank customer tackled the suspect and disarmed him. The police arrived immediately thereafter and took custody of the suspect. Ms. Martin was unharmed.

   Gardner's employer had a company rule forbidding armored truck drivers from leaving the truck unattended. Even if pulled over by someone who appears to be a police officer, drivers were instructed to show a card explaining that the driver would follow the police to the stationhouse. Gardner was fired for violating this absolute rule. He sued for wrongful discharge. What would be the arguments of the employer? Of the employee? Find out: *Gardner v. Loomis Armored Inc.*, 913 P.2d 377 (Washington 1996).

2. The 2001 Enron Corporate Responsibility Annual Report contains this statement:

   Enron employees … are trained to report without retribution anything they observe or discover that indicates our standards are not being met.

   In December 2001, using company equipment on company premises, an Enron employee posted a comment on an Internet message board revealing that Enron had paid $55 million in bonuses to its top people just before it filed for bankruptcy and laid off 4,000 workers. The employee who wrote this was fired. What ethical issues arise in this situation? Enron's headquarters are in Houston. In Texas, wrongful discharge claims succeed only when an employee has refused to perform an illegal act, so if this whistleblower sues, he would lose. What would be the legal result in Maryland? In New Jersey? In Montana?

3. How would each of these whistleblowers fare under the law in Maryland? New Jersey? Montana?

   a. William Scholtz was a security guard for Garden State Park. The park was hosting a prom when it received a bomb threat. Scholtz's supervisor told him to check the premises for a bomb, but he refused, claiming he had had no training in responding to bomb threats or in bomb detection. He was fired.

   b. DuPont produces Zonyl RP, a chemical that makes paper resistant to grease. After reading a 1987 study showing Zonyl could leach from paper coats into food at an unacceptable rate, chemical engineer Glenn Evers tried to persuade DuPont colleagues to notify customers and regulators. The company later learned that Zonyl breaks down into a substance that persists in the blood of humans, but by then the chemical was a best seller. When DuPont restructured in 2002, Evers was fired.

4. While an Assistant District Attorney in Brooklyn, Rob Reuland published a novel about working as a prosecutor. He was interviewed in his Homicide Bureau office by a reporter for *New York* magazine, and the resulting piece (highlighting young lawyers in the city) mentioned Reuland's upcoming book and quoted him as saying, "Brooklyn is the best place to be a homicide prosecutor" because "[w]e've got more dead bodies per square inch than anyplace else." Told by his supervisor that prominent politicians were outraged over his description of Brooklyn in the article, Reuland said he was just trying to explain why he enjoyed his job, and he offered to write a letter to the editor to make that clear. His attempt to do that—approved by his supervisor—stated:

> [T]his was not intended to be, nor is it, literally true. In fact Brooklyn's murder rate has declined more than 66 percent during the past decade. Even with the remarkable reduction, the loss of life remains high and still keeps a homicide prosecutor busy—the point of my hyperbolic remark.

Still, the District Attorney was not happy. He transferred Reuland out of the Homicide Bureau, a demotion. When Reuland did not receive positive performance reviews and his request to transfer was denied, he resigned. On what basis could Reuland sue? What would probably be the outcome of his case? Find out what it was: *Reuland v. Hynes* 460 F3d 409 (2d Cir. 2006).

5. Ten months before the Enron debacle, a 30-year-old reporter with *Fortune* magazine, Bethany McLean, wrote an expose of the company, called "Is Enron Overpriced?" The most disturbing fact she revealed was the absence of solid information in Enron's financial reports. Three Enron executives were flown to New York to try to convince the magazine not to publish the piece; Enron executive Jeffrey Skilling questioned Ms. McLean's research, calling her unethical; and Enron's CEO Kenneth Lay placed a call to the magazine's editor, claiming McLean was relying on a source who would benefit if Enron stock lost value. None of this pressure worked; the article was published anyway—although its message was largely ignored. What is at stake when corporate power attempts to silence the media?

6. Born in Mexico, Jose Castro illegally entered the United States in 1988, and got a job with Hoffman Plastic by showing false identification. In December 1988 the United Rubber, Cork, Linoleum and Plastic Workers of America, AFL-CIO started a union organizing campaign at his production plant, and Castro supported the effort, distributing authorization cards. In January 1989 Castro and others who had been involved in the organizing were laid off. The NLRB found that Castor's lay-off violated the law because Hoffman was attempting to "rid itself of known union supporters." In 2002, the Supreme Court ruled that as an undocumented "alien," Castro was not entitled to the monetary remedy (back pay) otherwise available under the National Labor Relations Act. Who are the stakeholders in this case? What impact does the ruling have on each of them? Suppose Castro had been fired after reporting health or safety violations in the workplace. Would a similar outcome—no whistleblower protection for an undocumented alien—apply?

7. The federal Whistleblower Protection Act of 1989 protects federal employees from retaliation for disclosing violations of law, gross mismanagement of public funds, abuse of authority or a substantial danger to public health or safety. But, since 1994, judicial interpretation of the WPA has made it hard for whistleblowers to win, and in May 2007,

a Labor Department ruling cast doubt on whether there would be any protection at all for environmental whistleblowing related to clean water, toxic substances, or hazardous waste. The House of Representatives, however, passed H.R. 985, the "Whistleblower Protection Enhancement Act" called by one supporter "the most significant breakthrough for whistleblower rights in history." In part, this legislation would change the result of a case such as *Garcetti v. Ceballos*.

Internet Assignment: Find out if a law has been passed by both houses and signed by the president to expand the protection of federal workers who blow the whistle. If so, what does it do to strengthen their rights?

8. Internet Assignment: Founded in 1977, the Government Accountability Project promotes "government and corporate accountability through advancing occupational free speech and ethical conduct, defending whistleblowers, and empowering citizen activists." What tips do they offer a would-be whistleblower? See http://www.whistleblower.org.

9. Harvard professor Joseph L. Badaracco, Jr. interviewed 30 graduates of Harvard's MBA program. These young managers were "dubious" about ethics codes and programs, explaining that the values contained in them "seemed inconsistent with 'what the company was about.'" Here, Badaracco summarizes what he learned:

> First, in many cases [they] received explicit instructions from their middle-manager bosses or felt strong pressures to do things they believed were sleazy, unethical, or sometimes illegal. Second, corporate ethics programs, codes of conduct, mission statements, hotlines, and the like provided little help. Third, many of the[m] believed that their company's executives were out of touch on ethical issues, either because they were too busy or because they sought to avoid responsibility. Fourth, the[y] resolved the dilemmas they faced largely on the basis of personal reflection and individual values, not through reliance on corporate credos, company loyalty, [or] the exhortations of senior executives.

Badaracco's interview subjects, who worked in banking, consulting, accounting, and advertising, came to believe they had to respond to the following "powerful organizational commandments:"

> First, performance is what really counts, so make your numbers. Second, be loyal and show us you're a team player. Third, don't break the law. Fourth, don't over-invest in ethical behavior.[30]

What do these findings suggest about the role of whistleblowers inside large corporations? Look back at the recent statistics about whistleblowing on p. 47. Do you see any items that seem to support these findings? That appear to challenge them?

CHAPTER **PROJECT**

Stakeholder Ethics Role Play

GUIDELINES: APPENDIX C

Name the stakeholders in this business ethics dilemma. Discuss possible choices for Nash in the light of law and ethical theory.

30 Joseph L. Badaracco, Jr. and Allen P. Webb, "Business Ethics: A View From The Trenches," *California Management Review*, Vol. 37, No. 2 (Winter 1995).

Desperate Air[31]

Desperate Air Corporation (DAC) flies routes along the U.S. East Coast. DAC acquired a number of hotels and undeveloped properties five years ago as part of a short-lived diversification strategy. DAC has recently experienced substantial losses, has a negative cash flow, and bankruptcy looms as a possibility unless high labor costs can be reduced and consumer confidence restored.

Benton Williams has just been brought in as CEO to revitalize DAC. Williams began by cutting back on middle management and by placing a one-year moratorium on hiring MBAs. Middle managers terminated by DAC and other airlines are having a tough time finding equivalent jobs.

DAC owns a large, undeveloped oceanfront property on the east coast of Florida. Williams directs George Nash, DAC's vice president of real estate, to find a buyer for the property to generate badly needed cash. After some effort, Nash identifies Fledgling Industries, a relatively new developer of retirement villas, as a good prospect. Fledgling is interested in finding a property on which it could build a complex of high-rise retirement condos featuring elaborate walking trails and outside recreational facilities.

DAC had conducted a full environmental audit of the property six months earlier and had discovered no problems. A copy of this report was given to the Fledgling representative, who also walked over the property and discovered no problems. The representative asked, "Anything I should know about?" Nash replied, "No problems."

As the negotiations progressed with Fledgling, Nash was approached by a longtime friend at DAC, Laura Devitt, who told him that there was now some highly toxic waste on the property. She said she heard this might be true through the rumor mill at the firm and that she had been curious enough to check things out. Walking around on the property one day, she had found several partially buried metal containers marked DANGER/BIOHAZARD. RADIOACTIVE MEDICAL WASTE. The containers were rusted where they were exposed; two were cracked and their liquid contents were seeping onto the ground. Laura told Nash she wanted him to know about this because she was worried that innocent people could be hurt if the sale went through.

Nash contacted Williams, but before he could mention the containers to him, Williams interrupted and told him it was vital that the sale closed and that it be done as soon as possible. Nash consulted with a DAC lawyer who told him that under Florida law it is not necessary to disclose the existence of hazardous waste on commercial property as long as there hasn't been a fraudulent misstatement about the condition of the property.

Nash was troubled. Should he mention the hazardous materials to the Fledgling representative before he closed the sale? He knew Fledgling had been considering some other similar properties, and Nash thought that if he mentioned the toxic spill problem Fledgling would probably not go through with the sale. At the least, disclosure could delay the sale for months while the spill was investigated and potential liability problems considered. Nash figured that he would be unlikely ever to deal with Fledgling again regarding future real estate deals because DAC did not own any other properties that fit Fledgling's business needs.

The question of whether to close the sale immediately bothered Nash enough that he talked to his wife about it, and then prayed about what to do.

---

31 This case was written by Professor Thomas Dunfee of the Wharton School at the University of Pennsylvania and is reprinted with his permission.

3 PRIVACY AND TECHNOLOGY

A wonderful fact to reflect upon, that every human creature is constituted to be that profound secret and mystery to every other. A solemn consideration, when I enter a great city by night, that every one of those darkly clustered houses encloses its own secret; that every room in every one of them encloses its own secret; that in every beating heart in the hundreds of thousands of breasts there is, in some of its imaginings, a secret to the heart nearest to it!

— CHARLES DICKENS

You already have zero privacy—get over it.

— SCOTT MCNEALY, CEO, SUN MICROSYSTEMS

There is indeed a whole lot a scannin' goin' on. People surreptitiously inter-cept, record, and disclose the usual suspects for the usual reasons, in the per-petual parade of human perfidy. Popular motivations are love, sex, drugs, crime, politics, business, and employment. And if we reflect, we quickly see that none of us is perfect and that all of us are potential victims. Who among us does not sometime, somewhere, have something they would prefer to keep to themselves?

— RODNEY A. SMOLLA, "INFORMATION AS CONTRABAND," 96 NW. UNIV. L REV 1099 (2002)

•

Human beings must experience a degree of privacy to thrive. Yet, as they act inside organizations, they frequently need information about one another, information that may be sensitive and confidential. Employers want to find out if their workers are productive and loyal. Corporations want to know the preferences of potential customers or the strategies of their competitors. Health insurers want access to patient medical histories and genetic profiles. Governments want to thwart terrorists. Tension between privacy and the need to know is heightened as computer technology revolutionizes information gathering. The process has never been so fast, so efficient, so omnipresent.

This chapter highlights the conflict between the sweeping power of technology to access and assemble information and the ongoing concerns about privacy we all share. Opening with a case involving the interception of e-mail by an employer, it broadens to look at electronic sur-veillance more generally, and at the legal framework that might address it. We read about the value of privacy, both for individuals and for communities. Next, we look at efforts employers are making to control employees' off-the-job behavior. Should employers be able to fire you for unhealthy habits? For dating someone who is married? We consider workplace testing of various types, such as psychological and drug tests. Readings on consumer privacy follow. We move on to explore constitutional privacy protection in the drug testing context. The chapter ends with a focus on the collection of sensitive health data through genetic testing.

Surveillance at Work

E-mail Interception

Ninety percent of all companies with more than 1,000 employees currently use e-mail, putting about 40 million workers on e-mail systems and sending some 60 billion messages annually. Because they use passcodes, employees may believe their e-mail messages are private, but the reality is that they are not. Even deleted messages are stored in archives easily accessible to employers and others. In 1996, a district court in Philadelphia was faced with the following situation. A Pillsbury employee and his supervisor were sending e-mail messages to one another. One message, referring to sales management, mentioned plans to "kill the back-stabbing bastards." Another message described a holiday party as the "Jim Jones Kool-Aid affair." These messages fell into their boss's hands, and both men were fired for sending "inappropriate and unprofessional comments" over Pillsbury's e-mail system. One of the employees sued, claiming he was "wrongfully discharged" when he lost his $62,500 per year job as a regional manager.

MICHAEL A. SMYTH v. THE PILLSBURY COMPANY

United States District Court, 1996

914 F. Supp. 97

WEINER, District Judge ✳

Defendant [Pillsbury Company] maintained an electronic mail communication system ("e-mail") in order to promote internal corporate communications between its employees. Defendant repeatedly assured its employees, including plaintiff, that all e-mail communications would remain confidential and privileged. Defendant further assured its employees, including plaintiff, that e-mail communications could not be intercepted and used by defendant against its employees as grounds for termination or reprimand.

In October 1994, plaintiff [Michael Smyth] received certain e-mail communications from his supervisor over defendant's e-mail system on his computer at home. In reliance on defendant's assurances regarding defendant's e-mail system, plaintiff responded and exchanged e-mails with his supervisor. At some later date, contrary to the assurances of confidentiality made by defendant, defendant, acting through its agents, servants and employees, intercepted plaintiff's private e-mail messages made in October 1994. On January 17, 1995, defendant notified plaintiff that it was terminating his employment ... for transmitting what it deemed to be inappropriate and unprofessional comments over defendant's e-mail system....

[Smyth argued wrongful discharge, claiming his employer had violated public policy by committing a tort known as "invasion of privacy." One version of invasion of privacy is called "intrusion." In the first step of his analysis, the judge defines the tort of "intrusion":]

"One who intentionally intrudes, physically or otherwise, upon the solitude or seclusion of another or his private affairs or concerns, is subject to liability to the other for invasion of his privacy, if the intrusion would be highly offensive to a reasonable person...."

[To determine if the facts of the case fit the definition above, the judge uses a "balancing test," weighing the employee's privacy interests against the employer's need to discover information.]

[W]e do not find a reasonable expectation of privacy in e-mail communications voluntarily made by an employee to his supervisor over the company e-mail system notwithstanding any assurances that such communications would not be intercepted by management. Once plaintiff communicated the alleged unprofessional comments to a second person (his supervisor) over an e-mail system which was apparently utilized by the entire company, any reasonable expectation of privacy was lost. Significantly, the defendant did not require plaintiff, as in the case of a urinalysis or personal property search, to disclose any personal information about himself. Rather, plaintiff voluntarily communicated the alleged unprofessional comments over the company e-mail system. We find no privacy interests in such communications.

Secondly, even if we found that an employee had a reasonable expectation of privacy in the contents of his e-mail communications over the company e-mail system, we do not find that a reasonable person would consider the defendant's interception of these communications to be a substantial and highly offensive invasion of his privacy…. [T]he company's interest in preventing inappropriate and unprofessional comments or even illegal activity over its e-mail system outweighs any privacy interest the employee may have in those comments.

In sum, we find that the defendant's actions did not tortiously invade the plaintiff's privacy and, therefore, did not violate public policy.

QUESTIONS

1. How does Judge Weiner explain why Michael Smyth lost any "reasonable expectation of privacy" in his e-mail comments?

2. Is there any difference between a password-protected message sent on company e-mail and a handwritten memo sealed in an envelope marked "private" sent through company mail? Consider the judge's reasons for his ruling that you articulated above. Would they also apply to the memo? Suppose Pillsbury began covert audio monitoring of the area near the coffee station in order to screen employee conversations on break time. How would the judge's reasoning apply?

3. From a Kantian perspective, how ethical were the actions of Smyth? Of Pillsbury? What appears to be the ethical framework underlying the judge's ruling?

4. Corporate culture varies, and with it, corporate surveillance policies. Some companies give notice to employees that their e-mail communications are not private. Kmart's policy, for example, introduced at every employee orientation, states that "misuse of the e-mail system could result in denial of access to the Kmart computing environment or dismissal." Apple Computers, on the other hand, has an explicit policy of not monitoring employee e-mail. What might be the advantages and disadvantages of such policies from an employee's viewpoint? An employer's?

5. Suppose you were responsible for developing a surveillance policy where you worked. How would you go about setting its parameters? How would you implement it?

More than 100 million people, about two-thirds of all employees, performed some of their work outside of the office as of 2006.[1] As laptop computers, cell phones, and other handheld communication devices make it possible for employees to do more and more work outside the physical confines of the traditional office—in transit and from home—the boundaries of work are no longer static. And increasingly, people work during hours that were once considered reserved for personal time. As of 2004, one-third of us keep in touch with work regularly outside normal working hours, and more than half of us work while on vacation.[2] Meanwhile U.S. employees work longer hours: 28 percent surpass a 40-hour week, and 8 percent put in more than 60 hours a week. The 2005 Census revealed that commuting time has been expanding too; we average over 100 hours a year just going to and from work.

1 IDC U.S. Mobile Worker Population Forecast and Analyses, 2002–2006.
2 Families and Work Institute study, "Over-Work in America." 2004.

6. As employees work longer hours, both onsite and offsite, and as the division between work and the rest of life becomes ever more blurred, should the balancing of interests articulated in the *Pillsbury* case change?

7. Hi-tech surveillance is not solely directed by employers at workers. American businesses have always been interested in capturing confidential information and trade secrets from competitors. Today, thanks to computer technology, they are able to spy on one another with more sophisticated means than ever before. What are some of the latest developments in this area? How far can a company go in this direction without crossing the line? Visit the Web site of the Society of Competitive Intelligence Professionals at http://www.scip.org.

8. Should educational institutions be free to randomly monitor student and faculty e-mail? What is your school's policy on e-mail privacy? Review it and discuss it with others. Are there elements of the policy that you would change, in light of what you have read? Rewrite it.

Electronic Surveillance: The Debate

Employers have long had an interest in scrutinizing their workforces. In the 1880s, Frederick Taylor invented an approach to industrial efficiency that broke each job into many separate, measurable components. He monitored every part of the process—time per task; hand and eye movements; spacing between workers, machines, and products—developing a system that gave managers the ability to track both the speed and the intensity of work very closely. And in the early twentieth century, Ford Motor Company hired social workers to investigate employees, to check that they had the right habits of cleanliness, thriftiness, and churchgoingness to deserve what was then an impressive $5/day wage. What is different about present-day workplace monitoring is the introduction of technology that allows workers to be observed secretly and in newly intrusive ways.

By 2003, 92 percent of employers were conducting some form of electronic monitoring of their employees.[3] According to a 2005 American Management Association survey, both the intensity and range of workplace surveillance is surging, from videotaping to monitoring of IM chat and blogging to GPS satellite tracking of cars and cell phones. Twenty-six percent of companies have terminated employees for misuse of the Internet; 25 percent for e-mail misuse. E-mail seems to be a special case, because one in five employers has had e-mail subpoenaed in recent years and 13 percent have been involved in lawsuits triggered by email. More than half of the companies responding to the survey—a rate up from 33 percent in 2001—said they monitor employees via videotape to counter theft. Video surveillance generally is on the rise—10 percent tape particular job categories; 6 percent tape all workers; 15 percent tape secretly.

Whereas most companies carry out electronic monitoring on a spot-check basis, the interest in the use of software that puts employees under continuous surveillance is growing.[4] Such software is evolving quickly and becoming increasingly sophisticated. Programs exist that can take surreptitious "screen shots" of employee computers or that can hunt for particular images. A product called Pornsweeper examines pictures attached to e-mails and picture files for anything that looks like flesh. Software can monitor keystrokes and can retrieve documents, even those that employees did not save. Telemate.Net can track Web site visits by individuals and rank them by categories—games, humor, pornography, cults, shopping, and job-hunting—instantly generating logs that reveal precisely who went where and when. SuperScout

---

3 2003 Center for Business Ethics at Bentley College, "Survey: 'You've Got Mail, and the Boss Knows.'"

4 Andrew Schulman, chief researcher for a 2001 Privacy Foundation study, reports that more than concerns over low productivity or vicarious liability, employers are driven to use continuous surveillance software because it is cheap. It costs less than $10/year to monitor each worker.

produces bar charts that show which workers are sending the longest e-messages, and who is sending or receiving the most e-mail. XVmail searches the actual text of e-mail messages.

Businesses justify electronic surveillance in a number of ways. It is a form of quality control, enabling supervisors to better correct and improve employee performance. It both measures and encourages efficiency. It enhances the completeness and fairness of personnel evaluations. It can uncover employee disloyalty, which can take the form of stealing tangible items, such as products and supplies, or intangibles, such as trade secrets. It can flag racially or sexually harassing e-messages. (In 1995, Chevron Corporation paid more than $2 million to settle claims brought by female employees who had received pornographic e-mail.)

Countering all this, employees claim that electronic monitoring puts them under dehumanizing pressure, in which computers, instead of people, judge their output. Because computers measure quantity better than quality, employees who work fast might look better than those who work best. The "electronic sweatshop," they say, causes psychological stress and physical symptoms.[5] Apart from the more measurable costs, employees emphasize their need to preserve at work what they expect to maintain elsewhere—a sense of dignity and self-respect.

Electronic Surveillance: The Law

America lacks a comprehensive, uniform legal standard protecting privacy. No express "right to privacy" was written into the U.S. Constitution, although the Supreme Court has interpreted the First, Fourth, Fifth, and Ninth Amendments as creating certain privacy rights that cannot be violated by the government. (Later in this chapter we explore one aspect, the right to be free of unreasonable government searches and seizures.)

In the private sector, privacy law is determined by a variety of federal and state statutes and by the common law of torts.[6] Employees may claim that electronic monitoring amounts to "intrusion," a variation on the tort of invasion of privacy. As the *Pillsbury* case indicates, intrusion involves invading another person's solitude in a manner considered highly offensive—unauthorized prying into a personal bank account, or a landlord bugging the wall of his tenants' bedroom, for example. Most courts consider two main factors: (1) the obnoxiousness of the means used to intrude; that is, whether it is a deviation from the normal, accepted means of discovering the relevant information; and (2) the reasons for intruding. In one Oregon case the employer had secretly taken 18 rolls of film of a worker suspected of filing a fraudulent worker's compensation claim. The film showed him taking out his trash, mowing his lawn, and otherwise looking fit and able. Dismissing his claim for intrusion, the court mentioned that once he filed his worker's compensation claim he had to expect a reasonable investigation.[7] Because electronic monitoring is now commonplace, it may be considered normal, if not accepted, and, as long as employers can point to a legitimate purpose for monitoring, it will be difficult for employees to win cases against them.

The 1968 Federal Wiretap Law, as amended by the Electronic Communications Privacy Act 1986 (ECPA), making it illegal to intercept, disclose, or access messages without authorization, would appear to protect workers from electronic eavesdropping. But there are a number of exemptions to the ECPA. For example, there is no protection for communications that are "readily accessible to the general public," such as public chat room exchanges. The law does not apply to the extent that employees give "consent" to monitoring, which would seem to

---

5 Peter Blackman and Barbara Franklin, "Blocking Big Brother: Proposed Law Limits Employers' Right to Snoop," *N.Y.L.J.*, August 19, 1993, p. 5, citing University of Wisconsin study that found monitored telecommunications workers suffered more depression, anxiety, and fatigue than their non-monitored counterparts at the same facility.

6 As of 2007, only two states, Connecticut and Delaware, had passed laws to protect employees against e-mail monitoring without notice. Conn. Gen. Stat. Sec. 31-48d, Del. Code tit. 19, § 705.

7 *McClain v. Boise Cascade Corporation*, 533 P.2d 343 (1975).

eliminate ECPA coverage in the many workplaces where people are told that their communications are not private. The ECPA also allows employers to listen in on communications made in the "ordinary course of business." In other words, where business interests such as efficiency or legal liability are at stake, the surveillance would be allowed.

The Value of Privacy

> *Privacy is much more than just a possible social technique for assuring this or that substantive interest ... it is necessarily related to ends and relations of the most fundamental sort: respect, love, friendship and trust. Privacy is not merely a good technique for furthering these fundamental relations, rather without privacy they are simply inconceivable. They require a context of privacy or the possibility of privacy for their existence.... To respect, love, trust, feel affection for others and to regard ourselves as the objects of love, trust and affection is at the heart of our notion of ourselves as persons among persons, and privacy is the necessary atmosphere for those attitudes and actions, as oxygen is for combustion.*
>
> — CHARLES FRIED, "PRIVACY," 77 YALE L.J. 475 (1968)

The following excerpt describes how privacy serves a set of important human needs. The author, Columbia University professor emeritus Alan Westin, now a corporate consultant on privacy issues, has been in the forefront of research on the effects of technology on privacy in our society, particularly in the workplace.

THE FUNCTIONS OF PRIVACY
ALAN WESTIN [8]

[T]he functions privacy performs for individuals in democratic societies ... can [be] ... grouped conveniently under four headings—personal autonomy, emotional release, self-evaluation, and limited and protected communication....

Personal Autonomy

In democratic societies there is a fundamental belief in the uniqueness of the individual, in his basic dignity and worth as a creature of God and a human being, and in the need to maintain social processes that safeguard his sacred individuality. Psychologists and sociologists have linked the development and maintenance of this sense of individuality to the human need for autonomy—the desire to avoid being manipulated or dominated wholly by others.

[Scholars describe a] "core self,"... pictured as an inner circle surrounded by a series of larger concentric circles. The inner circle shelters the individual's "ultimate secrets"—those hopes, fears, and prayers that are beyond sharing with anyone unless the individual comes under such stress that he must pour out these ultimate secrets to secure emotional relief.... The next circle outward contains "intimate secrets," those that can be willingly shared with close relations, confessors, or strangers who pass by and cannot

---

8 Reprinted with the permission of Scribner, an imprint of Simon and Schuster Adult Publishing Group, from "Privacy and Freedom" by Alan F. Westin. Copyright © 1967 by the Association of the Bar of City of New York..

injure. The next circle is open to members of the individual's friendship group. The series continues until it reaches the outer circles of casual conversation and physical expression that are open to all observers.

The most serious threat to the individual's autonomy is the possibility that someone may penetrate the inner zone and learn his ultimate secrets, either by physical or psychological means. Each person is aware of the gap between what he wants to be and what he actually is, between what the world sees of him and what he knows to be his much more complex reality. In addition, there are aspects of himself that the individual does not fully understand but is slowly exploring and shaping as he develops. Every individual lives behind a mask in this manner; indeed, the first etymological meaning of the word "person" was "mask"....

Emotional Release

Life in society generates such tensions for the individual that both physical and psychological health demand periods of privacy for various types of emotional release. At one level, such relaxation is required from the pressure of playing social roles.... On any given day a man may move through the roles of stern father, loving husband, car-pool comedian, skilled lathe operator, union steward, water-cooler flirt, and American Legion committee chairman—all psychologically different roles.... [N]o individual can play indefinitely, without relief, the variety of roles that life demands. There have to be moments "off stage" when the individual can be "himself": tender, angry, irritable, lustful, or dream-filled. Such moments may come in solitude; in the intimacy of family, peers or woman-to-woman and man-to-man relaxation; in the anonymity of park or street; or in a state of reserve while in a group. Privacy in this aspect gives individuals, from factory workers to Presidents, a chance to lay their masks aside for rest....

Another form of emotional release is provided by the protection privacy gives to minor non-compliance with social norms.... [A]lmost everyone does break some social or institutional norms—for example, violating traffic laws, breaking sexual mores, cheating on expense accounts, overstating income tax deductions, or smoking in restrooms when this is prohibited. Although society will usually punish the most flagrant abuses, it tolerates the great bulk of the violations as "permissible" deviations.... [I]f all transgressions were known—most persons in society would be under organizational discipline or in jail, or could be manipulated by threats of such action. The firm expectation of having privacy for permissible deviations is a distinguishing characteristic of life in a free society. At a lesser but still important level, privacy also allows individuals to deviate temporarily from social etiquette when alone or among intimates, as by putting feet on desks, cursing, letting one's face go slack, or scratching wherever one itches.

Another aspect of release is the "safety valve" function afforded by privacy. Most persons need to give vent to their anger at "the system," "city hall," "the boss," and various others who exercise authority over them, and to do this in the intimacy of family or friendship circles, or in private papers, without fear of being held responsible for such comments. This is very different from freedom of speech or press, which involves publicly voiced criticism without fear of interference by government....

Still another aspect of release through privacy arises in the management of bodily and sexual functions....

Self-Evaluation

Every individual needs to integrate his experiences into a meaningful pattern and to exert his individuality on events. To carry on such self-evaluation, privacy is essential. At the intellectual level, individuals need to process the information that is constantly bombarding them, information that cannot be processed while they are still "on the go...." This is particularly true of creative persons. Studies of creativity show that it is in reflective solitude and even "daydreaming" during moments of reserve that most creative "non-verbal" thought takes place. At such moments the individual runs ideas and impressions through his mind in a flow of associations; the active presence of others tends to inhibit this process....

The evaluative function of privacy also has a major moral dimension—the exercise of conscience by which the individual "repossesses himself." While people often consider the moral consequences of their acts during the course of daily affairs, it is primarily in periods of privacy that they take a moral inventory of ongoing conduct and measure current performance against personal ideals. For many persons this process is a religious exercise.... Even for an individual who is not a religious believer, privacy serves to bring the conscience into play, for, when alone, he must find a way to continue living with himself.

Limited and Protected Communication

The greatest threat to civilized social life would be a situation in which each individual was utterly candid in his communications with others, saying exactly what he knew or felt at all times. The havoc done to interpersonal relations by children, saints, mental patients, and adult "innocents" is legendary.

In real life, among mature persons all communication is partial and limited.... Limited communication is particularly vital in urban life, with its heightened stimulation, crowded environment, and continuous physical and psychological confrontations between individuals who do not know one another in the extended, softening fashion of small-town life....

Privacy for limited and protected communication has two general aspects. First, it provides the individual with the opportunities he needs for sharing confidences and intimacies with those he trusts.... "A friend," said Emerson, "is someone before ... [whom] I can think aloud." In addition, the individual often wants to secure counsel from persons with whom he does not have to live daily after disclosing his confidences. He seeks professionally objective advice from persons whose status in society promises that they will not later use his distress to take advantage of him. To protect freedom of limited communication, such relationships—with doctors, lawyers, ministers, psychiatrists, psychologists, and others are given varying but important degrees of legal privilege against forced disclosure. In its second general aspect, privacy through limited communication serves to set necessary boundaries of mental distance in interpersonal situations ranging from the most intimate to the most formal and public. In marriage, for example, husbands and wives need to retain islands of privacy in the midst of their intimacy if they are to preserve a saving respect and mystery in the relation.... In work situations, mental distance is necessary so that the relations of superior and subordinate do not slip into an intimacy which would create a lack of respect and an impediment to directions and correction....

Psychological distance is also used in crowded settings.... [A] complex but well-understood etiquette of privacy is part of our social scenario.... We learn to ignore people and to be ignored by them as a way of achieving privacy in subways, on streets, and in the "non-presence" of servants or children....

QUESTIONS

1. What are the functions of privacy, as described by Westin? For each, can you think of examples from your own experience?

2. Law professor and journalist Jeffrey Rosen, author of *The Unwanted Gaze: The Destruction of Privacy in America*,[9] offers this description of one of the primary values of privacy:

   Privacy protects us from being misdefined and judged out of context.... [W]hen your browsing habits or e-mail messages are exposed to strangers, you may be reduced, in

9 New York: Random House, 2000.

their eyes, to nothing more than the most salacious book you once read or the most vulgar joke you once told. And even if your Internet browsing isn't in any way embarrassing, you run the risk of being stereotyped as the kind of person who would read a particular book or listen to a particular song. Your public identity may be distorted by fragments of information that have little to do with how you define yourself. In a world where citizens are bombarded with information, people form impressions quickly, based on sound bites, and these brief impressions tend to oversimplify and misrepresent our complicated and often contradictory characters.

Does Westin come close to mentioning this aspect of privacy?

3. Which functions of privacy may have been served by the e-mail messages that Michael Smyth sent while working for Pillsbury?

4. To what extent can we describe privacy as an ethical imperative? Think of the *Smyth v. Pillsbury* scenario. Who are the most affected stakeholders? Under the utilitarian approach to ethics, was intercepting the e-mail the right thing to do? Now consider the case from the deontological perspective. Again, was Pillsbury's action ethical?

5. In 1890, in a first attempt to conceptualize privacy within the common law, U.S. federal judges Samuel Warren and Louis Brandeis described it as the right "to be let alone." They believed the law should not consider "a man's house as his castle" and then "open wide the back door" to invasions of privacy, particularly those enabled by the prying, gossip-mongering news media.[10] More recently, theorists have conceptualized privacy not so much as a right possessed by individuals, but more in terms of a public good, a benefit to society at large. Consider the Internet as an incubator of political awareness and debate, for instance. Legal scholar Paul Schwartz sees this potential, but warns:

   In the absence of strong rules for information privacy, Americans will hesitate to engage in cyberspace activities—including those that are most likely to promote democratic self-rule. Current polls already indicate an aversion on the part of some people to engage even in basic commercial activities on the Internet. Yet, deliberative democracy requires more than shoppers; it demands speakers and listeners. But who will speak or listen when this behavior leaves finely-grained data trails in a fashion that is difficult to understand or anticipate?... The Internet's interactive nature means that individuals on it simultaneously collect and transmit information. As a result, merely listening on the Internet becomes a speech-act. A visit to a Web site or a chat room generates a record of one's presence.... [O]ne leading computer handbook, the Internet Bible, concludes its description of the low level of privacy in cyberspace with the warning, "Think about the newsgroups you review or join—they say a lot about you."

   Schwartz goes on to argue that a vibrant democracy depends not only on robust public deliberation, but also on the ability of each person to figure out who they are and what they believe. This process of self-determination, he writes, is also compromised by lack of online privacy:

   George Orwell carried out the classic analysis of how surveillance can exert this negative pressure. In the novel 1984 ... he imagined a machine called the "telescreen." This omnipresent device broadcasted propaganda on a nonstop basis and allowed the state officials, the "Thought Police," to observe the populace. Computers on the Internet are reminiscent of the telescreen; under current conditions, it is impossible to know if and when the cyber-Thought Police are plugged in on any individual wire. To extend Orwell's thought, one can say that as habit becomes instinct and people on the Internet gain a sense that their every mouse click and key stroke might be observed, the necessary insulation for individual self-determination will vanish.[11]

---

10 "The Right to Privacy," 4 *Harv. L. Rev.* 193, 214 (1890).

11 "Privacy and Democracy in Cyberspace," 52 *Vand. L. Rev.* 1609 (1999).

Do you agree that privacy is essential to the flourishing of a healthy democracy? Do other areas of our collective life depend on privacy protection?

Lifestyle Control

When he opened up his assembly line 80 years ago, Henry Ford issued a booklet, called *Helpful Hints and Advice to Employees*, warning against drinking, gambling, borrowing money, taking in boarders, and poor hygiene, advising workers to "use plenty of soap and water in the home and upon their children, bathing frequently." As we read, Ford even employed 100 investigators to do door-to-door checks to make sure his advice was being followed. Today we find such a story quaint. We might think we have reached some sort of societal consensus that what employees do on their own time, away from the workplace, should be entirely their own business.

In 1968, then-chairman of IBM, son of its founder, Thomas Watson Jr. notified his managers that off-the-job behavior should concern them only when it impaired a person's ability to perform on the job. He wrote:

> The line that separates an individual's on-the-job business life from his other life as a private citizen is at times well-defined and at other times indistinct. But the line does exist, and you and I, as managers in IBM, must be able to recognize that line.... Our primary objective as IBM managers is to further the business of this company by leading our people properly and measuring quantity and quality of work and effectiveness on the job against clearly set standards of responsibility and compensation. This is performance—and performance is, in the final analysis, the one thing that the company can insist on from everyone....

The line that Tom Watson felt he could recognize and define has become much fuzzier since his memo was circulated at IBM. At this point, one of the most contested areas of workplace privacy involves the extent to which an employer may exercise control over a worker's life outside of working hours. Employers want to curb habits that drive up the cost of health care premiums.[12] From this perspective, smokers are much more expensive than nonsmokers.[13] and companies have tried to cut their losses with a number of strategies. Weyco, a Michigan-based, health-benefits management company, announced a draconian no smoking policy: Effective January 1, 2005, every employee who failed the mandatory nicotine test was terminated. Other firms use disincentives (Texas Instruments adds a monthly $10 surcharge on health insurance for employees who smoke); some offer incentives (Southern California Edison rebates each nonsmoking worker $120 annually). Policies like these have been aimed at a range of behaviors: Workers must keep their blood pressure and cholesterol at healthy levels, wear seat belts, and join corporate wellness programs. One Georgia developer will not employ anyone who engages in "high risk" recreational activities such as motorcycling or skydiving. The Best Lock Corporation will hire no one who admits to drinking. At the Borgata Casino in Atlantic City, New Jersey, bartenders and waitresses can be fired if they gain more than 7 percent of their body weight. Weigh-ins are mandatory with 90-day unpaid suspensions for violators. Exceptions are made for pregnancy and other valid medical reasons. "Borgata Babes" who miss their target weight after 90 days are fired.

Whereas companies say they are cutting health care costs and lowering rates of absenteeism in these ways, organizations such as the American Civil Liberties Union (ACLU) are troubled by this drift to control off-site behavior. Former ACLU president Ira Glasser has said:

---

12 Lifestyle-related illnesses are estimated to cost employers as much as $100 billion annually.

13 According to one Florida case, where a job applicant sued because Miami city government would not hire her as a smoker, health care and productivity costs of more than $4,611/year were cited as associated with employees who smoke. *Kurtz v. City of North Miami*, 653 So.2 1025 (S. C. Florida 1995).

If an employer believes your capacity to take care of yourself is in his interest, then you become like a piece of equipment. He gets to lock it up at night and control the temperature and make sure dust doesn't get into the machine, because what happens when it's not working affects how long it's going to last.

In fact, a peculiar alliance between the ACLU and the tobacco industry was extremely effective in lobbying state legislatures for laws that protect employees who smoke when they are not at work.[14] Today, a majority of states have some version of off-the-job privacy protection laws. In New York, for instance, it is illegal to fire an employee for engaging in off-hours sports, games, hobbies, exercise, reading, movie- or TV-watching.

This was the law at issue in the case that follows. Laurel Allen was married, but separated from her husband when she began dating Samuel Johnson, a co-worker at Wal-Mart. When the store manager found out, they were both fired. Wal-Mart's anti-fraternization policy prohibited such relationships as inconsistent with the company's "strongly held belief in and support of the family unit." The New York attorney general entered the case on behalf of the dating couple, alleging that firing them violated the state law protecting the employees' right to engage in off-duty, off-premises recreational activity.

STATE OF NEW YORK v. WAL-MART STORES, INC.

N.Y. App. Div., 1995

621 N.Y.S.2d 158

MERCURE, Justice. ✳

In February 1993, defendant discharged two of its employees for violating its "fraternization" policy, which is codified in defendant's 1989 *Associates Handbook* and prohibits a "dating relationship" between a married employee and another employee, other than his or her own spouse. In this action, plaintiff seeks reinstatement of the two employees with back pay upon the ground that their discharge violated [New York] Labor Law § 201-d(2)(c), which forbids employer discrimination against employees because of their participation in "legal recreational activities" pursued outside of work hours....

[The court must decide whether "a dating relationship" is meant to be included within the statutory definition of "recreational activities."]

[NY] Labor Law § 201-d(1)(b) defines "recreational activities" as meaning:

... any lawful, leisure-time activity, for which the employee receives no compensation and which is generally engaged in for recreational purposes, including but not limited to sports, games, hobbies, exercise, reading and the viewing of television, movies and similar material.

In our view, there is no justification for proceeding beyond the fundamental rule of construction that "[w]here words of a statute are free from ambiguity and express plainly, clearly and distinctly the legislative intent, resort may not be had to other means of interpretation".... To us, "dating" is entirely distinct from and, in fact, bears little resemblance to "recreational activity." Whether characterized as a relationship or an activity, an indispensable element of "dating," in fact its raison d'etre, is romance, either pursued or realized. For that reason, although a dating couple may go bowling and under the circumstances call that activity a "date," when two individuals lacking amorous interest in

---

14 By 1996, such laws were in effect in 28 states. Virginia, a "tobacco state," was the first to pass one. It reads: "No employee or applicant ... shall be required ... to smoke or use tobacco products on the job, or to abstain from smoking or using tobacco products outside of the course of his employment." *VA Code Ann.* 15.1-29, 18 (1990).

one another go bowling or engage in any other kind of "legal recreational activity," they are not "dating."

Moreover, even if [NY] Labor Law § 201-d(1)(b) was found to contain some ambiguity, application of the rules of statutory construction does not support [the trial court's] interpretation. We agree with defendant that ... the voluminous legislative history to the enactment, including memoranda issued in connection with the veto of two earlier more expansive bills, [shows] an obvious intent to limit the statutory protection to certain clearly defined categories of leisure-time activities. Further, in view of the specific inclusion of "sports, games, hobbies, exercise, reading and the viewing of television, movies and similar material" within the statutory definition of "recreational activities," ... personal relationships fall outside the scope of legislative intent....

[Order in defendant's favor affirmed.]

YESAWICH, Justice, dissenting. ✳

I respectfully dissent, for I find defendant's central thesis, apparently accepted by the majority, that the employment policy at issue only prohibits romantic entanglements and not other types of social interaction, to be wholly without merit. While the majority encumbers the word "dating" with an "amorous interest" component, there is nothing in defendant's fraternization policy, its application—defendant does not allege that its two former employees manifested an intimate or amatory attitude toward each other—or even in defendant's own definition of a "date", "a social engagement between persons of opposite sex" (*Webster's Ninth New Collegiate Dictionary*, 325 [1988]), that leads to such a conclusion.

More importantly, I do not agree that "dating," whether or not it involves romantic attachment, falls outside the general definition of "recreational activities" found in [the law]. The statute, by its terms, appears to encompass social activities, whether or not they have a romantic element, for it includes any lawful activity pursued for recreational purposes and undertaken during leisure time. Though no explicit definition of "recreational purposes" is contained in the statute, "recreation" is, in the words of one dictionary, "a means of refreshment or diversion" (*Webster's Ninth New Collegiate Dictionary*, 985 [1985]); social interaction surely qualifies as a "diversion...."

In my view, given the fact that the Legislature's primary intent in enacting Labor Law § 201-d was to curtail employers' ability to discriminate on the basis of activities that are pursued outside of work hours, and that have no bearing on one's ability to perform one's job, and concomitantly to guarantee employees a certain degree of freedom to conduct their lives as they please during nonworking hours, the narrow interpretation adopted by the majority is indefensible. Rather, the statute, and the term "recreational activities" in particular, should be construed as broadly as the definitional language allows, to effect its remedial purpose.... Here, the list, which includes vast categories such as "hobbies" and "sports," as well as very different types of activities (e.g., exercise, reading), appears to have been compiled with an eye toward extending the reach of the statute. This, coupled with the explicit directive that the definition is not to be limited to the examples given, provides further indication that the term "recreational activities" should be construed expansively.

QUESTIONS

1. The judges in this case—both majority and dissenting—are engaging in what is called **statutory construction**; they are determining the outcome of the case by trying to understand the meaning of the law passed by New York's legislature. Note the differences between them. One gives the statute a "broad" reading, the other gives it a "narrow" one. Which is which? What tools do the two judges use to interpret the law? Which interpretation do you think is most in keeping with the intent of the legislators?

2. Try to imagine yourself in Albany as this New York law was being debated. What policy is-sues might have been raised in favor of passing the law? Against?

3. Suppose you had the ability to rewrite the New York law, or even delete it from the stat-ute books. How would you change it?

4. **Internet Assignment:** For your state, find out if there is any legislation protecting employees' rights to engage in off-worksite activities. If so, are there any cases interpreting the law? Then, go back to the Montana Wrongful Discharge statute in Chapter 2. What similarities can you see between it and your state's law? What differences?

Testing

Are you a homosexual? Do you know of any reason why you could
be blackmailed? Do you get along with your spouse? Are you a communist?
Do you have any money in the bank? Have you ever stolen anything and
not been caught?

These are a few of the questions asked in a polygraph test used by the Coors Brewing Com-pany as a pre-employment screening device. The intrusive nature of that test was part of the reason for a wildcat strike at Coors in 1977. In 1986, as the U.S. Congress was considering a law that would make the use of polygraphs by employers illegal,[15] Coors replaced its poly-graph with a lengthy psychological test and background check.

Today, the use of such "pen and pencil" (as opposed to electronic polygraph) honesty or in-tegrity tests is common among employers. One major reason is that employee theft costs U.S. businesses about $10 billion annually. In addition, companies claim an interest in the ability to identify people who are not only competent and honest, but who also fit a certain psycholog-ical or moral profile.

KARRAKER v. RENT-A-CENTER, INC.

U.S. Court of Appeals, Seventh Circuit, 2005
411 F.3d 831

TERENCE T. EVANS, Circuit Judge. ☀
To prove their worth prior to the annual college draft, NFL teams test aspiring profes-sional football players' ability to run, catch, and throw. But that's not all. In addition to the physical tests, a draft prospect also takes up to 15 personality and knowledge tests....

This case involves a battery of nonphysical tests similar to some of those given by NFL teams, though the employees here applied for less glamorous, and far less well-pay-ing, positions. Steven, Michael, and Christopher Karraker are brothers who worked for Rent-A-Center (RAC), a chain of stores that offer appliances, furniture, and other house-hold goods on a rent-to-own basis.... Most new employees start as account managers.... [T]o secure a promotion ... an employee was required to take the APT Management

---

15 *The Polygraph Act of 1988* bans such tests except for security personnel and others in extremely sensitive positions. Applicants for police force jobs, for instance, are often faced with the kinds of intrusive questions asked in the Coors polygraph test.

Trainee-Executive Profile, which was made up of nine tests designed to measure math and language skills as well as interests and personality traits.

As part of the APT Test, the Karrakers and others were asked 502 questions from the Minnesota Multiphasic Personality Inventory (MMPI), a test RAC said it used to measure personality traits. But the MMPI does not simply measure such potentially relevant traits as whether someone works well in groups or is comfortable in a fast-paced office. Instead, the MMPI considers where an applicant falls on scales measuring traits such as depression, hypochondriasis, hysteria, paranoia, and mania. In fact, elevated scores on certain scales of the MMPI can be used in diagnoses of certain psychiatric disorders.

Applicants were asked whether the following statements were true or false:

"I see things or animals or people around me that others do not see."

"I commonly hear voices without knowing where they are coming from."

"At times I have fits of laughing and crying that I cannot control."

"My soul sometimes leaves my body."

"At one or more times in my life I felt that someone was making me do things by hypnotizing me."

"I have a habit of counting things that are not important such as bulbs on electric signs, and so forth."

All parts of the APT Test were scored together, and any applicant who had more than 12 "weighted deviations" was not considered for promotion. Thus, an applicant could be denied any chance for advancement simply because of his or her score on the MMPI. The Karrakers, who all had more than 12 deviations on the APT, sued on behalf of the employees at 106 Illinois RAC stores, claiming RAC's use of the MMPI as part of its testing program violated the Americans With Disabilities Act of 1990 (ADA). They also claimed that RAC failed to protect the confidentiality of the test results in violation of Illinois tort law....

Americans with disabilities often faced barriers to joining and succeeding in the workforce ... [including] attitudinal barriers resulting from unfounded stereotypes and prejudice. People with psychiatric disabilities have suffered as a result of such attitudinal barriers, with an employment rate dramatically lower than people without disabilities and far lower than people with other types of disabilities....

Congress enacted three provisions in Title I [of the ADA] which explicitly limit the ability of employers to use "medical examinations and inquiries" ... as a condition of employment: a prohibition against using pre-employment medical tests; a prohibition against the use of medical tests that lack job-relatedness and business necessity; and a prohibition against the use of tests which screen out (or tend to screen out) people with disabilities.

At its heart, the issue in this case is whether the MMPI fits the ADA's definition of a "medical examination"....

... Psychological tests that are "designed to identify a mental disorder or impairment" qualify as medical examinations, but psychological tests "that measure personality traits such as honesty, preferences, and habits" do not. Therefore, this case largely turns on whether the MMPI test is designed to reveal a mental impairment. RAC argues that, as it used the MMPI, the test only measured personality traits. For example, RAC argues in its brief that the MMPI does not test whether an applicant is clinically depressed, only "the extent to which the test subject is experiencing the kinds of feelings of 'depression' that everyone feels from time to time (e.g., when their favorite team loses the World Series)." Although that particular example seems odd to us (can an Illinois chain really fill its management positions if it won't promote disgruntled Cubs fans?), the logic behind it doesn't seem to add up, either. Repeating the claim at oral argument, RAC argued that the MMPI merely tested a "state of mood" and suggested that an applicant might, for example, score high on the depression scale because he lost his keys that morning. But why would RAC care if an applicant lost his keys the morning of the MMPI or took the test the day after another Cubs loss? Would RAC really want to exclude an employee from consideration for a promotion because he happened to feel sad on the wrong day? We see two possibilities: either the MMPI was a very poor predictor of an applicant's potential as a manager (which might be one reason it is no longer used by RAC), or it actually was designed to measure more than just an applicant's mood on a given day.

… Because it is designed, at least in part, to reveal mental illness and has the effect of hurting the employment prospects of one with a mental disability, we think the MMPI is best categorized as a medical examination. And even though the MMPI was only a part (albeit a significant part) of a battery of tests administered to employees looking to advance, its use, we conclude, violated the ADA….

The Karrakers also challenge the district court's dismissal of their tort claim based on the public disclosure of private facts. To prevail, they must show that private facts were made public and that the matter made public would be highly offensive to a reasonable person…. The publicity requirement is satisfied by disclosure to a limited number of people if those people have a special relationship with the plaintiff that makes the disclosure as devastating as disclosure to the public at large…. Disclosure to persons with a "natural and proper interest" in the information is not actionable.

… Much of the Karrakers' claim centered around RAC's handling of the test results, which they claim did not adequately protect their privacy. As the district court described, the test results were kept in a filing cabinet in personnel files, and anyone wishing to view the records needed permission to do so from someone in the payroll department. The filing cabinet was locked at night, and the records were eventually moved into a locked room. Although someone could have seen the test results sitting in the fax machine or in the personnel file, that possibility is not sufficient to support a claim….

[Held: Summary judgment for the plaintiffs on their claim that the MMPI is a medical examination under the ADA, and dismissing the public disclosure of private facts claim.]

QUESTIONS

1. What rights of privacy are created by the *Americans With Disabilities Act*? How does the ADA benefit people without disabilities?

2. The multi-million dollar psychological testing industry has been criticized for unreliability. In a case involving testing for jobs at Target Stores, for instance, expert witnesses had thrown into question both the validity and the reliability of the test used, called Psychscreen, which had a 61 percent false positive rate; in other words, more than 6 of every 10 *qualified* applicants failed it.[16]

Recent studies reveal a very low correlation between good tests results and effective performance at work. Some wonder if American employers put so much stock in psychological testing out of an urge to get a quick fix on something that is impossible to quantify. As one writer put it: "We have personality in the sense that we have a consistent pattern of behavior. But that pattern is complex … personality is contingent: it represents an interaction between our internal disposition and tendencies and the situation that we find ourselves in."[17] Assuming psychological testing is rife with problems, what could employers do instead to screen job applicants?

16 *Soroka v. Dayton Hudson Corporation*, 1 Cal Rptr.2d 77 (1991).
17 Malcolm Gladwell, "Personality Plus," *The New Yorker*, September 20, 2004.

3. In a 1982 Massachusetts case, salespeople for Bristol-Myers were fired for resisting an integrity test. Here the judge describes what happened:

The questionnaire, entitled Biographical Summary, sought information which, it represented, would be held in strict confidence. The subjects covered included business experience, education, family, home ownership, physical data, activities, and aims.... Questions ... concerned (a) serious illnesses, operations, accidents, or nervous disorders, (b) smoking and drinking habits, (c) off-the-job problems, and (d) principal worries, if any.... [Employee] Cort, however, gave limited answers, one of which he admitted was wrong. He was not married in 1960, 1961, and 1962. He listed his dog as a dependent. He gave no information, as the others did, about parents or siblings, if any.

Cort answered [other] questions ... largely in a flippant manner.... He wrote as to his principal strengths: "Able to leap tall bldg. at a single bound." As to his principal weaknesses: "Can't land on my feet." Activities in which he would prefer not to engage: "Filling in questions on forms of very personal nature that are no one's business but mine." He suggested "$1,000,000" as the income he would need to live the way he would like to. Answering concerning plans for the future, he wrote, "Depends on who reads this." He followed his questionnaire with a memorandum to his superiors asking the value to Bristol-Myers of answers to the following questions: "what medications I may be taking, the age and health of my mother and father, the occupations of my brothers and sisters, the value of my house and the amount of mortgage, whose support outside of my immediate family I contribute to, how much I smoke and drink each day, my wife's maiden name, and what personal problems I have outside of business."

The court decided Cort and his co-workers were at-will employees with no cause of action for privacy invasion:

Questions about family and home ownership were probably not of much significance to Bristol-Myers, but those questions were not improperly intrusive, sought information mostly available in public records, and ... were no more intrusive than those asked on an application for life insurance or for a bank loan.

— *Cort v. Bristol-Myers Co.,* 431 N.E. 2d 908 (1982).

Internet Assignment: In your state, are there any cases dealing with psychological or honesty testing? What was the outcome?

4. Some tests measure abilities:

- *Can you type 200 words a minute?*
- *Can you run 1.5 miles in 12 minutes?*
- *Are you comfortable using Excel?*

Clearly, employers need the results of ability tests to make good hiring and promotion decisions. More controversial is the use of another type of test, one that asks whether you are what you say you are. These are called authenticity tests:

- *You say you don't use illegal drugs, but are you really drug-free?*
- *You say you are honest, but are you really honest?*

In his 1993 book *Testing Testing: Social Consequences of the Examined Life,* anthropologist F. Allan Hanson explores this form of testing. He begins with history from the period before the scientific method, when authenticity tests took the form of torture and witch burning. He then moves forward to modern forms of testing for truth—the polygraph, honesty test, and urinalysis drug test. Hanson is concerned with the "metamessage," the message that is an inevitable byproduct of authenticity testing. He writes:

[T]he metamessage of distrust conveyed by the demand that employees take authenticity tests is unmistakable, and it often erodes loyalty and morale. Essentially they are

being told, regardless of your record of service, reliability, and safety, you are suspected of theft, dishonesty, or drug use, and that suspicion will be suspended only by your passing this test, and even if you pass, you will be trusted only until the next test. This engenders hostility against the company and may even spur some workers to take steps to confound or subvert the tests purely as a way to maintain a sense of autonomy and dignity in the face of a system that is aimed at systematically humiliating them…. Much more commonly, the metamessage … destroys employee motivation to take pride in one's work and perform at a high level and engenders a passive-aggressive response marked by smoldering resentment and diminished productivity.

Hanson goes on to mention the problem of false positives, where innocent people are wrongly judged guilty. Which ethical theory would attach significance to the points Hanson makes? Next, Hanson links his argument to a basic privacy concern:

To the claim that only those with something to hide need fear … authenticity tests, the proper response is that there is a little crook in all of us…. [Social interaction consists largely of a series of dramaturgical performances in which people don many masks in an effort to present themselves artfully—concealing certain elements of the self while highlighting and tinting others. The aim is to exercise some control over social situations by influencing others' perception of the self and thereby of the situation…. [A]uthenticity testing erodes this distinctive feature of social life. Whether test results are positive or negative is, at this level, irrelevant. The point is that testing opens the self to scrutiny and investigation in ways that the self is powerless to control. So far as the areas of knowledge covered by the tests are concerned, this transforms the person from autonomous subject to passive object.

What similarities to Alan Westin's description of the functions of privacy do you detect here? Some may claim that the fact that test results can be kept confidential changes the picture, but Hanson argues the reverse. For him, confidentiality is not a safeguard of privacy, but "yet another ingenious and highly effective technique for exercising power and discipline over the individual":

Although it is advertised as a protective measure for test takers, confidentiality completes the domination of test givers over test takers. It assures that each individual confronts the organizations that mandate testing utterly alone and therefore in the weakest possible state. Here disciplinary power has achieved the remarkable feat of perfecting the domination of people by dividing them and dealing with them singly, all the while convincing them that the arrangement is for their own good.

Do you agree with Hanson's analysis?

Consumer Privacy

Advertisers and publishers want a better eyeball, and a better eyeball is a more targeted eyeball.

— RICHARD BAUMER, PRESIDENT OF A COMPANY THAT SELLS ADS ON BEHALF OF WEB SITES

The big long-term concern about privacy is the surreptitious compilation of every site you click, every page you download, every product you order into a single database.

— MARC ROTENBERG, PRESIDENT, ELECTRONIC PRIVACY INFORMATION CENTER

According to a study by the research firm Privacy and American Business, 86 percent of Internet users want to be able to trade their personal data online as long as they are properly informed as to how the information would be used and are offered benefits in exchange for it. In the next case, bank customers object after their personal data was taken without their consent.

TIMOTHY v. CHASE MANHATTAN BANK

New York Supreme Court, 2002
741 N.Y.S.2d 100

The plaintiffs, who purport to represent a class of similarly-situated persons, are holders of credit cards and mortgages issued by Chase Manhattan Bank USA, N.A.…. The complaint alleges that Chase violated its commitment to protect customer privacy and confidentiality and not to share customer information with any unrelated third party…. This confidentiality commitment was contained in a printed document entitled "Customer Information Principles," which was distributed to the plaintiffs. Allegedly unbeknownst to the plaintiffs, without their consent and without giving the plaintiffs an opportunity to opt-out, Chase sold information to non-affiliated third-party vendors, including the plaintiffs' names, addresses, telephone numbers, account or loan numbers, credit card usage, and other financial data. The third-party vendors used this information and created lists of Chase customers, including the plaintiffs, who might be interested in their products or services. These lists were then provided to telemarketing and direct mail representatives to conduct solicitations. In return for the information, the third-party vendors agreed to pay Chase a commission (of up to 24% of the sale) in the event that a product or service offered were purchased….

To establish a cause of action under [New York's] General Business Law §349, a plaintiff must prove that the challenged act or practice was consumer-oriented, that it was misleading in a material way, and that the plaintiff suffered injury as a result of the deceptive act. Whether a representation or omission, the deceptive practice must be likely to mislead a reasonable consumer acting reasonably under the circumstances. In addition, to recover under the statute, a plaintiff must prove actual injury, though not necessarily pecuniary harm.

[T]he plaintiffs have not alleged, and cannot prove, any "actual injury" as is necessary under General Business Law §349 … [despite their claim that]:

> the products and services offered to class members as a result of [Chase's] practices of selling class members' confidential financial information included memberships in discount shoppers' clubs, emergency road service plans, dental and legal service plans, travel clubs, home and garden supply clubs, and credit card registration and magazine subscription services.

Thus, the "harm" at the heart of this purported class action, is that class members were merely offered products and services which they were free to decline. This does not qualify as actual harm.

The complaint does not allege a single instance where a named plaintiff or any class member suffered any actual harm due to the receipt of an unwanted telephone solicitation or a piece of junk mail.

[The state GBL claim was dismissed.]

The plaintiffs seek to recover damages for unjust enrichment based on the profits Chase earned as commissions on the purchases made by members of the plaintiffs' class. "To state a cause of action for unjust enrichment, a plaintiff must allege that it conferred a benefit upon the defendant, and that the defendant will obtain such benefit without adequately compensating plaintiff therefor" [cite] The plaintiffs failed to state a cause of action to recover damages for unjust enrichment since the members of the plaintiffs' class who made purchases of products and/or services received a benefit. There being no allegation that the benefits received were less than what these purchasers bargained for, it cannot be said that the commissions paid by the third-party vendors to Chase belong to the plaintiffs.

[The claim for unjust enrichment was also dismissed.]

QUESTIONS

1. Why was plaintiffs' claim under the New York General Business law dismissed? Their claim regarding unjust enrichment?

2. What similarities are there between this case and *Smyth v. Pillsbury*? Differences?

   Internet Assignment: Find out what happened when consumers sued American Express in Illinois for selling information much as Chase Manhattan had done in this case.

3. If you had to write a dissenting opinion to the *Timothy v. Chase Manhattan* case, what would you argue?

4. In August 2002, the New York attorney general sued Student Marketing Group (SMG) for violating the state's consumer protection laws. SMG had given surveys to high school teachers across the United States to be handed out to students, who would then fill in their names, e-mail addresses, age, gender, religious affiliation, ethnicity, grade-point average, and career interests. SMG claimed it was going to distribute this information to colleges and universities for admissions and financial aid purposes, but in fact they turned it over to marketers. How would you analyze this scenario from a utilitarian ethical perspective? A deontological one?

   Internet Assignment: What happened in this case?

5. The cost of errors in inventory management has been estimated as high as 500 billion dollars a year in the United States. Radio Frequency Identification (RFID), the technology which enabled British flight controllers in World War II to distinguish between friendly and enemy planes and which makes the EZ Pass system through highway tollbooths in some northeastern states possible, is the likely successor to bar code scanning. Tags can be almost as small as a grain of sand. Unlike the Universal Product Code used by bar code scanners, RFID does not require that the scanning device "see" the bars. Some RFID sensors can operate at 100 meters. And, unlike the Universal Product Code used by bar code scanners, the Electronic Product Code (EPC) can be programmed to add specific information that may have uses in product handling prior to sale and even in research concerning customer behavior after the purchase. It is the use of RFID technology to study customer behavior that has privacy groups concerned. An RFID trial in 2003 by Procter & Gamble triggered hidden cameras, which enabled researchers in Cincinnati to watch female customers handling lipstick in a Wal-Mart store in Oklahoma. As a California state senator said in reference to that incident, "How would you like it if…one day you realized your underwear was reporting on your whereabouts?" What are the ethical pros and cons of RFID?

6. Low-fare, no-frills JetBlue airlines had a scandal on its hands in the fall of 2003 when it admitted it had released information about more than one million of its passengers at the request of a private company working on antiterrorism with the Pentagon, Torch Concepts. The disclosure of customer names, addresses, phone numbers, and flight information was in violation of JetBlue's own privacy policy.

   Internet Assignment: What was the fallout of this incident? Investigation? Lawsuits?

7. **Internet Assignment:** Are U.S. consumers concerned about privacy as they shop online? Find a recent poll.

Europe vs. America: Dignity vs. Liberty

Yale law professor James Q. Whitman makes this broad distinction between conceptions of privacy in Europe versus America:

Continental privacy protections are, at their core, a form of protection of a right to respect and personal dignity. [They] ... are rights to one's image, name, and reputation, and ... to informational self-determination—the right to control the sorts of information disclosed about oneself ... all rights to control your public image—to guarantee that people see you the way you want to be seen. They are, as it were, rights to be shielded against unwanted public exposure—to be spared embarrassment or humiliation.

By contrast, America, in this as in so many things, is much more oriented toward values of liberty, liberty against the state. The American right to privacy still takes much of the form that it took in the eighteenth century: It is the right to freedom from intrusions by the state, especially in one's own home. The prime danger, from the American point of view, is that the ... [home] will be breached by government actors. American anxieties ... tend to be about maintaining a kind of private sovereignty within our own walls.[18]

Perhaps this distinction explains the strength of the protections given to personal information by the European Privacy Directive. A "Directive" protecting the privacy of personal information as it moves across national borders was passed by the European Union on July 24, 1995. Under the Privacy Directive, each member nation must pass laws guaranteeing that personal data gathered is accurate, up-to-date, relevant, and not excessive. Information collected may be used only for the purpose for which it was collected, and can be processed only with the consent of the subject, when required by law, or to protect the "public interest" or the "legitimate interests" of a third party, unless those interests are superseded by the "fundamental rights and freedoms of the data subject." The Directive sharply limits the collection of information about "racial or ethnic origin, political opinions, religious or philosophical beliefs, trade-union membership [or] concerning health or sex life." Data subjects must be informed that data will be taken about them, and must be notified how it will be used. Perhaps most striking of all, given the very different legal rules in the United States, the EU Directive gives Europeans the right of access to information collected about themselves, and the opportunity to correct inaccuracies. Further, each member nation must establish a data privacy "commissioner," and a national agency that monitors enforcement.

In 2006, EU regulators issued a report condemning a secret U.S. program of mass spying on the SWIFT (Society for Worldwide Interbank Financial Telecommunications) financial cooperative, as a violation of European law. EU officials found the financial prying was unauthorized, lacked checks and balances, and violated European privacy rules.

Privacy Under the Constitution

The right of the people to be secure in their persons, houses, papers and effects, against unreasonable searches and seizures, shall not be violated.

— FOURTH AMENDMENT, U.S. CONSTITUTION

18 "The Two Western Cultures of Privacy: Dignity v. Liberty," 113 Yale L. J. 1151 (2004).

Over the years, the Supreme Court has created three strands of privacy rights through its interpretation of various Constitutional Amendments, and their penumbras. One stops the government from interfering in the choices you make about your private family and sexual life—to use or not use birth control, or (for adults) to engage in consensual homosexual activity, for example—without government interference. Another prevents the government from publicizing the kind of information about ourselves that we consider most intimate—our medical and sexual histories for example. Finally, and of most importance to business, the Fourth Amendment protects the "reasonable expectations of privacy" of both individual and corporate citizens against unwarranted and unreasonable government searches or seizures. Whenever the government searches a person's body for drugs or alcohol, the TSA x-rays luggage at an airport, the health department inspects a restaurant, or a government agency searches business premises for evidence of wrongdoing, there is a potential Fourth Amendment "privacy" claim.

While the Fourth Amendment does protect citizens from "unreasonable searches," it is triggered only when the *government* is conducting a search; there is no constitutional protection against searches or surveillance by private corporations. And while government employees might argue that electronic surveillance is a "search" in violation of the Fourth Amendment, their constitutional rights are limited by a balancing test: Judges must decide which counts more weightily, an employee's privacy interest or the need of the government (as employer) to search.

That is why those who work for the government—public school teachers, IRS agents, police, firefighters, regulators at the FTC, and attorneys in the Justice Department, for example—can be subject to electronic surveillance and various types of testing as long as their employer's justification outweighs the individual's privacy interests.

In the next case, an applicant for a job in a city public library refuses to take a mandatory drug and alcohol test, and the city rescinds its offer of employment.

LANIER v. CITY OF WOODBURN

U. S. District Court, 2005
2005 WL 3050470 (D.Or.)

KING, J. ☀

On February 5, 2004, [Janet Lynn Lanier] applied for a "library page" position, which is a part-time, "at-will" position considered to be entry-level. Defendant Linda Sprauer, head of the library department, gave plaintiff a conditional offer of employment on February 23, 2004. Consistent with the City's policy, the City conditioned its offer of employment on a pre-employment drug and alcohol screening and upon plaintiff executing a Release and Waiver Form. This was done solely as a matter of policy and Sprauer had no particular suspicion that plaintiff had a problem with drugs or alcohol....[19]

Plaintiff wrote Sprauer that she wanted to accept the position of library page at the Woodburn Public Library, but would not submit to the post-offer, pre-employment drug or alcohol screening test because she believed it violated her constitutional and civil rights....

On March 30, 2004, Sprauer formally withdrew plaintiff's offer of employment.

The library page at the Woodburn Public Library is responsible for supervising juveniles and is occasionally at the desk in the youth services area of the library, [which] houses materials for children up through teenage youth for the community. Library page is the lowest job classification in the Woodburn Public Library; it is a part-time,

---

19 The City policy stated: "As a drug-free workplace, The City of Woodburn requires a pre-employment drug and alcohol screen for all prospective applicants. The candidate of choice for a City position must successfully pass the drug and alcohol screen as a condition of the job offer. The confirmed presence of any illegal drug or alcohol in a urine sample will be cause for disqualifying an applicant."

minimum wage, non-union, no-benefits position. The job, which requires manual tasks like shelving books, is usually filled by high school students.

Sprauer supported the addition of the drug and alcohol screening policy to the handbook because the community has numerous drug problems and the building is open to the public, including children....The City's drug and alcohol testing program does not apply to current employees of the City.

Legal Discussion

... Plaintiff alleges the City's drug and alcohol testing policy violates the Fourth Amendment of the United States Constitution. ...

The touchstone for determining the constitutionality of a search is its reasonableness, which requires balancing the intrusiveness of the search against its advancement of a legitimate government interest. Normally, reasonableness under the Fourth Amendment requires individualized suspicion. When the search is not based on individualized suspicion, "the proffered special need for drug testing must be substantial—important enough to override the individual's acknowledged privacy interest, sufficiently vital to suppress the Fourth Amendment's normal requirement of individualized suspicion." The Supreme Court directs courts to "undertake a context-specific inquiry, examining closely the competing private and public interests advanced by the parties."

The City claims it has a legitimate interest in having a drug-free workplace. Based on previous experience, department heads adopted the policy because they were concerned about employees under the influence of drugs. In addition, the City contends its interest is legitimate in light of the hazards of drug problems in the workplace—running the gamut from absenteeism to potential liability for employee actions. Balancing these interests against the fact that job applicants have a lower expectation of privacy than current employees and can choose not to apply for a position requiring drug testing, the City asserts its drug and alcohol screening does not violate the Fourth Amendment.

Plaintiff argues that the only substantial interest supporting drug testing is public safety, and the City's policy applies to all applicants who receive offers, regardless of whether the position is safety-sensitive. Plaintiff also challenges the evidence forming the basis for the City's statement that department heads adopted the policy because they were concerned about employees under the influence of drugs. According to plaintiff, a general desire to have a drug-free workplace is not a sufficiently legitimate interest.

Plaintiff relies principally on *Chandler v. Miller* (Supreme Court, 1997), while defendants cite *Willner v. Thornburgh*, (D.C.Cir.1991) and *Loder v. City of Glendale*, (Cal.1997). ...

In *Chandler*, the Supreme Court struck down a Georgia statute requiring candidates for state office to undergo a drug test; the statute violated the Fourth Amendment. The Court pointed out that Georgia "asserts no evidence of a drug problem among the State's elected officials, those officials typically do not perform high-risk, safety-sensitive tasks, and the required certification immediately aids no interdiction effort...." Protecting the state's image was not a constitutionally sufficient interest.

The Court also reviewed its precedent to evaluate what other rationales constitute important governmental interests. In *Skinner v. Railway Labor Executives' Assn.* (1989), the government had a vital interest in drug testing rail employees involved in train accidents or who violated certain safety rules, both for safety reasons and for collecting information about the causes of train accidents. In *National Treasury Employees v. Von Raab* (1989), the [Customs Office] drug testing program was implemented by an agency with an "almost unique mission" of drug interdiction, so employees involved in drug interdiction or employees who carried firearms could constitutionally be required to submit to a drug test. In *Vernonia School Dist.* (1995), a random drug testing program for high school students was necessary due to the "immediate crisis" of "a sharp increase in drug use" in the school district....

[The two cases offered as precedent by the City of Woodburn here were state court cases in which a drug testing policy was held to be constitutional, in part because it required job applicants, not current employees, to be tested. In the *Willner* case, the judge had stated: "The government's interest in detecting drug use is substantial at the pre-employment stage because … the applicant is an outsider"]

Both *Loder* and *Willner* were decided prior to *Chandler*, and in neither case did the court explore the government's actual prior experience with employees and drug use. Importantly, *Chandler* specifically identified this factor as a helpful one. The Court stated, "A demonstrated problem of drug abuse, while not in all cases necessary to the validity of a testing regime … would shore up an assertion of special need for a suspicionless general search program."

Here, although defendants claim they adopted the policy in response to concerns about employee drug use, they offer no concrete evidence to support their assertion…. In fact, Sprauer testified that in her 33 years with the library there was only one instance of an employee with a drug or alcohol problem:

> Q: Now, you said that the community has had numerous drug problems. In your 33 years in the Woodburn Public Library, has the staff or employees of the Woodburn Library Department had numerous drug problems?
> A: Not numerous. I have had a few instances.
> Q: And I'm not asking you to name names or invade anyone's privacy. But you are suggesting that you've had incidents in the past where you have had to discipline existing employees for drug and alcohol abuse?
> A: I had an existing employee who, two different times, went into a drug-alcohol rehabilitation program.
> Q: Other than that—or those incidents—what other drug or alcohol problems have you had—again within the staff and employees of the City of Woodburn Public Library?
> A: None that I recall.

This is not sufficient evidence of a concrete drug problem to warrant drug testing for all prospective employees.

Without concrete evidence of a drug problem, the City must point to another special need for testing all prospective employees. *Chandler* foreclosed defendants' argument that they have an interest in a drug-free workplace; merely desiring to preserve a certain image is not a constitutionally sufficient rationale. Furthermore, unlike *Skinner* or *Von Raab*, the City's policy is not directed at positions that involve safety-sensitive tasks, or involve interdiction of drugs. While there may be governmental interests besides these that would meet the special needs test, the City requires all applicants who receive job offers to take a drug test without regard to the particularized circumstances of the job.

Finally, I am not convinced that the City's interest in further scrutinizing an applicant by way of a drug test—to save costs in hiring and training, to ensure productivity, and to avoid third party liability—is a sufficiently special need under *Chandler*. However, even if it is, it is not a strong enough government interest to outweigh the applicant's reasonable expectation of privacy….

[D]efendants argue that an applicant has a reduced expectation of privacy as compared with a current employee because an applicant can choose whether or not to work for a drug-testing employer. ("If individuals view drug testing as an indignity to be avoided, they need only refrain from applying"). Nevertheless, even if an applicant has a reduced expectation of privacy as compared with a current employee, in balancing the interests in this case, the City's sole interest in what comes down to economic efficiency is insufficient to outweigh the burden upon individual privacy.

The City's policy is unreasonable, and therefore it violates the Fourth Amendment of the United States Constitution.

QUESTIONS

1. Under the Fourth Amendment analysis used by Judge King in this case, what does it take to justify a government drug testing program if there is no suspicion that a particular person to be tested is using illegal drugs?

2. Judges look to previously decided cases—called **precedent**—in order to find the appropriate rule of law and apply it to the **case at bar**. The process usually involves consideration of several precedent cases—some offered by the plaintiff, others by the defendant. In the legal discussion, judges explain why they have decided on which precedent to use. They often also explain why they have decided *not* to use the other precedent cases. This is called "distinguishing precedent." How did Judge King distinguish the *Willner* and *Loder* cases offered by the City of Woodburn here?

3. The judge agrees with the plaintiff that "a general desire to have a drug-free workplace is not a sufficiently legitimate interest" to justify a drug-testing program. Do you agree? Why shouldn't government employers be able to test for that reason alone?

4. Do you agree that there should be a difference between the treatment of prospective as opposed to current employees where drug testing is concerned?

5. At the time she was told about the drug and alcohol testing policy, Janet Lanier was also asked to sign a release, stating:

> *To facilitate the City of Woodburn's assessment of my fitness to serve in the position of Library Page, I hereby authorize the City of Woodburn, its officers, agents, assigns and employees to contact previous employers and other sources of information and to request, read, review or photocopy any and all information the City deems necessary to lawfully investigate my background for this position. This information may include, but is not limited to, my academic, residential, achievement, performance, attendance, disciplinary, employment history, and criminal history information.*
>
> *I hereby exonerate, release and discharge the City of Woodburn, its officers, agents and employees from any liability or damages that may result from furnishing the information requested, including any liability or damage pursuant to any state or federal laws.*
>
> *I specifically and permanently waive any rights I may have to review or inspect any and all of the information developed in this investigation.*

Although she offered to give the library her references and authorized Sprauer to contact them, and to gather any other information that was publicly available about her, Lanier refused to sign the release. Why do you think she did not want to sign it? What function of privacy mentioned by Alan Westin might be implicated here?

6. In 1987, the Supreme Court decided a case involving the search of a public employee's office. Magno Ortega, a psychiatrist at State Hospital, was suspected of stealing a computer and of sexually harassing female workers. While he was on vacation, his employer had his desk and file cabinets searched thoroughly. Investigators found, among other items, a valentine card, a book of love poetry, and a semi-nude photograph of a female doctor.

The Court found that this search did not violate the Fourth Amendment. It explained that the employment context itself both (1) lowered the employee's legitimate privacy expectations, and (2) created a strong need on the employer's part to discover work-related misconduct:

> *An office is seldom a private enclave free from entry by supervisors, other employees and business and personal invitees. Instead in many cases offices are continually entered by fellow employees and other visitors during the workday for conferences, consultations, and other work-related visits. Simply put—it is the nature of government offices that others … may have frequent access to an individual's office….*
> *While police … conduct searches for the primary purpose of obtaining evidence for use in criminal … proceedings, employers most frequently need to enter the offices*

and desks of their employees for legitimate work-related reasons wholly unrelated to il-legal conduct. Employers and supervisors are focused primarily on the need to complete the government agency's work in a prompt and efficient manner. An employer may have need for correspondence, or a file or report available only in an employee's office while the employee is away from the office. Or, as is alleged to have been the case here, employers may need to safeguard or identify state property or records in an office in connection with a pending investigation into suspected employee malfeasance.

Do you agree with the notion that people should have a reduced expectation of privacy when they are at work?

Privacy in Medical Information

Whatsoever things I see or hear concerning the life of men, in my attendance on the sick or even apart therefrom, which ought not to be noised about, I will keep silence thereon, counting such things to be as sacred secrets.

— HIPPOCRATIC OATH

One of the most disturbing flashpoints where technology has outstripped privacy protection involves the health care industry. Profoundly confidential medical information is accessible to thousands of strangers, as physicians, hospitals, HMOs, insurers, pharmacies, government agencies, pension funds, and employers find themselves generating and/or processing it.

Genetic testing of tiny amounts of human tissue—strands of hair, a few drops of blood—can reveal tremendous amounts of sensitive health data. In the next case, medical privacy issues come up in the context of genetic testing. A research facility in California required all job applicants to undergo health examinations to be eligible for clerical and administrative positions. The applicants, seven African-Americans and one Latino, had completed questionnaires and given blood and urine samples, but did not realize that theirs would be among those selected to be tested for such conditions as syphilis, sickle cell trait, and pregnancy. Here, the Ninth Circuit, in a case of first impression, must decide whether citizens have a right to genetic privacy.

NORMAN-BLOODSAW v. LAWRENCE BERKELEY LABORATORY

U.S. Court of Appeals, Ninth Circuit, 1997

135 F.3d 1260

REINHARDT, Circuit Judge. ☀

[The named plaintiffs] are current and former administrative and clerical employees of defendant Lawrence Berkeley Laboratory ("Lawrence"), a research facility operated … pursuant to a contract with the United States Department of Energy (the Department). The Department requires federal contractors such as Lawrence to establish an occupational medical program. Since 1981, it has required its contractors to perform "preplacement examinations" of employees as part of this program, and until 1995, it also required its contractors to offer their employees the option of subsequent "periodic health examinations." The mandatory preplacement examination occurs after the offer of employment but prior to the assumption of job duties. The Department actively oversees Lawrence's occupational health program, and, prior to 1992, specifically required syphilis testing as part of the preplacement examination.

[All but one of the named plaintiffs] received written offers of employment expressly conditioned upon a "medical examination…." All accepted these offers and underwent preplacement examinations…. In the course of these examinations, plaintiffs completed medical history questionnaires and provided blood and urine samples. The questionnaires asked, [among other things,] whether the patient had ever had any of sixty-one medical conditions, including "[s]ickle cell anemia,"[20] "[v]enereal disease," and, in the case of women, "[m]enstrual disorders."[21]

The blood and urine samples given by all employees during their preplacement examinations were tested for syphilis; in addition, certain samples were tested for sickle cell trait; and certain samples were tested for pregnancy. Lawrence discontinued syphilis testing in April 1993, pregnancy testing in December 1994, and sickle cell trait testing in June 1995. Defendants assert that they discontinued syphilis testing because of its limited usefulness in screening healthy populations, and that they discontinued sickle cell trait testing because, by that time, most African-American adults had already been tested at birth. Lawrence continues to perform pregnancy testing, but only on an optional basis. Defendants further contend that "for many years" signs posted in the health examination rooms and "more recently" in the reception area stated that the tests at issue would be administered.

Plaintiffs allege that the testing of their blood and urine samples for syphilis, sickle cell trait, and pregnancy occurred without their knowledge or consent, and without any subsequent notification that the tests had been conducted. They also allege that only black employees were tested for sickle cell trait and assert the obvious fact that only female employees were tested for pregnancy. Finally, they allege that Lawrence failed to provide safeguards to prevent the dissemination of the test results. They contend that they did not discover that the disputed tests had been conducted until approximately January 1995, and specifically deny that they observed any signs indicating that such tests would be performed. Plaintiffs do not allege that the defendants took any subsequent employment-related action on the basis of their test results, or that their test results have been disclosed to third parties.

On the basis of these factual allegations, plaintiffs contend … that the defendants violated the federal constitutional right to privacy by conducting the testing at issue, collecting and maintaining the results of the testing, and failing to provide adequate safeguards against disclosure of the results. They [also]contend that the testing violated their right to privacy under Article I, s 1 of the California Constitution. Finally, plaintiffs contend that Lawrence and the Regents violated Title VII by singling out black employees for sickle cell trait testing and by performing pregnancy testing on female employees generally.

Federal Constitutional Due Process Right of Privacy

The constitutionally protected privacy interest in avoiding disclosure of personal matters clearly encompasses medical information and its confidentiality. [cites] Although

---

20 Sickle cell anemia is a physical affliction in which a large proportion or majority of an individual's red blood cells become sickle-shaped. Sickle cell trait is a genetic condition in which an individual carries the gene that causes sickle cell anemia. The sickle cell gene is only semi-dominant; if the carrier of the gene is heterozygous (meaning that the gene is paired with a non-sickle cell gene), some of his or her red blood cells may sickle, but usually not to a sufficient degree to result in actual sickle cell anemia.

21 The section of the questionnaire also asks women if they have ever had abnormal pap smears and men if they have ever had prostate gland disorders.

cases defining the privacy interest in medical information have typically involved its disclosure to "third" parties, rather than the collection of information by illicit means, it goes without saying that the most basic violation possible involves the performance of unauthorized tests—that is, the non-consensual retrieval of previously unrevealed medical information that may be unknown even to plaintiffs. These tests may also be viewed as searches … that require Fourth Amendment scrutiny. Accordingly, we must balance the government's interest in conducting these particular tests against the plaintiffs' expectations of privacy. Furthermore, "application of the balancing test requires not only considering the degree of intrusiveness and the state's interests in requiring that intrusion, but also 'the efficacy of this [the state's] means for meeting' its needs."

One can think of few subject areas more personal and more likely to implicate privacy interests than that of one's health or genetic make-up…. Furthermore, the facts revealed by the tests are highly sensitive, even relative to other medical information. With respect to the testing of plaintiffs for syphilis and pregnancy, it is well established in this circuit "that the Constitution prohibits unregulated, unrestrained employer inquiries into personal sexual matters that have no bearing on job performance." The fact that one has syphilis is an intimate matter that pertains to one's sexual history and may invite tremendous amounts of social stigma. Pregnancy is likewise, for many, an intensely private matter, which also may pertain to one's sexual history and often carries far-reaching societal implications. Finally, the carrying of sickle cell trait can pertain to sensitive information about family history and reproductive decision making. Thus, the conditions tested for were aspects of one's health in which one enjoys the highest expectations of privacy.

[T]here was little, if any, "overlap" between what plaintiffs consented to and the testing at issue here…. That one has consented to a general medical examination does not abolish one's privacy right not to be tested for intimate, personal matters involving one's health—nor does consenting to giving blood or urine samples,[22] or filling out a questionnaire. As we have made clear, revealing one's personal knowledge as to whether one has a particular medical condition has nothing to do with one's expectations about actually being tested for that condition. Thus, the intrusion was by no means [insignificant]….

Title VII Claims

Section 703(a) of Title VII of the Civil Rights Act of 1964 provides that it is unlawful for any employer:

to fail or refuse to hire or to discharge any individual, or otherwise to discriminate against any individual with respect to his compensation, terms, conditions, or privileges of employment, because of such individual's race, color, religion, sex, or national origin….

The Pregnancy Discrimination Act further provides that discrimination on the basis of "sex" includes discrimination "on the basis of pregnancy, childbirth, or related medical conditions."

[P]laintiffs' Title VII claims fall neatly into a Title VII framework: Plaintiffs allege that black and female employees were singled out for additional nonconsensual testing and that defendants thus selectively invaded the privacy of certain employees on the basis of race, sex, and pregnancy.

It is well established that Title VII bars discrimination … in the "terms" and "conditions" under which individuals may obtain employment. See, e.g., *Griggs v. Duke Power*

---

22 Indeed, the Supreme Court has recognized that while the taking of a bodily fluid sample implicates one's privacy interests, "[t]he ensuing chemical analysis of the sample to obtain physiological data is a further intrusion of the tested employee's privacy interests." *Skinner v. Railway Labor Executives' Ass'n,* (1989) (allowing urine testing of railway workers for drugs).

Co. (1971) (facially neutral educational and testing requirements that are not reasonable measures of job performance and have disparate impact on hiring of minorities violate Title VII). Thus, for example, a requirement of preemployment health examinations imposed only on female employees, or a requirement of preemployment background security checks imposed only on black employees, would surely violate Title VII.

In this case, the term or condition for black employees was undergoing a test for sickle cell trait; for women it was undergoing a test for pregnancy. It is not disputed that the preplacement exams were, literally, a condition of employment: the offers of employment stated this explicitly. Thus, the employment of women and blacks at Lawrence was conditioned in part on allegedly unconstitutional invasions of privacy to which white and/or male employees were not subjected. An additional "term or condition" requiring an unconstitutional invasion of privacy is, without doubt, actionable under Title VII.[23]

[Judgment of the lower court dismissing the claims is reversed.]

QUESTIONS

1. On what basis did the Ninth Circuit find that the federal Constitution had been violated by the laboratory in this case? The federal Civil Rights Act?

2. Why do you think employers are interested in the results of genetic testing of their employees?

3. There have been many documented instances of employers and insurance companies denying health coverage based on knowledge of genetic dispositions.[24] The *Bloodsaw* case raises the specter of such data being gathered in a discriminatory way. Can you think of some of the other potential problems with genetic testing?

4. Does the type of testing that occurred in *Bloodsaw* violate the Americans With Disabilities Act?

Internet Assignment: Since the *Bloodsaw* case, Congress passed the Health Information Portability and Accountability Act, or HIPAA, which took effect in 2004. Would the type of testing that occurred in *Bloodsaw* violate the HIPAA statute?

5. Gary Avary worked for Burlington Northern Santa Fe Railroad, where he developed carpal tunnel syndrome. When he filed a Workers' Compensation claim, the railroad told him he had to have a medical exam. His wife, Janice, became suspicious when she found out that this exam required seven vials of his blood to be drawn. She went to the doctor's office and asked the medical workers what was going on. In this way she discovered that the company was having Gary genetically tested. Along with 36 other railroad workers in the same situation, Gary Avary sued his employer, claiming the testing was being done so that the railroad could blame "any future health problems on their genetic make-up, not the physical stress on the job."[25] What argument can you make that Avary's right to privacy was violated? How would his case be different if he had worked for the state transportation authority, instead of a privately owned railroad?

Internet Assignment: What was the outcome of this case?

---

23 An exception exists for pregnancy testing in those "instances in which ... pregnancy actually interferes with the employee's ability to perform the job." No such exception is asserted here.

24 A Georgetown University survey of people with genetic-based disorders in their families found that 43 percent claimed they were denied health insurance, life insurance, or a job because of disclosures of potential genetic problems.

25 "Genetic Tests Outpace Efforts to Safeguard People's Data

Genetic Testing in the NBA

In 1990, in a West Coast Tournament game, Loyola Marymount star, Hank Gathers dunked the basketball and collapsed on the floor. Two hours later he was dead. In 1993, in the first game of a playoff with the Charlotte Hornets, Boston Celtics star Reggie Lewis grabbed a rebound and fell down as if he had been shot. After exhaustive tests, Lewis seemed be O.K. Two months later, shooting baskets in a Boston gym, Reggie Lewis keeled over and died.

Both of these deaths were attributed to a heart condition known as hypertrophic cardiomyopathy (HCM). In May 2004, a genetic test for HCM became commercially available. The test is believed to detect genetic mutations that may account for 75 percent of HCM cases.

In 2001, the Chicago Bulls drafted a young high school senior named Eddy Curry. According to Andrew Rice, who has written a detailed article about the Eddy Curry case in the *Virginia Sports and Entertainment Law Journal*,[26] in the winter of 2004–2005, the Chicago Bulls were in their first playoff run since their glory days with Michael Jordan. At 6' 11", Curry was a dominant low-post player with an excellent field goal percentage. Warming up before a road game (this time, with the Charlotte Bobcats—the Hornets had moved to New Orleans), Curry felt sick and lightheaded. He was benched with an irregular heartbeat, and didn't play again with the Chicago Bulls.

The Bulls insisted that Curry be examined by several cardiologists. Only one cardiologist believed he had heart issues of any kind, but this doctor proposed the genetic test for HCM. A legal standoff ensued. Through his attorney, Curry claimed a right of privacy. The Bulls said they wanted to protect Eddy Curry, and backed this claim with an offer of $400,000 a year for 50 years, in the event that Curry tested positive. No federal statute seemed to give clear guidance; state laws were inconsistent; and the NBA's Collective Bargaining Agreement is moot on the subject of genetic testing. As Commissioner David Stern said, a ruling on genetic testing would make the NBA's hotly contested dress code seem simple.

In the end, the Bulls traded Curry to the New York Knicks. The Knicks' physician shied away from DNA testing. New York state law would have prohibited the Knicks from requiring the test. And Eddy Curry has played well for the New York Knicks. On April 19, 2007, Eddy Curry played through a hamstring injury, scoring 28 points and bringing down 8 rebounds in a win over the Charlotte Bobcats.

But, as Andrew Rice points out, genetic testing in the NBA remains a "hot button" issue.

Genetic Testing: Economics and Ethics

Ladies and gentlemen, progress is like a storekeeper. You can have anything you want, but you have to pay the price. You can have the telephone, but you will lose some of your privacy, and the charm of distance. You can have the airplane, but the birds will lose their wonder and the clouds will smell of gasoline.

— CLARENCE DARROW IN *INHERIT THE WIND*, ABOUT THE SCOPES TRIAL

With funding from the National Institute of Health, a diverse group of experts spent two years analyzing the role of genetic testing in disability insurance. The next reading was published in connection with their 2007 report.

THINKING ABOUT DISCRIMINATION
IN THE GENETIC AGE

PAUL STEVEN MILLER[27]

The information age has taken hold, and the genetic revolution is in full swing. With apologies to Aldous Huxley, we stand at the precipice of a brave new world.

…History has taught us that the wonders of science hold unique power to sway and seduce, and too often to corrupt, the course of human nature. James Watson [co-discoverer of the double helix] has urged that genetic progress in health can come only with a firm awareness of the potential for abuse. Whether the scientific community is mobilized to deride something as junk science or voodoo genetics may ultimately not matter. Sometimes public opinion and market forces prevail, regardless of whether something is scientifically rational.

As humanity charts a new course, it…must insist that genetic profiles in whatever form they take—remain in the control of the individual, and should never be used to violate fundamental human rights. The challenge for scientists, philosophers, ethicists, jurists, and policymakers is how to best balance the rights of the individual against the needs of society in this rapidly changing world.

Eugenics and Genetics

The U.S. Supreme Court legitimized state–sponsored sterilization in the name of eugenics in its landmark decision of *Buck v. Bell.* Carrie Buck was sent to the State Colony of Epileptics and the Feeble–Minded in Virginia to have a child conceived when she was raped by the nephew of her foster parents. At that time, Virginia permitted sexual sterilization when it was determined that a patient or "inmate" was afflicted with hereditary forms of insanity or imbecility. The authors of the law designed it to prevent the reproduction of "mentally defective" people in the best interest of the patient and society. Buck was ordered sterilized against her will. Dr. Albert Priddy (superintendent of the State Colony for Epileptics and Feeble–Minded) and Aubrey Strode (counsel for the State Colony and drafter of Virginia's sterilization law) chose Buck as the test case for the new law…. In its case, the State of Virginia simply analogized the forced sterilization to compulsory vaccinations.

In 1927, the U.S. Supreme Court…dismissed Buck's concerns. An employee of the Eugenics Record Office studied Buck's medical records and concluded that she exemplified the "shiftless, ignorant, and worthless class of anti–social whites in the South." Despite her appeals to the highest court in the land, Carrie Buck could not be spared from the cruelest corruption of Darwin's theories.

The Court emphasized that Carrie Buck was the daughter of a "feeble–minded" mother and the mother of an "illegitimate" feeble–minded daughter. Justice Oliver Wendell Holmes wrote in the opinion

It is better for all the world, if instead of waiting to execute degenerate offspring for crime, or to let them starve for their imbecility, society can prevent those who are manifestly unfit from continuing their kind. The principle that sustains compulsory

---

27 35 *J.L. Med. & Ethics* 47 (2007).

vaccination is broad enough to cover cutting the Fallopian tubes. Three generations of imbeciles are enough.

Years later in 1979, researchers determined that Carrie Buck, her sister, Doris, who was also sterilized, and her daughter, Vivian, all possessed standard intelligence. According to one report, this brand of pseudoscience permitted the forcible sterilization of 60,000 Americans in the 40 years after *Buck v. Bell*.

Genetic Discrimination in the Workplace

… Should an employer have access to this genetic information? Should the employer know a person's genetic information even if that person chooses not to know it? Where should the line be drawn between legitimate concerns about occupational safety and an individual's fundamental rights of privacy and self–determination? Should an employer be able to participate in, or influence these most personal questions and issues? What protections do employees have to ensure that their genetic information will not be misused?

The potential for genetic discrimination…defined as an employer taking an adverse employment action based upon an asymptomatic, genetic predisposition to a disease or medical condition [is real]…. Most genetic markers cannot predict that an individual will get sick, only that there is a greater likelihood that he or she will actually fall ill. It is important to keep in mind that our genes are only one part of our destiny….

It is difficult to know precisely how prevalent is the use of genetic testing in the workplace…. [T]here is a lack of empirical evidence measuring the extent to which, or for what purposes, employers presently seek genetic information about their employees or applicants….

… Craig Venter, the pioneering genetic scientist, has said that the fear of the misuse of genetic information by employers and insurers is the most significant barrier to genetic advances—greater than the inherent pitfalls that mark the journey to scientific discovery.

… In 1995, the U.S. Equal Employment Opportunity Commission (EEOC) … adopted the view that the ADA prohibits discrimination against workers based on their genetic makeup…. The EEOC's legal theory has never been tested in the courts….

In addition to [proposed] federal law, 34 states have enacted laws that, in one form or another, prohibit the use of genetic information in the workplace. These laws vary widely in form and breadth.

It is important to note that no genetic employment discrimination case has ever been decided, either in federal or state court. Indeed, there have only been a few charges of discrimination filed with the EEOC or the companion state agencies alleging genetic discrimination. However, in 2002, the EEOC filed a lawsuit against the Burlington Northern and Santa Fe Railroad, alleging genetic employment discrimination…in violation of the ADA.

… The EEOC alleged that Burlington Northern subjected its employees to surreptitious genetic testing. [The railroad] was testing to identify a genetic marker for carpal tunnel syndrome to address a high incidence of repetitive stress injuries among its employees. The EEOC further alleged that at least one employee was threatened with discipline and possible termination for refusing to take the genetic test once it was discovered.

Shortly after filing the case, the EEOC and Burlington Northern announced a mediated settlement in the amount of $2.2 million. The railroad also agreed to halt any genetic testing that may have been occurring at the company. While the result was overwhelmingly positive in that the EEOC achieved everything it sought in its lawsuit, by resolving the lawsuit informally, it was never necessary for the court to rule on the applicability of the ADA to the circumstances underlying the workers' complaints.

What was particularly interesting about the *Burlington Northern* case was that no one, not the business community, the employer groups, the scientists, the press, the politicians, nor even the talking heads on cable news programs thought that the surreptitious genetic testing of employees and adverse actions against those who had the "wrong genetic marker" should have been allowed.

With advances in genetic technology, we will soon realize that everyone has genetic predispositions for one genetic condition or another. Mapping the human genome changes the way we understand who is "normal" and who is "disabled." If we all have genetic misspellings, how do we define who is healthy and who is not? If we all have genetic conditions that are just waiting to express themselves in the future, aren't we all truly disabled? As we will all have knowledge of the potential genetic disorder that we each harbor, disabled people may no longer remain stigmatized as "the other" in society.

It is important to note that genetic mutations are not themselves all bad—even those that cause a disorder. The same genetic code that causes sickle cell anemia when inherited from both parents also confers immunity to malaria when inherited from only one. In the past, biological imperatives determined the importance of particular genetic mutations. People either survived to pass on their genes to their children or they did not. Because of advances in medical care and in our understanding of the mechanics of heredity, biological imperatives are less important. It is society that imparts value to genetic diversity, and until now, society has generally assigned a negative value to those mutations which in their expression diverge from the norm, however defined. What about those hidden markers that we will now learn each of us harbors? Are we going to be willing to allow employers to assign a negative value to such genetic markers even if they have no effect on one's ability to do a job? Such actions should be called illegal discrimination.

QUESTIONS

1. What does Professor Miller mean by "the cruelest corruption of Darwin's theories" in the Carrie Buck story?
2. Who are the stakeholders in the Burlington Railroad scenario? Identify the ethical issues.
3. Lewis Maltby began his career as a corporate attorney; later he managed an engineering company. His experiences with business and law combined with his personal interest in social policy led him to volunteer time with the ACLU. This led to his forming a nonprofit organization focused on the rights of employees. In a speech he gave in 2000,[28] Maltby warned:

> The knowledge we gain from the genetic revolution chips away at our very sense of community. Our willingness to think of ourselves as members of a community and to act as such has two deep roots. The first is that we are inherently social animals. Nature has wired us that way. The second is people have generally been better off as members of a community.
>
> But our sense of community is unraveling before our eyes. Millions of upper middle class parents have abandoned the public schools. This phenomenon is not limited to urban areas where the public schools leave much to be desired. Even in affluent communities, with excellent public schools, many middle class families send their children to private schools. We don't even live in the same towns anymore. When I grew up, there was a rich side of town and a poor side of town. But at least it was the same town and people freely crossed from one side of the tracks to another. But today we see the rise of gated communities. These private towns not only have their own police and other municipal services, but you can't even enter these new towns unless the security guard at the gate lets you in.

28 Lynda M. Fox, Aspen, Colorado: Memorial Keynote Address, University of Colorado Medical School, July 21, 2000.

Our growing ability to peer into the medical future only makes things worse. When we don't know who among us will be struck by calamity, it makes sense to stick together and take care of each other. But when we know that the curses of Job are likely to befall someone else rather than ourselves, our incentive to be a community diminishes. All of a sudden, we're not in the same boat anymore. The genetic revolution did not create this sea change. Widespread accumulation of wealth and growing economic inequality are the primary causes. But predictive genetics adds fuel to the fire. The greatest challenge we face entering a new century may be how to maintain our sense of community as the economic foundation of community disappears.

How does Maltby link the disintegration of community and the genetic testing phenomenon?

4. In 2001, only 1% of employers used genetic testing, primarily because of its high cost. Since then, genetic tests have become available for as little as $100, and direct-to-consumer testing is available over the Internet. How does that change the ethical calculus?

5. Under an executive order signed by President Bill Clinton in 2000, federal agencies cannot require genetic testing as a prerequisite for hiring federal employees or awarding the employees benefits and are banned from using genetic information in promotion decisions. Find out whether The Genetic Information and Nondiscrimination Act of 2005, a proposed federal law that would extend protection against to private employees has become law. If not, has other federal legislation aimed at genetic testing been adopted?

CHAPTER **PROBLEMS**

1. District Judge Larson begins his opinion in a recent case with an intriguing sentence:

   What are the legal boundaries of an employee's privacy in this interconnected, electronic-communication age, one in which thoughts and ideas that would have been spoken personally and privately in ages past are now instantly text-messaged to friends and family via handheld, computer-assisted electronic devices?

   The facts: A police department had a contract with Arch Wireless Operating Company, Inc. to provide its employees with pagers. Officers signed the department's equipment use policy, which clarified that any messages sent on city-owned computer equipment could be accessed and reviewed without notice, and that they "should have no expectation of privacy or confidentiality when using these resources." But the department also had an unofficial policy of not auditing the use of the pagers. And in practical terms, the department could only obtain data from employee pagers with the cooperation of Arch Wireless.

   As the bills for the pagers increased, the department reversed its informal policy and began auditing some of its SWAT team members' pager transcripts to determine to what extent overages were caused by personal use. Arch Wireless made the transcripts available. After reviewing them, the department determined that one of its employees had been using his pager for personal reasons, to transmit sexually explicit messages to his wife and girlfriend.

   a. Can you articulate any privacy claims the employees might make?

   b. **Internet Assignment:** Find out if making these messages accessible violated the federal Wiretap Act. *Quon v. Arch Wireless Operating Co., Inc.,* 145 F.Supp.2d 1116 (C.D. Cal., 2006).

2. James Gleick, in *What Just Happened*, writes this about privacy:

> *In public opinion surveys, Americans always favor privacy. Then they turn around and sell it cheaply. Most vehemently oppose any suggestion of a national identification system yet volunteer their telephone numbers and mothers' maiden names and even—grudgingly or not—their social security numbers to merchants bearing discounts or Web services offering "membership" privileges. For most, the abstract notion of privacy suggests a mystical, romantic cowboy-era set of freedoms. Yet in the real world it boils down to matters of small convenience. Certainly where other people's privacy is concerned, we seem willing to lower our standards. We have become a society with a cavernous appetite for news and gossip. Our era has replaced the tacit, eyes-averted civility of an earlier time with exhibitionism and prying. Even borderline public figures must get used to the nation's eyes in their bedrooms and pocketbooks. That's not Big Brother watching us. It's us.*

Do you agree that Americans seem to be willing to sell their own privacy cheaply while simultaneously craving private information about one another? If so, what role do you think technology has played in all of this? Can you imagine technology being used in new and different ways that might affect these trends?

3. Virginia Rulon-Miller had been an IBM employee for years, starting in 1967 as a receptionist in Philadelphia, and working her way up through a series of promotions to marketing manager in San Francisco by 1978. She began dating Matt Blum, who was an accountant with IBM when they met, but who left to work for a competitor. Ms. Rulon-Miller continued to see Mr. Blum and to flourish in her management position. In 1979 she received a $4,000 merit raise and was praised by her supervisor, Philip Callahan. Then one day Callahan left a message that he wanted to meet with her. Rulon-Miller testified:

> *I walked into Phil's office and he asked me to sit down and he said, Are you dating Matt Blum? and I said What? I was kind of surprised he would ask me and I said: Well, what difference does it make if I'm dating Matt Blum? ... And he said, well, something to the effect: I think we have a conflict of interest, or the appearance of a conflict of interest here. And I said, Well, gee, Phil, you've pointed out to me that there are no problems in the office because I am dating Matt Blum, and I don't really understand why that would have any, you know, pertinancy to my job. You said I am doing an okay job. I just got a raise. And he said: No and he said: I'll tell you what. He said: I'll give you a couple of days to a week. Think this whole thing over. I said: Think what over? And he said: You either stop dating Matt Blum or I'm going to take you out of your management job. And I was just kind of overwhelmed.*

The next day Callahan called her in again, told her "he had made up her mind for her," and when she protested, dismissed her....

Ms. Rulon-Miller sued and won $300,000—in large part (and ironically) due to IBM's own policy. Developed by its Chairman Thomas Watson, Jr. (see page 79), the policy protected her from exactly the kind of treatment she had received. According to Watson, there should be a clear distinction between an individual's on- and off-the-job life. Performance—"the one thing the company can insist on from everyone"—should be measured; private life should remain private. See *Rulon-Miller v. IBM*, 208 Cal.Rptr. 524 (1984).

Internet Assignment: Find a case from your state in which an employee claims an employer has overstepped the line between work and private life. What happened? What was the legal basis for the court's decision?

4. In June 1998, the FTC reported to Congress that 89 percent of 212 children's Web sites collected personal information about children without requiring some form of parental control over the process. According to a University of New Hampshire study, 20 percent of young people between the ages of 10 and 17 received unwanted sexual

solicitations online in 2000, and only a quarter of them told their parents. Nancy Willard, a psychologist-attorney who directs Responsible Netizen, has this to say about the invasion of a child's online privacy:

> The emergence of an understanding of the appropriate boundaries of personal privacy is clearly a developmental process, tied to the child's emerging cognitive development. Technically proficient children are using the Internet before they have the cognitive ability to appreciate the possible consequences of disclosure of personal information. Dot.com companies can use this to their advantage in seeking to mold the children's perceptions about personal privacy. They are able to accomplish this largely outside of parental influence because most parents do not know about the actions and intentions of these companies.
>
> Dot.com companies are asking children to disclose personal information and then using that information to develop a close relationship with the child for the purpose of influencing consumer behavior.... Children raised in such an environment will likely fail to develop an understanding of the appropriate boundaries of personal privacy. They will be extremely vulnerable to all manner of manipulation and exploitation, not only from corporate marketers, but also from scam artists, cults, and sexual predators.[29]

Do you agree that there are special concerns regarding privacy for children online?

Internet Assignment: Has there been a legislative response to this problem? Check http://www.ftc.gov.

5. Do Americans have a reasonable expectation of privacy that is violated when they are videotaped on public streets? In store dressing rooms? In motel rooms? In cybercafés? On what basis might they be challenged?

   When cybercafés began to proliferate in Garden Grove, California, they seemed to bring with them gang activity. The police chief pushed for some control, and the city council responded by passing a law that required cybercafés to install video surveillance systems that could be inspected by the city during business hours. When a California court denied a constitutional challenge to the video-surveillance law, one judge dissented:

   > Do my colleagues not realize the—there is no other word for it—Orwellian implications of their ruling today? They approve an ordinance which literally forces a "Big Brother" style telescreen to look over one's shoulder while accessing the Internet....
   > Cybercafes are not just your ordinary "retail establishment." ...
   > Cybercafes allow people who cannot afford computers ... the freedom of the press. They can post messages to the whole world, and, in theory (if they get enough "hits") can reach more people than read the hard copy of the New York Times every morning.... [They allow them] to access the global bulletin board of the Internet, i.e. the ability to receive what others have posted. Logging on is an exercise of free speech.
   > Consider that totalitarian governments have always cracked down on unrestricted access to the means of communication. When the Communists were in control of countries such as Albania and Bulgaria, each typewriter was licensed....
   > And consider that the governments of both Communist China and Vietnam have recently cracked down on cybercafes in an effort to curb the freedom of ideas that they promote—an effort that has entailed learning the identity of cybercafe owners....
   > Given the constitutional ramifications of the very nature of cybercafes, I will go so far as to say that there is an expectation of privacy even as to one's identity when using a cybercafe.... Vo v. City of Garden Grove, 9 Cal.Rptr.3d 257 (Court of Appeal, 2004) (Sills, Concurring and Dissenting).

   Create a constitutional analysis of the video surveillance requirement passed by Garden Grove.

29 "Capturing the 'Eyeballs' and 'E-wallets' of Captive Kids in School: Dot.com Invades Dot.edu," http://www.responsiblenetizen.org.

6. Since the Columbine tragedy, there has been a general crackdown on high school student freedoms, with the use of metal detectors, locker searches, Internet use monitoring, and even discipline of students for expressing their thoughts about violence. Drug testing is part of this trend. In 1995, the U.S. Supreme Court held that a high school could test its student athletes for drug use without violating their Fourth Amendment rights. The Court based this decision partly on the lowered expectation of privacy that would exist in a locker room shared by students who had volunteered to play football—in a school where the drug problem seemed centered on the football team.

   Internet Assignment: What about students in Tecumsah, Oklahoma, who have volunteered to sing in the choir, and who are not suspected of any drug-oriented activity? Do they have the right to resist school drug tests? Check the Supreme Court for 2002.

7. Internet Assignment: In the summer of 1995, Gail Nelson, an employee of Salem State College in Massachusetts, suffered a severe sunburn. Several times a day when she was alone in the office, she would go to the back area, unbutton her blouse and apply sunburn medication. After discovering that she had been videotaped by a hidden camera, she sued her employer for violating her Fourth Amendment rights. What happened? *Nelson v. Salem State College*, 845 N.E.2d 338 (MA 2006).

8. News broke in December 2005 that the National Security Agency (NSA) had been intercepting the phone calls and Internet communications of millions of U.S. citizens without warrants and in violation of the privacy safeguards established by Congress and the U.S. Constitution. The Electronic Frontier Foundation (EFF) brought a class-action lawsuit in January 2006 against AT&T, arguing it had given the NSA unchecked backdoor access to its communications network and its record databases. AT&T moved to dismiss the case, claiming it was immune from suit because it had been following the orders of government officials. The government also moved to dismiss the case, arguing that allowing it to proceed would necessarily reveal "state secrets," threatening national security. In July 2006, U.S. District Judge Vaughn Walker denied both defense motions, allowing the suit to go forward. Dismissing AT&T's immunity argument, he wrote: "AT&T cannot seriously contend that a reasonable entity in its position could have believed that the alleged domestic dragnet was legal." Regarding the government's secrecy argument, he wrote: "The compromise between liberty and security remains a difficult one. But dismissing this case at the outset would sacrifice liberty for no apparent enhancement of security."

   Internet Assignment: Find out what happened with the appeal to the 9th Circuit Court of Appeals.

9. In October 2005, IBM Chairman and CEO Sam Palmisano announced a new company policy preventing the use of genetic information in making personnel decisions. According to an article in *Business Week*:

   IBM's move is as much about smart business as it is about fair employment practices. Big Blue is a big player in medical-information technology, offering a variety of computing technologies for medical and pharmaceutical research. Among them: its powerful Blue Gene supercomputing system.

   IBM knows that if people think medical information will be used against them, they may resist getting the tests its clients are generating. And that could hamper growth of a key market. "This is going to be extraordinarily valuable to medicine," says Caroline Kovac, general manager of IBM health care and life sciences. "But it can't happen if patients don't have a high degree of confidence in the privacy of that information."[30]

---

30 Amy Barrett, "IBM's Smart Stance on Genetic Testing," October 11, 2005.

Evidently IBM's policy was the result of input from patient and other advocacy groups—and from its own employees, thousands of whom were participating in a multi-year research initiative run by National Geographic. This Genographic Project will generate a massive DNA database, making it possible for scientists to map how humans populated the earth. The employees who had volunteered DNA samples to the Project had expressed some concern to the firm's HR managers over how their data would be used.

Internet Assignment: Find out if any other companies have followed IBM's lead.

10. A computer system administrator for Qualcomm discovered that someone had hacked into the company's computer network. The FBI traced the intrusion to a computer on the University of Wisconsin network, and contacted the university's computer help desk. They in turn discovered that someone using a university-networked computer had gained access to the Mail2 server, which processed 250,000 e-mails a day for some 60,000 individuals on campus. Fearing that a shutdown of e-mail would wreak havoc, the campus administrator, Savoy, instead traced the source of intrusion: a computer used regularly to check the e-mail of Jerome Heckenkamp, a student who had once worked for computer services. Without a search warrant and without informing its owner, Savoy logged onto the computer for 15 minutes, determined it was the source of the hacking, and shut down its access to the campus e-mail system. Savoy then contacted Heckencamp, took a statement from him, copied his hard drive and gave both to the FBI. They used that evidence to get a search warrant, seized the computer and searched Heckenkamp's room. What violations of privacy occurred in this scenario? What arguments can you make that the following were justified: (a) the remote search of Heckenkamp's computer; (b) the image of Heckenkamp's hard drive; (c) the FBI seizure of the computer. *United States v. Heckenkamp*, 482 F.3d 1142 (9th Cir. 2007)

CHAPTER **PROJECT**

Mock Trial

GUIDELINES: APPENDIX D

My name is Lily Kim.

I am 35 years old, a divorced parent of two boys, and I have an advanced degree in molecular biology. I've been working for six years for a rapidly expanding biotechnology company called Greengenes. The company hired me because I had exactly the right training to do what they needed: research in the field of food irradiation. Treating food with small doses of radiation increases crop yields and nutritional value. I did my Ph.D. thesis in this area, so the position at Greengenes has been perfect for me. I started as head of one lab, but by last year I was supervising three labs—one in North Carolina, one in California, and one in Atlanta. There was a lot of travel involved, but I really loved my work, and I'd been receiving excellent performance evaluations and salary increases. Last year I made $200,000.

But here's the bad news. Last week Greengenes announced that it intended to do genetic testing on all of its full-time employees, no matter what their rank. The tests they want to run would isolate DNA from a few skin cells and ultimately detect whether a person has the genetic tendency to develop any serious disease in the future.

I know that DNA tests can be used to reveal this type of information, forecasting the ways people can get sick. Some people want to have themselves tested so they can try to prevent or minimize potential illnesses. Suppose they predict you are likely to get heart disease. You can take precautions—be extra careful of your diet and exercise, even go on blood thinners. But I'm not like that kind of person. *I don't want to know* if I am going to get—say—cancer! That's the kind of news I would really rather *not* get. I *don't want to know* whether or not I have a predisposition to get Alzheimer's disease! I want to live my life the best way I can, without trying to "play god" with my future. And I don't want anyone else to know my private health story either. What gives Greengenes the right to read my future? What business is it of theirs? And how do I know they'll keep secret whatever they find out about me? As a scientist I hate to admit it, but there are times when cutting-edge technology can be used clumsily, and the net result is not a benefit.

I've also heard of companies finding out that an employee might be a bad risk, and then deciding they don't want to carry the higher costs of health insurance. So they find an excuse to lay you off—it's easy to do. Suppose it turns out that I am genetically inclined to get cancer? Greengenes might start claiming I am underperforming, and that would be the end of my wonderful job. Once Greengenes has my data, I don't see how I can be certain the whole world won't find out—or at least the world of biotech companies. Which could mean I can't get another job—or health insurance. Imagine being unable to get insurance *because* you desperately need it?

So I told them I didn't want to be tested. The company responded immediately. I was called into the Human Resource office one day. There was someone there I didn't know—a Cary Packer. Packer wouldn't look me in the eye; said that Greengenes had a policy, a clear-cut rule, and because I was failing to obey it, I was to be terminated.

Now I am suing. I am concerned—not only for myself but for anyone else who is forced to make this kind of choice. Why should a company be able to demand that someone with a great background and a terrific job record reveal so much to keep their job? What controls are there on their use of that kind of information? If it is OK for employers to require genetic tests, what else can they force people to do? This is where technology is running away with privacy—it's just scary.

I am Cary Packer.

I am Human Resource manager of Greengenes, Inc. We are a new and flourishing company, one of only about 1,000 biotechnology companies worldwide. Biotechs are among the fastest growing companies of the twenty-first century. We are at the center of nearly every effort to improve healthcare, agriculture, industrial manufacturing, and the environment today.

Greengenes focuses on products for agricultural markets, on methods of altering plants to make them more beneficial for humans. We began operating in 1997 with about 20 employees; now, ten years later, we employ over 300. And almost all of the people we hire are experts, with advanced research or clinical backgrounds. Like software and computer companies, biotech employers like us attract top applicants through compensation packages that include stock options. And once we have made a hiring decision, we like to keep our employees happy, assuming they prove themselves to be valuable to us. We provide an on-site gym and squash courts, high-quality childcare at a reduced cost, and excellent health and retirement benefits. We believe that a happy workforce is an efficient one, and that it only makes good sense to do right by our employees.

As a high-tech company, we feel especially comfortable trusting in technology to help us make smart and efficient business decisions.

As part of that, we have decided to implement a policy of genetically testing everyone who works for the company. We feel we need to discover whether our people have the tendency to develop cancer and other life-threatening illnesses.

We have three simple reasons for this. First, we compete in a global marketplace, and many of our competitors are operating in countries where the government bears most of the cost of health care. But we are based in the United States, where the spiking costs of health care fall increasingly on employers. Our testing program is an effort to control losses in this area. Second, we want to employ the best, and the best means the best qualified, both mentally and physically. Employers should have the right to know if the people they hire, train, and trust with big responsibilities will someday become seriously ill and have their productive capacities cut short. This is nothing new—it's a matter of using technology that has existed for many years to give us a better handle on how to invest our resources.

The third reason we have for the testing is really for Ms. Kim's own good. Like many of our employees, Kim will be exposed to chemicals and radiation on the job. Not a lot—but even in small amounts those exposures could have nasty effects over the long term, especially if the person already has a tendency to become ill. Suppose an employee is susceptible to getting cancer? We may want to move her out of the lab and into some other division of the company. In this sense we would actually be doing her a favor. Of course, like any business, we have our shareholders' interests to consider. There's the potential to be sued at some later date by dozens of people who claim that they got cancer because we put them at risk on the job. Even when you win a case like that you lose in the court of public opinion.

We are sorry that Ms. Kim is so upset. But any employee who doesn't feel comfortable with our testing procedures should work somewhere else. It's a free country, after all!

VALUING DIVERSITY: STEREOTYPING VS. INCLUSION

4

Like and difference are quickening words, brooding and hatching. Better and worse are eggsucking words. They leave only the shell.

— Ursula Le Guin

The case is simple. A woman with pre-school children may not be employed, a man with pre-school children may. The distinguishing factor seems to be motherhood versus fatherhood. The question then arises: Is this sex-related? To the simple query, the answer is just as simple: Nobody—and this includes Judges, Solomonic or life tenured—has yet seen a male mother. A mother, to oversimplify the simplest biology, must then be a woman.

— Justice Brown, dissenting, Phillips v. Martin Marietta Corp.

The events of 9/11 made "immigrant" synonymous with "terrorist."

— Ruben J. Garcia, "Ghost Workers in an Interconnected World," (2003)

●

Despite civil rights laws barring discrimination and Supreme Court rulings that span half a century, the remnants of past practices survive. They can be seen in the difficulties that continue to plague small businesses owned by minorities and women, in the wage gap between men and women, people of color and whites, and in a national workforce in which jobs are still by and large segregated by race and gender. Stereotypes continue to create social and economic hardships for many in our society. In the first decade of the new millenium, the threat of terrorism and the globalization of business and labor have created new strains and concerns. In response to those stresses, a national debate has emerged over immigration policies and the rights of new citizens.

This chapter opens with a case that is one of the most controversial in years: the ruling by the high court of Massachusetts in favor of same-sex marriage. The Equal Protection Clause of the U.S. Constitution, and federal laws against discrimination based on race, sex, national origin, and disability provide the legal backdrop. Readings on the social construction of gender, the tension known as the work/life dilemma and the urgent need to come to grips with immigration round out the chapter.

In 2001, gay and lesbian couples in Massachusetts—including some who had lived together for many years—applied for licenses to marry. Denied by the town clerks, they filed a lawsuit seeking a judicial declaration that the Department of Public Health's policy violated the Massachusetts Constitution. When the lower court ruled against them, the plaintiffs appealed.

GOODRIDGE v. DEPARTMENT OF PUBLIC HEALTH

Supreme Judicial Court of Massachusetts, 2003
798 N.E.2d 941

MARSHALL, C. J. (with whom IRELAND and GREANEY, J. J. Concur) ☀

… Marriage is a vital social institution. The exclusive commitment of two individuals to each other nurtures love and mutual support; it brings stability to our society. For those who choose to marry, and for their children, marriage provides an abundance of legal, financial, and social benefits. In return it imposes weighty legal, financial, and social obligations. The question before us is whether, consistent with the Massachusetts Constitution, the Commonwealth may deny the protections, benefits, and obligations conferred by civil marriage to two individuals of the same sex who wish to marry. We conclude that it may not. The Massachusetts Constitution affirms the dignity and equality of all individuals. It forbids the creation of second-class citizens. In reaching our conclusion we have given full deference to the arguments made by the Commonwealth. But it has failed to identify any constitutionally adequate reason for denying civil marriage to same-sex couples.

We are mindful that our decision marks a change in the history of our marriage law. Many people hold deep-seated religious, moral, and ethical convictions that marriage should be limited to the union of one man and one woman, and that homosexual conduct is immoral. Many hold equally strong religious, moral, and ethical convictions that same-sex couples are entitled to be married, and that homosexual persons should be treated no differently than their heterosexual neighbors…. "Our obligation is to define the liberty of all, not to mandate our own moral code."[1]…

The plaintiffs are fourteen individuals from five Massachusetts counties. As of April 11, 2001 … Gloria Bailey, sixty years old, and Linda Davies, fifty-five years old, had been in a committed relationship for thirty years; … Hillary Goodridge, forty-four years old, and Julie Goodridge, forty-three years old, had been in a committed relationship for thirteen years and lived with their five-year-old daughter; … Gary Chalmers, thirty-five years old, and Richard Linnell, thirty-seven years old, had been in a committed relationship for thirteen years and lived with their eight-year-old daughter and Richard's mother….

The plaintiffs include business executives, lawyers, an investment banker, educators, therapists, and a computer engineer. Many are active in church, community, and school groups. They have employed such legal means as are available to them—for example, joint adoption, powers of attorney, and joint ownership of real property—to secure aspects of their relationships. Each plaintiff attests a desire to marry his or her partner in order to affirm publicly their commitment to each other and to secure the legal protections and benefits afforded to married couples and their children….

The benefits accessible only by way of a marriage license are enormous, touching nearly every aspect of life and death. The department states that "hundreds of statutes" are related to marriage and to marital benefits…. [S]ome of the statutory benefits conferred by the Legislature on those who enter into civil marriage include… : joint Massachusetts income tax filing; tenancy by the entirety (a form of ownership that provides certain protections against creditors and allows for the automatic descent of property to the surviving spouse without probate); extension of the benefit of the homestead

1 *Lawrence v. Texas*, 123 S.Ct. 2472, 2480 (2003) (Lawrence), quoting *Planned Parenthood of Southeastern Pa v. Casey*, 505 U.S. 833, 850 (1992) (obtained at http://news.findlaw.com/hdocs/docs/conlaw/goodridge111803opn.pdf).

protection… to one's spouse and children; [inheritance rights]… ; entitlement to wages owed to a deceased employee; eligibility to continue certain businesses of a deceased spouse; the right to share the medical policy of one's spouse; … access to veterans' spousal benefits and preferences; financial protections for spouses of … fire fighters, police officers, and prosecutors … killed in the performance of duty; [property rights upon divorce or separation]; … the right to bring claims for wrongful death and loss of consortium; … the presumptions of legitimacy and parentage of children born to a married couple; … evidentiary rights, such as the prohibition against spouses testifying against one another about their private conversations; … qualification for bereavement or medical leave to care for [relatives]… ; an automatic "family member" preference to make medical decisions for an incompetent or disabled spouse; … and the right to interment in the lot or tomb owned by one's deceased spouse….

It is undoubtedly for these concrete reasons, as well as for its intimately personal significance, that civil marriage has long been termed a "civil right." …

Without the right to marry—or more properly, the right to choose to marry—one is excluded from the full range of human experience and denied full protection of the laws for one's "avowed commitment to an intimate and lasting human relationship." …

For decades, indeed centuries, in much of this country (including Massachusetts) no lawful marriage was possible between white and black Americans. That long history availed not when the … United States Supreme Court … held that a statutory bar to interracial marriage violated the Fourteenth Amendment, *Loving v. Virginia*, (1967)….

The individual liberty and equality safeguards of the Massachusetts Constitution protect both "freedom from" unwarranted government intrusion into protected spheres of life and "freedom to" partake in benefits created by the State for the common good. Both freedoms are involved here. Whether and whom to marry, how to express sexual intimacy, and whether and how to establish a family—these are among the most basic of every individual's liberty and due process rights….

Under both the equality and liberty guarantees, regulatory authority must, at very least, serve "a legitimate purpose in a rational way."… Any law failing to satisfy the basic standards of rationality is void.

… The [lower court held] that "the state's interest in regulating marriage is based on the traditional concept that marriage's primary purpose is procreation." This is incorrect. Our laws of civil marriage do not privilege procreative heterosexual intercourse between married people above every other form of adult intimacy and every other means of creating a family…. Fertility is not a condition of marriage, nor is it grounds for divorce….

There is … no rational relationship between the marriage statute and the Commonwealth's proffered goal of protecting the "optimal" child rearing unit…. People in same-sex couples may be "excellent" parents. These couples have children for the reasons others do—to love them, to care for them, to nurture them…. Excluding same-sex couples from civil marriage will not make children of opposite-sex marriages more secure, but it does prevent children of same-sex couples from enjoying the immeasurable advantages that flow from the assurance of "a stable family structure in which children will be reared, educated, and socialized."

The department [also argues that] broadening civil marriage to include same-sex couples will trivialize or destroy the institution of marriage as it has historically been fashioned. Certainly our decision today marks a significant change in the definition of marriage as it has been inherited from the common law, and understood by many societies for centuries. But it does not disturb the fundamental value of marriage in our society.

Here, the plaintiffs seek only to be married, not to undermine the institution of civil marriage….

The history of constitutional law "is the story of the extension of constitutional rights and protections to people once ignored or excluded."… As a public institution and a right of fundamental importance, civil marriage is an evolving paradigm. The common law was exceptionally harsh toward women who became wives: a woman's legal identity all but evaporated into that of her husband.... Alarms about the imminent erosion of the "natural" order of marriage were sounded over ... the expansion of the rights of married women, and the introduction of "no-fault" divorce. Marriage has survived all of these transformations, and we have no doubt that marriage will continue to be a vibrant and revered institution.

The marriage ban works a deep and scarring hardship on a very real segment of the community for no rational reason. The absence of any reasonable relationship between, on the one hand, an absolute disqualification of same-sex couples who wish to enter into civil marriage and, on the other, protection of public health, safety, or general welfare, suggests that the marriage restriction is rooted in persistent prejudices against persons who are (or who are believed to be) homosexual. "The Constitution cannot control such prejudices but neither can it tolerate them...." Limiting the protections, benefits, and obligations of civil marriage to opposite-sex couples violates the basic premises of individual liberty and equality under law protected by the Massachusetts Constitution. [Held: the Department of Health policy denying marriage licenses to same-sex couples violates the Massachusetts Constitution.]

SPINA, J. (dissenting, with whom Sosman and Cordy, JJ., join). ☀

... The power to regulate marriage lies with the Legislature, not with the judiciary.... Today, the court has transformed its role as protector of individual rights into the role of creator of rights, and I respectfully dissent....

CORDY, J. (dissenting, with whom Spina and Sosman, JJ., join). ☀

...Because a conceivable rational basis exists upon which the Legislature could conclude that the marriage statute furthers the legitimate State purpose of ensuring, promoting, and supporting an optimal social structure for the bearing and raising of children, it is a valid exercise of the State's police power.

The marriage statute ... does not intrude on any right that the plaintiffs have to privacy in their choices regarding procreation, an intimate partner or sexual relations. The plaintiffs' right to privacy in such matters does not require that the State officially endorse their choices in order for the right to be constitutionally vindicated....

While the institution of marriage is deeply rooted in the history and traditions of our country and our State, the right to marry someone of the same sex is not. No matter how personal or intimate a decision to marry someone of the same sex might be, the right to make it is not guaranteed by the right of personal autonomy ... [nor by the] right to freedom of association....

Paramount among its many important functions, the institution of marriage has systematically provided for the regulation of heterosexual behavior, brought order to the resulting procreation, and ensured a stable family structure in which children will be reared, educated, and socialized.

... The alternative, a society without the institution of marriage, in which heterosexual intercourse, procreation, and child care are largely disconnected processes, would be chaotic....

It is undeniably true that dramatic historical shifts in our cultural, political, and economic landscape have altered some of our traditional notions about marriage, including the interpersonal dynamics within it, the range of responsibilities required of it as an institution, and the legal environment in which it exists. Nevertheless, the institution of marriage remains the principal weave of our social fabric.... A family defined by heterosexual marriage continues to be the most prevalent social structure into which the vast majority of children are born, nurtured, and prepared for productive participation in civil society.

It is difficult to imagine a State purpose more important and legitimate than ensuring, promoting, and supporting an optimal social structure within which to bear and raise children. At the very least, the marriage statute continues to serve this important State purpose….

… [T]he Legislature could conceivably conclude that declining to recognize same-sex marriages remains prudent until empirical questions about its impact on the upbringing of children are resolved….

As long as marriage is limited to opposite-sex couples who can at least theoretically procreate, society is able to communicate a consistent message to its citizens that marriage is a (normatively) necessary part of their procreative endeavor; that if they are to procreate, then society has endorsed the institution of marriage as the environment for it and for the subsequent rearing of their children; and that benefits are available explicitly to create a supportive and conducive atmosphere for those purposes. If society proceeds similarly to recognize marriages between same-sex couples who cannot procreate, it could be perceived as an abandonment of this claim, and might result in the mistaken view that civil marriage has little to do with procreation: just as the potential of procreation would not be necessary for a marriage to be valid, marriage would not be necessary for optimal procreation and child rearing to occur. In essence, the Legislature could conclude that the consequence of such a policy shift would be a diminution in society's ability to steer the acts of procreation and child rearing into their most optimal setting….[I dissent.]

QUESTIONS

1. On what basis does the majority strike down the Massachusetts marriage license law? How does the dissent respond?

2. **Internet Assignment:** The dissent mentions "empirical questions" about the impact of same-sex marriage on children. What can you find out about the impact—positive or negative—on those who have been raised by same-sex parents?

3. **Internet Assignment:** Find *Loving v. Virginia*, the 1967 Supreme Court case that held that statutes barring marriage across racial lines were unconstitutional. Did the Court employ any of the same arguments made by the majority in *Goodridge*?

4. In your view, what is marrige really about? An intimate relationship? An economic partnership? A way to raise children? An institution that allows the state to "privatize dependency" by making spouses legally responsible for caring for each other and their children? Which judge in *Goodridge* comes closest to your own vision? To what extent does your vision affect how you feel about same sex-marrlage?

5. Do you think the majority in *Goodridge* would have a problem with the following: (a) A statute declaring divorce illegal? (b) A law lowering the age for legitimate marriage to 11?

6. What impact would wide-scale recognition of same-sex marriage likely have on business?

7. **Internet Assignment:** In 2002, the Netherlands became the first country in the world to open up civil marriage to same-sex couples. Since then, Belgium, Canada, Denmark, Sweden, Iceland, Finland, France, Germany, and South Africa have allowed marriage-like partnerships. Find out how your state deals with same-sex marriages or partnerships.

Equal Protection

*[N]or shall any State deprive any person of life, liberty or property,
without due process of law; nor deny to any person within its jurisdiction
the equal protection of the law.*

— FOURTEENTH AMENDMENT, UNITED STATES CONSTITUTION

The Equal protection clause requires government to treat groups of people in the same situation similarly. As with all constitutional rights, however, the right to equal protection is not absolute. If government can show that it has strong enough justification for treating different—but "similarly situated"—groups unequally, it may do so. The justification the government must give varies depending on the type of discrimination involved.

Suppose the state of California passed a law that allowed all 16-year-olds, except those of Mexican ancestry, to apply for drivers' licenses. This law would discriminate between groups (Mexicans vs. non-Mexicans) that are similarly situated: They are all 16 years old, and they all want to get a driver's license. It distinguishes them based on a characteristic that people can do nothing to change, and one that has been used historically to oppress groups of people: their ethnicity. This kind of discrimination can only pass the standard of equal protection if California can show its law serves a very strong or **"compelling" state interest**, and if it is narrowly tailored to do so. In other words, if California can achieve its important goal(s) in a less discriminatory way, it must. This equal protection test is called **strict scrutiny**. It has been applied only to **suspect classifications**, such as race and ethnicity, and in cases where the classification infringes on such **fundamental freedoms** as the right of free speech or the right to vote. It sets such a high barrier that few cases in our entire history have met the strict scrutiny standard. The best known case was the *Korematsu* decision, in which the Supreme Court upheld an executive order issued by President Franklin Roosevelt that sent Japanese-Americans to live in internment camps during World War II.[2]

When the government discriminates in a way that is neither based on race nor ethnicity nor involves a fundamental right, equal protection analysis is much looser and permits the **state action** so long as it has a **rational relationship** to a valid government purpose. For example, suppose Chicago passed a law specifying that restaurants of more than 1,000 square feet must be inspected by the Department of Health twice a year, while smaller restaurants need be inspected only annually. The classification—larger versus smaller eating establishments—is not suspect, and there is no fundamental right to operate an unclean restaurant. The law will probably be upheld as well tailored to promote a legitimate state goal. Most legislation can pass the rational relationship test.

Some classifications—notably gender—receive what has come to be known as **intermediate** or **heightened scrutiny**, a level of judicial inquiry that falls somewhere between strict scrutiny and the minimal rational relationship. When government treats males one way and females another, the courts must determine if there is a substantial government reason for the difference. If not, it will rule that the classification violates equal protection.

* * * * *

I know this film well. "Easter '62" was the home movie Dr. Luce talked my parents into giving him. This was the film he screened each year for his students at Cornell University Medical School. This was the thirty-five second segment that, Luce insisted, proved out his theory that gender

---

2 *Korematsu v. United States*, 323 Y,S, 214 (1944). In an effort to ameliorate the results of this later-regretted decision, Congress in 1988 ordered $20,000 in reparations to be paid to each living survivor of the detention camps. 50 U.S.C. App. Sect. 1989(b) (1988).

identity is established early on in life. This was the film Dr. Luce showed to me, to tell me who I was. And who was that? Look at the screen. My mother is handing me a baby doll. I take the baby and hug it to my chest. Putting a toy bottle to the baby lips, I offer it milk.

— Jeffrey Eugenides, Middlesex[3]

* * * * *

When Elana Back was denied tenure as a school psychologist, the school district claimed it was because she lacked organizational and interpersonal skills. Back had a different perception: She claimed that the real reason had to do with stereotypes about mothers. That, she insisted, violated her constitutional right to equal protection of the laws.

BACK v. HASTINGS ON HUDSON UNION FREE SCHOOL

U.S. Court of Appeals, Second Circuit, 2004
365 F.3d 107

CALABRESI , Circuit Judge. ☀

… This appeal … poses an important question, one that strikes at the persistent "fault line between work and family—precisely where sex-based overgeneralization has been and remains strongest."… It asks whether stereotyping about the qualities of mothers is a form of gender discrimination, and whether this can be determined in the absence of evidence about how the employer in question treated fathers. We answer both questions in the affirmative.…

… [In her first two years as a school psychologist, Elana Back's supervisors] Brennan and Wishnie consistently gave her excellent evaluations. In her first annual evaluation, on a scale where the highest score was "outstanding," and the second highest score was "superior," Back was deemed "outstanding" and "superior" in almost all categories, and "average" in only one.… Narrative evaluations completed by Wishnie and Brennan during this time were also uniformly positive, [noting that she] … had "successfully adjusted to become a valued and valuable member of the school/community."…

Back asserts that things changed dramatically as her tenure review approached. The first allegedly discriminatory comments came … shortly after Back had returned from maternity leave, [when Back claims that Brennan] (a) inquired about how she was "planning on spacing [her] offspring," (b) said "[p]lease do not get pregnant until I retire," and (c) suggested that Back "wait until [her son] was in kindergarten to have another child."

Then, a few months into Back's third year at Hillside … Brennan allegedly told Back that she was expected to work until 4:30 p.m. every day, and asked "What's the big deal. You have a nanny. This is what you [have] to do to get tenure." Back replied that she did work these hours.… Brennan also indicated that Back should "maybe … reconsider whether [Back] could be a mother and do this job which [Brennan] characterized as administrative in nature," and that Brennan and Wishnie were "concerned that, if [Back] received tenure, [she] would work only until 3:15 p.m. and did not know how [she] could possibly do this job with children."

A few days later … Brennan allegedly told Back for the first time that she might not support Back's tenure because of what Back characterizes as minor errors that she made

3 (NY: Farrar, Strauss & Giroux, 2002) p. 226.

in a report.... [B]oth Brennan and Wishnie reportedly told Back that this was perhaps not the job or the school district for her if she had "little ones," and that it was "not possible for [her] to be a good mother and have this job." The two also allegedly remarked that it would be harder to fire Back if she had tenure, and wondered "whether my apparent commitment to my job was an act. They stated that once I obtained tenure, I would not show the same level of commitment I had shown because I had little ones at home. They expressed concerns about my child care arrangements, though these had never caused me conflict with school assignments."...

Back claims that in March, Brennan and Wishnie reiterated that her job was "not for a mother," that they were worried her performance was "just an 'act' until I got tenure," and that "because I was a young mother, I would not continue my commitment to the work place."...

... Individuals have a clear right, protected by the Fourteenth Amendment, to be free from discrimination on the basis of sex in public employment....

To show sex discrimination, Back relies upon a *Price Waterhouse* "stereotyping" theory. [The gender stereotypes method for proving same-sex sexual harassment is based on *Price Waterhouse v. Hopkins* (1989), a case in which the Supreme Court reviewed the sex discrimination claim of a woman who had been denied partnership in an accounting firm at least in part on the basis that she was "macho," "overcompensated for being a woman," needed "a course in charm school," was "masculine," and was "a lady using foul language." A partner advised the plaintiff that if she wished to improve her chances of earning partnership, she should "walk more femininely, talk more femininely, dress more femininely, wear make-up, have her hair styled, and wear jewelry."... The Court noted that "we are beyond the day when an employer could evaluate employees by assuming or insisting that they matched the stereotype associated with their group, for '[i]n forbidding employers to discriminate against individuals because of their sex, Congress intended to strike at the entire spectrum of disparate treatment of men and women resulting from sex stereotypes.'"...]

Accordingly, she argues that comments made about a woman's inability to combine work and motherhood are direct evidence of such discrimination....

... The principle of *Price Waterhouse* ... applies as much to the supposition that a woman *will* conform to a gender stereotype (and therefore will not, for example, be dedicated to her job), as to the supposition that a woman is unqualified for a position because she does *not* conform to a gender stereotype....

... [I]t takes no special training to discern stereotyping in the view that a woman cannot "be a good mother" and have a job that requires long hours, or in the statement that a mother who received tenure "would not show the same level of commitment [she] had shown because [she] had little ones at home." ...

Moreover, the Supreme Court itself recently took judicial notice of such stereotypes. In an opinion by Chief Justice Rehnquist, the Court concluded that stereotypes of this sort were strong and pervasive enough to justify prophylactic congressional action, in the form of the Family Medical Leave Act:

> *Stereotypes about women's domestic roles are reinforced by parallel stereotypes presuming a lack of domestic responsibilities for men. Because employers continued to regard the family as the woman's domain, they often denied men similar accommodations or discouraged them from taking leave. These mutually reinforcing stereotypes created a self-fulfilling cycle of discrimination that forced women to continue to assume the role of primary family caregiver, and fostered employers' stereotypical views about women's commitment to work and their value as employees. Those perceptions, in turn, Congress reasoned, lead to subtle discrimination that may be difficult to detect on a case-by-case basis.*

> — *NEVADA DEPT. OF HUMAN RESOURCES V. HIBBS, 123 S.CT. 1972 (2003)*

Hibbs makes pellucidly clear, however, that, at least where stereotypes are considered, the notions that mothers are insufficiently devoted to work, and that work and motherhood are incompatible, are properly considered to be, themselves, gender-based. *Hibbs* explicitly called the stereotype that "women's family duties trump those of the workplace" a "*gender* stereotype," and cited a number of state pregnancy and family leave acts—including laws that provided *only* pregnancy leave—as evidence of "pervasive sex-role stereotype that caring for family members is women's work."….

[We find that] stereotyping of women as caregivers can by itself and without more be evidence of an impermissible, sex-based motive.

QUESTIONS

1. How would you define stereotyping? What are some common stereotypes of women besides the one Elana Back had to confront? Of Hispanics? Asians? Muslims? African-Americans? What is the heart of the difference between stereotyping and outright discrimination?

2. Is there a difference—ethically speaking—between denying someone tenure because she is a woman and denying her tenure because she is a mother and might spend less time on her job responsibilities? Is it unethical to allow stereotypes to affect employment decisions? Why or why not?

3. **Internet Assignment:** Only those who are employed by the government can argue that the Constitution entitles them to equal protection in a situation like Elana Back's. Find a case in which a private sector employee claims discrimination or wrongful discharge based on stereotyping. On what law did the plaintiff rely? What happened?

4. Jewel Redhead taught fifth grade—one hour per day of Bible study, the rest secular subjects—at a Seventh Day Adventist school. In September of her fourth year, she told her principal she was pregnant. When Redhead told her principal she did not intend to marry the father, the school decided to terminate her ("pregnancy outside of marriage is evidence of fornication"). What legal arguments might Redhead make? How could the school defend itself? What ethical issues arise when discrimination occurs in a private, religious organization? *Redhead v. Conference of Seventh Day Adventists*, 440 F.Supp.2d 211(E.D. N.Y. 2006).

5. Feminist lawyer Nancy Dowd argues that "family is such a strong cultural construct it can change the law, but law cannot change family…. It may facilitate change or support change, but it cannot force change in family culture."[4] In the United States, nearly one-third of all families with minor children are single-parent families; marriage is neither a lifelong partnership nor the only form of committed partnership; there are increasing numbers of "independent" adoptions by persons other than a married husband and wife. All of these, she points out, are examples of "culture subverting [the legal definition of] family." Should the law be used to either support change that seems to be underway in family culture, or to stifle it?

Joan C. Williams directs the Program in Gender Work and Family at American University. In the following reading, she discusses some of what psychologists and sociologists have learned about stereotyping and cognitive bias against caregivers.

---

4 Nancy E. Dowd, "Law, Culture, and Family: The Transformative Power of Culture and the Limits of Law," 78 *Chi.-Kent L. Rev.* 785 (2003).

BEYOND THE GLASS CEILING: THE MATERNAL WALL AS A BARRIER TO GENDER EQUALITY

Joan C. Williams[5]

My subject is motherhood. More specifically, the intertwining of motherhood, economic vulnerability, and social stigma. We've all heard about the glass ceiling and I'm sad to say that the glass ceiling is alive and well in America. But most women never get near it because they are stopped long before by the maternal wall.

Over eighty percent of women become mothers. And although the wage gap between men and women is actually narrowing, the wage gap between mothers and other adults has actually risen in recent decades. Although young women now earn about ninety percent of the wages of men, mothers still earn only about sixty percent of the wages of fathers. This is what's called the family gap, as distinguished from the wage gap.

Much of this family gap stems from the ways we organize the relationship of market work to family work. We still define the ideal worker as someone who starts to work in early adulthood and works full-time, full force, for forty years straight, taking no time off for childbearing, childrearing, or really anything else. That's not an ungendered norm....

... [T]here is no federal statute that forbids discrimination against adults with caregiving responsibilities....

[Let me tell you about] two lawyers, a husband and wife, who worked for the same firm. After they had a baby, the wife was sent home like clockwork at 5:30—after all, she had a baby to take care of. The husband was kept late almost every night—after all, he had a family to support. That's called benevolent stereotyping. It's stereotyping done in a very different tone of voice than hostile stereotyping, but the effect is much the same: the employer polices men and women into traditionalist bread-winner/housewife roles— clearly an inappropriate role for an employer to play.

In the caregiver context, one key study by Susan Fiske and her colleagues ranked stereotypes by perceived competence. Fiske and her colleagues found that businesswomen were rated as very high in competence, similar to businessmen and millionaires. Housewives, on the other hand, were rated as very low in competence—similar to— (here I quote the researchers) the elderly, blind, "retarded," and "disabled."

To see how the caregiver stereotype operates in practice, let's recall the famous story of the Boston attorney who returned from maternity leave and found she was given the work of a paralegal. She said, "I wanted to say, 'Look I had a baby, not a lobotomy.'" What happened? She was taken out of the high competence "business woman" category and put into the low competence caregiver category.

Understanding this process is very important for understanding the kinds of problems mothers often experience at one of three particular moments in time: when they get pregnant, return from maternity leave, or go on a flexible work arrangement....

[Sociologists] ... compared the "good father" to the "good mother," and they found a lot of overlap. But they also found one key difference, in the time culture of parenthood. The "good mother" was viewed as someone who was always available to her children.... When a woman cuts back her hours, she may trigger stigma of various sorts and cease to be considered an ideal worker, at least she'll often be considered an ideal mother. The same is not true of many fathers. Nick Townsend ... pointed out that our ideals of fatherhood retain a strong

5 Source: Joan C. Williams, 26 T. Jefferson L. Rev. 1 (2003). This article was part of the 1st Annual Ruth Bader Ginsburg Lecture on Women and the Law Conference, Thomas Jefferson School of Law, April 25, 2003.

emphasis on fathers as the providers. And studies of masculinity…document how we still tie masculinity very tightly into the size of a paycheck. These studies help us understand why the chilly climate for mothers at work often becomes a frigid climate for fathers who take an active role in family care. This frigid climate can give rise to some troubling situations….

The stigma that's associated with flexible work arrangements also reflects various patterns of unexamined bias. [One person I interviewed told me:] "Before I went part-time and people called and found that I wasn't at my desk, they assumed I was somewhere else at a business meeting. But after I went part-time, the tendency was to assume that I wasn't there because of my part-time schedule, even if I was out at a meeting. Also, before I went part-time, people sort of gave me the benefit of the doubt. They assumed that I was giving them as fast a turn-around as was humanly possible. This stopped after I went part-time. Then they assumed that I wasn't doing things fast enough because of my part-time schedule." As a result, she said, she used to get top-of-the-scale performance reviews, but now she didn't, "even though, as far as I can tell, the quality of my work has not changed." Here we can identify three types of unexamined bias.

The first is attribution bias. When she was full-time and was not there, her co-workers attributed her absence to legitimate business reasons. But when she was part-time, and they found her not there, they attributed her absence to family reasons—even if she was at a business meeting.

The second kind of bias is called in-group favoritism. The in-group for this purpose is full-timers, and the out-group is part-timers, who are almost exclusively female. When the informant was in the in-group, she was given the benefit of the doubt. But after she went part-time, she was in the out-group and that stopped….

Finally … women employed part-time were viewed similar to "housewives."

The implication of all these studies is that the chilly climate for family caregivers at work, including the stigma that attaches to many part-time and other flexible work arrangements, stems in part from gender stereotyping….

QUESTIONS

1. Elsewhere in this reading, Williams asks: "Should feminists seek to empower in traditionally feminine roles or should they seek access to the preserves of masculinity?" What do you think? What would be involved in each goal?

2. According to Williams, how do employers define the "ideal worker"? How would you reinvent the ideal worker in an ungendered fashion? How might the law be used to support such a worker?

3. **Internet Assignment:** Find a company that has tried to create a corporate culture that supports men or women in part- or "flex" time employment. What are the characteristics of its program? Now check the company's financials. Is the "progressive" firm you've located also a successful one?

The Civil Rights Act of 1964

> *It shall be unlawful for an employer to fail or refuse to hire or to discharge any individual or otherwise discriminate against any individual with respect to his compensation terms, conditions, or privileges of employment because of such individual's race, color, religion, sex or national origin.*
>
> — TITLE VII, THE CIVIL RIGHTS ACT OF 1964[6]

---

6   42 U.S.C.A. Sect. 2000(e).

Gradually, over time, the courts began to expand the meaning of equal protection—ruling in *Brown v. Board of Education* in 1954, for example, that segregated schools were unequal. But the Constitution applies only to discrimination by government. For almost a century after the Civil War, there was no federal law against discrimination by private individuals or business firms, and state laws were uneven in their scope and application.

After a decade of protest against segregation and in the wake of the assassination of President John F. Kennedy, the U.S. Congress passed comprehensive civil rights legislation that, for the first time, would address discrimination on the part of private businesses and individuals. It outlawed discrimination in public accommodations (hotels, motels, restaurants), housing, public education, federally assisted programs, and employment.

Title VII, the provision dealing with employment, has no mention of the hot-button issues that emerged in the decades after its passage—affirmative action, sexual harassment, same-sex marriage. Its mandate appears to be relatively straightforward: to end discrimination. Yet Title VII has been interpreted as banning not only outright differential treatment, but also practices that appear to be neutral (height and weight standards, educational requirements, for example), but which disproportionately disadvantage members of one race, sex, or religion ("disparate impact discrimination"). It empowers courts to correct discrimination when they find it; to order companies to hire, promote, adjust raises or benefits, or otherwise compensate those who have been wronged.

Sex Discrimination

Sex, **gender**, and **sexuality** are terms whose meanings have been contested and re-conceptualized in the past few decades. Psychologists and feminist theorists, for example, generally use "sex" to refer to one's biological sex, labeling people "male" or "female" depending on their chromosomes, hormones, and anatomical features. Sex, they argue, is distinguishable from "gender" (whether one is masculine or feminine), because gender is the meaning that a particular society gives to one's sex. Whether one is "feminine" may depend, for example, on whether one takes care of children—even though, biologically, both males and females are capable of caring for children. This is often called the **social construction of gender**.

Interpreting the Civil Rights Act's ban on "discrimination on the basis of sex," courts have had to decide what Congress meant by sex. Federal courts have consistently held that "sex" refers to one's biological sex, whether discrimination occurred because one is male or female, or because of the kind of gender-stereotyping that Elana Back confronted. The statute has not been interpreted to protect against discrimination based on one's sexual orientation or affiliations (homosexuality, bisexuality, heterosexuality). This means that, except in those states and localities with laws banning discrimination based on sexual orientation, an employer can refuse to hire a woman because she is a lesbian, a man because he is gay.

* * * * *

The next case presents yet another nuance in the realm of sex discrimination. Peter Oiler alleges that he was fired from his job because he cross-dresses and impersonates a woman when he is off duty. This, he claims, illegally discriminates on the basis of sexual stereotyping.

OILER v. WINN-DIXIE LOUISIANA, INC.

U.S. District Court, Louisiana, 2002
2002 WL 31098541

AFRICK , District Judge.

In 1979, plaintiff, Peter Oiler, was hired by defendant, Winn-Dixie, as a loader. In 1981, he was promoted to yard truck driver and he later became a road truck driver. As a road truck driver, plaintiff delivered groceries from Winn-Dixie's grocery warehouse in Harahan, Louisiana, to grocery stores in southern and central Louisiana and Mississippi.

Plaintiff is a heterosexual man who has been married since 1977. The plaintiff is transgendered. He is not a transsexual and he does not intend to become a woman.... He is a male crossdresser [or] transvestite.

When he is not at work, plaintiff appears in public approximately one to three times per month wearing female clothing and accessories. In order to resemble a woman, plaintiff wears wigs and makeup, including concealer, eye shadow, foundation, and lipstick ... skirts, women's blouses, women's flat shoes, and nail polish. He shaves his face, arms, hands, and legs. He wears women's underwear and bras and he uses silicone prostheses to enlarge his breasts. When he is crossdressed as a woman, he adopts a female persona and he uses the name "Donna".

... While crossdressed, he attended support group meetings, dined at a variety of restaurants in Kenner and Metairie, visited night clubs, went to shopping malls, and occasionally attended church services. He was often accompanied by his wife and other friends, some of whom were also crossdressed.

On October 29, 1999, plaintiff told Gregg Miles, a Winn-Dixie supervisor, that he was transgendered.... [W]hen plaintiff did not resign voluntarily, Winn-Dixie discharged him ... because [of concerns that] if Winn-Dixie's customers learned of plaintiff's lifestyle, i.e., that he regularly crossdressed and impersonated a woman in public, they would shop elsewhere and Winn-Dixie would lose business. Plaintiff did not crossdress at work and he was not terminated because he violated any Winn-Dixie on-duty dress code. He was never told ... that he was being terminated for appearing or acting effeminate at work, i.e., for having effeminate mannerisms or a high voice. Nor did any Winn-Dixie manager ever tell plaintiff that he did not fit a male stereotype or assign him work that stereotypically would be performed by a female....

In *Ulane v. Eastern Airlines, Inc.* (7th Cir. 1984) a male airline pilot was fired when, following sex reassignment surgery, she attempted to return to work as a woman.... The *Ulane* court stated that:

> The phrase in Title VII prohibiting discrimination based on sex, in its plain meaning, implies that it is unlawful to discriminate against women because they are women and against men because they are men. The words of Title VII do not outlaw discrimination against a person who has a sexual identity disorder, i.e., a person born with a male body who believes himself to be a female, or a person born with a female body who believes herself to be male; a prohibition against discrimination based on an individual's sex is not synonymous with a prohibition based on an individual's sexual identity disorder or discontent with the sex into which they were born....

In 1964, when Title VII was adopted, there was no debate on the meaning of the phrase "sex." In the social climate of the early sixties, sexual identity and sexual orientation related issues remained shrouded in secrecy and individuals having such issues generally remained closeted. Thirty-eight years later, however, sexual identity and sexual orientation issues are no longer buried and they are discussed in the mainstream. Many individuals having such issues have opened wide the closet doors.

Despite the fact that the number of persons publicly acknowledging sexual orientation or gender or sexual identity issues has increased exponentially since the passage of Title VII, the meaning of the word "sex" in Title VII has never been clarified legislatively. From 1981 through 2001, thirty-one proposed bills have been introduced in the United States Senate and the House of Representatives which have attempted to amend Title VII and prohibit employment discrimination on the basis of affectional or sexual orientation. None have passed....

Plaintiff argues that his termination by Winn-Dixie was not due to his crossdressing as a result of his gender identity disorder, but because he did not conform to a gender stereotype....

After much thought and consideration of the undisputed facts of this case, the Court finds that this is not a situation where the plaintiff failed to conform to a gender stereotype. Plaintiff was not discharged because he did not act sufficiently masculine or because he exhibited traits normally valued in a female employee, but disparaged in a male employee. Rather, the plaintiff disguised himself as a person of a different sex and presented himself as a female for stress relief and to express his gender identity. The plaintiff was terminated because he is a man with a sexual or gender identity disorder who, in order to publicly disguise himself as a woman, wears women's clothing, shoes, underwear, breast prostheses, wigs, make-up, and nail polish, pretends to be a woman, and publicly identifies himself as a woman named "Donna."...

This is not just a matter of an employee of one sex exhibiting characteristics associated with the opposite sex. This is a matter of a person of one sex assuming the role of a person of the opposite sex....

In holding that defendant's actions are not proscribed by Title VII, the Court recognizes that many would disagree with the defendant's decision and its rationale. The plaintiff was a long-standing employee of the defendant. He never crossdressed at work and his crossdressing was not criminal or a threat to public safety.

Defendant's rationale for plaintiff's discharge may strike many as morally wrong. However, the function of this Court is not to raise the social conscience of defendant's upper level management, but to construe the law in accordance with proper statutory construction and judicial precedent. The Court is constrained by the framework of the remedial statute enacted by Congress and it cannot, therefore, afford the luxury of making a moral judgment.... [Held: plaintiff's suit is dismissed.]

QUESTIONS

1. On what basis did Oiler lose his case?

2. Assume that this case was appealed and that the appeals court agreed with Judge Africk. Write a dissenting opinion.

3. Women who worked for Winn-Dixie were allowed to wear jeans, plaid shirts, and work shoes while working in the warehouse or in refrigerated compartments. How might that information be used to make another kind of sex discrimination claim? What arguments might Winn-Dixie make to defend itself?

Sexual Harassment

Sexual harassment has a familiar ring today. But the notion that any type of private discrimination based on sex could be grounds for lawsuits was new at the time the Civil Rights Act of 1964 was under consideration by Congress. Then, opponents of the law attempted to block its passage by amending it to cover "sex," a ploy they believed would expose the whole concept of the law as absurd. Their strategy backfired; the Civil Rights Act did pass, and sex discrimination became illegal almost as an ironic afterthought. Yet the law made no mention of sexual harassment and never identified it as a form of sex discrimination. By the late 1970s, successful plaintiffs had convinced the courts that what feminist lawyer Catharine MacKinnon described as the "unwanted imposition of sexual requirements in the context of a relationship of unequal power" must indeed be classified as sex discrimination—an understanding that receives widespread support today.

Highlights in the Evolving Laws of Sexual Harassment

- **Congress Sets the Stage**: In 1964, Title VII of the Civil Rights Act was passed, outlawing discrimination in hiring, firing, and terms and conditions of employment based on race, color, religion, sex, or national origin. There is no mention of sexual harassment.

- **Early Lower Court Cases:** The first reported case of sexual harassment is filed by two women who resigned because of constant sexual advances from their boss. The court denied their claim, describing the supervisor's conduct as "nothing more than a personal proclivity, peculiarity or mannerism." *Corne v. Bausch & Lomb,* 380 F. Supp.161 (D. Ariz., 1975). But in a breakthrough case, a woman whose job was abolished after she repulsed the sexual advances of her boss sued and won. ("But for her womanhood the woman would not have lost her job.") *Barnes v. Costle,* 561 F.2d 983 (D. C. Cir. 1977).

- **EEOC Drafts Guidelines:** By 1980, EEOC announced that two types of illegal sexual harassment existed: **quid pro quo** and **hostile environment**. Quid pro quo refers to demands for sexual favors with threats attached; either the victim gives in or loses a tangible job benefit—even the job itself. Hostile environment refers to behavior that creates an intimidating or abusive workplace atmosphere.

- **Supreme Court Speaks:** Recognizing the hostile environment form of sexual harassment, the Supreme Court allows a suit where behavior is "sufficiently severe or pervasive to alter the conditions of the victim's employment and create an abusive working environment," in *Meritor Savings Bank v. Vinson,* 106 S.Ct. 2399 (1986). In a later case, the Supreme Court explains that a victim need not prove psychological injury to win, "so long as the environment would reasonably be perceived, and is perceived, as hostile or abusive." *Harris v. Forklift Systems,* 114 S.Ct. 367 (1993).

- **Supreme Court and Employer Liability:** The Court clarifies that employers are liable for misuse of supervisory authority—whether or not threats are carried out. Where tangible employment retaliation—for example, termination, demotion, or undesirable reassignment—is carried out or even threatened, the employer is automatically liable. In cases where a plaintiff claims a hostile environment exists, the employer can successfully defend by proving (1) it took reasonable care to prevent and correct promptly any sexually harassing behavior, and (2) the employee "unreasonably failed to take advantage of any preventive or corrective opportunities." *Faragher v. City of Boca Raton* 118 S.Ct. 2275 (1998) and *Burlington Industries v. Ellerth,* 118 S.Ct. 2257 (1998).

- **Same-Sex Harassment:** In 1999, the Supreme Court held that Title VII protects men as well as women, and that the fact that both plaintiff and defendant are of the same sex does not necessarily prevent a claim of sex discrimination. *Oncale v. Sundowner Offshore Services, Inc.,* 118 S.Ct. 998 (1999).

- **Constructive Discharge:** When a supervisor's official act precipitates a constructive discharge—making the abusive working environment so intolerable that a reasonble person would be compelled to resign—the employer is strictly liable ("aggravated hostile environment"). *Pennsylvania State Police v. Suders,* 124 S.Ct. 2342 (2004).

Hostile Environment: Proving a *Prima Facie* Case

What has been called "quid pro quo" harassment—sexual favors in exchange for something concrete such as a job or a raise—is generally easily identifiable as illegal sex discrimination and employers are automatically responsible for such "tangible" employment retaliation. Much harder to define and far more controversial are situations involving what has come to be known as "hostile environment" sexual harassment.

As is true in every civil lawsuit, a plaintiff's first burden is to demonstrate the *possibility* of winning by offering evidence to support each element of her claim. This is called a **prima facie** case. The defendant will then offer contrary evidence, witnesses who can discredit the plaintiff's allegations or support the defendant's own claims, and affirmative defenses. To make out a *prima facie* case of hostile environment sexual harassment, a plaintiff must show that (1) she is a **member of a protected group**, (2) she was the subject of **unwelcome** sexual harassment, (3) the harassment occurred **because of her sex**, and, in cases involving hostile environment, (4) the harassment was **sufficiently severe or pervasive** to alter the **terms and conditions** of her employment.

MEMBER OF A PROTECTED GROUP

The first element is easy to prove in most cases. The Supreme Court has made clear that men, as well as women, are "protected" by Title VII—so long as they are targeted based on their maleness or femaleness—and that a supervisor can be responsible for sexually harassing a person of the same sex. Each of the other elements, however, have created knotty problems for the lower courts.

UNWELCOMENESS

Plaintiffs must prove that the behavior that creates such an environment is not welcomed. As courts try to determine "welcomeness," they consider the entire range of circumstances. They may take into account, for example, a plaintiff's manner of speaking, behaving, or dressing. For a female plaintiff, this could mean that the tight fit of her sweaters or her taste in jokes may be viewed as "provocative," as inviting the behavior of which she complains. Even after-hours behavior could be examined: Does she go to bars alone? Have intimate relationships outside of marriage?

Some have argued that the standard used to measure hostile environment and whether a victim found it unwelcome is male-biased. While studies have repeatedly demonstrated that there is a great disparity between the way men and women view being approached sexually at work—men are typically flattered; women insulted—many in our society make the assumption that women tend to enjoy and welcome sexualized behavior. The law allows that assumption to be overcome, but the burden of proof is on the plaintiff. While in the context of a rape case the victim must prove non-consent, in the context of a claim of sexual harassment she must prove unwelcomeness.

Making such proof even more difficult is the tendency of females in our culture to avoid direct confrontation, to find ways to avoid conflict. In the following, a consultant who trained hundreds of New York City firefighters to identify and prevent sexual harassment describes how women typically deal with unwanted advances:

> [W]omen respond to sexually harassing behavior in a variety of reasonable ways. The coping strategy a woman selects depends on her personal style, the type of incident, and her expectation that the situation is susceptible to resolution.... Typical coping methods include: (1) denying the impact of the event, blocking it out; (2) avoiding the workplace or the harasser, for instance, by taking sick leave or otherwise being absent; (3) telling the harasser to stop; (4) engaging in joking or other banter in the language of the workplace in order to defuse the situation; and (5) threatening to make or actually making an informal or formal complaint....

Of these five categories, formal complaint is the most rare because the victim of harassment fears an escalation of the problem, retaliation from the harasser, and embarrassment in the process of reporting.... Victims also often fear that nothing will be done and they will be blamed for the incident.... Thus, the absence of reporting of sexual harassment incidents cannot be viewed as an absence of such incidents from the workplace....

An effective policy for controlling sexual harassment cannot rely on ad hoc incident-by-incident reporting and investigation....

A study by the Working Women's Institute found that ninety-six percent of sexual harassment victims experienced emotional stress.... Sexual harassment has a cumulative, eroding effect on the victim's well-being.... When women feel a need to maintain vigilance against the next incident of harassment, the stress is increased tremendously.... When women feel that their individual complaints will not change the work environment materially, the ensuing sense of despair further compounds the stress.

— TESTIMONY OF K. C. WAGNER[7]

BECAUSE OF ... ONE'S SEX

Since hostile environment suits are essentially claims of sex discrimination, a plaintiff must establish that whatever harassment took place did so "because of" her sex.

Christopher Vickers worked as a private officer on an all-male police force at the Fairfield Medical Center in Lancaster, Ohio. When his allegations of sex discrimination and harassment were ignored, he filed a complaint with the EEOC, and then a lawsuit. His case was dismissed before trial. In the case that follows, the appellate court must decide if Vickers should be allowed a trial. Judge Gibbons begins by describing the allegations set forth in Vickers' 71-page complaint as "a virtually day-by-day account" of alleged harassment that continued over a two-year period.

VICKERS v. FAIRFIELD MEDICAL CENTER
U.S. Court of Appeals, Sixth Circuit, 2005
453 F.3d 757

JULIA SMITH GIBBONS, Circuit Judge. ☀

...According to the complaint, Vickers befriended a male homosexual doctor at FMC and assisted him in an investigation regarding sexual misconduct.... Once his co-workers found out about the friendship, Vickers contends that [fellow officers Kory Dixon and Jon Mueller] "began making sexually based slurs and discriminating remarks and comments about Vickers, alleging that Vickers was 'gay' or homosexual, and questioning his masculinity." Vickers asserts that following a vacation in April 2002 to Florida with a male friend, Dixon's and Mueller's harassing comments and behavior increased. Vickers asserts that [Police Chief] Anderson witnessed the harassing behavior but took no action to stop it and frequently joined in the harassment....

... The allegations of harassment include impressing the word "FAG" on the second page of Vickers' report forms, frequent derogatory comments regarding Vickers' sexual preferences and activities, frequently calling Vickers a "fag," "gay," and other derogatory names, playing tape-recorded conversations in the office during which Vickers was ridiculed for being homosexual, subjecting Vickers to vulgar gestures, placing irritants and chemicals in Vickers' food and other personal property, using the nickname "Kiss" for Vickers, and making lewd remarks suggesting that Vickers provide them with sexual favors.

---

7 *Robinson v. Jacksonville Shipyards*, 760 F. Supp.1486 (M. D. Fla. 1991).

... [O]n several occasions, he was physically harassed by his co-workers.... [O]n October 20, 2002, Vickers and Mueller were conducting handcuff training. Dixon handcuffed Vickers and then simulated sex with Vickers while Anderson photographed this incident....

... [S]exual orientation is not a prohibited basis for discriminatory acts under Title VII. However, the Supreme Court has held that same-sex harassment is actionable under Title VII under certain circumstances.... Likewise, individuals who are perceived as or who identify as homosexuals are not barred from bringing a claim for sex discrimination under Title VII.

... Vickers relies on the theory of sex stereotyping adopted by the Supreme Court in *Price Waterhouse* to support both his sex discrimination and sexual harassment claims.... [In *Price Waterhouse*, t]he Supreme Court held that making employment decisions based on sex stereotyping, i.e., the degree to which an individual conforms to traditional notions of what is appropriate for one's gender, is actionable discrimination under Title VII....

Vickers contends that this theory of sex stereotyping supports his claim ... [because] in the eyes of his co-workers, his sexual practices, whether real or perceived, did not conform to the traditionally masculine role. Rather, in his supposed sexual practices, he behaved more like a woman.

We conclude that the theory of sex stereotyping under *Price Waterhouse* is not broad enough to encompass such a theory. The Supreme Court in *Price Waterhouse* focused principally on characteristics that were readily demonstrable in the workplace, such as the plaintiff's manner of walking and talking at work, as well as her work attire and her hairstyle.... By contrast, the gender non-conforming behavior which Vickers claims supports his theory of sex stereotyping is not behavior observed at work or affecting his job performance.... Rather, the harassment of which Vickers complains is more properly viewed as harassment based on Vickers' perceived homosexuality, rather than based on gender non-conformity.

[R]ecognition of Vickers' claim would have the effect of de facto amending Title VII to encompass sexual orientation as a prohibited basis for discrimination. In all likelihood, any discrimination based on sexual orientation would be actionable under a sex stereotyping theory if this claim is allowed to stand, as all homosexuals, by definition, fail to conform to traditional gender norms in their sexual practices.... While the harassment alleged by Vickers reflects conduct that is socially unacceptable and repugnant to workplace standards of proper treatment and civility, Vickers claim does not fit within the prohibitions of the law.

[A]n individual does not make out a claim of sexual harassment "merely because the words used have sexual content or connotations." Rather, "[t]he critical issue, Title VII's text indicates, is whether members of one sex are exposed to advantageous terms or conditions of employment to which members of the other sex are not exposed. [In, *Oncale*, a case involving a male plaintiff suing for sexual harassment by other males, The Supreme Court identified] three ways a male plaintiff could establish a hostile work environment claim based on same-sex harassment: (1) where the harasser making sexual advances is acting out of sexual desire; (2) where the harasser is motivated by general hostility to the presence of men in the workplace; and (3) where the plaintiff offers "direct comparative evidence about how the alleged harasser treated members of both sexes in a mixed—sex workplace." [Here, Vickers fails to allege any of these circumstances.] ...

[The trial court's dismissal of the complaint is affirmed.]

DAVID M. LAWSON, District Judge, dissenting. ☀

...The thrust of the opinion is that Vickers failed to plead that the harassment was based on sex because it had its roots in the harassers' perception that Vickers's private sexual practices were woman–like. The majority apparently believes that *Price Waterhouse* extends only to behavior and appearances that manifest themselves in the workplace, and not to private sexual conduct, beliefs, or practices that an employee might adopt or display elsewhere. It concludes, therefore, that Vickers's tormentors were motivated by Vickers's perceived homosexuality rather than an outward workplace manifestation of less-than-masculine gender characteristics.

I have no quarrel with the proposition that a careful distinction must be drawn between cases of gender stereotyping, which are actionable, and cases…that in reality seek protection for sexual–orientation discrimination, which are not. Nor do I believe that gender stereotyping is actionable per se under Title VII, although certainly it may constitute evidence of discrimination on the basis of sex. As Judge Posner of the Seventh Circuit pointed out:

> [T]here is a difference … between, on the one hand, using evidence of the plaintiff's failure to wear nail polish (or, if the plaintiff is a man, his using nail polish) to show that her sex played a role in the adverse employment action of which she complains, and, on the other hand, creating a subtype of sexual discrimination called "sex stereotyping," as if there were a federally protected right for male workers to wear nail polish and dresses and speak in falsetto and mince about in high heels, or for female ditchdiggers to strip to the waist in hot weather.…

However, these distinctions can be complicated [the line should not be drawn before there has been a trial.]

[The following are a few examples of allegations made by Vickers in his complaint that his was discriminated against because of the perception on nonconformity to gender norms.] … [O]n January 22, 2003, Dixon [warned] Mueller that Vickers was in a bad mood. Mueller said, "Maybe he is having a heavy (menstrual) flow day, huh?" Mueller then said to Vickers, "Why don't you pluck that tampon out and put a new pad in and lose some of that pressure?" … Mueller walked out of the office momentarily, returning with a sanitary napkin which he tried to rub in Vickers' face.… When Vickers returned to work on January 25, 2003, Mueller asked Vickers if his mood had improved.…

… [On another occasion] Mueller extended a tape measure to touch Vickers's crotch several times until Vickers got angry and told Mueller to stop. Anderson remarked that Vickers "must be tired, he's not in the mood to play." A few moments later, Dixon grabbed Vickers's breast and remarked "Kiss has titties."… In yet another instance, Anderson phoned the station, but when Vickers answered Anderson demanded to speak to "a real officer."…

These allegations, in my view, provide a basis for the inference that the plaintiff was perceived as effeminate and therefore unworthy to be considered "a real officer." The permissible conclusion that emerges is that the plaintiff was not tolerated—and the defendants made the workplace environment hostile—because the job required only "manly men," not woman-like ones or women themselves.…

[Because I believe the plaintiff should be allowed to go to trial, I respectfully dissent.]

QUESTIONS

1. How did the majority distinguish Vicker's claim from the plaintiff in the *Price-Waterhouse* case?

2. Is there an ethical difference between harassment based on stereotyes perceived as manifesting at work and those perceived as manifesting elsewhere?

3. A 16-year-old boy was harassed because his voice was soft, his physique slight, his hair long, and he wore an earring to work. Does he have a valid claim for sexual harassment? If so, on what basis?

4. What advice would you give to a young woman entering the workforce in terms of how best to present herself? A young man?

5. A directive of The European Union specifically outlaws discrmination based on sexual orientation. Is it time for U.S. law to do the same?

SUFFICIENTLY SEVERE OR PERVASIVE

Case law tells us that an employee does not have to put up with discriminatory intimidation, ridicule, and insult so severe or pervasive that it creates an abusive working environment. Courts are supposed to determine when this standard has been met by looking at all—the "totality" of—the circumstances including:

> [The] frequency of the discriminatory conduct; its severity; whether it is physically threatening or humiliating, or a mere offensive utterance; and whether it unreasonably interferes with an employee's work performance. [S]imple teasing, offhand comments, and isolated incidents (unless extremely serious) will not amount to discriminatory changes in the terms and conditions of employment.[8]

But, which factors to consider, and how to weigh them, is a matter of dispute among the various federal courts of appeals. One federal trial judge explains:

> The question of what is "sufficiently severe" sexual harassment is complicated because: (a) courts routinely remind plaintiffs that "Title VII is not a federal civility code," (b) the modern notion of acceptable behavior—as corroded by instant-gratification driven, cultural influences (e.g., lewd music, videos, and computer games, "perversity-programming" broadcast standards, White House "internal affairs" and perjurious coverups of same, etc.) has been coarsening over time; therefore, (c) what courts implicitly ask the "Title VII victim" to tolerate as mere "boorish behavior" or "workplace vulgarity" must, once placed in the contemporary context, account for any "Slouch Toward Gomorrah" societal norms might take.
>
> At the same time, this entire area of law is enervated by vague, almost circular standards… [I]if behavior offends the particular judge … then it must be "discriminatory."…
>
> [C]ourts decide what is "sufficiently severe" by resorting to "crudity comparables." That is, judges must compare the crudity and "lewdity" found in one case with that deemed sufficient to [allow the case to go to trial] in another.…
>
> As the case law has grown to show, determining the intensity/quantity of sexual gesturing, touching, bantering and innuendo that it takes to render a work environment sexually hostile is now no less difficult than "trying to nail a jellyfish to the wall." …[9]

*****

Vicki Schultz has been a strong advocate for changes that would make the workplace more equitable and hospitable to women. In the next reading, Schultz is critical of employer attempts to wipe out sexual harassment by harshly and promptly punishing harassers—a process she dubs "sanitization," and which she believes causes problems of its own, further distancing us from real solutions to gender inequality.

THE SANITIZED WORKPLACE

VICKI SCHULTZ[10]

… [T]he focus on sexual conduct has encouraged organizations to treat harassment as a stand-alone phenomenon—a problem of bad or boorish men who oppress or offend women—rather than as a symptom of larger patterns of sex segregation and inequality.…

---

8 *Harris v. Forklift Systems, Inc.*, 114 S. Ct. 367 (1993).

9 *Breda v. Wolf Camera, Inc.* 148 F.Supp.2d 1371 (S.D. Ga. 2001).

10 Source: Vicki Schultz, 112 *Yale L. J.* 2061 (2003). Reprinted by permission of The Yale Law Journal Company and William S. Hein Company from The Yale Law Journal, Vol. 112, 2061–2193.

... [T]he emphasis on eliminating sexual conduct encourages employees to articulate broader workplace harms as forms of sexual harassment, obscuring more structural problems that may be the true source of their disadvantage. Thus, women may complain about sexual jokes, when their real concern is a caste system that relegates them to low-status, low-pay positions.... Even more worrying is the prospect that some employees may make allegations of sexual harassment that disproportionately disadvantage racial and sexual minorities.... [W]hite women who enjoy sexual banter and flirtation with their white male coworkers may regard the same conduct as a form of sexual harassment when it comes from men of color. Heterosexual men who willingly engage in sexual horseplay with men whom they regard as heterosexual may be quick to label the same overtures as harassment when they come from openly gay men. [This suggests] that one-size-fits-all, acontextual prohibitions on sexual conduct may give individual employees, and management as a whole, too much power to enforce sexual conformity in the name of pursuing a project of gender equality that has been all but abandoned.

The truth is that managers cannot succeed in banishing sexuality from the workplace: They can only subject particular expressions of it to surveillance and discipline. Although some groups suffer more than others when this occurs, everyone loses.... With the decline of civil society, the workplace is one of the few arenas left in our society where people from different walks of life can come to know one another well. Because people who work together come into close contact with each other for extended periods for the purpose of achieving common goals, work fosters extraordinarily intimate relationships of both the sexually charged and the more platonic varieties.... We cannot expect diverse groups of people to form close bonds and alliances—whether sexual or nonsexual—if they must be concerned that reaching out to one another puts them at risk of losing their jobs or their reputations....

... The larger question is whether we as a society can value the workplace as a realm alive with personal intimacy, sexual energy, and "humanness" more broadly. The same impulse that would banish sexuality from the workplace also seeks to suppress other "irrational" life experiences such as birth and death, sickness and disability, aging and emotion of every kind. But the old Taylorist dream of the workplace as a sterile zone in which workers suspend all their human attributes while they train their energies solely on production doesn't begin to reflect the rich, multiple roles that work serves in people's lives. For most people, working isn't just a way to earn a livelihood. It's a way to contribute something to the larger society, to struggle against their limits, to make friends and form communities, to leave their imprint on the world, and to know themselves and others in a deep way.... [W]ork isn't simply a sphere of production. It is also a source of citizenship, community, and self-understanding.

... Just as individual employees may express themselves or embroider intimate relations through sexual language and conduct, so too may employees as a group resort to sexual interactions to alleviate stress or boredom on the job, to create vital forms of community and solidarity with each other, or to articulate resistance to oppressive management practices. Research suggests that workplace romance may even increase productivity in some circumstances.

Contrary to prevailing orthodoxy, such uses of workplace sexuality do not always harm or disadvantage women: A lot depends on the larger structural context in which the sexuality is expressed. As a well-accepted body of systematic social science research demonstrates, women who enter jobs in which they are significantly underrepresented often confront hostility and harassment from incumbent male workers, and in some settings the men use sexual conduct as a means of marking the women as "different" and out of place. However, a new body of sociological research suggests that women who work in more integrated, egalitarian settings often willingly participate and take pleasure in sexualized interactions—probably because their numerical strength gives them the power to help shape the sexual norms and culture to their own liking. Rather than presuming that women will always find sexual conduct offensive, this research suggests that we should ensure that women are fully integrated into equal jobs and positions of authority, thus giving them the power to decide for themselves what kind of work cultures they want to have.

… I would like to see organizations abandon sensitivity training in favor of incorporating their harassment policies into broader efforts to achieve integration and equality throughout the firm. Along similar lines, I urge that employers forgo measures to prohibit or discourage sexual or dating relationships among employees and refuse to intervene, just as they do with nonsexual friendships, unless there is clear evidence that a particular relationship is undermining specific organizational goals…. In my view, employees and supervisors should be free to work together to create a variety of different work cultures—including more and less sexualized ones—so long as that process occurs within a larger context of structural equality that provides all women and men the power to shape those cultures….

The contemporary drive to sanitize the workplace came about through a complex interplay of forces in which feminists, judges, HR managers, lawyers, and the news media all helped create an understanding that sexuality disadvantages women and disrupts productivity. In my view, we can only hope to halt the sanitization process by articulating a more appealing vision in which sexuality and intimacy can coexist with, and perhaps even enhance, gender equality and organizational rationality….

QUESTIONS

1. Schultz favors broad efforts to achieve integration and equality throughout the firm. What do you think she means by this? Can you give examples?

2. **Internet Assignment:** Schultz mentions "the old Taylorist dream of the workplace as a sterile zone." Who was Frederick Taylor? What about his life's achievement would lead Schultz to describe his dream as "sterile"? What is Schultz's vision of work?

Race, Religion, and National Origin

Sexual harassment is but one manifestation of illegal discrimination in the workplace. Indeed, cases involving racially intimidating and abusive conduct predate those involving gender and sexuality. More recently, there has been a rise in cases involving harassment and other forms of discriminaton based on religion, nationality, and immigration status.

This should not be surprising. During the past four decades, the United States has experienced the largest wave of immigration in its history, with at least one-third of new immigrants coming from Mexico. Census Bureau figures show that more than 10 percent of the 300 million people living in the United States in 2006 were born somewhere else. Increasingly, the new migrants are finding homes throughout the country from the upper Midwest to the Rocky Mountain states, as well as the more traditional landing spots along the coasts.

In an economy still adjusting to globalization, the information revolution, and the shift from production to services, there is widespread debate about the role of foreign-born workers. Here we look at one site of that contest: rules requiring English as the only language to be used at a workplace.

When the city of Altus, Oklahoma, adopted an English-only rule for it employees, 29 workers complained to the EEOC. All are Hispanic, the only significant national-origin minority group affected by the policy. All are bilingual, each speaking fluent English and Spanish. Unable to resolve the dispute, the EEOC granted them a right to sue. The trial court, however, threw out their case, granting summary judgment that would allow the city to enforce its new regulations. The employees appealed. Their claim: rights under Title VII of the Civil Rights Act of 1964 and the First Amendment to the U.S. Constitution were violated.

EEOC Guideline on English-Only Workplace Rules

1. an English-only rule that applies at all times is considered "a burdensome term and condition of employment," [in violation of Title VII] and

2. an English-only rule that applies only at certain times does not violate Title VII if the employer can justify the rule by showing business necessity.

Rationale for Rules

1. English-only policies may "create an atmosphere of inferiority, isolation, and intimidation" that could make a "discriminatory working environment";

2. English-only rules adversely impact employees with limited or no English skills … by denying them a privilege enjoyed by native English speakers: the opportunity to speak at work;

3. English-only rules create barriers to employment for employees with limited or no English skills;

4. English-only rules prevent bilingual employees whose first language is not English from speaking in their most effective language; and

5. the risk of discipline and termination for violating English-only rules falls disproportionately on bilingual employees as well as persons with limited English skills.

MALDONADO v. CITY OF ALTUS

U. S. Court of Appeals, Tenth Circuit, 2006
433 F.3d 1294

HARTZ , Circuit Judge. ✳

In the spring of 2002 the City's Street Commissioner, Defendant Holmes Willis, received a complaint that because Street Department employees were speaking Spanish, other employees could not understand what was being said on the City radio. Willis informed the City's Human Resources Director, Candy Richardson, of the complaint, and she advised Willis that he could direct his employees to speak only English when using the radio for City business.

Plaintiffs claim that Willis instead told the Street Department employees that they could not speak Spanish at work at all and informed them that the City would soon implement an official English-only policy....

In July 2002 the City promulgated the following official policy...

To insure effective communications among and between employees and various departments of the City, to prevent misunderstandings and to promote and enhance safe work practices, all work related and business communications during the work day shall be conducted in the English language with the exception of those circumstances where it is necessary or prudent to communicate with a citizen, business owner, organization or criminal suspect in his or her native language due to the person or entity's limited English language skills. The use of the English language during work hours and while engaged in City business includes face to face communication of work orders and directions as well as communications utilizing telephones, mobile telephones, cellular telephones, radios, computer or e-mail transmissions and all written forms of communications.... This policy does not apply to strictly private communications between co-workers while they are on approved lunch hours or breaks or before or after work hours while the employees are still on City property if City property is not being used for the communication ... [or to] strictly private communication between an employee and a family member.... Employees are encouraged to be sensitive to the feelings of their fellow employees, including a possible feeling of exclusion if a co-worker cannot understand what is being said in his or her presence when a language other than English is being utilized.

... Plaintiffs allege that the policy created a hostile environment for Hispanic employees, causing them "fear and uncertainty in their employment," and subjecting them to racial and ethnic taunting. They contend "that the English-only rule created a hostile environment because it pervasively—every hour of every work day—burdened, threatened and demeaned the [Plaintiffs] because of their Hispanic origin." Plaintiffs each stated in their affidavits:

The English-only policy affects my work environment every day. It reminds me every day that I am second-class and subject to rules for my employment that the Anglo employees are not subject to ...

Evidence of ethnic taunting included Plaintiffs' affidavits stating that they had "personally been teased and made the subject of jokes directly because of the English-only policy...." Plaintiff Tommy Sanchez testified in his deposition that ... other employees of the City of Altus "would pull up and laugh, start saying stuff in Spanish to us and said, 'They didn't tell us we couldn't stop. They just told you.'" Sanchez also testified that an Altus police officer taunted him about not being allowed to speak Spanish by saying, "Don't let me hear you talk Spanish." As evidence that such taunting was not unexpected by management, Lloyd Lopez recounted in his deposition that Street Commissioner Willis told ... him [and an Hispanic co-worker] that he was informing them of the English-only policy in private because Willis had concerns about "the other guys making fun of [them]."

I. Discussion of Civil Rights Violations: Disparate Impact

... One might say that Plaintiffs have not been subjected to an unlawful employment practice because they are treated identically to non-Hispanics. They claim no discrimination with respect to their pay or benefits, their hours of work, or their job duties. And every employee, not just Hispanics, must abide by the English-only policy....

[But in] *Griggs v. Duke Power Co.* (1971) the Supreme Court held that Title VII "proscribes not only overt discrimination but also practices that are fair in form, but discriminatory in operation." These kinds of claims, known as disparate-impact claims, "involve employment practices that are facially neutral in their treatment of different groups but that in fact fall more harshly on one group than another and cannot be justified by business necessity."

... Plaintiffs have produced evidence that the English-only policy created a hostile atmosphere for Hispanics in their workplace.... [A]ll the Plaintiffs stated that they had experienced ethnic taunting as a result of the policy and that the policy made them feel like second-class citizens ...

... [According to the Supreme Court in the *Griggs* case] the touchstone is business necessity. If an employment practice which operates to [discriminate against a protected minority] cannot be shown to be related to job performance, the practice is prohibited.

Defendants' evidence of business necessity in this case is scant. As observed by the district court, "[T]here was no written record of any communication problems, morale problems or safety problems resulting from the use of languages other than English prior to implementation of the policy." And there was little undocumented evidence. Defendants cited only one example of an employee's complaining about the use of Spanish prior to implementation of the policy…. [And city officials] could give no specific examples of safety problems resulting from the use of languages other than English…." Moreover, Plaintiffs produced evidence that the policy encompassed lunch hours, breaks, and private phone conversations; and Defendants conceded that there would be no business reason for such a restriction….

In our view, the record contains sufficient evidence of intent to create a hostile environment that the summary judgment on those claims must be set aside … [and the plaintiffs may proceed to trial on their Title VII claims.]

II. First Amendment claims

… Perhaps the City's English-only rule suffers from First Amendment shortcomings. But on the evidence and contentions presented by Plaintiffs, their challenge fails…. They have not shown that their speech precluded by the English-only rule includes communications on matters of public concern. Nor have they produced evidence that the English-only rule was intended to limit communications on matters of public concern [as required by the Supreme Court precedent case, *Pickering*.] …

Here, we do not question that Plaintiffs take pride in both their Hispanic heritage and their use of the Spanish language, nor do we question the importance of that pride. What we do question, because there is no supporting evidence, is that by speaking Spanish at work they were intending to communicate that pride, much less "to inform [an] issue [so] as to be helpful … in evaluating the conduct of government."… [Held: plaintiff's First Amendment claims are dismissed.]

SEYMOUR. J. , concurring [in Part I, Discrimination] and dissenting [in Part II, First Amendment.] ✳

… [I] part company with the majority in determining whether Plaintiffs' speech touched on a matter of public concern.…[It is] reasonable to assume that the alleged "content" of Plaintiffs' speech, namely, their choice to converse in Spanish rather than English, is pride in their cultural and ethnic identity and heritage. Plaintiffs have thus indicated that their desire to speak Spanish is, itself, a matter of public concern.

In arguing that their choice of language is itself a statement of public concern, Plaintiffs find support in *Hernandez v. New York* (1991), [where the Supreme Court] recognized the power of language (as well as a person's decision to speak a particular language as opposed to another) to convey special meaning as well as to engender conflict and disclose bigotry.

> … *[A] person's choice of language can convey a message–and a powerful one at that….[L]anguage choice and ethnic or cultural identity can be inextricably intertwined both in the mind of the speaker and in the minds of those who hear him….*

Before litigation challenging the legality of the City's English-only policy ever commenced…in a plea for understanding and reconciliation, Mr. Sanchez himself characterized the content of the prohibited speech as an expression of community identity and ethnic heritage, of solidarity and pride, in the face of contravening forces. In other words, an [apt] analogy may be wearing a tee-shirt proclaiming "proud to be a Yankees fan" to a rally for the Boston Red Sox, because that analogy describes the context as well as the content of the speech.

With respect to context, the record contains evidence of months of tension between Hispanic and non-Hispanic City employees. Prior to the adoption of the English-only policy, several Hispanic employees had filed complaints of discrimination and retaliation. The City, in response, had hired an outside human resources consultant…. Numerous individuals, both Hispanic and non-Hispanic, were involved in an on-going and evolving discussion on race relations, and that all levels of City government were involved, including the mayor, the City administrator, the City's director of human resources, and many City department heads and supervisors.... [T]he general public was aware of and interested in the English-only policy and its effects.... In one [news] article, the mayor was quoted as referring to the Spanish language as "garbage." That he later claimed in his deposition to have been misquoted is irrelevant to the question of whether his misquote further inflamed public debate over the English-only policy and its perceived intent. Moreover, the mayor's testimony that he eventually apologized to the City council for the misquote underscores the seriousness and the pervasiveness of the whole issue, namely, the apparently degenerating relations between Hispanics and non-Hispanics in the City of Altus. At a certain point then, this dispute evolved from a situation involving City employees to a wider discussion of discrimination, race relations, and the power of expressions of ethnic identity to elicit strong emotions on either side.

In sum, this is not a case about a single employee wearing a tee-shirt proclaiming "proud to be Hispanic!" or "proud to be Irish!" or "proud to be Vietnamese!" This is a case about a large group of employees (twenty-nine Hispanic City employees) desiring to wear such tee-shirts when an even larger number of their fellow employees are wearing (or perceived to be wearing) tee-shirts proclaiming "annoyed by Hispanics!" or "sick and tired of the Irish!" or "threatened by Vietnamese!" The record suggests this was a situation in which the right to speak one's chosen language became an expression of pride and resistance and identity....

... [I]t is important to remember what this case is not about. This is not a case involving the sole complaint of one employee in a City with no history of racial tensions. This not a case involving one employee's complaint against one or two of his supervisors. This is a case involving more than two dozen employees in a diverse workforce in a City with a recent history of racial and national origin discrimination complaints. This is a case in which the City, fully cognizant of that history, nonetheless adopted a broadly-sweeping policy that its director of human resources admitted in her deposition testimony could offend Hispanic employees and further inflame racial tensions. This is a case in which we have upheld, for summary judgment purposes, Plaintiffs' race and national origin discrimination claims against the City for restricting the very speech Plaintiffs want to use. In light of these facts, it seems incorrect to characterize Plaintiffs' expression of pride in their ethnic identity as reflecting merely "personal" or "internal" grievances. It is also difficult to see how that expression of pride does not add to the public debate on diversity or "sufficiently inform" the public that there are two equally vocal and passionate sides to that debate.... To the contrary, Plaintiffs' have expressed a desire to speak Spanish in order to sustain their community's history of linguistic and ethnic diversity and to preserve that history in the everyday details of their lives. The City's ban on Spanish from the work place creates a public space where Spanish speakers arguably do not feel welcome. In such a context, it is not hard to imagine the power of a simple "buenos dias" to convey resistance to that effort and hope for the future....

QUESTIONS

1. Who might be hurt by English-only rules? Who tends to benefit? Can such rules create or reinforce stereotypes?

2. Articulate the kind of discrimination claim made by the plaintiffs in this case. What will they have to prove at trial? How will the city defend itself? How important is it that plaintiffs are all bilingual?

3. Would there be a business necessity for requiring airline pilots to speak English in all air traffic communications within the United States? Having computer software salespeople speak English in all management meetings? What about an English-only rule for workers on a semiconductor assembly line, or an airline baggage handling area? Is there ever a business necessity for requiring English to be spoken during nonwork hours?

4. What reasons might an employer have for preferring to hire persons who don't speak English? How ethical would it be to prefer such persons for the reasons you have identified?

5. Title IX of the Civil Rights Act prohibits discrimination on the basis of race, color, religion, sex, or national origin in education. Should a school be allowed to prohibit students from speaking a language other than English in school? Should it matter whether it is a public or private school? See *Rubio v. Turner Unified School District No. 202*, 453 F. Supp.2d 1295 (D. Kansas, 2006).

6. Dissenting Judge Seymour mentions the history behind the adoption of the city's English-only policy, a history fraught with conflict. Can you think of a way this litigation might have been avoided? Suppose you were the HR consultant hired to lead discussions on a possible English-only policy for the city. Who would you try to bring into the conversation? How might you enable the different stakeholders to become active, respectful participants? What information might you want to access to assist their decision-making process?

Work/Life Balance

U.S. Family Realities

In 2000 31.1 percent of women compared to 19.5 percent of men earned poverty level wages or less.

Of the 72.3 million families reported in the 2000 U.S. Census, 7.4 million were headed by single mothers, 2.2 million run by single fathers.[11]

Since passage of the Family and Medical Leave Act in 1993, 42 percent of those taking leave have been men; roughly three of five U.S. workers meet the law's eligibility criteria.[12]

Some 3.3 million Americans over age 65 are severely impaired, requiring some kind of caregiving.[13] Two-thirds of those providing care for elders are employed.[14]

Two-fifths of all employed Americans work mostly at nonstandard times—in the evening, at night, on a rotating shift or during the weekend; single and low-educated mothers are more likely than married or better educated mothers to work nonstandard schedules.[15]

The average working woman in the United States spends about twice as much time as the average working man on household chores and the care of children. On average, men spend more time than women at their jobs and on leisure and sports.[16]

11 Marianne Sullivan, "Paid Sick Leave is Rare for Low Income Women," Women's eNews, May 10, 2004, 6., Jody Heyman, Alison Earle, Jeffrey Hayes, reporting on Harvard U. Project on Global Working Families and McGill U. Institute for Health & Social Policy, Feb. 2007 found at, http://www.womensnewsorg/article/cform/dynlaid/1809/context/archivewww.winningworkplaces.

12 Ibid.

13 Barbara R. Stucki and JaneMarie Mulvey, "Can Aging 'Boomers' Avoid Nursing Homes?" 83 *Consumer Research Mag.* 20, Aug 1, 2000.

14 Katherine Elizabeth Ulrich, "Insuring Family Risks: Suggestions for a National Family Policy and Wage Replacement," 14 *Yale J. L. & Feminism*, 1, 6 (2002).

15 Harriet B. Presser, "Working in a 24/7 Economy" (Russell Sage Foundation, N.Y., 2003), p.1.

16 Time-Use Survey, Bureau of Labor Statistics, Sept. 14, 2004, http://www.bls.gov/news/release/pdf/atus.pdf.

Some economists argue that the wage gap between men and women is explained neither by discrimination nor by occupational segregation, but by the fact that many women choose to spend more time with their families than developing their careers. They point to human capital studies showing that when workers take time off (for example, to have or raise children, to care for elderly parents) they earn less money than workers who don't interrupt their careers. Not surprisingly, it is more often women who leave their jobs, work part time and work less, and so earn lower wages.[17]

Other experts argue that the wage gap is not only a result of forms of discrmination, but is also affected by the degree to which women—more than men—must cope with work that takes place outside of the workplace, especially child and elder care. While some of this effort may be freely chosen, they believe, stereotyping and the lack of options factor in heavily.

Legislating Family Leave

While Title VII made it illegal for employers to discriminate on the basis of gender ("sex"), the courts interpreted it as allowing employers to single out and discriminate on the basis of pregnancy. In one highly criticized case, the Supreme Court upheld an employee disability plan that provided insurance for sickness and accidents, but excluded coverage for complications arising from pregnancy. The Court explained why Title VII's ban on sex discrimination was not violated:

> [A]n exclusion of pregnancy from a disability-benefits plan providing general coverage is not a gender-based discrimination at all.... [T]he selection of risks covered by the Plan did not operate, in fact to discriminate against women.... The Plan, in effect ... is nothing more than an insurance package, which covers some risks, but excludes others....[18]

Congress reacted to the Court's interpretation of Title VII by amending the law in 1978 to make it clear that discrimination on the basis of pregnancy was illegal. The amendments, known as the **Pregnancy Discrimination Act of 1978**, provide:

> Women affected by pregnancy, childbirth, and related medical conditions shall be treated the same for all employment-related purposes, including receipt of benefits under fringe benefit programs, as other persons not so affected but similar in their ability or inability to work.

Under this law, pregnant workers are to be treated like any other workers. But an argument can be made that a law that makes it illegal to fire a woman simply because she is pregnant does not go far enough. It affords no protection, for example, to a pregnant employee who is fired for excessive absenteeism by a company that similarly dismisses ill or injured workers who miss too many days at work. Nor does it address the need for time to care for a healthy newborn or accommodate other family responsibilities. In 1993, Congress passed, and President Clinton signed into law, the Family and Medical Leave Act, excerpted here:

FAMILY AND MEDICAL LEAVE ACT
29 United States Code Annotated 2601, et seq.

Findings and Purposes

1. the number of single-parent households and two-parent households in which the single parent or both parents work is increasing significantly;

---

17 H. Wenger, "Issue Briefing #155," April 24, 2001, Economic Policy Institute.
18 *General Electric Co. v. Gilbert*, 429 U.S. 125 (1976).

2. it is important for the development of children and the family unit that fathers and mothers be able to participate in early childrearing and the care of family members who have serious health conditions;

3. the lack of employment policies to accommodate working parents can force individuals to choose between job security and parenting;

4. there is inadequate job security for employees who have serious health conditions that prevent them from working for temporary periods;

5. due to the nature of the roles of men and women in our society, the primary responsibility for family caretaking often falls on women, and such responsibility affects the working lives of women more than it affects the working lives of men; and

6. employment standards that apply to one gender only have serious potential for encouraging employers to discriminate against employees and applicants for employment who are of that gender.

Leave Requirements

a. 1. Entitlement to leave

[A]n eligible employee shall be entitled to a total of 12 workweeks of leave during any 12-month period for one or more of the following:

A. Because of the birth of a son or daughter of the employee and in order to care for such son or daughter.

B. Because of the placement of a son or daughter with the employee for adoption or foster care.

C. In order to care for the spouse, or a son, daughter, or parent, of the employee, if such spouse, son, daughter, or parent has a serious health condition.

D. Because of a serious health condition that makes the employee unable to perform the functions of the position of such employee.

[Other sections of the law guarantee that an employee who returns from a leave can go back to his or her position, or one with equivalent benefits, pay, and employment conditions, without losing any benefits that had accrued prior to the leave, and without gaining any seniority while they were on leave. Employees become "eligible" after they have worked a specified number of hours for twelve months.]

Exceptions and Special Rules

[There are some exceptions. Those within a firm's top 10 percent of salaried employees within a 75-mile radius, for example, can be denied restoration to the job after a leave if:]

A. such denial is necessary to prevent substantial and grievous economic injury to the operations of the employer;

B. the employer notifies the employee of the intent of the employer to deny restoration on such basis at the time the employer determines that such injury would occur; and

C. in any case in which the leave has commenced, the employee elects not to return to employment after receiving such notice.

---

11 H. Wenger, "Issue Briefing #155," April 24, 2001, Economic Policy Institute.

12 *General Electric Co. v. Gilbert*, 429 U.S. 125 (1976).

[The law also provides that employees have a right to use their leave time by taking intermittent or reduced time health leaves if medically necessary. The employer, however, may temporarily transfer the employee to a different, comparably paid position. Leave for new-child care must be taken all at once, unless both employee and employer agree to some other arrangement. Employees must give whatever notice of their intention to give leave is possible and reasonable considering the circumstances (e.g., 30 days notice before birth or placement of an adopted child), and make reasonable efforts to schedule medical treatment to cause the least possible disruption to the employer. Employers are required to maintain coverage under group health plans for employees on leave.]

QUESTIONS

1. Look at the statutory provisions that explain the leave requirements. Do they seem well crafted to respond to the findings set forth by Congress in the law? Does the law require employers to give *paid* family or medical leave? Does it permit paid leave?

2. Does Congress address any stereotypes about caregivers? How responsive is the law to changes in our ideas about family? Who benefits from the law? Is anyone harmed? Can you think of any changes that would make it more responsive to the needs of caregivers?

3. **Internet Assignment:** Of 173 nations surveyed by Harvard/McGill Universities in 2007, only five did not provide some form of paid leave to all new mothers: Lesoto, Liberia, Papua New Guinea, Swaziland, and the United States. (a) Find out about an organization that advocates for or against such leave in the United States. What arguments do they give for their positions? Which is more persuasive? (b) In 2002, California became the first state to enact a comprehensive paid family leave law. The National Partnership for Women and Families has drafted a bill for a similar law. Find out the current status of the any law or proposals in your state.*

4. **Internet Assignment:** The Public Welfare Foundation reported that by 2007 at least 145 countries around the globe guaranteed workers paid sick days, although the United States was not among them. (a) Find out if that has changed. (b) Are there any laws or pending laws in your state that guarantee paid sick leave?

5. **Internet Assignment:** *Working Mother* magazine identified Citgroup, Eli Lilly, IBM, and PricewaterhouseCoopers as among the top family-friendly companies in 2007. Find a Web site for one of the top companies and compare its work/family programs and benefits to those of other companies in the same business sector. Is this a company you would want to work for? What are the relative merits of legislation such as the Family and Medical Leave Act versus purely voluntary efforts by business?

*Jody Heyman, Alison Earle, Jeffrey Hayes, reporting on Harvard U. Project on Global Working Families and McGill U. Institute for Health & Social Policy, Feb. 2007 found at http://www.winningworkplaces.

* * * * *

For almost three decades, American feminists have called for changes in the work/family paradigm that would help achieve gender equity. Yet, as the authors of the next reading argue, most proposals have overlooked certain realities of the labor market. Most importantly, Selmi and Cahn argue, there is not one labor market in the United States, but rather:

> [There are] really two, or perhaps three, very different labor markets—a small group of over-employed individuals and a larger group of underemployed individuals, including a substantial group of

Who Works

- Twenty-eight percent of the workforce have college degrees, fewer than 10 percent have advanced degrees.
- There are more families headed by single women, and more of those single mothers are in the workplace than ever before (21.9% workforce in 2000).

Working Hours

- Men average 42–43 hours/week, women average 35–36/week.
- Long hours (50 or more a week) are most common among professionals and managers, and more common among men than women.
- College-educated men (nearly 40%) are more likely to work long hours than men without college degrees (12%).
- College-educated women (20%) are more likely to work long hours than those with less than a high school degree (5%).
- White men tend to work more than nonwhite men.
- White women work the least among all women because more work part-time.
- Dual-income parents with children work a combined 3.3 hours less than couples without children; women reduce their hours more than men (childless men work .7 hours more, while childless women work 5.8 hours more).

Benefits

- Those with advanced degrees averaged $25.47/hour, while those with high school degrees earned $11.87/hour (2003).
- Fifty percent of white-collar workers use employer's health insurance, compared to 22 percent of service workers (2003).
- Few part-time workers have access to health care (9%).
- Full-time workers are more likely (60%) to have paid sick leave than part-time workers (16%); 59 million workers (49% of the workforce) have no paid sick leave.
- White-collar workers are more likely than others to have paid sick leave.
- More high-income female workers (7%) than blue-collar workers (2%) have access to employer-provided childcare; more white-collar workers have access to referral services.

women, with a third overlapping group of individuals who are undercompensated for the hours that they work. Importantly, most workers are unwilling, and unable, to trade income for fewer hours, in large part because they feel squeezed by the demands not just on their time but also on their income.

WOMEN IN THE WORKPLACE: WHICH WOMEN, WHICH AGENDA?

Michael Selmi, Naomi Cahn[19]

When we talk about women in the workplace, there is a tendency to speak in broad generalizations, and frequently our own experiences deeply influence those generalizations. This has been particularly true of the work and family literature that has blossomed in the last decade. That literature has brought greater attention to the difficulty so many women (and men) face in balancing the demands of their work and family obligations, particularly as the pressures on both ends of those scales has intensified. It appears that many employees today are working longer hours with less bargaining power, while parents scramble to provide their children with the means to stay ahead in an increasingly competitive educational environment. At the same time, much of the literature has focused on a small segment of women—typically professional women, lawyers, professors, or corporate executives…. The media has also demonstrated a disproportionate interest in the travails of professional women with a particular concentration on the phenomenon of professional women who leave the workforce to become full-time mothers.

As a result of the focus on professional women, the policy proposals many work-family scholars have advocated tend to reflect the interests, and the options, of those same women. The most frequently mentioned proposals—creating more and better part-time work, shorter work hours and greater workplace flexibility—are proposals that are of utility primarily to professional women, those, in other words, who can afford to trade less income for more family time. Even outside of specific proposals, virtually all of the current literature seeks to enable women to spend less time in the workplace.

We think this focus is misplaced for at least two reasons. The first reason is obvious: most women are not professionals; they are not lawyers, executives, professors, or even architects or advertising agents. Most women, like most men, toil in the lower economic strata, performing the service work that propels our economy with little hope of substantial advancement or power. In addition, the notion that middle class women have an easier time balancing work and family demands than their professional counterparts is simply wrong, and diverts attention from other more pressing issues…. [T]he fact that so many professional women have chosen their careers, and also have the means to obtain some balance between the demands of work and family–though it may not be their preferred balance–suggests that our policy choices should target those who have the fewest choices, those who have the fewest resources, rather than those who have the most.

In today's labor market, there are actually more underemployed women, women who would prefer to work longer hours as a means of obtaining more income, than overemployed women. Contrary to popular perception, the reality of working hours is that there has not been a substantial increase over the last two decades. Rather, the primary change in the workplace with respect to working hours has been that more women are working full-time jobs than they did in an earlier era. In other words, although most workers are not working substantially longer hours than in previous decades, more women are working hours associated with a full-time schedule, and this shift has inevitably created conflicts in work-life balance in ways that are difficult but predictable, particularly if our social norms outside of the workplace fail to evolve with the changing nature of the labor force. To the extent working women are expected to also fulfill the demands of the home, including childcare and housework, both men and women are likely to experience considerable stress in the course of seeking to achieve some sort of a work-life balance when women have less time to devote to the home. As has been widely chronicled, this is what has largely occurred—men continue to put in longer hours in the labor market and trail women by substantial margins in their efforts at home. Yet, the alternative of having women devote fewer hours in the labor market, as they frequently did before the 1970s, through part-time work, shorter workweeks, or flextime, is not a realistic option for most women, and even if it were, it is unlikely to lead to any measurable degree of workplace equality….

Rather than concentrating on policy options that would enable some women to spend more time out of the workplace…we offer policy proposals that are designed to allow women to spend more time in the workplace, or to spend the same amount of time with less worry and stress about their children during that time. Our proposals are to increase the length of the school day while providing more publicly financed before—and after—school programs; concentrate on changing the allocation of responsibilities within the home; and target domestic violence which both disproportionately affects lower-income income women and substantially interferes with their work obligations….

QUESTIONS

1. Much of the evidence that Selmi and Cahn use to support their arguments that work-family policies should focus on the needs of working class women is based on the findings reported in *The Time Divide*, by Jerry Jacobs and Kathleen Gerson, summarized in the box that precedes this reading. Review it to help you answer these questions. (a) Selmi and Cahn argue that "An entrenched feature of the labor market is that good jobs tend to be good across the board. Bad, or low-paying jobs, on the other hand, tend to have no significant advantages over higher-wage jobs." Do the statistics seem to support their claim? (b) What implications do these statistics have for work/life balance proposals that would create more part-time work? Selmi and Cahn point out that "Many European countries have far more extensive part-time sectors than the United States, and nowhere do we find a robust part-time market in which workers are not penalized in either wages or promotional opportunities for working part-time. Equally clear, wherever an extensive part-time market has been implemented, part-time work is almost exclusively the domain of women. And just as was true in the United States, many European part-time workers would like to work longer hours. In the Netherlands, which has the most extensive part-time sector in Europe, up to 40 percent of part-time workers would prefer to work longer hours."

2. Some have advocated shorter work weeks for all. Yet, as Selmi and Cahn point out, that has not worked well in Europe. In 1998, for example, lobbied by labor unions, the socialist government of France mandated a 35 hour work week at the same pay. By 2007, the system had unraveled and the socialists were voted out of power. Similar efforts have largely failed in Great Britain, and Germany has moved towards increasing work hours. Who would most benefit from such a move? Who might be harmed? What arguments can you make for or against laws expanding part-time work?

3. Selmi and Cahn mention a proposal that all primary caretaking parents receive an annual $5,000 grant that could be used for childcare, education, or retirement savings. Who would benefit from such a proposal? What about it seems fair? Unfair? How should such grants be funded?

4. What work/family problems might be resolved by restructuring the school day by, for example, extending it until 5:00 p.m.? Who would benefit? Who would be hurt?

5. Rates of domestic violence are higher for poorer women and for couples experiencing financial strain, and extremely high among women who receive welfare benefits. What impact might domestic violence have on the workplace?

6. The National Organization for Women estimates that 42 percent of private household services are provided by immigrants under arrangements that are often informal.[20] Would any of Selmi and Cahn's proposals help those women? If not, what should be done?

---

20 "Now Calls for Fair Immigration Reform," 3/7/07, at www.now.org.

Reasonable Accommodation
of Disabled Workers

Society first confined people with disabilities in almshouses, and then in institutions. Alone and ignored, people with disabling conditions experienced life in a Hobbesian state of nature: an existence, "solitary, poor, nasty, brutish, and short."... Until 1973, Chicago prohibited persons who were "deformed" and "unsightly" from exposing themselves to public view.... In 1975, when federal legislation finally required states receiving federal educational funds to serve all school-aged children with disabilities, 1.75 million children were not receiving any schooling, and an estimated 2.5 million were in programs that did not meet their needs.

— MARK C. WEBER[21]

Hailed by some as the most important legislation since the Civil Rights Acts of 1964, in 1990 Congress adopted the **Americans with Disabilities Act (ADA)**. Patterned on an earlier law that prohibited discrimination against persons with handicaps in government-funded programs, the ADA is a bold stroke to eliminate barriers in employment, education, housing, transportation, and public accommodations.

The ADA also takes aim at another problem: society's accumulated myths and fears about disability and disease. The law makes it illegal for employers to discriminate in hiring qualified persons who meet the legal defintion of disabled, and requires firms to make "reasonable accommodation" so that the disabled are given more opportunity to enter the mainstream.

The concept of reasonable accommodation is broad and flexible—but is not intended to impose an "undue hardship" on a business. It encompasses both physical changes to buildings (e.g., broadening aisles and doorways and lowering shelves to make them accessible to those in wheelchairs) and adjustments in the ways people work (e.g., flexible work schedules or modified job descriptions). While Title VII speaks of ending discrimination, the ADA does that and more: It sometimes requires employers to alter the jobs themselves.

Wherever reasonably possible, physical obstacles—the absence of ramps to enter buildings, narrow seating in theatres, the arrangement of furniture and machinery in some workplaces—must be replaced or altered to make business and public places accessible to disabled customers, clients, and employees.

The following definitions are excerpted from the law.

EQUAL OPPORTUNITY FOR INDIVIDUALS WITH DISABILITIES (AMERICANS WITH DISABILITIES ACT)
42 United States Code Annotated Sect. 12101

The term **disability** means, with respect to an individual (A) a physical or mental impairment that substantially limits one or more of the major life activities of such individual; (B) a record of such an impairment; or (C) being regarded as having such an impairment.

---

21 "Exile and the Kingdom: Integration, Harassment, and the Americans with Disabilities Act," 63 *Md. L. Rev.* 162 (2004).

The term **qualified individual with a disability** means an individual with a disability who, with or without reasonable accommodation, can perform the essential functions of the employment position that such individual holds or desires…. [C]onsideration shall be given to the employer's judgment as to what functions of a job are essential, and if an employer has prepared a written description before advertising or interviewing applicants for the job, this description shall be considered evidence of the essential functions of the job.

The term **reasonable accommodation** may include (A) making existing facilities used by employees readily accessible to and usable by individuals with disabilities; and (B) job restructuring, part-time or modified work schedules, reassignment to a vacant position, acquisition or modification of equipment or devices, appropriate adjustment or modifications of examinations, training materials or policies, the provision of qualified readers or interpreters, and other similar accommodations….

The term **undue hardship** means an action requiring significant difficulty or expense, when considered in light of the [following]: In determining whether an accommodation would impose an undue hardship on a covered entity, factors to be considered include (i) the nature and cost of the accommodation needed under this chapter; (ii) the overall financial resources of the facility or facilities involved in the provision of the reasonable accommodation; the number of persons employed at such facility; the effect on expenses and resources, or the impact otherwise of such accommodation upon the operation of the facility; (iii) the overall financial resources of the covered entity; the overall size of the business of a covered entity with respect to the number of its employees; the number, type, and location of its facilities; and (iv) the type of operation or operations of the covered entity, including the composition, structure, and functions of the workforce of such entity; the geographic separateness, administrative, or fiscal relationship of the facility or facilities in question to the covered entity.

QUESTIONS

1. During the past three decades, the courts have helped define the extent to which a particular business must change to accommodate the disabled. Consider the following: The National Federation of the Blind (NFB) is a nationwide, non-profit organization with some 50,000 members, most of whom are blind. Its mission is to aid the blind in their efforts to integrate themselves into society and to remove barriers and change social attitudes, stereotypes, and mistaken beliefs concerning the limitations created by blindness. Using JAWS screen reading software, Bruce Sexton, a legally blind man, can access the Internet to research products, compare prices, and make purchasing decisions. But when he tried to use Target.com—a Web site owned by the nationwide chain-store that enables customers to access information regarding Target store locations and hours, refill prescriptions, order photos, print coupons, and shop online—he could not make it work. Sexton and the NFB sued Target for violating the Americans with Disabilities Act. (a) What arguments can you make on behalf of Target? The blind plaintiffs? Find out what has happened in the actual case, *National Federation of the Blind v. Target Corporation*, 2007 WL 2846462 (N.D. Cal. 2007). (b) How important is it for the blind to be able to access ATMs independently? (See *Massachusetts v. ETrade Access Inc.*, 464 F.Supp.2d 52 [2006].)

2. **Internet Assignment:** In a lawsuit filed in 2006, the U.S. Treasury was accused of violating the Rehabilitation Act (the law that preceded the ADA) by failing to issue paper currency that was readily distinguishable by blind and visually impaired people. Of the 180 nations that issue paper currency, only the United States prints bills identical in size and color in all denominations. Raised symbols enable the blind to distinguish bills printed by Canada, Argentina, China, and Israel. New bills are constantly being printed—especially $1 bills—and the United States made major design changes in 1996. (a) Should the government do another

re-design to address the needs the blind or visually impaired? (b) Visit the NFDB Web site. What other issues are of concern to the blind and partially sighted?

3. Under the ADA, special rules apply to alcoholics and drug addicts. Alcoholism is considered an "impairment," although the law explicitly allows a company to hold an alcoholic to the same standards of behavior as other employees, even if her inability to perform is related to her alcoholism. Drug addicts cannot be penalized because of their status—or history—as addicts, but employers can refuse to hire or fire those who are "current users of illegal drugs." Like alcoholics, addicts can be held to the same standards and rules as other employees. Consider the case of Jose Hernandez. After testing positive for cocaine (a violation of workplace rules), he resigned from his job at Raytheon. Two years later, he reapplied for work at Raytheon and was turned down. Assuming his work record was otherwise good, was Raytheon justified—legally and/or ethically—in refusing to hire him? What argument can you make that it was illegal and/or unethical to refuse to rehire him? See *Raytheon v. Hernandez*, 540 U.S. 44, 124 S. Ct. 513 (2003).

4. **Internet Assignment:** Persons with mental illness are among the most stigmatized Americans. Yet there are few court cases finding ADA protection for mentally ill claimants. Locate a case involving an ADA claim based on mental disability. In what ways are mental impairments different from physical ones? How are they similar?

5. Under regulations promulgated by the EEOC to implement the ADA, a claimant cannot prove discrimination based on a "record of impairment" unless she can show her past impairment had substantially limited a major life activity. So, for example, a temporary stay in a psychiatric hospital, alone, would not be enough to establish that a person was protected under the ADA. Does that rule seem designed to further the goal of ending practices based on stereotypes about the disabled?

Equity in a Globalized Economy

Recently Arrived Migrants

March 2005[22]

- Naturalized citizens: 11.5 million
- Legal permanent residents: 10.5 million
- Temporary legal residents: 1.3 million
- Unauthorized migrants: 11.1 million
- Refuge arrivals: 2.6 million

continued

---

22 Based on findings of the Pew Hispanic Center, "Recently Arrived Migrants and the Congressional Debate on Immigration," (April 5, 2006) available on the website at http://www.pewhispanic.org.

March 2006

- Unauthorized migrants: 11.5 to 12 million

- 40 percent (4.4 million) of unauthorized migrants have been in the United States since 2000

- 250,000 migrants who arrived in the United States after 2000 are the spouses or children of unauthorized migrants who arrived earlier

- 56 percent of illegal immigrants come from Mexico

- A survey of Mexican migrants to the United States showed that only 23 percent had some form of photo ID issued by a U.S. government agency

- 48 percent of those surveyed are married or have a common law spouse; two-thirds of the married Mexican migrants live in the United States with their spouse.

- More than half of the Mexican migrants surveyed have children; a third of those children were left behind in Mexico; 78 percent report that they have relatives other than a spouse or children in the United States.

Ideas about what an equitable society looks like—and how to achieve it—remain hotly contested in this first decade of the twenty-first millennium. As we struggle for fairness on race, gender, and disability issues, we must also contend with deeply held but often contradictory feelings about those non-citizens who live among us, from guest workers to undocumented aliens.

An Immigration Reform Agenda for the 110th Congress
FAIR (Federation for American Immigration Reform)

- **Cut the Numbers**. The United States currently admits over one million legal permanent residents every year. This is equivalent to annually adding a city the size of Dallas, straining our communities, health care, education, and overall infrastructure. In fact, the *Associated Press* recently reported that New York City planners currently project the city's population growth will lead to an all-day rush hour by the year 2030. This level of immigration is unprecedented and unsustainable.... The number of legal immigrants is mainly the result of ever-expanding family-based preference system.

- **Secure the Borders**. The first step to solving our illegal immigration problem is to secure the border. The Census Bureau estimates that over 500,000 illegal aliens enter the United States every year. While this number is in part made up of visa over-stayers and not border-crossers, the fact is that over *one million* aliens are caught attempting to cross the U.S.-Mexico border every year. FAIR advocates the following border security measures:

    Extend fencing along the entire border and increase security on both borders

    Increase manpower (Border Patrol Agents, CBP Agents, etc.)

    Increase detention space by a minimum of 10,000 beds (end Catch-and-Release) ...

    Strengthen and clarify "hot pursuit" authority at border ...

- Apply Strong and Serious Worksite Enforcement. Hand in hand with securing the border is enhancing, and *enforcing*, penalties on employers who knowingly hire illegal aliens. There is broad agreement that the reason most illegal aliens come to the United States is to find work. Some employers seek to take advantage of illegal workers by employing them at sub-standard wages and increasing their profits. Their willingness to break the law by hiring illegal aliens creates demand for even more illegal aliens and only serves to depress wages for U.S. workers (including aliens here legally)....

- **Eliminate Document Fraud**. Document fraud is one of the primary ways illegal aliens manipulate the system to stay in the United States. Fake birth certificates, fake driver's licenses, and forged immigration documents enable illegal aliens to get work and in some instances claim benefits for which they are ineligible by law. Moreover, hundreds of thousands of false social security numbers are submitted to the Social Security Administration every year. For citizens and legal aliens whose social security numbers are stolen, the impact can be severe....

- **Reform Federal Agencies that Impact the Enforcement of Immigration Laws**. The federal agencies that administer our nation's guest worker programs do not take adequate measure to protect American workers. In addition, the federal agencies responsible for enforcing our nation's immigration laws do not share information that would uncover illegal immigration and have not closed systemic loopholes...FAIR advocates the following reforms:

  Reform tax laws so employers cannot use employment of illegal aliens to their advantage (i.e. deduction of wages and benefits)

  Provide increased resources for IRS to investigate and apply sanctions for fraudulent tax returns submitted by employers and aliens

  Impose stricter standards for the recruitment of U.S. workers and require that U.S. workers be given absolute preference in hiring and job security

  Protect wages and working conditions to maintain the standard of living of U.S. workers and eliminate an unfair economic advantage reaped by the employer for hiring illegal workers

  Eliminate State and Local Benefits to Illegal Aliens. The provision of benefits to illegal aliens is essentially a tax-payer subsidy of criminal behavior and only encourages more illegal immigration. The passage of the Illegal Immigration Reform and Immigrant Responsibility Act of 1996 made illegal aliens ineligible for most federally administered benefits, excepting certain emergency provisions, such as emergency medical care and assistance for battered aliens. However, many states have not passed legislation making illegal aliens ineligible for state and local benefits.... While the federal government cannot dictate to states what laws they adopt, Congress can refuse to allow federal taxpayer dollars to be sent to states that subsidize illegal immigration....

- **Oppose immigration legislation against our national interest**.... It is against our national interest to continue to import cheaper foreign labor to compete with U.S. workers (including legal aliens) and depress wages. Providing amnesty for illegal aliens is also against our interest because it rewards unlawful behavior, encourages more illegal immigration, and is fundamentally unfair to aliens who come to this country legally....

- **Oppose international agreements that impair U.S. sovereign control over immigration and border management issues**. One past example includes the North American Free Trade Agreement (NAFTA), which opened the flood gates and allowed big business to import cheap foreign labor en masse to take American jobs. A current example is the so-called NAFTA superhighway, the plan to create a 10-lane, limited-access highway running from Mexico to Canada. This superhighway would enable Asian manufacturers to ship containers full of goods to Mexican ports, unload them using Mexican labor (rather than U.S. labor) and put them on Mexican driven trucks (bypassing the Teamsters) which would then be driven into the United States. The goods would then be distributed through a new customs-free port in the U.S. operated by the Mexican and U.S. governments. FAIR opposes agreements such as these because they institutionalize the use of cheap foreign labor and are being made to cater to big business interests, not the interests of the American workers. FAIR also opposes these agreements because they complicate the process of effective border management....

THE INTERNATIONAL HUMAN RIGHTS OF NONCITIZEN WORKERS

MARIA PABON LOPEZ[23]

Doubtless in the United States today, the law regarding noncitizens and traditional civil rights law have met and forever changed each other's destiny. Ever–present questions over whether immigrants and other noncitizens fit into the national polity—so as to be afforded civil rights protections and the like—may now be definitively resolved.

Immigration law and civil rights law have met, for example, at the counter of a local driver's license bureau, where a noncitizen applicant is denied a driver's license because of his or her inability to prove lawful presence in the United States. They have met at the entrance to our country's schools, where large numbers of noncitizen children struggle for equal educational opportunity in the face of unequal economic funding in their schools at the K–12 level, and again in the halls of our universities, where the undocumented students face severe obstacles to obtaining post–secondary education because of their citizenship status. The laws have met in the interrogation rooms of the Department of Homeland Security, where thousands of citizens of Arab/Muslim countries residing in the United States have been legally required to attend interviews in a process called Special Registration.

Because the United States continues to be the land of opportunity, millions of non–citizens present in this country have much at stake in the intersection of immigration law—the law of who can and cannot enter the United States and who must leave—with alienage law and civil rights law, i.e., the statutory rights regime which came about following the political struggles for equality for African Americans during the 1960s....

... [I]t is my contention that the future of the civil rights of noncitizens in the United States lies in an international human rights paradigm, where, for example, (1) domestic [U.S.] courts hold actors accountable for their international human rights violations against noncitizens in the United States and (2) individuals and/or organizations take their grievances to international human rights bodies to protect the rights of noncitizens in the United States when domestic courts will not do so and the legislative process has failed to address the inequalities affecting the noncitizen's daily lives.

... Because of the sheer numbers of noncitizens—many of them undocumented—who come to the United States seeking work, the most important place where civil rights have met with immigration law in the United States today is in the workplace. The substandard and harmful conditions endured by noncitizen workers in the farms, urban lawns, suburban sweatshops and meatpacking plants of this country pose a direct challenge to our notions of decency, antidiscrimination and eradication of exploitation in the 21st century. For example, in a farm in California, immigrant women farmworkers were raped so often that the company's field was called "field del calzon" (Spanish for

---

23 44 Brandeis L.J.611, 2006, Maria Pabon Lopez, "The Intersection of Immigration Law and Civil Rights Law: Noncitizen Workers and the International Human Rights Paradigm."

"field of underwear"). And since most of these noncitizen workers are undocumented, domestic legal norms provide little or no effective recourse. Notwithstanding their immigration status, the legal condition of many of these workers as employees in this country should afford them civil or international human rights, even if they are undocumented.

At a time when constitutional colorblindness is being espoused and statewide racial privacy initiatives are being proposed, the importance of recognizing the context of equality and inequality for noncitizens, most often persons of color, is paramount. [It is time for] an international human rights approach to be applied to issues at the center of the intersection of immigration law, alienage law, and civil rights.

QUESTIONS

1. Who is FAIR? What influence have they had on the debate in Congress?

2. Who are the stakeholders in the immigration debate? Review FAIR's proposals. Who do they benefit? Harm?

3. FAIR recommends an addition of no more than 300,000 immigrants to the United States annually. What is the estimated number now arriving per year? What are the pros and cons of working with quotas or numbers to resolve this issue?

4. Illegal immigrants are not eligible for social security benefits or the earned income tax credit. Since 1996, however, they can get a special Immigrant Tax Identification Number (ITIN) that enables them to pay federal taxes without a social security number. In 2006 the IRS issued some 1.5 million ITINS, the most ever, and news outlets reported that spring 2007 saw an increase in federal tax filings from undocumented aliens. What are the pros and cons of this approach?

5. Pew Hispanic reports that in 2005, the 6.6 million illegal immigrant families in the United States had an average annual income of $29,000, and accounted for nearly $200 billion in purchasing power. But 30 million foreign workers—legal and illegal—are said to lack bank accounts. Citigroup Inc. and Bank of America have tried to tap into that market by making credit cards available without a social security number. (Other safeguards are in place, such as the requirement that an applicant have a Bank of America account in good standing for at least three months.) Nonprofit worker centers in Hempstead, Chicago, Los Angeles, and the New Labor Center in New Brunswick, New Jersey have begun to offer debit cards to immigrants. What problems are solved by such credit/debit cards? Created?

6. **Internet Assignment:** Find out what happened when the following practices were challenged in court. (a) In Freehold, New Jersey, Mamaroneck, New York, and Redondo Beach, California, Latino day laborers who solicit work are arrested or given tickets for loitering in public places. (b) Hazelton, a former coal-mining town in Pennsylvania, mandated English as the official language and adopted an ordinance withholding permits from companies who hired illegal immigrants. (c) Farmers Branch, a suburb of Dallas, Texas, banned renting apartments to illegal immigrants.

7. Consider the case of *Mohawk Industries v. Williams*, 465 F.3d 1277(11th Cir. 2006), where hourly workers accused the company of deliberately employing illegal immigrants in order to reduce labor costs, depress the wages of its legal workers and discourage workers' compensation claims. Should workers who are citizens or legal residents be allowed to sue an employer who knowingly employs illegal workers? What about competitors: Should they be allowed to sue on grounds of unfair competition?

8. Every state debated immigration issues in 2007, and 41 states adopted some kind of immigration laws, including restrictions on obtaining a driver's license and laws making restricting access to medical and other state aid. What arguments can you make for and against such state laws?

CHAPTER **PROBLEMS**

1. Employers are generally allowed to enforce dress and appearance standards so long as they do not discriminate on the basis of race, sex, religion, and so on. Gender-specific rules are acceptable if based on social norms, unless they place an unfair burden on one sex. So, for example, having a "business dress" rule that requires men to wear ties and women to wear dresses or skirts would be legal, but requiring only one sex to wear a uniform would not. What problems can you identify with any of the following? (a) A pizza company will make no exceptions to its rule that drivers must be clean shaven. Sixty percent of African-American men have a skin condition characterized by severely painful shaving bumps. The condition is cured by growing a beard. (b) UPS prohibits its workers from wearing dreadlocks. (c) Bank does not allow male employees to wear earrings. (d) Casino hires men and women as cocktail waiters. Women are required to wear three-inch high heels; men are allowed to wear any "dress shoe." (e) Imperial Palace hires only slim, young women and requires them to wear geisha-girl costumes to serve cocktails. But some of the waitresses have complained that the costumes are sexually provocative to customers and invite unwanted attention.

2. **Internet Assignment:** The kitchen manager who supervised Maria Torres repeatedly asked her to date him, called her at home, and made unwanted advances. When she refused, he increased her workload and cut her hours. What should the employer do next: investigate her complaint—or ask her to document her immigration status? See how the court ruled in *EEOC v. Perkins Restaurant and Bakery* 2007 WL 424323 (D.Minn.).

3. **Internet Assignment:** According to researchers for the Economic Policy Institute (EPI), U.S. employers expect employees to act as "unencumbered workers,"—that is, as employees who function as if they had a full-time partner or caregiver at home—ignoring the reality of an economy in which most mothers work and most married couples are dual wage-earners. Experiences in other countries can yield insights for new U.S. workplace policies, making it easier for American workers to balance the demands of career and family. In a report issued on January 9, 2002, EPI highlighted the findings of a study of global policies. Find and read the report. Which practices/policies would seem to be most likely to succeed in the United States?

4. **Internet Assignment:** Under the **Equal Pay Act** as interpreted by the courts, employers may not pay men and women different wages for doing the same job except to the extent that wage differentials are based on seniority, merit, or factors "other than sex." Title VII of the Civil Rights Act of 1964 prohibits discrimination in pay and other compensation based on race, sex, color, religion, or national origin. Yet there are still wage gaps. The National Coalition for Pay Equity, working since 1979 to eliminate sex- and race-based wage discrimination and to achieve pay equity, reported these statistics on its Web site in spring 2007:

Women's earnings in 2005 were 77% of men's, leaving the wage gap statistically unchanged from last year, while wages declined for the third consecutive year for women and the second consecutive year for men. Based on the median earnings of full-time, year-round workers, women's earnings were $31,858, a drop of 1.3%, and men's earnings were $41,386, a drop of 1.8%, according to revised 2004 data. Median earnings for women of color continue to be lower, in general, than earnings for men as a whole. In 2005, the earnings for African American women were $29,672, 71.7% of men's earnings, and for Latinas $24,214, 58.5% of men's, both slight gains, while Asian American women's earnings were $36,092, 87.2% of men's, a slight drop from last year.

   a. Check out the Web site of the National Coalition for Pay Equity. What is the current status of the proposed Fair Pay Act?

   b. What are the current race and gender income/wage disparitites?

5. By 2007, 145 cities and counties across the nation had enacted "living-wage bills," generally requiring those businesses that receive government contracts to pay wages higher than the legal minimum wage. Maryland's living wage law requires employers with state contracts to pay workers at least $8.50/hour—higher in some parts of the state, and higher than the state minimum wage ($6.15 an hour, one dollar higher than the federal floor). Nonprofit groups and small businesses (i.e., those with 10 or fewer workers) with state contracts worth less than $500,00 are exempt. Who will benefit most from such laws? Who might be harmed by them? What arguments can you make for and against living wage laws?

6. **Internet Assignment:** As this book goes to press, Wal-Mart is defending itself in the largest civil rights lawsuit ever. A class-action on behalf of approximately one and a half million women nationwide accuses Wal-Mart of sex discrimination in its employment practices. Find out about *Dukes v. Wal-Mart* and compare and contrast it to the class action brought by eight women brokers against Morgan Stanley. The suit against the Wall Street firm was settled in April 2007 when Morgan Stanley agreed to pay $46 million. What evidence do these cases give that there is still a glass ceiling in the United States? What are their implications for smashing it?

7. J. L. Josephs worked as a service technician for Pacific Bell, visiting customers' homes to provide assistance. When Pacific Bell discovered that Josephs had a criminal record ("not guilty of murder by reason of insanity"), he was terminated. Josephs sued, claiming discrimination in violation of the ADA. What will he have to prove to win? How should Pacific Bell defend itself? See *Josephs v. Pacific Bell*, 2006 U.S.App.Lex. 8695 (9th th Cir.).

8. **Internet Assignment:** The H-1B Visa program allows highly skilled noncitizens to work in the United States for three years (renewable for three additional years). The 2007 cap for H-1B Visas was 65,000 workers a year. Historically, about half of the H-1B visa holders eventually get permanent resident ("green") card status. Most of the companies requesting such visas are high-tech, many based in India. Microsoft's Bill Gates praised this magnet for uniquely skilled workers as a boon for the American economy. But in a report published by the Economic Policy Institute in March 2007, Ronil Hira countered that the visa has accelerated the pace of offshore outsourcing of computing work. Visa holders assess a U.S.-based client's needs and specifications, but the work of software coding itself is most often done in India. (a) Find out how well holders of H-1B visas are being compensated. What impact would you expect such visas to have on compensation for citizens and permanent residents? (b) In 2007, visas for unskilled workers were capped at 10,000, while some 65,000 H-1B visas were available. Is it fair to favor skilled workers over unskilled ones? (c) How will newly adopted or proposed changes in the immigration law impact those seeking to come to the United States for work?

9. The flip side of immigration—emmigration—involves the flow out of a country. In fall 2006, *The New York Times* reported on a growing phenomenon: American college graduates moving to India to accept high-paying jobs in the technology field. Is that fair to native-born engineers in India?

10. **Internet Assignment:** In 2001, Human Rights Watch released a report entitled "Hidden in the Home: Abuse of Domestic Workers with Special Visas in the United States." Special visas allow foreigners to live in the United States and work for diplomats and

international organizations (e.g., OAS). Almost all of them are women, and the abuses documented include median workdays of 14 hours, median wages of $2.14/hour (including room and board), and claims that workers have been slapped, yelled at, and sexually assaulted by their employers. What action, if any, has been taken by the United States to ameliorate this problem? What action should be taken?

CHAPTER **PROJECT**

Alternative Dispute Resolution: Accommodating Parents

GUIDELINES, APPENDIX E

Witness Statement for Donna Coke, the ER Nurse:

When I had our third child, my husband and I planned things carefully. He's a full-time student, so it made sense that he'd stay home taking care of the kids, and I'd go back to work and support us.

As a nurse, I know experts strongly recommend breast-feeding as the healthiest way to nourish infants. I've learned there is real evidence showing that children who have been breast-fed for at least a year turn out physically and psychologically healthier than other children. So I made a decision to breast feed our baby Meghan. I took the two months maternity leave, and then I was ready to go back to work. Using a breast pump, I expressed enough milk in a bottle for the baby to be fed while I was at work. But the first night we tried this, the baby wouldn't accept the bottle. She started yelling and shaking—my husband called all upset. I could hear her screaming in the background. I had to tell my supervisor Lee Gibbon that there was a family emergency, and I had to go home that night.

The next day, my supervisor met me as I was coming in. She asked,"What are you going to do about the situation?" I told her that my husband and I had come up with an idea: He'd drive the baby up to the ER entrance door each time I'm on mid-shift break, and I'd go out and sit in the car and feed the baby. My supervisor didn't go for this. She said my patients might need me. I said, "Hey, other nurses go outside the building for their breaks. They smoke cigarettes, they go shopping. You don't do anything to stop them." She said, "This isn't going to work." So I made other suggestions. I even told her I'd be willing to go to part-time. She didn't really answer me. She said, "Go home. I need to think this over."

I called the next day and Gibbons told me that she didn't think I should come back until she had figured out a better solution. She said she'd call me but she didn't. It's been almost five months now, and they still haven't called me, not even to tell me I won't be called back in. I can't believe they are making me make a choice between caring for my baby and caring for my patients. I loved my job, and we need me to have that job. I was good at it, just like I'm good at being a mother. I think I should have a right to breast feed—that Meghan has the right to be breast-fed. I think we should sue the hospital.

Witness Statement: Lee Gibbon, the Supervisor:

Donna Coke is an excellent nurse. I'd never argue with that. But what I do argue with is her assumption that she should be accommodated by the hospital on this. Donna made a choice to breast feed her baby. She has a right to do that. What she doesn't have a right to do is force her employer to make allowances for that choice. She and her husband have to live with it. When Donna came in to tell me she wanted special arrangements to feed her baby in the parking lot at break, it took me 15 seconds to imagine all the ways that plan could go wrong. What if her baby demanded more time than Donna's break allowed? What if the baby was not ready to feed when Donna was on break? Anything can happen with small babies, we all know that. Donna and her husband seemed to expect the hospital—and its critically ill patients—to cut her some slack. We just aren't in a position to do that. This is a business, no different from any place else. If women keep on expecting the government to protect them in every single individual situation like this, where will it end? Pretty soon we'll be hearing from women, that they should have extra paid time off to go to PTA meetings, because evidence shows that children whose mothers are involved in schools do better academically—and psychologically! It's time we stopped acting like victims all the time and took on the world of work like everyone else. We can handle it. In fact, it would serve the cause of feminism better if we women got to proving that we too know how to "take it like a man!"

WORKERS RIGHTS AS HUMAN RIGHTS:

Health and Safety in the Workplace

5

There was another interesting set of statistics that a person might have gathered in Packingtown—those of the various afflictions of the workers.... [E]ach one of these lesser industries was a separate little inferno, in its way as horrible as the killing-beds, the source and fountain of them all. The workers in each of them had their own peculiar diseases. And the wandering visitor might be skeptical about all the swindles, but he could not be skeptical about these, for the worker bore the evidence of them about on his own person—generally he had only to hold out his hand.

— UPTON SINCLAIR, THE JUNGLE (1906)

Labour is not a Commodity.

— PHILADELPHIA DECLARATION OF THE INTERNATIONAL LABOUR ORGANIZATION (1994)

For most people in our society, work is unavoidable. If individual workers find themselves facing unacceptable occupation risks they cannot simply withdraw from the market.... Adequate information is often lacking; the power to insist on less risk does not exist; and there is no possibility of mobility. These limitations on choices characterize occupational as opposed to recreational or aesthetic risks.

— MARK MCCARTHY, (1982)[1]

•

From the time of the industrial revolution through today's increasingly global economy, there has been little consensus in the United States regarding the appropriate balance between risk and security in the workplace. Just how healthy and safe must a workplace be? Whose responsibility is it to set the standards to minimize harm to life, limb, and pocketbook caused by industrial accidents, occupational disease, and toxic exposure? Free-market economists believe regulation tends to stifle competition and detract from efficiency, while reformers look to the state to rein in the harshest effects of unrestrained capitalism. Some are wary of both big business and big government, arguing for maximal freedom for individuals. Similar debates arise on a transnational scale: some would allow national standards to prevail while others favor universal norms and guidance from international organizations.

---

1 Mark McCarthy, "A Review of Some Normative and Conceptual Issues in Occupational Safety and Health," 9 *Boston College Env'tl Affairs L. Rev.* 773, 778–80 (1980–82).

This chapter begins with perspectives on work-related risks—both the avoidable and the unavoidable. The legal backdrop includes laws designed to compensate those who suffer occupational harms, and the watershed Occupational Health and Safety Act of 1970, embodying a national policy to reduce or prevent them from occurring. In the final section we explore the twenty-first century global dimensions of workplace health and safety.

Confronting Risk in the Work Environment: The WTC Cleanup

In November 2004 an Army National Guard medic filed a class action against the Environmental Protection Agency (EPA), the White House Council on Environmental Quality, and the Occupational Safety and Health Administration (OSHA) on behalf of all those who worked in the immediate vicinity of the World Trade Center from September 11, 2001 to October 31, 2001. The plaintiff claimed that statements in EPA press releases issued in the wake of the disaster were made (1) to speed work at the site, (2) with the knowledge they were false or misleading, and (3) with deliberate indifference to the health risks of the workers. The court must decide if those allegations are enough to allow plaintiffs to move to the next step—a trial.

LOMBARDI v. WHITMAN
United States Court of Appeal, Second Circuit, 2007
485 F.3d 73

JACOBS, Chief Judge. ☀

The collapse of the World Trade Center towers on [September 11, 2001] generated a cloud of debris that coated the surrounding buildings and streets of Lower Manhattan with concrete dust, asbestos, lead, and other building materials. Fires within the wreckage burned for months, emitting various metals and particulate matter in addition to such potentially harmful substances as dioxin, polychlorinated biphenyls (PCBs), volatile organic compounds and polycyclic aromatic hydrocarbons.

The plaintiffs arrived at the site on September 11 or in the days soon after: John Lombardi is a … medic; Roberto Ramos, Jr. is an Emergency Services Officer in the New York City Corrections Department; Hasan A. Muhammad is an Emergency Services Captain … ; Rafael A. Garcia is a Deputy U.S. Marshal; and Thomas E. Carlstrom is a paramedic…. They participated in search, rescue, and clean–up work at the site, with little or no equipment to protect their lungs. They were not told by their employers or any government official about the health risks posed by the dangerous contaminants in the air, and they thought they could work at the site with little or no respiratory protection based on the information available to them, including statements of government officials indicating that Lower Manhattan's air quality presented no significant health risks to the public.

… A September 13, 2001, EPA press release, [i] indicated that initial environmental tests done at the site after the terrorist attacks were "very reassuring about potential exposure of rescue crews and the public to environmental contaminants"; [ii] concluded that the results of "[a]dditional sampling of both ambient air quality and dust particles … in lower Manhattan … were uniformly acceptable"; and [iii] expressed the EPA's intent to work with other agencies and rescue workers to provide respiratory equipment and to make sure they observed appropriate safety precautions—assistance that the plaintiffs allege (to their knowledge) never materialized.

… A September 16 EPA press release reported additional good news:

"[N]ew samples confirm previous reports that ambient air quality meets OSHA standards and consequently is not a cause for public concern.... EPA has found variable asbestos levels in bulk debris and dust on the ground, but EPA continues to believe that there is no significant health risk to the general public in the coming days...."

... [A] September 18 press release [by the EPA] reported ... that the "vast majority" of air samples taken near the site measured harmful substances at below maximum acceptable levels.... [T]he highest asbestos levels were close to the site itself, where rescue and cleanup workers were supposedly being supplied with adequate equipment....

In fact, according to the EPA Inspector General, 25 percent of the bulk dust samples taken up to that point recorded asbestos at levels representing a significant health risk. ...

... [A] September 12 internal EPA email directed that all statements to the media were to be cleared by the National Security Council [through the CEQ] before release ... and in response to the CEQ's suggestions ... the EPA [i] removed a reference to recent test samples that recorded higher asbestos levels than those in previous samples and [ii] added a quote from John L. Henshaw of OSHA assuring that it was safe to go to work in Lower Manhattan ....*

Under the Due Process Clause of the Fifth Amendment of the Constitution, "[n]o person shall ... be deprived of life, liberty, or property, without due process of law." This clause has been interpreted as a "protection of the individual against arbitrary action of government...." [But] government action resulting in bodily harm is not a substantive due process violation unless "the government action was 'so egregious, so outrageous, that it may fairly be said to shock the contemporary conscience.'"

Only an affirmative act can amount to a violation of substantive due process, because the Due Process Clause "is phrased as a limitation on the State's power to act, not as a guarantee of certain minimal levels of safety and security." ... It is not enough to allege that a government actor failed to protect an individual from a known danger of bodily harm or failed to warn the individual of that danger. So, to the extent the plaintiffs here allege that the defendants had an affirmative duty to prevent them from suffering exposure to environmental contaminants, their claims must fail. They cannot rely on the EPA's failure to instruct workers to wear particular equipment, its failure to explain the exact limitations of its knowledge of the health effects of the airborne substances that were present, or its failure to explain the limitations of its testing technologies.

But the complaint goes further; it alleges that defendants' affirmative assurances that the air in Lower Manhattan was safe to breathe created a false sense of security that induced site workers to forgo protective measures, thereby creating a danger where otherwise one would not have existed. "[I]n exceptional circumstances a governmental entity may have a constitutional obligation to provide ... protection, either because of a special relationship with an individual, or because the governmental entity itself has created or increased the danger to the individual." The plaintiffs allege no "special relationship" between them and federal officials.... They plead that their reliance on the government's misrepresentations induced them to forgo available safeguards, and thus characterize the harm as a state created danger....

[Plaintiffs' allegations allow the court to assume that defendant's optimistic statements caused them to experience a false sense of security that led to the harmful exposures.] But, [i]n order to shock the conscience and trigger a violation of substantive due process, official conduct must be outrageous and egregious under the circumstances; it must be truly "brutal and offensive to human dignity...."

... [D]eliberate indifference that shocks in one environment may not be so patently egregious in another....

The complaint ... recognizes what everyone knows: that one essential government function in the wake of disaster is to put the affected community on a normal footing, i.e., to avoid panic, keep order, restore services, repair infrastructure, and preserve the economy.

If anything, the importance of the EPA's mission counsels against broad constitutional liability in this situation: the risk of such liability will tend to inhibit EPA officials in making difficult decisions about how to disseminate information to the public in an environmental emergency ... [and] officials might default to silence in the face of the public's urgent need for information....

Can the goals of a government policy possibly outweigh a known risk of loss of life or bodily harm? The EPA and other federal agencies often must decide whether to regulate particular conduct by taking into account whether the risk to the potentially affected population will be acceptable. Such decisions require an exercise of the conscience, but such decisions cannot be deemed egregious, conscience–shocking, and "arbitrary in the constitutional sense," merely because they contemplate some likelihood of bodily harm.

... When great harm is likely to befall someone no matter what a government official does, the allocation of risk may be a burden on the conscience of the one who must make such decisions, but does not shock the contemporary conscience.

These principles apply notwithstanding the great service rendered by those who repaired New York, the heroism of those who entered the site when it was unstable and on fire, and the serious health consequences that are plausibly alleged in the complaint.

[HELD:] Because the conduct at issue here does not shock the conscience, there was no constitutional violation. [The lower court's dismissal of the case is affirmed.]

QUESTIONS

1. Plaintiffs did not allege that the defendants acted with evil intent to harm them. On what basis, then, did they claim that defendants were responsible for the harm they suffered? Why does the court dismiss that claim?

2. Do you agree with Judge Jacobs that the assurances given by the EPA were not "conscience shocking"?

3. In a sense, the judge's ruling here is in sync with the "no duty to rescue" rule discussed in Chapter 1. Which exception to the rule did the plaintiffs hope to use?

4. Is there anything the EPA could have done to avoid the "rock and the hard place," for example, something that would have protected the rescue workers more effectively without making a bad situation worse?

5. Identify the ethical issues that arise in this case for (a) rescue workers, (b) EPA officials, and (c) Judge Jacobs.

6. In the immediate aftermath of the collapse of the Twin Towers, it was fair to assume that there were safety risks at the site. Whose responsibility should it be to pay for the treatment expenses of those who were exposed to toxins while cleaning up the WTC site? Is your answer the same for those who were "on the job" at the time, and those who volunteered to help? (b) Kenneth R. Feinberg, a lawyer, served as administrator of the September 11 Victim Compensation Fund. He oversaw the distribution of more than $7 billion to the families of those who died in the WTC attacks, and rescue and cleanup workers who had already been diagnosed with respiratory ailments. He has proposed that a similar fund—with contributions from charities and contractors added, along with public money—be established to compensate people who were diagnosed after the initial disbursements. By the end of 2006, officials were warning that the $40 million set aside for treatment of rescue workers, volunteers, and firefighters would run out. Who are the stakeholders in this scenario? Who should pay for ongoing medical costs associated with the WTC cleanup?

7. **Internet Assignment** In another suit growing out of the WTC disaster, workers sued the City of New York, the Port Authority, and more than 100 private contractors working at the site, claiming that those in charge of the clean up had emphasized speed over safety. In October 2006, a federal judge allowed the suit to go forward, ruling that immunity defenses should be evaluated on a case-by-case basis. Find out whether any defendants have since been dismissed from *In re: World Trade Center Disaster Site Litigation*, 456 F.Supp.2d (2006). What is the current status of the case?

8. **Internet Assignment** New concerns about the harms caused by the cleanup of the World Trade Center site surfaced during the summer of 2007. The National Institute for Occupational Safety and Health estimated that treating sick and injured workers from the site costs more than $195 million a year. The New York City Department of Health and Mental Hygiene reported that rescue and recovery workers at ground zero had developed asthma at 12 times the normal rate, with rates increasing the longer workers remained at ground zero. In October 2007, investigative reporters for the *New York Times* questioned the accuracy of some of the health reports issued by the Selikoff Center for Occupational and Environmental Medicine, which has received millions of dollars in federal funding and examined some 20,000 workers exposed at the site. What has been the response to these reports?

*"Our tests show that it is safe for New Yorkers to go back to work in New York's financial district ... Keeping the streets clean and being careful not to track dust into buildings will help protect workers from remaining debris."

* * * * *

Risks never exist in isolation. They are part of systems. For that reason, any effort to reduce a single risk will have a range of consequences, some of them likely unintended....

If the Occupational Safety and Health Administration ("OSHA") increases regulation of benzene, a carcinogenic substance, it might lead companies to use a less safe, or perhaps even an unsafe, substitute; it might also decrease the wages of affected workers, and decrease the number of jobs in the relevant industry. People who have less money, and who are unemployed, tend to live shorter lives and hence occupational regulation might, under certain circumstances, sacrifice more lives than it saves. Of course the unintended consequences of risk regulation might be desirable rather than undesirable as, for example, when regulation spurs new pollution-control technologies.

— Cass R. Sunstein[2]

From sudden accidents with dangerous machinery on the assembly line to the gradual onset of carpal tunnel syndrome from repetitive motions such as data processing or butchering, workers face a wide array of risks. Many of the worst hazards are invisible, like the chemical exposures that threaten the reproductive capacities of both men and women. Those who work in dry cleaners and laundries face carbon disulfide and benzene. Health workers—in hospitals, clinics, and dentist offices—are exposed to infectious diseases and radiation from X-ray machines. Mercury, cadmium, coal tar, carbon tetrachloride, and vinyl chloride are risks for production line workers. Computer assemblers breathe toxic dust; taxi drivers breathe carbon monoxide.

In the following case, the court must weigh an individual's willingness to risk his own health against a company's efforts to ensure a safe working environment.

2 "Cost-Benefit Default Principles," 99 *Mich. L. Rev.* 1651 (2001).

ECHAZABAL v. CHEVRON USA, INC.

United States Court of Appeals, Ninth Circuit, 2000

226 F.3d 1063

REINHARDT, Circuit Judge. ☀

Mario Echazabal first began working at Chevron's oil refinery in El Segundo, California in 1972. Employed by various maintenance contractors, he worked at the refinery, primarily in the coker unit, nearly continuously until 1996, when the events that gave rise to this litigation occurred.

In 1992, Echazabal applied to work directly for Chevron at the same coker unit location.... A preemployment physical examination conducted by Chevron's regional physician revealed that Echazabal's liver was releasing certain enzymes at a higher than normal level. Based on these results, Chevron concluded that Echazabal's liver might be damaged by exposure to the solvents and chemicals present in the coker unit. For that reason, Chevron rescinded its job offer. Nevertheless, Echazabal continued to work for Irwin, a maintenance contractor, throughout the refinery including at the coker unit. Chevron made no effort to have him removed from his assignment.

In 1995, Echazabal again applied to Chevron for a position at the coker unit. Again, the job offer was rescinded because of the risk that his liver would be damaged if he worked in the coker unit. This time, however, Chevron wrote Irwin and asked that it "immediately remove Mr. Echazabal from [the] refinery or place him in a position that eliminates his exposure to solvents/chemicals."

[Echazabal claimed that Chevron's refusal to allow him to work in the coker unit was illegal discrimination under the Americans with Disabilities Act (ADA) based on his disability—his diagnosed Hepatitis C. Chevron disagreed with Echazabal's interpretation of a provision in the ADA that creates what is called the "direct threat defense." Here, Chevron argued, it did not have to allow Echazabal to work in the coker unit because his presence would present a "direct threat" to his own health. The court disagrees:]

The direct threat defense permits employers to impose a "requirement that an individual shall not pose a direct threat to the health or safety of other individuals in the workplace." On its face, the provision does not include direct threats to the health or safety of the disabled individual himself....

Although we need not rely on it, the legislative history of the ADA also supports the conclusion that the direct threat provision does not include threats to oneself. The term "direct threat" is used hundreds of times throughout the ADA's legislative history in the final conference report, the various committee reports and hearings, and the floor debate.... In nearly every instance in which the term appears, it is accompanied by a reference to the threat to "others" or to "other individuals in the workplace." Not once is the term accompanied by a reference to threats to the disabled person himself....

Congress's decision not to include threats to one's own health or safety in the direct threat defense makes good sense in light of the principles that underlie the ADA in particular and federal employment discrimination law in general.... [T]he ADA was designed in part to prohibit discrimination against individuals with disabilities that takes the form of paternalism....

More generally, courts have interpreted federal employment discrimination statutes to prohibit paternalistic employment policies.... In *Johnson Controls*, the Court ... held that the threats of lead exposure to female employees' own reproductive health did not justify the employer's decision to exclude women from certain positions at a battery manufacturing plant. Given Congress's decision in the Title VII context to allow all individuals to decide for themselves whether to put their own health and safety at risk, it should come as no surprise that it would enact legislation allowing the same freedom of choice to disabled individuals.

Chevron suggests that we must ignore Congress's clear intent because forcing employers to hire individuals who pose a risk to their own health or safety would expose employers to tort liability.... [G]iven that the ADA prohibits employers from refusing to hire individuals solely on the ground that their health or safety may be threatened by the job, state tort law would likely be preempted if it interfered with this requirement. Moreover, we note that Chevron's concern over an award of damages reflects a fear that hiring a disabled individual will cost more than hiring an individual without any disabilities. The extra cost of employing disabled individuals does not in itself provide an affirmative defense to a discriminatory refusal to hire those individuals....

[W]e conclude that the ADA's direct threat defense means what it says: it permits employers to impose a requirement that their employees not pose a significant risk to the health or safety of other individuals in the workplace. It does not permit employers to shut disabled individuals out of jobs on the ground that, by working in the jobs at issue, they may put their own health or safety at risk. Conscious of the history of paternalistic rules that have often excluded disabled individuals from the workplace, Congress concluded that disabled persons should be afforded the opportunity to decide for themselves what risks to undertake. The district court's grant of summary judgment to Chevron on Echazabal's ADA claim is reversed.

TROTT , Circuit Judge, dissenting. ☀

Mario Echazabal sues over not getting a job handling liver-toxic substances, i.e., "hydrocarbon liquids and vapors, acid, caustic, refinery waste water and sludge, petroleum solvents, oils, greases, and chlorine bleach." He was denied the job because he suffers from a chronic, uncorrectable, and life-threatening viral liver disease, Hepatitis C, that most likely will be aggravated by exposure to these hazardous materials to the extent that his life will be endangered.

[Under the ADA, employers are not required to hire disabled individuals unless they are "otherwise qualified" to handle the "essential functions" of the job.] ... Mr. Echazabal simply is not "otherwise qualified" for the work he seeks. Why? Because the job most probably will endanger his life. I do not understand how we can claim he can perform the essential functions of the position he seeks when precisely because of his disability, those functions may kill him. To ignore this reality is bizarre....

Our law books, both state and federal, overflow with statutes and rules designed by representative governments to protect workers from harm long before we rejected the idea that workers toil at their own peril in the workplace. "Paternalism" here is just an abstract out-of-place label of no analytical help. Whether paternalism or maternalism, the concept is pernicious when it is allowed to dislodge longstanding laws mandating workplace safety. That battle was fought and lost long ago in our legislatures. In many jurisdictions, it is a crime knowingly to subject workers to life-endangering conditions.... In effect, we repeal these laws with respect to [Echazabal], and to other workers in similar situations. So much for OSHA. Now, our laws give less protection to workers known to be in danger than they afford to those who are not. That seems upside down and backwards. Precisely the workers who need protection can sue because they receive what they need....

Chevron correctly points out that the majority's holding leads to absurd results: a steelworker who develops vertigo can keep his job constructing high rise buildings; a power saw operator with narcolepsy or epilepsy must be allowed to operate his saw; and a person allergic to bees is entitled to be hired as a beekeeper....

I believe it would be an undue hardship to require an employer to place an employee in a life-threatening situation. Such a rule would require employers knowingly to endanger workers. The legal peril involved is obvious, and as a simple human to human matter, such a moral burden is unconscionable.

QUESTIONS

1. Look again at the facts offered by both the majority and the dissent. Why do you think Echazabal was willing to risk his health by working in the coker unit? Assuming he had a complete grasp of the risks involved, is it ethical to allow him to work there? For this, re-examine the frameworks for ethical decision making in Chapter 1.

2. Chevron gave certain reasons for refusing to allow Echazabal to work in the coker unit. Name them. Can you think of any other reasons the company may have had for that decision?

3. **Internet Assignment** On appeal, the Supreme Court reversed. Justice Souter explained why: "The EEOC was certainly acting within the reasonable zone when it saw a difference between rejecting workplace paternalism and ignoring specific and documented risks to the employee himself, even if the employee would take his chances for the sake of getting a job." *Chevron USA Inc. v. Echazabal*, 536 U.S. 73, 122 S.Ct. 2045 (2002). The "direct threat defense" is allowable, according to the Court, when it is based on a "'reasonable medical judgment that relies on the most current medical knowledge and/or the best available objective evidence,' and upon an expressly 'individualized assessment of the individual's present ability to safely perform the essential functions of the job....'" Find out how the lower courts applied the test when they revisited *Echazabal* on remand from the Supreme Court. Are you satisfied that Chevron's decisions were not based on the kind of pretextual stereotypes at which the ADA is aimed?

4. In this case, we see both the company and the employee between a rock and a hard place. Echazabal must choose to either further endanger his health or lose a coveted opportunity, while Chevron is caught between liability under the ADA and liability for unsafe work conditions. Suppose you were a top manager inside Chevron, responsible for strategic planning on workplace safety. Is there anything you and your firm could do to prevent or minimize the risk of this type of scenario from developing in the future?

5. Mentioned in the *Echazabal* case is *International Union v. Johnson Controls*, 111 S.Ct. 1196, a 1991 Supreme Court decision in which, again, a company was accused of paternalism for restricting access to hazardous jobs. In *Johnson Controls*, fertile women were not permitted to work on a battery-making production line where exposure to lead could cause harm to their offspring. The Supreme Court held that this restriction amounted to illegal sex discrimination under Title VII, stating that the female workers should "not be forced to choose between having a child and having a job." The company had argued it was concerned about harm to future generations, but the Court wrote: "Decisions about the welfare of future children must be left to the parents who conceive, bear, support and raise them rather than to the employers who hire those parents." Is there a group of stakeholders (affected individuals) whose preferences have not been considered in the *Johnson Controls* case? How might the absence of such voices alter an ethical analysis of this situation?

The State of Workplace Health and Safety in 2007

More than 4.2 million nonfatal workplace injuries and illnesses were reported in 2005 (Bureau of Labor Standards, http://www.bls.gov).

5,734 persons lost their lives due to work-related injuries in 2005, 5,214 in private industries (Bureau of Labor Statistics, http://www.bls.gov); most fatalities: construction industry.

It is estimated that 50,000–60,000 workers die each year from occupational diseases (*Death on the Job: The Toll of Neglect April 2007*, available at www.aflcio.org).

Hispanic and Latino workers suffer disproportionately high numbers of fatal workplace injuries; of 917 Hispanic and Latino workers whose deaths were counted as workplace fatalities in 2005, 625 were foreign-born, 292 native-born (Bureau of Labor Statistics, http://www.bls.gov).

Less than one-third of the costs of occupational illness and injuries are paid by employer-funded workers' compensation; 20 percent are paid by Medicaid/Medicare; most costs are borne by workers and their families (*Immigrant Workers at Risk*, 2005, available at www.aflcio.org).

At current staffing and inspection levels, one inspection of every workplace under federal OSHA's jurisdiction would take 133 years.

Occupational Safety and Health Administration (OSHA)

> *I build ships for a living. When I'm working on a particular job and the company needs something done fast, they tell me to go to work without the staging and the service I need to do the work safely. When they don't need a job done right away, then I get service. Sometimes it takes longer to provide me with a staging than it does for me to do the job itself, so when they want it fast, safety goes by the wayside....*
>
> — CHARLEY RICHARDSON, SHIPBUILDER'S LOCAL 5 QUINCY, MASSACHUSETTS, 1985[3]

> *The guiding principle regarding OSHA penalties must be this: it should cost an employer more to break the law than to observe it.*
>
> — NANCY LESSIN, MASS. COALITION FOR OSH

The primary focus of lawsuits, such as that brought on behalf of WTC workers, and compensation schemes such as workers' compensation—described later in this chapter—is on paying those who have been injured or made ill. But this is not the only possible approach to workplace safety. From their earliest days, labor unions have sought greater protections for their members. During the 1937 National Silicosis Conference, for example, industry representatives

---

3 From a panel discussion published in "Chemical Hazards at Work: Whose Business?" 9 *Harvard Env't Law Rev.* 331, 351–2 (1985).

argued that because exposure to silicon dust was being minimized and minimal exposure was not disabling, there was no longer a real crisis. Representing organized labor, John Frey of the American Federation of Labor disagreed. As historians Rosner and Markowitz explain:

> Frey argued silicosis was a problem for workers even before they became disabled ... because any silica in the lungs was pathological.... He maintained that ... emphasis on disability and impairment led management to rely on pre-employment physicals and periodic screening as a means of denying employment or firing diseased workers.... The real issue was not to eliminate diseased workers from the workplace but to "eliminate the silica from the air, and prevent additional infections."
>
> Unlike industry spokespeople, who sought to reduce the problem of silicosis to an engineering and cost-benefit issue that balanced the health of the work force against the cost to industry, Frey based his argument upon the older public health reformers' analysis, which emphasized protecting communities rather than individuals. "Silicosis is an industrial disease which can be eliminated as effectively as typhoid germs can be removed from the city's drinking water." ... The cost of protecting the work force was a public obligation.... Just as modern city administrators had decided that the very high cost of purifying the water supply was justified by the improvements in health of the population, so too the cost of purifying the work environment was justified by the need to protect all workers from risk of contracting a preventable condition.[4]

The union perspective did not prevail. It would be another 40 years before the AFL's goal of an expanded federal responsibility for workplace regulation and standard-setting would be realized.

With the adoption of the **Occupational Safety and Health Act of 1970** (OSH Act),[5] the United States began to address the need to prevent, or minimize, workplace accidents and health hazards.

The OSH Act created a general duty on the part of every covered employer to maintain a work environment free from "recognized hazards causing or likely to cause death or serious physical harm to employees." It also created a federal agency, the Occupational Safety and Health Administration (OSHA), empowered to oversee safety and health standards, by enforcing the general duty clause and by writing and enforcing detailed health and safety standards for each industry.

In the more than three decades of its existence, OSHA's responsibility grew, as the number of workers expanded from 58 million in 3.5 million workplaces in 1970, to more than 111 million employed at 7.25 million workplaces in 2007. While the International Labor Union sets a benchmark of one labor inspector for every 10,000 workers, there were only 2,112 federal and state inspectors—or one for every 63,670 workers—in the United States in 2006.

Dr. Michael Silverstein, worked as the assistant director for industrial safety and health for the state of Washington for eight years. In 2007 Silverstein posted a draft paper to stimulate critical discussion about the future of workplace safety and health in the United States. He begins the paper by crediting the OSH Act as a "major step up the ladder of worker rights and public health protection," reducing overall injury and death rates since 1973. But he believes these data mask serious ongoing problems. In Silverstein's words, "Getting workers home safe and sound is not just a matter of statistics but one of fairness, justice and human rights."

---

4 David Rosner and Gerald Markowitz, *Deadly Dust: Silicosis and the Politics of Occupational Disease in Twentieth Century America* (Princeton U. Press, 1991).

5 29 U.S.C. Sections 651–678 (1970).

WORKING IN HARM'S WAY: GETTING HOME SAFE AND SOUND? OSHA AT THIRTY FIVE[6]

MICHAEL SILVERSTEIN

… Thirty five years after the Act, much is left undone. A worker still becomes injured or ill on the job every 2.5 seconds and these injuries and illnesses have disproportionate, unfair impact in especially high risk industries and among groups of disadvantaged workers.…

[O]verall national rates for workplace injuries and deaths have declined since 1973, due at least in part to activities set in motion by the OSH Act, but these improvements mask serious remaining problems that have been resistant to change. … [T]he rate of more severe cases (those resulting in days away from work or restricted work) has stayed almost flat.… The number of fatal work injuries among Hispanic workers, particularly those who were foreign born, has nearly doubled in less than fifteen years. This is partly because the numbers of immigrants in the workplace has been increasing, but also because Hispanic workers are concentrated in especially dangerous jobs and have work fatality rates greater than the national average.…

… These deaths and injuries are not random accidents. They are predictable and preventable. They target the most vulnerable and least privileged, the recent immigrants, day laborers, farmworkers and others who work under the worst conditions and are subjected to the highest risks:

[Silverstein notes high-risk employment faced by truck drivers, construction workers, nurses aides, and farmworkers. He also cites meat and poultry industry employees as having to contend not only with the risk of severe physical injury, but with employers who make it hard for them to collect workers' compensation, and who crush any efforts by a mainly immigrant labor force to organize into unions.]

It is unconscionable that in the most advanced economy in the world our modern offices, hospitals and factories operate side by side with sweatshops and industrial jungles that should exist only in novels about an earlier era.

Workers today are confronted with four types of risks on the job.

First, many dangers, such as falls from roofs or amputations from unguarded machinery, were widely recognized when the OSH Act was adopted in 1970 and should have been eliminated years ago. Simple means of correcting some of these hazards have actually been well understood for more than two thousand years, as Herodotus described the prevention of fatal trench collapses in his history of the Persian Wars. [cite omitted]

Second, today's workers face hazards present in 1970 but not fully appreciated by those who wrote the OSH Act, like the forceful exertions, repetitive movements and awkward postures that can cause the work related musculoskeletal disorders which account for more than 30% of all worker compensation claims and affect workers in virtually every industry and occupation. [cite omitted] Other examples include workplace violence and biohazards.

Third are genuinely new hazards that have entered the workplace since 1970 such as diacetyl and other food flavorings that cause bronchiolitis obliterans ("popcorn lung") [cite omitted] or modern metalworking fluids that cause hypersensitivity pneumonitis. [cite omitted]

---

6 Silverstein, at www. SKAPP.org.

Fourth, changes in the political, economic, and legal landscape of work since 1970 have brought new safety and health challenges. Globalized businesses, downsized manufacturing, increased outsourcing, reduced pension security, erosion of labor laws, an aging workforce, declining unionization, and growing numbers of recent immigrant workers have altered the nature and experience of work....

Coping with this vast array of workplace risks, even just those well recognized in 1970, would have required a full national commitment to fund OSHA adequately and to implement it vigorously. However, the effectiveness and legitimacy of the regulatory and enforcement system established by the OSH Act was challenged almost immediately. ... The business community was angered at the way OSHA's first inspectors began issuing thousands of citations for nonserious violations and labor representatives were equally angered by OSHA's failure to identify and cite serious ones. The situation worsened when OSHA turned hundreds of old and sometimes laughably trivial or obsolete consensus standards into enforceable rules, exposing the new agency to public ridicule.

... The agency's political problems were compounded by trivially small appropriations and an operational strategy of using its tiny staff to inspect one workplace at a time and to regulate one new hazard at a time....

Off to this bad start OSHA has never been out of the political spotlight and has never received the funding or achieved the impact Congress intended. Even OSHA's right wing critics have recognized OSHA's impotence. Writing for the CATO Institute, Kniesner and Leeth observed:

> OSHA inspectors frequently overlook dangerous working conditions, and even when they find serious health and safety violations, inspectors often cannot compel firms to eliminate the hazards discovered. To encourage timely compliance, administrators often slash assessed penalties, further reducing the already minor economic incentives for firms to observe health and safety standards. Firms realize that it is unlikely that they will be inspected ... and if they are inspected, firms can avoid paying severe fines by simply agreeing to abide by OSHA's regulations in the future ... OSHA is about 1/20th the size of the EPA. The federal government has six times more fish and game inspectors than workplace health and safety inspectors ...

OSHA has become essentially invisible and irrelevant to most employers.... Nothing has better illustrated the consequences of this than OSHA's astonishing inability or unwillingness to use its authority to protect thousands of public and private sector workers engaged in emergency response and recovery efforts after the 911 attack on the World Trade Center and the near destruction of New Orleans by Hurricane Katrina. Huge numbers of World Trade Center workers and community members are now showing evidence of preventable lung disease, paying the price for OSHA's decision to provide advice about respiratory protection but not to enforce its rules. The aftermath of 911 and Katrina revealed other stubborn problems: thousands of public employees not covered by the OSH Act; overlapping and ambiguous government jurisdictions; thousands of immigrant and temporary employees without clearly defined or stable employer-employee relationships; and the lack of basic rules for safety and health management programs, medical surveillance, exposure assessment or ergonomics....

[The OSHA model for command and control regulation] correctly presumes market imperfections so significant that government intervention is necessary for worker protection. It also correctly presumes that state governments by themselves without federal oversight cannot be counted on to provide the level and consistency of protection needed to ensure fairness and equity....

… OSHA rules have resulted in reduced exposures and illnesses, in some cases by stimulating significant changes in workplace organization and technology.… OSHA has given unions tools that enhance their ability to get the attention of a company or an entire industry and to thereby get more mileage out of their own representational and organizing functions. And the very adoption of the OSH Act created a new baseline of national expectations about the nature of work, evident by the entire subculture of professional and advocacy organizations, research centers, and training institutions that emerged and matured, along with a marketplace for safety and health products and materials.…

[But] the most effective tool provided by the OSH Act—enforcement—falls far short of what is needed. While there is evidence that injuries decline in workplaces that have been inspected by OSHA, there is little evidence that OSHA inspections have a rippling effect on injury prevention in other similar workplaces that have not been inspected.… The penalty structure in the OSH Act has also limited the agency's deterrent impact on employer behavior. The average penalty for a serious violation of the OSH Act (one involving substantial probability of death or serious physical harm) was less than $900 in 2005. Average penalties for willful violations have averaged $30,000 to $40,000 over the past few years.… In 2005 ten cases where a willful violation resulted in a worker death were referred by the U.S. Department of Labor to the Justice Department for possible criminal prosecution.… [A 1978] summary of regulatory effectiveness … still seems pertinent today:

> … *Employers at whom the sanctions are aimed—those who will correct violations only if it is economically profitable for them to do so—are not being affected. Thus the current sanctions antagonize employers who attempt to obey the law, while having little impact on those employers who will obey the law only if it is economically profitable. [cite omitted.]*

Second, there is little if any evidence, other than self serving anecdotes, that OSHA's consultation services and other voluntary programs, accounting for 28% of its budget in 2003, have had any measurable impact on workplace hazards, injuries or illnesses.

Third, … the system is designed such that resources will never … come close to being sufficient. The law relies on the threat of a government inspection to motivate employers to comply with rules. Yet, with eight million workplaces and 2000 federal and state inspectors able to conduct about 100,000 inspections a year, each workplace can expect an inspection once every 88 years.… Other statutory problems include: 8.5 million state and local public employees lack OSHA coverage; there are no mandatory deadlines for timely rulemaking; penalty levels are too low to command respect from most employers; individual workers who have been harmed by violations of the OSH Act have no private right of action in the courts; and OSHA inspectors do not have the right to shut down dangerous jobs.

Fourth, the OSH Act was written in an era when employment relationships were significantly different from those of today. In 1970 employees were significantly more likely than today to hold a long term job with a single, stable employer and to be represented by a labor union.… Today's employment landscape—characterized by transnational manufacturing and services, global outsourcing, contingent and temporary employment, and a significant shadow economy of underground, off the book business dealings—is increasingly resistant to the tools of the OSH Act and may require very different approaches.…

QUESTIONS

1. What special risks are faced by workers in the twenty-first century U.S. labor force, according to Silverstein?

2. What are the serious flaws in the OSH Act according to Silverstein?

3. What ethical issues are touched upon in Silverstein's report?

4. **Internet Assignment** Silverstein posted his paper on www.defendingscience.org, the Web site for Scientific Knowledge and Public Policy (SKAPP.) Dedicated to "transparent decision-making that draws on the best science to protect public health," SKAPP writers are expected to be careful to document their findings. (a) Find the complete draft of Silverstein's paper and read the footnotes that have been omitted from this excerpt. To what extent does he cite evidence to support his claims? (b) What other papers can you find on the SKAPP Web site that address the abuse/misuse of science in making public policy?

5. **Internet Assignment** From 2000 through 2007, under the Bush administration, OSHA issued the fewest significant health and safety standards in its history. It imposed only one major safety rule, involving electrical safety; the one important health standard—setting permissible exposure limits for hexavalent chromium—was ordered by a federal court, and has already been criticized as too weak by the plaintiff, Public Citizen. Proposed regulations were withdrawn and no action was taken on even those risks identified by the administration as most pressing: dust from silica and noise known to cause increasing numbers of construction workers to lose their hearing. Find out about Edwin G. Foulke, Jr., head of OSHA in 2007. What did he do before he took on the job of the nation's top health and safety administrator? What is his philosophy of government and government regulation? What do critics say about him?

6. As an alternative to a system that regulates one hazard at a time and sends government inspectors to one workplace at a time, Silverstein proposes a generic rule requiring employers to implement comprehensive safety and health programs to reduce injury and illness, and to obtain an annual written certification that their firm had been inspected by a third party for compliance with all OSHA requirements. What would be the advantages and disadvantages of this approach?

7. Should the OSH Act be amended to include protection for any of the following categories of workers: (a) public employees, (b) farmworkers, and (c) independent contractors? Why or why not?

When three workers at a construction site were killed at a gas line explosion, both OSHA and the Texas state health department investigated. The OSHA inspector found numerous violations. The most serious was a finding that Erik K. Ho, the owner of the building, had willfully violated his general duty to provide a safe workplace when he ordered a subcontractor to tap into an unmarked pipeline. On behalf of OSHA, Elaine Chao, secretary of labor—with overall responsibility for OSHA—issued 39 violations against Ho. She also issued violations against Houston Fruitland and Ho Ho Ho Express, two corporations closely tied to Ho.

Asked to enforce the citations, the Occupational Health and Safety Review Commission instead vacated the most serious. Chao appealed. Below, the appeals court explains why it will not overturn the Commission's rulings.

CHAO v. OCCUPATIONAL SAFETY AND HEALTH REVIEW COMMISSION

U. S. Court of Appeals, Fifth Circuit, 2005,

401 F.3d 355

DeMOSS, Circuit Judge. ✳

Background

... On October 27, 1997, Ho individually purchased a defunct hospital and medical office building in Houston to develop the property as residential housing. Ho knew there was asbestos onsite. He was also aware that any alteration to asbestos–containing materials was to be handled by personnel licensed and registered with the Texas Department of Health ("TDH"). Ho instead hired Manuel Escobedo and Corston Tate, whose work he had previously used, to do the renovations. Escobedo hired 11 Mexican nationals, who were illegal immigrants, to assist. Renovations, including the removal of asbestos, started in January 1998.

At most, the workers were occasionally given dust masks not suitable for protection against asbestos. They were not issued protective clothing. Ho also did not provide a respiratory protection program, conduct medical surveillance, conduct asbestos monitoring, implement adequate ventilation or debris removal, inform the workers of the presence and hazards of asbestos, or provide any training whatsoever. There is no dispute that Ho was aware of the worksite conditions; he visited almost every day.

On February 2, 1998, a city inspector visited the worksite. After observing the conditions, he issued a stop–work order citing the possibility of exposure to asbestos, requiring that city approval be given before work could resume. Ho then began negotiating with a licensed contractor, Alamo Environmental, to remove the asbestos....

However, during this period of negotiation, Ho had resumed work at the site under the same conditions, except that he directed all work be performed at night. The workers ate, and some lived, at the site. The workers had no potable water and only one portable toilet.... Ho continued to visit the worksite and was aware of these conditions.

Asbestos removal continued in this fashion until March 10, 1998. On March 11, 1998, as Ho had directed, daytime work resumed at the site. Ho had been informed that either the sprinkler system or fire hydrant valves had not been turned off and thus remained available for use. To wash out the building, Ho directed Tate to tap into an unmarked valve believed to be a water line. It turned out to be a gas line. An explosion later occurred when Tate started his truck; it injured Tate and two workers. On March 12, 1998, workers were summoned to Ho's office where they were given releases to sign, acknowledging receipt of $1000 as full payment for their work, and acknowledging receipt of $100 to release Ho from any claims that might arise from the explosion and fire. The releases were written in English, but an interpreter translated them for the workers.

After the explosion, TDH conducted an investigation. Samples of debris and the ambient air at the worksite showed levels of asbestos in excess of federal and state standards. The state notified Ho that the site remained unsafe and needed to be sealed by qualified personnel. Again, Ho used the same workers to install plywood over the windows and did not give them any protective equipment....

Piercing the Corporate Veil

[The secretary of labor challenges the Commissions' findings regarding the corporate entities, Ho Ho Ho Express and Houston Fruitland, Inc. The court begins by explaining the concept of "piercing the corporate veil."]

In the typical corporate veil piercing scenario, the corporate veil is pierced such that individual shareholders can be held liable for corporate acts. Here, the purpose of piercing the corporate veils of Ho Ho Ho Express, Inc. and Houston Fruitland, Inc. would be to hold the corporations liable for the acts of their individual shareholder, Ho. Therefore, this case presents a "reverse corporate veil piercing" situation. "This slight variation is of no consequence, however, because the end result under both views is the same—two separate entities merge into one for liability purposes." If alter ego is shown, courts reverse pierce the corporate veil to treat the individual and the corporation as "one and the same."

[In a precedent case involving a natural gas contract dispute, the Fifth Circuit] determined that an alter ego relationship for purposes of reverse veil piercing applies where "there is such unity between corporation and individual that the separateness of the corporation has ceased." Factors involved in this test for an alter ego relationship include:

> [T]he total dealings of the corporation and the individual, including the degree to which corporate formalities have been followed and corporate and individual property have been kept separately, the amount of financial interest, ownership and control the individual maintains over the corporation, and whether the corporation has been used for personal purposes.

[Next the appellate court considers the evidence in the record that led the Commission to rule that Houston Fruitland and Ho Ho Ho Express are not the alter egos of defendant Ho.]

… The Secretary's contention that Ho Ho Ho Express and Houston Fruitland were "nothing more than incorporated pocketbooks for Ho's personal use" is unfounded. Although Ho clearly involved some of the corporate entities' finances in his hospital project, the record evidence indicates that Ho as the individual in charge of this particular renovation project remained distinct from the [corporations] as ongoing, formalized fruit sale and delivery entities.

While there is evidence that Ho played a role in the corporate Ho Respondents' day-to-day operations, and Ho's personal assistant employed by Ho Ho Ho Express ran some errands for Ho concerning the renovation project, Houston Fruitland and Ho Ho Ho Express still maintained entirely separate corporate identities, tax identities, bank accounts, and legitimate business operations.… [T]he record evidence here indicates that the [corporations] had a limited financial stake in Ho's renovation project, not that they functioned as his alter egos on the renovation project.

Although Ho borrowed from the [corporations] for financing of the hospital project, an admittedly personal pursuit, the record evidence indicates distinct debit ledger entries and some repayment to the corporations by Ho.… Moreover, there is no evidence that the corporate entities were ever treated or confused as one and the same with the individual Ho or his personal dealings.…

We find substantial evidence in the record adequately supporting … the Commission's findings that Ho Ho Ho Express and Houston Fruitland were not alter egos of Ho to support reverse corporate piercing.

Willful Violation of the General Duty Clause

[Next, the court must decide whether the Commission properly overturned the secretary's finding that Ho willfully violated the OSH Act's general duty clause.]

OSH Act requires employers to free their workplaces of "recognized hazards that are causing or are likely to cause death or serious physical harm to … employees." The specific general duty citation here arose from the explosion of natural gas released by tapping an unmarked valve. A willful violation is one committed voluntarily, with either intentional disregard of, or plain indifference to, OSH Act requirements. . . . In contrast, "[t]he gravamen of a serious violation is the presence of a 'substantial probability' that a particular violation could result in death or serious physical harm." The employer's intent to violate an OSH Act standard is irrelevant to find a serious violation. . . .

Though Ho's pattern of illegal work practices may have been conscious, and his asbestos–related OSH Act violations found to be willful, this does not compel a finding of willfulness as to his specific instruction to open the unmarked valve. Therefore, because the Commission's legal determination as to Ho's lack of willfulness was neither arbitrary, capricious, nor an abuse of discretion, and accords with law, we accept its conclusion.

[HELD: Commission's decision is affirmed.]

EMILIO M. GARZA, Circuit Judge, dissenting: ☀

. . . Courts need to look beyond formalities and records to determine the true economic relationship between the entities. . . . In *Jon–T Chemicals*, the court dismissed the formality of recording paid expenses as loans because "whenever [one company] could not pay its bills, [the other company] did so by writing a check." The companies shared an accounting department and "funds were transferred between the different [companies'] accounts in order to cover deficiencies." That is precisely what happened here. The Ho Entities shared one bookkeeper who notified Ho when one account was deficient; Ho would then transfer the funds to cover the deficiency of the other company.

The evidence shows that Ho has complete control over the Ho Entities. Ho owns two-thirds of the stock and is president of both companies. The Ho Entities advanced the vast majority of Ho's personal investment of the property. In addition, the Ho Entities provided funds for the workers' wages and for supplies and equipment. Converting a hospital into residential units has nothing to do with the Ho Entities' business purposes of transportation and fruit sales. While the frequent transfers among the Ho Entities and Ho were documented as debts, there were no loan documents, no interest due, no schedule for repayment and no representation of debt repayment. Accordingly, I believe that substantial evidence supports a finding that the Ho Entities were Ho's alter egos. . . .

. . . Ho conceded that tapping into an unmarked pipe at a demolition site was a "recognized hazard." Instructing his employees to tap an unmarked pipe a "recognized hazard" evidences a plain indifference to the General Duty Clause. Even without the benefit of hindsight, it is self–evident that tapping an unmarked pipe is "likely to cause death or serious physical harm." Therefore, the Commission abused its discretion by finding Ho's violation of the General Duty Clause "serious" instead of "willful." Accordingly, I would vacate the Commission's order reducing the General Duty Clause violation to serious from willful.

For the above stated reasons, I respectfully dissent.

QUESTIONS

1. What is meant by "piercing the corporate veil?" On what basis did the majority decide that the corporate veil need not be pierced in this case? How does the dissent respond?

2. What is required for a "willful" violation of the OSH Act's general duty clause? For a "serious" violation? Why does the majority uphold the Commission's rule that the violation in this case was not willful? On what basis would the dissent have reversed the Commission's holding?

3. What difference does it make to the story of this case that the workers involved were illegal immigrants? Does it make any difference to the legal analysis? Do you think it should?

Corporate Criminal Liability

Employers have rarely been held criminally responsible for even the most egregious workplace injuries and deaths.

For most of its history, OSHA rarely invoked its legal authority to bring criminal actions. Convictions were relatively few, and penalties light. Of the 170,000 workplace deaths recorded between 1982 and 2002 (1,242 of which were found by OSHA to involve willful violations of law by employers), only 16 convictions involved jail time. Employers faced $106 million in civil OSHA fines and jail sentences totalling less than 30 years for all workplace deaths from 1982–2002; 20 years of those jail terms were attributable to a 1991 chicken-plant fire in North Carolina that killed 25 workers. In contrast, in 1991 alone, 72 persons were jailed for a total of 256 years for violating environmental protection laws.[7]

In the face of weak criminal enforcement at the federal level, some state prosecutors sought indictments under state criminal laws to address the most horrific situations. The first state prosecution, *People v. O'Neil* [8] was brought after a worker extracting silver from used x-ray film died of cyanide poisoning. The employees of that company, most of whom were non–English-speaking illegal immigrants, were deceived about the hazards of working with cyanide. They were working in an area with inadequate ventilation and were supplied with virtually none of the safety equipment required by law. Both the company and its owners were initially found guilty of murder, but the convictions were overturned on technical grounds, in 1990.

Relatively few employers have been convicted under any state criminal codes. The president, plant manager, and foreman of Chicago-Magnet were charged with aggravated battery when they exposed 42 employees to poisonous and stupefying substances in the workplace. But, after the longest trial in Illinois history, they were acquitted. In another widely publicized case, *People v. Pymm Thermometer*, a jury found the owners of a Brooklyn-based silver reclamation company guilty of assault with a deadly weapon for knowingly exposing workers to mercury. Their sentence: weekend jail for six months and a $10,000 fine.

The one exception is in California, where the state runs its own workplace safety program— as do almost half of the states. A special California-OSHA unit, mostly made up of former police officers, investigates every workplace death or serious injury and reports deliberate safety violations to local prosecutors. California has prosecuted more employers for safety violations than all of the other states combined and has a workplace death rate substantially lower than the rest of the nation.[9]

Beginning in 2005, OSHA and the EPA joined with a select group of Justice Department prosecutors to prosecute the most flagrant workplace safety violators under existing laws, including environmental laws and federal criminal statutes usually reserved for white-collar and racketeering cases. The government touted an early achievement of this new partnership: a guilty plea by Shell Oil to negligently endangering workers and committing environmental crimes. Shell was ordered to pay a $10 million fine and was sentenced to three years' probation. In the first trial emerging from the new strategy, a federal jury found four managers and Atlantic States Cast Iron Pipe Company—owned by McWane Inc., an Alabama-based conglomerate with an extensive record of safety and environmental violations—guilty of conspiring to evade workplace safety and environmental laws. The illegal actions included lying to

7 David Barstow, "When Workers Die," *The New York Times*, December 22, 2003.

8 550 N.E.2d 109 (Ill. App. Ct. 1990).

9 See David Barstow, "California Leads in Making Employer Pay for Job Deaths," *The New York Times*, December 23, 2003, p. A1.

regulators, tampering with evidence and silencing employees faced with dangerous working conditions. In 2006, the Department of Labor referred eleven enforcement cases to the Justice Department for criminal prosecution.

Safety Concerns in the Global Economy

As capital, labor, and data cross national boundaries with increasing ease, products may be designed in one country, built in another (with components from still others), and then marketed around the world. Few would quarrel with the International Covenant on Economic, Social and Cultural Rights—that everyone has a right to safe and healthy working conditions, to form and join trade unions, to take other appropriate steps to safeguard the right to a livelihood. Yet, as the next series of readings makes clear, there is little consensus as to how to ensure those rights.

Twenty-First Century Slavery

> *Fundamentally, there are only two ways of coordinating the economic activity of millions. One is central direction involving the use of coercion— the technique of the army and of the modern totalitarian state. The other is voluntary cooperation of individuals—the technique of the marketplace.*
>
> — MILTON FRIEDMAN (1962)

> *Sweatshop exploitation is modern globalized capitalism stripped bare.*
>
> — HTTP://WWW.NOSWEAT.ORG.UK (2004)

There are an estimated 27 millions slaves in the world today, more than ever before in human history. Kevin Bales, a scholar and activist trying to build a global coalition to end slavery, explains that this count does not include sweatshop workers or those who are just extremely poor, but "people who are controlled by violence, who cannot walk away." While this is a definition that would encompass slavery in the American pre-Civil War South, Bales notes the important difference between slavery then and now:

> *Historically, the investment of purchasing a slave gave incentive for the master to provide a minimum standard of care, to ensure the slave would be healthy enough to work and generate profit for the long term. Today, slaves are extremely cheap and abundant, and thus disposable. Today the interest is not in "owning" slaves, only in controlling them—through violence or the threat of. A slave is exploited for as long as he or she is profitable; then discarded.*

The lack of legal ownership, Bales has written, is a benefit to slaveholders today, "because they get total control without any responsibility for what they own."

In the following interview, Kevin Bales discusses modern slavery, and what can be done to end it. He begins by talking about why we are facing a situation where there are so many so-called "disposable people":

> *Vulnerability is the key here. When subsistence farmers are driven out of the countryside because they've been replaced by cash crop agribusiness, and they end up in cardboard shacks in shantytowns around developing world cities.... They don't have their temple or church, their extended family or the village network—all that gets lost.... [T]hey're economically vulnerable because they can't get work.... They're physically vulnerable because they can't protect themselves from people who have weapons, and they're legally vulnerable because the police won't enforce the law....*

SLAVERY: ALIVE AND THRIVING IN THE WORLD TODAY

Interview with Kevin Bales[10]

What Are the Most Typical Types of Modern Slavery?

Debt bondage is the most common kind of enslavement around the world, concentrating in South Asia, [most commonly] … "collateral" debt bondage: when you borrow money, you and all of your family … become collateral…. In India I've met families in their fourth generation of bondage—a great-grandfather borrowed $20 worth of rupees … and because the family and all their work is collateral against the debt, there's no way that you can get the money to pay it back….

In the developing world, particularly in small communities that are not necessarily literate, a person's word and reputation are extremely important to them. It means that there's a culture of honesty … and slaveholders will use that to trick people, to talk to them in a way that makes it sound like there's just a loan … and it's all fair…. [Even though they] … recognize the fact they're enslaved, they feel a responsibility to keep their word….

What Are Some Examples of Modern Slavery?

Thailand is an excellent example because it has gone through rapid changes and is highly integrated into the global economy. Here you have young women enslaved into brothels who clearly demonstrate the impact of the low cost of slaves. In world terms, they're pretty expensive—one of these women, 14 to 15 years old, costs $800 to $2,000. At that price, and because they are forced to have sex with ten to 15 people a day— what is really a kind of serial rape—they generate enormous profits, something like 850 percent profit a year for the people who procured them. But these girls … only last two, three or four years. They become HIV positive or a cocktail of sexually transmitted diseases, they are brutalized or their mental health diminishes to the point where they can't function anymore, or all of those things mixed together. So after three or four years, they are, in a sense, useless and are just thrown away….

It Seems so Far Removed, How Does Slavery Touch Our Own Lives?

… When you go to Wal-Mart, for example, the stuff you find there is really cheap, so cheap that if you think about it, you think how on earth could this be?

In Brazil, we know that people are enslaved making charcoal used by the steel industry, which is a major export from Brazil. We know that American companies are invested in Brazilian steel and in the land where forests are destroyed to make charcoal. American companies are invested in beef and timber from Brazil; and slaves are used to log timber and to prepare the land for the cattle and care for them and so forth. There's two, three, five—who knows how many—links in that chain, and it's hard for us to actually trace them.

There's a parallel here with multinational corporations that subcontract out to factories using sweatshop labor, which distances them from exploitation and shifts the blame.

Slavery is even further down the line than the factories. It occurs in very small units; you rarely—if ever—find a factory full of slaves. The factory may be a sweatshop, but the raw materials or bits coming into a factory may have come up from slave labor.

---

10 "Slavery: Alive and Thriving in the World Today" Interview with Kevin Bales by Rachel Cernansky from *Satya Magazine*, January 2003.

Can You Give a More Specific Example of How Slavery is Linked to Our Daily Lives?

Cocoa's an easy one—the Ivory Coast is the world's largest exporter of cocoa, and it flows directly into the U.S.… [We've] discovered horrific enslavement of young men, mostly economic migrants from Mali, who'd come down looking for work and had been forced into slavery on farms growing cocoa.…

Hasn't Legislation Related to that Been Passed by Congress?

This is extremely interesting. There was an amendment that would have required labeling of chocolate as slave-free; but it was withdrawn because it would have been impossible to determine—it's this problem again of tracing the product chains. It is currently impossible to determine precisely which cocoa is slave-free. Anybody who has that label wouldn't actually be able to prove that. It was also withdrawn because the chocolate industry agreed to work directly with human rights groups, anti-slavery organizations, and trade unions to eradicate the problem.… Now we finally have an industry that says, Yes, we take moral, economic, social responsibility for our product chain.…

[A]nti-Globalization Activists … Attack the Globalized Economy for Driving the Bottom Line at the Expense of Human Rights. Is Slavery the Epitome of that Type of Human Exploitation?

… Slavery is not essential to the global economy. The productive capacity of slaves, as I calculate it, is something like $13 billion a year in the global economy, which is nothing.… There's a positive side to globalization as well.… [T]he concepts of human rights are becoming globalized.… [W]hen I'm in rural India, where people are illiterate, and they blurt out in English, "Universal Declaration of Human Rights." They know what it means—they don't know precisely what those English words mean, but they think about human rights.

What Are International Bodies Doing?

There's a new UN convention on human trafficking giving every country that adopts it … an agreed definition of what they're working on and suggests ways for it to be effective. A lot of countries are rewriting their laws so that they match each other's.

How Receptive Has the U.S. Government Been? What Kind of Success Have You Seen?

… Administrations change, but … the people who actually manage the projects and programs, who work overseas, or work in the customs service to inspect for slave-made goods—to them it doesn't matter which political party's in power. They're trying very hard, they're doing very good things about slavery.

What Do You See as Hope for Change?

The number of slaves is very high, but the cost of actually helping people out of slavery is very low. Sending an activist around India, for example, to talk to people about alternatives to their bondage is very cheap. When the resources are there it can be done. It may sound crazy after talking about such huge numbers, but with sufficient mobilization this really could be the generation that brings slavery virtually to an end—for the first time in human history.…

QUESTIONS

1. What impact might global slavery have on the health and safety conditions of ordinary workers?

2. **Internet Assignment** According to Bales, there are some 150,000 to 200,000 slaves in the United States. Find out what kinds of work they are doing. Is anything being done to

abolish this trade? Start at http://www.iAbolish.org, the Web portal of the American Anti-Slavery Group.

3. **Internet Assignment** In 2007, the American Civil Liberties Union (ACLU) filed suit against Maj. Waleed Al Saleh, a Kuwaiti diplomat living in Virginia, and his wife for allegedly keeping domestic workers as slaves, and the Kuwaiti government for enabling the abuse. Varsha Sabhanani and Mahender Sabhanani, a couple who operate a worldwide perfume business were arrested in May 2007 and charged with keeping two Indonesian women as slaves in their luxurious Long Island home. Find out what happened in these suits.

4. **Internet Assignment** Elsewhere in this interview, Bales talks about the fair trade movement as a means of altering the demand component of the global economic equation, and of helping to eradicate modern slavery. What is the fair trade movement? How exactly might its activities impact slavery today?

5. In the mid-1990s villagers brought suit against the multinational energy giant, Unocal, for atrocities committed during the laying of a pipeline in Southeast Asia. There were allegations of forced land compensation and forced labor, with the Myanmar military threatening to kill those who would resist. There was testimony that one man was shot as he tried to escape the project, and in retaliation his wife and child were thrown into a fire; the baby died. Other witnesses described how villagers who would not work or who became too weak to work were summarily executed.

Plaintiffs brought suit under a federal statute, the Alien Tort Claims Act (ATCA), which allows non-citizens to sue in the U.S. courts for wrongs committed in violation of the law of nations. The defendants in most ATCA cases are foreign states or officials. For example, the statute was the basis of large—though uncollected—awards for human rights abuses committed by the former dictator of the Philippines Ferdinand Marcos and the Bosnian Serb leader Radovan Karadic. The case against Unocal, however, was an attempt to hold global business interests responsible for allowing human rights violations to occur. The claim was that the firm knowingly looked the other way as the military regime in Myanmar oversaw the construction of their pipeline, using rape and torture to intimidate the local villagers into working on the project.

As the *Unocal* case was ongoing, in 2004 the U.S. Supreme Court held that ATCA cases had to involve human rights violations that are "specific, universal and obligatory" under international law—crimes like genocide, enslavement, or torture. Both sides in the *Unocal* case described the Supreme Court ruling as boding well for them. Defense attorneys stated that, in the absence of any direct involvement in atrocities, their clients were not responsible under ATCA, whereas plaintiffs' lawyer Dan Stormer forecasted the case would move on to trial: "We have slavery, we have torture, we have crimes against humanity as part of our claim. They can pound the table all they want but we are going to get to argue this case." The outcome of the case against Unocal would be closely watched, partly because several other corporations were facing charges under ATCA, including ExxonMobil, Royal Dutch/Shell, and ChevronTexaco.

1. Is there any ethical theory we have looked at that you could use to justify the use of U.S. courts to punish corporations for indirect involvement in human rights abuses?

2. **Internet Assignment** Press reports in December 2004 indicated that Unocal had settled the suits in California state and federal courts. What can you find out about the settlement terms?

The International Battle Against Sweatshop Labor

During the 1990s, student and labor activists fueled an international movement to end sweatshop labor. Tactics ranged from lobbying efforts and boycotts to street demonstrations during meetings of such established free trade groups as the World Trade Organization (WTO) and the International Monetary Fund (IMF). American-based multinationals have responded to such pressure in a variety of ways.

Nike, for example, engaged in a public relations campaign to enhance its image. Some activists, however, were not convinced that genuine change was underway. Claiming that Nike's press releases and letters to newspaper editors misrepresented the actual working conditions under which its products were made, one activist sued Nike for unlawful and unfair business practices and false advertising.

KASKY v. NIKE
Court of Appeals, California, 2000
93 Cal. Rptr. 2d 854

SWAGER , Associate Justice. ☀

Nike, Inc., a marketer of athletic shoes and sports apparel, has grown into a large multinational enterprise through a marketing strategy centering on a favorable brand image, which is associated with a distinctive logo and the advertising slogan, "Just do it." To maintain this image, the company invests heavily in advertising and brand promotion, spending no less than $978,251,000 for the year ending May 31, 1997. The promotional activities include product sponsorship agreements with celebrity athletes, professional athletic teams, and numerous college athletic teams....

Like other major marketers of athletic shoes and sports apparel, Nike contracts for the manufacture of its products in countries with low labor costs. In Nike's case, the actual production facilities are owned by South Korean and Taiwanese companies that manufacture the products under contract with Nike. The bulk of Nike products are manufactured in China, Thailand, and Indonesia, though some components or products involving more complex technology are manufactured in South Korea or Taiwan. In 1995, a Korean company opened up a major new facility in Vietnam, giving that country also a significant share of Nike's production. The record indicates that between 300,000 and 500,000 workers are employed in Asian factories producing Nike products. The complaint alleges that the vast majority of these workers are women under the age of 24.

The company has sought to foster the appearance and reality of good working conditions in the Asian factories producing its products. All contractors are required to sign a Memorandum of Understanding that, in general, commits them to comply with local laws regarding minimum wage, overtime, child labor, holidays and vacations, insurance benefits, working conditions, and other similar matters and to maintain records documenting their compliance. To assure compliance, the company conducts spot audits of labor and environmental conditions by accounting firms. Early in 1997, Nike retained a consulting firm, co-chaired by Andrew Young, the former ambassador to the United Nations, to carry out an independent evaluation of the labor practices in Nike factories. After visits to 12 factories, Young issued a report that commented favorably on working conditions in the factories and found no evidence of widespread abuse or mistreatment of workers.

Nevertheless, Nike was beset in 1996 and 1997 with a series of reports on working conditions in its factories that contrasted sharply with the favorable view in the Young report. An accounting firm's spot audit of the large Vietnamese factory, which was leaked to the press by a disgruntled employee, reported widespread violations of local regulations and atmospheric pollution causing respiratory problems in 77 percent of the workers.... And the Hong Kong Christian Industrial Committee released an extensively documented study of several Chinese factories, including three used by Nike, which reported 11- to 12-hour work days, compulsory overtime, violation of minimum wage laws, exposure to dangerous levels of dust and toxic fumes, and employment of workers under the age of 16.

These reports put Nike under an unusual degree of public scrutiny as a company exemplifying a perceived social evil associated with economic globalization the exploitation of young female workers in poor countries....

Nike countered with a public relations campaign that defended the benefits of its Asian factories to host countries and sought to portray the company as being in the vanguard of responsible corporations seeking to maintain adequate labor standards in overseas facilities....

The complaint alleges that, in the course of this public relations campaign, Nike made a series of six misrepresentations regarding its labor practices including ... that Nike products are made in accordance with applicable laws and regulations governing health and safety conditions....

[These misrepresentations, plaintiff claimed, constituted unlawful and unfair business practices and false advertising. Next, the court addresses the defense raised by Nike: that its press releases are protected by the First Amendment to the Constitution.]

Since extending First Amendment protection to commercial speech ... the United States Supreme Court has "been careful to distinguish commercial speech from speech at the First Amendment's core.... A line of decisions ... has sanctioned restraints on commercial speech that is false, deceptive or misleading....

[T]he speech at issue here was intended to promote a favorable corporate image of the company so as to induce consumers to buy its products. A Nike executive expressed this business objective in a letter to the editor [of a newspaper]: "Consumers ... want to know they support companies with good products and practices.... During the shopping season, we encourage shoppers to remember that Nike is the industry's leader in improving factory conditions."

[W]e think that a public relations campaign focusing on corporate image, such as that at issue here, calls for a different analysis than that applying to product advertisement.

[T]he case at bar lies in familiar First Amendment territory—public dialogue on a matter of public concern. Though drafted in terms of commercial speech, the complaint in fact seeks judicial intervention in a public debate.

The "heart of the First Amendment's protection" lies in "the liberty to discuss publicly and truthfully all matters of public concern....

Nike exemplifies the perceived evils or benefits of labor practices associated with the processes of economic globalization.... Nike's strong corporate image and widespread consumer market places its labor practices in the context of a broader debate about the social implications of employing low-cost foreign labor for manufacturing functions once performed by domestic workers. We take judicial notice that this debate has given rise to urgent calls for action ranging from international labor standards to consumer boycotts. Information about the labor practices at Nike's overseas plants thus constitutes data relevant to a controversy of great public interest in our times.

Freedom of "expression on public issues" has always rested on the highest rung of the hierarchy of First Amendment values.... The constitutional safeguard ... "was fashioned to assure unfettered interchange of ideas for the bringing about of political and social changes desired by the people." And, it represents a "profound national commitment to the principle that debate on public issues should be uninhibited, robust, and wide-open.... "

It follows that "under the free speech guaranty the validity and truth of declarations in political disputes over issues of public interest must be resolved by the public and not by a judge." …

The fact that Nike has an economic motivation in defending its corporate image from such criticism does not alter the significance of the speech to the "listeners" the consumers or other members of the public concerned with labor practices attending the process of economic globalization.

[The court affirms the decision of the trial judge to dismiss the complaint against Nike].

QUESTIONS

1. The court refused to order Nike to cease its public relations campaign. Why?

2. The Supreme Court of California reversed this case. "Because the messages in question were directed by a commercial speaker to a commercial audience, and because they made representations of fact about the speaker's own business operations for purposes of promoting sales of its product," the majority found they were commercial speech, subject to California's ban on false advertising. Dissenters argued that the ruling would prohibit a business from speaking out on issues of public importance or from vigorously defending its own labor practices. *Kasky v. Nike, Inc.*, 119 Cal.Rptr. 2d 296 (2002). What arguments can you make to defend the decision of the lower court? Of the state's Supreme Court? Frame your argument in terms of ethical theory.

3. **Internet Assignment** After granting a right to appeal, the United States Supreme Court issued a one-sentence unsigned order declaring that *certiorari* had been "improvidently granted." In other words, the matter was left to the California courts, where Nike would have to defend itself against Kasky's claim that it was guilty of false advertisement.. Instead, in September 2003 the company agreed to pay $1.5 million to the Fair Labor Association to settle the case. In a joint statement, Nike and the FLA said the money would be used for worker education and to develop a global standard on corporate responsibility. Find out what progress has been made.

4. At the time of the settlement, Nike indicated that it would not disseminate its corporate responsibility report outside the company and would continue to limit its participation in public events and media engagements in California. Use ethical theory to defend Nike's decisions.

5. **Internet Assignment** In September 2005, toy and garment workers from Bangladesh, China, Indonesia, Nicaragua, and Swaziland brought a class-action suit against Wal-Mart in California. The plaintiffs claimed to be third-party beneficiaries to a contract between Wal-Mart Stores and its suppliers, the factories where the plaintiffs worked. All of Wal-Mart's foreign suppliers had signed Wal-Mart's Code of Conduct ("Standards for Suppliers Agreement"). The Code, and basic human rights were violated, the plaintiffs argued, when they were forced to endure sweatshop conditions detrimental to their health and safety. And, since Wal-Mart could have—but didn't—leverage its economic power to force better conditions for them, the company should be held accountable. The plaintiffs were joined by American union workers for competitors to Wal-Mart, who claimed they were harmed by Wal-Mart's failure to enforce its suppliers' promise to pay minimum and prevailing wages. (a) Find out what has happened to this suit, *Doe v. Wal-Mart Store*, filed by the International Labor Rights Fund (http://www.ILRF.org). (b) Has the ILRF brought any other suits to enforce safer and healthier working conditions around the globe?

6. **Internet Assignment** Nosweatapparel.com is a "virtual mall" where all the vendors sell goods made by union workers. American Apparel, a company that moved from Mexico to Los

Angeles in 2001, publicizes its sweat-free ethos by including photo essays of immigrant cutters and sewers at work in its catalog. Find out about current trends in the global movement against sweatshop labor.

Compensation for Workplace Injury and Illness

Under even the best of circumstances, workplace injuries and illnesses are not going to disappear entirely. Most often in the United States, those who suffer such harms must look to workers' compensation or similar statutory remedies. What happens, however, if the injured employee is someone whose presence in the United States has not been legally sanctioned? That is the issue to be resolved in the next case.

MADEIRA v. AFFORDABLE HOUSING FOUNDATION, INC.

United States Court of Appeals, Second Circuit, 2006

469 F.3d 219

RAGGI , Circuit Judge. ✳

… Plaintiff Jose Raimundo is a citizen of Brazil who illegally entered the United States in 1998. In Brazil, Madeira had worked in a factory earning approximately $175 per month; he had also labored briefly on his parents' farm without formal remuneration. In the United States, Madeira fared better, working consistently as a construction laborer, largely through the efforts of his brother, Paulo Miranda. As a supervisor for C & L, Miranda had authority to hire workers to perform that party's subcontracts. In the years prior to the accident here at issue, Madeira was earning approximately $15 per hour in the United States and working as many as 50 hours per week.

… Although Madeira was generally paid in cash for his work, he testified that he paid income taxes on his earnings by using a taxpayer identification number…. Madeira further stated that, sometime in 2000, he attempted to legitimize his work status by applying for a Social Security card and work permit but, at the time of trial in 2004, those applications had not yet been acted on.

On June 20, 2001, while working as a roofer for C & L, Madeira fell from the top of a building at a development site in Monroe, New York, sustaining serious injuries that required four surgeries and more than three months' hospitalization. At the time of trial, Madeira was still substantially disabled, particularly in walking.

Following his accident, Madeira … [sued] Affordable, the owner of the construction site, and Mountain, the development's general contractor, for their alleged failure to provide adequate safety equipment at the work site in violation of New York's "Scaffold Law."

… The jury proceeded to find both Affordable and Mountain liable … [and] awarded Madeira $638,671.63 in total compensatory damages, consisting of $92,651.63 in incurred expenses; $46,000 for past pain and suffering; $40,020 in past lost earnings; $230,000 for future pain and suffering (over the course of forty–two years); and $230,000 for future lost earnings (over the course of twenty–six years)…. Only the past and future lost earnings awards are at issue on this appeal. From the fact that the future lost earnings award represents far more than Madeira would likely have earned in Brazil in the specified twenty–six years, but considerably less than he could have earned in the United States over the same time, one can reasonably infer that the jury concluded that, but for his injury, Madeira would have remained and worked in the United States, but only for a limited period....

In reviewing the joint challenge raised by Affordable, Mountain, and Silva to the damages awarded Madeira ... we note at the outset that no party here disputes the fact of Madeira's injury ... or Madeira's right to be compensated for incurred expenses and past and future pain and suffering. Instead, Affordable, Mountain, and Silva dispute only Madeira's recovery of lost earnings.

... Appellants submit that, if an injured undocumented worker can recover any lost earnings, it is only at the rates he could have earned in his native country....

It is well established that the states enjoy "broad authority under their police powers to regulate ... employment relationship[s] to protect workers within the State." ... This includes "the power to enact 'laws affecting occupational health and safety.'" ... Pursuant to this power, New York, like many states, has enacted various laws to compensate workers who sustain workplace injuries.

Most obviously, New York's Workers' Compensation Law requires employers to "pay or provide compensation [to employees] for their disability or death from injury arising out of and in the course of the employment without regard to fault as a cause of the injury." ... This "statute was designed to provide a swift and sure source of benefits to the injured employee." ... "The price for these secure benefits is the [employee's] loss of the common–law tort action [against his employer] in which greater benefits might be obtained."

New York does not, however, rely only on workers' compensation awards to promote workplace safety and compensate injury. Mindful of the particular dangers of construction work, the state has long imposed absolute liability for personal injury on those site owners and general contractors who fail to provide adequate safety equipment to all persons working at construction sites.... This liability applies regardless of the fact that the injured worker may be in the direct employ of a party other than the defendant contractor or owner. As the New York Court of Appeals recently explained, [N.Y. Labor Law] seeks to place "ultimate responsibility for safety practices at building construction sites where such responsibility actually belongs, on the owner and general contractor, instead of on workers, who are scarcely in a position to protect themselves from accident. ... "

New York law not only holds site owners and general contractors absolutely liable for personal injuries resulting from a violation of [its Labor Law]; it specifically extends the protections of that law to injured undocumented workers.

[The courts have created a legal rule known as **federal preemption**, based on the Supremacy Clause of the U.S. Constitution ("The Laws of the United States ... shall be the supreme Law of the Land."). Under this legal doctrine, Congress can "preempt" an area of law by specifically indicating that states may not adopt their own legislation. Where Congress has not specifically deprived the states of power to act, however, the courts must determine whether or not state laws are "preempted." Here, defendants argue that the federal immigration law preempts New York state law allowing undocumented workers injured in construction accidents to recover compensatory damages for lost United States earnings. The court, however, disagrees]

The federal government exercises supreme power in the field of foreign affairs, including "immigration, naturalization and deportation." ...

[The Immigration Reform Control Act of 1986, or IRCA] makes it unlawful for employers knowingly to hire unauthorized aliens. To ensure against such hiring, IRCA mandates employer verification of the legal status of persons hired. Employers who fail to check their workers' immigration status or who fail to keep eligibility records face civil fines.

Employers who engage in a pattern or practice of knowingly employing undocumented aliens are subject to criminal penalties.

… Not until IRCA was itself amended in 1990 did Congress provide for penalties and sanctions to be imposed directly on undocumented workers who sought employment in the United States…. Even then, however, Congress made IRCA's new sanctions applicable only to aliens who knowingly or recklessly used false documents to obtain employment. It did not otherwise prohibit undocumented aliens from seeking or maintaining employment.

… Congress can convey its clear and manifest intent to preempt the exercise of state police power in three ways. First, Congress may explicitly state that it intends to preempt a state law…. Second, even absent any such explicit statement, Congress's preemptive intent may be implied "where the scheme of federal regulation is sufficiently comprehensive to make reasonable the inference that Congress 'left no room' for supplementary state regulation," in short, where Congress has manifested an intent for federal law to occupy the field…. Finally, Congress's preemptive intent may be implied from the fact that state law so conflicts with federal law that … "compliance with both federal and state regulations is a physical impossibility," …

… It is not physically impossible to comply with both IRCA and New York labor law, and appellants have failed convincingly to demonstrate that New York law, as applied in this case, stands as a definite and positive obstacle to the accomplishment and execution of the full purposes and objectives of Congress. Accordingly, we reject appellants' claim of conflict preemption as without merit and uphold the damages awarded at the first phase of trial.

QUESTIONS

1. Under what law did Madeira seek damages? On what basis did the company object? What reasons does the Court give for allowing the plaintiff to claim damages despite his status as an undocumented immigrant?

2. In a concurring opinion, Chief Judge Walker suggested that juries might better calculate lost future wages based on the likelihood that an illegal alien would obtain authorization to work, rather than the likelihood that she would evade immigration enforcement agencies. What difference would that make?

Workers' Compensation

Although Madiera's suit was based on a New York labor law that specifically protects construction workers, most often workplace injuries are covered by generally applicable workers' compensation statutes. Workers' compensation schemes were adopted in the United States during the period 1911–1925, first in the more industrialized states and gradually throughout the nation. Effective in ameliorating some of the conflict between management and employees over the social and economic costs of accidental injuries, the details varied from state to state. In general, however, they were designed to provide a limited, "no-fault" recovery.

Firms contribute to a fund that is used to pay benefits to employees accidentally injured in the workplace. Instead of suing, an employee's legal task is simplified; she need only file a claim indicating that she was hurt in the course of her employment; she need not prove the company was negligent, nor can the company raise any of the traditional defenses to negligence to defeat the claim.

Employers are willing to accept this approach because there is a trade-off: if workers' compensation covers an injury, the employee cannot choose to bring a negligence suit, hoping a jury will award large damages. This is the **exclusivity rule**, so-called because the employee's only—or "exclusive"—remedy lies with workers' compensation. Payments are set by a formula that generally provides less than the actual wages lost, and no provision is made for the kind of award that could reach high numbers in a tort suit—pain and suffering, loss of consortium, or punitive damages.

Today, workers' compensation is widely criticized as anachronistic and unworkable. Besides the claim that the exclusivity rule is unfair where harm is intentional, there are other contentious issues: whether an injury occurred in the "course of employment;" whether a work-related disability is whole or partial, temporary or permanent; and whether an employer should pay for items not covered by workers' compensation statutes, such as property damage or mental anguish in the absence of physical harm. Whenever these issues arise, there is a chance that one party will insist on judicial resolution. In some states, workers' compensation cases languish in the courts for as many as 10 years. And, critics point out, because most disability, health, and life insurance policies offer far more extensive coverage than the limited amounts available under workers' compensation, many firms are required to carry liability insurance to cover acts of negligence, forcing them to pay separate premiums for duplicative policies that may not even provide employees with the intended coverage

Exporting Hazards

In the final reading in this chapter we consider the migration of technologies, rather than people, from the developed world to the developing world. In it, Henry Shue provides a framework for analyzing the ethics of exporting old, unsafe technology to developing nations.

EXPORTING HAZARDS

HENRY SHUE[11]

[A] general statement of the liberal no-harm principle is, "It is wrong to inflict avoidable harm upon other people, and it ought often to be prohibited by law." While harming oneself may sometimes be immoral, it is harming others that ought generally to be illegal....

No one may hurt or endanger others, except in cases of genuine necessity, in the course of justified warfare, in punishment for heinous crime, or in other quite special circumstances. Even the most one-sided advocates of freedom have rarely advocated the freedom to injure and danger....

[Shue discusses the argument that the general no-harm principle does not apply where the costs of exporting old, unsafe technology is overbalanced by the benefit to foreign workers. He distinguishes mere costs from true "harms," which he finds unacceptable.]

Yes, it is granted, there are costs to the foreign workers in the form of new dangers to health and safety, but there are also new benefits that are, so to speak, part of the same package. And—this is the point—although the costs to the workers are undeniably real ... the benefits are real too and they are greater than the costs.... The worker might be safer sitting at home, but he or she might also be unemployed....

[A cost, according to Shue, is a true harm when it involves all six of the following factors:]

---

11   Source: "Exporting Hazards," by Henry Shue, is reprinted from *Boundaries: National Autonomy & Its Limits*, P. Brown and H. Shue, eds. (New Jersey: Rowan & Littlefield, 1981).

The first factor is that the damage done is physical: it is life, limb and vitality that are at stake, not, for example, reputation or life style only, but the adequate, continued functioning of parts of one's body....

Second, the potential damage is not simply physical; it is serious, possibly fatal.... The bodily threat is to vital organs. Some of the malignancies are still untreatable and certainly fatal.

Third, besides being serious physical damage, the damage that is risked is irreversible. It does not "clear up," and damaged portions do not grow back....

[Fourth], the potential physical damage to the workers is undetectable for the victim without a level of medical care to which the workers have no access and [fifth] is unpredictable for the victim, even probabilistically, without a level of knowledge to which the workers have no access....

[Sixth,] the undetectability and unpredictability are avoidable at the choice of the firm's management.... This double point is simple but quite significant: people poor enough to work readily in the conditions we are considering will not have enough money—even if doctors are available, which is unlikely given the low effective demand—to afford routine medical examinations.... So "early detection by a doctor is out of the question.... This is what I mean by saying the damage is undetectable for the victim: it is, for the person who has undergone it, discoverable only when it is so serious as to interfere with normal overall functioning, if not to threaten life. It is readily detectable by a physician with standard X-ray equipment. This is why the damage seems to be avoidably undetectable....

Even people who have never before seen or heard about mining ... do not need to be told that shafts sometimes collapse and so might this one.... But they would not—and generations of miners did not—realize that there is such a thing as "black lung" and that they might well be developing it.... This fifth factor is that potential victims do not know, and cannot figure out for themselves, how high the risk is, although their employers know the probabilities and keep them quiet. Thus, once again, we appear to have avoidable unpredictability....

[Finally, Shue addresses the argument that, even if harm is being inflicted in a manner that ought to be stopped, it cannot be the responsibility of individual firms acting alone to stop it: This would amount to a form of forced heroics or martyrdom. Again, Shue finds this position unpersuasive.]

It may be also be suggested that firms are not in the business of protecting the interests of their workers, except when this is a means to their own goals ... [and that] if the government of a poor country wants the citizens of the country to enjoy safer workplaces, the government ought to impose uniform standards upon all firms, instead of expecting isolated firms to raise their own costs while their competitors are allowed to undercut them by retaining the cheaper, less safe technology....

[B]ut no institution, including the corporation, has a general license to inflict harm, even if the infliction of harm holds down production costs. In order to maintain otherwise one must reject the traditional liberal no-harm principle. Protecting people against harm is another matter.... What the corporation is being asked to do is simply not to inflict harm: not to prefer to a safer process a manufacturing process that harms a higher percentage of the people subjected to it than other readily available processes do.

Second, the national governments of poor countries that try to protect their workers against such harms face precisely the same problem that the firms invoke—and the governments face it because of the reasoning that the firms use. They first complain that they cannot be expected to go it alone (by unilaterally introducing more expensive, safer processes) because this would put them at a competitive disadvantage. But governments of poor countries that compete for foreign investment face an exactly analogous choice....

[In the final section of this piece, Shue discusses the allocation of responsibility for preventing harms.]

Whom does this leave to defend the victims of the harm who at present cannot defend themselves? It leaves us, fellow American consumers. Why us, or, to be precise, why me?

To some degree the question answers itself. Why should I defend defenseless human beings? Because they are human beings and they are defenseless....

But there are additional ... reasons. The main reason why one particular Samaritan must decide whether to do "good" is no better a reason than that this Samaritan happened to come along this road at this time, when (a) the victim was already in the ditch and (b) the previous travelers had already passed by on the other side of the road. To this Samaritan's "why me?" there is no cosmic explanation, and there is no better answer than: "You are here and therefore in a position to help this victim—is there a stronger claim upon you now?"

The firm that has retained control ... of the harmful process [that] has inflicted the wound, and the victim's own government has usually passed by on the other side of the road. Whoever is next in a position to assist the victim has some obligation to do so, irrespective of whether he or she was previously involved, unless some stronger obligation overrides. A previous involvement with the case is not required. Call this responsibility through ability—ability to make a positive difference.

We have been considering a case in which products consumed by U.S. purchasers and formerly made by U.S. workers are now made by Mexican workers as the result of a U.S.-based firm's decision to continue to use a less safe process to which U.S. workers cannot legally be subjected. United States consumers are hardly Samaritans who just happen to be passing by an asbestos factory on the other side of the border. We pay lower prices, suffer less inflation, etc., because the health costs of the retention of the less safe technology are now borne by the Mexican workers and Mexican society. It is true, that most of us did not ask to have this arrangement made. But once we understand it, we are no longer unwilling (because unknowing) beneficiaries. We now must choose whether to continue to accept these benefits on these terms. In such situations, knowledge is not only power but also responsibility, because it places us in a position to act. Call this responsibility through complicity—complicity by continuing acceptance of benefits.

QUESTIONS

1. According to Shue, what are the six indicators that a "cost" is actually a "harm" where use of foreign labor is concerned? What does he mean by describing a harm as "unavoidably undetectable"?

2. What does Shue mean when he writes that poor countries face an "analogous choice" as they compete for foreign investment?

3. Shue mentions (a) responsibility through ability and (b) responsibility through complicity. Consider the *Unocal* case. Did the company possess either form of responsibility in Myanmar? What could it have done that would be in line with the "no-harm principle?"

4. Who do you think bears responsibility for the maintenance of safe working conditions in American-owned firms located in foreign countries: the workers themselves? The corporate owners or managers? The foreign government? The U.S. government? An international safety and health organization? The individual U.S. consumer?

5. What do you think Shue would say about the actions of the EPA and other officials during the clean up of the WTC?

CHAPTER **PROBLEMS**

1. Mining is one of the most dangerous industries in the world. During 2006 in the United States alone, 45 coal miners died on the job. The most widely publicized deaths came from a January 2006 explosion in the Sago Mine in West Virginia, where a delayed rescue effort killed twelve men and severely injured the lone survivor. Three weeks later a conveyer belt fire in the Aracoma Alma Mine—also in West Virginia—killed two others. In the decade preceding these disasters, the national budget for Mine Safety and Health Administration had been cut by $2.8 million, leading to the loss of 183 staff members.

   The Sago Mine disaster was attributed to a combination of natural and man-made causes: a lightning strike touched off the methane blast, mine operators did not monitor methane levels inside the sealed section of the mine, and seals used to close off that inactive section were not strong enough to withstand the blast. Searchers did not reach the team trapped inside the mine for 40 hours.

   Investigators into the deaths at the Aracoma Alma mine concluded that a previous fire had not been reported, a fire alarm did not work, a critical wall was missing, a waterline had no water in it, and an automatic fire sprinkler was missing. The deaths may have been caused, in part, by difficulty donning breathing devices. After the disaster, the Bush administration reinstated a Clinton-era proposed safety standard for breathing devices that the Bush administration had withdrawn in 2001.

   Federal investigators missed obvious problems before both accidents.

   Internet Assignment Find out what actions were taken against the owners of the Sago Mine and International Coal Group, the owner of the Aracoma Alma Mine. Have any lawsuits been filed? What has West Virginia done to make mining safer? The federal government?

2. How much discretion should government agencies have to not make rules? Consider the following: In 1989, the Mine Safety and Health Administration (MSHA) proposed a comprehensive rule that would establish lists of hazardous substances: Permissible Exposure Limits (PELs) for more than 600 chemical substances that might be present in a mine, 165 of which would have been regulated for the first time. While one phase of the rule was adopted after public hearings and comments in 1994, the MSHA withdrew the remainder of its rule in September 2002. Its primary reason was the "result of changes in agency priorities." The United Mine Workers union challenged the withdrawal of the proposed Air Quality Rule as arbitrary and capricious.

   Internet Assignment Find out what happened in *International Union, United Mine Workers of America v. United States Department of Labor*, 358 F. 3d 40 (D.C.Cir. 2004).

3. Homicide is the leading cause of workplace fatalities in five states, the nation's capitol, and New York City. Street-front shops in high-crime areas, convenience stores, and taxicabs are particularly high-risk sites. Across the nation in 2005 564 homicides occurred when the victims were at work. (a) What obligation, if any, should an employer have to protect employees from intentional assaults by other employees? (b) Should workers' compensation laws cover workplace assault and battery?

   In recent years, OSHA has made workplace violence a major priority.

   Internet Assignment In 1996, OSHA published guidelines for workplace violence prevention at night retail establishments. What has OSHA done since then? In Philadelphia in 2007, a group of industrial companies installed high-resolution cameras that feed video to the local police to help catch muggers. Other companies use internal security. What are the ethical issues that arise with such surveillance? What other steps have been taken by businesses?

4. In what some have called the "feminization of migration," increasing proportions—probably close to half—of the world's 120 million legal and illegal migrants are believed to be women, who overwhelmingly take up work as maids, domestics, and nannies.

> *Imagine you are locked away in a strange home. You do not speak your captor's language. On the rare occasions when you are escorted off the premises, you are forbidden to speak to anyone. You are often fed the leftover food of the children you are required to watch while completing your around-the-clock household duties. You have never been paid for your labors, and the woman of the house physically abuses you. While the scenario seems to hark back to an earlier time in U.S. history, it describes Noreena Nesa's recent working conditions in the Washington, D.C. area. Tucked behind the manicured lawns and closed doors of our wealthiest residents live some of the most vulnerable people in the United States: abused migrant domestic workers, who are sometimes the victims of slavery and human trafficking.*
>
> — Joy M. Zarembka, "America's Dirty Work: Migrant Maids and Modern-Day Slavery"[12]

The extremes—slavery and human trafficking—are criminal offenses that can be prosecuted and punished. (The Thirteenth Amendment to the U.S. Constitution bans slavery and involuntary servitude.) But more common abuses—long hours, inadequate pay, unsafe conditions in the home itself—are difficult to police since domestic servants are not covered by most American labor laws. Should they be?

5. What would be the costs/benefits of each of the following proposals: (a) Permitting workers whose employers have endangered them to sue for violating the OSH Act; (b) Creating labor/management safety and health committees to allow workers on the shop floor to participate in finding and fixing hazards, with authority to shut down dangerous operations; (c) Making business licenses contingent on some measure of safety and health performance, such as achieving a specified level or reduction in workplace injury rates?

6. In July 2006, immigration officials from the Department of Homeland Security ran a sting operation in which they posed as OSHA officials. When construction workers showed up at a "mandatory OSHA meeting" at the Seymour Johnson Air Force Base in North Carolina, the immigration officers arrested 48 workers and processed them for deportation. Is there anything unethical about using safety and health programs as a ruse to deport undocumented immigrant workers?

7. Flammable liquids overflowed at BP's Texas City oil refinery in 2005, creating a cloud of vapor that ignited, killing 15 workers and injuring 170. This was not the only fatal accident at BP during the last 30 years, yet OSHA had made only one full safety-management inspection at the refinery, in 1998. (Nationally, OSHA had only enough resources to do nine such inspections in targeted industries between 1995–2005.) However, a U.S. Chemical Safety and Hazard Investigation Board report, headed by former Secretary of State James A. Baker, put most of the blame for the blast on the company. Cost cutting, weak leadership, and a "decentralized management system and entrepreneurial culture" which left safety processes to the discretion of managers all contributed. Overworked employees did not report accidents and safety concerns for fear of repercussions. Internal company audits were more concerned about compliance with the law than ensuring safety. Which of these problems can be changed by voluntary actions on the part of the

12 *Global Woman: Nannies, Maids, and Sex Workers in the New Economy*, Barbara Ehrenreich and Arlie Russell Hochschild, eds. (NY: Henry Holt, 2002).

corporation? Do any require changes in the law or allocation of tax revenues? How would a socially responsible corporation respond to this report?

8. Is collective bargaining by unions a better way to improve workplace safety and health than pervasive government regulation? Law professor Thomas Kohler thinks so. Despite the pervasiveness of anti-union attitudes and low union membership, Kohler argues we need unions in a time when wage and earnings distribution has become increasingly unequal and the middle class has shrunk. He writes:

> Along with these developments has come a significant loosening of the employment bond. So-called contingent employment arrangements—part-time, temporary and contract arrangements—are on the rise, and many analysts expect the number of part-time employees to double in the next few years. These "just-in-time" employees typically have at best highly restricted claims to pension, health and other benefits incident to employment....
> [He looks, as well, at developments on the international level:]
> ... [T]he remarkable transformation of what used to be called the Easternbloc was spearheaded by an independent trade-union movement, which improbably survived despite the forces arrayed against it. Nor were the Poles left to go it alone. At a time when our own government took a wait-and-see attitude, the AFL-CIO and other unaffiliated American unions supported Solidarity from the first with funds, equipment and expertise. American unions also lobbied Western governments on Solidarity's behalf, and worked to keep the Polish situation before the public's eye.... There is also a pronounced tendency today to overlook, or to be absolutely unaware of, the domestic contributions made by the union movement. The support of unions, for example, was crucial to the passage of the Civil Rights Act of 1964. Unions also have been in the forefront of efforts to improve workplace safety and public health and to ensure pay equality for the sexes....

Kohler speculates that unions might be more valued if people better understood the importance of collective bargaining. It is, he argues, a system of "private-law making." This is important because:

> Individuals and societies alike become and remain self-governing only by repeatedly and regularly engaging in acts of self-government. It is the habit that sustains the condition.... [I]t is through their involvement in the collective bargaining process that average citizens can take part in deciding the law that most directly determines the details of their daily lives.[13]

Internet Assignment (a) Find the most recent annual report, *Death on the Job: The Toll of Neglect*, posted each April on the AFL-CIO's Web site . What do you learn about the current status of occupational health and safety in your state? (b) Find out what other unions are doing today to support safe and healthy workplaces in the United States and abroad.

9. A 2005 survey of day laborers found more than 117,600 people typically gather at more than 500 hiring sites, most looking for jobs in construction, landscaping, and home repairs. The workers are mostly undocumented—primarily from Latina—frequently underpaid, and often subject to dangerous working conditions. (According to the study, 73 percent were placed in hazardous working conditions: digging ditches, working with chemicals, or on roofs or scaffolding, and 20 percent had suffered injuries requiring medical attention during the previous year.[14] Is there anything wrong with offering day labor

---

13 Thomas C. Kohler, "Civic Virtue at Work: Unions as Seedbeds of the Civic Virtues," 36 *B.C. L. Rev.* 279 (1995).

14 Steven Greenhouse, "Broad Survey of Day Laborers Finds High Level of Injuries and Pay Violations," *The New York Times*, January 22, 2006, p. 20.

to poor people? To immigrants? To undocumented immigrants? If so, how should such work get done?

10. **Internet Assignment** Ergonomic injuries are one of the most prevalent occupational hazards. In 2005, musculoskeletal disorders accounted for nearly one-third of all workplace injuries. A general ergonomics standard issued by OSHA after almost a decade of litigation was abandoned by the Bush administration in 2003, with the promise of a more comprehensive approach. Find out the current status of ergonomics injuries and efforts to prevent them.

CHAPTER **PROJECT**

Red Gold

Gerry Mullen, CEO of Red Lobster restaurants, looked up from his computer screen, feeling a bad headache coming on. In the top executive position for just two years, Mullen had been adjusting to the pace and the workload fairly well, but what he had just read made him feel like this was his first day on the job.

It was an e-mail from Red Lobster's vice president for public relations, Terry Modotti. One of Modotti's main responsibilities was to continually check the media for anything that mentioned the company—anything at all. On constant alert, Modotti and her team sifted through the good, the bad, and the ugly—but especially the ugly. You could never be too quick when it came to responding to negative media exposure. That was why, Modotti had written in her e-mail, Gerry should read the attached file as soon as possible. Evidently the low price of the delicious lobster that is the star feature of a Red Lobster menu came with a very high price tag—in human and environmental terms. Here is a summary of what Gerry read:

* * * * *

La Mosquitia, known as the Mosquito Coast, is on the Caribbean side of Honduras and Nicaragua. Its tropical climate supports some of the richest biodiversity on the planet. But it is also a place of tremendous suffering. Most of the young men of this area are being killed and maimed to make lobster available at cheap prices to consumers in the United States.

The 50,000 people of the Mosquito Coast, descended from native tribes and escaped African slaves, are extremely poor, illiterate, and have few options for economic survival. They can get involved in drug smuggling, prostitution—or they can dive for lobster. Ninety percent of the income earned in this region comes from lobster diving, and it is the Miskito men who do it. They call themselves "buzos" or "divers." They deal with the middlemen, the sacabuzos (meaning "fetch a diver,") men in clean white shirts with clipboards who give them $50 advances and sign them up for two- to three-week stints on the lobster boats.

Lobster fishing, a $50 million industry on the Mosquito Coast, has changed radically over the last 30 years. It was once possible to wade out a few feet and simply reach down into the clear blue-green water to catch lobster; but since the 1990s lobster have been over-harvested and are seriously depleted. These days, strapped into antiquated scuba tanks and breathing through clogged regulators, the buzos must dive up to 130 feet for lobster. Every year, they must go out further and stay down longer. The work is especially dangerous because there are no medical or decompression facilities on the boats, and no equipment to assist the divers as they make their way back to the surface. As a result, buzos commonly develop decompression sickness, known as the bends.[15] This is an excruciatingly painful condition that begins with paralysis and ends in slow death. Men who are stricken while the boat is still at sea are often simply left below deck to suffer, untreated. In a form of mercy killing, fellow divers may even vote to throw a stricken diver overboard if he should develop the illness in the early days of a cruise. Rarely does a boat return without someone dead or severely paralyzed, and without the rest of its crew suffering with some less severe form of paralysis. The problem is now an epidemic. According to a World Bank report, "close to 100% of divers show symptoms of neurological damage—presumably due to inadequate decompression."

Men in a typical Mosquito Coast village can only shake hands weakly. Most limp. Almost everyone has lost a brother, an uncle, a husband to the bends. In a location with no modern medical infrastructure, those who have been afflicted have nowhere to go for rehab. They don't even have wheelchairs. Stricken divers lie on straw mats or blankets on the floors of their huts, waiting to die, easily becoming victims of urinary tract infections, skin ailments or cuts, and gangrene. But young buzos continue to sign up, dive, and come home to die. One factor may be a strong tradition of "machismo." Miskitos have a reputation for stubbornness, for taking bravery to extremes—and are proud of it. Risky dives are a rite of passage for young buzos, who might boast, for example, of surfacing from 150 feet with a pierced ear drum. Too, for as long as he can survive it, a skilled buzo can make a decent living on the boats. A 100-lb. box of lobster sells for $10 to $12 wholesale. After the sacabuzos, boat captains, and fish processors take their cuts off the top, the buzo will get what remains—about $2 per pound. This can amount to $300 per two-week shift.

A quick comparison to the standards for North American recreational divers, who are trained and equipped to avoid decompression sickness: Dives below 60 feet are considered deep dives, and must be limited. Four to five dives a day at this depth would be pushing it. The buzos on the Mosquito Coast will typically go deeper than 100 feet an average of 13 times a day, every day for two or three weeks.

Boat captains have a reputation for cruelty, fighting in court to avoid making any payments to injured buzos or to the families of those who die. One buzo, after four years of diving, became seriously afflicted with the bends. He contacted his boat owner to ask for help. The captain swore at him and hung up.

Higher up in the lobster industry are the food processors, those companies that receive and package lobster for export. Their owners are millionaires. One owner—Albert Jackson—used his fortune to build a sport-dive resort called Fantasy Island, complete with a local dwarf.

The sad situation on the Mosquito Coast has not gone unnoticed. A non-profit organization, Sub Ocean Safety or SOS, was founded by an individual from North America, Bob Izdepski. A commercial diver with some 30 years' experience, Izdepski became aware of the Mosquito Coast situation and was appalled:

> I had my epiphany. I understood that I was a diver, I made my living as a diver, that diving was my life. And what was going on in La Miskitia was the moral Armageddon of the diving world, a slow-motion underwater genocide. I stood on the beach and felt the blinding light of human obligation.

Funding SOS himself, Izdepski decided to help the divers by installing decompression chambers—the only ones on the Mosquito Coast—12 foot long metal capsules where underwater conditions can be simulated, allowing divers to be gradually "brought to the surface." The trouble is, they should be used within 5 minutes of surfacing, and the buzos don't reach these

---

15 "Due to increased pressure below the surface of the sea, air in a submerged body becomes decompressed. When a diver ascends, the denser air begins to expand, forming bubbles in the bloodstream. If a diver surfaces too quickly, or goes down too often, these nitrogen-rich bubbles can block capillaries, cutting off oxygen to the brain and leading to tissue damage, paralysis, or death."—Mark Jacobson, "Hunt for Red Gold," *OnEarth Magazine*, Fall 2004.

chambers until they come ashore many hours too late. Izdepski would like to see regulations on diving—control over the number of dives per day, safety equipment on the boats, and a limit on the lobster season to maintain the lobster population. There is no indication, however, that local or national Honduran or Nicaraguan governmental authorities are about to effectively regulate the lobster industry. Paul Raymond, with an organization that oversees seafood imports to the United States, says:

> There is a sense of lawlessness along the Mosquito Coast, especially in the lobster business. If you look hard enough you'll find major abuses in almost all the big seafood import companies. Not that anyone is really looking. Policing by the locals is almost nonexistent.

Raymond points out that his organization monitors the size of lobster sold to the United States, but has no power to deal with the diving situation.

> There's no law against diving for lobster, not in Nicaragua, not in Honduras, not in the United States. The fact is, lobster diving is a human rights issue, and human rights are beyond our jurisdiction.

Red Lobster is owned by Darden Restaurants, Inc., which also runs the Olive Garden chain and is the biggest "casual dining" company in the world. Darden has been consistently profitable over recent years (2000 to 2005), with net earnings in 2004 of $291 million. Both sales and earnings per share have been climbing every year since 2000. Red Lobster helped set up one of the first lobster processing plants on the Mosquito Coast in the mid 1970s, contracting for exclusive buying rights for five years. Red Lobster, still the biggest single purchaser of lobster from the area, began making deals with several of the larger boat owners on the Mosquito Coast in the early 1990s.

* * * * *

Gerry Mullen was feeling confused. He was proud of his company. With over 670 restaurants and over 63,000 employees in North America, Red Lobster sales in the last year had reached $2.4 billion, making it one of the flagship brands for Darden Restaurants. According to nationwide polls taken by an industry magazine, diners had voted Red Lobster as the best seafood restaurant for 17 years. What was the key to this kind of success? Gerry wondered if it was the company's marketing strategy. People love to eat lobster not only because it tastes fantastic, but because it makes them feel special. A $9.95 lobster fest puts a delicious luxury meal within range of every pocketbook, every family. This strategy—making everyone feel like a king—played into the great American Dream. It was smart, and it was working.

Then Gerry scanned back over what he had just read. He could see inconsistencies between that information and Red Lobster's advertising slogan, "Share the Love." But he wasn't sure what to do about it. There were those happy customers to think about … and the shareholders.

Advise Gerry Mullen. What options does he have? Describe the advantages and disadvantages of each. Then tell him which would be the right course of action for him to take, and why. Explain your reasons fully.

RED GOLD DEBATE

Representing one of the following—Divers/Boat Captains/Mopawi/SOS/Darden Restaurants/Red Lobster customers—you and your partner will spar with the other groups. The rest of the class will represent a fictional organization—the United Nations World Trade World Health Commission.

Format

1. **Opening Statements.** Each stakeholder pair will give an opening statement, explaining their perspective on the Red Gold controversy. Introduce yourself, and your role in the

situation. Then justify your role, using as many facts as possible. You have up to and no more than five minutes to do this. You can share the time or one of you can do it all. You will not be interrupted during your opening, but you will be penalized for going over the time limit.

Order for opening statements:

1. SOS

2. Boat captains

3. Divers

4. Darden Restaurants, Inc.

5. Mopawi

6. Red Lobster customers

2. **Q&A.** For the next 20 minutes you will be asking questions of other stakeholders, and fielding questions from them. You and your partner should prepare some pointed, provocative questions for some of the other stakeholders. (Make a list of your questions, indicating for each question which other group you would ask it of. For top grades, you and your partner should have six to eight tough questions for "opponent" stakeholder groups. Rank order them according to their importance.

3. **Open Discussion.** In the time remaining, you will take questions from the UNWTWHC (the rest of the class).

4. **Grading.** You and your partner will be graded on how well you argued for your stakeholder position, and how well your presentation, questions, and responses to questions reflect the research you did on the Red Gold situation. Begin by reading the attached articles and read Chapters 5 and 6 for relevant items. You'll earn extra points for making connections to the textbook.

Suggestions for Roles

SOS: You are the opening presenters. The class depends on you to set the stage. You could do this by role-playing Bob Izdepski and telling the story as he would tell it. You are explaining the whole thing from your perspective. Try not to give too much of the information that might best be covered by Mopawi and the divers (who will more or less overlap with your interests).

Boat Captains: You are described as "cruel" at some points in this controversy, but of course you need to put as positive a spin on your role as possible. You might emphasize that if it weren't for the lobster diving, the Miskito "buzos" would have no way to earn a living, explaining the horrible alternatives they realistically face. You could point the finger at other stakeholders, such as the ultimate consumers, who create the demand for cheap lobster. You could compare your profits with those of the giant food wholesalers, or with Darden Restaurants, and so on—they are benefiting even more! Be aggressive! There's no doubt that you are recruiting the divers to do dangerous work, so you must find creative ways to justify your role.

Divers: You are the "buzos." Try to get inside their skin, to imagine their lives, and the choices they must make. Think about their history, and how they are a macho, independent culture. It seems like the buzos have a sort of love/hate relationship to the lobster diving they do; please portray that.

Darden Restaurants: As you justify your role in the controversial lobster industry, you might point out that you aren't the only large company involved in the lobster trade, and that if you pull out, not only will there be negative consequences for many of the stakeholders, but another huge corporate interest will simply rush in to replace you. Pull out all the arguments that support the fact of your involvement; express them clearly.

Mopawi: You are an NGO (non-governmental organization) concerned with making positive social change. As part of your opening statement, please give some background information about the land and the people of the Mosquito Coast area, detailing how the Miskito people survive, what their options are, and what they might be. It is important that you illuminate any environmental aspects of the Red Gold controversy also.

Red Lobster Consumers: Go to a Red Lobster restaurant and interview a few people, to help you determine how to represent the consumer viewpoint in the debate. You may be able to get people leaving the restaurant to answer a handful of questions to help you as a student with an assignment! Here are some thoughts on what you could ask, but feel free to change this:

- Why do you like to eat at Red Lobster?
- Do you know that the supply of lobster is being depleted by overharvesting?
- Knowing this, will you avoid eating lobster in the future?
- Did you know that lobster divers risk their health/lives to harvest lobster because they are not given proper equipment?
- Does that information change your interest in eating here?
- Would you pay more for lobster here if you knew the extra cost would go to increase the divers' safety?

6 SUSTAINABLE ECONOMIES:

Global Environmental Protection

God, who hath given the world to men in common, hath also given them reason to make use of it to the best advantage of life, and convenience. The earth, and all that is therein, is given to men for the support and comfort of their being.

— JOHN LOCKE

[My] story is of all life…and of us two-leggeds sharing in it with the four-leggeds and the wings of the air, and all green things; for these are children of one mother and their father is one Spirit.

— BLACK ELK

We need to have our senses transgressed, and to find life pasturing freely where we never wander.

— HENRY DAVID THOREAU

•

We begin this chapter with what has been termed a "landmark" Supreme Court case on environmental legislation and global climate change, decided in May 2007. We then focus on the legal response to environmental concerns in the United States: from the comprehensive legislative approach launched in the 1970s, to more recent trends in which there is interplay between the public and the private sector, with market incentives playing a role in regulation, and the possibility of government incentives sparking innovation.

A selection of readings presents different philosophical points of view on the relationship between humans and their natural surroundings. We resume the legal theme with a case in which environmental regulation is arguably a "taking" of property requiring "just compensation" under the Fifth Amendment to the U.S. Constitution.

We end with a reading about environmental justice and global free trade.

Global Climate Change: A Landmark Supreme Court Case

In 1970, when the first Earth Day sparked environmental legislation—the National Environmental Protection Act, the Clean Air Act amendments, the Clean Water Act—public dialog in the United States about the effect human activity might be having on the natural world was focused on problems at home: Love Canal, where buried hazardous waste endangered a residential community, contaminants in our rivers and lakes, and daily smog reports, warning of immediate risks from polluted air within our cities.

Today, world leaders are struggling to address global environmental concerns, with climate change in the forefront. And at this point, we have alarming data. By drilling through sheets of Antarctic ice and extracting core samples, scientists have plotted the level of carbon dioxide in the "ancient air" on a virtually year-by-year basis for the past 420,000 years. By monitoring relatively unpolluted air in an observatory in Hawaii, we have been able to track carbon dioxide levels since 1959. The ice core analysis reveals that carbon dioxide levels in the earth's air were never, over the past 420,000 years, greater than 300 parts per million. In 1959, the Hawaii readings came to 316; by 1970, 325; and by 2006, 382 parts per million, a level believed to be the highest concentration of carbon dioxide in the atmosphere in 20 million years.

Since the 1980s, scientists have been documenting not only significant increases in carbon dioxide levels, but also a rise in global temperatures. They now believe these two trends are related: Carbon dioxide and other heat-trapping gases function like the top of a greenhouse, trapping solar energy and preventing the escape of reflected heat. There is general agreement across the scientific community that this process is causing global climate change.

In 1999 a coalition of private organizations, including Friends of the Earth, Greenpeace USA, California Solar Industries Association and Bio Fuels America, petitioned the Environmental Protection Agency (EPA), the agency responsible for implementing federal environmental laws, to regulate automobile greenhouse gas emissions under the Clean Air Act. Their claim: Climate change will have serious adverse effects on human health and the environment.

More than a year later, the EPA asked for public comment on "any scientific, technical, legal, economic or other" aspects of these issues. It received over 50,000 comments over the next five months. The Bush administration requested help from the National Research Council "in identifying the areas in the science of climate change where there are the greatest certainties and uncertainties." In 2001, the NRC produced a report that concluded, "[g]reenhouse gases are accumulating in Earth's atmosphere as a result of human activities, causing surface air temperatures and subsurface ocean temperatures to rise. Temperatures are, in fact, rising."

Yet, in September 2003, the EPA refused to regulate greenhouse gases. Petitioners appealed; by this time they had been joined by many other organizations and several states—California, Maine, and Massachusetts among them—and cities—Washington DC, New York City, and Baltimore. The case was decided by the Supreme Court in 2007.

MASSACHUSETTS v. EPA
U.S. Supreme Court, 2007
127 S.Ct. 1438

Justice STEVENS delivered the opinion of the Court.

Calling global warming "the most pressing environmental challenge of our time," a group of States, local governments, and private organizations, alleged … that the Environmental Protection Agency (EPA) has abdicated its responsibility under the Clean Air Act to regulate the emissions of four greenhouse gases, including carbon dioxide. Specifically, petitioners asked us to answer two questions concerning the meaning of § 202(a)(1) of the Act: whether EPA has the statutory authority to regulate greenhouse gas emissions from new motor vehicles; and if so, whether its stated reasons for refusing to do so are consistent with the statute.

[The Court here discusses the rationale the EPA gave for refusing to exercise its rule-making power.]

EPA reasoned that climate change had its own "political history": Congress designed the original Clean Air Act to address local air pollutants rather than a substance that "is fairly consistent in its concentration throughout the world's atmosphere," declined in 1990 to enact proposed amendments to force EPA to set carbon dioxide emission standards for motor vehicles, and addressed global climate change in other [anti-ozone] legislation. Because of this political history EPA concluded that climate change was so important that unless Congress spoke with exacting specificity, it could not have meant the agency to address it.

... EPA [also argued] ... that greenhouse gases cannot be "air pollutants" within the meaning of the Act.... The agency [argued] that if carbon dioxide were an air pollutant, the only feasible method of reducing tailpipe emissions would be to improve fuel economy. But because Congress has already created fuel economy standards subject to Department of Transportation administration, EPA regulation would either conflict with those standards or be superfluous.

Even assuming that it had authority over greenhouse gases, EPA explained why it would refuse to exercise that authority. The agency recogniz[ed] that the concentration of greenhouse gases has dramatically increased as a result of human activities, and acknowledged the attendant increase in global surface air temperatures. EPA nevertheless [cited] the NRC Report's statement that a causal link between the two "cannot be unequivocally established." Given that residual uncertainty, EPA concluded that regulating greenhouse gas emissions would be unwise.

The agency ... characterized any EPA regulation of motor-vehicle emissions as a "piecemeal approach" to climate change, [which] would conflict with the President's "comprehensive approach" to the problem. That approach involves ... support for technological innovation, [for] voluntary private-sector reductions in greenhouse gas emissions, and further research on climate change—not actual regulation.... [U]nilateral EPA regulation of motor-vehicle greenhouse gas emissions might also hamper the President's ability to persuade key developing countries to reduce greenhouse gas emissions.

[The Court now must resolve a preliminary issue known as "standing." When a petitioner lacks standing, a case cannot proceed to its underlying issues or "merits." Standing is based on language from Article III of the Constitution, which limits federal court jurisdiction to "Cases" and "Controversies." The notion is that only when a person or entity has suffered a particular harm can there be a remedy sought within the judicial system. The Court must determine if any of the petitioning organizations that sued to make the EPA rule in this case can point to an injury that would satisfy this threshold issue of standing.]

"[T]he gist of the question of standing" is whether petitioners have [a sufficiently] "personal stake in the outcome of the controversy."... As Justice Kennedy explained in ... *Lujan v. Defenders of Wildlife* [landmark standing case decided by the Supreme Court in 1992]:

> *While it does not matter how many persons have been injured by the challenged action, the party bringing suit must show that the action injures him in a concrete and personal way. This requirement...preserves the vitality of the adversarial process by assuring both that the parties before the court have an actual ... stake in the outcome, and that the legal questions presented ... will be resolved, not in the rarified atmosphere of a debating society, but in a concrete factual context conducive to a realistic appreciation of the consequences of judicial action.*

[While acknowledging the *Lujan* case requires a petitioner to demonstrate a specific injury that is "actual or imminent," that can be traced to the defendant, and that is likely to be remedied by a favorable decision, the Court here relaxes the *Lujan* standard. It does this in part because there is a "procedural right" under the Clean Air Act to challenge the EPA for "arbitrary and capricious" actions. It also reasons that one of the petitioners in this case is "a sovereign State and not, as it was in Lujan, a private individual."]

When a State enters the Union, it surrenders certain sovereign prerogatives. Massachusetts cannot invade Rhode Island to force reductions in greenhouse gas emissions, it cannot negotiate an emissions treaty with China or India, and in some circumstances the exercise of its police powers to reduce in-state motor-vehicle emissions might well be pre-empted....

These sovereign prerogatives are now lodged in the Federal Government, and Congress has ordered EPA to protect Massachusetts (among others) by prescribing [emissions] standards.

[Citing the consensus of scientific experts, the Court finds that Massachusetts has indeed suffered an "injury" sufficient for purposes of standing:]

"Global warming threatens (among other things) a precipitate rise in sea levels by the end of the century, "severe and irreversible changes to natural ecosystems" ... and an increase in the spread of disease.... [R]ising ocean temperatures may contribute to the ferocity of hurricanes.[1]... Global sea levels rose somewhere between 10 and 20 centimeters over the 20th century as a result of global warming. These rising seas have already begun to swallow Massachusetts' coastal land. Because the Commonwealth "owns a substantial portion of the state's coastal property,"[2] it has alleged a particularized injury in its capacity as a landowner. The severity of that injury will only increase over the course of the next century: If sea levels continue to rise as predicted, ... a significant fraction of coastal property will be "either permanently lost through inundation or temporarily lost through periodic storm surge and flooding events." Remediation costs alone, petitioners allege, could run well into the hundreds of millions of dollars.

[Continuing with the standing analysis, the Court finds that regulation of greenhouse gases would help prevent these injuries to Massachusetts.]

EPA ... maintains that its decision not to regulate greenhouse gas emissions from new motor vehicles contributes so insignificantly to petitioners' injuries that the agency cannot be ha[u]led into federal court to answer for them. For the same reason, EPA does not believe that any realistic possibility exists that the relief petitioners seek would mitigate global climate change and remedy their injuries. That is especially so because predicted increases in greenhouse gas emissions from developing nations, particularly China and India, are likely to offset any marginal domestic decrease.

But ... [a]gencies, like legislatures, do not generally resolve massive problems in one fell regulatory swoop. They instead whittle away at them over time, refining their preferred approach as circumstances change....

And reducing domestic automobile emissions is hardly a tentative step.... [T]he United States transportation sector emits an enormous quantity of carbon dioxide into the atmosphere ... more than 1.7 billion metric tons in 1999 alone. That accounts for more than 6% of worldwide carbon dioxide emissions.... Considering just emissions

---

1   [The 2004] affidavit-drafted more than a year in advance of Hurricane Katrina was eerily prescient. Immediately after discussing the "particular concern" that climate change might cause an "increase in the wind speed and peak rate of precipitation of major tropical cyclones (i.e., hurricanes and typhoons)," [it] noted that "[s]oil compaction, sea level rise and recurrent storms are destroying approximately 20-30 square miles of Louisiana wetlands each year. These wetlands serve as a 'shock absorber' for storm surges that could inundate New Orleans, significantly enhancing the risk to a major urban population."

2   For example, the [Massachusetts Department of Conservation and Recreation] owns, operates and maintains approximately ... 53 coastal state parks, beaches, reservations, and wildlife sanctuaries ... sporting and recreational facilities in coastal areas..., including numerous pools, skating rinks, playgrounds, playing fields, former coastal fortifications, public stages, museums, bike trails, tennis courts, boathouses and boat ramps and landings. Associated with these coastal properties and facilities is a significant amount of infrastructure....

from the transportation sector, which represent less than one-third of this country's total carbon dioxide emissions, the United States would still rank as the third-largest emitter of carbon dioxide in the world, outpaced only by the European Union and China....

[Finally, the Court discusses whether regulating greenhouse gases is likely to remedy the problems faced by Massachusetts.]

... Because of the enormity of the potential consequences associated with man-made climate change, the fact that the effectiveness of a remedy might be delayed during the (relatively short) time it takes for a new motor-vehicle fleet to replace an older one is essentially irrelevant. Nor is it dispositive that developing countries such as China and India are poised to increase greenhouse gas emissions substantially over the next century: A reduction in domestic emissions would slow the pace of global emissions increases, no matter what happens elsewhere.

We ... attach ... significance to EPA's "agree[ment] with ... President [Bush] that 'we must address the issue of global climate change,'" and to EPA's ardent support for various voluntary emission-reduction programs, As Judge Tatel observed in dissent [in the prior round of this case], "EPA would presumably not bother with such efforts if it thought emissions reductions would have no discernable impact on future global warming."

[Having determined that the petitioners have standing to pursue their claim, the Court now considers the underlying "merits" of the case. It begins by acknowledging the limits of "judicial review" in circumstances like these, where courts are reviewing the decision of a federal agency. This caution should be especially in evidence where an agency has decided not to enforce one of its rules. And here, EPA has refused to make a rule at all.]

[T]he first question is whether § 202(a)(1) of the Clean Air Act authorizes EPA to regulate greenhouse gas emissions from new motor vehicles in the event that it forms a "judgment" that such emissions contribute to climate change. We have little trouble concluding that it does. In relevant part, § 202(a)(1) provides that EPA "shall by regulation prescribe ... standards applicable to the emission of any air pollutant from any class or classes of new motor vehicles or new motor vehicle engines, which in [the Administrator's] judgment cause, or contribute to, air pollution which may reasonably be anticipated to endanger public health or welfare."

... The Clean Air Act's sweeping definition of "air pollutant" includes "any air pollution agent or combination of such agents, including any physical, chemical ... substance or matter which is emitted into or otherwise enters the ambient air...." On its face, the definition embraces all airborne compounds of whatever stripe, and underscores that intent through the repeated use of the word "any." Carbon dioxide, methane, nitrous oxide, and hydrofluorocarbons are without a doubt "physical [and] chemical ... substance[s] which [are] emitted into ... the ambient air." The statute is unambiguous....

EPA finally argues that it cannot regulate carbon dioxide emissions from motor vehicles because doing so would require it to tighten mileage standards, a job (according to EPA) that Congress has assigned to DOT. But that DOT sets mileage standards in no way licenses EPA to shirk its environmental responsibilities. EPA has been charged with protecting the public's "health" and "welfare," a statutory obligation wholly independent of DOT's mandate to promote energy efficiency. The two obligations may overlap, but there is no reason to think the two agencies cannot both administer their obligations....

While the Congresses that drafted [the Clean Air Act] might not have appreciated the possibility that burning fossil fuels could lead to global warming, they did understand that without regulatory flexibility, changing circumstances and scientific developments would soon render the Clean Air Act obsolete. The broad language of [the CAA] reflects an intentional effort to confer the flexibility necessary to forestall such obsolescence.

[Even if the EPA had the authority to regulate greenhouse gases, it argued that it would be unwise to do so. The Court goes on to deal with this argument.]

The EPA has refused to comply with this clear statutory command. Instead, it has offered a laundry list of reasons not to regulate....

Although we have neither the expertise nor the authority to evaluate these policy judgments, it is evident they have nothing to do with whether greenhouse gas emissions contribute to climate change. Still less do they amount to a reasoned justification for declining to form a scientific judgment....

In short, EPA has offered no reasoned explanation for its refusal to decide whether greenhouse gases cause or contribute to climate change. Its action was therefore "arbitrary, capricious, ... or otherwise not in accordance with law."... We hold only that EPA must ground its reasons for action or inaction in the statute.

The judgment of the Court of Appeals is reversed, and the case is remanded for further proceedings consistent with this opinion.

It is so ordered.

Chief Justice ROBERTS, with whom Justice SCALIA, Justice THOMAS, and

Justice ALITO join, dissenting. ※

Global warming may be a "crisis," even "the most pressing environmental problem of our time." [Redress] of grievances of the sort at issue here, [however], "is the function of Congress and the Chief Executive," not the federal courts.

[Chief Justice Roberts does not agree that the application of the test for standing should be relaxed for a state. He does not see any "actual and imminent injury," as called for in the *Lujan* case. Whether global warming is the cause of any diminishment of the Massachusetts coastline is "pure conjecture," he argues; threatened harm does not satisfy the standing requirements of the Constitution. Roberts also disputes the majority's willingness to find a causal connection between any injury to Massachusetts and regulation of motor vehicle emissions, not to mention global warming.]

The Court ignores the complexities of global warming.... Because local greenhouse gas emissions disperse throughout the atmosphere and remain there for anywhere from 50 to 200 years, it is global emissions data that are relevant. According to one of petitioners' declarations, domestic motor vehicles contribute about 6 percent of global carbon dioxide emissions and 4 percent of global greenhouse gas emissions. The amount of global emissions at issue here is smaller still; the Clean Air Act [would] cover only new motor vehicles, ... so petitioners' desired emission standards might reduce only a fraction of 4 percent of global emissions.

[Roberts argues the link between EPA regulation and any coastal degradation is even weaker in the light of global climate change, which "necessarily involves a complex web of economic and physical factors."]

Petitioners are never able to trace their alleged injuries back through this complex web to the fractional amount of global emissions that might have been limited with EPA standards. In light of the bit-part domestic new motor vehicle greenhouse gas emissions have played in what petitioners describe as a 150-year global phenomenon, and the myriad additional factors bearing on petitioners' alleged injury—the loss of Massachusetts coastal land—the connection is far too speculative....

[Overall, Roberts strongly disputes the notion that Massachusetts has standing to sue in this case.]

[P]etitioners' true goal for this litigation may be more symbolic than anything else. The constitutional role of the courts, however, is to decide concrete cases—not to serve as a convenient forum for policy debates.

I respectfully dissent.

Justice SCALIA with whom Chief Justice ROBERTS, Justice THOMAS, and

Justice ALITO join, dissenting. ✺

[Justice Scalia begins by quoting the EPA.]

"A sensible regulatory scheme would require that all significant sources and sinks of [greenhouse gas] emissions be considered in deciding how best to achieve any needed emission reductions.... Unilateral EPA regulation of motor vehicle [greenhouse gas] emissions could also weaken U.S. efforts to persuade developing countries to reduce the [greenhouse gas] intensity of their economies. Considering the large populations and growing economies of some developing countries ... any potential benefit of EPA regulation could be lost to the extent [they] decided to let their emissions significantly increase in view of U.S. emissions reductions. Unavoidably, climate change raises important foreign policy issues, and it is the President's prerogative to address them.

The reasons the EPA gave are surely considerations executive agencies regularly take into account (and ought to take into account) when deciding whether to consider entering a new field: the impact such entry would have on other Executive Branch programs and on foreign policy.

[Scalia also challenges the certainty of the science behind the petitioner's argument. He quotes the EPA:]

"The science of climate change is extraordinarily complex and still evolving. Although there have been substantial advances in climate change science, there continue to be important uncertainties in our understanding of the factors that may affect future climate change and how it should be addressed.... [T]he understanding of the relationships between weather/climate and human health is in its infancy and therefore the health consequences of climate change are poorly understood.

[Finally, Scalia attacks the majority's interpretation of "pollution." Only if greenhouse gases are agents of "air pollution" would the EPA have the authority to regulate them under the Clean Air Act.]

[Under the majority's interpretation,] everything airborne, from Frisbees to flatulence, qualifies as an "air pollutant." This reading of the statute defies common sense.

[T]he term "air pollution" is not itself defined by the CAA; EPA began with the commonsense observation that the "[p]roblems associated with atmospheric concentrations of CO_2," bear little resemblance to what would naturally be termed "air pollution."

... Since the inception of the Act, EPA has used these provisions to address air pollution problems that occur primarily at ground level or near the surface of the earth. This has meant setting [air quality standards] for concentrations of ozone, carbon monoxide, particulate matter and other substances in the air near the surface of the earth, not higher in the atmosphere.... CO_2, by contrast, is fairly consistent in concentration throughout the world's atmosphere up to approximately the lower stratosphere."

In other words, regulating the buildup of CO_2 and other greenhouse gases in the upper reaches of the atmosphere, which is alleged to be causing global climate change, is not akin to regulating the concentration of some substance that is polluting the air.

... No matter how important the underlying policy issues at stake, this Court has no business substituting its own desired outcome for the reasoned judgment of the responsible agency.

QUESTIONS

1. Why, in the majority opinion of Justice Stevens, is the "standing" of the petitioners enhanced by the fact that they include the Commonwealth of Massachusetts? Why, according to Chief Justice Roberts' dissent, do the petitioners lack standing?

2. According to the majority, why is the EPA's decision not to exercise its rulemaking function "arbitrary and capricious?" Why does dissenting Justice Scalia disagree?

3. According to Osha Gray Davidson, in an article in *Mother Jones* magazine called "Dirty Secrets" published in 2003:

> [T]he White House has all but denied the existence of what may be the most serious environmental problem of our time, global warming. After campaigning on a promise to reduce emissions of the greenhouse gas carbon dioxide, Bush made an abrupt about-face once elected, calling his earlier pledge "a mistake" and announcing that he would not regulate CO_2 emissions from power plants.... Since then, the White House has censored scientific reports that mentioned the subject ... and even, at the behest of ExxonMobil, engineered the ouster of the scientist who chaired the United Nations Intergovernmental Panel on Climate Change.

Internet Assignment Investigate Davidson's claims about censorship by the Bush administration. Were scientific reports on global warming changed or kept from the public? What reports were they? If they were changed, how? If language was omitted, what language? Did the U.S. government act to unseat the scientist who chaired the U.N. panel on climate change? Did it take any other actions to sway public knowledge about global warming?

Source: Osha Gray Davidson, "Dirty Secrets," *Mother Jones*, September/October 2003. Copyright © 2003 Foundation for National Progress. Reprinted by permission

4. **Internet Assignment** Immediately after this case was decided, on May 14, 2007, President Bush directed the EPA to come up with plan to reduce carbon dioxide emissions. What specific approach did he suggest? How were his suggestions criticized? Find out how the EPA has responded.

5. On September 20, 2006, the State of California sued General Motors and five other automakers for damages relating to the greenhouse gas emissions of their vehicles.
Internet Assignment How is this suit similar to *Massachusetts v. EPA*? What arguments do the automobile manufacturers make to have the suit dismissed? What is the current status of the California case?

6. In Kyoto, Japan in 1995, the United Nations adopted protocols assigning limits to greenhouse gas emissions for developed countries. The Kyoto Protocol was signed by 130 countries, but in 1997, the United States Senate passed a unanimous resolution refusing to adopt it.
Internet Assignment What were the arguments against adopting the Kyoto Protocol?

7. Many states are now ahead of the federal government in responding to the problem of greenhouse gas emissions.
Internet Assignment Locate the California Climate Action Registry. How many states have now joined with California in tracking green house gas emissions? What is the difference between the state-based registry and the U.S. Department of Energy's reporting system?

8. Many cities are also ahead of the federal government on this issue. Cities cover one percent of the Earth's surface but generate 80 percent of the anthropogenic (human-caused) heat-trapping greenhouse gases.
Internet Assignment Locate the Large Cities Climate Summit of 2007. What strategies can cities adopt independent of their state and federal governments to reduce emissions of greenhouse gases?

9. The World Meteorological Organization (WMO) and the United Nations Environment Programme (UNEP) established the Intergovernmental Panel on Climate Change (IPCC) in 1988. On May 4, 2007, in Bangkok, the IPCC released its most recent report.
Internet Assignment Browse quickly online through this 36-page report and summarize the strategies the authors recommend national governments take to most effectively reduce greenhouse gas emissions.

Environmental Protection Strategies

> *Thirty five years ago, our nation awoke to the health and environmental impacts of rampant and highly visible pollution—rivers so contaminated that they caught on fire, entire towns built upon sites so toxic that the only recourse was to abandon them, and air pollution so thick that in some cities people had to change their shirts twice a day.*
>
> — EPA ADMINISTRATOR JOHNSON AT THE 35-YEAR CELEBRATION

Statutory Law

The first Earth Day—April 22, 1970—created the political climate that would lead to a new federal agency, the Environmental Protection Agency (EPA), and a series of laws protecting the environment. Over the ensuing years, the legislative framework in the United States—federal, state, and local regulations addressing pollution of the air, water, and land—grew to be the most comprehensive in the world. Yet this regulatory network is relatively new and, as of this writing, the head of the EPA is still not a cabinet-level position. Below we briefly describe several federal environmental laws.

- The **Clean Air Act of 1970**[3] regulates the emission of pollutants into the atmosphere. Under this law, national ambient air-quality standards (NAAQs) are set, and the release of certain major pollutants—particulates, toxins, and compounds that deplete stratospheric ozone, contribute to acid rain, and are dangerous to human health—are limited. The Clean Air Act is carried out and monitored by the states, which must submit "state implementation plans" (SIPS) for approval by the EPA. The 1990 amendments address "nonattainment" areas, the parts of the country that are not in compliance with the NAAQs, and set new deadlines—from 5 to 20 years for compliance on ozone, for example.

- The **Clean Water Act (CWA)**[4] sets a goal of ending the discharge of pollutants into navigable waters, and provides federal funding for sewage treatment plants nationwide. Although CWA requires discharge permits, an April 2006 report by the Public Interest Research Group (PIRG) revealed that more than 62 percent of all major facilities discharged pollution in excess of their permits at least once between January 1, 2003 and June 30, 2004.[5] In May 2007, PIRG reported that 10.9 billion gallons of untreated sewage had been poured into Lake Erie in 2005.

- A 2006 Supreme Court decision, *Rapanos v. U.S.*, narrowed the definitions of navigable waters and wetlands covered by the law, as did an executive decision by President Bush to remove small streams and wetlands from the protection of the law. As this book goes to press, a bipartisan group in Congress has responded by proposing the Clean Water Restoration Act of 2007.

- The **Resource Conservation and Recovery Act (RCRA)**[6] sets up a "cradle-to-grave" program for the control of hazardous waste, regulating labeling, containers, transport, and disposal sites.

---

3 42 U.S.C. 7401 (1998).

4 33 U.S.C. sec. 7413(a)(2)(Supp. V 1993).

5 Environmental Laboratory Washington Report, Vol. 15, No.8, April 23, 2004.

6 42 U.S.C. Sec. 6901-6992k (1988 & Supp. V 1993).

- The **Comprehensive Environmental Response, Compensation, and Liability Act (CERCLA)**[7] is a liability scheme rather than a monitoring program. CERCLA created a $1.6 billion fund—**Superfund**—to finance the cleanup of toxic waste sites. For decades the government would collect from polluting companies to reimburse Superfund, but under the Bush administration most of the resources for cleanup will come from taxpayers. **Potentially responsible parties** include (1) owners or operators of hazardous waste sites, (2) those who owned or operated the sites when the hazardous material was deposited, (3) the "generators," or those who create the wastes, and (4) the transporters—those who carry it to the sites.

Other environmental laws deal with endangered species; pesticides; coastal management; the timber, mining, and oil industries; marine life; and so on. For many of these statutes, the federal version of each is either mirrored or implemented by legislation at the state level. The EPA homepage, http://www.epa.gov, updates statutes and regulations.

Market-Based Incentives

By 2005, after 35 years overseeing 13 extremely complicated laws, the EPA could boast of many accomplishments. The number of Americans served by modern sewage treatment plants doubled. Sewage flow into waterways was cut by about one-third, and the proportion of waterways meeting clean water standards rose from 36 to 72 percent. Air pollution decreased over 50 percent—while our population increased by 40 percent, energy consumption increased 47 percent, and the gross domestic product increased 187 percent. Some 600,000 acres of contaminated land were restored. The work still to be done by the EPA, though, is enormous, and differs somewhat from the kind of task it first faced. In the early years the agency dealt mainly with the type of environmental degradation—dirty smoke emitted from factory smokestacks, Love Canals, oil spills—that was blatant, and traceable to a few major industrial sources. At this point the problems are more insidious and diffuse. They are generated by large firms but also by thousands of small businesses, by millions of individual consumers—and they surface here and transnationally as threats to forests, oceans, biodiversity, and to global climate itself.

Over recent years, the comprehensive statutory scheme designed to protect our environment has come under attack. Its critics have been generally unopposed to the concept of environmental protection. Rather, they became convinced that the so-called "command and control" regulatory network was too complex, expensive, and inflexible. Some believed that costly regulation diminished the global competitiveness of American firms and was inefficient. Instead of forcing polluters to comply with preset governmental standards, they argued, why not integrate the profit motive into the mechanism for environmental protection, to drive change more effectively?

Such thinking was behind the **tradeable permit system** for sulfur dioxide emissions authorized by the 1990 Amendments to the Clean Air Act. Sulfur dioxide is a key culprit in producing acid rain, which not only defaces buildings, but lowers the pH levels in lakes, making them uninhabitable for fish and plants. Under the tradeable permit plan, the EPA auctions a set number of sulfur dioxide emission allowances annually, with each allowance permitting one ton of emissions. Companies can then use up their allowances for that year (by releasing sulfur dioxide), save them for future use, or sell their allowances to other companies. In this way pollution reduction can occur in the most efficient way possible, because firms for whom emission reduction is cheapest have the incentive to do more than meet the minimum standards, while those for whom it is too expensive to improve pollution controls will purchase

7 42 U.S.C. Sec. 9601-9675 (1988 & Supp. V 1993). Amended in 1984 and 1986.

more permits. Meanwhile, the overall emissions levels are held constant. While the so called "cap-and-trade" system appears to offer a desirable way to reduce certain pollutants, such as sulfur dioxide and smog, it may not be the best way to handle others. Mercury, for example, affects the nervous system and is particularly harmful to children and developing fetuses. When the Bush administration extended the concept to mercury emissions, critics warned that the new rule would allow mercury "hot spots" to persist around such sites as power plants that might choose to buy the right to emit mercury instead of installing technology to avoid mercury emissions. A few states, notably New York, New Jersey and Pennsylvania, adopted state emissions plans that prohibit trading of mercury pollution credits, and environmentalists urged the EPA to create a national mercury monitoring network.

Through the 1990s and early 2000s, regulators took advantage of "carrots" (market-based incentives) as well as "sticks" (injunctions, penalties) to bring environmental goals into focus.

At the same time, increasingly, environmentalists have sought to work more closely with business. Forty years after the Environmental Defense Fund was founded by the lawyers whose suit led to the banning of DDT, EDF highlights its Director of Corporate Partnerships on its Web page. Gwen Ruta, a chemical engineer with both private industry and government experience, describes her philosophy:

> To change America, you need to engage America's corporations. Environmental Defense brings about change not through confrontation, but through partnership with powerful market leaders. We approached FedEx, for instance, with a goal of transforming truck technology in America. FedEx rose to the challenge and together we developed ambitious performance goals and commissioned new powertrains. Today, our hybrid trucks run 57% farther on a gallon of fuel and reduce the particulates that cause cancer and respiratory illness by 96%. As we anticipated, other fleets have begun to follow FedEx's lead, including Coca-Cola, PG&E and the U.S. Postal Service.
>
> It is not just altruism that moves major corporations to join us: Rather, our scientists, economists and engineers quantify the benefits of improving efficiency and reducing waste. As McDonald's vice president Bob Langert recently wrote on his corporate blog: "Environmental Defense is probably the best nongovernmental organization to find the intersection between profit and planet.

Zerofootprint

In spring 2007, Zerofootprint, a nonprofit group that provides information and services to combat global warming collaborated with with Business Objects, a company that makes business intelligence software to produce a new Web site: http://www.Zerofootprint.net. Check it out to see what you as an individual can do to reduce carbon emissions.

Green Capitalism

> The lesson is plain: pollution prevention works; pollution control does not. Only where production technology has been changed to eliminate the pollutant has the environment been substantially improved. Where it remains unchanged, where an attempt is made to trap the pollutant in an appended control device—the automobile's catalytic converter or the power plant's scrubber—environmental improvement is modest or nil. When a pollutant

is attacked at the point of origin, it can be eliminated. But once it is pro-
duced, it is too late.

— Barry Commoner, 1989

Noted television journalist Bill Moyers speaks with Hunter Lovins in the next segment, taken from his show *Now With Bill Moyers*, aired on PBS on January 18, 2002. Lovins co-founded the Rocky Mountain Institute, an organization that describes itself as "independent, non-adversarial and transideological," with a mission to look to the free market system for ways to solve the energy needs of our society while sustaining the natural environment. As Moyers begins this interview, he asks Lovins if she believes the energy problem is a matter of U.S. dependence on foreign oil.

BILL MOYERS INTERVIEW WITH HUNTER LOVINS

Lovins: People tend to define the energy problem as we're running out. And therefore we have to get more energy of any type from any source. In fact, the world is awash in energy.

As Pogo once said "we're confronted by insurmountable opportunities." What we really ought to be doing is choosing the best technologies to meet our needs for energy services at the least cost, in the ways that are most benign. And when you ask the question that way, the answer comes up energy efficiency and the various diverse renewable supplies of energy, which are what's winning in the marketplace today.

Moyers: The marketplace? You think the market can get us there?

Lovins: The market will absolutely get us there. Markets do work, but it will take a while. And if we care about getting off of imported oil, there are ways to do that. For example, just increasing the efficiency with which our cars burn gasoline by about three miles a gallon would eliminate our need to import any oil from the Mideast.

Moyers: But you hear all this talk in Washington that the answer to getting off dependence on oil is to develop fossil fuels at home. We'll use our oil to be free of foreign oil.

Lovins: The United States uses about 25% of the world's oil. We have reserves of about 3% or less. You do the math.

What has been proposed, for example, of drilling in the Arctic National Wildlife Refuge—assume that all the oil that the proponents hope is there is, in fact, there and it can be lifted economically. Those are two big assumptions that are probably not true. Assume they're true. It would provide about 1% of the oil that this country needs.

Moyers: For how long?

Lovins: For maybe a decade or so. Not very long.

Moyers: So it's not going to really liberate us from Middle Eastern oil.

Lovins: No. Now maybe the Gulf War in the early '90s was fought for other reasons. But myself, I think if Kuwait only grew broccoli, we would not have had our young men and women there in 0.7-mile-per-gallon tanks and 17-feet-per-gallon aircraft carriers. And if we had put our people in 32-mile-a-gallon cars, we wouldn't have needed any oil from the Middle East at all.

Moyers: And immediately, after 9/11, someone I respect very much in the environmental community called and said, "You know, this proves that our dependence on foreign oil, fossil fuels, is the Achilles Heel of American foreign policy." Do you think that's true?

Lovins: Clearly, our dependence on imported oil is costing us a lot of money; and it certainly contributed to that. And it's unnecessary.

Communities across the country have demonstrated alternatives. About ten years ago, Sacramento, California, voted to shut down its then-operating nuclear plant because it wasn't operating very well and it was costing a lot. That cut off about half the capacity to that community.

Instead, the utility invested in efficiency and in a diverse array of supply—solar, a little bit of wind, fuel cells, co-generation—all of this was relatively small scale, but collectively it made up all the energy they needed. Ten years later, the economics are in; the community is healthier. It has generated about $185 million, just this investment in efficiency and new supply. And it has generated hundreds of new jobs....

Some of the American companies [are developing renewable energy resources. T]ake a look at Shell Oil, which recently created Shell Hydrogen. And as the head of it, Don Hubert, said the Stone Age didn't end because we ran out of stones; the Oil Age won't end because we ran out of oil. And Shell recently announced the end of oil and the beginning of the transition to Shell being an energy company supplying renewable energy—there's Shell renewables—and to ultimately an economy based on hydrogen. This would be a much more benign economy to have.

Hydrogen is the most plentiful element in the universe other than perhaps stupidity.

Now, suppose you drove a car that's powered by hydrogen. And most of the big car companies have hydrogen car programs already well in development. You will start to see hydrogen cars on the road within the next three to four years. So you drive your hydrogen car up to the building that has the fuel cell in it and the reformer making hydrogen. You plug your car into the reformer to get your hydrogen and into the grid. Your car, which has previously been an idle large asset, is now making electricity and selling it to the grid at the real time price, making you money.

The car fleet running around on the road is probably about ten times the generating capacity of all of the power plants of the electric utilities. You could displace all fossil plants just with this one measure. And these technologies exist and they're entering the marketplace.

Moyers: So the answer, as I read you, is not to hug a tree if you want to save the environment, but to hug an economist.

Lovins: (laughs) ... Hug an entrepreneur. Hug somebody who's bringing these technologies into the marketplace and making money doing it.

QUESTIONS

1. **Internet Assignment** What can you find regarding hydrogen-powered, bio-fuel powered or electronic cars? Which form of alternative power holds the most promise? In which do automakers seem to be most invested? Is the trend even across U.S., European, and Japanese manufacturers?

2. **Internet Assignment** Check out the Xebra electric car. Check out Philly CarShare. Find other recent green business applications. What applications can you find in the public sector?

3. **Internet Assignment** In the summer of 2004, the Apollo Alliance, a coalition of labor, community, business, and environmental groups, released a study finding that if the United States invested $30 billion a year over 10 years in energy efficiency—updating older factories and using renewable fuels, for example—3.3 million jobs, $905 billion in personal income, and $284 billion in energy savings would result. While there would be losses in the fossil fuel industries, America would dramatically reduce dependence on foreign oil and the economy would gain 10 times more jobs overall. Is the federal government moving in this direction now?
Source: Now With Bill Moyers, aired on PBS on January 18, 2002.

Velib: Making Money and Saving the Environment

In 2007, 20,000 bicycles were placed at 1,000 stations throughout Paris, in an experiment called Velib, which aims to change the transportation landscape of that city. Users can pick up and use the bikes, and then drop them off at any one of the conveniently located stations. An advertising firm is financing the project in exchange for exclusive rights to use some 1,600 urban billboards. The city will actually make money on the deal—about $46 million over 10 years—while users pay an annual fee of about $50. The first half hour of any trip is free; additional half hours costs about $2 each.

In Lyon, where a similar bicycle program has been a great success, there are now 50,000 subscribers and 4,000 bikes. Bicycle use has increased 30 percent and car use is down four percent, reversing the previous trend where automobile use was on a steady rise. Lyon calculates its program has prevented 3,000 tons of carbon monoxide from being emitted.

Citywide bicycle programs are increasingly popular in Europe. They already exist in Dublin, Brussels, Marseille, Vienna and in several smaller cities. Celine Lepault, who directs the Parisian program from the mayor's office, has already received requests for information from places like Sydney, Australia and Rio de Janeiro, Brazil.

Corporate Governance: Shareholder Activism

Shareholders have the right to attempt to influence the actions of management. They can do this by putting nonbinding proposals forward—called resolutions—to be voted upon at annual shareholder meetings. Until the 1970s, shareholder resolutions tended to focus on bottom-line concerns. But in 1971, the Episcopal Church filed the first church-sponsored shareholder resolution, challenging General Motor's operations in the apartheid regime in South Africa, and sparking others to make proposals related to corporate social responsibility. Today, shareholder activism continues to grow, with proposals each year on a range of issues, from executive compensation to diversity to the environment.

THE PROXY SYSTEM

In advance of each annual meeting, shareholders are sent form ballots listing the items that are up for vote, including membership on the board of directors, choice of an outside auditor, and resolutions brought by the board or shareholders. Each share of stock generally counts as one vote.[8] Shareholders have the right to come to the annual meetings in person to cast their ballots, but few do. If they prefer, shareholders can vote by returning the "proxy card" that is mailed along with the notice of the meeting. The board of directors has the right to vote the shares of those who neither appear nor return a completed proxy vote. Given the large number of individuals who own stock in the typical publicly owned corporation, few of whom have a big block of shares, this system assures corporate control of the majority of the votes.

PRELIMINARY MANAGEMENT RESISTANCE

Getting a shareholder resolution voted upon is not automatic. Management may strongly disagree with the proposal, and has the right to write a statement in opposition (with no length

---

8 Most states permit corporations to issue several classes of stock. Traditionally, only common stock had voting rights, although that law has changed in some states.

limit) that will appear on the ballot ("proxy statement"), effectively killing the proposal. In the face of outright opposition from management, shareholder proposals are often withdrawn before a vote.

BROAD POLICY PROPOSALS ONLY

According to SEC rules regarding shareholder proposals, there are 13 circumstances under which a corporation may "omit" or ignore the resolution.[9] For example, resolutions may not deal with "the conduct of the ordinary business operations" of a company. This means that shareholders may not make proposals dealing with how the firm is actually run, but may only offer suggestions regarding overall corporate policy. Shareholders may propose that the company review its human resource policies with regard to homosexuals, for example, but may not propose that human resource personnel hire a certain proportion of gay men and women. Shareholders may propose that a company conduct an audit of its practices regarding recycling and renewable energy use, but they may not offer specifics outlining how it would carry out such a plan.

In the wake of Enron and other corporate scandals, large institutional investors—controlling the pension funds for employees of an entire city or state, for example—have taken a self-protective interest in corporate governance, and in the shareholder resolution process. For example, they have focused on the fact that, in many firms, the CEO is also the chairman of the board, creating an inherent conflict of interest: The legal, fiduciary, and ethical obligations belonging to top management can be at odds with those of the board, with its watchdog function. In a sharply contested proxy fight in 2004, institutional investors backed a proposal that Walt Disney, Inc. oust its CEO Michael Eisner. He was removed as CEO—although he remained as chairman of Disney's board.

MERE RECOMMENDATIONS, BUT WITH MORAL AUTHORITY

Even if a proposal makes it onto the ballot, and even if an impressive proportion of shareholders votes for it, the result is merely advisory—or "nonbinding." Management still has the right to respond to the issue in some different way, or to ignore the resolution altogether. However, most corporate boards realize the appropriateness of making some kind of compromise with popular shareholder measures, and shareholder resolutions have been an effective means of forcing change even in the absence of majority shareholder approval. Recently, resolutions have brought on changes in corporate governance, accounting practices,. and environmental policies. For example, in 2003, Ford Motor Company opened a dialogue with sponsors of a shareholder proposal that the company report on its greenhouse gas emissions; at Occidental Petroleum shareholders agreed to withdraw their proposal once the company promised to report its carbon emissions and climate change data more fully. Spurred on by environmental organizations and socially conscious investment funds, shareholders filed dozens of global warming resolutions with U.S. firms in 2004, a trend that appears to be building. Many of these proposals garnered upwards of 20 percent approval, a high proportion, given the process.

Below is a sample shareholder resolution. It was put forward in 2004 by investors in American International Group, Inc. (AIG—Chubb Insurance its subsidiary), requesting that it assess the risks to its business presented by global climate change. The lead sponsors included "socially responsible" investment funds.[10] The insurance company decided to omit this resolution from its proxy statement.

9 17 Code of Federal Regulations (CFR) Ch. II, Sec. 240.14a-8.

10 (Walden Asset Management, Calvert Asset Management Company, Progressive Investment Management), religious investors (Community Church of New York, Congregation of the Sisters of St. Joseph of Brighton), environmental groups (Conservation Land Trust, Tides Foundation) and government pension funds (State of Connecticut Treasurer's Office, State of Maine, Office of the Treasurer).

Shareholder Resolution on Climate Change

Resolved:

The shareholders request that the Board of Directors prepare a report, at reasonable cost and omitting proprietary information, made available to shareholders by September 30, 2004, providing a comprehensive assessment of Chubb's strategies to address the impacts of climate change on its business.

Supporting Statements:

- We believe the human contribution to climate change has become widely accepted among the scientific community. Legislation, regulation, litigation, and other responses to climate change seem likely.

- "In global warming, we are facing an enormous risk to the U.S. economy and retirement finds that Wall Street has so far chosen to ignore." (Philip Angelides, Treasurer of California)....

- In November 2003, as a part of the Carbon Disclosure Project, 87 institutional investors representing over $9 trillion in assets wrote to the 500 largest companies by market capitalization asking for relevant information concerning greenhouse gas emissions. According to the Project Coordinator, "There are potential business risks and opportunities related to actions stemming from climate change that have implications for the value of shareholdings in corporations worldwide."

- Munich Re's 2002 Annual Report states that climate related catastrophes are the greatest cost to the industry. Of the 35 largest natural catastrophes that cost insurers over €1 billion, only two were not climate related. Climate change may lead to increased erratic and extreme weather events, resulting in serious environmental and public health impacts.

- Swiss Re sees inaction on climate change as a possible liability for directors and officers (D&O), and is considering potential coverage implications for insured companies that do not address climate change risks. As D&O liability insurance is a significant part of Chubb's business, we believe investors should know how the company is addressing this issue.

- We believe proactive behavior in the European Union, Japan and elsewhere may put U.S. companies at a competitive disadvantage globally. Of 84 signatories to the United Nations Environmental Programme Financial Initiatives Insurance Industry Initiative, only three are North American companies. Chubb is not a signatory.

- "Catastrophe insurers can't simply extrapolate past experience. If there is truly 'global warming,' for example, the odds would shift, since tiny changes in atmospheric conditions can produce momentous changes in weather patterns." (Warren Buffet, Chairman, Berkshire Hathaway, 1993)

- With property and casualty customers in 29 countries, we believe Chubb is exposed to climate risks....

Chubb's Annual Report has, since 1997, stated under the heading *Catastrophe Exposure*, "We also continue to explore and analyze credible scientific evidence, including the impact of global climate change, that may affect our potential exposure under insurance policies." Chubb has not responded to investor requests for additional information.

Insuring Against Global Climate Change

Insurance companies have multiple reasons to be concerned about global warming. Keyed in as they are to weather and damage trends, they have already experienced heavy claims post-Katrina and post-Kyrill, a hurricane that swept through a wide area of Europe in January 2007, killing 47 people and wrecking hundreds of thousands of homes in half a dozen countries. European insurers have begun to follow their U.S. counterparts, increasing rates and scaling back coverage in anticipation of further weather extremes, the result of climate change.

But should the insurance industry be doing more, using its financial muscle to support green business innovation? A few firms offer discounts for drivers with hybrid cars or for those who limit their driving. Some give price breaks to companies with energy efficient buildings. Some, like AXA of France, are taking a step further by cutting back on investments in companies that are environmental offenders, purchasing stock in eco-friendly firms instead.

Yet according to Jeremy Leggett, former chief scientist for Greenpeace UK and now chief executive of a renewable energy company in London, overall the industry lacks a strategic focus on low-carbon investments, which he labels "dysfunctional to the point of being suicidal."

Environmental Philosophy

And the fear of you and the dread of you shall be upon every beast of the earth, and upon every fowl of the air, upon all that moveth upon the earth and upon all the fishes of the sea; into your hand are they delivered. Every moving thing that liveth shall be meat for you; even as the green herb have I given you all things.

— GOD TO NOAH, GENESIS 9: 2-3

Every man ... has an equal right of pursuing and taking to his own use all such creatures as are [wild].

— W. BLACKSTONE, COMMENTARIES 411 (1766)

The quotes above reflect the traditional Western Judeo-Christian understanding of the virtually unqualified right of men to control, to own, to "take" whatever can be taken from the natural world. In the late seventeenth century, political theorist John Locke wrote a justification of the natural right of each person, by dint of the labor he invested in it, to unlimited private property. Locke's thinking would greatly influence those who conceptualized and brought into existence the modern liberal democratic state, particularly those who established the American Republic.

SECOND TREATISE OF GOVERNMENT

JOHN LOCKE

Of Property

§ 27. Though the earth, and all inferior creatures, be common to all men, yet every man has a property in his own person: this no body has any right to but himself. The labour of his body, and the work of his hands, we may say, are properly his. Whatsoever then he removes out of the state that nature hath provided, and left it in, he hath mixed his labour with, and joined to it something that is his own, and thereby makes it his property. It being by him removed from the common state nature hath placed it in, it hath by this labour something annexed to it, that excludes the common right of other men: for this labour being the unquestionable property of the labourer, no man but he can have a right to what that is once joined to, at least where there is enough, and as good, left in common for others.

§ 28. He that is nourished by the acorns he picked up under an oak, or the apples he gathered from the trees in the wood, has certainly appropriated them to himself.... That labour put a distinction between them and common: that added something to them more than nature, the common mother of all, had done; and so they became his private right....

§ 30 ... [W]hat fish any one catches in the ocean, that great and still remaining common of mankind ... is by the labour that removes it out of that common state nature left it in, made his property.... And ... the hare that any one is hunting, is thought his who pursues her during the chase ... whoever has employed so much labour ... as to find and pursue her, has thereby removed her from the state of nature, wherein she was common, and hath begun a property....

§ 32 ... As much land as a man tills, plants, improves, cultivates, and can use the product of so much is his property. He by his labour does, as it were, inclose it from the common. Nor will it invalidate his right, to say every body else has an equal title to it; and therefore he cannot appropriate, he cannot inclose, without the consent of all his fellow-commoners, all mankind.... God and his reason commanded him to subdue the earth, i.e. to improve it for the benefit of life....

§ 33. Nor was the appropriation of any parcel of land, by improving it, any prejudice to any other man, since there was still enough, and as good left.... So that, in effect, there was never the less left for others because of his inclosure for himself: for he that leaves as much as another can make use of, does as good as take nothing at all. No body could think himself injured by the drinking of another man, though he took a good draught, who had a whole river of the same water left him to quench his thirst....

§ 46. The greatest part of things really useful to the life of man, and such as the necessity of subsisting made the first commoners of the world look after, as it doth the Americans now, are generally things of short duration; such as, if they are not consumed by use, will decay and perish of themselves: gold, silver and diamonds, are things that fancy or agreement hath put the value on, more than real use, and the necessary support of life. Now of those good things which nature hath provided in common, every one had a right ... to as much as he could use, and property in all that he could effect with his labour; all that his industry could extend to, to alter from the state nature had put it in, was his. He that gathered a hundred bushels of acorns or apples, had thereby a property in them, they were his goods as soon as gathered. He was only to look, that he used them before they spoiled, else he took more than his share, and robbed others. And indeed it was a foolish thing, as well as dishonest, to hoard up more than he could make use of. If he gave away a part to any body else, so that it perished not uselessly in his possession, these he also made use of. And if he also bartered away plums that would have rotted in a week, for nuts that would last good for his eating a whole year, he did no injury; he wasted not the common stock; destroyed no part of the portion of goods that belonged to others, so long as nothing perished uselessly in his hands. Again, if he would give his nuts for a piece of metal, pleased with its colour; or exchange his sheep for shells, or wool for a sparkling pebble or a diamond, and keep those by him all his life, he invaded not the right of others, he might heap up as much of these durable things as he pleased; the exceeding of the bounds of his just property not lying in the largeness of his possession, but the perishing of any thing uselessly in it.

§ 47. And thus came in the use of money....

Of Paternal Power

§ 57. So that, however it may be mistaken, the end of law is not to abolish or restrain, but to preserve and enlarge freedom: for in all the states of created beings capable of laws, where there is no law, there is no freedom: for liberty is to be free from restraint and violence from others; which cannot be, where there is no law: but freedom is not, as we are told, a liberty for every man to do what he wishes: (for who could be free, when every other man's humour might domineer over him?) but a liberty to dispose, and order as he wishes, his person, actions, possessions, and his whole property, within the allowance of those laws under which he is, and therein not to be subject to the arbitrary will of another, but freely follow his own....

Of the Ends of Political Society and Government

§ 123. If man in the state of nature be so free, as has been said; if he be absolute lord of his own person and possessions, equal to the greatest, and subject to no body, why will he part with his freedom? Why will he give up this empire, and subject himself to the dominion and control of any other power? To which it is obvious to answer, that though in the state of nature he hath such a right, yet the enjoyment of it is very uncertain, and constantly exposed to the invasion of others: for all being kings as much as he...and the greater part no strict observers of equity and justice, the enjoyment of the property he has in this state is very unsafe, very unsecure. This makes him willing to quit a condition, which, however free, is full of fears and continual dangers: and it is not without reason, that he seeks out, and is willing to join in society with others....

§ 124. The great and chief end, therefore, of men's uniting into commonwealths, and putting themselves under government, is the preservation of their property....

Of the Extent of the Legislative Power

§ 138. Thirdly, The supreme power cannot take from any man any part of his property without his own consent: for the preservation of property being the end of government, and that for which men enter into society, it necessarily supposes and requires, that the people should have property, without which they must be supposed to lose that, by entering into society, which was the end for which they entered into it; too gross an absurdity for any man to own. Men therefore in society having property, they have such a right to the goods, which by the law of the community are theirs, that no body hath a right to take their substance or any part of it from them, without their own consent: without this they have no property at all; for I have truly no property in that which another can by right take from me, when he pleases, against my consent. Hence it is a mistake to think, that the supreme or legislative power of any commonwealth, can do what it will, and dispose of the estates of the subject arbitrarily, or take any part of them at pleasure....

QUESTIONS

1. According to Locke, what gives a person the right to own property? Is there any limitation on that right?

2. Why does Locke believe people form government?

Deep Ecology

> *A human being is part of the [W]hole,... a part limited by time and space. We experience ourself... as something separated from the rest—a kind of optical delusion of our consciousness. This delusion is a kind of prison for us, restricting us to our personal desires and to affection for a few persons nearest to us. Our task must be to free ourselves from this prison by widening our circle of compassion.*

— ALBERT EINSTEIN

Science and common sense tell us that human communities are ultimately deeply embedded within the natural world, that we must understand and nourish our interconnectedness with nature because our survival depends upon it. Businesses, just like other human groupings, depend on the continued existence of the natural world for the resources that allow them to continue. One way to understand the need for sustainable development, then, is purely instrumental. That is, the natural world is of value to humankind because humankind wants to use it to meet its various needs—material, and also psychological, spiritual. Some would go further and place environmentalism on a rights-based foundation. Although the U.S. Constitution does not name the right to a livable environment, arguably we each have such a right.[11]

Whether viewed as a means to human ends or as a right we each possess, we tend to conceptualize the importance of preservation of our natural world in terms of what it means to human beings. This is an **androcentric** perspective, experiencing, explaining, and reasoning always from the human vantage point.

Some criticize this human-centeredness, and urge that we become **biocentric** in our approach to the environment. For them, the ethical stance is one that values the continued existence of the entire natural world for its own sake, not because of anything it can do for us. Supporters of what is sometimes called **deep ecology** insist that the rich diversity of life in all forms has intrinsic value, and that human beings have no right to threaten or reduce it, but rather have the obligation to change policies and behaviors that do so.

---

11 Some states have amended their constitutions to mention such rights. The *Constitution of Pennsylvania*, for instance, now reads:

The people have a right to clean air, pure water, and to the preservation of the natural, scenic, historic and aesthetic values of the environment. Pennsylvania's natural resources . . . are the common property of all the people, including generations yet to come. As trustee of these resources, the Commonwealth shall preserve and maintain them for the benefit of all the people.

A SAND COUNTY ALMANAC
Aldo Leopold

Wilderness

For the first time in the history of the human species, two changes are now impending. One is the exhaustion of wilderness in the more habitable portions of the globe. The other is the world-wide hybridization of cultures through modern transport and industrialization. Neither can be prevented, and perhaps should not be, but the question arises whether, by some slight amelioration of the impending changes, certain values can be preserved that would otherwise be lost.

To the laborer in the sweat of his labor, the raw stuff on his anvil is an adversary to be conquered. So was wilderness an adversary to the pioneer.

But to the laborer in repose, able for the moment to cast a philosophical eye on his world, that same raw stuff is something to be loved and cherished, because it gives definition and meaning to his life.

This is a plea for the preservation of some tag-ends of wilderness, as museum pieces, for the edification of those who may one day wish to see, feel, or study the origins of their cultural inheritance.

The Ethical Sequence

This extension of ethics, so far studied only by philosophers, is actually a process in ecological evolution. Its sequences may be described in ecological as well as in philosophical terms. An ethic, ecologically, is a limitation on freedom of action in the struggle for existence. An ethic, philosophically, is a differentiation of social from anti-social conduct. These are two definitions of one thing. The thing has its origin in the tendency of interdependent individuals or groups to evolve modes of co-operation. The ecologist calls these symbioses. Politics and economics are advanced symbioses in which the original free-for-all competition has been replaced, in part, by co-operative mechanisms with an ethical content.

The complexity of co-operative mechanisms has increased with population density, and with the efficiency of tools. It was simpler, for example, to define the anti-social uses of sticks and stones in the days of the mastodons than of bullets and billboards in the age of motors.

There is as yet no ethic dealing with mans' relation to land and to the animals and plants which grow upon it. Land, like Odysseus' slave-girls, is still property. The land-relation is still strictly economic, entailing privileges but not obligations.

Individual thinkers since the days of Ezekiel and Isaiah have asserted that the despoliation of land is not only inexpedient but wrong. Society, however, has not yet affirmed their belief. I regard the present conservation movement as the embryo of such an affirmation.

Animal instincts are modes of guidance for the individual in meeting such situations. Ethics are possibly a kind of community instinct in-the-making.

The Community Concept

All ethics so far evolved rest upon a single premise: that the individual is a member of a community of interdependent parts. His instincts prompt him to compete for his place in that community, but his ethics prompt him also to co-operate (perhaps in order that there may be a place to compete for).

The land ethic simply enlarges the boundaries of the community to include soils, waters, plants, and animals, or collectively: the land.

This sounds simple: do we not already sing our love for and obligation to the land of the free and the home of the brave? Yes, but just what and whom do we love? Certainly not the soil, which we are sending helter-skelter downriver. Certainly not the waters, which we assume have no function except to turn turbines, float barges, and carry off sewage. Certainly not the plants, of which we exterminate whole communities without batting an eye. Certainly not the animals, of which we have already extirpated many of the largest and most beautiful species. A land ethic of course cannot prevent the alteration, management, and use of these "resources," but it does affirm their right to continued existence, and, at least in spots, their continued existence in a natural state.

In short, a land ethic changes the role of Homo sapiens from conqueror of the land-community to plain member and citizen of it. It implies respect for his fellow-members, and also respect for the community as such.

In human history, we have learned (I hope) that the conqueror role is eventually self-defeating. Why? Because it is implicit in such a role that the conqueror knows…just what makes the community clock tick, and just what and who is valuable, and what and who is worthless, in community life. It always turns out that he knows neither, and this is why his conquests eventually defeat themselves….

Source: Aldo Leopold "A Sand County Almanac: and Sketches Here and There." Copyright © 1949, 1953, 1966, renewed 1977 and 1981 by Oxford University Press, Inc. Used by permission of Oxford University Press, Inc.

Free Market Ideology

A being has rights only if it is a rational, free moral agent with the ability to regulate and guide its life in accordance with some overall conception it chooses to accept.

— ROBERT NOZICK

WHY I AM NOT AN ENVIRONMENTALIST

STEVEN E. LANDSBURG[12]

Economics is the science of competing preferences. Environmentalism goes beyond science when it elevates matters of *preference* to matters of *morality*. A proposal to pave a wilderness and put up a parking lot is an occasion for conflict between those who prefer wilderness and those who prefer convenient parking. In the ensuing struggle, each side attempts to impose its preferences by manipulating the political and economic systems. Because one side must win and one side must lose, the battle is hard-fought and sometimes bitter. All of this is to be expected….

Economics forces us to confront a fundamental symmetry. The conflict arises because each side wants to allocate the same resource in a different way. Jack wants his woodland at the expense of Jill's parking space and Jill wants her parking space at the expense of Jack's woodland. The formulation is morally neutral and should serve as a warning against assigning exalted moral status to either Jack or Jill.

The symmetries run deeper. Environmentalists claim that wilderness should take precedence over parking because a decision to pave is "irrevocable." Of course they are right, but they overlook the fact that a decision *not* to pave is *equally* irrevocable. Unless we pave today, my opportunity to park tomorrow is lost as irretrievably as tomorrow itself will be lost. The ability to park in a more distant future might be a quite inadequate substitute for that lost opportunity.

A variation on the environmentalist theme is that we owe the wilderness option not to ourselves but to future generations. But do we have any reason to think that future generations will prefer inheriting the wilderness to inheriting the profits from the parking lot? That is one of the first questions that would be raised in any honest scientific inquiry.

Another variation is that the parking lot's developer is motivated by profits, not preferences. To this there are two replies. First, the developer's profits are generated by his customers' preferences; the ultimate conflict is not with the developer but with those who prefer to park. Second, the implication of the argument is that a preference for a profit is somehow morally inferior to a preference for a wilderness, which is just the sort of posturing that the argument was designed to avoid.

It seems to me that the "irrevocability" argument, the "future generations" argument, and the "preferences not profits" argument all rely on false distinctions that wither before honest scrutiny....

The hallmark of science is a commitment to follow arguments to their logical conclusions; the hallmark of certain kinds of religion is a slick appeal to logic followed by a hasty retreat if it points in an unexpected direction. Environmentalists can quote reams of statistics on the importance of trees and then jump to the conclusion that recycling paper is a good idea. But the opposite conclusion makes equal sense. I am sure that if we found a way to recycle beef, the population of cattle would go down, not up. If you want ranchers to keep a lot of cattle, you should eat a lot of beef. Recycling paper eliminates the incentive for paper companies to plant more trees and can cause forests to shrink. If you want large forests, your best strategy might be to use paper as wastefully as possible—or lobby for subsidies to the logging industry. Mention this to an environmentalist. My own experience is that you will be met with some equivalent of the beatific smile of a door-to-door evangelist stumped by an unexpected challenge, but secure in his grasp of Divine Revelation.

This suggests that environmentalists—at least the ones I have met—have no real interest in maintaining the tree population. If they did, they would seriously inquire into the long-term effects of recycling. I suspect that they don't want to do that because their real concern is with the ritual of recycling itself, not with its consequences. The underlying need to sacrifice, and to compel others to sacrifice, is a fundamentally religious impulse.

Environmentalists call on us to ban carcinogenic pesticides. They choose to overlook the consequence that when pesticides are banned, fruits and vegetables become more expensive, people eat fewer of them, and cancer rates consequently rise. If they really wanted to reduce cancer rates, they would weigh this effect in the balance.

Environmentalism has its apocalyptic side. Species extinctions, we are told, have consequences that are entirely unpredictable, making them too dangerous to risk. But unpredictability cuts both ways. One lesson of economics is that the less we know, the more useful it is to experiment. If we are completely ignorant about the effects of extinction, we can pick up a lot of valuable knowledge by wiping out a few species to see what happens. I doubt that scientists really *are* completely ignorant in this area; what interests me is the environmentalists' willingness to *plead* complete ignorance when it suits their purposes and to retreat when confronted with an unexpected consequence of their own position.

In October 1992 an entirely new species of monkey was discovered in the Amazon rain forest and touted in the news media as a case study in why the rain forests must be preserved. My own response was rather in the opposite direction. I lived a long time without knowing about this monkey and never missed it. Its discovery didn't enrich my life, and if it had gone extinct without ever being discovered, I doubt that I would have missed very much.

There are other species I care more about, maybe because I have fond memories of them from the zoo or from childhood storybooks. Lions, for example. I would be sorry to see lions disappear, to the point where I might be willing to pay up to about $50 a year to preserve them. I don't think I'd pay much more than that. If lions mean less to you than they do to me, I accept our difference and will not condemn you as a sinner. If they mean more to you than to me, I hope you will extend the same courtesy.

In the current political climate, it is frequently taken as an axiom that the U.S. government should concern itself with the welfare of Americans first; it is also frequently taken as an axiom that air pollution is always and everywhere a bad thing. You might, then, have expected a general chorus of approval when the chief economist of the World Bank suggested that it might be a good thing to relocate high-pollution industries to Third World countries. To most economists, this is a self-evident opportunity to make not just Americans but *everybody* better off. People in wealthy countries can afford to sacrifice some income for the luxury of cleaner air; people in poorer countries are happy to breathe inferior air in exchange for the opportunity to improve their incomes. But when the bank economist's observation was leaked to the media, parts of the environmental community went ballistic. To them, pollution is a form of sin. They seek not to improve our welfare, but to save our souls....

Biodiversity and Habitat Preservation

Extinction is irreversible, we lose diversity, beauty, a genetic resource, a natural wonder, a souvenir of the past. But more underlies these, really a religious reason. Life is a sacred thing, and we ought not to be careless about it. This applies not only to experienced life, but to preservation of the lesser zoological and botanical species. Species enter and exit the natural theater, but only over geologic time and selected to fit evolving habitats. Individuals have their intrinsic worth, but particular individuals come and go, while that wave of life in which they participate overleaps the single lifespan millions of times.[13]

ROLSTON HOLMES III

At this point in history, the destruction of habitat is the primary cause of species loss, not the actual hunting and killing of individual creatures. Although poachers still hunt the rare black rhino, for instance,[14] much more damage to animals, birds, fish and plants occurs indirectly, as the rapidly expanding human population of the globe makes way for itself and its drive for a high-consumption existence. This is why habitat preservation is so important—the maintenance of wetlands, forests, prairies, oceans, and rivers that naturally cleanse the water, air, and soil.

In the 1995 Supreme Court case *Babbitt v. Sweet Home*, loggers who had lost income and jobs for the sake of preserving the northern spotted owl and the red-cockaded woodpecker argued that the Endangered Species Act should not be interpreted to protect habitat—in this situation the ancient woods where the birds lived—but should be used only to keep people from hunting and killing the birds themselves. The Supreme Court disagreed. Describing the ESA as "the most comprehensive legislation for the preservation of endangered species ever enacted by any nation," the Court ruled that it could indeed cover habitat. Dissenting, Justice Scalia argued for a more narrow interpretation of the ESA. The law prevented outright killing of individual

continued

13 Environmental Ethics: Duties to and Values in the Natural World (Temple University PressPhiladelphia, 1988).

14 Not that these "truly egregious, even macabre" hunting practices don't still happen, including "the decimation of tigers to produce tiger penis soup at $300 a plate." Christopher Stone, "What to Do about Biodiversity: Property Rights, Public Goods, and the Earth's Biological Riches," 68 S. Cal L. Rev. March 1995, p. 592.

endangered creatures, but if government wanted to go further and protect habitat on privately owned land, it should use government funds to buy that land and set it aside for conservation purposes. To do otherwise would "impose unfairness to the point of financial ruin—not just upon the rich, but upon the simplest farmer who finds his land conscripted to national zoological use." Scalia refused to view the destruction of breeding grounds as the equivalent of injury to the species:

[S]urely the only harm to the individual animal from impairment of [the breeding function] is not the failure of issue (which harms only the issue), but the psychic harm of perceiving that it will leave this world with no issue (assuming, of course, that the animal in question, perhaps an endangered species of slug, is capable of such painful sentiments). If it includes that psychic harm, then why not the psychic harm of not being able to frolic about—so that the draining of a pond used for an endangered animal's recreation, but in no way essential to its survival, would be prohibited by the Act?

It was just this point that Justice O'Connor had taken up in her concurring opinion. "Breeding, feeding, and sheltering are what animals do," she wrote:

To raze the last remaining ground on which the piping plover currently breeds, thereby making it impossible for any piping plovers to reproduce, would obviously injure the population (causing the species' extinction in a generation). But by completely preventing breeding, it would also injure the individual living bird, in the same way that sterilizing the creature injures the individual living bird. To "injure" is, among other things, "to impair." [O'Connor quotes Webster's Dictionary.] One need not subscribe to theories of "psychic harm," to recognize that to make it impossible for an animal to reproduce is to impair its most essential physical functions and to render that animal, and its genetic material, biologically obsolete. This, in my view, is actual injury.[15]

Private Property, Regulation, and the Constitution

The **Fifth Amendment** to the U.S. Constitution states that "private property [may not] be taken for public use, without **just compensation**." The power to take private property for public use is called **eminent domain**. It may be exercised by local as well as federal and state government. Historically it has enabled public projects—such as the construction of highways, utility lines, parks and rapid transit systems—to move forward in spite of private property interests that might otherwise have blocked them. Suppose your state government determines that the most appropriate route for a new expressway is right through your living room. Your family may not refuse to cooperate with the state, but the state must pay your family for this "taking" of your property; government should not be able to force a small number of citizens to bear the brunt of activities that benefit the public generally.

The Fifth Amendment is the only part of the Constitution that explicitly protects private property owners' economic interests, and it has been an important battleground over the years as courts have had to define "public use," "just compensation," and, especially in recent environmental cases, the concept of a "**taking**."

15 *Babbitt v. Sweet Home*, 115 S.Ct. 2407 (1995).

Early cases typically dealt with the confiscation of private land—as in the highway example above. By the early twentieth century, though, many of the conflicts involved local zoning laws that prevented owners from enjoying economically optimal use of their property. In a 1926 case,[16] for instance, land that had been zoned for industrial development was restricted by a new zoning ordinance to residential use, reducing its value to the owner by 75 percent. Yet the Supreme Court found that this did not amount to a taking, and the city did not have to compensate the owner for it. The Court viewed the rezoning as an exercise of the **police power**, the power of state and local governments to make laws for public health, safety, and welfare. Pointing out that commercial use of land might, in shifting circumstances under that police power, wear out its welcome and become a **nuisance**, the Court wrote:

> *A nuisance may be merely a right thing in the wrong place—like a pig in the parlor instead of in the barnyard.*[17]

The result in *Euclid* was reached by balancing public benefits against private loss brought on by the regulation. In a more recent test of the police power to zone, the Supreme Court held that the benefit to the public derived from preserving the beauty and historic value of a train station in New York City outweighed the cost imposed on the private owner who had planned the construction of a 53-story building on top of it.[18] Again, there was no "taking," and no need to compensate the owner.

Since the passage of the National Environmental Protection Act in 1970, **regulatory takings** challenges have been brought by private property owners who believe that environmental regulations unfairly burden them as individuals with the costs of protecting our natural resources. Here is how these cases have arisen: a government regulation designed to protect the environment impinges on an owner's freedom to use that property in some way. For instance, farmers are directed not to use certain pesticides harmful to groundwater, ranchers are told they must put their cattle at risk to protect grizzly bears, the owners of "wetlands," the marshes that harbor delicate ecosystems crucial to the natural cleansing cycle, are directed not to drain or build on their land. In each situation, the owner alleges that the environmental regulation is the equivalent of a "taking," and demands compensation. Environmentalists view these claims with alarm because, if they succeed, they have the potential of undercutting the entire regulatory network; government will not be able to afford to regulate.

In the next case, the Supreme Court deals with one of these challenges, and in the process recasts its mechanism for defining a taking under the Fifth Amendment.

LUCAS v. SOUTH CAROLINA COASTAL COUNCIL

Supreme Court of the United States, 1992
112 S.Ct. 2886

Justice SCALIA delivered the opinion of the Court. ✳

In 1986, David H. Lucas paid $975,000 for two residential lots on the Isle of Palms ... South Carolina, on which he intended to build single-family homes. In 1988, however, the South Carolina Legislature enacted the Beachfront Management Act (Act), which had the direct effect of barring [him] from erecting any permanent habitable structures on his

---

16 Village of Euclid v. Ambler Realty Co., 272 U.S. 365 (1926).

17 In the *Euclid* case, the pig did not wander into the parlor. By varying the zoning, the town was moving its "parlor" to surround the "pig." Even so, the Supreme Court held that a common law "nuisance" existed.

18 Penn Central Transportation Co. v. New York City, 98 S.Ct. 2646 (1978).

two parcels.... This case requires us to decide whether the Act's dramatic effect on the economic value of Lucas's lots accomplished a taking of private property under the Fifth and Fourteenth Amendments requiring the payment of "just compensation."

South Carolina's expressed interest in intensively managing development activities in the so-called "coastal zone" dates from 1977 when, in the aftermath of Congress's passage of the federal Coastal Zone Management Act of 1972, the legislature enacted a Coastal Zone Management Act of its own. [This law] required owners of coastal zone land that qualified as a "critical area" (defined in the legislation to include beaches and immediately adjacent sand dunes), to obtain a permit from the newly created South Carolina Coastal Council prior to committing the land to a [new use].

In the late 1970s, Lucas and others began extensive residential development of the Isle of Palms, a barrier island situated eastward of the City of Charleston.... Lucas in 1986 purchased the two lots at issue in this litigation.... No portion of the lots, which were located approximately 300 feet from the beach, qualified as a "critical area" under the 1977 Act; accordingly, at the time Lucas acquired these parcels, he was not legally obliged to obtain a permit from the Council in advance of any development activity. His intention with respect to the lots was to do what the owners of the immediately adjacent parcels had already done: erect single-family residences. He commissioned architectural drawings for this purpose.

[But in 1988 new legislation directed the Council to create a line beyond which no "occupiable improvements" could be built. When this "baseline" was drawn, Lucas found he was prohibited from building on his land.]

[In *Pennsylvania Coal Co. v. Mahon* (1922), Justice Holmes recognized] that ... if ... the uses of private property were subject to unbridled, uncompensated qualification under the police power, "the natural tendency of human nature [would be] to extend the qualification more and more until at last private property disappear[ed]." These considerations gave birth in that case to the oft-cited maxim that, "while property may be regulated to a certain extent, if regulation goes too far it will be recognized as a taking."

[The Court explains that in the 70 years since the *Mahon* case, it has avoided the use of any "set formula" for determining "how far is too far," instead examining the specific facts of each case.]

We have, however, described at least two discrete categories of regulatory action as compensable without case-specific inquiry into the public interest advanced in support of the restraint. The first encompasses regulations that compel the property owner to suffer a physical "invasion" of his property. In general (at least with regard to permanent invasions), no matter how minute the intrusion, and no matter how weighty the public purpose behind it, we have required compensation. For example, in *Loretto v. Teleprompter Manhattan CATV Corp.* (1982), we determined that New York's law requiring landlords to allow television cable companies to emplace cable facilities in their apartment buildings constituted a taking, even though the facilities occupied at most only 1 1/2 cubic feet of the landlords' property.

The second situation ... is where regulation denies all economically beneficial or productive use of land....

[R]egulations that leave the owner of land without economically beneficial or productive options for its use—typically, as here, by requiring land to be left substantially in its natural state—carry with them a heightened risk that private property is being pressed into some form of public service under the guise of mitigating serious public harm....

We think, in short, that there are good reasons for our frequently expressed belief that when the owner of real property has been called upon to sacrifice *all* economically beneficial uses in the name of the common good, that is, to leave his property economically idle, he has suffered a taking....

[There are many precedent cases establishing that government may halt a use of property that is harmful to the public without paying compensation to the owner.

However, Scalia argues, since none of those precedents involved regulations that completely removed all economic value from the land, that principle does not apply to the case before him. In *Lucas*-like situations, he reasons, the regulation must count as a taking—unless it simply forbids a use already forbidden under the common law.]

On this analysis, the owner of a lake bed, for example, would not be entitled to compensation when he is denied the requisite permit to engage in a landfilling operation that would have the effect of flooding others' land. Nor the corporate owner of a nuclear generating plant, when it is directed to remove all improvements from its land upon discovery that the plant sits astride an earthquake fault. Such regulatory action may well have the effect of eliminating the land's only economically productive use, but it does not proscribe a productive use that was previously permissible under relevant property and nuisance principles. The use of these properties for what are now expressly prohibited purposes was always unlawful, and … it was open to the State at any point to make the implication of those background principles of nuisance and property law explicit….When, however, a regulation that declares "off-limits" all economically productive or beneficial uses of land goes beyond what the relevant background principles would dictate, compensation must be paid to sustain it.

The "total taking" inquiry we require today will ordinarily entail (as the application of state nuisance law ordinarily entails) analysis of, among other things, the degree of harm to public lands and resources, or adjacent private property, posed by the claimant's proposed activities, the social value of the claimant's activities and their suitability to the locality in question, and the relative ease with which the alleged harm can be avoided through measures taken by the claimant and the government (or adjacent private landowners) alike. The fact that a particular use has long been engaged in by similarly situated owners ordinarily imports a lack of any common-law prohibition (though changed circumstances or new knowledge may make what was previously permissible no longer so). So also does the fact that other landowners, similarly situated, are permitted to continue the use denied to the claimant.

[Judgment against Lucas is reversed. The case goes back to the state courts to determine if common law principles would prevent him from building on his property. If not, he must be compensated for the environmental restriction.]

Justice KENNEDY concurring in the judgment. ✳

The rights conferred by the Takings Clause and the police power of the State may co-exist without conflict. Property is bought and sold, investments are made, subject to the State's power to regulate. Where a taking is alleged from regulations which deprive the property of all value, the test must be whether the deprivation is contrary to reasonable, investment-backed expectations….

In my view, reasonable expectations must be understood in light of the whole of our legal tradition. The common law of nuisance is too narrow a confine for the exercise of regulatory power in a complex and interdependent society.

Justice BLACKMUN, dissenting. ✳

Today the Court launches a missile to kill a mouse.

The State of South Carolina prohibited Lucas from building a permanent structure on his property from 1988 to 1990. Relying on an unreviewed (and implausible) state trial court finding that this restriction left Lucas' property valueless, this Court granted review to determine whether compensation must be paid in cases where the State prohibits all economic use of real estate….

I, like the Court, will give far greater attention to this case than its narrow scope suggests—not because I can intercept the Court's missile, or save the targeted mouse, but because I hope perhaps to limit the collateral damage.

In 1972 Congress passed the Coastal Zone Management Act. The Act was designed to provide States with money and incentives to carry out Congress' goal of protecting the public from shoreline erosion and coastal hazards. In the 1980 Amendments to the Act, Congress directed States to enhance their coastal programs by "[p]reventing or significantly reducing threats to life and the destruction of property by eliminating development and redevelopment in high-hazard areas."

South Carolina began implementing the congressional directive by enacting the South Carolina Coastal Zone Management Act of 1977. Under the 1977 Act, any construction activity in what was designated the "critical area" required a permit from the Council, and the construction of any habitable structure was prohibited. The 1977 critical area was relatively narrow.

This effort did not stop the loss of shoreline. In October 1986, the Council appointed a "Blue Ribbon Committee on Beachfront Management" to investigate beach erosion and propose possible solutions. In March 1987, the Committee found that South Carolina's beaches were "critically eroding," and proposed land-use restrictions. In response, South Carolina enacted the Beachfront Management Act on July 1, 1988. The 1988 Act did not change the uses permitted within the designated critical areas. Rather, it enlarged those areas to encompass the distance from the mean high watermark to a setback line established on the basis of "the best scientific and historical data" available.

Petitioner Lucas is a contractor, manager, and part owner of the Wild Dune development on the Isle of Palms. He has lived there since 1978. In December 1986, he purchased two of the last four pieces of vacant property in the development. The area is notoriously unstable. In roughly half of the last 40 years, all or part of petitioner's property was part of the beach or flooded twice daily by the ebb and flow of the tide. Between 1957 and 1963, petitioner's property was under water.... Between 1981 and 1983, the Isle of Palms issued 12 emergency orders for sandbagging to protect property in the Wild Dune development. Determining that local habitable structures were in imminent danger of collapse, the Council issued permits for two rock revetments to protect condominium developments near petitioner's property from erosion; one of the revetments extends more than halfway onto one of his lots....

The Court creates new Takings jurisprudence based on the trial court's finding that the property had lost all economic value. This finding is almost certainly erroneous. [Lucas] can still enjoy other attributes of ownership, such as the right to exclude others, "one of the most essential sticks in the bundle of rights that are commonly characterized as property." [Lucas] can picnic, swim, camp in a tent or live on the property in a moveable trailer.... Petitioner also retains the right to [sell] the land, which would have value for neighbors and for those prepared to enjoy proximity to the ocean without a house....

The Court ... takes the opportunity to create a new scheme for regulations that eliminate all economic value. From now on, there is a categorical rule finding these regulations to be a taking unless the use they prohibit is a background common-law nuisance....

I first question the Court's rationale in creating a category that obviates a "case-specific inquiry into the public interest advanced," if all economic value has been lost. If one fact about the Court's taking jurisprudence can be stated without contradiction, it is that "the particular circumstances of each case" determine whether a specific restriction will be rendered invalid by the government's failure to pay compensation. This is so because ... the ultimate conclusion "necessarily requires a weighing of private and public interests." When the government regulation prevents the owner from any economically valuable use of his property, the private interest is unquestionably substantial, but we have never before held that no public interest can outweigh it....

This Court repeatedly has recognized the ability of government, in certain circumstances, to regulate property without compensation no matter how adverse the financial effect on the owner may be. More than a century ago, the Court explicitly upheld the right of States to prohibit uses of property injurious to public health, safety, or welfare without paying compensation ... *Mugler v. Kansas* (1887). On this basis, the Court upheld an ordinance effectively prohibiting operation of a previously lawful brewery, although the "establishments will become of no value as property." *Mugler* was only the beginning in a long line of cases.... In *Miller v. Schoene* (1928), the Court held that the Fifth Amendment did not require Virginia to pay compensation to the owner of cedar trees ordered destroyed to prevent a disease from spreading to nearby apple orchards....

In none of the cases did the Court suggest that the right of a State to prohibit certain activities without paying compensation turned on the availability of some residual valuable use. Instead, the cases depended on whether the government interest was sufficient to prohibit the activity, given the significant private cost....

[T]he Court seems to treat history as a grab-bag of principles, to be adopted where they support the Court's theory, and ignored where they do not.

QUESTIONS

1. The image of David Lucas that emerges from majority Justice Scalia's description is strikingly different from the one that Justice Blackmun creates in his dissent. What are the two contrasting stories in this case? Do you think that when Lucas bought the land at issue here, in 1986, he had reason to know that by building on it he would soon be the owner of a "pig in a parlor"?

2. According to the majority, what two types of regulatory action automatically trigger compensation as takings, without a court needing to examine the circumstances in a case-specific way? Why does the dissent object to this approach?

3. Included in the bundle of rights that go with land ownership are those of occupation, use, and sale. When something is done to affect those rights—making them less valuable to the owner—the common law allows a suit for nuisance. A nuisance is an activity or condition that creates an unreasonable interference with a person's use and enjoyment of property. So, for example, a nuisance is created when a service station allows gasoline to leak from its holding tanks onto adjourning residential property[19] or when a farmer's seasonal irrigation system spews waste water onto his neighbors' farmlands.[20] What role does nuisance play in the majority opinion in this case? In the other *Lucas* opinions?

4. A ballot initiative passed by Oregon voters in the November 2004 election reverses a trend in that state, which has some of the most restrictive land-use rules in the country. The new measure allows owners to prove that zoning or environmental regulations will reduce the investment value of their property, forcing the government to either compensate them for those losses or exempt them from the rules. Describing Oregon's strict regulation, co-author of the ballot measure Ross Day said, "If Enron does something like this, people call it theft. If Oregon does it, they call it land-use planning." Think of a way to counter his point.

---

19 *Golovach v. Bellmont*, 4 A.D.3d 730 (App.Div, N.Y. 2004); *Felton Oil Company v. Gee*, 2004 WL 119486 (Ark. 2004).

● Environmental Justice

Environmental justice refers to the ethical issues at the intersection of race/class discrimination and environmental harm or reform, as people who have suffered from discrimination or poverty are affected differently than the rest of the population, arguing that they are unfairly exposed to more environmental harms, and/or less able to gain access to important information. In general, they claim they are unfairly prevented from participating in decisions that deeply affect their health and safety in environmentally related matters.

The movement gained momentum in the 1980s, soon after a controversy that developed in North Carolina, when a largely African-American neighborhood was used as a dumping site for thousands of tons of toxic soil. The incident began in 1978 when a contractor decided to spray gallons of PCB-contaminated oil along rural highways at night instead of taking it to a recycling facility. (The contractor would go on to spend a short time in prison.) Faced with an environmental nightmare, in 1982 the governor directed that the soil at the roadsides be moved to a rural landfill about 60 miles from Raleigh, pending clean up when technology became available. The people living near the location where this landfill was being created believed their county had been selected because it was mostly African-American and poor. Protests began, with some people lying in the road to prevent trucks from dumping. Eventually, environmental officials admitted that the site was not ideal for hydrological reasons, and the controversy heightened, with charges of "environmental racism" made. The site was not decontaminated until 2004.

* * *

In 2001, the state environmental agency issued permits to a cement processing facility in Camden, New Jersey. About half of the people living in this mostly African-American area were children, and more than half were living at or below the poverty line. Some health data for the community are as follows:

- The age-adjusted rate of death of black females in Camden County from asthma was over three times the rate of death for white females from asthma in Camden County;

- The age-adjusted rate of death of black males in Camden County from asthma was over six times the rate of death for white males from asthma in Camden County.

- The self-reported asthma rate for Waterfront South residents was 33 percent, more than twice the self-reported rate of asthma in other parts of the City of Camden.

The people in South Camden called for an injunction to rescind the permits and halt the cement factory project, concerned that it would add to the air pollution from which they already disproportionately suffered. *South Camden Citizens v. New Jersey Department of Environmental Protection* was a groundbreaking case, representing the first time civil rights law was applied in the context of environmental justice. It was the first time a federal judge ruled that a state agency, as a recipient of federal funds, had an obligation to investigate the ways a private project might have unfair and discriminatory effects on a subset of the community. When this case was appealed to the Third Circuit,[21] a record number of **amicus** ("friend of the court") briefs were filed on behalf of all litigants. Both business and civil rights groups had a high stake in the outcome.

continued

20 *King v. Van Setten*, 2004 WL 1447736 (Mont. 2004).

The community won the first round of the case, in federal district court in 2001. On appeal, the Third Circuit found that the plaintiffs had no right to enforce Title VI's unless they could prove *intentional* discrimination.

* * *

Camden is not the only relatively powerless minority community with a concentration of heavily polluting industrial sites. In recent years toxic waste operators have considered Indian reservations and developing countries as potential disposal sites. Sometimes environmental justice advocates are able to pressure their way towards a more equitable outcome. Living through decades of industrial explosions and toxic leaks from the Royal Dutch/Shell-affiliated plants near her neighborhood in Norco, Louisiana—and watching cancer rates there rise sharply—brought Margie Eugene-Richard to the point of activism. She spearheaded negotiations that, by 2002, resulted in Shell buying the homes of the mostly low-income African-Americans in her community, enabling them to move away. Shell also agreed to upgrade its Norco facilities.

Globalization, Fairness, and the Environment

Vandana Shiva is a well-known activist for sustainable development and social justice. She holds a doctorate in theoretical physics, and in 1993 she received the prestigious Right Livelihood Award, an alternative to the Nobel Prize.[22] She writes and lectures about the damage done to democracy and to the natural environment by corporate globalization. This essay illuminates the essence of her critique. She begins by identifying what she calls the "myths of globalization." One myth is that trade integration will lead to a world where "everyone will have more goods, everyone will consume goods without limits, and everyone will be happy." This "trickle-down" theory, she writes, wrongly assumes that free trade will eventually benefit all, even the poor. A corollary "myth," according to Shiva, is that globalization is the path not only to universal prosperity, but to environmental stability: "The poor are hungry and will destroy the environment; only rich people will protect the environment; when everyone's rich the environment will prosper." In the essay that follows Shiva debunks these beliefs.

THE MYTHS OF GLOBALIZATION EXPOSED: ADVANCING TOWARD LIVING DEMOCRACY

VANDANA SHIVA[23]

[In India w]e were repeatedly told by organizations such as the International Monetary Fund (IMF) and the World Bank that Third World countries should not grow staple crops. They did not have competitive advantage, and the comparative advantage of feeding themselves should wait upon the development of a new market for farmers from the Midwest of the United States. In the meantime, Third World nations should grow flowers and shrimp and vegetables. If you look at any trade agreement-based structural adjustment prescription for any Third World country in the last decade, that is what it is supposed to do.

Basic or subsistence foods are, in general, low-valued goods. Shrimp and flowers are high-value commodities, so you can supposedly sell them on the export markets, and

---

22 Given annually by the Swedish parliament, the Right Livelihood Awards focus on visionary work on behalf of the planet and its people.

23 From James Gustave Speth, ed., *Worlds Apart: Globalization and the Environment* (Washington, DC: Island Press, 2003).

make a lot of money, with which your country can buy food, and so have growth. Unfortunately, it does not work that way, because when every country starts to grow shrimp, shrimp become cheap. When you import products such as rice and meat, they keep rising in cost. In India, we have had a fourfold rise in food prices in recent years, this in a country where 300 million are already hungry, where 90 percent of the income of the poor was for buying food. If they were already spending 90 percent buying food and were half-fed, when the food is four times more costly, you can imagine what they are doing—eating less. That is where malnutrition [and disease] comes from....

This industry has been moved [from temperate zones] to the Third World by the global food corporations partly because of the environmental costs, which are heavy.... In trying to recreate the sea on land, using huge pumps to bring seawater into fields, there is the danger of seepage: The sea water seeps into the local groundwater, and soon the area has no drinking water. I came to know about this issue because the women in the costal area of India started to destroy the shrimp farm ponds in protest, and when they were arrested, they wrote to me and said, "We've done this, we think it is an environmental problem ... come and help us." So I came to investigate and saw major environmental disaster areas: coconut trees dying and paddy fields wiped out because of salinization....

Swedish environmentalists have done a tremendous job of assessing these shrimp farms and their environmental footprints. These studies, and ours in India, have examined the destruction of agriculture, water, and mangroves. Only 13 percent of the feed given to a shrimp converts into protein. The rest goes to waste and becomes pollution, which is then pumped out daily into the sea and, of course, is degrading sea fisheries. So more fishermen lose their occupations.... For every dollar traded globally by exporting shrimp, between seven to ten dollars is destroyed locally in resources. Shrimp farming also required that you catch 15 times more fish at sea than the weight of shrimp that will be produced: the sea fish are used to make the food fed to the farmed shrimp. Thus a "sustainable" industry requires even more unsustainable sea fishing. There are many such shadow costs to globalized industries....

The Danish Environmental Ministry did a fascinating study some years ago that showed that 1 kilogram of food traded globally generates 10 kilograms of carbon dioxide. Thus, imports that replace local crops have the shadow cost of increased carbon emissions.... The Gujarat earthquake of January 2001 followed the Orissa cyclone of 2000, a storm of about 300 kilometers per hour. India never had cyclones of that kind of speed before. We did a study and found that it was approximately 50 percent higher in speed than past cyclones.... Because the shrimp farms had destroyed the costal mangroves, there was no natural buffer. As a result, the Orissa cyclone had a serious impact, and communities that had never been affected in the past did not know how to deal with it. Thirty thousand people died, along with about 1000,000 cattle. To the degree that global climate events may be linked to the environmental destruction brought about by globalization—and I believe that this link will be increasingly well demonstrated—we will see a vicious cycle: more globalized trade leading to more global environmental destruction that will require more global trade, and so on.

The government of India is now proposing a superhighway around the coast. We already have a highway and a train track. The new superhighway's only advantage would be that it is even closer to the sea and therefore it would supposedly save a few cents per ton in the transport of goods. [But] what happens when you have a highway wall 40 feet high hit by a cyclone driving a tidal wave 50 feet high: All that salt water sits on the inland side of the road and cannot drain out. We have already have examples of seawater rendering agricultural land infertile in this way; a new superhighway, combined with continuing climate change, is a recipe for further disasters.

Globalization has definitely meant the globalization of nonsustainable industrial agricultural, such as higher use of pesticides and more expensive seeds, which means debt, unpayable debt in the context of national poverty. In India, the land of karma, where we always believed that things got sorted out in the next janam (rebirth), for the first time people realize that we have to sort it out today with the moneylender. And who is the moneylender? The agent of the same global company that sells the pesticide and the seed. So, in India we see multinational corporations serving as moneylender and seed/pesticide agent in one, withdrawing traditional low-interest credit—another destructive element of globalization. These private moneylenders/sales agents charge for credit at 30 percent to 100 percent.... This is absolutely outrageous.... [M]ore than twenty thousand peasants have been driven to suicide due to high costs of seeds and pesticides in a deregulated market for agricultural inputs....

I want to stress that none of this can happen without real violence against people.... In protests against the aquaculture movement, six people were shot dead in various parts of India by the police. These numbers may seem small on their face, but they indicate a much larger population driven to the edge by undemocratic changes imposed on them from without and an increasing level of state-sanctioned repression in response to legitimate protest. In 1993, before the conclusion of the Uruguay Round, we saw a protest of half a million farmers in Bangalore, basically telling the Indian government not to sign the treaty because it would destroy our agriculture, upon which 75 percent of Indians depend.... Almost every day there is a protest somewhere in India, and some are dealt with violently by corporate security forces and the police.... I believe that protest is the first step in resistance but that the second and bigger step is building concrete alternatives institutionally in both production systems and consumption systems.

... [H]ow do we make the transition to sustainability? We are in an unstable situation in which three upside-down pyramids—our global economic system, our global political system, and our global environmental systems—have the least powerful in their shadows. The economic pyramid assigns high value to markets, but little or none to local economies. Regarding the environmental pyramid, most natural resources should remain unexploited, to maintain nature's vital processes; instead, most natural resources are being sucked into global markets. Little is being left for the sustenance of the people, and next to nothing is being left for nature's maintenance. In politics, democracy requires that people be empowered locally because that is where they can truly act and influence, and through local action address national issues. People want secure ways to influence their representatives. Since most people live and work at local levels, that is where the democracy should be the strongest.... [W]hat should be a tip of the political pyramid is now at the base, a far-reaching erosion of democratic power at the national and local levels.

These three upside-down pyramids need to be put back in order because they are thoroughly unstable, ready to fall at any time. Our current global systems are explosive—economically, environmentally, and politically.

For me, the use of the term "sustainability" is very clear. It is the maintenance of the ecosystem over time so that our rivers are not dead, our lakes are not polluted, our species are not extinct. It is also social sustainability: People must be able to maintain their cultures and diversity, maintain their livelihoods, and maintain their economic security. We have to bring nature and people into the picture.

The way we have started in India is through a movement we called the "Jaya-Panchayat," which means, literally, "living democracy." It is spreading like wildfire. We started it in twenty villages. We have reached four thousand villages in a year, and they are shaping their own systems of what they call free colonies, freedom zones. We will not have patents on life, we seek to resurrect sustainable systems that we had, and we will learn to advance new, sustainable technologies.

The success in India that we have had with the Panchayat grows out of three things. First, we have a constitutional amendment recognizing decentralized democracy as the highest form of democracy, one where the local village community or town community has more powers than the parliamentarians regarding major areas of the law, especially natural resources use, development planning, and the like. It is an example of true self-rule;

the people in these communities are saying, "We rule in our village and we will negotiate with government about what powers we want to delegate to them." The national government makes decisions on the basis of the principle of subsidiarity already enshrined in our constitution. And global investments and trade have to respect local democracy....

Second, the Panchayati-Raj is an elected body, and a panchayat by law has to have 30 percent women ... a more inclusive, less sexist, more balanced form of governance.

[Third], we are widening that concept to converge with the deep consciousness that we call "Vasudhaiv Kutumbkam," the earth community. This is not just the panchayat in the formal sense but the panchayat in the ecological sense of community, of all lives that must work together. The building of these new freedom zones, which ensure the protection of all species as well as the livelihoods of the poor, is creating a new potential and challenging the idea that you need to destroy the planet before you can save it. A new vision of a globalized world can come out of this potential; a globalization based not on free trade (that is not free) or open markets (which are not open), but on the true community of living things on a living planet.

QUESTIONS

1. Outline the many faceted harms associated with shrimp aquaculture in India.

2. According to Shiva, rampant globalization has created "three upside-down pyramids." What are they?
Source: "The Myths of Globalization Exposed: Advancing Toward Living Democracy" by Vandana Shiva.

CHAPTER **PROBLEMS**

1. In the summer of 2007, the G-8 nations (Britain, Canada, France, Germany, Italy, Japan, Russia, and the United States) met at a summit. With an eye on the 2012 expiration of the Kyoto Protocol, German Chancellor Angela Merkel and Japanese Prime Minister Shinzo Abe, leaders of the third and second largest world economies, pressed the leader of the largest, George W. Bush, to join them in strengthening an international response to climate change. Pointing to a U.N. report joined by more than 2,000 scientists estimating that, to prevent global temperatures from spiking to disastrous levels, greenhouse gases would have to be drastically limited within eight years, they argued that the developed nations should agree to set specific targets—such as a 50 percent cut in emissions by 2050. President Bush for years had been publicly skeptical of the science of global climate change, challenging the notion that it was caused by human activity, and had led U.S. resistance to signing the Kyoto Protocol. But in June 2007 he altered his approach somewhat. While acknowledging the importance of addressing climate change, he would draw the line at accepting specific targets for reducing greenhouse gas emissions. Instead, he called for a meeting of the most polluting nations, with the goal of crafting a plan for reducing—not capping—emissions.
Internet Assignment What happened? Have the world's heaviest polluters, including top polluter the United States, been able to reach an agreement? Have fast-developing nations like China and India signed on? Will the developed countries help them with new green technologies?

2. One approach to environmental protection involves creative use of taxes. Traditionally, we tax many of the things we value; we levy taxes on paychecks, income, property, sales, and businesses. But because taxation tends to discourage productive activity, why not use the power to tax for what it is: a reverse incentive? Why not, many argue, tax that which we

do *not* value, such as pollution, congestion, sprawl, and resource depletion? Nine European governments do just that: Reducing taxes on the "goods," they instead tax the "bads," like toxic waste. This is called "tax shifting." A "green tax" is one that uses government taxing power to build sustainable economies and benefit the environment.

Internet Assignment Find an example of green taxes or environmental tax shifting, both in the United States and abroad. Compare the two. Which seems to offer the most promising solution? Which scheme generates "the greatest good for the greatest number"?

Consider these three means of controlling air pollution:

- Fines levied on companies that exceed set emission levels
- Taxing emissions
- Allowing a tradeable permit system for emissions

Compare and contrast the three approaches. Which would you want in your neighborhood? Which would you favor if you owned a polluting business?

3. *Massachusetts vs. EPA* focuses on reduction of greenhouse gas emissions by new cars and trucks. But there are many strategies not touched upon in this case that will reduce vehicle emissions. Consider that in the next 30 years, 70 million new homes will be built in the United States alone.

   Internet Assignment Find the Congress for the New Urbanism and PlaNYC. What reduction in greenhouse gas emissions takes place when people choose an urban, as opposed to an ex-urban, lifestyle?

4. More than 20 states now require that utility companies derive a certain fixed percentage of their energy from renewable sources. Government has encouraged the private sector in the past with incentives and subsidies: In the mid-nineteenth century Congress gave railroad companies the land to build transcontinental rail networks and commissioned the first telegraph lines; in the twentieth century, the federal government financed the research that led to the creation of the Internet; in the twenty-first century, government continues to encourage alternative technologies.

   Internet Assignment Find out what Daniel Yergin, chairman of Cambridge Energy Research Associates, has dubbed the "bouillabaisse of incentives, mandates, subsidies and related … ingredients" that government entities are offering the private enterprise to help them go green. What government policies seem to be the most innovative? Most effective at achieving sustainability goals? Identify the stakeholders in the government subsidy context. Who benefits, and who is harmed?

5. Daniel Kammen, founder of the Energy and Resources Group in the Goldman School of Public Policy at the University of California, Berkeley, describes three waves of environmentalism. The first wave, he says, involved such prophets as Rachel Carson, the author of the mid-twentieth century book Silent Spring, which first raised the alarm on environmental harms, recognizing the problem. The second stage, according to Kammen, has been the regulatory effort of such bills as the Clean Air Act and the Clean Water Act. But, Kammen says, we need a third wave which will involve leaders with a "charismatic megaphone." Two such leaders are Al Gore and Virgin Airlines founder, Richard Branson.

   Internet Assignment Describe the terms of the $25 million dollar Virgin Earth Prize offered by Gore and Branson.

6. In 1990 the nonprofit organization Ceres was founded, envisioning "a world in which business and capital markets promote the well being of society and the protection of the earth's biological systems and ressources." Today it maintains a Web site identifiying itself as "Investors and Environmentalists for Sustainable Prosperity.

   "Internet Assignment Log on to the Ceres Web site (http://www.ceres.org) to answer the following:

- What is the Global Reporting Initiative (GRI)? How many companies have signed on?
- What is the Investor Network on Climate Risk (INCR)?
- What new Ceres projects have been initiated in the past year?

7. The World Trade Organization (WTO) was established in 1995 pursuant to the Uruguay Round of negotiations under the GATT to ensure the "optimal use of the world's resources in accordance with the objective of sustainable development. During the Doha Round of negotiations, the WTO discussed ways to promote global trade in vulnerable natural resources, such as forest products and endangered fish species.
Internet Assignment Find out what environmentalists have to say about the WTO's balancing of free trade and preservation of resources by checking out such groups as the World Wildlife Fund (http://www.wwf.org), the Friends of the Earth (http://www.foe.org), or Greenpeace (http://www.greenpeace.org). How do the proponents of free trade respond?

8. Species have been disappearing into extinction since they first existed on this planet, but the last 100 years have seen the rate of extinction leap alarmingly. At the time of the dinosaurs it is estimated that one species became extinct every 1,000 years, while today we lose one every day. The predictions are dismal: Within 30 years we will have lost 15 to 20 percent of all forms of life. Extinction should worry us for both practical and philosophical reasons. More than 50 percent of our pharmaceuticals come from various species. Until the bark of Pacific yew was discovered to contain a cure for ovarian cancer, it was considered a worthless scrub tree, and was almost wiped out. We do not know what other precious essences are yet to be discovered in the multitude of species now existing, but scientists are sure that by ruining their habitats, we are cheating ourselves and our descendants of their benefits. In fact, it seems likely that the more exotically diverse habitats, such as those in the rain forests, are likely to yield, if gradually, substances of highest priority for human well being.

The federal **Endangered Species Act (ESA)** went into effect in 1973. Of the 1,304 U.S. species that have been listed for protection since the law was passed, 12 were recovered by 2005, including the American bald eagle. Of the more than 568 animal species on the list in 2005, approximately 39 percent are either stable or improving. Still, there have been sporadic efforts to repeal the law.
Internet Assignment What is the current status of the Endangered Species Act?

9. Internet Assignment Despite widespread consensus among the vast majority of the world's scientists—and a majority of the Supreme Court—that global warming is happening, that it has serious negative impacts on human health and the environment, and that human activity is one of its causes, many still want to blunt that message. The Global Climate Coalition, for example, ran a multi-million dollar ad campaign in the late 1990s arguing that the Kyoto Protocol would severely undermine the U.S. economy. Find out what you can about the now-disbanded Global Climate Coalition. Who were they? What were their goals? Find out what you can about the following organizations who are skeptical about taking action to slow global warming:

- George Marshall Institute
- Science and Environmental Policy Project (SEPP)
- Greening Earth Society

Who funds them? Investigate the individuals who are prominent within the organizations. What is their expertise? What awards or achievements do they possess that would lend them credibility on this issue? If they have done research, how was it funded? Try www.sourcewatch.org, a project of the Center for Media and Democracy or the Integrity in Science project at www.cspinet.org. Ask the same questions of the Center for Media and Democracy and the Integrity in Science project.

10. **Internet Assignment** Find out what you can about indigenous environmental activists in other countries. What has been going on, for example, with the Mapuche Indians' fight for control of the forests on their ancestral lands in Chile? What was the result of the "water wars" in the Cochabamba region of Bolivia?

CHAPTER **PROJECT**

Business Ethics Fairy Tales

Many business analysts now believe that it makes economic sense for companies to embrace environmentally friendly strategies. As Zoe Knight, senior director of socially responsible investment at Merrill Lynch in London, puts it, "The benefits of addressing environmental issues now outweigh the costs. A shift has occurred whereby business will be rewarded by adopting a proactive stance." As established companies are learning to think green, green technology is on the rise, with venture capital firms seeking out innovative entrepreneurs. For the purposes of this exercise, a fairy tale is a story about how a single company was able to accomplish something "socially responsible" in the context of environmental quality. You will need to find an example of a company that has done what Milton Friedman would rail against—an activity that is not designed solely to increase stockholder return on investment, but is instead designed to benefit stakeholders who are not stockholders. The example you choose may, in fact, enhance the company's image and/or its bottom line, but the point of the exercise is to tell the story of a business that focused on environmentally and socially responsible goals, and achieved them. The class will be divided into teams. Each team will research and then tell a business ethics "fairy tale." Then the class will vote to select the best team product.

THE CONTEST

This is a contest, on two levels. First, your team is competing to locate the fairy tale you wish to tell. [24] Choose carefully—don't rush it. Consider a small- or medium-sized company, and try to find one whose story has not been told as often as Ben & Jerry's. (Nonprofits don't count, for purposes of this assignment.) You may want to do some "dirt-digging" on a company before your team selects it. A company's own public relations description of its achievements may look wonderful, but often a little research reveals another reality. One Web site that offers a perspective that is not susceptible to greenwashing is http://www.corpwatch.org. The second level of competition involves presenting your fairy tale to the rest of the class. Your team can tell its tale by making an oral report, distributing a written report, or by constructing a Web site. Once everyone has reviewed all the fairy tales, the class votes to see which team has done the best job, based on the evaluative criteria listed below.

EVALUATIVE CRITERIA

1. **Effectiveness:** The company's program appears to be well designed to address the goal it is trying to meet. (Evidence that the company is succeeding in its efforts would help.)
2. **Ethical consistency:** The company's behavior in any area of its enterprise does not appear to undercut its fairy tale project. The project itself has substance beyond pure greenwashing. (This is where checking for critical commentary matters.)
3. **Originality:** The company's efforts are unusual or fresh in some way.
4. **Presentation:** The fairy tale is told clearly and colorfully.

---

24 To avoid duplication, communicate to your instructor in advance for approval of your selection.

7

MARKETING AND TECHNOLOGY:

Choice and Manipulation

*The drive for material goods ... may be less admirable than a differ-
ent...set of goals. The fact is that the system works, and that it does both
motivate and reward people. If it appears to critics that the motivations are
inferior, and rewards are vulgar, it must be remembered that at least the people have their own choice of what these rewards will be.... It is essentially a
democratic system, and the freedom of individual choice makes it valuable
to the people who do the choosing.*

— JOHN CRICHTON, MORALS AND ETHICS IN ADVERTISING[1]

*It was like, "iCanBuy.com, your parents can give you an allowance and you
can just go and buy whatever you want." And I said, "ooh, that sounds
cool!"*

— TORI CLIFFORD, 12 YEARS OLD

A decade ago, more than $200 billion was spent annually on advertising in the United States,
much of it focused on television where the average American viewed close to 20,000 ads annually. Today, marketers have a broader range of options as mobile phones and the Internet
have become the media of choice in what some call a "digital centric landscape." *U.S.A. Today*
estimates that marketers will spend $33 billion on online advertising, close to 8 percent of
total global ad expenditures in 2007. By 2010, those numbers are expected to increase to $63
billion, representing 13.2 percent of global ad spending. New channels are constantly being created by an advertising industry whose spending continues to outstrip the growth of the world
economy by one-third.

This chapter begins with the U.S. constitutional protection available to advertisers—their
right to free "commercial speech." In the first case, this right challenges a law banning the sale
to pharmaceutical firms of data on doctors' prescribing practices, one example of the many
ways in which technology has altered the landscape of marketing.

We move on to consider consumer demand: Is it created and sustained by the advertising
industry, or is it already present, just waiting to be educated and informed by advertising?

The chapter continues by introducing legislation responsive to deception in advertising,
the Federal Trade Commission and Lanham Acts. The advertising business regulates itself,

---

1 In *Ethics, Morality and the Media: Reflections on American Culture*, Lee Thayer, Ed. (New York: Hastings House, 1980), p.
113.

and we include a recent revision of the Association of American Advertising Agencies' Standards of Practice.

In classical microeconomic terms, wages and prices fluctuate in response to millions of preferences expressed by consumers as they make their purchasing choices. But do some marketing strategies warp optimal marketplace functions by manipulating consumer perceptions? We read about the marketing of junk food to children in light of rising obesity rates, and about the tobacco industry, where advertising and public relations techniques have successfully reconfigured consumer perception of risk. In the same vein, a case dealing with direct-to-consumer advertising of birth control sustains the health-related theme of this chapter.

We are witnessing a sea change in marketing, where what matters is not so much the relative qualities of a product or service, but rather the mystique of its *brand*. In the last reading, we consider the impact branding may be having on our entire society, as the line between "corporate sponsors and sponsored culture" blurs.

Commercial Speech

Freedom of speech is guaranteed by the First Amendment of the U.S. Constitution, but for much of our history, from the persecution of abolitionists in the nineteenth century to the jailing of socialists in the early twentieth century, the public expression of offensive or unpopular opinion could be lawfully silenced. Not until the 1920s did legal doctrines protecting speech, *particularly* when offensive or unpopular, begin to gel in the courts. Today, unless it is deemed defamatory, obscene, or likely to incite violence, expression—including artistic and symbolic expression—is protected in what has been dubbed "the marketplace of ideas."

Initially the Supreme Court refused to apply expanded First Amendment protection to advertising, or "**commercial speech**," distinguishing between the marketplace of ideas and the marketplace of goods and services. Then, in 1976, a group of discount pharmacies in Virginia claimed that a state law that prevented them from advertising cut-rate drug prices violated their First Amendment rights. The Supreme Court agreed. Apart from the advertisers' economic interest, the Court recognized the consumers' interest in hearing what the advertisers had to say. "[T]hose whom the suppression of prescription drug price information hits the hardest are the poor, the sick and particularly the aged," it wrote. So, in *Virginia Board*,[2] the Court appeared to link the "right to receive information and ideas" with the traditional values that underlie free speech, as if well-educated consumers were the equivalent of well-educated voters. Commercial speech was protected mainly to ensure that "numerous private economic decisions" would be made on as well-informed a basis as possible. In contrast to pure speech, though, commercial speech was considered "hardier," better able to bounce back if regulated: "Since advertising is the *sine qua non* of commercial profits, there is little likelihood of its being chilled."

Two years after the *Virginia Board* case, the Supreme Court again struck down a state law as a violation of the First Amendment rights of a commercial speaker. In *First National Bank v. Bellotti*,[3] a Massachusetts bank wanted to publicize its opposition to proposed legislation for a graduated income tax. State law made it a crime for a corporation to advertise to influence voters on issues that did not "materially affect" its business, adding that no law regarding taxation would "materially affect" a corporation. The Supreme Court held that this law infringed upon the bank's First Amendment rights. Drawing from its reasoning in *Virginia Board*, it found the law limited the "stock of information from which the public may draw." And, in another case upholding the right to First Amendment protection for commercial speech—this

2   *Virginia State Board of Pharmacy v. Virginia Citizens Consumer Council, Inc.*, 96 S.Ct. 1817 (1976).

3   435 U.S. 765 (1978).

time for lawyers' advertising—the Court stated that regulation restricting the flow of information to consumers fosters the "assump[tion] that the public is not sophisticated enough to realize the limitations of advertising, and that the public is better kept in ignorance than trusted with correct but incomplete information."[4]

In the following case, a federal judge must decide a commercial speech claim in the pharmaceutical marketing context. As Judge Barbadoro explains:

> A lucrative market has developed... for data... [on] the prescribing practices of...[doctors]. Pharmacies acquire...[this] data in the ordinary course of business. Data mining companies such as the plaintiffs in this case...purchase the prescription data, remove information identifying patients before it leaves the pharmacy, combine what remains with data from other sources, and sell the combined data to interested purchasers....

The "interested purchasers," mainly pharmaceutical companies, then use the data to refine the technique known as "detailing" the personal visits of sales reps to doctors.

In part out of concern for the way detailing contributed to escalating health care costs, the New Hampshire legislature passed a law prohibiting the sale of "prescriber-identifiable data." Two data compiling firms sued, arguing the ban violated their consitutional rights to freedom of speech.

IMS HEALTH INC. ET. AL. v. KELLY AYOTTE, ATTORNEY GENERAL OF NEW HAMPSHIRE

United States District Court, New Hampshire, 2007
2007 WL 1244077

Paul Barbadoro, District Judge. ❋

Approximately 1.4 million licensed health care providers are authorized to write prescriptions in the United States for approximately 8,000 different pharmaceutical products in various forms, strengths, and doses. These prescriptions are filled by approximately 54,000 retail pharmacies and other licensed medical facilities throughout the United States.

...For each prescription filled, a record is kept that includes the name of the patient, information identifying the prescriber, the name, dosage, and quantity of the prescribed drug, and the date the prescription was filled. If the pharmacy is part of a larger organization with multiple retail outlets, each outlet's prescription data is ultimately aggregated with data from other outlets and stored in a central location.

IMS and Verispan are the world's leading providers of information, research, and analysis to the pharmaceutical and health care industries. IMS...purchases prescriber information from approximately 100 different suppliers. Verispan, a company roughly one-tenth the size of IMS, obtains its information from approximately thirty to forty suppliers. Plaintiffs collectively acquire and analyze data from billions of prescription transactions per year throughout the United States.

...To comply with state and federal laws protecting patient privacy, participating pharmacies allow plaintiffs to install software on their computers that encrypts any information identifying patients before it is transferred to plaintiffs' computers...where it is combined with data from other sources and made available to plaintiffs' customers....

[P]laintiffs add value to prescriber-identifiable data [by] combin[ing] it with prescriber reference information. This allows plaintiffs to, among other things, match each

4 *Bates v. State Bar of Arizona*, 97 S.Ct. 2691 (1977).

prescription to the correct prescriber, identify and use the prescriber's correct name, and address, specialty, and other professional information about the prescriber to the prescription data. Prescriber reference files are created using information obtained from various sources, including the American Medical Association's ("AMA") Physician Masterfile.... Plaintiffs use the data, together with the reference file data, to produce a variety of patient de-identified databases.

The AMA recently adopted a program that gives participating...[doctors] the power to limit access to their prescribing information ("the Prescribing Data Restriction Program" or "PDRP"). Under the PDRP, pharmaceutical companies are permitted to acquire prescriber-identifiable data for participating providers but they may not share the information with their sales representatives. IMS and Verispan participate in the PDRP and require their customers to abide by its terms.

....Pharmaceutical companies commit vast resources to the marketing of prescription drugs. In 2000, the pharmaceutical industry spent approximately $15.7 billion on marketing, $4 billion of which was dedicated to direct-to-physician strategies. More recent estimates suggest the industry currently spends between $25 billion and $30 billion per year on marketing. The large pharmaceutical companies spend roughly 30 percent of their revenues on promotion, marketing, and administration, while spending only approximately 13 percent on research and development.

Pharmaceutical companies market to both consumers and prescribers.... Among the companies'...marketing practices that are most relevant to this case are their efforts to enlist the support of "thought leaders" in the medical community and their use of "detailing" to persuade individual...[doctors] to prescribe specific brand-name drugs.

Thought leaders are physicians and researchers whose views are accorded special weight in the medical community. Pharmaceutical companies...sponsor...their research [and] retain them to serve as consultants and speakers, and entertaining them at dinners and other events....

Detailing

Pharmaceutical detailing generally involves the provision of promotional and educational information during face-to-face contact between sales representatives and... [doctors].

Pharmaceutical companies strictly control the information that detailers are authorized to present on their behalf. Although sales representatives generally provide prescribers with accurate information,... [a] 1995 study published in the *Journal of the American Medical Association* concluded that 11 percent of the in-person statements made to physicians by pharmaceutical sales representatives contradicted information that was readily available to them....

...Published reports estimate that the total annual retail value of sampled drugs exceeds $11 billion. Product sampling programs...facilitate access to prescribers. They also promote sales by allowing prescribers to become familiar with the sampled drugs and by increasing the likelihood that patients will continue to request prescriptions for sampled drugs after their samples have been consumed.... Many physicians accept samples because it allows them to provide free medications to patients who might not otherwise be able to afford them.

Gifts, Meals and Other Inducements

Prescribers are often reluctant to meet with sales representatives. In an effort to overcome this reluctance, sales representatives provide health care providers and their staffs with small gifts, free meals, and other inducements....

The Pharmaceutical Research and Manufacturers of America ("PhRMA") has adopted a voluntary...[code] in an effort to address public concern with gift-giving by sales representatives. The 56-page [code]...permits members to hire...[doctors] to serve as consultants and speakers,...it discourages members from otherwise offering inducements directly to health care providers unless either the value of what is provided is insubstantial (less than $100) and the inducement is primarily for the benefit of patients, or the value of the inducement is minimal and the inducement is directly related to the provider's practice....

...Pharmaceutical companies are not obligated to follow the PhRMA Code in New Hampshire. Nevertheless, the United States Department of Health and Human Services has endorsed the Code...[with these words]: "[a]lthough compliance with the PhRMA Code will not protect a manufacturer as a matter of law under the anti-kickback statute, it will substantially reduce the risk of fraud and abuse and help demonstrate a good faith effort to comply with the applicable federal health care program requirements."

Detailing can be an effective marketing technique for brand-name drugs. It works by, among other things: (i) building name recognition among prescribers for the drug being detailed; (ii) providing information about the drug to prescribers in a form that is designed to be persuasive; and (iii) providing inducements to providers consisting of free samples, small gifts, and meals....

...Detailing is generally used only to market prescription drugs that are entitled to patent protection. After the patents on a brand-name drug expire,...detailing is no longer seen as...cost-effective....

Pharmaceutical companies continue to heavily market brand-name drugs as treatments for conditions that can also be treated with generic alternatives that are not bioequivalent.... [T]hose patients who achieve the same benefits from a non-bioequivalent generic medication can save money by substituting the non-bioequivalent generic medication for [the more expensive] branded alternative.

Uses of Prescriber-Identifiable Information in Detailing

Pharmaceutical companies use prescriber-identifiable data to...identify "early adopters" who...are disposed to prescribe new medications. They also...identify...[doctors] who have recently changed their prescribing practices with respect to specific drugs, those who are prescribing large quantities of the [detailed] drugs,...and those who are prescribing competing drugs....

Pharmaceutical companies use prescriber-identifiable data to tailor their...messages to specific...[doctors]. For example, a sales representative might mention...that the drug she is detailing does not have a specific side effect that is associated with a competing drug that the health care provider is currently prescribing....

Yet another use of prescriber-identifiable data is to measure the effectiveness of detailing. Companies use the data to identify the ratio of brand-name to generic drugs prescribed, assess the success of or resistance to detailer visits, and measure the effectiveness of larger marketing campaigns....

The Statute

The Prescription Information Law...expressly prohibit[ing] the transmission or use of both patient-identifiable data and prescriber-identifiable data for certain commercial purposes,[5]...[was] signed into law on June 30, 2006...[and] is the first of its kind in the United States....

---

5 The pertinent language of the statute reads: Records relative to prescription information containing patient-identifiable and prescriber-identifiable data shall not be licensed, transferred, used, or sold by any pharmacy benefits manager, insurance company, electronic transmission intermediary, retail, mail order, or Internet pharmacy or other similar entity, for any commercial purpose, except for the limited purposes of pharmacy reimbursement; formulary compliance; care management; utilization review by a health care provider; the patient's insurance provider or the agent of either; health care research; or as otherwise provided by law. Commercial purpose includes, but is not limited to, advertising, marketing, promotion, or any activity that could be used to influence sales or market share of a pharmaceutical product, influence or evaluate the prescribing behavior of an individual health care professional, or evaluate the effectiveness of a professional pharmaceutical detailing sales force....

According to the law's legislative history, [it was passed] to protect patient and physician privacy and to save the State, consumers, and businesses money by reducing health care costs....

[At a legislative hearing] Representative Pamela Price...claimed that a one-year supply of the branded drug Dynacirc would cost Medicaid $1,047, while a one-year supply of the generic drug Verapamil would cost Medicaid only $162. Because Medicaid insures a hundred thousand patients, she said, the potential cost savings could be substantial.

...Based [on her reading of several studies, Price] concluded that detailing causes public mistrust of prescriber decisions...and the provision of incomplete and/or misleading information to prescribers. [She]...criticized [the AMA and PhRMA guidelines] as overly narrow, vague, discretionary, and lacking in enforcement mechanisms....

According to testimony offered at this hearing, some detailers use prescriber-identifiable information to put improper pressure on prescribers. One anecdote shared by a nurse practitioner...highlights this alleged problem.

> For the past several months, a drug rep has been bringing coffee to our office on Tuesday mornings. We have never asked her to continue doing this since we have a coffee pot, and we routinely make coffee for our staff and our patients. But she does it anyway, which is very nice of her. She calls this "Two for Tuesday." The problem is that every week she also says to me, "If you don't write 2 more prescriptions for my brand today, I'm not going to be able to continue bringing coffee." I prescribe her drug when it is right for my patients. There are many times when it is not right.
>
> We feel pressure from her to prescribe her product even though we have never asked her to bring coffee. This may sound like a small thing, but I feel that since she knows exactly how many prescriptions I write each week for her drug versus the competition, she is expecting a quid pro quo.[6]

LEGAL ANALYSIS

Does the Challenged Statute Restrict "Speech"?

[The New Hampshire Attorney General first argues that the state ban does not trigger the First Amendment, because it restricts mere factual information, not protected speech.]

The challenged law restricts speech by preventing pharmaceutical companies from using prescriber-identifiable information both to identify a specific audience for their marketing efforts and to refine their marketing messages. Such laws are subject to First Amendment scrutiny because they affect both the speaker's ability to communicate with his intended audience and the audience's right to receive information. Accordingly, I reject the Attorney General's argument that the Prescription Information Law is not subject to the First Amendment....

[The judge now applies the legal analysis found in the 1980 landmark Supreme Court case *Central Hudson Gas & Electric Corp. v. Public Service Comm'n.*]

Truthful commercial speech that does not promote unlawful activity can be limited under *Central Hudson* only if it "(1) is in support of a substantial government interest, (2) 'directly advances the government interest asserted,' and (3) 'is not more extensive than is necessary to serve that interest.'..."

---

6 A similar anecdote, as described in a January 2006 article in *The New York Times*, was also included in the legislative record. According to the article, a district manager for a pharmaceutical company sent an e-mail to detailers in which she stated that "[o]ur goal is 50 or more scripts per week for each territory. If you are not achieving this goal, ask yourself if those doctors that you have such great relationships with are being fair to you. Hold them accountable for all of the time, samples, lunches, dinners, programs, and past preceptorships that you have provided or paid for and get the business!! You can do it!!"

Is Protecting Prescriber Privacy a Substantial Governmental Interest?

[The Attorney General argues that the government has two interests that are substantial: an interest in protecting doctor's privacy, and an interest in containing health costs. The court rejects the first argument.]

... [The Attorney General argues] that pharmaceutical companies are using the data to help persuade doctors to make inadvisable prescribing decisions. In short, what the Attorney General claims as a distinct interest in protecting prescriber privacy is nothing more than a restatement of her contentions that the law can be justified because it prevents pharmaceutical companies from using prescriber-identifiable data in ways that undermine public health and increase health care costs. Accordingly, I reject the Attorney General's argument that the law can be justified on the distinct basis that it promotes prescriber privacy.

[On the assumption that New Hampshire's interests in promoting public health and in containing health care costs are "substantial," however, the judge now discusses whether the other elements of the *Central Hudson* test are met here.]

Does the Prescription Information Law Directly Advance the State's Interests in Promoting Public Health and Containing Health Care Costs?

... The [AG's] chain of reasoning ... begins with the major premise that prescriber-identifiable data allows pharmaceutical companies to target health care providers for marketing and tailor marketing messages in ways that make detailing more persuasive. Next, it assumes that because prescriber-identifiable data makes detailing more persuasive, it inevitably leads to more prescriptions for brand-name drugs when compared with generic alternatives because only branded drugs are detailed. Finally, it assumes that any increase in the number of prescriptions written for brand-name drugs when compared to generic alternatives harms the public health and increases health care costs because branded drugs often turn out to be more harmful than generic alternatives and almost always are more expensive. Accordingly, a ban on the use of prescriber-identifiable data for marketing purposes promotes public health and contains health care costs by prohibiting pharmaceutical companies from using prescriber-identifiable data to promote the sale of brand-name drugs.

... Any general claim that the public health is undermined when the effectiveness of detailing for brand-name drugs is increased depends upon the counterintuitive and unproven proposition that, on balance, brand-name drugs are more injurious to the public health than generic alternatives. ... [The State's] argument is unpersuasive because the record does not establish either that early adopters are more likely to be influenced by detailing than other health care providers or that new drugs are generally more injurious to the public health than existing medications. Accordingly, the Attorney General has failed to prove that the Prescription Information Law directly promotes public health.

... The Attorney General appears to assume that any health care cost savings that will result from a ban on the use of prescriber-identifiable data can be achieved without compromising patient care. However, this proposition is far from self-evident. Non-bioequivalent generic drugs are not always as effective as brand-name alternatives. ... Yet, a ban on the use of prescriber-identifiable data affects both helpful and harmful brand-name prescribing practices in the same way. Because the Attorney General has failed to prove that any reductions in health care costs that may result from a ban on the use of prescriber-identifiable data can be achieved without compromising patient care, I am unable to endorse her argument that the Prescription Information Law can be justified as a cost containment measure.

[At this point the judge notes that no one is arguing that prescriber data is false or misleading. It is true information, and case law has "previously rejected the notion that the Government has an interest in preventing the dissemination of truthful commercial information in order to prevent members of the public from making bad decisions with the information."]

"[B]ans against truthful, non-misleading commercial speech...usually rest solely on the offensive assumption that the public will respond 'irrationally' to the truth. The First Amendment directs us to be especially skeptical of regulations that seek to keep people in the dark for what the government perceives to be their own good." Health care providers are highly trained professionals who are committed to working in the public interest. They certainly are more able than the general public to evaluate truthful pharmaceutical marketing messages. Accordingly, the State simply does not have a substantial interest in shielding them from sales techniques that enhance the effectiveness of truthful and non-misleading marketing information. Instead, if the State is concerned that truthful detailing is causing health care providers to make inadvisable prescribing decisions, "the remedy to be applied is more speech, not enforced silence."

[Having found that the law fails to directly promote public health or to directly control health care costs, the judge goes on to discuss the final aspect of the *Central Hudson* test.]

Is the Prescription Information Law More Extensive than Necessary to Serve the State's Substantial Interests?

Even the harshest critics of pharmaceutical detailing acknowledge that it is sometimes used in ways that benefit public health.... The Prescription Information Law, however, does not discriminate between beneficial detailing and harmful detailing. Instead, it imposes a sweeping ban on the use of prescriber-identifiable information to enhance the effectiveness and efficiency of all detailing....

[T]here are a number of ways in which the State can address the concerns that underlie the Prescription Information Law without restricting protected speech. First, if legislators are concerned that pharmaceutical companies are improperly using samples, gifts, meals, and other inducements to promote inadvisable prescribing practices, they can address this perceived problem by following other states that have adopted laws that limit such practices.

Second, if legislators fear that pharmaceutical detailing is simply too effective...they can require the State to enter the intellectual marketplace in several different ways with competing information that will help health care providers balance and place in context the sales messages that detailers deliver.... [T]hey can require the State to prepare and distribute "best practice" [prescribing] guidelines;... to develop counter-detailing programs that make health care providers aware of the cost implications of their prescribing decisions; or they can require health care providers to regularly participate in continuing medical education programs [that provide] information concerning the advantages and disadvantages of prescribing generic drugs rather than brand-name drugs.

Finally, if legislators are concerned that pharmaceutical companies are using prescriber-identifiable data to drive up Medicaid drug costs, they can address the issue directly by properly implementing a Medicaid Pharmacy Program that takes into account the cost-effectiveness of brand-name drugs when compared with non-bioequivalent generic alternatives.... [T]he State can prevent unnecessary expenditures on brand-name drugs simply by subjecting such drugs to prior authorization and rejecting requests to prescribe them when they are not medically necessary.

Conclusion

...Because the Prescription Information Law restricts constitutionally protected speech without directly serving the State's substantial interests and because alternatives exist that would achieve the State's interests as well or better without restricting speech, the law cannot be enforced to the extent that it purports to restrict the transfer or use of prescriber-identifiable data. Plaintiffs' request for declaratory relief and a permanent injunction are granted.

So ordered.

QUESTIONS

1. What is involved in "detailing" a drug? Identify the various stakeholders involved in detailing. How does each benefit from the practice? How are they harmed?

2. How does the acquisition of prescription information facilitate the marketing of branded drugs? Why did the state of New Hampshire want to limit the practice? On what grounds did the court overturn the New Hampshire law?

3. A state-supported program in Pennsylvania called PACE, pays a team of doctors to assess multiple scientific studies in order to give physicians objective information regarding the costs and benefits of various types of treatments. This so-called "academic detailing program" helps doctors decide which drugs are most effective and most cost-effective. Suppose the federal government supported this kind of program nationwide, and banned all pharmaceutical detailing. Would this regulation pass the *Central Hudson* test?

4. New Hampshire's Attorney General claimed to have a "substantial state interest" in protecting prescriber privacy by "limiting unwarranted intrusions into the decision-making process of prescribing physicians…." Review Chapter 3, focusing on the Alan Westin article "The Functions of Privacy." What aspects of privacy might arguably be at risk when prescribing data is being accessed, packaged, and sold as here? Who are the stakeholders? What ethical issues arise?

5. Judge Barbadoro writes: "If legislators are concerned that pharmaceutical companies are improperly using samples, gifts, meals, and other inducements to promote inadvisable prescribing practices, they can address this perceived problem by following other states that have adopted laws that limit such practices. "
Internet Assignment Find a state law designed to control detailing excesses. Try to assess its effectiveness. Look for enforcement actions.

6. During the legislative hearing, New Hampshire state representative Price submitted a research paper written by a health care advocate for California Public Interest Research Group (CALPIRG), Emily Clayton. Find this paper at http://calpirg.org. Read it; then write a dissenting opinion for *IMS v. Ayotte*.

7. In May 2004 Pfizer paid a $430 fine and pled guilty to criminal charges over the marketing by its subsidiary Warner-Lambert of a drug called Neurontin. The marketing strategy was to pay doctors tens of thousands of dollars each if they would agree to give talks to groups of other doctors, explaining that Neurontin, which had been approved for epilepsy, could be prescribed for several other ("off label") uses. One of these physician/lecturers was paid more than $300,000; others, including some from prestigious medical schools, received more than $100,000 each. Neurontin became a top-selling drug, producing $2 billion in sales as doctors prescribed it for a range of maladies, including bipolar disorder and restless-leg syndrome.[7] Such scandals seemed to flood the news in 2004, leading to a

---

7 "I want you out there every day selling Neurontin. . . . Pain management, now that's money. We don't want to share these patients with everybody, we want them on Neurontin only. We want their whole drug budget—not a quarter, not half—the whole thing. . . . Hold their hand and whisper in their ear: 'Neurontin for pain, Neurontin for everything.' I don't want to see a single patient coming off Neurontin before they've been up to at least 4,800 milligrams a day. I don't want to hear that safety crap, either. Have you tried Neurontin? Every one of you should take one just to see there's nothing. It's a great drug!" (Transcript of a whistleblower lawsuit filed against Pfizer and Warner-Lambert in 1996, and unsealed in 2003.)

government crackdown on the marketing techniques of the pharmaceutical industry, with nearly every global drug company receiving subpoenas.

What would an ethical analysis of these marketing strategies look like from a free market perspective? From the point of view of a utilitarian? A deontologist? A virtue ethicist? A proponent of the ethic of care?

Native Americans and Malt Liquor Advertising

In 1993,[8] Hornell Brewing Company decided to adopt the name Crazy Horse for one of its products, a malt liquor. This decision sparked anger among Native Americans—and their sympathizers in Washington DC. Crazy Horse was a greatly respected Oglala Sioux known for his spiritual qualities; the use of his name to sell alcohol seemed particularly outrageous in the light of a documented rate of alcoholism among Native Americans six times that of the general population. After a heated debate, Congress passed a law prohibiting the use of the name Crazy Horse on alcoholic beverages. Hornell then sued, arguing the ban violated the company's free speech rights.

Applying the *Central Hudson* test, the district judge had no difficulty finding a "substantial government interest" in protecting the health and welfare of an afflicted community, stating, "Native American infants are twenty times more likely than other United States infants of being born with fetal alcohol syndrome." Yet he was not convinced that a ban on the Crazy Horse label would "directly advance" such a worthy goal:

> Indeed, the legislative record as to the offensiveness of the Crazy Horse label would seem as likely to suggest the contrary proposition, that Native Americans would be discouraged from consuming an alcoholic beverage that dishonors the name of a revered Native American leader....
>
> The government asks the Court to make a leap of faith and logic... by concluding that because advertising may increase consumption and a product label is a form of advertising, the mere use of the Crazy Horse label product will enhance consumption. It is true that... a product label is a form of advertising. But that is not to say that a product label, standing alone, can have a remotely comparable effect on product consumption as would all advertising, such as print ads, billboards, and radio and television commercials.

And as for the final *Central Hudson* requirement, that a law must be tailored to fit the identified need, and be "no more extensive than necessary to further the government's interest," the judge wrote:

> The prohibition prevents use of the label anywhere simply to protect a relatively small segment of the population. The prohibition is not, as it could have been, limited to Native American reservations or narrow geographic areas where there is a demonstrably high concentration of Native Americans.
>
> Nor does this sweeping prohibition take into account sensible alternatives... such as education programs to inform Native Americans of the dangers of alcohol [or] an additional warning on the Crazy Horse bottle informing Native Americans of the dangers of alcohol or of the high incidence of alcoholism and its effects in Native American communities.... With obvious alternatives available that do not hinder speech in any way, or hinder it far less, the statute is not, by any means, a reasonable fit.

continued

8 *Hornell Brewing Co., Inc. v. Brady*, 819 F.Supp. 1227 (U.S. Dist. Ct. NY.) 1993.

As the court found the label ban unconstitutional as a violation of the First Amendment, it took the trouble to explain that it did not condone or endorse Hornell's choice of Crazy Horse to name its new malt liquor:

> The Court can well appreciate that the use of the name of a revered Native American leader, who preached sobriety and resisted exploitation under the hand of the United States government, is offensive and may be viewed as an exploitation of Native Americans throughout this country. The choice may be particularly insensitive given the ample documentation of alcohol abuse and its destructive results among Native Americans. Nevertheless, a price we pay in this country for ordered liberty is that we are often exposed to that which is offensive to some, perhaps even to many. It is from our exposure to all that is different that we best learn to address it, change it, and sometimes tolerate and appreciate it. "Freedom of speech may best serve its high purpose when it induces a condition of unrest, creates dissatisfaction with conditions as they are, or even stirs people to anger."

The judge concluded by suggesting that those upset by the Crazy Horse label do what another judge recommended when a restaurant in Toledo, Ohio decided to call itself *Sambo's*:

> If they are offended…not only can they refuse to patronize the plaintiffs, but they, too, can erect signs, carry placards, or publish advertisements designed to persuade others to refuse to patronize the plaintiffs. That is what freedom of speech is all about.

Advertising and Economics

> *Left wing economists, ever eager to snatch the scourge from the hand of God, hold that advertising tempts people to squander money on things they don't need. Who are these elitists to decide what you need? Do you need a dishwasher? Do you need a deodorant? Do you need a trip to Rome? I feel no qualms of conscience about persuading you to do that. [B]uying things can be one of life's more innocent pleasures, whether you need them or not. Remember your euphoria when you bought your first car?*
>
> — DAVID OGILVY, OGILVY ON ADVERTISING

> *[T]he illusion arises that it is good to accumulate it without limit. By doing so, man harms both the community and himself because, concentrating on such a narrow aim, he deprives his soul and spirit of larger and more rewarding experiences.*
>
> — ARISTOTLE

> *Advertising ministers to the spiritual side of trade.…It is a great power…part of the greater work of the regeneration and redemption of mankind.*
>
> — CALVIN COOLIDGE, 1926

Which came first, the advertising or the consumer craving? And what's wrong with consumer craving? Is advertising destructive of our polity? Or is it an essential driver of a healthy economy, even a form of artistic expression?

THE DEPENDENCE EFFECT

John Kenneth Galbraith[9]

The theory of consumer demand, as it is now widely accepted, is based on two broad propositions, neither of them quite explicit but both extremely important for the present value system of economists. The first is that the urgency of wants does not diminish appreciably as more of them are satisfied or, to put the matter more precisely, to the extent that this happens it is not demonstrable and not a matter of any interest to economists or for economic policy. When man has satisfied his physical needs, then psychologically grounded desires take over. These can never be satisfied or, in any case, no progress can be proved. The concept of satiation has very little standing in economics. It is neither useful nor scientific to speculate on the comparative cravings of the stomach and the mind.

The second proposition is that wants originate in the personality of the consumer....

Were it so that a man on arising each morning was assailed by demons which instilled in him a passion sometimes for silk shirts, sometimes for kitchenware, sometimes for chamber-pots, and sometimes for orange squash, there would be every reason to applaud the effort to find the goods, however odd, that quenched this flame. But should it be that his passion was the result of his first having cultivated the demons, and should it also be that this effort to allay it stirred the demons to ever greater and greater effort, there would be question as to how rational was his solution. Unless restrained by conventional attitudes, he might wonder if the solution lay with more goods or fewer demons.

So it is that if production creates the wants it seeks to satisfy...then the urgency of the wants can no longer be used to defend the urgency of the production. Production only fills a void that it has itself created....

The even more direct link between production and wants is provided by the institutions of modern advertising and salesmanship. These cannot be reconciled with the notion of independently determined desires, for their central function is to create desires— to bring into being wants that previously did not exist. This is accomplished by the producer of the goods or at his behest. A broad empirical relationship exists between what is spent on production of consumers' goods and what is spent in synthesizing the desires for that production. A new consumer product must be introduced with a suitable advertising campaign to arouse an interest in it. The path for an expansion of output must be paved by a suitable expansion in the advertising budget. Outlays for the manufacturing of a product are not more important in the strategy of modern business enterprise than outlays for the manufacturing of demand for the product. None of this is novel. All would be regarded as elementary by the most retarded student in the nation's most primitive school of business administration....

But such integration means recognizing that wants are dependent on production. It accords to the producer the function both of making the goods and of making the desires for them. It recognizes that production, not only passively through emulation, but actively through advertising and related activities, creates the want it seeks to satisfy.

The businessman and the lay reader will be puzzled over the emphasis which I give to a seemingly obvious point. The point is indeed obvious. But it is one which, to a singular degree, economists have resisted. They have sensed, as the layman does not, the damage to established ideas which lurks in these relationships. As a result, incredibly, they

9 From John Kenneth Galbraith, *The Affluent Society* (Boston: Houghton Mifflin, 1958). Copyright 1958, 1969, 1978, 1984 by John Kenneth Galbraith. Reprinted by permission of Houghton Mifflin Company. All rights reserved. Galbraith is a Harvard University economist.

have closed their eyes (and ears) to the most obtrusive of all economic phenomena, namely modern want creation.

This is not to say that the evidence affirming the dependence of wants on advertising has been entirely ignored. It is one reason why advertising has so long been regarded with such uneasiness by economists. Here is something which cannot be accommodated easily to existing theory. More pervious scholars have speculated on the urgency of desires which are so obviously the fruit of such expensively contrived campaigns for popular attention. Is a new breakfast cereal or detergent so much wanted if so much must be spent to compel in the consumer the sense of want? But there has been little tendency to go on to examine the implications of this for the theory of consumer demand and even less for the importance of production and productive efficiency. These have remained sacrosanct. More often the uneasiness has been manifested in a general disapproval of advertising and advertising men, leading to the occasional suggestion that they shouldn't exist. Such suggestions have usually been ill received. . . .

The fact that wants can be synthesized by advertising, catalyzed by salesmanship, and shaped by the discreet manipulations of the persuaders shows that they are not very urgent. A man who is hungry need never be told of his need for food. If he is inspired by his appetite, he is immune to the influence of Messrs. Batten, Barton, Durstine and Osborn. The latter are effective only with those who are so far removed from physical want that they do not already know what they want. In this state alone men are open to persuasion. . . .

As a society becomes increasingly affluent, wants are increasingly created by the process by which they are satisfied. This may operate passively. Increases in consumption, the counterpart of increases in production, act by suggestion or emulation to create wants. Or producers may proceed actively to create wants through advertising and salesmanship. Wants thus come to depend on output. In technical terms it can no longer be assumed that welfare is greater at an all-round higher level of production than at a lower one. It may be the same. The higher level of production has, merely, a higher level of want creation necessitating a higher level of want satisfaction. There will be frequent occasion to refer to the way wants depend on the process by which they are satisfied. It will be convenient to call it the Dependence Effect. . . .

The final problem of the productive society is what it produces. This manifests itself in an implacable tendency to provide an opulent supply of some things and a niggardly yield of others. This disparity carries to the point where it is a cause of social discomfort and social unhealth. The line which divides our area of wealth from our area of poverty is roughly that which divides privately produced and marketed goods and services from publicly rendered services. Our wealth in the first is not only in startling contrast with the meagerness of the latter, but our wealth in privately produced goods is, to a marked degree, the cause of crisis in the supply of public services. For we have failed to see the importance, indeed the urgent need, of maintaining a balance between the two.

This disparity between our flow of private and public goods and services is no matter of subjective judgment. On the contrary, it is the source of the most extensive comment which only stops short of the direct contrast being made here. In the years following World War II, the papers of any major city—those of New York were an excellent example—told daily of the shortages and shortcomings in the elementary municipal and metropolitan services. The schools were old and overcrowded. The police force was under strength and underpaid. The parks and playgrounds were insufficient. . . . Internal transportation was overcrowded, unhealthful, and dirty. So was the air. . . .

The family which takes its mauve and cerise, air-conditioned, power-steered, and power-braked car out for a tour passes through cities that are badly paved, made hideous by litter, blighted buildings, billboards, and posts for wires that should long since have been put underground. They pass on into a countryside that has been rendered largely invisible by commercial art. (The goods which the latter advertise have an absolute priority in our value system. Such aesthetic considerations as a view of the countryside accordingly come second. On such matters we are consistent.) They picnic on exquisitely packaged food from a portable icebox by a polluted stream and go on to spend the night at a park which is a menace to public health and morals. Just before dozing off on an air-mattress, beneath a nylon tent, amid the stench of decaying refuse, they may reflect vaguely on the curious unevenness of their blessings. Is this, indeed, the American genius?....

The case for social balance has, so far, been put negatively. Failure to keep public services in minimal relation to private production and use of goods is a cause of social disorder or impairs economic performance. The matter may now be put affirmatively. By failing to exploit the opportunity to expand public production we are missing opportunities for enjoyment which otherwise we might have had. Presumably a community can be as well rewarded by buying better schools or better parks as by buying bigger cars. By concentrating on the latter rather than the former it is failing to maximize its satisfactions....

The conventional wisdom holds that the community, large or small, makes a decision as to how much it will devote to its public services. This decision is arrived at by democratic process. Subject to the imperfections and uncertainties of democracy, people decide how much of their private income and goods they will surrender in order to have public services of which they are in greater need. Thus there is a balance, however rough, in the enjoyments to be had from private goods and services and those rendered by public authority.

It will be obvious, however, that this view depends on the notion of independently determined consumer wants. In such a world one could with some reason defend the doctrine that the consumer, as a voter, makes an independent choice between public and private goods. But given the dependence effect—given that consumer wants are created by the process by which they are satisfied—the consumer makes no such choice. He is subject to the forces of advertising and emulating by which production creates its own demand. Advertising operates exclusively, and emulation mainly, on behalf of privately produced goods and services. Since management and emulative effects operate on behalf of private production, public services will have an inherent tendency to lag behind. Car demand which is expensively synthesized will inevitably have a much larger claim on income than parks or public health or even roads where no such influence operates. The engines of mass communication, in their highest state of development, assail the eyes and ears of the community on behalf of more beer but not of more schools. Even in the conventional wisdom it will scarcely be contended that this leads to an equal choice between the two.

The competition is especially unequal for new products and services. Every corner of the public psyche is canvassed by some of the nation's most talented citizens it see if the desire for some merchantable product can be cultivated. No similar process operates on behalf of the non-merchantable services of the state.... The scientist or engineer or advertising man who devotes himself to developing a new carburetor, cleanser, or depilatory for which the public recognizes no need and will feel none until an advertising campaign arouses it, is one of the valued members of our society. A politician or a public servant who dreams up a new public service is a wastrel. Few public offenses are more reprehensible.

So much for the influences which operate on the decision between public and private production. The calm decision between public and private consumption pictured by the conventional wisdom is, in fact, a remarkable example of the error which arises from viewing social behavior out of context. The inherent tendency will always be for public services to fall behind private production. We have here the first of the causes of social imbalance.

QUESTIONS

1. What are the two assumptions of consumer demand theory as Galbraith explains it? How does Galbraith undermine those assumptions?

2. According to Galbraith, the notion that production is dependent on consumer demand, which is dependent on advertising, is dangerous, because most economists would sense "the damage to established ideas which lurks in these relationships." What does he mean by this?

3. Some would say that advertising does not create the desire to buy things, but simply taps into desires that already exist within us. According to Professor Hugh Rank, "If advertisers are often accused of peddling dreams, we must recognize first that they are *our* dreams: they are all genuine human desires; they are the benefits we seek." Do you agree?

4. Galbraith writes that we are paralyzed by a blitz "on behalf of more beer but not of more schools." Do you agree with him that advertising affects us so that we don't "want"—don't vote for—more and improved public goods and services? What would Milton Friedman and other free market economists say to this? How might a utilitarian thinker respond?

Federal Versus Industry Self-Regulation

The Federal Trade Commission

The Federal Trade Commission (FTC), one of the first federal agencies, has two broad mandates: to promote competition through its enforcement of the Sherman and Clayton Antitrust Acts, and to protect consumers. The agency was established by the Federal Trade Act of 1914, which outlawed "unfair methods of competition and unfair or deceptive acts and practices," including false or misleading advertising. Since then, the FTC has issued detailed regulations that outline its interpretation of the FTC Act and later consumer-protection laws.

Deceptive advertising claims are those likely to mislead reasonable consumers, causing them to change their conduct. These can take several forms. Obvious, or "express" claims must be truthful. An ad that appears to offer firsthand evidence of a product's qualities, for example, must be what it appears to be. The FTC pursued Campbell's Soup Company for having ad photos taken in which glass marbles were added to the bottom of bowls of soup, making it seem like they were brimming with vegetables.[10]

Advertisers are responsible, too, for suggested, or "implied" claims—the misleading messages that consumers are led to believe. In one case, the makers of Anacin invited consumers to discover whether "medically proven" Anacin would "work better" for them. While it was true the company had proved that Anacin contained more aspirin than other nonprescription analgesics, and that Anacin was as effective as its leading competitor, the ad was deceptive because it left the reasonable consumer with the wrong impression that Anacin had been "medically proven" to work better than any other analgesic.[11]

Some ads that are literally true are deceptive because of what they *don't* say; they fail to disclose information a consumer would consider important. Internet service providers America

---

10 *In re Campbell's Soup Co.*, 77 FTC 664 (1970).

11 *American Home Products Corp. v. FTC*, 695 F.2d 681 (3d Cir. 1982).

Online (AOL), Prodigy, and CompuServe, for example, were all accused of deceptive advertising when their offers of "free trials" failed to mention that after the trial period, consumers would be automatically enrolled—and charged a monthly membership fee—unless they affirmatively cancelled during the free period.

Endorsements and testimonials must reflect the honest opinions or findings of the endorser. Ads that feature a named man identified as an "ordinary consumer" are deceptive unless, for example, his experience with weight loss is typical of what users of the product generally achieve. When an ad suggests that an endorser is an expert, she must have relevant expert qualifications and experience. It would be deceptive, for example, to have an "engineer" endorse a car if she were a chemical engineer and not an automotive engineer.

The FTC will typically investigate a complaint and attempt to settle it. One possible result is a **consent decree** that stops the ad from appearing. For example, the manufacturer of a well-known aerosol spray deodorant promoted the product as "ozone-friendly" because it did not contain or produce chlorofluorocarbons during its manufacture. What it failed to reveal was that butane, another air pollutant, was used as a substitute. The FTC barred the company from making "green" claims for products that add to air pollution. Where necessary, advertisers may be required to run new ads to correct misinformation in the original ad.

Recently, the FTC has made consumer privacy a priority, bringing eleven spyware enforcement actions between 2005 and 2007. In one case, the Commission settled with Zango, Inc., a company that provided advertising software programs ("adware") that monitored consumers' Internet use in order to display targeted pop-up ads. Without notice or consent, the company installed adware on millions of computers, often as part of an offer of free screensavers, peer-to-peer file sharing software, or games. Hard to identify, locate or remove, the adware delivered billions of pop-up ads. As part of the settlement, Zango agreed to disgorge $3 million in profits. *In the Matter of Zango, Inc.*, FTC File No. 052 3130 (Nov. 3, 2006).

Deceptive and unfair spam practices have been an FTC target since 1987. The largest civil penalty for illegal spam resulted from a March 2006 settlement with Jumpstart Technologies. Accused of promising "free" movie tickets to consumers if they divulged the e-mail addresses of several friends and then repeatedly e-mailed those friends using the consumer's own e-mail address, Jumpstart agreed to pay a $900,000 civil penalty and promised not to engage in future e-mail campaigns with deceptive sender information or content. *United States v. Jumpstart Techs., LLC*, No. C-06-2079 (MHP) (N.D. Cal. filed Mar. 22, 2006).

Many claim the FTC's process is much too slow; its preferred method of confronting false and misleading advertising is to proceed on a case-by-case basis, and a single case may take as long as 20 years to wend its way through the system.

The following case was brought by the FTC against a company and its owner for making false and deceptive claims on Spanish-language television, as it advertised that its product would eliminate cellulite.

FTC v. SILUETA DISTRIBUTORS, INC. AND STANLEY KLAVIR
United States District Court, California, 1995
1995 WL 215313

ARMSTRONG, District Judge.
Defendants promoted the sale of a product known as Sistema Silueta through advertisement broadcasts on KDTV, Channel 14, and on other Spanish-language stations across the country. Sistema Silueta consists of a moisture lotion and diuretic tablets.... [T]he advertisement represents that Sistema Silueta will eliminate cellulite from the body and that consumer testimonials support this assertion.

The Sistema Silueta advertisement features an unidentified man sitting on the edge of a desk, positioned in front of book-lined shelves. The man states: "I would like to talk to you for a few moments. Sistema Silueta is the scientific miracle of the moment." During this introduction, there is a subscript which reads: "We do not specify a determined weight loss with this product." The subscript disappears as the man continues: "Silueta is an astonishing treatment in two steps which penetrates the skin and attacks and dissolves the fat cells which are the cause of those ugly cellulite bumps, and later expels them from your body."

The commercial then switches to a swimsuit-clad woman who states: "We all know that neither diets nor strenuous exercises can get rid of cellulite, but with Sistema Silueta I did achieve it when I applied it on those areas I wanted to reduce." During the time the woman speaks, there is a subscript that reads: "To lose weight with this product, you need to eat less and follow the instructions."

The advertisement then moves into its third phase, which is comprised of illustration and narration. The illustration is of an overweight woman's body in a swimsuit. The figure rubs a cream onto corpulent and bumpy thighs. The figure then transforms and becomes thin. The next illustration apparently represents fat cells. Arrows are depicted entering into the spaces between the fat cells and the cells become smaller. Then a liquid pours over the picture, apparently washing the residue away. During this illustration phase, the narration is as follows: Step number one—the Silueta cream penetrates underneath the surface of the skin breaking those fat and cellulite deposits and converts them into liquids that step number two takes care of by expelling them from your body.

The advertisement then returns to the unidentified man's office. He is now sitting behind the desk and the swimsuit-clad woman is perched on the edge of the desk. The woman states: "Nothing could be easier. Start today to get the figure you have always dreamed about." During this last scene, there is a subscript that reads: "Testimonials on file."

At this point, the advertisement shows an 800 number. When a consumer calls the 800 number, the consumer is told that it is possible to order the Sistema Silueta products by C.O.D. Although the advertised cost of the Sistema Silueta regimen is $34.95 plus $5.00 shipping and handling, the C.O.D. cost of the regimen is $43.95.

Liability

Section 5(a) of the FTC Act declares unlawful "unfair or deceptive acts or practices in or affecting commerce" and empowers the Federal Trade Commission (the "Commission") to prevent such acts or practices. Section 12 of the FTC Act is specifically directed to false advertising. This section prohibits the dissemination of "any false advertisement" in order to induce the purchase of "food, drugs, devices, or cosmetics...." The FTC Act defines "false advertisement" as "an advertisement, other than labeling, which is misleading in a material respect." An advertisement is misleading or deceptive if (1) there is a representation, omission, or practice that (2) is likely to mislead consumers acting reasonably under the circumstances, and (3) the representation, omission, or practice is material. Express product claims are presumed to be material. Furthermore, the use of a consumer endorsement violates Section 5 if the endorsement misrepresents that the alleged results are what consumers typically achieve.

FTC asserts that defendants' advertisement violated the FTC Act because it expressly and falsely represented that Sistema Silueta will eliminate cellulite, that Sistema Silueta has caused cellulite elimination in actual use, and that consumer testimonials support the conclusion that Sistema Silueta eliminates cellulite. Because these representations were expressly made in the advertisement, the materiality of the representations is presumed. Furthermore, because these representations relate to the very reason a consumer would purchase the product (i.e., to eliminate cellulite), these representations, if false, would clearly mislead consumers acting reasonably under the circumstances. Thus, the only issue here is whether the representations are false....

Plaintiff provides ample evidence by way of expert declaration testimony establishing that Sistema Silueta cannot eliminate cellulite. This evidence reveals that the "cream is nothing more than a moisturizer, the ingredients of which are those found in body lotions and creams generally." Furthermore, the diuretic tablets contain an herbal diuretic that cannot cause the loss of cellulite, only water loss, which will be replaced immediately upon the ingestion of water.

Because defendants have presented no evidence contradicting plaintiff's contentions regarding any of the three representations, no genuine issue of fact exists as to whether defendants' Sistema Silueta advertisement was false and violated the FTC Act. Thus, this Court grants summary judgment in favor of plaintiff on this issue.

Klavir's Liability

Klavir asserts that he is not individually liable for the violations because he did not know and should not have known of the misrepresentations. Klavir maintains that he bought Silueta from Juan Perez, who created the advertisement for Sistema Silueta. Klavir claims that Perez stated he had verified the statements in the advertisement and Klavir had no reason to believe that Perez's verification was not accurate. Klavir claims that, except for products returned under the money-back guarantee, Klavir received no complaints about the product. Finally, he asserts that, as soon as plaintiff notified him of possible infractions of the FTC Act, defendants voluntarily stopped advertising the product. Based on these contentions, Klavir disclaims any individual liability in this case.

The policy behind the imposition of individual liability is to ensure that an individual defendant does not benefit from deceptive activity and then hide behind the corporation. Individual liability...can be predicated either on (1) having participated directly in the violative conduct, or (2) having had the authority to control the conduct. The parties do not dispute Klavir's authority to control Silueta's conduct, as he is the sole owner of Silueta. Disputed here is the issue of whether Klavir must have had knowledge of the conduct before liability attached....

... Courts requiring a showing of knowledge before imposition of individual liability apply the following standard: The Commission must show that the individual defendant possessed one of the following: (1) actual knowledge of material misrepresentations, (2) reckless indifference to the truth or falsity of such misrepresentations, or (3) an awareness of a high probability of fraud along with an intentional avoidance of truth....

The evidence presented here reveals that 63 percent of the consumers who ordered Sistema Silueta returned the product. Such an extraordinarily high rate of return should have placed Klavir on notice that the product did not eliminate cellulite as claimed by the advertisements. This evidence causes the Court to conclude that Klavir acted with a reckless indifference to the truth or falsity of the advertisement's misrepresentations, or, at a minimum, that Klavir had an awareness of a high probability of fraud and intentionally avoided the truth. Consequently, the Court finds that imposition of individual liability on Klavir is appropriate....

Before moving on, the Court addresses Klavir's assertions that his reasonable reliance on the alleged verification made by Perez saves him from individual liability. The Court finds Klavir's argument to be unpersuasive for several reasons.... [N]othing in the record establishes Perez as a reliable source for an endorsement of Sistema Silueta.... [I]t was unreasonable for Klavir to rely on Perez's alleged verification, as this took place during a sales transaction between Klavir and Perez. It is unlikely that Perez would have informed Klavir, a prospective purchaser, that the advertisement was deceptive.... [T]he evidence reveals that the advertisement being challenged here was not the one created by Perez, but was one that was materially altered by Klavir. Klavir significantly edited the advertisement from a 1-minute running time to a 30-second running time. Finally, good faith reliance on another's representation is no defense to liability under the FTC Act.

[The defendant also objected to the remedy the government was seeking: not just a permanent injunction preventing Klavir from deceptively selling his product, but also "restitution and disgorgement," forcing him to give back his profits. The court ruled against Klavir on this issue also. Restitution and disgorgement are intended to prevent unjust enrichment, that is, to keep a company from benefiting from a deceptive trade practice. Klavir's firm had shipped 10,399 units of Silueta, but 6,546 were returned. Multiplying the unreturned shipments by the cost of each unit, the court required Klavir to "disgorge" $169,339.35. Then, using names and addresses provided by the defendant, the government would reimburse cheated consumers and keep in the U.S. Treasury whatever was left over.]

QUESTIONS

1. Why did Klavir claim he was not liable as an individual? How did the court respond? Note the treatment of Klavir's relationship with Perez, the creator of the actual ad. Why couldn't Klavir shift the responsibility for the Silueta commercial to Perez?

2. If you are led into making a contract by fraud or deception, you may sue to rescind the agreement and get your money back. Given that each of the misled customers for Silueta could have brought such a claim and won, do we need the FTC to pursue false advertisers also?

3. In the wake of September 11, the FTC has sent warnings to dozens of Web sites, ordering them to stop making unsubstantiated claims that their products would protect consumers from bioterrorism. Peddling such items as gas masks, mail sterilizers, protective suits, biohazard test kits, and a device called the "deGERMinator," which supposedly kills anthrax with ultraviolet light, the sites were told that they could be shut down, fined, or forced to reimburse their customers.
   Internet Assignment What action has been taken since then by the FTC? Has the Food and Drug Administration (FDA) done anything to aid consumers?

4. **Internet Assignment** Go to the FTC Web site, http://www.ftc.gov. Look for Advertising Policy Statements and Guidance. How does the agency define "deception"? "Unfairness"? What guidance is offered regarding advertising and marketing on the Internet?

Lanham Act

The Lanham Act was passed by Congress in 1946, one of a series of laws regulating business that were passed in reaction to the Great Depression. While the focus of the Lanham Act is trademark registration and protection, Section 43(a) gives competitors the right to sue for false or misleading advertising damaging to them. It has been interpreted to allow suits for false claims about either a company's own products or those of its rivals, and to include not only traditional advertising campaigns but infomercials, labels, and messages on telephone-answering systems.

To succeed under the Lanham Act, a plaintiff must prove that the defendant made a "factual misrepresentation" about a product or service, something more than sales "puffery." (The claim that a pregnancy test kit works "in as fast as ten minutes" is asserted as a fact and must be true. The claim that a pregnancy test kit is "the most advanced equipment available" is considered mere puffery, a general statement inflating the positive quality of what is for sale.) If a company can show that its rival's ads are actually false, or likely to confuse consumers, it can win a court order stopping the ads; to win money damages it must prove that it actually lost customers because of a rival's misleading claims.[12]

GlaxoSmithKline Consumer Healthcare (GSKCH) is in the nicotine replacement therapy (NRT) market. GSKCH sells two products—Nicorette, a nicotine gum, and a skin-patch called NicoDerm CQ. In 2002, it aired two TV commercials aimed at its competitor, Pharmacia, maker of Nicotrol.

The first ad, "Revised Tough Decision," features an actor portraying a consumer deciding whether to buy Nicorette or Nicotrol. A voice-over asks: "Trying to quit smoking? According to the labels, Nicorette gum can be used whenever you need it, day or night. Nicotrol's patch can only be worn for 16 hours." Superimposed text at the bottom of the screen reads: "Use anytime. Use as directed." The announcer then states: "So much for flexibility," after which the actor chooses Nicorette. The second commercial, "Revised Smart Choice" contrasts NicoDerm and Nicotrol, based on several criteria involving consumer preferences. At the end, the announcer states "more doctors prefer the patch that gives you the choice."

Pharmacia went to court seeking to stop the ad campaign, claiming that GSKCH was violating the Lanham Act. In the case that follows, the court must decide (1) whether it is likely that GSKCH violated the law and, (2) if so, whether the court should preliminarily enjoin the ad, pending a full trial.

PHARMACIA CORPORATION v. GLAXOSMITHKLINE CONSUMER HEALTHCARE

United States District Court, D. New Jersey, 2003
292 F.Supp.2d 594

COOPER, District Judge. ✳

... A Lanham Act false or misleading statement may be proved in one of two ways. The plaintiff must show that "the commercial message or statement is either (1) literally false or (2) literally true or ambiguous, but has the tendency to deceive consumers."... [In cases of the second kind, plaintiff must show that a substantial portion of consumers actually understand the ad to be making the misleading claim, by producing] evidence that consumers are actually misled by the defendant's statements....

[Discussion of Pharmacia's Likelihood of Success in Proving its Lanham Act Claims]

[The court begins by assessing Pharmacia's claims that GSKCH's ad violates the Lanham Act. The first is that the "Revised Tough Decision" ad makes an expressly false claim about Nicorette:]

While the ad tells viewers that the label states Nicorette may be used any time the consumer needs it, Pharmacia argues, the label in actuality places limitations on when Nicorette may be used. Specifically...the label instructs consumers to refrain from chewing Nicorette while eating or drinking...cautions users not to continuously chew one piece after another, and not to use more than 24 pieces per day. Pharmacia asserts that these various restrictions render "Revised Tough Decision" literally false because there are significant periods of each day during which a user may not chew Nicorette.

---

12 Every state has its own laws banning unfair trade and consumer fraud. While federal law must be enforced by the FTC (FTC Act) or by lawsuits brought by an injured competitor (Lanham Act), some state laws, often referred to as "little FTC Acts" allow individuals harmed by false ads to sue. In addition, state tort laws offer remedies to consumers who have been harmed by the way a product has been marketed.

[The court must decide whether the claim is literally false—a "per se" violation—or merely ambiguous.]

... If the statement in question does not make an unambiguous claim, there is no Lanham Act violation absent a showing of actual consumer deception. The Court must look at the commercial as a whole when making its assessment.... ("A determination of literal falsity rests on an analysis of the message in context.")

The Court finds that GSKCH's statement makes an ambiguous claim..."Revised Tough Decision" as a whole conveys the message that Nicorette is a more flexible aid to quitting smoking than Nicotrol. Within this context, we further find that the statement "According to the labels, Nicorette gum can be used whenever you need it, day or night" makes an ambiguous claim. One viewer could understand the commercial to claim that Nicorette's label allows consumers to use Nicorette at times when they would be unable to use Nicotrol. Alternatively, another viewer might conclude that GSKCH is claiming that the label permits users to chew the gum whenever they feel like it, even during a meal. The statement is open to interpretation.

... [Without evidence of actual consumer confusion we] will not preliminarily enjoin GSKCH from showing "Revised Tough Decision."

Pharmacia also alleges that "Revised Smart Choice" runs afoul of the Lanham Act because it makes the expressly false claim that doctors prefer NicoDerm [because it] offers the choice of being worn for either 16 or 24 hours....

We find...that GSKCH does not have any evidence to support its claim that doctors prefer NicoDerm over Nicotrol because it offers choice, and therefore that claim is *per se* false.

[Is Pharmacia Entitled to a Preliminary Injunction?]

[Having decided that Pharmacia has made a strong case that GSKCH violated the Lanham Act, the court must decide how fair it is to award a preliminary injunction.]

Harm to Pharmacia

Pharmacia can establish irreparable harm if it can "demonstrate a significant risk that [it] will experience harm that cannot adequately be compensated after the fact by monetary damages....We find that GSKCH's own research demonstrates that a commercial nearly identical to "Revised Smart Choice" was effective at eroding Nicotrol's position in the market in 1996, and that this format was revived because GSKCH believed it would work just as well again. These findings establish a significant risk of harm to Pharmacia, because Pharmacia will likely lose market share if GSKCH is free to air "Revised Smart Choice."

Harm to GSKCH

Pharmacia must also demonstrate that the potential harm it faces without injunctive relief outweighs the harm [GSKCH] will suffer should an injunction issue....To the extent GSKCH is injured by an injunction...that injury was caused by GSKCH's own misconduct in making a false claim. The Court therefore discounts any such harm. The likely loss of market share Pharmacia faces without injunctive relief outweighs any harm to GSKCH caused by granting preliminary relief.

Public Interest

The final factor in the preliminary injunction inquiry is whether "the public interest favors issuing the injunction." Pharmacia urges that there is a strong public policy against the dissemination of false and misleading advertising. The Court finds that the case law in the Third Circuit supports this contention, especially in the context of OTC drug advertising....

There is a public consideration that counsels against granting an injunction, however. The public has a strong interest in free competition....The injunctive power of the courts should not be misused by manufacturers attempting to stifle the free market that is the cornerstone of our economy. Courts should therefore be wary of producers' pleas for injunctive relief against the advertisements of their close competitors.

We nevertheless find that "[t]he public interest in truthful advertising is obviously served by a court's prohibition of advertising that is plainly false."

Equitable Considerations

… GSKCH asserts that Pharmacia has itself engaged in false advertising, and thus Pharmacia's motion should be denied under the doctrine of unclean hands.

GSKCH argues that Pharmacia comes before the Court with unclean hands because in an October 2002 press release Pharmacia stated that Nicotrol was the only 16-hour patch in the NRT market. GSKCH contends that this statement (which, the Court finds, is false because NicoDerm is also approved for 16-hour use) should preclude Pharmacia from enjoining "Revised Smart Choice."

The Court disagrees. First, GSKCH has not alleged that Pharmacia's statement caused it injury, which is a predicate to application of the unclean hands doctrine. Second…the nexus between Pharmacia's statement and GSKCH's claim in "Revised Smart Choice" is too remote. Pharmacia's claim that Nicotrol is the only 16-hour patch was made in a mere press release. The claim did not disparage NicoDerm. In contrast, [the false claim in] "Revised Smart Choice" directly attacks Nicotrol. Further, GSKCH's false statement was made in a recurring television commercial aimed at influencing millions of consumers. This is a far cry from a single press release. Pharmacia's one false statement "does not excuse current deceptive and misleading advertisements to the public."

QUESTIONS

1. On what basis does the court conclude that GSKCH likely violated the Lanham Act?

2. What public interests are at stake in this case?

Industry Self-Regulation

The advertising industry has established a number of mechanisms for self-regulation, including the PhRMA code, mentioned in the first case in this chapter. Some commentators believe this voluntary approach is more effective than government regulation. For instance, all ad campaigns undergo a review process as they are conceptualized, both by the client (usually represented by a group of lawyers and other technical people) and the ad agency. Concern remains that the nature of the client/agency relationship can complicate thoughtful efforts to monitor the line between truth-telling and deception. Think of the way Perez interacted with Klavir in the *Silueta* case.

The National Advertising Division (NAD) of the Council of the Better Business Bureau is the official self-policing mechanism of the advertising industry. Set up in 1971 to preempt what might have been harsher government interference, NAD investigates about 180 disputes annually and resolves 98 percent of them. In about half the cases the challenged company is let off the hook, and the rest of the time the client company changes or agrees to stop the ad. The two percent of cases not resolved are appealed to the National Advertising Review Board (NARB), which uses standards close to those of the FTC and Lanham Acts. Although NAD and NARB have no enforcement power, they can threaten to send a case to the FTC for government investigation, and they have been successful in stemming the flow of the most openly deceptive and misleading advertising.

In 1990, the American Association of Advertising Agencies adopted the following revision of its own guidelines.

Standards of Practice

We hold that the responsibility of advertising agencies is to be a constructive force in business.

We hold that, to discharge this responsibility, advertising agencies must recognize an obligation, not only to their clients, but to the public, the media they employ, and to each other. As a business, the advertising agency must operate within the framework of competition. It is recognized that keen and vigorous competition, honestly conducted, is necessary to the growth and health of American business. However, unethical competitive practices in the advertising agency business lead to financial waste, dilution of service, diversion of manpower, loss of prestige, and tend to weaken the public confidence....

To these ends the American Association of Advertising Agencies has adopted the following Creative Code....

Creative Code

We the members of the American Association of Advertising Agencies, in addition to supporting and obeying the laws of legal regulations pertaining to advertising, undertake to extend and broaden the application of high ethical standards. Specifically, we will not knowingly create advertising that contains:

a. **False or misleading statements or exaggerations, visual or verbal**

b. **Testimonials that do not reflect the real opinion of the individual(s) involved**

c. **Price claims that are misleading**

d. **Claims insufficiently supported or that distort the true meaning or practicable application of statements made by professional or scientific authority**

e. **Statements, suggestions, or pictures offensive to public decency or minority segments of the population**

We recognize that there are areas that are subject to honestly different interpretation and judgment. Nevertheless, we agree not to recommend to an advertiser, and to discourage the use of, advertising that is in poor or questionable taste or that is deliberately irritating....

QUESTIONS

1. Television advertising for children has come under attack for many reasons. One is that small children have difficulty distinguishing between program content and advertising. There are also concerns that children are exposed to too much—to an avalanche of ads. In the late 1970s, the FTC recommended a series of changes, including banning all television advertising directed at children under the age of eight, and banning all television advertising for sugared food products directed at children between the ages of eight and twelve. This proposal was withdrawn after critics dubbed the FTC "National Nanny."[13] Do the AAAA Standards above address this issue?

2. Internet Assignment Find out about interactive Web sites directed at children, like Webkinz, WeeWorld or Club Penguin. Investigate. How do they engage children? How do they advertise? Now locate a set of industry standards that address advertising targeting children. Do the Web sites conform to those standards?

---

13 A bill decreasing the number of commercial minutes permitted in shows directed at children, vetoed by Reagan, was passed by Congress during the Bush administration. It limits these commercials to 10.5 minutes per hour on weekends and 12 minutes per hour on weekdays.

Children, Obesity, and Marketing Junk Food

The World Heath Organization estimates that obesity affects 22 million children under the age of five worldwide. Data from a 1999-2000 U.S. government study revealed since 1980 more than 30 percent of children from six to eleven had become overweight or were at risk for being overweight—a doubling. In the same period, among adolescents the rate had tripled.[14] Overweight children are at risk for hypertension, asthma, and Type 2 diabetes, previously mainly a disease of adulthood.

At the same time the so-called "obesity epidemic" has been escalating, an unprecedented burst of spending on marketing targeting children has occurred. In 1983, television was the primary venue for ads to children, and corporations spent $100 million. Today that figure ranges between $10 and $12 billion, and it is spent in radically pervasive ways.

The following article was written by sociology professor Juliet B. Schor, author of *Born to Buy: The Commercialized Child and the New Consumer Culture*, and Margaret Ford, an honors sociology undergraduate, both of Boston College. They describe the dilemma at the intersection of these trends in vivid terms. They begin by noting how, more than ever before, children are involved "in media, celebrity, shopping and other consumer practices."

FROM TASTES GREAT TO COOL: CHILDREN'S FOOD MARKETING AND THE RISE OF THE SYMBOLIC

JULIET B. SCHOR
and
MARGARET FORD[15]

The Commercialization of Childhood

As their participation in consumer markets has grown, children have become increasingly attractive targets for advertisers. This is partly driven by their high media use. According to the 2005 Kaiser Family Foundation study of children and media use, the average eight to eighteen year old is currently exposed to eight-and-a-half hours of media a day, almost all of which is "commercial" media. Actual media time (as opposed to media exposure, which double counts periods when more than one medium is being used simultaneously) is six hours and twenty-one minutes. Younger children, for whom the most recent data are not available, also have very high levels of media use. In a 1999 Kaiser study, children aged two to thirteen were found to watch more than two hours of television per day, and their total media time was five and a half hours of per day. Although pre-school children tend to have lower television viewing than school-aged children, 25% of them have televisions in their bedrooms, and watch an average of two hours a day. Viewing time and exposure to junk food marketing is much higher for low-income children as well as racial and ethnic minority children, groups which also have higher rates of obesity and obesity-related illnesses. For example, in the 2005 study, black children were found to watch an average of four hours and five minutes of TV daily, compared to two hours forty-five minutes for white children....

---

14 Cynthia Ogden et. al., "Prevalence and Trends in Overweight Among Children and Adolescents, 1999-2000," JAMA, Oct. 9, 2002, at 1728. The CDC defines "overweight" as having a Body Mass Index (BMI) in the 95th percentile or more; "at risk" of being overweight refers to a BMI at the 85th percentile or above.

15 35 *Journal of Law Medicine and Ethics* 10 (Spring 2007).

[A] 1996 content analysis of Saturday morning cartoons[16] found that 63% of the 353 advertisements in this time slot were for food products. Among... nearly 1,400 food ads studied between 1972 and 1996, there were no commercials advertising fruits and vegetables with the exception of a few Public Service Announcements. (The lack of fruit and vegetable advertising is due to the fact that almost none, with the prominent exception of Chiquita Bananas, are branded.)

Children are also heavily exposed to food ads during prime time viewing hours. A 1998 content analysis during the top-ranked prime-time shows for children aged two to eleven found that 23% of the commercials were for food, and 40% of those were for fast-food restaurants.[17] Excluding fast-foods, 41% of the advertised foods were in the fats, oils and sweets category of the United States Department of Agriculture's food pyramid....

Food marketing to children has moved beyond the television set, however. Packaging has become a form of advertisement, as companies [put] food into "cool" new containers or [add] licensed characters, games, and ads for other branded foods. Another marketing strategy is product placement, in which food companies pay producers of music videos, radio, books, comic strips, songs, plays, and movies to place the product in the setting.... Product placements... cannot be zapped out, unlike 30-second spots.

Another common promotional technique for food is giveaways, or premiums.... McDonald's Happy Meals are arguably the most successful marketing strategy in human history, and are credited with turning a visit to a fast food restaurant into a favored activity for children. The current prize for the Happy Meal is a "fun game piece" from the Disney movie Pirates of the Caribbean, which was released in the summer of 2006 to record box office revenues, and is part of a ten-year global marketing agreement Disney signed with McDonald's in 1996.

Character licensing has also become pervasive, especially for major movie releases. For example, breakfast cereal Cap'n Crunch launched a campaign with Warner Brother's 2006 Superman, creating a new cereal called "Superman Crunch" with advertisements for the movie on the box as well as in the television commercials.... Harry Potter famously "sold out," according to some, by cross-promoting with Coca-Cola.

Food corporations are also collaborating with toy companies and book publishers to launch lines of branded books and toys, especially to pre-school aged children. Amazon.com sells more than 40 children's branded food counting and reading books such as: The M&M's Brand Counting Book..., Hershey's Kisses Addition Book, and Reese's Math Fun: Addition 1 to 9. Other branded products include Barbie dressed in a McDonald's employee outfit, and Easy-Bake Ovens with food preparation sets from Oreo, Chips Ahoy, Pop Tarts, M&M's Cookies, and Pizza Hut....

Junk food also appears to have made its way into upscale tween fashions, with a trendy line by a company called "Junk Food Clothing" which sells expensive t-shirts featuring sweets and other food products.

Food companies are also sponsoring events, such as music group tours, where they advertise heavily.... Food companies run promotional tours that give away free product samples on the streets of major cities with specially outfitted vehicles. PopTarts sent the world's largest (branded) climbing wall touring the country for years. Motts juices sponsors concert tours by the musical group the Wiggles. Nabisco Nilla Wafers sponsored a

---

16 M. Gamble and N. Cotuga, "A Quarter Century of TV Food Advertising Targeted at Children," *American Journal of Human Behavior* 23 (1999): 26–267, at 263.

17 C. Byrd-Bredbenner and D. Grasso, "Prime-Time Health: An Analysis of Health Content in Television Commercials Broadcast During Programs Viewed Heavily by Children," *International Electronic Journal of Health Education* 2 (1999): 159–169.

banana pudding pie eating contest at theme parks around the country…. Nestlé sponsored a "fun zone" with a number of musical groups at theme parks, air shows, fairs, camps, zoos, and sporting events, and Kellogg's has done an in-line skating tour to push its Cinnamon Krunchers to tween males.

A related tactic is viral, or peer-to-peer, marketing. Children are enlisted to serve as "brand representatives" to other kids, to talk up the product, give out free samples, and help create buzz. Although originally used more for music releases, fashion, and shoes, viral marketing is now common with food products as well. Viral marketing firms enlist children to be in regular relationship with them, by constructing programs that give them titles (one firm uses the title "secret agent"), and keep in email contact The Girls Intelligence Agency gets tween girls, beginning at about age eight, to set up slumber parties at their homes to test and give out products. Procter and Gamble's viral marketing arm, Tremor, has a reported 240,000 young people touting its products in everyday settings. Viral marketing is an increasingly popular form of marketing in the children and teen marketplace.

The Internet is another rapidly growing advertising venue…. [T]he first extensive analysis of internet food marketing [in 2005]…reported 85% of food brands that advertise through television have branded websites marketing to children online. Internet advertising provides a more extensive and deeper participation by children since they are viewing the product for an unlimited and extended period of time through several different marketing vehicles. These include advergames, [on 73% of sites] which integrate the food product or characters associated with the brand, promotions or sweepstakes, clubs, email listservs, and software which allows the child to view television commercials online. [V]iral marketing…was found on 64% of the sites…. Only about half (51%) of the websites had nutrition information and only 18% of the websites followed [the Children's Advertising Review Unit[18]] specific guidelines that state that any advertising content must be clearly identified.[19]

Schools have also become a centerpiece of the marketing arsenal. In…2000, more than one-third of elementary schools, half of middle and junior high schools, and close to three-fourths of senior high schools had contracts giving soft drink companies the rights to sell their product at school. Fast food companies have gotten in on the action with incentive programs linked to educational activities. These include McDonald's "McSpellit Club" and Pizza Hut's "Book it." By using free or discounted foods as an incentive, the companies reward children for reading or getting perfect scores on spelling tests. Another major marketing effort in schools is through Channel One, which delivers a current events program plus two minutes of pure ads, to 38% of middle and high schools in the U.S. Until recently, there has been a high proportion of food ads on Channel One…. Food marketing to children has literally become a major part of public school curriculum….

Deteriorating Diets and Rising Obesity

Children's diets are now significantly deviating from the recommended diet. There has also been a dramatic rise in soft drink consumption. Between 1965 and 1996, the per capita daily soft drink consumption for boys aged eleven to eighteen rose from 179g to 520g, and from 148g to 337g for girls…. A…study…found a 60% increased risk of developing childhood obesity in middle-school aged children for every additional serving of soft drink consumed after controlling for potentially confounding factors.

18 CARU is the children's arm of the advertising industry's self-regulation program and evaluates child-directed advertising and promotional material in all media.

19 E. Moore, *It's Child's Play: Advergaming and Online Marketing of Food to Children* (Menlo Park CA: Henry J. Kaiser Family Foundation, 2006).

Another important change is the growth of meals eaten outside the home, and fast food consumption in particular. In the late 1970's, children ate 17% of their meals away from home and fast food accounted for 2% of their energy intake. By the mid to late 1990s, those figures had increased to 30% and 10%.... [A]n average large-sized fast food meal contains about 2200 kcal, an amount that requires running a complete marathon to burn off.[20]

Obesity rates among children have grown rapidly....

Different Approaches to Advertising Effectiveness

...Children's marketers typically... [seem to assume] a set of innate "needs" and attempt to create ads whose message is that the product will satisfy the need. Needs include love, mastery, power, and glamour. Food advertisers are also heavy users of reward models in which toys, prizes, or other "premia" are given in return for purchase.... It is also likely that food advertisers know much more about how to stimulate desire than they share with outsiders. Almost all of their research is proprietary and unavailable to academic researchers....

The Shift from Product Attributes to Symbolic Messages in Children's Marketing

In its early decades (1950s-1980s), children's advertising was low-budget, drew on little research or creative talent, and tended to follow well-established formulae. Children were not a lucrative market.... In general, commercials conveyed intrinsic product benefits. Toy commercials tended to show children playing with the toy, and focused on the things it could do. This strategy is part of what got many toy companies and their ad agencies into legal trouble in the 1960s and 1970s—the ads frequently portrayed toys doing things they really could not. In the case of food, the intrinsic product benefit approach meant that the ad promised the food would taste good. The implicit advertising model was thus either the economists' informational one, or a latent stimulus/response approach in which product characteristics were assumed to trigger desire. Symbolic messaging was rare.

In contrast, adult-oriented advertising had already begun to reject the intrinsic product benefit model in the 1960s and 1970s. This was partly due to the realities of marketing commodities in a mass consumer society. If, for example, Coke and Pepsi or Nike and Reebok barely differ in terms of real product attributes, other advertising strategies are necessary to avoid damaging price cutting. In the earlier decades of the 20th century, advertisers had turned to crude appeals to status positioning and consumer insecurities (for example, consumers' fears of body odor or social isolation) to market these types of goods. But these messages became less effective as consumers' skepticism of advertising, particularly hard-sell techniques of industries such as automobiles, began to grow in the late 1950s and 1960s. Often dubbed the "creative revolution," advertisers turned instead to more symbolically and culturally-driven messages, building brand value on the basis of popularly-held cultural traits. They stressed brand image with campaigns designed to convince consumers that Nike equals power and athleticism or Pepsi is the brand of youth rebellion.

As Thomas Frank[21] has argued, the core of the creative revolution was an appeal to non-conformity and the counter-cultural quality of "cool." The association of a brand with "coolness" became a common strategy in adult and teen marketing....

20 C. B. Ebbeling, D. B. Pawlak, and D. S. Ludwig, "Childhood Obesity: Public Health Crisis, Common Sense Cure," *Lancet* 260 (2002): 473–82.

21 T. Frank, *The Conquest of Cool* (Chicago: Chicago University Press, 1997).

Specific Themes in Symbolic Marketing: Junk Food as Oppositional

...[C]ool is an expansive category, which takes on a variety of specific meanings....[P]erhaps the most important of its manifestations is the message that oppositional attitudes are cool, that junk food is oppositional, and that therefore junk food is cool This issue has been posed most intriguingly by anthropologist Allison James, whose research was triggered by the accidental finding that the British word for children's sweets, "kets," means "rubbish" in adult dialect. "It is thus of great significance that something which is despised and regarded as diseased and inedible by the adult world should be given great prestige as a particularly desirable form of food by the child...."

Food advertisers have become sophisticated anthropologists.... Their ads build on basic social relationships and the connections of food to those relationships, and their power derives from these symbolic meanings.... [I]n our preliminary analysis of 55 commercials, 29 included both adult and child characters.

These [adult/child] ads often portray children and adults as occupying separate and frequently oppositional symbolic spaces. The strategy typically aligns the marketer (or the company) with the audience, and against adults. This "anti-adultism" is evident in commercial messages in which adults are portrayed as stupid, uncool, boring, nerdy, out of touch, controlling, or evil. Ads often transport children to adult-free utopian spaces, devoid of the unwelcome stresses and pressures caused by adults. Classic examples of this technique include a Starburst (candy) commercial in a classroom which goes back and forth between a drab, black-and-white format in which a very nerdy teacher is facing the class and in control, to a riotous, colorful party atmosphere of candy consumption when his back is turned and the students assume control over the classroom. A recent Captain Crunch cereal commercial portrays an ominous, "battle-axe" babysitter arriving to two defiant children. Of course they conquer her with the aid of the cereal....

Junk Food as a "Drug"

...The association of junk foods with energy, power, physiological transformation or an altered state is another common tactic.

... When one of the authors (Schor) sat in on focus groups with tweens for a sugary drink, she found that the children talked about their desire to get "hyper," or to "bounce off the walls." They said they wanted Coke because it has "caffeine." They were well versed in and took great delight in the transformative properties of sugar and caffeine. Not surprisingly, the soft drink companies have heavily promoted the concepts of high-energy and hyper. Pepsi's Mountain Dew, with its Code Red brand, is one example, with its themes of extreme sports and excess. So is the rise of "energy drinks" such as Red Bull, with their high levels of caffeine and appeals to youth.

[J]unk food is to a certain extent being positioned symbolically to children as a "drug...." The association to drugs is partly based on the transformative physiological processes associated with high-sugar foods, in which they produce positive sensations (as drugs do), make the user feel differently. An example is a Dunkin' Donuts commercial showing bored people in an office. The scene is re-run after they drink a smoothie and their mood has switched to happy....

A second theme is that junk foods are increasingly being marked by adults as dangerous...Like many drugs, the pleasurability of junk food is acknowledged, but it is seen to be addictive, and its ingestion is accompanied by serious bad consequences (obesity, diabetes, ill-health). Ads recognize this forbidden fruit dimension of the product in order to enhance its desirability to young viewers.... On the other hand, this is a double-edged sword for marketers, because there are countervailing reasons to portray their foods as healthy and wholesome. They are involved in a delicate balancing act between raising the appeal of their products by associating them with the qualities of pleasure and danger, and at the same time attempting to avoid associations of disease and decay.

[While cigarette smoking also is socially coded as "cool", t]he relationship between tobacco and junk food is not merely symbolic. Since Philip Morris acquired Seven-Up in 1978, tobacco companies have owned some of the nation's largest junk food marketers. These include the 1988 purchase of Kraft, also by Philip Morris, the 1989 buyout of Nabisco by tobacco company R. J. Reynolds, and its subsequent 2000 acquisition by Philip Morris. Philip Morris has also acquired cereal-maker General Foods, Swiss confectioner Suchard, Taco Bell, and Miller Brewing Company. Significantly, participants from the legal fights against tobacco are now active (on both sides) in struggles about junk food marketing to children, and newspaper headlines have drawn the connection. "Is Junk Food the New Tobacco?" became a frequent refrain in 2003 as the conflict about junk food began to heat up.

Connections to Existing Research

….[S]tudies look[ ] at how children respond to parental restrictions or disapproval of junk foods and discovers what is colloquially known as the "forbidden fruit syndrome"—forbidden foods are more desirable. For example, [researchers] have found that maternal restrictions on high-fat, high-sugar foods lead daughters to increase their consumption of these foods when they are in environments where access is unlimited.[22] …. Another study found that pre-school children are more attracted to foods that are not available to them, and that the effect was stronger with children whose mothers were more restrictive.[23] A third found that five-year-old girls are inclined to do the opposite of what they think their parents desire with respect to junk food consumption.[24]

The Debate about Food Marketing to Children

Since the publication, in late 2001, of the Surgeon General's report on the obesity epidemic, the debate about junk food marketing has heated up on a number of fronts. Medical professionals, children's advocates and parents began to organize against in-school junk food marketing.…Soft drinks, which research had shown to have a unique impact on obesity, have been singled out for attention. School districts began to reject exclusive contracts with Coke and Pepsi.… A number of lawsuits have also been filed, claiming damages from companies such as McDonald's, for marketing harmful and addictive food to children. In Massachusetts, the Center for Science in the Public Interest has initiated a legal process against Kellogg and Viacom, parent company of Nickelodeon, a major children's food marketer, accusing them of harm associated with excessive levels of food advertising.

The food industry responded to these attacks with a multi-pronged strategy. Companies were aggressive in attempting to deflect attention from food, arguing that lack of exercise was the reason for rising obesity, not their products. Coke and Pepsi began sponsoring fitness activities, and McDonald's handed out free pedometers. This was reminiscent of Big Tobacco's longstanding claims that tobacco does not cause lung cancer. Indeed, the food companies' initial responses to their opponents followed the tobacco strategy fairly faithfully. The food industry, which gives heavily to Congress and the Bush Administration, enlisted the latter to promote its position, which the Administration has

---

22 J. O. Fisher and L. L. Birch, "Mothers' Child-Feeding Practices Influence Daughters' Eating and Weight," *American Journal of Clinical Nutrition* 71 (2000): 1054–1061.

23 J. O. Fisher and L. L. Birch, "Restricting Access to Palatable Foods Affects Children's Behavioral Response, Food Selection, and Intake," *American Journal of Clinical Nutrition* 69 (1999): 1264–1272, as cited in M. B. Schwartz and R. Puhl, "Childhood Obesity: A Societal Problem to Solve," *The International Association for the Study of Obesity: Obesity Reviews* 4 (2003): 57–71.

24 J. L. Carper, J. O. Fisher, and L. L. Birch, "Young Girls' Emerging Dietary Restraint and Disinhibition Are Related to Parental Control in Child Feeding," *Appetite* 35 (2000): 121–129, as cited in M. B. Schwartz and R. Puhl, "Childhood Obesity: A Societal Problem to Solve," *The International Association for the Study of Obesity: Obesity Reviews* 4 (2003): 57–71.

done, both domestically and abroad. In 2001, the Administration undermined a World Health Organization (WHO) anti-obesity initiative. The restaurant and beverage companies also founded and generously funded a political front-group, the Center for Consumer Freedom, which ridicules public health activists (calling them "food fascists"), and argues that efforts to curb obesity are anti-freedom.

More recently, some companies have realized that they cannot afford the negative reputation associated with making children fat, so they have downplayed their initial claims that food doesn't matter, and tried to position themselves as part of the solution to the obesity epidemic. Kraft gained headlines by claiming that it would stop in-school activities, and the marketing of the least nutritious of its brands, such as Oreos, to young children. McDonald's, Pepsi, and others have introduced new, "healthier" products. Soft drink companies are trying to sell sweetened fruit drinks and energy drinks, perhaps hoping that consumers will (mistakenly) think these are significantly different from sodas.

Industry has also argued in favor of, and begun to practice pro-nutrition advertising to children… [But] there are reasons to think this is a problematic response…. Both the marketers' deliberate symbolic positioning of their products as forbidden and oppositional, and parents' or health professionals' coding of them as unhealthy (diseased) may make these products particularly desirable, and render their opposites (healthy foods) unpalatable….

Along these lines, the track record of both family and in-school intervention programs which focus on behavior modification and pro-nutritional messaging suggests that these are relatively ineffective strategies. However, one documented intervention that has yielded reduced BMI for youth is an in-school television reduction program. Whether the positive results from this study are due to reduced ad exposure, activity substitution, lower food consumption during television viewing, or other benefits is not known….

QUESTIONS

1. Describe the evolution from the "intrinsic product benefit" model for advertising and the "creative revolution." According to the authors, why did the change occur?

2. Many argue that the health dangers associated with consuming junk food are obvious and well known, and when people eat junk food they are merely exercising their freedom to choose. How would the authors respond to this claim?

3. Many argue that parents have primary responsibility for their children's eating habits, and that marketers should not be blamed for rising rates of obesity among the young. How would the authors respond?

4. Junk food marketing proliferates in low-income communities, on billboards, store signs, targeted television, and radio. The same communities tend to have limited access to affordable healthy food, and—no surprise—higher obesity rates. This confluence of factors, along with recent studies showing African-American and Hispanic populations are more genetically disposed to obesity and diabetes than others, has driven grassroots strategies to raise awareness and change food choice behavior. The first step is often "food assessment," with people investigating their own neighborhoods for advertising saturation and lack of fresh food available.
   Internet Assignment Find out what happened in Los Angeles with Community Action on Food Environments (CAFÉ). What do you think of community engagement strategies as a means of combating the effects of junk food marketing?

5. **Internet Assignment** Ashley Pelman and Jazlen Bradley, minor customers of McDonald's, claimed to have increased risk of becoming obese and developing diabetes and other medical problems as a result of the company's advertising, which gave the false impression

that its food was healthy and nutritious. What happened with this case? *Pelman v. McDonald's*, 396 F.3d 508 (N.Y.), 2005.

6. The nonprofit group Children NOW has testified before the FTC advocating for a ban on interactive advertising to children. Commercial Alert advocates for a ban on all junk food sales in schools.

   a. Put each of these strategies for limiting commercial speech through the *Central Hudson* test outlines in the *IMS* case at the beginning if this chapter. Would either one be constitutional?

   b. Working with a partner or a small group, determine what kind of information you would need in order to justify a regulation of junk food advertising under *Central Hudson*. Then try to write a law that would pass that test.

7. As the authors indicate, the public schools have been hotbeds of activism on this issue. Parents and advocacy groups have fought Channel One,[25] and banned junk food and soda. According to a 2004 U.S. Government Accountability Office report, "13 states ha[d] established laws addressing commercial activities in public schools, and at least 25 states [were] considering such legislation."

   a. Find out if your high school uses or has ever used Channel One. If it was taken out, find out how that happened.

   b. **Internet Assignment** Find out if your state has junk food legislation for its public schools.

   c. Administrators often point to the much-needed funds and in-kind corporate resources that marketing in schools generate, while critics argue that the benefits promised are not always realized, and are not worth it, where junk food is advertised. What do you think? What ethical issues arise in this controversy?

8. In this article, the Center for Consumer Freedom is described as "a political front group."

   a. **Internet Assignment** Locate the Center for Consumer Freedom Web site. Read some of its articles. Do they seem well-researched and reliable? Why/why not? What can you find out about how this organization is funded?

   b. What ethical values underlie the CCF arguments?

9. Other countries have regulated advertising to children. More than a decade ago, for example, Sweden banned advertising to children under the age of twelve. In 2001 the mayor of Rio de Janeiro issued a decree restricting all outdoor ads for food, drink, and tobacco within 200 meters from schools and hospitals; the city has also banned all soda and fast food ads in its schools. In March 2005, as news of the childhood obesity epidemic was breaking in the U.S. media, Democratic Senator Tom Harkin of Iowa announced that he would introduce bills, one that would empower the FTC to regulate ads to children, and another that would allow the Secretary of Agriculture to prevent branded food items in schools. **Internet Assignment** Find out what happened. Were these bills ever introduced? Are there any current efforts underway at the federal level to regulate marketing to children in the United States?

10. Threatened by parents and advocacy groups with an obesity lawsuit, Kellogg announced new nutritional standards in June 2007. A single serving of any Kellogg product will

---

25 As of 2007, Channel One has lost most of its advertisers, and is dependent on federal anti-drug and military recruitment ads.

contain not more than 200 calories, have no trans fats, and have limited sodium and sugar content. As of the time of the announcement, the company admitted that half of its products failed those standards, but Kellogg made a commitment that by 2008 all of them would meet the new guidelines. The company also promised to stop marketing to children under twelve and to stop offering branded toys.

a. What reservations might the authors have about Kellogg's announcement?

b. **Internet Assignment** Has Kellogg met its commitments?

Direct-to-Consumer Pharmaceutical Advertising

The Tobacco Story

Harvard Law School professors Jon Hanson and Douglas Kysar's article, "A Case Study in Market Manipulation: The Tobacco Industry,"[26] asks whether the free market is not in fact prone to distortions caused by advertising and marketing techniques that influence how consumers perceive risk. They focus on the tobacco industry as an example of this syndrome for several reasons.

Firstly, the industry's enormous cash flow from repeat purchases of tobacco products allows the industry to spend unparalleled amounts of money on the tools of manipulation—including marketing research, promotion, public relations, and advertising. Second, the public has for some time been aware that tobacco products may pose serious health risks. That awareness, coupled with the fact that cigarettes are far and away the most dangerous consumer product marketed today, means that the incentive for manufacturer manipulation of risk perceptions is perhaps nowhere more strongly felt than in the cigarette industry. Third, the concentrated nature of the industry might have a catalytic effect on the industry's ability to manipulate.

Hanson and Kysar discuss the creation of demand for cigarettes as a matter of "conveying to smokers a sense of independence, autonomy, and sexuality." Once research connecting smoking with serious health problems became public knowledge, the tobacco industry worked to discredit it, doing everything its power to turn scientific findings into a "controversy." They also promoted filter tip and low tar "safer" cigarettes. And in the 1970s they became particularly innovative and aggressive about recruiting new smokers—the young. As Hanson and Kysar write:

Indeed, examination of industry documents reveals a near obsession with marketing to the "pre-smoker."

continued

---

26 Jon D. Hanson & Douglas A. Kysar, Jon Hanson is a professor at Harvard Law School; Douglas Kysar is a graduate of Harvard Law School. This excerpt is from their article, "Taking Behavioralism Seriously: Some Evidence of Market Manipulation," 112 *Harv. L. Rev. 1420* (May 1999). Reprinted by permission of Harvard Law Review via Copyright Clearance Center.

The industry's chief strategy for capturing this "pre-smoker" market is pervasive, relentless advertising. Cigarettes are among the most promoted consumer products in the United States. The FTC reported to Congress that domestic cigarette advertising and promotional expenditures rose from close to $4 billion in 1990 to more than $6 billion in 1993. Tobacco imagery—product brand names, logos, and advertising messages—is ubiquitous. It can be found on or in everything from billboards to magazines, and from city buses to race cars. The effect is to convey the message "to young people that tobacco use is desirable, socially acceptable, safe, healthy, and prevalent." In fact, young people tend to buy the most heavily advertised cigarette brands, whereas many adults buy more generic or value-based cigarette brands, which have little or no image-based advertising....

In 1967...new advertisement campaigns [such as Philip Morris' for Virginia Slims] specifically targeting young girls coincided with a 110% jump in twelve-year-old starters....

Tobacco advertising has been restricted in the United States to some extent as a result of a multi-billion dollar settlement of a lawsuit brought by the attorneys general of most states, claiming that the industry should reimburse them for health care costs associated with caring for smokers.

Compare tobacco with junk food. Which product is more harmful? Why? What similarities can you identify between the marketing strategies of the two industries? How does their behavior compare as they found themselves under public health scrutiny? Should any regulatory response be the same for both tobacco and junk food? Explain.

This chapter began with a case involving pharmaceutical sales techniques aimed at those who prescribe medications. This one looks at the other end of the spectrum in drug sales, marketing aimed at consumers. It was brought by a group of women who had experienced problems with the contraceptive Norplant, an FDA-approved reversible contraceptive that can prevent pregnancy for up to five years. Wyeth Laboratories marketed Norplant heavily to women rather than doctors, advertising on television and in women's magazines such as *Glamour*, *Mademoiselle*, and *Cosmopolitan*. The plaintiffs claim that these ads touted the convenience and simplicity of Norplant, and that none carried warnings of side effects, which, as enumerated by the majority judge in this appeal, included "weight gain, headaches, dizziness, nausea, diarrhea, acne, vomiting, fatigue, facial hair growth, numbness in the arms and legs, irregular menstruation, hair loss, leg cramps, anxiety and nervousness, vision problems, anemia, mood swings and depression, [and] high blood pressure." In addition, there were complications with removal of the Norplant device. Plaintiffs point to research published in medical journals. One study reported that Norplant removal was difficult for one-third of women and painful 40 percent of the time. Another found that doctors experienced difficulty in removing the implant in more than half of all instances.

SARAY PEREZ v. WYETH LABORATORIES INC.

Supreme Court of New Jersey, 1999

734 A.2d 1245

O'HERN, Judge. ☀

Our medical-legal jurisprudence is based on images of health care that no longer exist. At an earlier time, medical advice was received in the doctor's office from a physician who most likely made house calls if needed. The patient usually paid a small sum of money to the doctor. Neighborhood pharmacists compounded prescribed medicines…It is safe to say that the prevailing attitude of law and medicine was that the "doctor knows best."

Pharmaceutical manufacturers never advertised their products to patients, but rather directed all sales efforts at physicians.…

For good or ill, that has all changed. Medical services are in large measure provided by managed care organizations. Medicines are purchased in the pharmacy department of supermarkets and often paid for by third-party providers. Drug manufacturers now directly advertise products to consumers on the radio, television, the Internet, billboards on public transportation, and in magazines.…The question in this case, broadly stated, is whether our law should follow these changes in the marketplace or reflect the images of the past.…

Direct-to-Consumer Advertising

It is paradoxical that so pedestrian a concern as male-pattern baldness should have signaled the beginning of direct-to-consumer marketing of prescription drugs. Upjohn Company became the first drug manufacturer to advertise directly to consumers when it advertised for Rogaine, a hair-loss treatment. The ad targeted male consumers by posing the question, "Can an emerging bald spot…damage your ability to get along with others, influence your chance of obtaining a job or date or even interfere with your job performance?"…

Advertising for Rogaine was the tip of the iceberg.…[The court later mentions medicine for allergies, nail fungus, hypertension, and depression.]

Pressure on consumers is an integral part of drug manufacturers' marketing strategy. From 1995 to 1996, drug companies increased advertising directed to consumers by ninety percent. In 1997, advertising costs of pharmaceutical products surpassed the half-billion dollar mark for the first time, "easily outpacing promotional efforts directed to physicians.…" These efforts…[have been] extremely successful.…As of December 1998, "because of its testimonials" in print and broadcast media by renowned personalities, sales of a product that treats male impotence had increased to $788 million, with approximately 7.5 million prescriptions having been written.

[To highlight why the medical establishment has been troubled by DTC advertising, the majority next quotes from the 1999 *Harvard Law Review* article about the tobacco industry cited on p. 216:]

> The American Medical Association (AMA) has long maintained a policy in opposition to product-specific prescription ads aimed at consumers. A 1992 study by the Annals of Internal Medicine reports that a peer review of 109 prescription ads found 92 per cent of the advertisements lacking in some manner. The difficulties that accompany this [type of advertising] practice are manifest. "The marketing gimmick used by the drug manufacturer often provides the consumer with a diluted variation of the risks associated with the drug product." Even without such manipulation, "[t]elevision spots lasting 30 or 60 seconds are not conducive to 'fair balance' [in presentation of risks]." Given such constraints, pharmaceutical ads often contain warnings of a general nature. However, "[r]esearch indicates that general warnings (for example, see your doctor) in [DTC ads] do not give the consumer a sufficient understanding of the risks inherent in product use." Consumers often interpret such warnings as a "general reassurance" that their condition can be treated, rather than as a requirement that "specific vigilance" is needed to protect them from product risks.[27]

---

27 Jon D. Hanson and Douglas A. Kaysar, "Taking Behaviorism Seriously: Some Evidence of Market Manipulation," 112 *Harv. L. Rev.* 1420 (1999).

[Traditionally, companies had a legal duty to warn consumers directly of dangers associated with their products. An exception developed however, in the area of pharmaceutical drugs: Manufacturers do not have to warn consumers as long as they have warned physicians adequately. This **Learned Intermediary Rule** made sense in the "doctor knows best" world described at the start of this case, a setting where consumers are dependent upon their doctors for advice and information about prescription drugs.]

[T]he respected Judge John Minor Wisdom explained the rationale behind the learned intermediary doctrine. His perspective reflects the then-prevalent attitude about doctor-patient relationships:

> This special standard for prescription drugs is an understandable exception to the Restatement's general rule that one who markets goods must warn foreseeable ultimate users of dangers inherent in [the] products....Prescription drugs are likely to be complex medicines, esoteric in formula and varied in effect. As a medical expert, the prescribing physician can take into account the propensities of the drug, as well as the susceptibilities of [the] patient. [The physician's] task [is to weigh] the benefits of any medication against its potential dangers. The choice [the physician] makes is an informed one, an individualized medical judgment bottomed on a knowledge of both patient and palliative. Pharmaceutical companies then, who must warn ultimate purchasers of dangers inherent in patent drugs sold over the counter, in selling prescription drugs are required to warn only the prescribing physician, who acts as a "learned intermediary" between manufacturer and consumer. [Reyes v. Wyeth Labs, Inc. 498 F.2d 1264 (5th Cir. 1974)]

A more recent review summarized the theoretical bases for the doctrine as based on four considerations.

> First, courts do not wish to intrude upon the doctor-patient relationship. From this perspective, warnings that contradict information supplied by the physician will undermine the patient's trust in the physician's judgment. Second, physicians may be in a superior position to convey meaningful information to their patients, as they must do to satisfy their duty to secure informed consent. Third, drug manufacturers lack effective means to communicate directly with patients, making it necessary to rely on physicians to convey the relevant information. Unlike [over the counter products], pharmacists usually dispense prescription drugs from bulk containers rather than as unit-of-use packages in which the manufacturer may have enclosed labeling. Finally, because of the complexity of risk information about prescription drugs, comprehension problems would complicate any effort by manufacturers to translate physician labeling for lay patients....

These premises...are all (with the possible exception of the last) absent in the direct-to-consumer advertising of prescription drugs.

First, with rare and wonderful exceptions, the "Norman Rockwell" image of the family doctor no longer exists...

Second, because managed care has reduced the time allotted per patient, physicians have considerably less time to inform patients of the risks and benefits of a drug. "In a 1997 survey of 1,000 patients, the FDA found that only one-third had received information from their doctors about the dangerous side effects of drugs they were taking."

Third, having spent $1.3 billion on advertising in 1998, drug manufacturers can hardly be said to "lack effective means to communicate directly with patients," when their advertising campaigns can pay off in close to billions....

... Concerns regarding patients' communication with and access to physicians are magnified in the context of medicines and medical devices furnished to women for reproductive decisions. In *MacDonald v. Ortho Pharmaceutical Corp.*, 475 N.E.2d 65 (1985), the plaintiff's use of oral contraceptives allegedly resulted in a stroke. The Massachusetts

Supreme Court explained several reasons why contraceptives differ from other prescription drugs and thus "warrant the imposition of a common law duty on the manufacturer to warn users directly of associated risks." For example, after the patient receives the prescription, she consults with the physician to receive a prescription annually, leaving her an infrequent opportunity to "explore her questions and concerns about the medication with the prescribing physician." [And] because oral contraceptives are drugs personally selected by the patient, a prescription is often not the result of a physician's skilled balancing of individual benefits and risks but originates, instead, as a product of patient choice. Thus, "the physician is relegated to a...passive role."

... When a patient is the target of direct marketing, one would think, at a minimum, that the law would require that the patient not be misinformed about the product. It is one thing not to inform a patient about the potential side effects of a product; it is another thing to misinform the patient by deliberately withholding potential side effects while marketing the product as an efficacious solution to a serious health problem. Further, when one considers that many of these "life-style" drugs or elective treatments cause significant side effects without any curative effect, increased consumer protection becomes imperative, because these drugs are, by definition, not medically necessary....

The direct marketing of drugs to consumers generates a corresponding duty requiring manufacturers to warn of defects in the product. The FDA has established a comprehensive regulatory scheme for direct-to-consumer marketing of pharmaceutical products....

[The majority holds that the plaintiffs can argue in tort that the manufacturers of Norplant misinformed them, substantially "contributing to their use of a defective pharmaceutical product...."]

POLLOCK, Judge, dissenting. ☀

Norplant is not an over-the-counter drug; it can be obtained only with a doctor's prescription. To insert Norplant, a physician or other health-care professional anesthetizes an area in a patient's upper arm, makes a one-eighth-inch incision, and implants six capsules just below the patient's skin. Similar surgery is required to remove the capsules.

The use of Norplant thus requires the significant involvement of the prescribing physician. Even Norman Rockwell would recognize the procedure as one performed in accordance with the traditional physician-patient relationship.... The invasiveness of the Norplant procedure, moreover, would give any patient pause and a physician cause to evaluate the risks....

The majority identifies four premises underlying the learned intermediary doctrine that it asserts are inapplicable when a manufacturer advertises the drug directly to consumers.... Contrary to the majority, those four considerations remain relevant to the implantation of Norplant.

First, the Norplant System must be implanted surgically. Implicit in the performance of a surgical procedure is respect for the physician-patient relationship. "[T]he physician is in the best position to take into account the propensities of the drug and the susceptibilities of the patient, and to give a highly individualized warning to the ultimate user based on the physician's specialized knowledge." Second, the physician is the only person who can communicate with the patient to obtain the patient's informed consent to the procedure. Third, a pharmaceutical company, such as Wyeth, cannot provide an adequate warning to each individual consumer about the potential side-effects and risks associated with the device. Each patient has individualized risks associated with surgical procedures. Lastly, the Norplant implant, far more than other birth control devices, is a complex contraceptive system that requires detailed instructions and warnings.

QUESTIONS

1. What is the Learned Intermediary Rule? Explain the context in which it became law.

2. On what legal grounds does the majority believe that the Learned Intermediary Rule does not apply where drugs are advertised directly to consumers? How does the dissent view this issue?

3. **Internet Assignment** In the European Community, direct-to-consumer advertising of prescription drugs is prohibited. What, if anything, is recommended to regulate DTC ads by consumer advocates in the United States?

4. One theme of the *Perez* case is the degree to which consumers today are active, aware, and taking responsibility for their own health, rather than passive and in awe of medical expertise. Direct-to-consumer advertising—estimated at $58 billion as of 2005—is premised on the notion that consumers will be driven to want certain prescription drugs, and to ask for them by name when they see their doctors.

   a. From a consumer perspective, what are the pros and cons of DTC advertising?

   b. Who are the major stakeholders in the pharmaceutical direct-to-consumer scenario? Does this type of marketing create "the greatest happiness for the greatest number," in utilitarian terms? What might a deontological thinker say about DTC marketing?

The Branding of Culture

In her provocative book *No Logo*, journalist and media commentator Naomi Klein claims that a fundamental shift has occurred—from marketing as advertising of products to marketing itself as the product—to the pre-eminence of "the brand." She sees this shift as having profound consequences for every aspect of our culture.

NO LOGO

Naomi Klein

The Beginning of the Brand

It's helpful to go back briefly and look at where the idea of branding first began. Though the words are often used interchangeably, branding and advertising are not the same process....Think of the brand as the core meaning of the modern corporation, and of the advertisement as one vehicle used to convey that meaning to the world. The first mass-marketing campaigns, starting in the second half of the nineteenth century, had more to do with advertising than with branding as we understand it today. Faced with a range of recently invented products—the radio, phonograph, car, light bulb and so on—advertisers had more pressing tasks than creating a brand identity for any given corporation; first, they had to change the way people lived their lives. Ads had to inform consumers about the existence of some new invention, then convince them that their lives would be better if they used [it].

[Klein explains how, in the ad campaigns of the late nineteenth and early twentieth centuries, ads were more descriptive than persuasive, and rivals were not mentioned in the copy. Then things began to change.]

By the end of the 1940s, there was a burgeoning awareness that a brand wasn't just a mascot or a catchphrase or a picture printed on the label of a company's product; the company as a whole could have a brand identity....

The search for the true meaning of brands—or the "brand essence," as it is often called—gradually took the agencies away from individual products and their attributes and toward a psychological/anthropological examination of what brands means to the culture and to people's lives.

[She goes on to tell how, for companies like Nike, Apple, the Body Shop, Disney, Levi's and Starbucks, the branding process was becoming more important than the actual products.]

They integrated the idea of branding into the very fabric of their companies. Their corporate cultures were so tight and cloistered that to outsiders they appeared to be a cross between fraternity house, religious cult and sanitarium. Everything was an ad for the brand: bizarre lexicons for describing employees (partners, baristas, team players, crew members), company chants, superstar CEOs, fanatical attention to design consistency, a propensity for monument-building, and New Age mission statements....

[As Klein sees it, the new marketplace is marked by two important developments: "The deeply unhip big-box bargain stores that provide the essentials of life and monopolize a disproportionate share of the market (Wal-Mart, et al.) and the extra-premium 'attitude' brands that provide the essentials of lifestyle and monopolize ever-expanding stretches of cultural space (Nike, et al.)."]

Nike, for example, is leveraging the deep emotional connection that people have with sports and fitness. With Starbucks, we see how coffee has woven itself into the fabric of people's lives, and that's our opportunity for emotional leverage....A great brand raises the bar—it adds a greater sense of purpose to the experience, whether it's the challenge to do your best in sports and fitness or the affirmation that the cup of coffee you're drinking really matters....

The Brand Expands

The effect, if not always the original intent, of advanced branding is to nudge the hosting culture into the background and make the brand the star. It is not to sponsor culture but to be the culture. And why shouldn't it be? If brands are not products but ideas, attitudes, values and experiences, why can't they be culture too?...

The project of transforming culture into little more than a collection of brand-extensions-in-waiting would not have been possible without the deregulation and privatization policies of the past three decades....[I]n the U.S. under Ronald Regan and in Britain under Margaret Thatcher (and in many other parts of the world as well), corporate taxes were dramatically lowered, a move that eroded the tax base and gradually starved out the public sector. As government spending dwindled, schools, museums and broadcasters were desperate to make up their budget shortfalls and thus ripe for partnerships with private corporations. It also didn't hurt that the political climate during this time ensured that there was almost no vocabulary to speak passionately about the value of a non-commercialized public sphere. This was the time of the Big Government bogeyman and deficit hysteria, when any political move that was not overtly designed to increase the freedom of corporations was vilified.... It was against this backdrop that, in rapid order, sponsorship went from being a rare occurrence (in the 1970s) to an exploding growth industry (by the mid-eighties)....

[Klein goes on to discuss the notion of "cool."]

Just as the history of cool in America is really (as many have argued) a history of African-American culture—from jazz and blues to rock and roll and rap—for many of the superbrands, cool hunting simply means black-culture hunting. Which is why the cool hunters' first stop was the basketball courts of America's poorest neighborhoods....

Tommy Hilfiger: To the Ghetto and Back Again

Tommy Hilfiger, even more than Nike or Adidas, has turned the harnessing of ghetto cool into a mass-marketing science. Hilfiger forged a formula that has since been imitated by Polo, Nautica, Munsingwear (thanks to Puff Daddy's fondness for the penguin logo) and several other clothing companies looking for a short cut to making it at the suburban mall and inner-city attitude.

...Hilfiger ads are a tangle of Cape Cod multiculturalism: scrubbed black faces lounging with their windswept white brothers and sisters in that great country club in the sky, and always against the backdrop of a billowing American flag. "By respecting one another we can reach all cultures and communities," the company says. "We promote...the concept of living the American dream." But the hard facts of Tommy's interracial financial success have less to do with finding common ground between cultures than with the power and mythology embedded in America's deep racial segregation.

Tommy Hilfiger started off squarely as white-preppy wear in the tradition of Ralph Lauren and Lacoste. But the designer soon realized that his clothes also had a peculiar cachet in the inner cities, where the hip-hop philosophy of "living large" saw poor and working-class kids acquiring status in the ghetto by adopting the gear and accoutrements of prohibitively costly leisure activities, such as skiing, golfing, even boating. Perhaps to better position his brand within this urban fantasy, Hilfiger began to associate his clothes more consciously with these sports, shooting ads at yacht clubs, beaches and other nautical locales. At the same time, the clothes themselves were redesigned to appeal more directly to the hip-hop aesthetic. Cultural theorist Paul Smith described the shift as "bolder colors, bigger and baggier styles, more hoods and cords, and more prominence for logos and the Hilfiger name." He also plied rap artists like Snoop Dogg with free clothes and, walking the tightrope between the yacht and the ghetto, launched a line of Tommy Hilfiger beepers.

Once Tommy was firmly established as a ghetto thing, the real selling could begin— not just to the comparatively small market of poor inner-city youth but to the much larger market of middle-class white and Asian kids who mimic black style in everything from lingo to sports to music. Company sales reached $847 million in 1998—up from a paltry 53 million in 1991 when Hilfiger was still, as Smith puts it, "Young Republican clothing." Like so much of cool hunting, Hilfiger's marketing journey feeds off the alienation of the heart of America's race relations: selling white youth on their fetishization of black style, and black youth on their fetishization of white wealth.

QUESTIONS

1. How does Klein distinguish the following: marketing, advertising, branding? Which does she view as dominant today?

2. Compare Klein's article to the Galbraith reading at the beginning of this chapter. To what extent does Klein's analysis overlap or support Galbraith's? Does it contradict Galbraith in any way?

3. Klein attributes Tommy Hilfiger's financial success to the "power and mythology embedded in America's deep racial segregation." What does she mean by this? Can you argue against that view?

4. One of Klein's concerns is the blurring of the distinction between advertising and media content. Recent Nike commercials, for example, are lengthy MTV spots that appear to be music videos. In April 2001, one such ad ran for two-and-a-half minutes with a funk-music sound track. Further confusing the sponsored/nonsponsored divide, the basketball players in the ad are both professional and so-called streetball players. The commercial has

nothing in it that is overtly selling, in fact. For just one moment a player thrusts a basket-ball with the Nike swoosh logo at the camera. "It doesn't have any shoe shots," says the creative director of this ad. "It's more about celebrating the game. We were interested in something that would turn kids on to basketball so they would pick up the ball and play. We wanted to communicate that basketball is a game about freedom and self-expression and individuality. "What, if anything, is wrong with a marketing strategy like this? Do any ethical issues occur to you?

Source: Excerpts from "No Logo" by Naomi Klein. Copyright 1999. NY: St. Martin's Press.

CHAPTER **PROBLEMS**

1. Beginning in the 1990s, with their research pipelines drying up, the major players in the pharmaceutical industry moved to sustain profits by fighting to extend patent periods, by advertising direct-to-consumers, and by raising drug prices. The facts of a case filed recently in California reflect a blend of these strategies: As the patent for AstraZeneca's blockbuster drug for acid reflux, Prilosec, ran out, the company spent millions to persuade consumers that their new and eight-times-more-expensive product, Nexium, was more effective in treating acid reflux than Prilosec in its generic, over-the-counter form. As of late 2004, Nexium was AstraZenenca's best selling product, ranked seventh among all prescription drug sales in the United States. With a $257 million blitz to promote Nexium, the "purple pill," in 2003, the company outspent all other pharmaceutical drug campaigns that year. AstraZeneca was sued by a coalition including senior citizens groups and the AFL-CIO. (This was the first time the union joined litigation aimed at controlling health care costs.) The plaintiffs argued that the Nexium ads were deceptive.

   a. What law would be the basis for their claim? What would they have to prove to win?

   b. What actions might the government have taken?

   c. Internet Assignment Find out what happened in the actual case.

2. In the wake of public scrutiny and industry self-regulation of pharmaceutical detailing practices, the focus has shifted to "simple one-on-one human rapport." As *The New York Times* reported in 2005:

   Anyone who has seen the parade of sales representatives through a doctor's waiting room has probably noticed that they are frequently female and invariably good looking. Less recognized is the fact that a good many are recruited from the cheerleading ranks.
   Known for their athleticism, postage-stamp skirts and persuasive enthusiasm, cheerleaders have many qualities the drug industry looks for in its sales force. Some keep their pompoms active, like Onya, a sculptured former college cheerleader. On Sundays she works the sidelines for the Washington Redskins. But weekdays find her urging gynecologists to prescribe a treatment for vaginal yeast infection.

   The article goes on to quote a cheerleading advisor at the University of Kentucky, who gets regular calls from drug company recruiters. He explains why his team is in demand:

   Exaggerated motions, exaggerated smiles, exaggerated enthusiasm—they learn those things, and they can get people to do what they want.

Former cheerleaders—female and male—are evidently joining the ranks of pharmaceutical sales reps in large numbers, and they walk into good salaries: $50,000 to $60,000 a year with bonuses, and a car. The companies deny that they are hiring based on sex appeal. As one executive puts it:

Obviously, people hired for the work have to be extroverts, a good conversationalist, a pleasant person to talk to; but that has nothing to do with looks, it's the personality.[28]

Are there ethical issues here?[29]

3. **Internet Assignment** In recent years, the U.S. Supreme Court and lower federal courts have been dealing with several First Amendment challenges to regulation of tobacco and alcohol ads. In 2002, a community college's ban on ads on its property for alcohol, tobacco, guns, and illegal drugs was found to violate the First Amendment. Using a legal search database, find out how the *Central Hudson* test was applied in the following cases:

   a. The city of Baltimore passed an ordinance banning billboard advertising of alcoholic beverages and cigarettes near schools and playgrounds.

   b. The state of Rhode Island passed a law banning the mention of price from all advertising of alcoholic beverages.

   c. The New York State Liquor Authority banned the Bad Frog Brewery label that showed a frog with the second of its four unwebbed fingers extended in a gesture of insult.

4. In the 1990s R.J. Reynolds Tobacco planned to test market a new brand of menthol cigarettes to African-Americans in Philadelphia. The Urban Coalition got wind of this and launched a protest.

   Internet Assignment Find out what happened.

5. What is the "aesthetic appeal" of advertising? Consider this:

During recent years, in certain circles, the surest way to silence a would-be critic of advertising has been to cite its artistic achievements. Whatever we may think of the products or the sponsors, this argument runs, we have to admit that those creative types in the agencies are . . . clever, sometimes even brilliant. The only influence—far from sinister—they have exercised has been to enliven our cultural atmosphere with staccato visual and verbal rhythms of the commercial vernacular. . . .

Since the late nineteenth century, advertising has given people who like to write, draw, or shoot film the opportunity to get paid regularly (maybe even well) for it. The industry has attracted many extraordinarily talented people. These artists and writers have served, in a sense, as emissaries between social universes, the agency-client world and the wider population; art and big business; museums and commercial culture. They have worked various boundaries, sometimes creatively reconnecting aesthetics and everyday life, more often conforming out of the necessity of agency organization. Whatever their accomplishments, they deserve more than a passing glance. . . .[30]

And this:

Like advertising, poetry's purpose is to influence an audience; to affect its perceptions and sensibilities; perhaps even to change its mind. . . . [P]oetry's intent is to convince and seduce. In the service

28 Stephanie Saul, "Cheerleaders Pep Up Drug Sales," *The New York Times*, November 28, 2005.

29 *Khademi v. S. Orange Co. College*, 194 F. Supp. 2d 1011 (Cal. 2002).

30 Jackson Lears, *Fables of Abundance: A Cultural History of Advertising in America* (New York: Basic Books, 1994), pp. 261–262.

of that intent, it employs without guilt or fear of criticism all the arcane tools of distortion that the literary mind can devise. Keats does not offer a truthful engineering description of his Grecian urn. He offers, instead...a lyrical, exaggerated, distorted, and palpably false description. And he is thoroughly applauded for it, as are all other artists, in whatever medium, who do precisely the same thing successfully.

    Commerce...takes essentially the same liberties with reality...as the artists, except that commerce calls its creations advertising....As with art, the purpose is to influence the audience by creating illusions, symbols, and implications that promise more than pure functionality....[31]

Is certain advertising art? Is all advertising art? None of it?

6. In 1980, roughly one-third of all biomedical research was funded by the pharmaceutical industry. As government support declined, the industry stepped in, and by 2000 it funded nearly two-thirds of such work. The industry also provides much of the advertising that supports the publication of professional medical journals, such as the *New England Journal of Medicine*. A 1998 study of medical journal editorials about a controversial group of blood pressure medications found that those who favored the drugs were much more likely to have (undisclosed) financial ties to the drug manufacturers than those who were critical. The industry is also entwined in the regulatory apparatus: In the summer of 2004 a federal panel recommended that Americans at risk of heart disease should radically reduce their cholesterol levels from previous estimates. Most of the members of the panel had financial ties to the pharmaceutical companies that make "statins," new drugs that lower cholesterol.

    a. What ethical concerns do these links between industry, the medical profession, and government raise? Can you think of any ways to protect consumers from any harms that might result?

    b. **Internet Assignment** Find out what reforms have been proposed by Public Citizen. Find out what you can about Public Citizen (who supports it, its record, etc.).

    c. Find out who opposes the efforts of Public Citizen and why.

7. According to the Surgeon General, the causes of childhood obesity in the United States are unhealthy eating, insufficient physical activity, and genetics. With a team of your classmates, come up with a policy recommendation that addresses all three of these factors.

8. In 1998, Coca-Cola held a contest inviting high-school students to devise promotional ideas for the company. A prize of $500 would go to the school with the best PR strategy. Greenbriar High in Evans, Georgia, was the winner. On "Coke Day," students were to attend lectures from visiting company executives, wear Coke t-shirts to school and pose for a group photograph, spelling out the word Coke with their bodies. Senior Mike Cameron decided to play a prank. Just as the group formation photo was about to be taken, he removed his outer shirt to reveal a Pepsi t-shirt. He was suspended for being rude and disruptive. The principal explained: "We had the regional president of Coca-Cola here and people flew in from Atlanta to do us the honor of being resource speakers." Is there anything ethically troubling about this story? Is there a distinction between paid advertisements in schools and corporate sponsorship of the content of education? What would happen if Mike sued for violation of his First Amendment rights?

    Internet Assignment Find out what happened when he did.

---

31 Theodore Levitt, "The Morality (?) of Advertising," *Harv. Bus. Rev.* 48 (July–August 1970), p. 85.

9. By 2030 tobacco will be the biggest cause of death, killing about 10 million people annually. The fastest growing population of smokers exists in the developing world. In China, for example, there are an estimated 300 million smokers—one-third of its adult population and triple the number of 20 years ago. In the Philippines, 73 percent of adults and half the children ages 7 to 17 smoke. Africa has never been thought of as a primary growth region for smoking, but Philip Morris' profit there has been increasing at the rate of 20 percent a year. And in India, where only 12 percent of people smoke, both R. J. R. Reynolds and Philip Morris are now a presence, trying to tap the last major virgin market for tobacco consumption.

   a. What ethical considerations arise when tobacco companies market their products in developing countries?

   b. **Internet Assignment** The first world treaty dealing with public health went into effect in February 2005. The Framework Convention on Tobacco Control bans all tobacco advertising, promotion, and sponsorship. Find out which countries ratified the treaty. Is the United States a signatory? Why or why not? What can you find out about the likely effectiveness of this global effort to reign in tobacco marketing?

10. The chic political and cultural Web logs (blogs) run by Gawker Media receive some 400,000 to 700,000 visitors monthly. Recently Gawker began blogging on behalf of big advertisers like Nike. For its advertorial blog "The Art of Speed," Nike provided several short films on the theme of speed and Gawker contributed commentary and layout. A Nike representative called the Gawker blog audience "the right community. It may be small but it's an important and influential group."

    Internet Assignment Find any blog site containing advertising. What kind of buzz is the sponsor trying to generate? How would you describe the connection between the company's branding and its blogging?

11. New York's Metropolitan Transportation Authority proposes to sell naming rights to bridges and to rail and subway stations to corporate advertisers. Meanwhile, in Rome, city planners have been very successful raising funds for restoring ancient buildings and monuments by selling advertising space. Billboards hang on scaffolding while a structure is being renovated. In the summer of 2004, 50 important sites with aging facades were available to the highest advertising bidder—including the Pantheon—while a huge (and very suggestive) billboard advertising Glam Shine lipstick hung over the Spanish Steps. Is this a win-win situation? What are the ethics of mixing public and private imperatives in this way? Where should the line be drawn?

12. A young, attractive couple is hanging around in Times Square. They are wearing backpacks, and they have with them a Sony-Ericsson cellular telephone with a digital camera attached. Approaching a passerby, the young man of the couple smiles and says: "Would you take a picture of me and my girlfriend?" Almost everyone is willing to, and as they do, he explains how the new gadget works. "It's easy. Look. Just push this button. This is so sweet. I just got it...." Soon the passerby is intrigued with the cell phone too. And although she'll never find out, the passerby has just had an encounter with two paid operatives in a "viral marketing" campaign, promoting a product like a virus spreads disease—silently but effectively. How would you feel if the attractive person who flirted with you at a bar asking for a light for a cigarette turned out to be hawking that cigarette? Does stealth marketing seem unethical to you?

CHAPTER **PROJECT**

Legislative Hearing: Hard Liquor Advertising on Network Television

GUIDELINES, APPENDIX F

In 1948, the makers of distilled spirits placed a voluntary ban on television ads. In 1996, the industry lifted its ban, and in December 2001, a spot promoting designated drivers on behalf of Smirnoff Vodka ran on NBC's *Saturday Night Live*. Liquor ads had been appearing on cable and local TV, but this was the first breakthrough into the networks. NBC has its own 19-point guideline for hard liquor ads. They may appear only on shows where at least 85 percent of the audience is 21 years and older; they cannot promote drinking as a "mark of adulthood" or a "rite of passage"; and they cannot show the actual consumption of liquor, for instance. But many are arguing that the stakes are too high to trust industry self-regulation.

You will be representing an interest group testifying before a congressional commerce committee on the question of whether government regulation should control liquor ads on TV.

Spokespeople:

- Seagram's president, representing the industry
- NBC president, representing the networks
- ACLU representative, free speech advocate
- American Medical Association (AMA) president
- Mothers Against Drunk Drivers (MADD) representative
- Reverend Jesse Brown, African-American activist against tobacco and alcohol advertising to blacks
- Republican congressperson
- Democratic congressperson
- Head of the Commerce Committee

8 RISK ALLOCATION: PRODUCTS LIABILITY

Our duty is "[t]o sustain, to repair, to beautify this noble pile" that is the common law.

— WILLIAM BLACKSTONE[1]

Consumers by definition, include us all. They are the largest economic group, affecting and affected by almost every public and private economic decision. Yet they are the only important group...whose views are often not heard.

— PRESIDENT JOHN F. KENNEDY, DECLARATION TO U.S. CONGRESS (1962)

Virtually every product is dangerous in some manner and to some extent, at least when put to certain uses. But most such dangers are simple facts of physics, chemistry, or biology. There is no reasonable way to avoid them. For such natural risks of life, product users, rather than product suppliers, properly bear responsibility for avoiding and insuring against any injuries that may result.

— DAVID OWEN (2004)[2]

●

For centuries, the phrase ***caveat emptor*** ("buyer beware") dominated the law in Britain and the United States, warning that most sellers made no enforceable promises with regard to their goods. By the middle of the twentieth century, the common law had shifted, allowing those injured by dangerous products to hold both sellers and manufacturers accountable. Today, tort law, the Uniform Commercial Code (UCC) provisions regarding contract warranties, and government agencies such as the Food and Drug Administration (FDA) all play a role in assuring product safety. In the past few decades, class action suits on behalf of thousands, sometimes hundreds of thousands, of injured plaintiffs have been brought against entire industries found to have hidden the known risks of their products: asbestos, tobacco, and lead.

The chapter opens with this newest twist in the effort to hold the makers of unsafe products accountable: using the "nuisance" law against manufacturers. We then explore both the legal backdrop and the policy debates that product liability litigation has wrought. We close

---

1 4 William Blackstone, *Commentaries* (435 – 6).

2 David G. Owen, "Proof of Product Defect," 93 *Ky. LJ.* 1 (2004-05).

with an examination of government regulation and its limitations in this era of global free trade; for example, a loaf of Sara Lee™ whole grain white bread contains ingredients from India, the Netherlands, China, Switzerland—along with honey from either Vietnam, Brazil, Uruguay, Canada, or Mexico and wheat gluten supplied by France, Poland, Russia, or Australia.

Unsafe Products

Lead, a naturally occurring metal with a wide variety of purposes in products from batteries to paint, glassware, and plastics, has been linked to serious health problems.

In 2001, the City of Newark, New Jersey, filed a complaint against manufacturers and distributors of lead paints, seeking the cost of detecting and removing lead paint from homes and buildings, of providing medical care to residents affected with lead poisoning, and of developing programs to educate residents about the dangers of lead paint. Later joined by 26 other municipalities and counties, the plaintiffs relied on a number of legal theories. Most significantly, they claimed that the makers of lead paint created a **public nuisance** for which they should be held financially responsible. Below, the Supreme Court of New Jersey explains why it is dismissing their complaint.

IN RE LEAD PAINT LITIGATION

Supreme Court of New Jersey, 2007

924 A.2d 484

Justice HOENS delivered the opinion of the Court. ❋

... The most recent annual report prepared by the New Jersey Department of Health and Senior Services (DHSS) describes lead paint and the risk it poses as follows:

> When absorbed into the human body, lead affects the blood, kidneys and nervous system. Lead's effects on the nervous system are particularly serious and can cause learning disabilities, hyperactivity, decreased hearing, mental retardation and possible death. Lead is particularly hazardous to children between six months and six years of age because their neurological system and organs are still developing. ...

...Although lead–based paint was banned in the United States in 1978, most homes constructed in the United States before 1978 contain some lead paint, and lead exposure in children today most commonly results from their "chronic ingestion of lead–contaminated dust." Despite the decline in average blood lead levels among the population of the United States, as of 2000, the Centers for Disease Control considered childhood lead exposure to be "a major environmental health problem." ...

[Next, the court looks at the common law tort of public nuisance.]

...Originally, public nuisance was created as a criminal offense, which was used to allow public officials, acting in the place of the sovereign, to prosecute individuals or require abatement of activities considered to be harmful to the public.... [T]he historical focus of public nuisance prosecutions included attacking such behaviors as "keeping diseased animals or the maintenance of a pond breeding malarial mosquitoes,...storage of explosives,...[operating] houses of prostitution,...[causing] loud and disturbing noises,...disseminat[ing] bad odors, dust and smoke,...[and] obstruction of a public highway or a navigable stream." ...

Essential to the concept of public nuisance, as illustrated by these historical examples, is the "interference with the interests of the community at large."

…[T]he Legislature addressed the lead paint problem in a manner completely in accord with our historical notions of public nuisance. By attaching a criminal penalty, by ordering an abatement through a public entity, and by maintaining a focus on the owner of premises as the actor responsible for the public nuisance itself, the Legislature's approach remained tethered to the historical bases that have defined public nuisance dating back centuries….

[Next, the majority explains why it is the property owners, not the lead-paint makers, who are responsible for creating a public nuisance.]

[New Jersey passed its own Lead Paint Act (LPA) in 1971. One part of the statutory scheme focuses on abatement of lead paint in buildings, paid for largely by property owners who must pay higher inspection fees and can be sued by a local health department that removes the lead paint. Separate provisions of the law create programs to address the health concerns arising from lead exposure. HMOs, hospitals, and insurers are required to provide or cover blood lead screening and treatment for lead-related disorders.]

…The Lead Paint Act's focus on owners maintains the traditional public nuisance theory's link to the conduct of an actor, generally in a particular location….

…[O]ne cannot…argue persuasively that the conduct of defendants in distributing [the paint], at the time when they did, bears the necessary link to the current health crisis. Absent that link, the claims of plaintiffs cannot sound in public nuisance…[without stretching] the theory to the point of creating strict liability to be imposed on manufacturers of ordinary consumer products which, although legal when sold, and although sold no more recently than a quarter of a century ago, have become dangerous through deterioration and poor maintenance by the purchasers.

… We cannot help but agree with the observation that, were we to find a cause of action here, "nuisance law 'would become a monster that would devour in one gulp the entire law of tort.'"

[Held: Claims against paint companies are dismissed.]

Chief Justice ZAZZALI, dissenting.

…Lead paint is a deadly toxin that permeates the structural environment of this State. The effects of lead poisoning are well-documented:

> *Lead is highly toxic and affects virtually every system of the body. At high exposure levels, lead poisoning can cause coma, convulsions, and death. While adults can suffer from excessive lead exposures, the groups most at risk are fetuses, infants, and children under age six. At low levels, the neurotoxic effects of lead have the greatest impact on children's developing brains and nervous systems, causing reductions in IQ and attention span, reading and learning disabilities, hyperactivity, and behavioral problems….However, the vast majority of childhood lead–poisoning cases go undiagnosed and untreated, since most poisoned children have no obvious symptoms.*

Children need not ingest lead paint directly to be at risk. Because lead does not "dissipate, biodegrade, or decay," all lead paint not properly extracted remains in the State's environment, and children are not safe from exposure simply because their residence has been decontaminated….The usual wear and tear associated with the use of walls, windows, and doors introduces the toxin into our environment…The federal Department of Housing and Urban Development, therefore, has identified lead poisoning as "the most common environmental disease of young children, eclipsing all other environmental health hazards found in the residential environment."

...Children from underprivileged communities are most at risk because of the prevalence of older, dilapidated buildings within their communities.... Statistically, low–income children are eight times more likely to be poisoned than children from other income brackets, and an estimated sixty percent of all poisoned children are on Medicaid.

Adding to the crisis are the logistical difficulties associated with abating lead paint contamination.... [I]n 2003, the Legislature noted that "because of the age of New Jersey's housing stock, our State is among the states with the most serious risk of exposure from previous residential use of lead–based paint."...

Most significant, however, is the staggering cost of decontamination. In 2001 [A state task force] estimated that it would cost New Jersey $50 billion to abate lead paint contamination.... The cost to private property owners is also prohibitive, with the decontamination of a single apartment costing as much as $12,000.

In sum, New Jersey's residential environment is infected with a deadly toxin that affects our most vulnerable and cherished citizens: our children.

...[The Lead Paint Act's] purpose is to ensure appropriate governmental regulation of lead paint removal and detection. Nowhere does the Lead Paint Act express an intention to foreclose pre–existing common law remedies [such as the public nuisance tort] that would supplement the eradication of lead paint....

...The Lead Paint Act and the public nuisance doctrine are complementary....

...[In a part of the case not included above, the majority of the court found that the plaintiffs' only remedy was under the state Product Liability Act, or PLA. In the remainder of this dissenting opinion, Judge Zazzali explains why he believes the PLA does not apply.]

Plaintiffs' allegation that defendants intentionally polluted residential buildings is a fitting example of an environmental tort. Defendants manufactured toxic lead pigment for application to New Jersey's buildings. Plaintiffs allege that defendants were aware of lead's toxicity and knowingly introduced it into the structural environment of this State. Consequently, lead paint permeates many of our residences. I see no significant distinction between the scenario presented in this appeal and traditional environmental torts where pollutants are introduced into some other aspect of the physical environment, such as the air or water....

In my view, *Stevenson v. Keene Corp.*, (1993) [a case permitting a lawsuit against an asbestos company] is controlling in this appeal.... There is no meaningful difference between the manufacturing of asbestos and the production of toxic lead pigment.

...Here, the injured parties are also not consumers, but unsuspecting children who are exposed to ambient lead pollutants decades after the paint was originally purchased by consumers. What remains is an environmental disaster that poisons innocent children. The environmental tort exception to the Products Liability Act was intended to apply in such circumstances.

...[The application of the public nuisance doctrine by the majority of the court] conflicts with sound policies underlying public nuisance principles and, more important, permits those allegedly responsible for contaminating New Jersey to avoid responsibility for curing the infection....

The majority correctly notes that the "conduct that has given rise to the public health crisis is, in point of fact, poor maintenance of premises...."

However, that perspective sidesteps the harsh reality of the lead paint crisis. Decades ago, lead paint was applied to buildings throughout this State. As the harmful effects of lead paint became public, those who could afford its removal or proper maintenance did so. The dangerous lead paint that remains in our physical environment exists primarily in underprivileged, residential communities where home owners and municipalities cannot afford the exorbitant costs of decontamination.... Those citizens and communities should not be portrayed as the cause of a public health crisis; they are the victims. More important, defendants should not be shielded from liability by recasting the reality of the lead paint problem. If plaintiffs' allegations are proven true, defendants should bear the burden of remediation.

...One purpose of the law, particularly the common law of torts, is to provide a corrective mechanism for injustice.... It is our responsibility to ensure that formalistic distinctions and outdated definitions do not thwart justice....Our duty is "[t]o sustain, to repair, to beautify this noble pile" that is the common law. [William Blackstone.]

The tragedy of the lead paint crisis is that it was and is entirely preventable. The only impediment to purging New Jersey of lead paint is the financial cost. The majority's holding unfairly places the cost of abatement on taxpayers and private property owners, while sheltering those responsible for creating the problem. Because the common law doctrine of public nuisance is an appropriate means of shifting the cost of abatement to those who unfairly profited at the expense of the general public, I respectfully dissent.

QUESTIONS

1. According to the majority, the plaintiffs have not properly alleged a tort of public nuisance. Why not? Why does the dissent disagree?

2. Both majority and dissent point to the historical basis and purpose of law, specifically the tort of public nuisance. How would allowing this case to go forward distort the historical tort, according to the majority? How would it further the "corrective" and "preventive" functions of the tort?

3. How should society deal with a problem like the lead exposure to children described in this case? Is it fair to go after the manufacturers years after their products were sold and used? To expect the property owners to bear the clean-up costs? Who are the stakeholders in this scenario? What ethical issues surface as you identify potential solutions?

The Debate Over Tort Reform

Tort law is public law in disguise.

— Leon Greene (1959)[3]

The use of nuisance lawsuits to address injuries caused by dangerous products has become a lightning rod for proponents and opponents of "tort reform." Victor E. Schwartz, a partner in a law firm that defends businesses, is a well-known advocate for tort reform. His co-author is also an attorney at Shook, Hardy & Bacon L.L.P. They argue that public nuisance theory is being misused by self-interested lawyers, and that it was "not developed to allow private citizens the power to stop or abate conduct, to allow government to grow its coffers, to spread the risk of an enterprise, or to punish defendants."

---

3 Leon Greene, "Tort Law Public Law in Disguise," 38 *Tex. L. Rev.* 1 (1959).

THE LAW OF PUBLIC NUISANCE: MAINTAINING RATIONAL BOUNDARIES ON A RATIONAL TORT[4]

VICTOR E. SCHWARTZ AND PHIL GOLDBERG

Introduction

The current effort to expand public nuisance theory to provide sanctions against manufacturers of lawful products is disconcerting because it would fundamentally change the entire character of public nuisance doctrine, as well as undermine products liability law. Not surprisingly, the targets involve "unpopular" products, such as asbestos, guns, tobacco, lead paint...and others....

Tobacco Litigation

The watershed event for product-based litigation in public nuisance theory came out of the lawsuits filed by state attorneys general against numerous manufacturers of tobacco products. These lawsuits, which "sought reimbursement of state expenditures for Medicaid and other medical programs" for smokers, included several novel applications of recovery theories....[Some] included public nuisance claims, marking the first time that public nuisance was used in mass actions in products litigation....

In 1998, the state attorneys general settled all of their claims with the manufacturers of tobacco products in what was called the Master Settlement Agreement (MSA). The MSA resulted in the transfer of $246 billion to the states and the plaintiffs' firms hired to bring the litigation. Nothing in the MSA indicated that the sale, distribution, and promotion of tobacco products constituted a public nuisance, but some of the lawsuits covered by the settlement contained public nuisance claims. Even though no court validated the use of public nuisance theory in the tobacco litigation, the use of public nuisance theory quickly became a misleading aspect of the state attorney general tobacco litigation legend. Given the sheer size of the award and resulting attorneys' fees, it is not surprising that, since the MSA, governments and plaintiffs' lawyers have attempted to apply public nuisance theory against many other industries of product manufacturers.

Firearms Litigation

The use of public nuisance theory in firearms litigation was a direct outgrowth of the MSA tobacco legend. Professor David Kairys, who taught at the Beasley School of Law at Temple University, worked with some cities to file public nuisance claims against gun manufacturers....

In his first cases, Professor Kairys made an important and clever change in how public nuisance theory would be applied. The alleged public nuisance would not be "in the manufacture of guns [or] in the existence or sale of guns," but in the marketing and distribution practices and policies of the manufacturers. Specifically, the plaintiffs alleged that the manufacturers facilitated the illegal secondary market for firearms, thereby interfering with the public health of the community. As in most attempts to stretch public nuisance theory, this new application was accepted by a few maverick courts but rejected by most....

Lead Pigment and Paint Litigation

Lead pigment and paint public nuisance suits grew out of failed attempts by personal injury lawyers to recover under products liability law....

---

4 45 Washburn L.J. 541 (2006).

Litigation against the product manufacturers began in the mid-1980s when Ralph Nader formed an alliance of contingency fee lawyers and filed strict products liability lawsuits. Those cases failed because plaintiffs could not satisfy the basic standards of products liability law...

In 1999, personal injury lawyers from the law firm Motley Rice convinced the Attorney General of Rhode Island to partner with them in commencing a government public nuisance action against the former lead companies; the case would be brought on a contingency fee basis. The alleged public nuisance was the mere presence of lead paint in homes and buildings. Armed with the power of the sovereign, Mr. Motley sought the costs of removing lead paint from every building in Rhode Island that contained it. He even boasted that he would "bring the entire lead paint industry to its knees." Since filing that case in 1999, the plaintiffs' bar has partnered with public entities to bring public nuisance claims on behalf of several states, counties, and municipalities. [While the jury ruled in favor of the defendants, the trial judge overturned their verdict, rendering a judgment for the Rhode Island plaintiffs.]...

Public Policy

[Next, Schwartz and Goldberg argue that products liability is the right body of law for product-based claims.]

The underlying principles of products liability balance the interests of consumers, manufacturers and suppliers, and the public at large by facilitating plaintiffs' recovery and providing manufacturers with an incentive to exercise due care in making their products....

[The writers are concerned that public nuisance theory does not require that a plaintiff prove a "defect" existed, and they argue that "defect is the conceptual linchpin that holds products liability law together."]

The reason that public nuisance theory is so alluring to the personal injury bar is because it would negate the traditional products liability requirement of proving defect. Plaintiffs also may be able to circumvent defenses based on their own conduct and statutes of limitation....

The result would be "staggering": "The manufacturer's liability will turn not on whether the product was defective, but whether its legal marketing and distribution system somehow promoted the use of its product by 'criminals and underage end users.'"...

Another potential danger in allowing public nuisance claims against product manufacturers is that courts would "use [their] injunctive powers to mandate the redesign of" products and regulate "business methods." Consider, for example, reports that lawyers may bring public nuisance claims against food manufacturers for people's consumption habits that have led to obesity....Former [Clinton appointee] Labor Secretary Robert Reich has called such regulation through litigation "faux legislation, which sacrifices democracy."

This practice is being used against several industries. For example, a number of purported public nuisance class actions have been filed against manufacturers of alcoholic beverages by parents seeking the money that their children illegally spent on alcohol. These parents allege that industry advertisements constitute a public nuisance, notwithstanding the conclusions of the U.S. Federal Trade Commission that the advertisements properly target adults of legal drinking age and that any regulation on advertising could violate the companies' First Amendment right to free speech....

Another tactic used by personal injury lawyers in the name of industry reform is the underwriting of state public nuisance actions in exchange for a portion of the proceeds through contingency fee arrangements. The use of private, contingency fee lawyers in government public nuisance claims, however, improperly combines private monetary motivations with government police power....As the California Supreme Court recognized in striking down such an arrangement, government public nuisance cases involve "a balancing of interests" and "a delicate weighing of values" that "demands the representative of the government to be absolutely neutral.... Any financial arrangement that would tempt the government attorney to tip the scale cannot be tolerated."

The authors of the following, attorneys at the Center for Constitutional Litigation, have a different perspective. In their view, civil lawsuits are a way for ordinary people to hold corporations accountable.

BLAME IT ON THE BEE GEES: THE ATTACK ON TRIAL LAWYERS AND CIVIL JUSTICE

ROBERT S. PECK AND

JOHN VAIL[5]

Blame it on the Bee Gees. Or disco in general. Or the water. But something in the '70s led the country away from good sense about music, and something led the country away from good sense about justice, too.

In the '60s Dr. Martin Luther King, Jr. told America, "the arc of the moral universe is long, but it bends toward justice." Certainly, legal history is characterized by a broadening of access to justice, as well as a recognition that a person's right to a day in court is virtually an American birthright. In the '70s, some straight-thinking Americans decided they could not tolerate that arc. "[L]iability insurers, product manufacturers, and other repeat-play tort defendants began a concerted effort to enact laws that would limit tort liability that they contended had run amok." Their work continues, funded at rates that would make a defense contractor blush....

Why attack the remedial imperative? Corporations—artificial persons—want an ever bigger piece of the pie that feeds real persons. They promote the idea that the civil justice system is simply a tool to serve the economy, and that trial lawyers are harbingers of economic ruin. The role of the civil justice system as glue that holds the polity together is denigrated or forgotten, and trial lawyers are portrayed as enemies of the good—sometimes, literally, as terrorists.

Those who campaign for tort reform and against trial lawyers see courts as one-way streets, available for their efforts to hold others accountable, but never to hold themselves accountable. Their rhetoric refers to meritorious lawsuits—those where liability was successfully established—as "frivolous," and blames wealth-redistributing juries and complicit judges for falling under the sway of heartstring-pulling trial lawyers.

From the earliest stages of the "tort wars," a half-century ago, the insurance industry set its sights on trial lawyers. Trial lawyers' success in increasing payouts on automobile claims had captured their ire. The damage to insurers' economic bottom lines inspired a creative campaign to use all available media—the press, movies, and even television sitcoms—to reinforce the public's unsavory image of trial lawyers.

...[T]he campaign attempted to tap into preexisting antipathy toward lawyers and courts to further a private, corporate-driven economic agenda that increasingly became a political agenda. This preexisting suspicion of the legal profession is so deeply rooted

5 51 *N.Y.L.Sch.L.Rev.* 373 (2006-07).

that even colonial Americans referred to members of the profession as "bloodsuckers," "pick-pockets," "windbags," and "smooth-tongued rogues."...

Yet, for all its sound and fury about trial lawyers, the campaign is really one against the nature of our civil justice system, where corporate bosses must stand on an equal footing with the "unwashed masses" and suffer the ignominy that comes from being held accountable by those who lack their education, wealth, political clout, or status in the community. The attack on trial lawyers, at bottom, is merely a surrogate for the real object of their disaffection: the civil justice system and its accommodation of peoples' claims....

The Attack on Contingency Fees

If representing the rank-and-file were not potentially profitable, there would be no need to seek various types of tort reform to render it unprofitable. For that reason, the contingency fee, the key to the courthouse for those who cannot afford to pay for legal representation upfront, is under constant attack—with the attack focused on the capacity of the fees to generate trial lawyer "wealth."

It is no coincidence that the contingency fee aligns counsel's interests with that of the client. As eloquently stated by Judge Frank Easterbrook:

> ...The lawyer gains only to the extent his client gains. This interest-alignment device is not perfect.... But [an] imperfect-alignment of interests is better than a conflict of interests, which hourly fees may create.

Pennsylvania Justice Michael A. Musmanno agreed and famously declared:

> If it were not for contingent fees, indigent victims of tortious accidents would be subject to the unbridled, self-willed partisanship of their tortfeasors. The person who has, without fault on his part, been injured and who, because of his injury, is unable to work, and has a large family to support, and has no money to engage a lawyer, would be at the mercy of the person who disabled him because, being in a superior economic position, the injuring person could force on his victim, desperately in need of money to keep the candle of life burning in himself and his dependent ones, a wholly unconscionable meager sum in settlement or even refuse to pay him anything at all. Any society, and especially a democratic one, worthy of respect in the spectrum of civilization, should never tolerate such a victimization of the weak by the mighty.

In the view of those who attack the system, this alignment of interests is precisely the problem—it enables lawsuits that otherwise never would be filed.... It is not those who cannot otherwise afford a lawyer who protest the contingency fee system. Rather, these attacks are mounted by frequent defendants and insurers. That, in itself, is telling....

QUESTIONS

1. On what basis do Schwartz and Goldberg object to the kind of nuisance suit brought by Camden, New Jersey against paint-companies? How would Peck and Vail argue in favor of such suits?

2. Lead-paint nuisance suits filed in Milwaukee, St. Louis, and Santa Clara County have all been dismissed; Rhode Island remains the site of the lone victory. In spring 2007, Ohio became the second state to file a lead paint suit.

   Internet Assignment Find out if there have been any suits involving lead paint brought in your state. On what basis did plaintiffs claim relief? How did the court rule?

3. **Internet Assignment** Peck and Vail argue that the insurance industry and business defendants are leading the charge on tort reform, and are largely responsible for media attacks on lawyers and the contingent fee system. Look for some evidence of that. Find an article that takes this position and try to track down its source.

4. **Internet Assignment** The Department of Justice sued Philip Morris, R.J. Reynolds, Brown & Williamson, and others in the late 1990s in the largest civil racketeering suit in history. In 2006, federal district court judge Gladys Kessler ruled in favor of the government, finding that companies had defrauded the American public through deceptive marketing practices. What do you think Peck and Vail would say about that? How might Schwartz and Goldberg respond? Find out what has happened to the case on appeal. What has happened in other class action suits against the tobacco companies brought under various state consumer protection laws? *United States v. Philip Morris U.S.A.*, 449 F. Supp.2d 1 (D.D.C. 2006).

Importing Lead-Painted Toys[6]

DAVID LEONHART

A typical Thomas the Tank Engine story is a little morality play about hubris. The stories take place on the fictional Island of Sodor, where train cars with faces and personalities go about their work.

Almost inevitably, one of the trains tries to run too fast or pull too many boxcars and ends up in a big mess. By the end of the story, though, he comes to understand what he has done wrong. As the last line of "A Big Day for Thomas" puts it, "Thomas had already learned not to make the same mistake again."

An English clergyman named Wilbert Awdry invented the talking trains in the 1940s, while trying to entertain his son Christopher, who was laid up with the measles. The first book was published in 1945, and a new one followed every year until 1972, when Mr. Awdry retired. In the 1980s, the Thomas stories became a hit television series. These days, millions of little toy Thomas trains are sold every year around the world.

...[T]he toy trains are manufactured in China, and one of the factories that makes them has been using lead paint for the last couple of years. So [in June 2007], the United States government urged parents to confiscate 26 different kinds of Thomas toys. The manufacturer, the RC2 Corporation, asked that customers mail back the toys and promised to send lead-free replacements within six to eight weeks.

But this isn't really about replacing toy trains. It is about the realities of offshoring, and it doesn't yet have a tidy Thomas-style ending.

Over the last two decades or so, American companies have generally followed a two-pronged outsourcing strategy. First, the companies have tried to move as much of their manufacturing as possible to places where wages are just a fraction of what they are here. Second, the companies have distanced themselves from their overseas production. They usually don't own the factories and refuse to say much about them.

[James Fallows visited Sehnzhen, a Chinese city of eight million people, where many of the world's best known companies produce their goods, for a story in *The Atlantic Monthly*. He was not allowed to identify any of the factories with a specific brand.]...

continued

6 David Leonhardt, "Economix: A Lesson That Thomas Could Teach," *The New York Times*, June 20, 2007.

"In decades of reporting on military matters, I have rarely encountered people as concerned about keeping secrets as the buyers and suppliers who meet in Shenzhen and similar cities," he wrote.

This secrecy brings a number of advantages. It keeps competitors from finding out tricks of the trade. It keeps consumers from discovering that their $100 brand-name shirt comes from the same assembly line as a $40 generic version. And it prevents activists from criticizing a company for the working conditions in a factory where its products are made. The companies get the cost advantages of outsourcing without the publicity disadvantages.

In the days since the Thomas recall was announced, the company that owns the Thomas brand, HIT Entertainment, has stuck to this script. HIT is an English company that holds the rights to a number of popular characters, including Barney and Bob the Builder, and then licenses the toy manufacturing to companies like RC2.

Except for a small link on the Thomas Web site to RC2's recall announcement, HIT has otherwise acted as if it has nothing to do with the situation. Its executives haven't even said that they regret having been promoting toys with lead paint in them. They haven't said anything publicly.

When I suggested to the company's public relations agency, Bender/Helper Impact, that this might not be the smartest approach, the agency e-mailed me a two-sentence unsigned statement. It said that HIT appreciated the concerns of its customers and was working with RC2 on the recall, but that the recall was "clearly RC2's responsibility."

In effect, HIT has outsourced Thomas's image, one of its most valuable assets, to RC2. And RC2 has offered a case study of how not to deal with a crisis, which is all the more amazing when you consider that the company also makes toys for giants like Disney, Nickelodeon and Sesame Street.

…Most important of all, the company hasn't yet explained how the lead got into the trains or what it's doing to avoid a repeat. Like their counterparts at HIT, the RC2 executives have stayed silent.

Battening down the hatches might very well work if this were a scandal about sweatshop conditions. Fairly or not, Americans have a limited attention span when it comes to human rights problems on the other side of the world. But the prospect of lead paint in your child's nervous system tends to focus the mind.

The fact that the executives at HIT and RC2 haven't grasped the difference shows how out of date the corporate script on outsourcing has become. In many businesses, outsourcing has simply grown too big to stay behind the curtain. What happens in Chinese factories determines how good—how reliable and how safe—many products are. So there is no way for executives to distance themselves from China without also distancing themselves from their own product.

The government clearly needs to play a role here by inspecting more of the items coming into this country. Perversely, the Consumer Product Safety Commission has fewer employees than it did 20 years ago when there were far fewer imports.

But there is also reason to hope that basic competition will take care of some of the safety problems now being exported from China. Adrian J. Slywotzky, the management writer and consultant, argues that smart companies are starting to realize that they are better off knowing what happens in their factories. Nike, for instance, began to get more involved with its overseas suppliers after it was criticized on human rights grounds, but as a result, the company has also figured out how to get products to market more quickly….

[I]t does seem likely that consumers will eventually punish a company that ducks responsibility for the safety of its products….

Evolution of Products Liability Law

The early common law had allowed some exceptions to the general rule of *caveat emptor* (buyer beware), most notably for food products. In Britain, an Act of Parliament in 1266 made it a crime to sell "corrupt wine and victuals," and American law required those who sold food intended for immediate consumption to ensure its safety or pay damages to anyone injured by it. But, prior to the twentieth century, most people injured by defective goods had little legal recourse.

The most important remedy was a suit for **breach of warranty** against those who sold unfit goods, a legal theory described as a "freak hybrid, 'born of the illicit intercourse of tort and contract,' and partaking the characteristics of both."[7] For centuries, however, those claims were limited by a legal doctrine called "privity of contract," a rule that a buyer could sue only the entity from whom she purchased the item, not anyone further up the chain of commerce, such as a wholesale distributor or the actual manufacturer. Negligence (tort) claims against companies who breached their legal duty to be reasonably careful in the design, manufacture, and packaging of goods were hard to prove and easy for companies to defend against.

Breach of Warranty and the Uniform Commercial Code

The modern American law of contracts is found in the **Uniform Commercial Code (UCC)**, first written in 1952 and later adopted by every state in the United States as the basic law governing the sale of goods. Under the UCC, every merchant who sells a product automatically promises that it is fit for its ordinary purpose.[8] Food should not be contaminated, hair dye should not cause one's hair to fall out, rungs of ladders should not splinter, televisions should not explode. A merchant[9] who does not intend to make such a promise must adhere to specific rules in order to disclaim that implied warranty of merchantability.[10] A seller's promise that goods are fit for their ordinary purpose can be enforced not only by the purchaser, but by members of her household as well. In some states, the warranty extends even further, protecting not only the purchaser, family, and household, but "any person who may reasonably be expected to use, consume or be affected by the goods and who is injured" as a result of the breach.[11] Historically, an injured party could sue only her immediate seller ("privity of contract" was required for a breach of contract or warranty suit), but that requirement is no longer a bar and a buyer can sue retailers, wholesalers, and manufacturers when goods are not as promised.

Contract law is primarily designed to encourage commerce by assuring those who freely enter into agreements that the law will protect their expectations. If one side reneges on its bargain, the other can go to court to seek a remedy, giving her the benefit of the bargain struck.

Since the UCC rests on a fundamental belief in the freedom to contract, the law encourages commercial parties to decide when they enter into an agreement what remedy will be available if either side breaches. If they don't make such provisions, courts deal with any breach of contract "dispassionately," giving the injured party the financial benefit it expected under the agreement—a combination of what are known as general and incidental damages. At times, the plaintiff may also win what are called "special" or consequential damages, covering the

7   William J. Prosser, John W. Wade, and Victor E. Schwartz, *Torts: Cases and Materials*, 7th ed. (New York: Foundation Press, 1982), p. 743.

8   UCC 2-314.

9   Under the UCC 2-104, a merchant is a person who deals in goods of the kind involved in the sale, for example, a car manufacturer or a car dealer when he or she sells cars; or a person whose occupation indicates that she has special knowledge or skill regarding goods involved, for example, an optometrist selling glasses; or someone who hires a merchant to act on his behalf, such as a middleperson.

10 UCC 2-316 and Magnuson-Moss Warranty Act, 15 U.S.C. 2301, *et. seq.*

11 UCC 2-318.

economic costs that are a "consequence" of the breach, such as lost profits while a business is shut down because a seller failed to deliver a needed machine. But juries are not free to compensate the winner for pain and suffering, or to award punitive damages or attorneys' fees.

* * * *

Transport Corporation of America, Inc. (TCA) operates a national trucking business out of Minnesota. In 1989, TCA decided to update the computer system it used to process incoming orders, issue dispatching assignments, and store all distribution records. TCA purchased an IBM computer system for $541,313.38 from ICC, a company that produces software and resells IBM computers. A year after the system was installed, it failed. Although it was ultimately repaired, TCA was without it for almost 34 hours, and sued both the manufacturer (IBM) and the seller (ICC) on various tort and contract theories.

The lower court dismissed the suit before trial, finding that the economic loss doctrine barred the tort claims, and that the plaintiff was not entitled to any damages for breach of contract because the computer had been repaired. The appellate court agreed, explaining why in the following excerpt.

TRANSPORT CORPORATION OF AMERICAN v. IBM

U.S. Court of Appeals, Eighth Circuit, 1994

30 F.3d 953

McMILLAN, Circuit Judge. ✻

On December 19, 1990…the computer system went down and one of the disk drives revealed an error code. TCA properly contacted IBM, and IBM dispatched a service person. Although TCA requested a replacement disk drive, the error code indicated that the service procedure was not to replace any components but to analyze the disk drive. TCA had restarted the computer system and did not want to shut it down for the IBM service procedure. IBM informed TCA that replacement was not necessary under the limited warranty of repair or replace, and agreed to return on December 22, 1990, to analyze the disk drive. On December 21, 1990, the same disk drive completely failed, resulting in the computer system being inoperable until December 22, 1990.

TCA alleges that the cumulative down-time for the computer system as a result of the disk drive failure was 33.91 hours. This includes the time to replace the disk drive, reload the electronic backup data and manually reenter data which had been entered between 2:00 a.m. and the time the system failed. TCA alleges that it incurred a business interruption loss in the amount of $473,079.46 ($468,514.46 for loss of income; $4,565.00 for loss of data and replacement media).

Economic Loss Doctrine

Minnesota courts have consistently held that the UCC should apply to commercial transactions where the product merely failed to live up to expectations and the damage did not result from a hazardous condition…. Because failure of the disk drive was contemplated by the parties and the damage was limited in scope to the computer system (into which the disk drive and its data were integrated), TCA must look exclusively to the UCC for its remedy.

IBM's Disclaimer of Implied Warranties

TCA next argues that because it was not a party to the negotiations between ICC and IBM, it is not bound by the terms of the remarketer agreement, including IBM's disclaimer of implied warranties….

The UCC as adopted in Minnesota has a privity provision that operates to extend all warranties, express or implied, to third parties who may reasonably be expected to use the warranted goods…. The seller can disclaim implied warranties…[and these disclaimers] are extended to third party purchasers [like the plaintiff]….

The remarketer agreement between IBM and ICC included a disclaimer of "ALL OTHER WARRANTIES, EXPRESS OR IMPLIED, INCLUDING, BUT NOT LIMITED TO, THE IMPLIED WARRANTIES OF MERCHANTABILITY AND FITNESS FOR A PARTICULAR PURPOSE." As the district court correctly noted, this language complies with the requirements of [the UCC] (that is, it was in writing, conspicuous and mentioned merchantability) and thus effectively disclaimed all implied warranties.

IBM's Limited Remedy of Repair or Replace

[Next, the court must decide whether or not to enforce the "exclusive remedy" created by the parties to deal with a possible breach of contract. The UCC provides that the remedy should be enforced unless it "fails of its essential purpose."] Under Minnesota law, "[a]n exclusive remedy fails of its essential purpose if circumstances arise to deprive the limiting clause of its meaning or one party of the substantial value of its bargain."…A repair or replace clause does not fail of its essential purpose so long as repairs are made each time a defect arises….

ICC's Disclaimer of Consequential Damages Liability

[Under the UCC a] seller may limit or exclude consequential damages unless the limitation is unconscionable…. The UCC encourages negotiated agreements in commercial transactions, including warranties and limitations…. An exclusion of consequential damages set forth in advance in a commercial agreement between experienced business parties represents a bargained-for allocation of risk that is conscionable as a matter of law….

In the agreement between ICC and TCA, TCA expressly agreed to an ICC disclaimer that stated in part "IN NO EVENT SHALL ICC BE LIABLE FOR ANY INDIRECT, SPECIAL OR CONSEQUENTIAL DAMAGES SUCH AS LOSSES OF ANTICIPATED PROFIT OR OTHER ECONOMIC LOSS IN CONNECTION WITH…THIS AGREEMENT."

[T]he disclaimer of consequential damages was not unconscionable and…the damages claimed by TCA, for business interruption losses and replacement media, were consequential damages. Furthermore, TCA and ICC were sophisticated business entities of relatively equal bargaining power. ICC's disclaimer was not unconscionable and TCA is therefore precluded from recovering consequential damages….

[Judgment for ICC is affirmed].

QUESTIONS

1. On what grounds did the court determine that Transport Corporation was not entitled to money damages? What should the plaintiff have done to better protect itself?

2. While it is common for businesses to limit damages, as IBM did in this case, the UCC makes it **unconscionable** (shocking to the conscience) to limit damages for personal injury in the sale of products to consumers. So, for example, Ford could not give a warranty that limited its responsibility for injuries caused by a defect in one of its vehicles. Does it seem fair to distinguish consumer from commercial transactions in this way? To allow courts to "rewrite" a deal that two parties freely entered?

The Tort of Strict Product Liability

New York Court of Appeals Justice Benjamin Cardozo is widely considered the first to recognize that a person injured by a unsafe product might bring a lawsuit based on negligence. In the early twentieth century he wrote an important decision, *MacPherson v. Buick Motor Co.*, allowing an injured person to sue the manufacturer of a car for a defect in its wheel. The wheel was wooden; when its spokes crumbled, the car collapsed and the plaintiff was thrown out and injured. Instead of suing the seller from whom he bought the car for breach of contract, the plantiff sued the manufacturer for negligence. The jury ruled in his favor. On appeal, the court agreed that Buick was negligent since the car's "defects could have been discovered by a reasonable inspection, and that inspection was omittted."[12]

To win a suit for negligence, a plaintiff must establish that the defendant breached its duty of care, creating an unreasonable risk of harm, and that such careless behavior was the proximate cause of the plaintiff's injury. This is often difficult. Generally, a company will not be found negligent if it adhered to industry standards or the "state of the art" with regard to the engineering, selection of materials, production processes, assembly, and marketing of its product. Proof of reasonable quality control procedures is usually sufficient to negate a charge of negligence. A firm can also defend itself or limit the amount of damages it must pay by showing that its negligence was not the only cause of the injury—a car accident caused in part by faulty brakes and in part by drunk driving, for example—or that the plaintiff contributed to her own harm, either by assuming a known risk or acting carelessly.

And then, in 1944, a waitress injured when a bottle of Coca-Cola exploded in her face sued the local bottling company and won. This time, the jury was convinced of the company's negligence, and the California Supreme Court upheld its verdict. The most important part of the case, however, was the language of concurring Justice Traynor, which foreshadowed the development of the law of products liability:

> [I]t should now be recognized that a manufacturer incurs an absolute liability when an article that he has placed on the market...proves to have a defect that causes injury.... [P]ublic policy demands that responsibility be fixed wherever it will most effectively reduce the hazards...in defective products. [T]he manufacturer can anticipate some hazards and guard against the recurrence of others, as the public cannot....[13]

Eventually, the full California Supreme Court came to agree with Traynor. In a 1963 case, it adopted the rule that manufacturers should be strictly liable for selling defective products.[14] This new legal theory, referred to as the doctrine of **strict liability**, made it easier for injured persons to sue and harder for manufacturers to defend themselves. Described in Section 402A of the ***Restatement of Torts (Second),***[15] strict liability recognizes that there are times when losses must be allocated between two "innocent" parties: the consumer who was hurt while using a product properly and the company that was not negligent (careless) in creating it. It places the responsibility on the company for reasons articulated here by a noted legal scholar, Prosser in "The Fall of the Citadel":

> The public interest in human safety requires the maximum possible protection for the user of the product, and those best able to afford it are the suppliers.... By placing their goods upon the market, the suppliers represent to the public that they are suitable and safe for use; and by packaging, advertising and otherwise, they do everything they can to induce that belief.[16]

---

12 *MacPherson v. Buick Motor Co.*, 111 N.E. 1050 (N.Y. 1916).

13 *Escola v. Coca-Cola Bottling Company of Fresno*, 50 P.2d 436 (Cal. 1944).

14 *Greenman v. Yuba Power Products, Inc.*, 377 P.2d 897 (Cal. 1963).

15 The **Restatement of Law** is an attempt by legal scholars to summarize and "restate" the common law based on judicial precedents from around the country. Today, there is a **Third Restatement of Torts**. However, most states continue to follow the **Second Restatement of Torts**.

16 William Prosser, "The Fall of the Citadel," 50 *Minn. L. Rev.* 791, 799 (1966).

Restatement of Torts (Second) Section 402A

1. One who sells any product in a defective condition unreasonably dangerous to the user or consumer or to his property is subject to liability for physical harm thereby caused to the ultimate user or consumer or to his property, if

   a. the seller is engaged in the business of selling such a product, and

   b. it is expected to and does reach the user or consumer without substantial change in the condition in which it is sold.

2. The rule stated in Subsection (1) applies although

   a. the seller has exercised all possible care in the preparation and sale of the product, and

   b. the user or consumer has not bought the product from or entered into any contractual relation with the seller.

Most states have adopted Section 402A of the Restatement, finding sellers liable for defective product designs, manufacturing ("production") defects, and failure to warn. In each case, the focus is not on the company's behavior (as it is in negligence law), but on whether the product itself is defective and unreasonably unsafe.

For example, a company may hire qualified engineers who design a new car using standard techniques. No one was negligent, yet the company produced a model that causes injury. Under the *Restatement (Second) of Torts*, a jury might conclude that there was a design defect because the harmful nature of the product outweighs its usefulness.

Or the design of a car may be perfectly safe, but something in the way a particular car is assembled causes injury—an undetected weakness in a sheet of aluminum or a glitch leading to an improperly assembled component, for example. While we expect companies to implement good quality control systems, we know that some production defects will occasionally slip through the cracks of a manufacturing process. Once again, strict liability burdens the company, not the consumer, with the loss, even when the company was not negligent.

A third kind of defect involves products that cannot be made completely safe but can be made safer by appropriately warning the consumer. The inadequate information about possible side effects of a drug or of the absence of other potential danger posed by a product may result in a manufacturer's strict liability for failure to warn. This was the main defect in the *Norplant* case discussed in Chapter 7.

In different jurisdictions, interpretations of the *Restatements of Torts* may vary. In every state, a person who claims injury from a defective product must prove that the product was the proximate (or legal) cause of his harm. If the injury results from some alteration in the product (e.g., by the consumer or by someone who serviced it), the seller is not held responsible. Most states allow companies to defend themselves by proving that the plaintiff misused or abused the product in a way that the manufacturer could not have foreseen.

The *Restatement (Second)* did not define "defective and unreasonably dangerous product," so state courts had to create their own definitions. Under what is called the "consumer expectation" test, a product is defectively dangerous if it is dangerous to an extent beyond that which would be contemplated by the ordinary consumer who purchased it with the ordinary knowledge common to the community as to the product's characteristics. Alternatively, under the danger-utility approach adopted in some states, a product is defective if, but only if, the magnitude of the danger outweighs the utility of the product. The theory underlying this approach is that virtually all products have both risks and benefits and that there is no way to go about evaluating hazards intelligently without weighing risk against utility.

Market-Share Liability

Some "reformers" have identified **market-share** or **enterprise liability** as an area that needs reform. Enterprise liability was first used by a California court in a case against eleven of the many drug companies involved in the sale of the synthetic hormone diethyl stilbestrol (DES). Discovered by British researchers in 1937, DES was never patented. In the 1940s, twelve American drug manufacturers agreed to cooperate with each other to bring it to market. They pooled all clinical data pertaining to DES and used literature written by Eli Lilly Company as the model for their package inserts. On the basis of two studies by independent researchers indicating that DES prevented miscarriages in a significant percentage of high-risk pregnancies, Lilly and other drug companies sought FDA approval of the drug. The studies were criticized by some: they lacked controls, later studies could not replicate their findings, and scientists were beginning to discover that drugs ingested by a pregnant woman crossed her placenta and might injure the fetus. Still, none of the drug companies ever used animals or humans to test the effects of DES on the fetus.

Once approved by the FDA, DES was marketed to pharmacists and doctors from 1947 to 1971. It was sold as a generic, because all DES was of identical chemical composition. Druggists usually filled prescriptions from whatever was on hand. Few records were kept, and women taking the drug seldom had any way of knowing which firm had manufactured it. During the 24 years that DES was sold for use in pregnancy, approximately 300 makers produced it, entering and leaving the market continuously. Eli Lilly was one of the major producers, selling in bulk to other drug companies for use under their own names and acquiring close to 45 percent of the DES market.

By 1971, studies had established the harmful effects on DES on the daughters of mothers who took the drug. Specifically, tests indicated that DES caused vaginal cancer and adenosis, a precancerous vaginal or cervical growth requiring extensive monitoring. The FDA banned DES.

When Jane Sindell developed adenoids and a malignant bladder tumor, she blamed it on the DES her mother had taken during pregnancy. But her mother had no idea which company had provided the actual dosage she had ingested. On behalf of California girls and women who "may have been exposed to DES before birth and who may or may not know that fact or the dangers to which they were exposed," Jane Sindell brought a class action suit against eleven drug companies, including Abbott Labs and Eli Lilly. The court allowed the suit to go forward, reasoning that it was fair to hold responsible any company involved in the "enterprise of selling DES" that had acquired a substantial share of the national market during the relevant time period; it was not the plaintiffs' fault that they could not pinpoint which company had made which doses of the drug. The court removed from the suit only those market share defendants who could prove that they could not possibly have made the ingested drugs.[17]

Contract Law and Tort Law

It is not uncommon for lawyers to file suit against all potential defendants (e.g., immediate seller, shipper, manufacturer, component parts maker) on several potential theories (breach of contract, negligence, and strict liability.) During the **pre-trial discovery** phase of litigation,

---

17 *Sindell v. Abbott Laboratories*, 607 P.2d 924 (Cal. 1980).

plaintiffs can gather information about the production process, injury records, and documents indicating who knew what and when, all of which help sort out which party or parties are most likely responsible. The rules of litigation make one or another cause of action more advantageous in particular situations. In most states, for example, the time for bringing a suit ("**statute of limitations**") differs for tort and contract cases. And, in all states, the general rules regarding remedies are fundamentally different for contract cases, where successful plaintiffs are generally limited to damages that would give them the "benefit of their bargain," and tort cases, where damages are more open-ended.

In June 9, 1986, Nancy Denny slammed on the brakes of her Ford Bronco II in an effort to avoid a deer that had walked directly into the path of her vehicle. The Bronco rolled over, and Denny was severely injured. She sued Ford, asserting negligence, strict product liability, and breach of implied warranty under the Uniform Commercial Code. The jury came back with a mixed verdict; the Bronco was not unreasonably dangerous and defective, so there was no tort liability. But, they found, Ford had violated the implied warranty of merchantability by selling Denny a vehicle that was not fit for its ordinary purpose. In the excerpts below, the highest court in New York has to decide whether the two legal theories—a tort action for strict product liability and a contract action for implied warranty—are really one and the same.

DENNY v. FORD MOTOR COMPANY

Court of Appeals of New York, 1995
639 N.Y.S.2d 250

TITONE, Judge. ※

The trial evidence centered on the particular characteristics of utility vehicles, which are generally made for off-road use on unpaved and often rugged terrain. Such use sometimes necessitates climbing over obstacles such as fallen logs and rocks....

Plaintiffs introduced evidence at trial to show that small utility vehicles in general, and the Bronco II in particular, present a significantly higher risk of rollover accidents than do ordinary passenger automobiles...[and] that the Bronco II had a low stability index attributable to its high center of gravity and relatively narrow track width. The vehicle's shorter wheel base and suspension system were additional factors contributing to its instability. Ford had made minor design changes in an effort to achieve a higher stability index, but, according to plaintiffs' proof, none of the changes produced a significant improvement in the vehicle's stability.

Ford argued at trial that the design features of which plaintiffs complained were necessary to the vehicle's off-road capabilities. According to Ford, the vehicle had been intended to be used as an off-road vehicle and had not been designed to be sold as a conventional passenger automobile. Ford's own engineer stated that he would not recommend the Bronco II to someone whose primary interest was to use it as a passenger car, since the features of a four-wheel-drive utility vehicle were not helpful for that purpose and the vehicle's design made it inherently less stable.

Despite the engineer's testimony, plaintiffs introduced a Ford marketing manual which predicted that many buyers would be attracted to the Bronco II because utility vehicles were "suitable to contemporary life styles" and were "considered fashionable" in some suburban areas. According to this manual, the sales presentation of the Bronco II should take into account the vehicle's "suitab[ility] for commuting and for suburban and city driving." Additionally, the vehicle's ability to switch between two-wheel and four-wheel drive would "be particularly appealing to women who may be concerned about driving in snow and ice with their children." Plaintiffs both testified that the perceived safety benefits of its four-wheel-drive capacity were what attracted them to the Bronco II. They were not at all interested in its off-road use.

Although the products liability theory sounding in tort and the breach of implied warranty theory authorized by the UCC coexist and are often invoked in tandem, the core element of "defect" is subtly different in the two causes of action.... [T]he New York standard for determining the existence of a design defect [in strict liability cases] has required an assessment of whether "if the design defect were known at the time of manufacture, a reasonable person would conclude that the utility of the product did not outweigh the risk inherent in marketing a product designed in that manner." This standard demands an inquiry into such factors as (1) the product's utility to the public as a whole, (2) its utility to the individual user, (3) the likelihood that the product will cause injury, (4) the availability of a safer design, (5) the possibility of designing and manufacturing the product so that it is safer but remains functional and reasonably priced, (6) the degree of awareness of the product's potential danger that can reasonably be attributed to the injured user, and (7) the manufacturer's ability to spread the cost of any safety-related design changes.... The above-described analysis is rooted in a recognition that there are both risks and benefits associated with many products and that there are instances in which a product's inherent dangers cannot be eliminated without simultaneously compromising or completely nullifying its benefits.... In such circumstances, a weighing of the product's benefits against its risks is an appropriate and necessary component of the liability assessment under the policy-based principles associated with tort law.

[T]he risk/utility balancing test is a "negligence-inspired" approach, since it invites the parties to adduce proof about the manufacturer's choices and ultimately requires the fact finder to make "a judgment about [the manufacturer's] judgment."...

It is this negligence-like risk/benefit component of the defect element that differentiates strict products liability claims from UCC-based breach of implied warranty claims....

While the strict products concept of a product that is "not reasonably safe" requires a weighing of the product's dangers against its over-all advantages, the UCC's concept of a "defective" product requires an inquiry only into whether the product in question was "fit for the ordinary purposes for which such goods are used."... The latter inquiry focuses on the expectations for the performance of the product when used in the customary, usual and reasonably foreseeable manners. The cause of action is one involving true "strict" liability, since recovery may be had upon a showing that the product was not minimally safe for its expected purpose without regard to the feasibility of alternative designs or the manufacturer's "reasonableness" in marketing it in that unsafe condition.

[Next, the court explains the distinction in terms of the history of the two doctrines: Implied warranty originated in contract law, "which directs its attention to the purchaser's disappointed expectations," while tort actions have traditionally been concerned with "social policy and risk allocation by means other than those dictated by the marketplace."]

As a practical matter, the distinction between the defect concepts in tort law and in implied warranty theory may have little or no effect in most cases. In this case, however, the nature of the proof and the way in which the fact issues were litigated demonstrates how the two causes of action can diverge. In the trial court, Ford took the position that the design features of which plaintiffs complain, i.e., the Bronco II's high center of gravity, narrow track width, short wheel base and specially tailored suspension system, were important to preserving the vehicle's ability to drive over the highly irregular terrain that typifies off-road travel. Ford's proof in this regard was relevant to the strict products liability risk/utility equation, which required the fact finder to determine whether the Bronco II's value as an off-road vehicle outweighed the risk of the rollover accidents that could occur when the vehicle was used for other driving tasks.

On the other hand, plaintiffs' proof focused, in part, on the sale of the Bronco II for suburban driving and everyday road travel. Plaintiffs also adduced proof that the Bronco II's design characteristics made it unusually susceptible to rollover accidents when used on paved roads. All of this evidence was useful in showing that routine highway and street driving was the "ordinary purpose" for which the Bronco II was sold and that it was not "fit" or safe for that purpose.

Thus, under the evidence in this case, a rational fact finder could have simultaneously concluded that the Bronco II's utility as an off-road vehicle outweighed the risk of injury resulting from rollover accidents and that the vehicle was not safe for the "ordinary purpose" of daily driving for which it was marketed and sold.... Importantly, what makes this case distinctive is that the "ordinary purpose" for which the product was marketed and sold to the plaintiff was not the same as the utility against which the risk was to be weighed. It is these unusual circumstances that give practical significance to the ordinarily theoretical difference between the defect concepts in tort and statutory breach of implied warranty causes of action....

SIMONS, Judge, dissenting. ☀

In my judgment, the consumer expectation standard, appropriate to commercial sales transactions, has no place in personal injury litigation alleging a design defect and may result in imposing absolute liability on marketers of consumers' products. Whether a product has been defectively designed should be determined in a personal injury action by a risk/utility analysis....

[T]he word "defect" has no clear legal meaning....

The jury having concluded that the Bronco II was not defective for strict products liability purposes, could not logically conclude that it was defective for warranty purposes.... The warranty claim in this case was for tortious personal injury and rests on the underlying "social concern [for] the protection of human life and property, not regularity in commercial exchange."... As such, it should be governed by tort rules, not contract rules....

Accordingly, I dissent.

QUESTIONS

1. What did Nancy Denny think she was buying? What did she buy? On what legal theories did she sue? On what basis did she win?

2. Elsewhere in the decision, dissenting Judge Simons argues that the majority imposes a kind of absolute liability on a manufacturer. Is he right? What might Ford have done differently?

3. Compare this case to the *Norplant* case in Chapter 7. What similarities/differences do you see in the marketing campaigns? In the lawsuits?

Economic Loss Doctrine

In some states, legal options may be limited by what is known as the "economic loss" doctrine. This rule, barring a party from bringing a tort suit if the only loss suffered is economic, was applied in the *Transport Corporation* case and is one reason why AOL loses the following case.

AOL released a software package, AOL 5.0, in October 1999, marketing it as "risk free," "easy to use," and providing "superior benefits." But, according to thousands of subscribers, AOL 5.0 interfered with their system's communications settings so that they could no longer connect to other ISPs, run non-AOL email programs, or connect to local networks. By adding or altering hundreds of files on the user's system, AOL 5.0 was said to cause instability. Subscribers could not remove the software without doing further harm to their computers.

By January 2000, multiple class action suits had been filed by AOL subscribers claiming they had lost data, software systems, work, time, money, and the use of their computers thanks to AOL 5.0. When AOL called on its insurance company to defend the suits, St. Paul refused. The stated reason: the kinds of harms alleged by the plaintiffs were not covered under AOL's commercial general liability [CGL] policy. To force St. Paul to fulfill its "duty to defend," AOL sued. St. Paul defended itself by arguing that its responsibility was limited to claims that AOL had caused harm to tangible property.

AMERICA ONLINE, INC., v. ST. PAUL MERCURY INSURANCE CO.

United States District Court, E.D. Va., 2002
207 F.Supp. 2d 459

LEE, District Judge. ☀

For the reasons stated below, the Court holds that St. Paul does not have an obligation to defend AOL.... An insurance policy is a contract, and like any other contract the Court is bound by the plain terms of the agreement and cannot rewrite the policy to bind the parties to obligations they did not consent to. If there is any ambiguity in the terms to be interpreted, Virginia law instructs that ambiguity to be construed against the insurer. An insurer's duty to defend attaches whenever a complaint alleges claims that if proven would fall within the risk covered by the policy.

The Terms of the Policy

[AOL's insurance] Policy states... that St. Paul will "pay amounts [AOL] is legally required to pay as damages for covered bodily injury, property damage, or premises damage.... caused by an event [i.e. an accident]." Property damage is defined as "physical damage to tangible property of others, including all resulting loss of use of that property; or loss of use of tangible property of others that isn't physically damaged."...

The Policy sets forth certain events that are excluded from coverage. For instance, the Policy will not "cover bodily injury or property damage that's expected or intended by [AOL]" [or that results from AOL's] faulty or dangerous products or completed work....

Property Damage under the Policy and the Complaint

...[The Complaint] alleges that AOL 5.0 damaged consumers' computers, damaged their software, damaged their data, damaged their computers' operating systems, and caused the loss of data and the loss of use of the computers.

Tangible Property

[First, the court must decide if there is any harm alleged to tangible property.]

...Black's Law Dictionary defines "tangible" as:

Having or possessing physical form. Capable of being touched and seen; perceptible to the touch; tactile; palpable; capable of being possessed or realized; readily apprehensible by the mind; real; substantial . . . .

As [this definition makes] clear, the plain and ordinary meaning of the word tangible is something that is capable of being touched or perceptible to the senses. Computer data, software, and systems do not have or possess physical form and are therefore not tangible property as understood by the Policy.

. . . A "bit" on a computer disk or hard drive is not palpable. Electrical impulses that carry computer data may be observable with the aid of a computer, but they are invisible to the human eye . . . . An ordinary person understands the term "tangible" to include something she can touch, such as a chair or a book, not an imperceptible piece of data or software that can only be perceived with the help of a computer . . . .

In light of . . . established case-law, the Court holds that the Policy does not cover damage to computer data, software and systems because such items are not tangible property.

However . . . [a] computer is the "medium that holds" the data, the software and the systems; unlike its cargo, the computer can be "perceived, identified or valued." [It] therefore qualifies as tangible property under the Policy.

Physical Damage

[Next, the Court must determine if there was "physical damage" to plaintiffs' computers.] . . . [The] complaint is rife with allegations that AOL 5.0 physically damaged consumers' computer data and systems. But these claims go to the "brains" of the computer, not its physical make-up . . . .

The allegations of injury to the computer itself are more properly characterized as a loss of use of the computer. Viewed in this light, there is no "physical" damage alleged to the plaintiffs' computers in the common understanding of the word. There is nothing physical about the loss of use or access to a computer. . . .

[However, one kind of damage is covered by the insurance policy:] . . . AOL 5.0 caused the loss of use of plaintiffs' computers and computer functionality . . . [by causing] consumers' computers to freeze preventing consumers from accessing and using their computers . . . .

[Next the court must decide whether the damage to consumers' computers is excluded from coverage because it was the result of AOL's faulty or dangerous product.]

Impaired Property Exemption

. . . The crux of the Complaint is that the loss of computer use was caused by AOL 5.0, . . . a "faulty or dangerous" product. . . . "AOL 5.0 had been rushed to the market- . . . while it still included substantial bugs and incompatibility with numerous applications and operating systems;" "By installing AOL 5.0, consumers unknowingly exposed their computer systems and software to a defectively designed and/or unreasonably dangerous software installation process that causes serious injury; and "The product was defective in its design." . . . [The court finds that the lost use of the computer is not covered by AOL's insurance policy.]

Holding otherwise would eviscerate the common law "economic loss" rule. The economic loss rule generally bars claims in tort for economic losses, limiting recovery for such losses to the law of contract.

. . . Similar to the defective data in *Transport Corp.*, once incorporated into plaintiffs' computer systems, AOL 5.0 was a defective component part that caused plaintiffs' computers to malfunction in the form of crashing or freezing. The only losses flowing from plaintiffs' computer crashes were purely economic and did not constitute losses to other property.

[**Held:** Because of the economic loss rule, St. Paul has no duty to defend.]

QUESTIONS

1. What is "the economic loss doctrine"? How did it apply to AOL? To Transport Corporation?

2. Is there anything AOL could have done to better protect itself in the process of making an insurance deal? What could it have done in the process of making/selling its software?

Punitive Damages

> ...[The role tort law plays in this country] is uniquely American. A mass tort case is a passion or morality play. It speaks to the conscience of the country and asks whether we have gone badly astray. It examines values and probes motives; and when it is completed, it has a cathartic effect. When courts speak of punitive damages as reflecting a sense of outrage, they utter an important truth: when society bears witness to truly outrageous conduct it must react. Swift and certain justice is necessary not only because it will deter future wrongdoers, but also because it substantiates society's intolerance for malevolent corporate behavior that brings injury to thousands.
>
> — AARON TWERSKI 1994[18]

Under the common law of torts, juries are free to award an injured plaintiff all sorts of damages, not only to compensate for damaged property or out-of-pocket medical expenses, but for pain and suffering, and significantly, punitive damages designed to punish companies who disregard safety, to create incentives to make safer products and deter similar wrongdoing in the future. It is common for plaintiffs' lawyers to frame their products liability suits as tort cases, claiming that a manufacturer was negligent in designing, producing, or marketing the product and/or that even a nonnegligent manufacturer should be held strictly liable to the injured party as a matter of public policy. While some state laws limit the amount of punitive damages a jury can award, others leave the jury free to award hundreds of thousands—even millions—of dollars to punish serious wrongdoing.

In the 1980s, Ford's Pinto and Mustang models were involved in a variety of lawsuits, both civil and criminal. In one of the Pinto cases, plaintiffs won not only compensatory damages, but also $3.5 million in punitive damages. The trial lasted six months and included the testimony of a former Ford executive who had been forced into early retirement because he had spoken out on safety. In the following excerpt, the appellate court affirms the verdict against Ford.

GRIMSHAW v. FORD MOTOR COMPANY

California Court of Appeals, Fourth District, 1981
174 Cal. Rptr. 348

Tamura, Acting Presiding Justice. ❈

A 1972 Ford Pinto hatchback automobile unexpectedly stalled on a freeway, erupting into flames when it was rear ended by a car proceeding in the same direction. Mrs. Lilly Gray, the driver of the Pinto, suffered fatal burns and 13-year-old Richard Grimshaw, a

18 Aaron Twerski, Introduction to "Symposium on Punitive Damages Awards in Products Liability Litigation: Strong Medicine or Poison Pill?" 39 *Vill. L. Rev.* 353 (1994).

passenger in the Pinto, suffered severe and permanently disfiguring burns on his face and entire body....

Design of the Pinto Fuel System

In 1968, Ford began designing a new subcompact automobile which ultimately became the Pinto. Mr. Iacocca, then a Ford Vice President, conceived the project and was its moving force. Ford's objective was to build a car at or below 2,000 pounds to sell for no more than $2,000.

Ordinarily marketing surveys and preliminary engineering studies precede the styling of a new automobile line. Pinto, however, was a rush project, so that styling preceded engineering and dictated engineering design to a greater degree than usual. Among the engineering decisions dictated by styling was the placement of the fuel tank. It was then the preferred practice in Europe and Japan to locate the gas tank over the rear axle in subcompacts because a small vehicle has less "crush space" between the rear axle and the bumper than larger cars. The Pinto's styling, however, required the tank to be placed behind the rear axle leaving only 9 or 10 inches of "crush space," far less than in any other American automobile or Ford overseas subcompact. In addition, the Pinto was designed so that its bumper was little more than a chrome strip, less substantial than the bumper of any other American car produced then or later. The Pinto's rear structure also lacked reinforcing members known as "hat sections" (2 longitudinal side members) and horizontal cross-members running between them such as were found in cars of larger unitized construction and in all automobiles produced by Ford's overseas operations. The absence of the reinforcing members rendered the Pinto less crush resistant than other vehicles. Finally, the differential housing selected for the Pinto had an exposed flange and a line of exposed bolt heads. These protrusions were sufficient to puncture a gas tank driven forward against the differential upon rear impact.

Crash Tests

During the development of the Pinto, prototypes were built and tested.... The crash tests revealed that the Pinto's fuel system as designed could not meet the 20-mile-per-hour proposed [federal] standard.... Tests conducted by Ford on...modified or reinforced mechanical Pinto prototypes, proved safe at speeds at which the Pinto failed....

The Cost to Remedy Design Deficiencies

When a prototype failed the fuel system integrity test, the standard of care for engineers in the industry was to redesign and retest it. The vulnerability of the production Pinto's fuel tank at speeds of 20 and 30-miles-per-hour fixed barrier tests could have been remedied by inexpensive "fixes," but Ford produced and sold the Pinto to the public without doing anything to remedy the defects. Design changes that would have enhanced the integrity of the fuel tank system at relatively little cost per car included the following: a single shock absorbent "flak suit" to protect the tank at $4; a tank within a tank and placement of the tank over the axle at $5.08 to $5.79; a nylon bladder within the tank at $5.25 to $8; placement of the tank over the axle surrounded with a protective barrier at a cost of $9.95 per car.... Equipping the car with a reinforced rear structure, smooth axle, improved bumper and additional crush space at a total cost of $15.30 would have made the fuel tank safe in a 34- to 38-mile-per-hour rear end collision by a vehicle the size of the Ford Galaxie.... If the tank had been located over the rear axle, it would have been safe in a rear impact at 50 miles per hour or more.

Management's Decision to Go Forward with Knowledge of Defects

Ford's Product Planning Committee, whose members included Mr. Iacocca, Mr. Robert Alexander, and Mr. Harold MacDonald, Ford's Group Vice President of Car Engineering, approved the Pinto's concept and made the decision to go forward with the project.... As the project approached actual production, the engineers responsible for the components of the project "signed off" to their immediate supervisors who in turn "signed off" to their superiors and so on up the chain of command until the entire project was approved for public release by Vice Presidents Alexander and MacDonald and ultimately by Mr. Iacocca. The Pinto crash tests results had been forwarded up the chain of command to the ultimate decision-makers and were known to the Ford officials who decided to go forward with production.

Harley Copp, a former Ford engineer and executive in charge of the crash testing program, testified that the highest level of Ford's management made the decision to go forward with the production of the Pinto, knowing that the gas tank was vulnerable to puncture and rupture at low rear impact speeds creating a significant risk of death or injury from fire and knowing that "fixes" were feasible at nominal cost. He testified that management's decision was based on the cost savings which would inure from omitting or delaying the "fixes"....

[The court addresses Ford's claim that the jury should not have been permitted to award punitive damages in this case because Ford lacked the "malice" required by the California punitive damages statute:]

Ford argues that "malice"...requires...evil motive, an intention to injure the person harmed and that the term is therefore conceptually incompatible with an unintentional tort such as the manufacture and marketing of a defectively designed product.

[But] numerous California cases...have interpreted the term "malice"...to include...conduct evincing "a conscious disregard of the probability that the actor's conduct will result in injury to others...."

The primary purposes of punitive damages are punishment and deterrence of like conduct by the wrongdoer and others.... In the traditional noncommercial intentional tort, compensatory damages alone may serve as an effective deterrent against future wrongful conduct but in commerce related torts, the manufacturer may find it more profitable to treat compensatory damages as a part of the cost of doing business rather than to remedy the defect.... Governmental safety standards and the criminal law have failed to provide adequate consumer protection against the manufacture and distribution of defective products.... Punitive damages thus remain as the most effective remedy for consumer protection against defectively designed mass produced articles. They provide a motive for private individuals to enforce rules of law and enable them to recoup the expenses of doing so which can be considerable and not otherwise recoverable....

Ford complains that the punitive award is far greater than the maximum penalty that may be imposed under California or federal law prohibiting the sale of defective automobiles or other products.... It is precisely because monetary penalties under government regulations prescribing business standards or the criminal law are so inadequate and ineffective as deterrents against a manufacturer and distributor of mass produced defective products that punitive damages must be of sufficient amount to discourage such practices....

[Judgment for plaintiffs affirmed.]

QUESTIONS

1. Why did the jury award punitive damages against Ford? On what basis does the court uphold the punitive damages award? Ford argued that the amount should be limited by the California and federal guidelines setting maximum fines for selling defective products. Can you think of any other arguments against leveling large punitive damage awards? What arguments can you make for and against an award of punitive damages in the latex glove case?

2. An internal Ford memo, entitled "Fatalities Associated With Crash Induced Fuel Leakage and Fires," estimated the "benefits" and "costs" of design changes as follows:

Benefits: Savings—180 burn deaths, 180 serious burn injuries, and 2,100 burned vehicles
Unit cost—$200,000 per death, $67,000 per injury, $700 per vehicle[19]

Total benefits: 180 × ($200,000) plus
                180 × ($67,000) plus
                2,100 × ($700) = $49.53 million

Costs: Sales—11 million cars, 1.5 million light trucks

Unit cost—$11 per car, $11 per truck

Total costs: 11,000,000 × ($11) plus
             1,500,000 × ($11) = $137.5 million

Assume you are a safety engineer at Ford, consulted as to the wisdom of adding $11 to the cost of manufacturing the Pinto. What recommendation would you make? Can you make use of ethical theory to argue in defense of it? Against it?

3. Would punitive damages be justified in the following case? Holmes was injured in 1999 when his Ford Explorer, equipped with its original Firestone radial tires, rolled over. A Web site posted by Public Citizen, a non-profit consumer advocacy group, included a "Chronology of Firestone/Ford Knowledge of Tire Safety Defect" which described Ford and Firestone memos and letters, and actions taken by governmental agencies, which showed that Firestone knew about the tread separation problem long before the tires were recalled. "Ford and Firestone were experiencing problems with these tires in other countries with warm climates during the 1990s. The first lawsuit alleging a tread separation of this tire on an Explorer was filed in 1992. In 1996 there were memos from two different state agencies in Arizona warning state employees that these tires were suffering tread separations, and that Firestone was replacing some of the tires." Should Holmes be allowed to re-open his case to argue for punitive damages? *Holmes v. Bridgestone/Firestone, Inc.,* 891 So.2d 1188 (Fl. 2005). Source: Fred Baron, "President's Page: Firestone/Ford Makes the Case for the Tort System," 36 Trial 9 (November 2000). Excerpted with permission of TRIAL (November 2000). Copyright by the Association of Trial Lawyers of America; Fred Baron.

4. Suppose the jury had the option of putting Lee Iacocca, Robert Alexander, and Harold MacDonald in prison for their decision regarding the Pinto design. What are the pros and cons of meting out criminal sentences as compared to issuing punitive damage awards?

5. In 1979, Ford, indicted for manslaughter, was one of the first corporations to face such charges based on a defective product. In the mid-1990s, the crash of a ValuJet airplane in the Florida Everglades again led to criminal charges. This time, however, the defendant was not the airline or its manufacturer, but SabreTech, a maintenance company. SabreTech was charged with mislabeling hazardous waste (used oxygen generators) and delivering it to the plane that crashed.

    Internet Assignment What happened in these cases? Find any other criminal cases brought against companies. What happened to the companies?

---

19 The $200,000 value attributed to the loss of life was based on a study of the National Highway Traffic Safety Administration, which included in its estimate such items as medical costs, pain and suffering, funeral expenses, and lost productivity.

Is There a Litigation Crisis?[20]

- From 1996 to 2006, state tort litigation dropped 10 percent. In 2001, state courts handled just over 100 million cases; of those, most were criminal cases: only 17.1 million were civil, of which 67 percent were tort claims.

- In fiscal year 2002–2003, only 2 percent of all federal tort cases went to trial, and only 5.2 percent of state cases did; plaintiffs won 34 percent of their product liability cases.

- In state tort trials, the median damage award has gone from $64,000 in 1992 to $28,000; fewer than 20 percent of successful plaintiffs received $250,000 or more.

- Plaintiffs won more often in judge trials than they did in jury trials—54 percent to 46 percent.

- In state courthouses, only 6 percent of successful tort plaintiffs received punitive damages; punitive damages are most likely to be awarded in slander/libel cases (58%) and cases involving intentional torts (36%), not in negligence or strict liability cases.

- Courts are primarily overcrowded because of increasing criminal caseloads; the majority of civil trials are handled within 24 months.

- Businesses file four times as many lawsuits as individuals represented by trial lawyers do.

- Businesses that pay their lawyers an hourly fee are 69 percent more likely to be sanctioned for bringing frivolous lawsuits.

- Of the top 10 jury awards in 2003, eight were business–against–business suits (e.g., intellectual property disputes, indemnification of pollution cases, real estate development, trade secrets litigation, and general corporate bad faith cases). The largest damages award the Bureau of Justice Statistics tracked in a civil case was $90 million, which a Dallas jury awarded in a business dispute.

Manufacturer Liability for Consumer Uses

A product is not in a defective condition when it is safe for normal handling and consumption. If the injury results from abnormal handling. as where a bottled beverage is knocked against a radiator to remove the cap, or from abnormal preparation for use, as where too much salt is added to food, or from abnormal consumption, as where a child eats too much candy and is made ill, the seller is not liable. Restatement (2d) of Torts.

In most states, a seller can defend itself by proving that the consumer's use of its product was an abnormal one, unanticipated by the seller. As you read the next case, ask yourself this question: Was this an unanticipated "abuse" of an otherwise safe drug? The drug involved is OxyContin, an opium derivative ("opioid") first approved by the FDA in 1995 for the treatment of cancer pain.

20 Carmel Sileo and David Ratcliff, "The Myth of the Litigation Crisis: Straight Talk about Torts, When It Comes to Tort 'Reform,' Cutting Through the Fog Can Be Difficult. That's Why We've Gone to the Source: Statisticians and Researchers Who Keep a Running Tally of Who's Going to Court, Why, and What Happens When They Get There," 42JUL *Trial* 42 (July 2006)

FOISTER v. PURDUE PHARMA, L.P.

U.S. District Court, Kentucky, 2003
295 F.Supp.2d 693

Reeves, District Judge. ☀

Background

…OxyContin is a prescription narcotic intended to help individuals with moderate to severe pain…. It is illegal to use or sell OxyContin without a valid prescription.

…In 1994, the Department of Health and Human Services issued clinical guidelines encouraging the use of opioids to treat pain in cancer patients. A year later, the FDA approved the use of OxyContin to treat moderate and severe pain….

[But some individuals learned that by crushing the pills they] were able to unlock the full narcotic effect of the [opioids in OxyContin]…. As word of this procedure spread, abuse of OxyContin proliferated. Abuse of the drug in this manner has been particularly problematic in remote, rural areas such as Eastern Kentucky…[because] they're home to large populations of disabled and chronically ill people who are in need of pain relief; they're marked by high unemployment and a lack of economic opportunity; they're remote, far from the network of Interstates and metropolises through which heroin and cocaine travel; and they're areas where prescription drugs have been abused—though in much smaller numbers—in the past…(cites omitted).

As discussed below, the plaintiffs used OxyContin at various times for both legitimate and illegitimate purposes…. All purportedly suffered serious and debilitating side effects; namely, addiction to the drug. Two claim that their relatives were killed by OxyContin. They allege, *inter alia*, that Purdue did not adequately warn them of the side effects.

…Rodney Howard ("Howard") is 30 years of age and is also a resident of Pathfork, Kentucky. After working for six years in the coal mines and two years operating a logging business, Howard became gravely ill with Crohn's disease. His pain is severe and his prognosis is grim. In treating his pain, Howard has been prescribed Lorcet, Tylox and Demerol.

Howard was first prescribed OxyContin in January 2000. A month later, he began ignoring his doctor's order to take only two pills a day and began increasing his dosage. By March of that year, he was taking OxyContin orally every 60 to 90 minutes. Around that time, Howard began crushing the pills and taking them intravenously through a portacath that had previously been inserted into his chest to assist in the administration of Demerol. When his doctor discovered that Howard had been injecting OxyContin in this fashion, the doctor ordered the portacath removed….

…When Howard's heavy pill habit could not be supported by his prescriptions, he purchased most of his pills illegally….

Amy Foister ("Foister") is a 58-year-old resident of Manchester, Kentucky. She was employed as a welder until she sustained a back injury in March 1972…. To treat her pain, Foister was prescribed, at various times, Valium, Empirin/Codeine, Tylenol/Codeine, [and beginning in July 2000, OxyContin]…. In March 2001, her doctor refused to write any more OxyContin prescriptions due to the "misuse of the meds in our community." In lieu of OxyContin, he prescribed her Valium and Lortab. Foister apparently discontinued her use of OxyContin in March of 2001 and experienced some symptoms of withdrawal for a three to four week period…[but] was not "addicted" to OxyContin.

Legal Analysis

As the Supreme Court of Kentucky determined in *Monsanto Co. v. Reed* (1997), "a manufacturer is not liable when the injuries result from the mutilation or alteration of the [product]. Such intervening conduct severs any causal connection between the product and the injury…". Here, seven of the eight plaintiffs…intentionally altered the OxyContin pills and used them in an illegal and unauthorized manner. These plaintiffs either chewed, snorted or injected their pills…overdosed the drug with regularity…[and] clearly ignored the directions that accompanied OxyContin prescriptions. At the relevant times, the package insert for OxyContin stated, in bold letters:

> WARNINGS
> OxyContin…TABLETS ARE TO BE SWALLOWED WHOLE, AND ARE NOT TO BE BROKEN, CHEWED OR CRUSHED. TAKING BROKEN, CHEWED OR CRUSHED OxyContin TABLETS COULD LEAD TO THE RAPID RELEASE AND ABSORPTION OF A POTENTIALLY TOXIC DOSE OF OXYCODONE.

The warning was repeated later in the insert. Indeed, most of the plaintiffs admitted that they knew that altering the pills could be dangerous.

OxyContin, as approved for use by the FDA, is not unreasonably dangerous when used as directed. Like any drug, however, there are possibilities for abuse. Even "mild" drugs such as aspirin and acetaminophen can be dangerous if used improperly. Such drugs, however, are not unreasonably dangerous simply because they may be harmful if ingested in significant quantities or ingested in an illegal manner. The seven plaintiffs who improperly altered the pills fundamentally changed the characteristics of OxyContin. In effect, they created a different drug. Moreover, in most instances their alteration also included significant overuse of the pills.

The plaintiffs have presented no proof to suggest that the drug would have been unreasonably dangerous absent its illegal alteration. Indeed, the drug's FDA approval indicates that OxyContin is reasonably safe when used as directed. Therefore, the plaintiffs have not demonstrated that OxyContin is the proximate cause of addiction and withdrawal symptoms for people using the drug illegally. The proximate cause of any alleged injury in such circumstances is the alteration and/or abuse of the drug, not the drug itself….

…In Kentucky, a plaintiff may not recover in a legal or equitable proceeding when the basis for such an action rests on their own illegal conduct….

[T]he seven plaintiffs that procured and used OxyContin illegally may not recover in this action. These parties…are left with the dilemma which they created….

The Learned Intermediary Doctrine

…The learned intermediary doctrine provides that once a drug manufacturer has warned physicians of the dangers of the drug, the pharmacy's liability is cut off by the physician's knowledge…. In this case, Purdue argues that it warned prescribing physicians of all relevant side-effects and possible abuses. Thus, if the learned intermediary doctrine applies, the defendants' liability is cut-off by the doctor's knowledge.

> This court agrees…that Kentucky will likely adopt the "learned intermediary doctrine," as the *Restatement (Third) of Torts and numerous other jurisdictions have done*….

The lengthy and technical warnings provided by pharmaceutical manufacturers are much less useful to patients than the considerate, patient-specific instructions offered by physicians. Physicians are in the best position to determine whether the patient understands the benefits and risks and thus is in the best position to provide the necessary warnings. When it is clear that a patient does not understand the risks involved, the physician can explain them in a different manner until it is clear that the patient comprehends the potential complications.

Pharmaceutical companies, on the other hand, have no direct contacts with patients. Indeed, in many instances the patients may not be able to read the printed warnings provided by pharmaceutical companies, either because they cannot read English or because they cannot read at all. In sum, the physician is in the best position to pass on relevant risks. Thus, a pharmaceutical company must simply ensure that the physician is made aware of the known risks. Doing so absolves it of liability for failure to warn....

[Judgment for Purdue Pharma, the maker of OxyContin.]

QUESTIONS

1. How do the plaintiffs in the OxyContin case compare to the cigarette smoker who continues to smoke, despite reading Surgeon General warnings, and then develops lung cancer? Are they similar or different in their moral culpability? In their legal rights and responsibilities?

2. Faced with an opportunity to overturn the learned intermediary rule, the Kentucky court chose not to. Compare the court's reasoning to that in the New Jersey case involving Norplant that was discussed in Chapter 7. Which is more persuasive to you? Why? To what extent do the judgments seem to reflect differences in state populations?

3. The attorney general for West Virginia sued Purdue Pharma in 2001, charging the company with aggressively marketing OxyContin and deliberately hiding its addictive qualities from doctors. In November 2004, the parties settled. The lawsuit was dropped in return for Purdue Pharma's promise to spend $10 million on drug abuse and education programs in West Virginia. What argument can you make in favor of injured plaintiffs suing as opposed to suits by state attorneys general? By states?

   Internet Assignment Find out about other lawsuits against Purdue Pharma. Which outcomes seem preferable from an ethical perspective?

4. In 2007, Purdue Pharma and three of its top executives—President Michael Friedman, Howard K. Udell, its top lawyer, and former medical director Dr. Paul D. Goldenheim—agreed to pay $634.5 million in penalties to resolve a false marketing charge growing out of the company's sale of OxyContin. Part of the sentence required the former executives to serve 400 hours each of community service in drug treatment programs. News outlets reported that the penalty, the largest ever paid by a drug company, represented nearly 90 percent of the profits Purdue Pharma initially made from the sale of OxyContin. Do you think this plea agreement is fair, even though the executives will serve no jail time?

Vioxx

Vioxx, a nonsteroidal anti–inflammatory drug ("NSAID") was introduced to the market in 1999, approved for relief from menstrual cramps and pain caused by osteoarthritis. Its maker, Merck, promoted Vioxx as a painkiller with a safety profile superior to other NSAIDs, such as aspirin, ibuprofen, and naproxen. Traditional NSAIDs operate by inhibiting two enzymes, Cox-1 and Cox-2. Significantly, Vioxx did not inhibit Cox-1, diminishing the risk of a deteriorated stomach lining and gastrointestinal problems such as perforations and bleeds associated with suppressing Cox-1.

At its peak, Vioxx was a $2.5 billion-a-year blockbuster for Merck.

But there were problems with the drug. In a press release issued in 2000, and again in a submission to the FDA, Merck presented the results of one study comparing Vioxx with naproxen. This "VIGOR" study showed thrombotic events, including heart attack, occurred in more patients in the Vioxx treatment group than in the naproxen treatment group. Merck attributed this outcome to a "cardioprotective effect of naproxen" (also known as the "naproxen hypothesis") rather than to an increased risk of heart attack due to Vioxx. The VIGOR study initiated a public debate and extensive coverage in the press, scientific publications such as JAMA, and financial analysts about the cause of the increased risk (Naproxin hypothesis or Vioxx hazard?).

Meanwhile, Merck touted Vioxx's "excellent safety profile" and "favorable cardiovascular safety profile" in numerous press releases and public statements.

The first product liability class action was filed on May 29, 2001 in the United States District Court for the Eastern District of New York, alleging that "[a]s demonstrated by Merck's own research, users of Vioxx were four times as likely to suffer heart attacks as compared to other less expensive medications, or combinations thereof. ... Nonetheless, Merck ... [has] taken no affirmative steps to communicate this critical information." The company was accused of failing to warn, failing to perform adequate testing prior to marketing the drug, and that it knew or should have known that Vioxx posed a greater risk to patients.

In September 2001 the FDA entered, and fueled, the public debate by issuing a Warning Letter to Merck concerning the company's promotion of Vioxx. The letter admonished Merck for misrepresenting the safety profile of Vioxx, downplaying the cardiovascular findings of its VIGOR study, and explaining the results by offering the naproxen hypothesis as if it were based in fact. Merck was ordered to cease its misleading promotion and to issue a letter to doctors to correct false information it had disseminated.

More lawsuits were filed immediately after the publication of the FDA Warning Letter. One, a consumer fraud class action lawsuit filed in New Jersey state court, claimed the New Jersey-based Merck had violated the state's Consumer Fraud Act by engaging in unconscionable commercial practices, when it "omitted, suppressed, or concealed material facts concerning the dangers and risks associated with the use of Vioxx, including, but not limited to, the risks of serious damage from cardiovascular problems." Merck was accused of deliberately downplaying the risks of Vioxx.

By the end of 2003, Vioxx-related securities class action suits had been filed against Merck. Investors claimed that the company's failure to disclose material information about the cardiovascular risks of Vioxx had inflated the price of Merck's stock, leading to financial loss when the truth was revealed and the stock price fell.

Finally, in fall 2004, in the midst of another study on Vioxx, Merck voluntarily withdrew the drug from the market based on data observed in that test and the availability of alternative therapies. During its five years on the market, some 20 million Americans took Vioxx. Epidemiologists estimate the drug may have caused 100,000 heart attacks.

Merck spent an estimated $285 million defending itself in 2005 alone. Only a handful of cases have actually gone to trial, with Merck winning as many as it has lost. One jury found that Vioxx did not cause the heart attack suffered by 68-year-old Elaine Doherty of New Jersey; another awarded $13 million to 77-year-old John McDarby, who had a heart attack after taking Vioxx for 4 years; Merck lost a jury verdict in Louisiana, and won in California. As this book goes to press, plaintiffs are considering whether to accept Merck's offer to pay $4.85 billion to settle as many as 47,000 pending Vioxx suits.

Government Regulation of Product Safety

Some government agencies, such as OSHA, are located within a particular executive department like the Department of Labor, headed by persons who serve at the pleasure of the president. These are known as executive agencies. "Independent administrative agencies" are not within any particular branch of government. They are considered independent because they are headed by a board of commissioners who are appointed for a specific term and can be removed early only for cause defined by Congress.

The record of direct government regulation of product safety by the major independent agencies—Consumer Product Safety Commission (CPSC), Food and Drug Administration (FDA), and the Environmental Protection Agency (EPA)—is spotty at best. And, not surprisingly, independent agencies are often caught in a crossfire of criticism from both consumer groups and business interests.

While the Internet is beginning to change the public face of the agencies,[21] it remains to be seen whether easier access to records, the status of actions, and advice for consumers and businesses alike will lead to greater confidence in agency regulatory work.

The Consumer Product Safety Commission (CPSC)

The Consumer Product Safety Act of 1972 created the CPSC as an independent federal regulatory agency to protect consumers from unreasonable risk of injury, illness, or death from unsafe products. Underfunded by Congress (which has funded only three of five potential commissioners since 1987) and unsure of its mission, the agency was once described by consumer advocate Ralph Nader as "dormant for 15 years." Empowered by law to ban products, seek court-ordered recalls of hazardous products, and set mandatory standards, the CPSC has relied instead primarily on voluntary standards. It was not until 2006 that the agency promulgated its first major safety standard, when it set minimum safeguards to protect mattresses from open flames and fires caused by cigarettes.

Increasingly, the 15,000 types of consumer products over which the CPSC has jurisdiction are imported. In 2006, a record number of recalls—467—involved products made in China. Indeed, in recent years, nearly 60 percent of all product recalls came from China, including all 24 toys recalled for safety reasons in the United States in 2006. From January to July 2007 the CPSC lacked a chair and was unable to vote because it lacked a quorum. Finally, in July 2007, in response to a public outcry over product safety, acting chair Nancy A. Nord began work on regulatory proposals that would mandate broader inspections of imports and stiffer penalties for ignoring safety rules.

The CPSC runs a hotline for reporting dangerous products and product-related injuries, and highlights current concerns on its Web site, http://cpsc.gov.

Food and Drug Administration (FDA)

The role of the FDA, created by the 1906 Pure Food and Drug Act to prevent illegal distribution of misbranded and adulterated food and drugs has expanded over the years, mostly in response to high profile tragedies. In 1938, for example, an early "wonder drug" marketed for strep throat in children, Elixir of Sulfanilamide, was laced with a chemical used in antifreeze

---

21 For example, figuring out which government entity has responsibility for a particular kind of product once made it difficult to get information on product recalls. Today, recall information is easily accessed on http://www.recalls.gov, which links to those agencies with statutory authority to issue recalls, the FDA, CPSC, EPA, National Highway Traffic Safety Administration (NHTSA), U.S. Coast Guard, and Department of Agriculture.

and killed 107 people. Public outrage led Congress to expand the FDA's responsibilities to include oversight of cosmetics and therapeutic devices, and to authorize the agency to require companies to prove the safety of drugs before they could be marketed. Today the agency's jurisdiction extends to other products: dietary supplements, food additives, blood products, and those that emit radiation, such as microwaves and cellphones. Once again, its effectiveness in fulfilling its mission to "protect public health by helping safe and effective products, reach the market in a timely way and monitoring products for continued safety" is being seriously questioned.

In the early 2000s, while the FDA campaigned to discourage Americans from purchasing drugs from Canada or over the Internet—warning of the dangers of counterfeit or unregulated drugs—news events highlighted the safety risks of FDA-approved drugs: the cardiovascular risks of Vioxx; an increased risk of suicide for children and adolescents taking Paxil and other antidepressents; kidney failure linked to cholesterol-lowering drugs. Consumer advocates pointed to a weakness in FDA oversight of drug safety: problems that surface in drugs already on the market. In response, the FDA created a Drug Safety Oversight Board in 2005. But a congressional Government Accountability Office (GAO) report issued in March 2006[22] recommended further reform. The GAO wanted "more meat on the bone" to address the continued lack of systematic tracking and resolution of safety issues. It blamed lack of communication between two offices within the FDA and financial conflicts of interest,[23] and called for FDA authority to require postmarket studies.

In March 2007, the agency acted to reform itself, issuing guidelines barring advisors with more than $50,000 invested in FDA-regulated drug or medical device companies. Two months later, the Senate passed a bipartisan bill that would increase the fees paid by drug makers to help finance the work of the FDA, and enhance the agency's power to enforce its rules, allowing it to impose fines on companies that violated a drug safety plan or ran false or misleading ads. Critics of the bill pointed to a rider that maintained the current ban on imported drugs, but most predicted that it would become law.

The other major prong of FDA responsibility—assuring the safety of the American food supply—has become an almost impossible task for the underfunded, overworked agency. In the mid-1990s, consumer "health-consciousness" led the agency to look at the burgeoning supply of nutritional supplements—it banned ephedra in 2004—and to exercise its new power to review the health claims of food products.

A decade later, attention refocused on the basics: meat, fish, dairy, and produce. When 200 people became ill from E. coli tainted spinach in 2006, the agency issued voluntary guidelines for handling produce. Critics noted that from 2001 to 2007, the only significant food safety regulations adopted by the FDA were those ordered by Congress. During that time, the corner grocery store had become a truly global market. With 1,750 food inspectors at ports and domestic food-production plants, the FDA inspectors could sample only a relatively small number—20,662 shipments—and visually inspect an additional 115,000—of the roughly 9 million imports to the United States.

China, the world's third-largest exporter of food, sending 199,000 shipments to the United States in 2006, was the source of contaminated pet food and of toxic toothpaste discovered in spring 2007. Around the same time, federal inspectors also found melamine-laced ingredients for fish feed made in Toledo, Ohio. Calls for further overhaul of the FDA were loud and furious.

---

22 Government Accountability Office, "Improvement Needed in FDA's Postmarket Decision-Making and Oversight Process," GAO-06-402 (March 31, 2006).

23 The prestigious *Journal of the American Medical Association* reported earlier in 2006 that one quarter of the FDA's expert consultants had conflicts of interest that might taint the approval process.

In July 2007, as some members of Congress pushed for stronger measures against Chinese imports to the United States, the FDA asserted itself. It effectively banned the import of five seafood products, including shrimp, catfish, and eels, from the world's leading seafood exporter after repeatedly finding fish from China were contaminated with banned chemicals, unsafe additives, pesticides, and carcinogens. As this book goes to press, the debate on the FDA's effectiveness in an increasingly complex global marketplace continues.

Environmental Protection Agency (EPA)

When the EPA was created in 1970, responsibility for oversight of pesticides shifted from the FDA to the new agency. Today, through the Federal Insecticide, Fungicide, and Rodenticide Act (FIFRA), the EPA is responsible for licensing and registering pesticides, herbicides, and rodenticides for use in "strict accordance with label directions, based on review of scientific studies." By law, pest-killers must not pose unreasonable risks to human health or the environment. In addition, anyone planning to import pesticides for use in the United States must notify the EPA.

National Highway Traffic Safety Administration (NHTSA)

Created in 1970 as part of the U.S. Department of Transportation, the NHTSA's mission is to reduce deaths, injuries, and economic losses resulting from motor vehicle crashes by setting and enforcing safety performance standards, investigating defects, conducting research, and educating the public. Despite this broad mandate, its specific powers are limited. The agency has no way to track safety-related problems unless it is notified by the affected industry. In the 1990s, hundreds of people were killed or injured in roll-over accidents caused by tread-separation on Bridgestone and Firestone tires. But the NHTSA was not notified of the tread problem by either the carmakers or the tiremakers until the companies had been sued. Finally, in 2000, the NHTSA recalled 6.5 million tires.

In June 2007, on the heels of the reports of problems with toys and food imported from China, the NHTSA ordered a recall of 450,000 tires imported from China. The problem: Tread separation seemingly caused two vehicle rollovers, killing two and injuring two others. Again, it was only after a suit was filed that the manufacturer came forward, acknowledging that a "gum strip" was missing from the production process.

The NHTSA posts safety reports at http://www.nhtsa.dot.gov; its critics' perspective can be found at http://www.citizen.org, the Web site of Public Citizen, a consumer-advocate group founded by Ralph Nader and now led by former-NHTSA head, Joan Claybrooke.

The Need for Reform

The non-profit Consumers Union (CU), publisher of *Consumer Reports*, tests products, publicizes safety issues, and works with government agencies and Congress to improve standards and compliance. Sally Greenberg, an attorney at CU explains: "We try to make sure there is a balance within federal agencies, because we know the manufacturers have a lot more people, a lot more money, and are in a position to wield more power [than consumers]." Her co-author, Janell Mayo Duncan, once counsel to the FDA, and now at CU, describes CU's mission as 'Test, Inform, Protect." They discuss weaknesses in the regulatory agencies in the following interview by Sara Hoffman Jurand, Associate Editor of *Trial* magazine.

ARE GOVERNMENT REGULATORY AGENCIES DOING ENOUGH TO ENSURE THAT CONSUMER PRODUCTS ARE SAFE?

AN INTERVIEW WITH SALLY GREENBERG AND JANELL MAYO DUNCAN[24]

TRIAL: *Why do government standards sometimes fall short of our safety expectations? What other interests are agencies considering when they lower their standards?*

DUNCAN: Government regulators are always under pressure from industry to regulate as little as possible, and there's a dearth of consumer voices to push a consumer agenda. Manufacturers have considerable resources to lobby Congress and the agencies.

GREENBERG: Moreover, agency decisions are too often a victim of political considerations. The auto industry, for example, is a potent force at NHTSA, which is part of the Department of Transportation and answers directly to the president. You have political appointees in leadership roles at the agencies and a legendary revolving door. And then you also have people who've been working at these agencies for many years, and some are, quite simply, bureaucrats who are not comfortable with swift, decisive action. Finally, too often there are statutes that prevent agencies from taking swift action.

For example, under the CPSC's Freedom of Information Act (FOIA) provisions, the agency has to notify the manufacturer and give it time to review the FOIA request before the agency can release information to the public. There are many roadblocks to getting the safest possible regulations in place.

DUNCAN: I think it depends on the people in the agency—for instance, who is truly safety conscious and who is not. But there are policy glitches in the system that are not allowing even the bold people to do what they need to do.

GREENBERG: There certainly are many dedicated staff doing good work in safety agencies, but ultimately, decisions are made at the top. Political or "cost benefit" considerations can block needed safety-oriented actions.

For example, why wouldn't the CPSC require safety registration cards with baby and nursery products—cribs, strollers, playpens, swings? Children's lives are at stake, and at 50 cents or so per card, that's not too high a price to pay.

The CPSC votes to reject these child product registrations. The companies said, "We can't do it, it's too expensive"; meanwhile, they keep vast stores of marketing information on their customer base. So why can't they make it easy for customers to register and, in the event of a safety hazard, let the customer know and likely save a child's life?

TRIAL: *Let's talk specifically about NHTSA....*

GREENBERG: NHTSA's standards are inadequate in a number of areas; any honest observer can see that. Vehicles should be manufactured with a strong emphasis on safety—strong sides, strong roofs, safety in all crash testing, effective seat belts and air bags, and more stability to prevent rollover.

Why hadn't NHTSA fixed the tire standard until the Ford/Firestone crisis erupted in 2002? Why don't most rollover-prone vehicles have roofs that don't collapse? Why are we just now getting to tougher side-impact standards?...

---

24 "Governing Product Safety: Are Government Regulatory Agencies Doing Enough to Ensure that Consumer Products Are Safe? Two Attorneys from Consumers Union Discuss the System's Weaknesses and Needed Improvements," 40-NOV *Trial* 26 (2004).

Although NHTSA has been weak in a number of areas, it has done many other good things. It implemented a rollover-resistance test, which we supported, though we're not yet happy with how that information has been presented to consumers. If a vehicle tips up and fails the test, it can still get three stars out of five. We ask, why mask its poor performance? But this program also detected that the Saturn Vue's suspension was faulty and now GM has recalled the vehicle. So stability testing has helped protect consumers from a potentially hazardous vehicle.

TRIAL: *Some consumer advocates complain that even though an agency acted, it did so too slowly or didn't do enough. A good example is the EPA and pressure-treated wood [containing arsenic. The EPA recently completed a "voluntary phase-out" of the product, but the agency did not require a recall or rehabilitation of the structures that are already in parks and backyards.] Is slow action better than no action at all, and are there ways to make agencies take more timely action?*

GREENBERG: Obviously taking some action is better than doing nothing, but you have to ask, if an agency has known about a problem for 15 years, what steps has it taken to address the problem in that period?

It's the same with the CPSC and [its failure to adopt stronger] fire safety standards. The agency's history is slow action or no action. Meanwhile, children are getting burned by flammable upholstered furniture—hundreds of people die in such fires each year, and from bedding fires, et cetera....

DUNCAN: Especially for a vulnerable population. We're talking about arsenic-treated wood on playgrounds. There's really no excuse for not acting as soon as possible after the risk has been identified when untold numbers of children could be involved....

TRIAL: *Should consumers be able to hold manufacturers to a higher safety standard than the government agencies require?*

GREENBERG: Yes, they should. Companies often fall back on the excuse "Well, it meets government standards." But government standards, to the extent they exist, are a floor; they are not a ceiling....

For example, with roof crush in rollover situations, just because the government hasn't upgraded the standard in decades, this doesn't mean that roofs are as strong as they need to be. Just because the government doesn't have a rollover standard doesn't mean manufacturers don't have a role to play in preventing rollovers.

If manufacturers know there are ways to make consumers safer, they ought to be held to implementing that knowledge in their product designs. They are, we are pleased to note, installing anti-rollover technology in more and more SUVs, and doing so voluntarily because the public has become keenly aware that SUVs are more rollover-prone than cars. Having anti-rollover technology in SUVs helps sell these vehicles and, by the way, safety has become one of the top considerations for car buyers, unlike 20 years ago....

TRIAL: *Critics claim politics influenced the CPSC's decision not to recall Daisy BB guns. Do you think the appointment of agency directors affects how agencies regulate product safety?*

GREENBERG: Sometimes, and in this case I would say it did. I'm sorry to say that it appears as if two commissioners worried too much about the manufacturer and not enough about the safety of consumers. And that isn't the mandate of the agency. It was clear, from the CPSC's opinion and from the press afterwards, that the deciding factor was that the company had said it might go bankrupt if it had to conduct a recall, because it would be a big, costly recall.

Probably the best thing I read was from [dissenting] Commissioner Thomas Moore, who said that this is not the "manufacturer product protection" commission or the "manufacturer economic well-being" commission, this is the Consumer Product

Safety Commission; I'm mandated to protect consumers. He added that this decision was based on a reliance on the company's arguments that it might suffer economically. We agree. We don't think that's appropriate.

DUNCAN: If a company sells a product that is unreasonably dangerous or defective, then it really should not be in business. And in this case it did look like there was a lot of tortured analysis to get to the conclusion that there was some way to handle this other than a recall.

QUESTIONS

1. What are the relative merits of government regulation versus litigation? What arguments can you make that one or both of those mechanisms for assuring our safety needs to be reformed?

2. **Internet Assignment** Choose one of the federal agencies with some responsibility for monitoring product safety, such as the FDA, EPA, NHTSA, or CPSC. Find out about the backgrounds of those persons with policy-making power within the agency, including education, work experience in both the public and private sectors, and political affiliations. Do you detect any potential conflicts of interest? How responsive have they been to public concerns? To issues raised by lawmakers? To problems voiced by the industry they regulate? What guidelines would you suggest for appointments to such positions in the future?

CHAPTER **PROBLEMS**

1. Talon-G is a rat poison made by ICI Americas and sold only to professional pest control companies. The poison was registered by the EPA and packaged in a container with EPA-approved labeling that displayed warnings cautioning users to keep it out of the reach of children, that it might be harmful or fatal if swallowed, and to store it in its original container in a location inaccessible to children. ICI could have—but didn't—make the poison safer by adding an emetic that would cause any human ingesting it to immediately vomit, thereby expelling the poison (rats do not have a vomit reflex). Alternatively, ICI could have added bitrex, an aversive agent used in a variety of products since the late 1970s that makes the poison taste bad to children but would not keep rats from eating it.

   a. Assume that an exterminator stores leftover Talon-G in an unmarked container. A nine-year-old child finds and eats the poison, thinking it is candy. Several days later, the child dies. On what basis might the child's family bring a lawsuit?

   b. What defenses might be raised?

   c. Assuming that the labels met EPA requirements for warning labels, are there policy reasons for refusing to allow a suit against ICI? See *Banks v. ICI Americas, Inc.* 45 S. E.2d 671 (Ga. 1994).

   d. **Internet Assignment** Check http://www.epa.gov to find out about the EPA Consumer Labeling Initiative. Is this a good strategy for minimizing harm to humans from dangerous products? What else might be needed?

2. While his mother was sleeping, a two-year-old child retrieved a disposable butane lighter from his mother's purse atop the family refrigerator and used it to start a fire. The child, a sibling, and the sleeping mother were all killed. The lighter had no child-

resistant features, and those representing a third child, who managed to escape from the house, brought suit against the maker. Analyze the case using the language of both tort and contract. How does it compare to the Talon-G scenario described previously? See *Phillips v. Cricket Lighters*, 2004 WL 1277978 (Pa. Super.).

3. As we learned in Chapter 7, obesity—especially childhood obesity—has become a national health scandal. In December 2003 Xenical became the first drug specifically approved by the FDA for the treatment of obesity in adolescents. In the past few years lawsuits have been brought—and settled—against McDonalds (for failing to disclose the use of beef fat in its French fries), DeConna Ice Cream Company (for understating fat and calorie content of its ice cream), Robert's American Gourmet Foods (for understating fat and calorie content in its cheese snacks), Kraft (for failing to disclose that Oreo cookies contained trans fatty acids), and the New York City school system (for serving nonnutritious food in the schools).

    Internet Assignment What changes can you detect in the food industry since the spate of lawsuits against them?

4. Silicone gel breast implants were introduced to the U.S. market in the 1960s. In 1992, after reports that they leaked silicone into women's bodies and endangered their health, the FDA took the devices off the market and restricted the use of implants to clinical trials. During the next 14 years, women continued to get other kinds of breast implants. (Public Citizen estimates that 80 percent of the 300,000 implants done in the United States each year are for cosmetic reasons.) Then, in fall 2006, the agency announced that the implants were "safe and effective," approving their use for breast augmentation in women 22 and older, and for breast reconstruction in women of any age. The makers were required to conduct a long-term (10-year) safety study on some 40,000 women. Prior to the lifting of the ban, the FDA had received a letter from a scientist, an ex-employee of one of the two companies later approved for implants, Mentor Corp. in which he accused the company of withholding data from the FDA about seepage and rupture problems. What ethical issues arise in this scenario?

5. Consider the following: Linda Green began her career as a health care worker in 1978, following hospital rules that required her to wear protective gloves while attending patients. For more than a decade she wore nearly 40 pairs of cornstarch powdered latex gloves, made by Smith & Nephew (S&N), during every shift. In 1989, Green began suffering various health problems: her hands became red, cracked, and sore, and began peeling. No matter what she did, the rash continued, and eventually spread to her upper trunk and neck. She began experiencing chronic cold-like symptoms such as a runny nose and watery eyes. Green's symptoms grew increasingly severe, eventually culminating in an acute shortness of breath, coughing, and tightening of the throat. In the mid-1990s experts began to understand that some people become "sensitized" to latex through allergic reactions. Subsequent exposure may cause the person to develop progressively worse reactions, including irreversible asthma. Occasionally hypersensitivity may trigger anaphylactic shock, a life-threatening reaction to even a small exposure. Once she understood her own reaction to the gloves, Green sued S&N. What kinds of lawsuits might she bring? What will she have to prove to win? How might S&N defend itself?

    Internet Assignment Find out what happened in this suit. *Green v. Smith & Nephew AHP, Inc.*, 629 N.W.2d 727 (Wis. 2001).

6. In July 2007, Zheng Xiaoyu, one of the most powerful regulators in China, was executed after confessing to accepting gifts and bribes from drug companies over the eight years he headed China's equivalent of the FDA. During Zheng's tenure, his agency approved over 150,000 applications for new drugs, at least six of which were fake, under a system he

created. In 2002, the Chinese began to investigate charges of corruption among various drug officials. In addition to bribery, Zheng was found guilty of derilection of duty for failing to police the drug industry and his subordinates and of creating regulatory schemes that allowed dangerous drugs to come to market. On execution day, the government announced that it was dismantling the drug approval system Zheng had created.

Internet Assignment Find out what changes have taken place in China to ensure greater safety of both food and drugs. What changes have taken place in the United States to assure that imports, from China and elsewhere, are safer?

7. DDT is a cheap way to eliminate insects that threaten crops and people—including mosquitoes that spread malaria. Because it accumulates in the food chain and causes harm to humans and animals, its use has been banned in the United States since 1972. However, 23 nations continue to use it for malaria control, although most countries no longer use DDT for agricultural purposes. Alternative pesticides—such as pyrethroids—are almost two to three times more costly. By 1999, only three nations—China, Mexico, and India—still produced and exported DDT. However, when the United Nations considered a worldwide ban on DDT as part of a plan to minimize the use of 12 toxic chemicals ("persistent organic pollutants"), some members of the public health community were alarmed. There was a resurgence of mosquito-borne malaria, with some 300 to 500 million new cases a year. Drugs to treat malaria are expensive and increasingly ineffective against the disease. Use ethical theory to articulate a response to this dilemma.

8. Health agencies are looking to artemisinin, a new drug derived from sweet wormwood isolated by Chinese scientists to fight malaria. Used in combination with other drugs, it can be a powerful treatment. But 18 companies from around the world make artemisinin in a one-drug form that can be sold cheaply to the developing world where people with fevers often buy drugs without knowing for sure they have malaria. Fearing misuse would create an incurable strain of malaria, the World Health Organization demanded companies stop selling the drug in its monotherapy form. What ethical issues arise here?

9. An Oregon jury awarded $79.5 million in punitive damages to the widow of a heavy cigarette smoker who died of smoking-related lung cancer. The judgment against Philip Morris was reduced to $32 million by the judge. On appeal, the U.S. Supreme Court overturned the punitive damage award as a taking of property from the defendant without due process of law. While such damages may be imposed to punish unlawful conduct and deter its repetition, they may not be arbitrary nor grossly excessive, according to Justice Breyer. Due process forbids a state to use a punitive damages award to punish a defendant for injury that it inflicts upon nonparties, as the jury appeared to do in this case. What does this mean? *Philip Morris USA v. Williams* 127 S.Ct. 1057 (2007). In dissent, Justices Ginsberg and Thomas argued that the punishment is based on how reprehensible the conduct was—and the more people injured, the more reprehensible the conduct.

Internet Assignment Find out about existing or pending legislation on punitive damages in your state.

10. Biotech medicines—proteins made by modifying the DNA of bacteria, yeast or mammal cells and infused into sick patients—are the fastest growing category of health spending. Sales reached $40 billion in 2006, when reports indicated there were more than 400 biotech products being synthesized to treat cancer, AIDS, diabetes, Alzheimers, and a hundred other diseases. The manufacture of biotechs is more complex and costly than conventional medicine, and the cost to patients can run as high as $25,000–50,000 a year. Some members of Congress have introduced legislation that would give consumers access to lower-cost copies; one would authorize the FDA to approve safe, lower-cost

versions of biotechnology drugs without the full range of tests normally required for new products. Who are the stakeholders who will be affected by such legislation? What arguments can you make for or against it?

CHAPTER **PROJECT**

Legislative Activism

1. For this project, you are asked to identify a proposed regulation related to product safety and to submit a written comment for or against the proposed rule.

   - Begin by going to the Web site of any of the major government regulatory agencies with responsibility for product safety (the National Highway Transportation Safety Administration at http://www.nhtsa.gov, the Environmental Protection Agency at http://www.epa.gov, the Consumer Product Safety Commission at http://www.cpsc.gov, the Food and Drug Administration at http://www.fda.gov, or the Federal Trade Commission at http://www.ftc.gov).

   - Once you have selected a government agency, locate its docket of proposed regulations. Choose one on a topic that interests you, and read through the proposal.

   - Learn as much as you can about the debate for and against the proposed regulation. Check out such consumer advocacy groups as http://www.citizen.org, http://www.consumersunion.org, or Friends of the Earth at http://www.foe.org. Find the business perspectives through popular business publications, by using a database such as abinform, or through a trade association such as http://www.Phrma.org (pharmaceutical industry).

   - Take a position for or against the new regulation, and submit a written comment to the regulatory agency that has proposed it. E-mail a copy of your comment to your professor.

9 OWNERSHIP AND CREATIVITY:

Intellectual Property

As for piracy, I love to be pirated. It is the greatest compliment an author can have. The wholesale piracy of Democracy was the single real triumph of my life. Anyone may steal what he likes from me.

— Henry Brooks Adams, 1905[1]

At its best, the Knowledge Society involves all members of a community in knowledge creation and utilization. [It] is not only about technological innovations, but also about human beings, their personal growth, and their individual creativity, experience and participation.

— The United Nations, "Understanding Knowledge Societies" (2003)

•

Intellectual property (IP) is the work product of the human mind. Novels, paintings, computer programs, songs, and inventions are all examples. IP differs from other kinds of property (land, buildings, stocks, consumer goods) in several key ways. While often expensive and time consuming to generate, intellectual property can be quickly and easily copied. Unlike tangible items whose use has physical limitations—only one person can drive a car at a time; a pie can be divided into only so many slices—the number of persons who can use any one item of intellectual property is boundless. A painting hung in a museum or reproduced in art books or on the Internet can be viewed by many; a poem or song can be endlessly repeated and enjoyed; the same software program can run on computers throughout the world.

The legal framework that protects intellectual property has evolved over the years, as lawmakers have sought to promote commercial progress and enrich culture by rewarding inventors and creative people for their efforts.

Today, IP law is the focus of controversy, not only in the business and legal communities, but among the general public. As intellectual property has become key to U.S. hegemony in the world economy, legal protections for those owning patents and copyright have been greatly expanded—often in conflict with the norms of cyberspace, whose founders freely shared and borrowed creative works, claiming "information wants to be free." Business interests warn that sharing has economic costs: the Business Software Alliance (BSA) estimates global losses from software piracy at $11 billion annually, with more than $6.9 billion lost in the United States alone in 2005. As this book goes to press, The Coalition Against Counterfeiting and Piracy is urging stronger U.S. government action to stop trafficking in pirated and counterfeit goods, claiming it costs the U.S. economy between $200 and $250 billion and

---

1 Letter, July 11, 1905, to Brooks Adams. *Letters*, Vol. 2, Worthington Chauncy Ford, Ed. (Houghton Mifflin, 1938).

750,000 lost jobs per year.[2] Patent law—once too technical and obscure for most of the public to notice—now commands headlines, with 440,000 inventors filing patent applications in the United States in 2006 and more than 20 percent of human genes already patented.

In this chapter, we explore some critical IP issues, beginning with one of the stickiest problems: downloading music from the Internet. The legal background is both traditional copyright law and relatively recent changes under the Digital Millennium Copyright Act. Then we turn to other kinds of IP: misappropriation, trademark, patents, and trade secrets. The ethical focus of the chapter centers on finding a delicate balance between protecting individual inventiveness and stimulating a vibrant shared culture. We end with a discussion of the globalization of IP law through the TRIPS agreement and a challenge to remake IP law to enhance human rights.

Copyright Law

Article 1, Section 8 of the U.S. Constitution empowers Congress to pass legislation "to promote the progress of science and (the) useful arts by securing for limited Times to authors and inventors the exclusive right to their respective Writings and Discoveries."

The congressional report on the Copyright Act of 1909 articulates the tension underlying intellectual property protection in our legal system:

> *In enacting copyright law Congress must consider … two questions: First, how much will the legislation stimulate the producer and so benefit the public, and second, how much will the monopoly granted be detrimental to the public? The granting of such exclusive rights, under the proper terms and conditions, confers a benefit upon the public that outweighs the evils of the temporary monopoly.*

Tension between private and public interests, between encouraging and rewarding individual creators—authors, composers, software engineers—and improving upon, borrowing, or critiquing their works has remained a constant in an otherwise evolving legal landscape.

Music

If a song means a lot to you, imagine what it means to us.

— ARTISTS AGAINST PIRACY

Online music sharing is now almost ubiquitous. In 1999 a 19-year-old college dropout, Shawn Fanning, released computer code that allowed his friends to share their collections of digitalized music (MP3 files). By July 2000, some five million users had visited the Napster site, and the Recording Industry Association of America (RIAA) began its campaign to stop illegal downloading. One tool in its arsenal was to use copyright law. As federal trial court Judge Patel saw it, the RIAA suit to shut down Napster was really about "the boundary between sharing and theft, personal use and the unauthorized worldwide distribution of copyrighted music and sound recordings." While Patel and the federal appellate court in California agreed with the recording industry that Napster illegally contributed to copyright infringement, further appeals and technical difficulties delayed the dismantling of its services.

In the meantime, music swapping had planted itself firmly in the culture. Napster-like Web sites became popular. The newer ones—Grokster, StreamCast, Morpheus—allowed one user to to receive music directly from other users, unlike Napster, which gave its users access

---

2 See http://www.uschamber.com/ncf/initiatives/counterfeiting.htm (Web site visiting August 31, 2007).

to Napster's online clearinghouse containing millions of songs. Now joined by the movie industry, RIAA stood its ground.

In the case that follows, a group of copyright holders (MGM, other motion picture studios, recording companies, songwriters, and music publishers) take on Grokster and other peer-to-peer networks, alleging they knowingly and intentionally distributed their software to enable users to violate copyright laws. The Supreme Court must decide when the distributor of such a product is liable for the way others use it.

METRO-GOLDWIN-MAYER STUDIOS INC. v. GROKSTER, LTD.
United States Supreme Court, 2005
125 S.Ct. 2764

Justice SOUTER. ❋

Given [their]…security, cost, and efficiency, peer–to–peer networks are employed to store and distribute electronic files by universities, government agencies, corporations, and libraries, among others….

[A study by an MGM-commissioned statistician] showed that nearly 90% of the files available for download on the FastTrack system were copyrighted works. Grokster and StreamCast dispute this figure…. They also argue that potential noninfringing uses of their software are significant in kind, even if infrequent in practice. Some musical performers, for example, have gained new audiences by distributing their copyrighted works for free across peer–to–peer networks, and some distributors of unprotected content have used peer–to–peer networks to disseminate files, Shakespeare being an example. Indeed, StreamCast has given Morpheus users the opportunity to download the briefs in this very case, though their popularity has not been quantified.

…MGM's evidence gives reason to think that the vast majority of users' downloads are acts of infringement, and because well over 100 million copies of the software in question are known to have been downloaded, and billions of files are shared across the FastTrack and Gnutella networks each month, the probable scope of copyright infringement is staggering….

Grokster and StreamCast are not…merely passive recipients of information about infringing use. The record is replete with evidence that from the moment Grokster and StreamCast began to distribute their free software, each one clearly voiced the objective that recipients use it to download copyrighted works, and each took active steps to encourage infringement.

…Internal company documents indicate that StreamCast hoped to attract large numbers of former Napster users if that company was shut down by court order or otherwise, and that StreamCast planned to be the next Napster. A kit developed by StreamCast to be delivered to advertisers, for example, contained press articles about StreamCast's potential to capture former Napster users, and it introduced itself to some potential advertisers as a company "which is similar to what Napster was."…An internal e–mail from a company executive stated: "We have put this network in place so that when Napster pulls the plug on their free service…or if the Court orders them shut down prior to that…we will be positioned to capture the flood of their 32 million users that will be actively looking for an alternative."

Thus, StreamCast developed promotional materials to market its service as the best Napster alternative…. StreamCast even planned to flaunt the illegal uses of its software; when it launched the OpenNap network, the chief technology officer of the company averred that "[t]he goal is to get in trouble with the law and get sued. It's the best way to get in the new[s]."...

The evidence that Grokster sought to capture the market of former Napster users is sparser but revealing, for Grokster launched its own OpenNap system called Swaptor and inserted digital codes into its Web site so that computer users using Web search engines to look for "Napster" or "[f]ree filesharing" would be directed to the Grokster Web site, where they could download the Grokster software....

...Morpheus in fact allowed users to search specifically for "Top 40" songs, which were inevitably copyrighted. Similarly, Grokster sent users a newsletter promoting its ability to provide particular, popular copyrighted materials....

... [T]he business models employed by Grokster and StreamCast confirm that their principal object was use of their software to download copyrighted works. Grokster and StreamCast receive no revenue from users, who obtain the software itself for nothing. Instead, both companies generate income by selling advertising space, and they stream the advertising to Grokster and Morpheus users while they are employing the programs. As the number of users of each program increases, advertising opportunities become worth more. While there is doubtless some demand for free Shakespeare, the evidence shows that substantive volume is a function of free access to copyrighted work. Users seeking Top 40 songs, for example, or the latest release by Modest Mouse, are certain to be far more numerous than those seeking a free Decameron, and Grokster and Stream-Cast translated that demand into dollars.

Finally, there is no evidence that either company made an effort to filter copyrighted material from users' downloads or otherwise impede the sharing of copyrighted files. Although Grokster appears to have sent e-mails warning users about infringing content when it received threatening notice from the copyright holders, it never blocked anyone from continuing to use its software to share copyrighted files. StreamCast not only rejected another company's offer of help to monitor infringement, but blocked the Internet Protocol addresses of entities it believed were trying to engage in such monitoring on its networks....

[Next, Justice Souter addresses the balance between the values of "supporting creative pursuits through copyright protection and promoting innovation in new communication technologies by limiting the incidence of liability for copyright infringement." He writes: "The more artistic protection is favored, the more technological innovation may be discouraged; the administration of copyright law is an exercise in managing the trade–off." Grokster did not directly infringe on anyone's copyright].

The argument for imposing indirect liability in this case is, however, a powerful one, given the number of infringing downloads that occur every day using StreamCast's and Grokster's software. When a widely shared service or product is used to commit infringement, it may be impossible to enforce rights in the protected work effectively against all direct infringers, the only practical alternative being to go against the distributor of the copying device for secondary liability on a theory of contributory or vicarious infringement....

One infringes contributorily by intentionally inducing or encouraging direct infringement, and infringes vicariously by profiting from direct infringement while declining to exercise a right to stop or limit it. [T]hese doctrines of secondary liability emerged from common law principles and are well established in the law....

Evidence of "active steps...taken to encourage direct infringement," such as advertising an infringing use or instructing how to engage in an infringing use, show an affirmative intent that the product be used to infringe, and a showing that infringement was encouraged overcomes the law's reluctance to find liability when a defendant merely sells a commercial product suitable for some lawful use....

…We adopt [the inducement rule for copyright], holding that one who distributes a device with the object of promoting its use to infringe copyright, as shown by clear expression or other affirmative steps taken to foster infringement, is liable for the resulting acts of infringement by third parties. We are, of course, mindful of the need to keep from trenching on regular commerce or discouraging the development of technologies with lawful and unlawful potential.… [M]ere knowledge of infringing potential or of actual infringing uses would not be enough here to subject a distributor to liability. Nor would ordinary acts incident to product distribution, such as offering customers technical support or product updates, support liability in themselves. The inducement rule, instead, premises liability on purposeful, culpable expression and conduct, and thus does nothing to compromise legitimate commerce or discourage innovation having a lawful promise.

…Three features of this evidence of intent are particularly notable. First, each company showed itself to be aiming to satisfy a known source of demand for copyright infringement, the market comprising former Napster users.…

Second, this evidence of unlawful objective is given added significance by MGM's showing that neither company attempted to develop filtering tools or other mechanisms to diminish the infringing activity using their software.…

Third, … [i]t is useful to recall that StreamCast and Grokster make money by selling advertising space, by directing ads to the screens of computers employing their software. As the record shows, the more the software is used, the more ads are sent out and the greater the advertising revenue becomes. Since the extent of the software's use determines the gain to the distributors, the commercial sense of their enterprise turns on high–volume use, which the record shows is infringing. This evidence alone would not justify an inference of unlawful intent, but viewed in the context of the entire record its import is clear.

The unlawful objective is unmistakable… [Held: Summary judgment for Grokster is reversed and case remanded.].

QUESTIONS

1. What reasons does Souter give for finding Grokster, Streamcast, and Morpheus liable for "inducing" violations of copyright law?

2. What ethical issues surface in the marketing and business strategies of those firms?

3. Two decades before Napster, the movie industry tried to ban a then-novel product called a Betamax video recorder made by Sony. Their claim: every time a VCR was used to tape a copyrighted program shown on TV, the user violated the copyright law. By supplying the means to do so, knowing full well what would happen, Sony was contributing to the infringement. But when the evidence showed that most owners used their VCRs for "time-shifting"—taping a program to watch at a more convenient time—the Court ruled against Sony. There was nothing wrong with time-shifting, the Court found, making VCRs "capable of commercially significant noninfringing uses." Under those circumstances, the manufacturer could not be faulted solely on the basis of its sale and distribution of the product. *Sony Corp. of America v. Universal City Studios, Inc.,* 464 U.S. 417, 104 S.Ct. 774, 78 L.Ed.2d 574 (1984).

    When the Court ruled against Grokster, without overruling the *Sony* precedent, Justice Ginsberg called for a re-writing of *Sony*. Concurring Justice Breyer disagreed:

    … *Sony's* rule, as I interpret it, has provided entrepreneurs with needed assurance that they will be shielded from copyright liability as they bring valuable new technologies to market.

Sony's rule is clear. That clarity allows those who develop new products that are capable of substantial noninfringing uses to know, [beforehand], that distribution of their product will not yield massive monetary liability. At the same time, it helps deter them from distributing products that have no other real function than—or that are specifically intended for—copyright infringement, deterrence that the Court's holding today reinforces (by adding a weapon to the copyright holder's legal arsenal).

Sony's rule is strongly technology protecting. The rule deliberately makes it difficult for courts to find secondary liability where new technology is at issue.... *Sony* thereby recognizes that the copyright laws are not intended to discourage or to control the emergence of new technologies, including (perhaps especially) those that help disseminate information and ideas more broadly or more efficiently. Thus *Sony*'s rule shelters VCRs, typewriters, tape recorders, photocopiers, computers, cassette players, compact disc burners, digital video recorders, MP3 players, Internet search engines, and peer–to–peer software...[but not] descramblers....

Sony's rule is forward looking. It does not confine its scope to a static snapshot of a product's current uses (thereby threatening technologies that have undeveloped future markets). Rather, as the VCR example makes clear, a product's market can evolve dramatically over time....

a. How does peer-to-peer software differ from a VCR? Do those technological differences seem ethically significant to you? The differences in use?

b. Do you agree with where Justice Breyer has drawn the line here? Why or why not?

4. According to the Business Software Alliance (BSA), globally, 35 percent of the software loaded on personal computers in 2007 was unlicensed. To counter one of the biggest sources of the problem, BSA raised the bounty it offers to those who identify employees who pirate software in the workplace to $1 million in July 2007. Is there an ethical distinction between illegally downloaded music and unlicensed software?

Online Piracy or Culture Jamming?

> *The enigma is this: If our property can be infinitely reproduced and instantaneously distributed all over the planet without cost, without our knowledge, without its even leaving our possession, how can we protect it? How are we going to get paid for the work we do with our minds? And, if we can't get paid, what will assure the continued creation and distribution of such work?*
>
> — JOHN PERRY BARLOW[3]

As the practice of music file sharing evolved, so too did efforts to stop it—using technology, the law, and the market. The major technology players joined together in various ways to improve what is known as "digital rights management," systems for building copy-protection into CDs and DVDs and for providing secure and compensated methods for lawful digital sharing. Sony, Apple, and Realnetworks created Apple iTunes to compete with Microsoft's "Windows Media Rights." Intel and Nokia joined a global consortium to create "Project

---

3 John Perry Barlow, "The Economy of Ideas: A Framework for Patents and Copyrights in the Digital Age," http://www.wired.com/wired/archive/2.03/economy.ideas.html.

Hudson," enabling handheld devices to be used to share movies or music files on a limited basis. All had the same goal: to find a technological solution that would limit what they called "online piracy."

In a wave of lawsuits, RIAA joined with the music industry to sue individual users. Unable to identify them initially, they sent "John Doe" subpoenas to the major Internet service providers—AOL, Verizon, and so on—to learn the names of those who were downloading music. Privacy advocates and cybertarians were alarmed, but the suits had an impact: They alerted parents and school administrators to the practice and within six months, reportedly, the number of people swapping files online dropped by half.

Some critics, like the experimental music and art collective known as Negativland, argued that the problem is not infringement on rights, but rather the current structure of a music industry controlled by a handful of transnational corporations, and the increasingly rigid legal regime of copyright.[4]

Unwilling to simply forego profits, the content providers looked to the market as well. By late 2001, the five multinational companies that dominated the recording industry had introduced their own online (paid) music services. Today, Ruckus Network allows college students to download songs for free, with restrictions. Supported by ads on its Web site and on the software used to download music, Ruckus persuaded music labels to license their music at reduced royalty fees. In 2007, a new, bottom-up, cooperative record label was created by 1980's rock star Robin Gibb of BeeGees fame and David Ferguson, who heads the British Academy of Composers and Authors, the organization that collects royalty fees on behalf of musicians. Their Academy Recordings struck a deal with Apple's iTunes and an ad-supported British music download service, We7, backed by rock artist Peter Gabriel.

Yet, we might ask, should we be rethinking the norms and values that underly our definition of intellectual property? Perhaps Negativland's view of the world as "a freely usable public domain" is more consistent with the way culture is created? Or, perhaps there is a more complex way to view intellectual property, as suggested in the next reading by political scientist and feminist scholar Deborah Halbert. Halbert seeks to "make visible the underlying masculine assumption existing in our construction of intellectual property" and to highlight the ways intellectual property has historically benefited men more than women.

FEMINIST INTERPRETATIONS OF INTELLECTUAL PROPERTY

DEBORA HALBERT[5]

...Two examples help highlight the values associated with women's creative work and can lead to an alternative view of the way intellectual property may look from a gendered perspective. The first example highlights the difference between craft and industrialized knowledge and illustrates the differences in knowledge construction. Knitting has long been considered a craft enterprise associated with women's work. Virtually all knitters are women. There is a long history of sharing patterns among knitters, knitting is often communicated from parent or grandparent to child, and knitting circles were a popular method of doing productive labor while enjoying the company of other women. Within the past few years, knitters have noticed changes in the world of knitting. Where once patterns were published in easy-to-share formats with little concern

---

4 Negativland, "Two Relationships to a Cultural Public Domain," 66 *Law & Contemp. Probs. 239* (2003). This article is also available at http://law.duke.edu/journals/66LCPNegativland.

5 14 Am. U.J. *Gender Soc. Pol'y & L.* 431 (2006).

for copyright, today's knitting patterns come with strict prohibitions regarding sharing, copying, and producing knitted material for commercial purposes.

In other words, copyright has entered the world of knitting patterns, a world assumed by many involved as a communal source of knowledge to share. Patterns have been appropriated into the larger industrialized process of publishing for profit....

While the knitting circles and community remain primarily female (public and shared), the ownership of knowledge about patterns has been appropriated into the dominant mode of production—it has been privatized. Patterns are sold, not to further the culture of knitting, but to maximize profit....

It is important to note that women (who need not be feminists) may operate in either paradigm and that many of those constructing these copyrighted patterns are women. Feminists, however, would argue that the women's way of knowing, illustrated by the tradition of knitting, should be used as the source for articulating and understanding a different method of constructing knowledge—one not contingent upon the abstract individual and original author, but one centered in relationships of care. After all, the pattern is only part of the creative process. The individual who does the knitting makes changes to the design, picks the colors of the yarn, and invests her unique motivation into the knitting process. The creative act of knitting transcends the pattern; yet, as copyright invades and colonizes this space, its users attempt to appropriate for themselves the claim to original creativity and seek to control the activity well beyond the construction of a pattern.

Quilting provides a second example of "intellectual property" that developed outside the productive world of abstract authorship and within the framework of a network of sharing and care.... Quilts are increasingly read as women's history because the knowledge sewed into their patterns not only tells stories of the women who made them, but transformations in quilting also mark changes in the status of women over time.

... In the nineteenth century, quilt-making was just one example of women's work considered essential to the household, serving very functional purposes. Quilts were not assigned the status of "original" given that the primary purpose of quilting was functional, therefore they could not earn copyright protection. As the position of women within the household changed during the nineteenth century, so did the focus on sewing and quilting. Even as most productive jobs were moving outside the household, the "cult of domesticity" prescribed sewing as an essential aspect of women's work.... [and] the essence of the "feminine."...

Instead of simply providing functional blankets, women now also quilted more intricate patterns and designs. These designs were taken from popular magazines and defined as works of "leisure" for women. Women who quilted became status symbols for their husbands because they had the time to spend on quilting instead of working.... Unlike early utilitarian quilt production, these more artistic quilts could be bought as kits, but there is no evidence they were treated as works of authorship in the same sense as literary works of the same period....

Unlike the notion of the romantic author that had emerged to assert ownership of the written text, the culture of quilting remained collective and integrated into the everyday lives of women. Women came together and developed friendships over quilts. Multiple women would work on a single quilt, thus confounding our modern understanding of authorship.... Certainly, the creative work of a quilt is similar to that of any other form of authorship. The designs reflect originality, and the sophisticated use of color to create the intended effect is an artistic talent. However, their creation as collective projects, as gifts, and always with the intent of care, suggests another model for authorship.

Quilts often include stories sewn into their squares, they utilize important knowledge of textiles and appliqué techniques, and they have served important political and cultural functions.... Additionally, because quilts were historically created within the culture of feminine sharing, issues of authorship were not associated with the abstract notion of author protected by copyright. Certainly, women took great pride in the creation of these quilts, but these quilts existed within a different paradigm of ownership—one that attempted to solidify connections between people, not divide people by property boundaries.

Both quilting and knitting, primarily women's ways of creating, have existed outside copyright law and developed as collective enterprises, perhaps because the romantic author and the desire for profit were not central to the process of creation....

...Once one stops privileging the abstract and rational and seeks out the relational in cultural creation and innovation, it is clear that a paradigm of intellectual property that creates rigid boundaries to sharing stands in the way of a relational approach to knowledge creation, one in which care and the work of the heart can play a role. A feminist critique from this perspective is a quite radical critique of the boundaries established by intellectual property law, which typically are boundaries that seek only to divide and control instead of facilitate exchange....

QUESTIONS

1. According to Halbert, why are quilting and knitting traditionally outside the realm of copyright protection? How and why is that changing? Why don't crafts like these fit inside the copyright paradigm?

2. What values underlie authorship in the traditional literary context? In crafts like knitting and quilting?

3. Is there a clear divide between crafts, which produce useful objects and are often created by anonymous collective effort, and "fine art and literature," which tend to be without practical usefulness and are created by known individual efforts? Can you think of examples that cross over? Does copyright protection make sense for such kinds of creativity?

4. Identify the various stakeholders in the online music-swapping controversy created by Napster and its progeny. How ethical are these services from a free market perspective? A utilitarian or deontological one? What would a feminist interpretation bring to the table?

Traditional Copyright Law

In vain we call old notions fudge,
And bend our conscience to our dealing;
The Ten Commandments will not budge,
And stealing will continue stealing.

— MOTTO OF THE AMERICAN COPYRIGHT LEAGUE, 1885

Our first federal copyright law gave exclusive rights to the authors of maps, charts, and books for 14 years. During the term of copyright—now extended to 70 years beyond the author's life—the copyright holder controls the right to reproduce and distribute her work. Under today's law, ideas that are "fixed in a tangible medium of expression"—such as photographs, paintings, music, movies, and computer programs—can be copyrighted, and their authors generally gain rights lasting 70 years beyond the author's life. The right attaches when the author first makes her work public, signing, dating, and using the © symbol to claim ownership. Registration with the Federal Copyright Office, necessary to sue to enforce copyright, is relatively easy; all that is required is a registration form, a fee, and a copy (or copies) of the material.

To establish **copyright infringement,** a plaintiff must prove ownership by showing that the work as a whole is original and that she has complied with statutory formalities and that the defendant copied the plaintiff's work. To do this, the owner must establish that the alleged infringer had access to the copyrighted work and that the offending and copyrighted works are so similar that the court may infer there was actual copying. The plaintiff must then prove that the copying was so extensive that it rendered the offending and copyrighted works substantially similar.

U.S. Copyright Law Highlights

1790: First U.S. copyright law; protection available only for "maps, charts and books,"—not music—for a 14-year term.

1831: Copyright Act amended to expand protection to musical compositions.

1909: Compulsory licensing scheme and a royalty rate created for "phonorecords."

1912: Copyright Act amended to expand protection to motion pictures.

1914: American Society for Composers and Publishers (ASCAP) formed.

1971: Copyright Act amended to extend limited protection to recordings.

1976: Major revision to U.S. copyright law; protection extended to all creations "fixed in tangible medium of expression"—including radio and television.

1984: Sony v. Betamax; Supreme Court rules that use of VCRs by home viewers to "time-shift" television shows is a "fair use" that does not violate copyright law.

1994: United States signs international treaty, Trade-Related Aspects of Intellectual Property (TRIPS); Congress creates penalties for bootlegging audio recordings of live performances and music videos.

1995: Digital Rights in Sound Recordings Act gives exclusive rights to holders of sound recordings to public play of digital versions.

1998: Digital Millennium Copyright Act (DMCA) bans technologies that circumvent anti-piracy measures or otherwise facilitate infringement.

1998: Sonny Bono Copyright Term Extension Act (CTEA) extends the period protecting all copyrights 20 years to author's life plus 70 years; and to 95 years for "works for hire" where copyright is held by a corporation.

Fair Use

In truth, in literature, in science and in art, there are, and can be, few, if any, things, which, in an abstract sense, are strictly new and original throughout. Every book in literature, science and art, borrows, and must necessarily borrow, and use much which was well known and used before. No man creates a new language for himself, at least if he be a wise man, in writing a book. He contents himself with the use of language already known and used and understood by others. No man writes exclusively from his own thoughts, unaided and uninstructed by the thoughts of others. The thoughts of every man are, more or less, a combination of what other men have thought and expressed, although they may be modified, exalted, or improved by his own genius or reflection.... Virgil borrowed much from Homer; Bacon drew from earlier as well as contemporary minds; Coke exhausted all the known learning of his profession; and even Shakespeare and Milton, so justly and proudly our boast as the brightest originals would be found to have gathered much from the abundant stores of current knowledge and classical studies in their days.

— JUSTICE STORY, EMERSON V. DAVIES[6]

In a lawsuit for copyright infringement, a defendant can avoid liability by successfully arguing **fair use**. This defense to copyright claims is based on the notion that the free flow of ideas at times requires quoting or otherwise borrowing from a copyrighted work. This can happen, for example, when critics review books, when news reporters use video clips, or when teachers make copies of articles for classroom use.[7]

＊＊＊＊＊

Panorama Records makes and sells karaoke CDs of top hits, in packets (refered to as CD +G) that contain a "graphic element," text of the lyrics that scroll across the screen as the music (without vocals) plays. Zomba Enterprises, a music publishing company, holds the copyrights to songs performed by 98 Degrees, Backstreet Boys, *NSYNC, and Britney Spears, among others. When Zomba discovered that Panorama's karaoke packages included copies of music it owned, it sent a cease-and-desist letter, offering a license to use the music on specified terms. Instead of responding, Panorama kept selling its CDs, and Zomba sued. Panorama defended itself by claiming "fair use."

ZOMBA ENTERPRISES, INC. v. PANORAMA RECORDS, INC

United States Court of Appeals, Sixth Circuit, 2007
491 F.3d 574

Karen Nelson Moore, Circuit Judge. ☀

From Japan to the United States and beyond, karaoke is wildly popular. Countless people have lined up at various venues to perform their favorite songs with, and in front of, their friends. But few participants (with the possible exception of IP lawyers) ever stop to consider the intellectual property regime governing karaoke.

Panorama Records, Inc. ("Panorama"), a purveyor of karaoke discs, resembles the majority of these participants. It entered the business of recording and selling karaoke discs without considering whether doing so infringed the intellectual property rights of others. Before long, this lack of foresight caught up with Panorama.

The elements of a copyright-infringement claim are (1) ownership of the copyright by the plaintiff and (2) copying by the defendant. Panorama disputes neither element. Instead, it claims that the fair-use doctrine affirmative defense precludes liability.

...The purpose of the fair-use doctrine is to ensure that courts "avoid rigid application of the copyright statute when, on occasion, it would stifle the very creativity which that law is designed to foster.... Accordingly, § 107 of the Copyright Act provides that

---

6　8 F.Cas. 615 (Cir.Ct., D. Mass., 1845) (Justice Story).

7　"The fair use of a copyrighted work...for purposes such as criticism, comment, news reporting, teaching (including multiple copies for classroom use), scholarship, or research, is not an infringement of copyright." 17 U.S.C. Sect. 107.

"the fair use of a copyrighted work…for purposes such as criticism, comment, news reporting, teaching (including multiple copies for classroom use), scholarship, or research, is not an infringement of copyright." It further instructs district courts to consider the following factors in analyzing a claim of fair use:

1. the purpose and character of the use, including whether such use is of a commercial nature or is for nonprofit educational purposes;

2. the nature of the copyrighted work;

3. the amount and substantiality of the portion used in relation to the copyrighted work as a whole; and

4. the effect of the use upon the potential market for or value of the copyrighted work.

a. Purpose and Character of the Use

In evaluating the purpose and character of the use of the work at issue, we consider whether the new work is "transformative," and whether the use of that work is for commercial or noncommercial purposes. The central purpose of this investigation [into purpose and character of use] is to see…whether the new work merely "supersede[s] the objects" of the original creation, or instead adds something new, with a further purpose or different character, altering the first with new expression, meaning, or message; it asks, in other words, whether and to what extent the new work is "transformative."…

As an initial matter, Panorama's use of the compositions is only minimally, if at all, transformative. Although Panorama created its own recordings of these songs, the hired musicians did not "change the words or music."… Unlike a parody, a facsimile recording of a copyrighted composition adds nothing new to the original and accordingly has virtually no transformative value.…

The crux of Panorama's fair-use argument is its assertion that its use was transformative because its karaoke packages are used for "teaching."… [But] Panorama's own description of karaoke…undermines its assertion regarding "teaching": "Karaoke is primarily thought of as a form of *entertainment* that allows anyone to grab a microphone, hop on stage, and live out their fantasies of performing as famous music stars."… Moreover, the record is bereft of evidence indicating that Panorama's products are used for teaching *at all* (e.g., invoices showing sales to schools, advertisements aimed at educators, affidavits from teachers, etc.).

More importantly though, the end-user's utilization of the product is largely irrelevant; instead, the focus is on whether alleged infringer's use is transformative and/or commercial. In *Princeton University Press*, we considered a copyright suit against a college-town copy shop that copied portions of books and then sold [them]…to students in "coursepacks." We rejected the copy shop's fair-use defense, concluding that the defendant's copying was a commercial use, even though the students ultimately used the copies for educational purposes. To reach this conclusion, we emphasized that "the use of the materials by the students is not the use that the publishers are challenging." Instead, the publishers were challenging "the duplication of copyrighted materials for sale by a for-profit corporation that has decided to maximize its profits…by declining to pay the royalties requested by the holders of the copyrights."

Quite similarly, Zomba does not challenge karaoke crooners' renditions (atrocious or otherwise) of the relevant compositions, but rather Panorama's decision to copy these songs onto CD+Gs and then distribute them without paying royalties. Like the copying at issue in *Princeton University Press*, Panorama's manufacturing and selling the karaoke packages at issue "was performed on a profit-making basis by a commercial enterprise." Accordingly, Panorama's use is commercial in nature, a fact militating against its fair-use defense.

b. The Nature of the Copyrighted Work

The second [factor]…calls for recognition that some works are closer to the core of intended copyright protection than others," and accordingly are entitled to stronger protection. Like the musical composition in *Campbell* (Roy Orbison's "Oh, Pretty Woman"), the compositions of pop songs here at issue "fall within the core of the copyright's protective purposes." Accordingly, this factor militates against a finding of fair use.

c. The Amount and Substantiality of the Portion Used

As the *Princeton University Press* court recognized, "the larger the volume … of what is taken, the greater the affront to the interests of the copyright owner, and the less likely that a taking will qualify as a fair use." Here, Panorama acknowledges that it copied the entire compositions. It hired studio musicians to play the songs as closely as possible to the original performers, and distributed copies of their efforts. Additionally, it copied the lyrics, in both an auditory (on the tracks containing vocals) and a visual (on the graphics display) fashion. Because Panorama copied the relevant compositions in their entirety, this factor, too, cuts against Panorama's fair-use defense.

d. Effect on the Potential Market for the Copyrighted Work

Finally, we consider the effect on the potential market for licensing of the relevant musical compositions. Regarding the allocation of proof for this factor, we have held that when the copying at issue is commercial in nature, the alleged infringer bears the burden of proving the "market effect" factor. Here, Panorama has failed to sustain its burden of proving that its copying does not adversely affect the market value of Zomba's copyrights.

…[T]he record illustrates that Zomba has previously licensed (and continues to license) its musical compositions to purveyors of karaoke products. It follows, then, that market harm is a given, as Panorama's unlicensed copying deprived Zomba of licensing revenues it otherwise would have received. Further, there can be no doubt that Panorama's practices, if they became widespread throughout the karaoke industry, would have a deleterious effect on the potential market for licenses to Zomba's songs. Accordingly, Panorama cannot show that its copying passes the market-harm test, and this factor, like the other three, militates in favor of rejecting its fair-use defense.

Because all four fair-use factors indicate that Panorama's copying was not a fair use, we conclude that the district court correctly rejected this defense and concluded that Panorama infringed Zomba's copyrights.

QUESTIONS

1. Why does Panorama lose this case? Does the outcome seem fair to you?

2. Using the factors of analysis from the *Zomba* case, determine which of the following would be a fair use of copyrighted material:

   a. A seventh-grade teacher clips an article from the morning newspaper and makes copies for her class to discuss.

   b. A college professor collects chapters from various books and brings them to the local copy center to have them made into a "Class Anthology." She reuses the same anthology for three years.

   c. Same as above, but instead of going to the local copy center, the professor scans the articles and posts them on the course Web site.

   d. A student selects several essays from an online magazine to include in a 50-page term paper, with no mention of their authors.

   e. Same as above, but the student properly attributes each essay to its rightful author.

    f. A literary critic quotes from six short stories in a scathing review of a popular author's newest collection.

    g. A painter, inspired by the poetry of a Pulitzer-prize winning poet, shows his work in a gallery installation in which he posts a different poem next to each of his two dozen paintings; the gallery publishes a guide to the show that includes the text of the poems and photos of the paintings. Neither had permission of the poet.

    h. Same as before, except that it is a student visiting an art gallery for the first time who decides to publish online his own "guide to the show."

3. A parody—a literary or artistic work that imitates the characteristic style of an author or a work for comic effort or ridicule—is a classic example of a fair use. Parodies are considered "transformative" because they provide social benefit, shedding light on an earlier work while creating a new one. By definition, there must be some connection between the original work and the parody that borrows from it:

> [T]he heart of any parodist's claim to quote from existing material is the use of some elements of a prior author's composition to create a new one that, at least in part, comments on that author's works [Campbell v. Acuff-Rose Music, Inc. 510 U.S. 569 (1994)]

Which of the following should qualify as fair use parodies?

    a. Artist Mark Napler created a "Barbie" Web site, using digital images and text that commented on Barbie as a cultural icon. In an interactive section, visitors could share what Barbie meant to them as they were growing up. There was also an "Alternative Barbies" section, a behind-the-scenes look at the seamy underbelly of Barbie's world, including digitally altered "Fat and Ugly Barbie" and "Mentally Challenged Barbie." Mattel, Inc., maker of Barbie and owner of the trademark, threatened to sue Napler.

    b. From his fake news desk on Comedy Central's *The Daily Show,* Jon Stewart used a six-second excerpt from Sandra Kane's public access TV show to mock public access television, and commented on videotaped clips from network news reports.

4. An Internet user who types "naked female body" into the Google Image search engine will see thumbnail images of photo files posted on other Web sites, including the pornographic "Perfect 10" Web site. While these small images reside on Google's servers, clicking on them directs the user to the full-size image, and a frame of the original Web site appears on the Google screen.

    a. What argument does Perfect 10 have against Google? How might Google defend itself?

    b. **Internet Assignment** Find out how the Ninth Circuit ruled in the actual case.

Digital Millennium Copyright Act

> *"[F]or all I know, the monks had a fit when Gutenberg made his press."*

— JUSTICE STEPHEN BREYER, ORAL ARGUMENT IN METRO-GOLDWYN-MAYER STUDIOS, INC. V. GROKSTER, LTD. (2005).

Once experts figured out how to digitalize movies, filmmakers found themselves in a quandary. The quality of DVDs is superior to that of videotapes, opening the door to a potentially lucrative market of home viewers. But, just as VCRs make it easy to tape a movie shown on TV, computers make it easy to copy a DVD. As the next case explains, the film industry tried to build digital walls, such as encryption codes and password protections, to prevent piracy.

At the same time, they lobbied Congress for laws to make it easier to police the unlawful distribution of DVDs by combating piracy in its earlier stages, before the work was even copied. The Digital Millennium Copyright Act (DMCA) did just what the industry had hoped for: It targeted both pirates who would circumvent digital walls and anyone who would traffic in a technology primarily designed to circumvent a digital wall.

In the next case, eight motion picture studios invoke their rights under the anti-trafficking provisions of the DMCA to stop Internet Web site owners from posting computer software to decrypt DVD movies or from linking to other Web sites that made decryption software available. The defendant, publisher of a hacker magazine and its affiliated Web site,[8] argues that the DMCA violates the First Amendment.

UNIVERSAL CITY STUDIOS, INC. v. ERIC CORLEY

U.S. Court of Appeals, Second Circuit, 2001
273 F.3d 429

Newman, Circuit Judge. ✳

The improved quality of a movie in a digital format brings with it the risk that a virtually perfect copy … can be readily made at the click of a computer control and instantly distributed to countless recipients throughout the world over the Internet.…

[To minimize the piracy threat, the entertainment industry] enlisted the help of members of the consumer electronics and computer industries who in mid-1996 developed the Content Scramble System ("CSS") … an encryption scheme that employs an algorithm configured by a set of "keys" to encrypt a DVD's contents.… [For a fee, the studios licensed these player keys to DVD-makers, who were obliged to keep them confidential and prevent any transmission from a DVD drive to any "internal recording device" such as a computer hard drive.]

With encryption technology and licensing agreements in hand, the studios began releasing movies on DVDs in 1997, and DVDs quickly gained in popularity, becoming a significant source of studio revenue.…

In September 1999, Jon Johansen, a Norwegian teenager, collaborating with two unidentified individuals he met on the Internet, reverse-engineered a licensed DVD player … and culled from it the player keys and other information necessary to decrypt CSS.… Johansen wrote a decryption program executable on Microsoft's operating system. That program was called, appropriately enough, "DeCSS."

If a user runs the DeCSS program … with a DVD in the computer's disk drive, DeCSS will decrypt the DVD's CSS protection, allowing the user to copy the DVD's files and place the copy on the user's hard drive. The result is a very large computer file that can be played … and copied, manipulated, and transferred just like any other computer file.…

Johansen posted the executable object code, but not the source code, for DeCSS on his web site. Within months … DeCSS was widely available on the Internet, in both object code and various forms of source code.

In November 1999, [Defendant] Corley wrote and placed on his web site, 2600.com, an article about the DeCSS phenomenon. His web site is an auxiliary to the print magazine, *2600: The Hacker Quarterly*, which Corley has been publishing since 1984.… [T]he

---

8 The court describes the hacker community as one that "includes serious computer-science scholars conducting research on protection techniques, computer buffs intrigued by the challenge of trying to circumvent access-limiting devices or perhaps hoping to promote security by exposing flaws in protection techniques, mischief-makers interested in disrupting computer operations, and thieves, including copyright infringers who want to acquire copyrighted material (for personal use or resale) without paying for it."

focus of the publications is on the vulnerability of computer security systems, and more specifically, how to exploit that vulnerability in order to circumvent the security systems. Representative articles explain how to steal an Internet domain name and how to break into the computer systems at Federal Express. . . .

Corley's article about DeCSS detailed how CSS was cracked, and described the movie industry's efforts to shut down web sites posting DeCSS. It also explained that DeCSS could be used to copy DVDs. At the end of the article, [he] posted copies of the [computer] object and source code of DeCSS . . . [because] "in a journalistic world you have to show your evidence" . . . [and] links . . . to other web sites where DeCSS could be found. . . .

[In the next section, the court addresses Corley's defense: that the DMCA violates the First Amendment. First, the court must decide whether DeCSS code is "protected speech":]

Communication does not lose constitutional protection as "speech" simply because it is expressed in the language of computer code. Mathematical formulae and musical scores are written in "code," i.e., symbolic notations not comprehensible to the uninitiated, and yet both are covered by the First Amendment. If someone chose to write a novel entirely in computer object code by using strings of 1's and 0's for each letter of each word, the resulting work would be no different for constitutional purposes than if it had been written in English. . . .

Computer programs are not exempted from the category of First Amendment speech simply because their instructions require use of a computer. A recipe is no less "speech" because it calls for the use of an oven, and a musical score is no less "speech" because it specifies performance on an electric guitar. . . .

Having concluded that computer code conveying information is "speech" within the meaning of the First Amendment, we next consider, to a limited extent, the scope of the protection that code enjoys. . . .

[The court then quotes approvingly from the trial judge's opinion that:]

> Society increasingly depends upon technological means of controlling access to digital files and systems, whether they are military computers, bank records, academic records, copyrighted works or something else entirely. There are far too many who, given any opportunity, will bypass security measures, some for the sheer joy of doing it, some for innocuous reasons, and others for more malevolent purposes. Given the virtually instantaneous and worldwide dissemination widely available via the Internet, the only rational assumption is that once a computer program capable of bypassing such an access control system is disseminated, it will be used. . . .

There was a time when copyright infringement could be dealt with quite adequately by focusing on the infringing act. If someone wished to make and sell high quality but unauthorized copies of a copyrighted book, for example, the infringer needed a printing press. The copyright holder, once aware of the appearance of infringing copies, usually was able to trace the copies up the chain of distribution, find and prosecute the infringer, and shut off the infringement at the source.

In principle, the digital world is very different. Once a decryption program like DeCSS is written, it quickly can be sent all over the world. Every recipient is capable not only of decrypting and perfectly copying plaintiffs' copyrighted DVDs, but also of retransmitting perfect copies of DeCSS and thus enabling every recipient to do the same. They likewise are capable of transmitting perfect copies of the decrypted DVD. The process potentially is exponential rather than linear. . . .

In considering the scope of First Amendment protection for a decryption program like DeCSS, we must recognize that the essential purpose of encryption code is to prevent unauthorized access. Owners of all property rights are entitled to prohibit access to their property by unauthorized persons. Homeowners can install locks on the doors of their houses. Custodians of valuables can place them in safes.... These and similar security devices can be circumvented. Burglars can use skeleton keys to open door locks. Thieves can obtain the combinations to safes....

Our case concerns a security device, CSS computer code, that prevents access by unauthorized persons to DVD movies.... CSS is like a lock on a homeowner's door, a combination of a safe, or a security device attached to a store's products.

DeCSS is computer code that can decrypt CSS. In its basic function, it is like a skeleton key that can open a locked door [or] a combination that can open a safe....

[R]egulation of decryption code like DeCSS is challenged in this case because DeCSS differs from a skeleton key in one important respect: it not only is capable of performing the function of unlocking the encrypted DVD movie, it also is a form of communication.... As a communication, the DeCSS code has a claim to being "speech," and as "speech," it has a claim to being protected by the First Amendment.... [But] the capacity of a decryption program like DeCSS to accomplish unauthorized indeed, unlawful access to [copyrighted] materials ... must inform and limit the scope of its First Amendment protection....

[Held: An injunction against posting DeCSS on the Web or linking to other Web sites that contain DeCSS is warranted. The posting restriction is justified because the government has a substantial interest in preventing unauthorized access to encrypted copyright material, and there is no less restrictive way of preventing instantaneous worldwide distribution of the decryption code. The ban on posting links is needed to regulate the "opportunity instantly to enable anyone anywhere to gain unauthorized access to copyrighted movies on DVDs."]

QUESTIONS

1. What is DeCSS? What was the defendant's legal claim, and why did he lose this case?

2. Is there a difference, ethically, between the copyright infringing activity of a music file-sharing service and those who use it? Between a hacker like Johansen who created DeCSS, Corley who disseminated it, and someone who accesses and uses it to watch a movie? Is it fair that copyright law, for the most part, is enforced against the Groksters and Corleys of the digital world?

3. Under the DMCA, nonprofit educational service providers (e.g., state colleges) are protected when a faculty member or graduate student infringes copyright while teaching or researching if three conditions are met: (i) the activities do not involve providing recommended or instructional materials for a course taught at the institution within the preceding 3-year period; (ii) within that same time, the university received no more than two notifications of claimed infringement by the same person; and (iii) the institution provides all users with information regarding compliance with copyright law. The individual faculty member or graduate student, however, can be found liable.

   a. Why do you think the law does not apply to undergraduate infringement? Should it?

   b. Find out whether, and how, your school informs Internet users of their obligations to comply with copyright law, and evaluate its effectiveness.

4. Are any of the following in violation of the DMCA? (a) 24-year-old Jorge Romero allegedly uploaded the first four episodes of the TV show *24* to the Internet and posted links to the pirated content on other Web sites to make it easier for viewers to find them. (b) YouTVpc.com and Peekvid.com provide users with menus of links to video clips that are stored on other Web sites' computer servers. Many of those video clips are protected by copyright.

5. Viacom made news headlines when it sued YouTube and its owner, Google, for more than $1 billion, claiming YouTube had not done enough to prevent its users from posting

thousands of copyrighted videoclips to its site.

Internet Assignment Find out what has happened with this lawsuit.

6. When a hacker unearthed the string of 32 digits and letters that comprise a new antipiracy code, AACS, from his movie-playing software in February 2007, he posted it on a Web bulletin board. The code spread among tech-savvy users via blogs and technology Web sites. When the code's owner (the Advanced Access Content System Licensing Administrator), sent notices to "cease and desist" posting the code in violation of the DMCA, the hacker community resisted. One 24-year-old musician improvised a melody to accompany his singing of the code and posted his song to YouTube. A Washington engineer created a Web page featuring the code, "obscured in an encrypted format that only insiders could appreciate." Is this, in the words of one news reporter, "a lesson in mob power on the Internet and the futility of censorship in the digital world"?[9]

Joint Copyrights and Collective Rights

American copyright law creates a bundle of rights for the owner, including the right to reproduce, distribute, perform, display, or adapt the work. As with other property, the owner can sell or license some or all of her rights. Unknown authors of new books, for example, may contract to sell their copyright in exchange for royalties paid by a company that publishes the book. Others may agree to give up some, but not all, of their rights.

The copyright statute attempts to divide rights between an individual creator and the publisher of what is called a "collective work." Newspapers, magazines, and this textbook are examples. Angela R. Riley, author of the next reading, retains her copyright interest in the article she wrote, although Cengage Learning holds the copyright in the overall work, *Law and Ethics in the Business Environment*. Movies, too, are collective works to which musicians, screenwriters, cinematographers, and producers all make varied contributions—with the producer holding the collective copyright, and the composer, for example, retaining her copyright to the background music.

But what if the separate individual contributions to a creation are not so easily teased apart? The author of the next reading tells the "story of one indigenous group's search to recover collectivity" through recognition of their rights, as a tribe, to cultural property.

RECOVERING COLLECTIVITY

ANGELA R. RILEY[10]

In 1996 the German rock group, Enigma, spent thirty-two weeks on Billboard Magazine's International Top 100 Chart, turning the new genre of "world-beat" music into a household name. The United States, quick to recognize the mesmerizing quality and marketing potential of the music, selected Enigma's hit single, *Return to Innocence*, as the background theme for television broadcast advertisements of the 1996 Olympic Summer Games. Meanwhile, far in the southern region of the island nation of Taiwan, the Ami people, Taiwan's largest surviving indigenous tribe, mourn the desecration and exploitation of a sacred tribal creation which has its roots in thousands of years of Ami tradition.

---

9 Brad Stone, "Antipiracy Code, Once a Secret, Spreads on Web," *The New York Times*, p. A-1, May 3, 2007.

10 Angela R. Riley, "Recovering Collectivity: Group Rights to Intellectual Property in Indigenous Communities." This article originally appeared in 18 *Cardozo Arts & Ent. L.J.* 175 (2000). Reprinted by permission.

Lifvon Guo, an Ami tribal elder, has spent most of his life as a keeper of Ami traditional folksongs. Lifvon quit school at the age of ten to tend to the animals and the crops. He then committed his captivating voice to the preservation of the ancestral songs of his culture as a tribal singer for almost seventy years…. Because the Ami language has not been transcribed in written form, oral tradition is the only method by which the tribe has transmitted cultural knowledge, religion, stories, and personal narratives for thousands of years. For his continued devotion to the passing down of Ami works, Lifvon is highly renowned within his tribe, but, until recently, he had little contact or familiarity with the world outside his indigenous community. That is, until he received a telephone call from a friend in Taipei, informing him that Taipei radio was broadcasting a song in which Lifvon was singing an Ami chant. Lifvon soon learned that a recording of him singing the Ami *Song of Joy* had been pirated and digitally incorporated into a popular "world beat" tune known as *Return to Innocence*, of which over five million copies were eventually sold worldwide.

With the help of friends, Lifvon struggled to reconstruct the events leading up to the international fame of Enigma, and the Ami "contribution" that had made it possible. The answer lay in a performance invitation made by the Ministries of Culture of Taiwan and France in which Lifvon and his wife, along with about thirty other indigenous singers from Taiwan, were invited to perform their songs in music halls across Europe. For a month they traveled, giving group performances of aboriginal music, which were recorded without their knowledge or consent. The recordings from the concerts were published on compact disc a year later, and eventually fell into the hands of German music mogul Michael Cretu (known in the industry as "Enigma"), who was scouring recordings of "tribal performances" in hopes of finding the perfect piece to integrate into his own music. Cretu was immediately mesmerized with Lifvon's haunting voice, and he purchased the "rights" to the chant from an arm of the French Cultural Ministry. The Ami people never received recognition or payment for the use of the song. In fact, until the phone call, tribal members had no knowledge the appropriation had ever occurred.

Thus, *Return to Innocence* was created, an ethereal song that mixes the Ami aboriginal chant, sung by Lifvon, and modern dance beats to create a new, cutting-edge sound in the record industry, now known as "world beat." *Innocence* appears on Enigma's second album, *Cross of Changes*.

Though the Ami realize a serious injustice has occurred, they also know that current copyright law offers no protection for communally created indigenous works. As a result, the tribe is constrained to observe a piece of its history and culture slip from its grasp. Not only must the Ami confront the futility of challenging the initial infringement, but they are also powerless to determine the fate of the recordings, reap the rewards of their own creation, or control resulting violations of tribal law and blatant distortions of their work….

[This account] is a complicated commentary on the state of indigenous peoples across the globe, their relationship to formal legal systems, and the resulting gap that lingers between the Indian world view and Western law. Indigenous works fail to fulfill individualistic notions of property rights that underlie the structure of Western law, and these works are thus omitted from intellectual property regimes. The focus of current copyright doctrine on rigid individualism devalues and trivializes conceptions of communal property that are deeply embedded in the institutions and norms of indigenous societies. This flagrant dismissal of non-Western viewpoints in the creation, consideration, and interpretation of copyright law keeps indigenous creations unprotected and vulnerable to mass appropriation and exploitation.

This paper contends that only a group rights model of ownership of intangible property will adequately protect the works of indigenous peoples from an ever-encroaching dominant society. The validation of communal property seeks to bring collaborative, inter-generational tribal creations within the scope of copyright protection....

Copyright protection is geared towards the printed word, and societies that transcend this limitation through oral transmission fall entirely outside the sphere of Anglo-American copyright protection.... The very nature of Native artistic expression works that are created inter-generationally, built upon fluid conceptions of revision and creativity, and seldom recorded in a tangible medium (notwithstanding the collective memory of its peoples) precludes copyright protection. The result is an entire body of artistic and literary expression that is being generated by groups already surviving on the very margins of society, prevented from enjoying freedom from infringement, appropriation, and callous distortion.

The Ami's *Song of Joy* must satisfy the Copyright Act's three essential requirements in order to earn protection as a musical composition under the Act. The work must demonstrate originality, production by a clearly defined "author," and must be expressed through a "fixed" and "tangible medium."

Though it is clearly established that to be original, a work need only demonstrate a *de minimis* quantum of creativity, *Song of Joy* nevertheless falls short of the applicable standard. The work simply cannot be said to be "independently created by the author." Placing the question of authorship aside, even if Lifvon created *Song of Joy,* he indisputably did not create it independently. The very essence of the song's communal nature defies the notion of "originality."

The Romantic-inspired conception of "originality" is in strict opposition to indigenous notions of creation. The current law, "with its emphasis on rewarding and safeguarding 'originality,' has lost sight of the cultural value of what might be called 'serial collaborations' works such as those resulting from successive elaborations of an idea or text by a series of creative workers, occurring perhaps over years or decades." For the Ami, ascertaining the creation instance is virtually impossible. The song might have existed for as long as the Ami peoples themselves. Lifvon's purpose is to carry the song to future generations of Ami members, thus conveying its significance and import to those who came after him, just as he learned it from the Ami tribal singers who came before him. Knowledge transmission in indigenous communities, a heritage involving centuries of maintaining culturally revered stories in song, implies that even the most basic elements of copyright law remain unfulfilled.

[I]n the seventy years in which Lifvon has been singing, his esteemed role in the Ami community has been defined not only by his inspiring voice, but by his ability to modify the chants, guaranteeing their endurance through time....

Storytelling to Native peoples is about more than entertainment, or even education. It is a vital and necessary component of continued life, the life of the tribe and the life of the world itself. Creation stories are told ritually to ensure the continued existence of the world.... Storytelling in the Indian world occurs through songs, chants, narratives, and ceremonies which are kept sacred in the community, but which are not compelled to remain unchanged. Variation on the storytelling by the storyteller is the work of imagination, not contradiction.

In an indigenous society, concepts of creativity and originality rely on notions of fluidity not seen in the Western world. By its very nature, oral tradition is a passing down, a handing off, of creative expression. A work can be reborn and recreated each time it is sung; it takes on the needs of the tribe, defined and redefined by its keepers and by the purposes for which it is called upon. Without recognition of group rights to communal property, it is virtually impossible to frame indigenous works in the monolithic scheme of current copyright law....

Because only an "author" is entitled to copyright protection, the meaning of the term is of great importance.... [T]he Romantic archetype has lent to copyright doctrine a conception of the author as lone genius, whose work breaks from tradition and does not receive increased importance or validity through connections to prior creations....

The resulting definition of authorship exists in direct opposition to the communal methods of creativity symbolizing the structure of Native communities, which place the origins of tribal works in the group, not the individual....

Designating a clearly identified "author" [essential for copyright protection] in the case of *Song of Joy*, as with most indigenous creations, is inconceivable....

The most likely scenario is that there never existed a clearly delineated "author" or "authors" of the song. In indigenous societies, many members believe that ceremonies, music, and stories are communicated to the tribe by the Creator.... Thus, in whatever manner the inspiration for *Song of Joy* was conceived, known methods of transmission among indigenous peoples indicates that the song does "belong" and has always "belonged" to the tribe as a whole....

[T]he sanctity of the work itself derives, in part, from the import placed on the collective creation of the piece. The group product in the indigenous society is the medium through which all tribal members, living, dead and unborn, speak their voice and become a part of the tribal way....

Denying copyright protection to works not "fixed in a tangible medium" results in the devastating exclusion of an entire realm of indigenous creations, as the use of oral tradition spans almost every Native community in existence....

[Riley recommends legal protection that embraces a "group-rights model" of copyright law that would protect collaborative inter-generational tribal creations.]

To fully embrace the group rights model, implicit in which there is a profoundly non-Western conception of ownership, there must exist a common belief among group members that they are "normatively bound to each other such that each does not act simply for herself or himself but each plays her or his part in effectuating [a] shared normative understanding." For many Native peoples, tribal affiliation is precisely this sort of commitment.... For individuals within these distinct groups, flourishing in the world as a person is intimately related to cultural identity.

Identity in the indigenous world is inextricably linked to community structure. But identity for tribal peoples reaches further, to form a forceful nexus between the group and its cultural property. For a tribe, the authority to control that property is essential for group survival, as it links its very existence to collective creations. Cultural property situates indigenous people in a historical context, tying them to the place from which they came and the point of their creation. Tribal members become linked to the goods of the tribe: turtle rattles, trickster narratives, religious bundles often resulting in a commitment to the objects outside of themselves; this commitment is the Native peoples' definition of what life is about.

For a tribe, determining the destiny of collective property, particularly that which is sacred and intended solely for use and practice within the collective, is a crucial element of self-determination. The legal enforcement of a group model of invention and ownership would support self-determination principles, not only by protecting indigenous works from theft and exploitation, but by placing the sanctity of tribal cultural property back into the hands of indigenous peoples, affirming their ability to determine themselves as a people through their culture. When a group has exclusive authority to prescribe the employment of its most valuable creations, the entire community flourishes and benefits. Most importantly, the group-rights model of ownership takes into account the Indian world view by providing a foundation for "intergenerational justice." Preserving the divine nature of cultural works and sheltering them from the market demonstrates Indian respect for those who have walked on, and sets the work aside for use and honor by future generations.

QUESTIONS

1. What are the three elements that make a work eligible for copyright? How does the Ami *Song of Joy* fail each?

2. How would Riley modify the law of copyright? Why?

3. Think back to the ethical frameworks in Chapter 1. Which of these support the legal protection of tribal cultural property? Explain.

4. Suppose that, instead of a single payment to Lifvon for one song, you wanted to set up a system to fairly compensate indigenous people whenever their culture became the basis for a new work of art. What might that system look like? Who should control it?

5. Riley argues that the infringement of collective rights is only the first violation against Native peoples:

> Beyond appropriation lies the distortion and misrepresentation of tribal creations as they are freely picked up by non-Natives and openly exploited for capital gain, playing into Westerners' fetish-ism with Native works, but without recognition or compensation going to the Native communities.

Compare the distortion that occurs in "borrowing" indigenous work to other kinds of borrowing, such as music sampling or the creation of jigsaw puzzles and mouse pads out of reproductions of well-known paintings.

6. How might Debora Halbert, author of the reading on the *Feminist Interpretations of Intellectual Property*, respond to this reading?

Public Domain

While Riley looks to create protection for "group" rights, some argue we should be moving in the opposite direction, reducing private control of culture and preserving more for our common, public use. Material that is always freely usable by anyone, without permission, is said to be "in the public domain." Free-floating "ideas"—as opposed to expressions that have been "fixed"—and government writings, such as judicial opinions, are available to anyone. Too, when copyrights expire, protected works are said to return to the **public domain**.

Lawrence Lessig, author of the next reading, is concerned about the diminishing public domain. After telling two stories, he goes on to explain that we have experienced a "technological inversion," such that the old values embedded in our copyright laws no longer make sense.

THE CREATIVE COMMONS

LAWRENCE LESSIG[11]

Everyone has heard of the Brothers Grimm. They wrote fairy tales. If you are like I was, you probably think that they wrote wonderful and happy fairy tales—the sort of stories children ought to be raised on. That's a mistake. The Grimm fairy tales are, as the name suggests, quite grim: awful, bloody, moralistic stories that should be kept far from

---

11 "The Creative Commons" by Lawrence Lessig from *Florida Law Review*, Vol. 55, 2003, p. 763. Reprinted by permission of Florida Law Review.

any healthy childhood. Yet you are likely to believe that these stories are wonderful and happy, because they have been retold to us by an amazing creator called Disney.

Walt Disney took these stories and retold them in just the way our founders imagined that our culture would grow. He took the stories, and retold them in a way that would speak to his time. And most important for my purposes here, he could retell them because these stories lived in the public domain. Their copyright protections had lapsed. And they had lapsed because copyrights, in America at least, are for a "limited time" only. That limitation in turn builds a kind of creative commons: a resource from which anyone can draw and add and build upon because the Constitution guarantees the law's protection will end.

We can think of this "creative commons," this public domain from which others may draw, as a lawyer-free zone. No one can control what you do with material there, meaning you need never speak to a lawyer to draw material from there. The public domain is thus a resource that requires the permission of no one. And it is a resource that creators throughout history have drawn upon freely.

[But under today's law, with copyright extending 70 years beyond the life of an author, or 100 years if owned by a company as a "work for hire"] … no one can do to the Disney Corporation what Disney did to the Brothers Grimm. …

[Lessig tells another story, this one about AIBO, a robot dog created by Sony that sells for roughly $1,300.]

… As with any dog, ownership gives you the right to take the dog home and teach it how to behave—at least within limits.

One fan of the AIBO dog learned something about these limits. He took his Sony AIBO dog apart to understand how it worked. He tinkered with the dog. And after tinkering with the dog, he figured out how the code instructed the dog to operate, and he wanted his dog to operate in a somewhat different way. He wanted to teach his dog to dance jazz. On his website, aibopet.com, this fan of the AIBO taught others how to tinker with their pet. And one particular bit of tinkering would enable the AIBO dog to dance jazz. …

[W]hen the owner of aibopet.com posted this little hack on his website, he got a letter from the Sony Corporation: "Your site contains information providing the means to circumvent AIBO ware's copy protection protocol constituting a violation of the anti-circumvention provisions of a law called the Digital Millennium Copyright Act." …

[To understand these stories, Lessig writes, we need to look at the technological inversion that has occurred in the United States:]

… [The original values of our copyright law] protected the public domain. They enabled a vibrant cultural commons. Yet changing technology and changing law is increasingly enclosing that commons. Tools built into the architecture of cyberspace are defeating a tradition of balanced freedom that defined our past. Yet the law has not yet recognized this inversion. …

The Framers granted authors a very limited set of rights. … Our outrage at China notwithstanding, we should not forget that until 1891, American copyright law did not protect foreign copyrights. We were born a pirate nation.

In the first ten years of this copyright regime, there were some 13,000 titles that were published. Yet there were less than 1,000 copyright registrations. The aim of the original copyright regulation was to control publishers. In 1790, there were 127 publishers. This law was a tiny regulation of a tiny part of early American culture.

Most culture thus remained free of any copyright regulation. You could take a book and write an abridgement … translate the book … turn it into a play … physically write out every word in that book and give it to your friends without any regulation of copyright law. The culture was free in a sense that is increasingly being demanded in debates about culture today: there was a freedom to Disnify culture, as Disney did to the Brothers Grimm … and a freedom to tinker with the content that one finds without fear of committing a federal crime, as the fans of the AIBO wanted.

We could say, following a recent Apple ad campaign, that in our past, there was a freedom to "Rip, Mix, and Burn" culture. Regulation protected against unfair competition, but that regulation left people to develop their culture as they wished.

That past has now changed. It first changed because the law has changed. [Today, the law protects] essentially any creative work reduced to a tangible form … [and does so] automatically.

More important than these changes in law are the changes effected by technology. Think about the life of a book.… The publisher can't control what I do with a printed book because there is no way to control pages separated from the publisher. And not only can they not control what I do physically with the book, the law, copyright law, affirmatively limits the ability of the publisher to do anything to the book, once the book is sold.

But compare then a book in cyberspace. I have … in my Adobe eBook Reader … *Middlemarch*—a work that is in the public domain. Even though this uncopyrighted book is in some senses free, it's not free in the Adobe eBook Reader.… [Limited p]ermission is granted to me to read this book aloud … I may copy ten text sections into the computer's clipboard memory every ten days … [and] print ten pages everyday using my computer. And here is the most embarrassing example: my most recent book, *The Future of Ideas*. My publisher released it stating I'm not allowed to copy any text sections into the memory, I'm not allowed to print any pages, and don't try to use your computer to read my book aloud, it's an offense of copyright law. Freedoms I would have with a real book get erased when this book is made virtual.

Now what makes these protections possible? In part what makes it possible is just the code built into the Adobe eBook Reader. The technology gives the publisher a control over an eBook that no publisher could ever have had over a regular book. And because of this control, the *use* of an eBook is regulated … [instead of] the publishing of copyrighted material.…

These controls increasingly mean that the ability to take what defines our culture and include it in an expression about our culture is permitted only with a license from the content owner. Free culture is thus transformed into licensed culture. The freedom to remake and retell our culture thus increasingly depends upon the permission of someone else. The freedom to Disnify is undermined. The freedom to counter-tell stories is weakened. The freedom to tinker, especially for the technologist to tinker, is threatened.

QUESTIONS

1. If you had the power to rewrite the law of copyright, would you want to? If so, give it a try. It may be more productive to work with a classmate or two. If not, write a critique of the revisions proposed by one or more of your classmates.
   Internet Assignment Find out what the recording industry and RIAA attorney Hilary Rosen thinks of the creative commons license.

2. **Internet Assignment** Find out what you can about Lessig. What background does he bring to the debate about expanding or limiting IP rights? Who are his supporters? Detractors? What has he written or spoken about since 2003 when this article was published?

3. Is a Creative Commons license really "the middle ground" sought by all sides? In 2004, *Wired* magazine distributed some 750,000 free copies of a compilation CD featuring the Beastie Boys, David Byrne and others, entitled "The Wired CD: Rip. Sample. Mash. Share," with permission of the artists, as an experimental implementation of the Creative Commons license. What are the benefits/risks of a notice that reads "some rights reserved"?

4. Since the 1970s, Project Gutenberg has been creating a full-text, online archive of public domain books, amassing some 21,000 works by April 2007. The Internet Archive makes available, for free, texts—from Project Gutenberg, other libraries around the world, and the arpnet—audio, films, Web sites, and software.

Internet Assignment Visit its Web site to learn about recent controversies involving the Internet Archive.

5. Apple and Microsoft have copyrighted their operating systems. This means, for example, that a software engineer who wants to write a program to run on Windows must pay Microsoft for a license to use its Windows code. Another operating system, Linux, is not copyrighted and can be freely copied. Since the 1980s, self-styled hacker Richard Stallman has promoted a "copyleft" license through his foundation, GNU. Known as a General Public License (GPL), it allows anyone to see, modify, or redistribute the underlying computer source code as long as they publish their changes when they redistribute the software. In June 2007, Stallman's Free Software Foundation released a new version, GPL3. Anyone who contributes to GPL3-licensed software automatically licenses others to use any underlying patents. Those who buy a device that uses GPL software, like TiVo, should be free to change the software. As the Free Software Web site explains:

> Some devices are designed to deny users access to install or run modified versions of the software inside them, although the manufacturer can do so. This is fundamentally incompatible with the aim of protecting users' freedom to change the software.... Therefore, we have designed this version of the GPL to prohibit the practice for those [products made for individual use.] ... [W]e stand ready to extend this provision ... in future versions of the GPL, as needed to protect the freedom of users.

More than 30,000 projects relied on GPL1 and GPL2, including some run by IBM and Novell.

Internet Assignment Find out how this newest version of free software has been received. Who has been critical of it, and why?

Beyond Copyright: Misappropriation, Trademark, Patents, and Trade Secrets

As the reading on collective indigenous culture suggests, not every good idea is—or can be—fixed in the kinds of "tangible expressions" that can be copyrighted. Nor is federal copyright law the only source of protection for intellectual property. The following case involves a claim of misappropriation under California's state law.

WHITE v. SAMSUNG AND DEUTSCH ASSOCIATES

U.S. Court of Appeals, Ninth Circuit, 1992
971 F.2d 1395

Goodwin, Senior Circuit Judge. ☀

Plaintiff Vanna White is the hostess of "Wheel of Fortune," one of the most popular game shows in television history. An estimated forty million people watch the program daily. Capitalizing on the fame which her participation in the show has bestowed on her, White markets her identity to various advertisers.

The dispute in this case arose out of a series of advertisements prepared for Samsung by Deutsch. The series ran in at least half a dozen publications with widespread, and in some cases national, circulation.

… Each [ad] depicted a current item from popular culture and a Samsung electronic product. Each was set in the twenty-first century and conveyed the message that the Samsung product would still be in use by that time. By hypothesizing outrageous future outcomes for the cultural items, the ads created humorous effects. For example, one lampooned current popular notions of an unhealthy diet by depicting a raw steak with the caption: "Revealed to be health food. 2010 A.D.…."

The advertisement which prompted the current dispute was for Samsung videocassette recorders (VCRs). The ad depicted a robot, dressed in a wig, gown, and jewelry which Deutsch consciously selected to resemble White's hair and dress. The robot was posed next to a game board which is instantly recognizable as the Wheel of Fortune game show set, in a stance for which White is famous. The caption of the ad read: "Longest-running game show. 2012 A.D.…."

[The court must determine whether the defendants have violated Ms. White's common law right of publicity, by "appropriat[ing her] name or likeness to [their] advantage, commercially or otherwise" without her consent. Since they had not actually used Vanna White's name or her real likeness in the ad, defendants argued they did not "appropriate" her. But the Court decided not to limit the manner of appropriation in this way.]

[T]he most popular celebrities are not only the most attractive to advertisers, but also the easiest to evoke without resorting to obvious means such as name, likeness, or voice.

Consider a hypothetical advertisement which depicts a mechanical robot with male features, an African-American complexion, and a bald head. The robot is wearing black hightop Air Jordan basketball sneakers, and a red basketball uniform with black trim, baggy shorts, and the number 23 (though not revealing "Bulls" or "Jordan" lettering). The ad depicts the robot dunking a basketball one-handed, stiff-armed, legs extended like open scissors, and tongue hanging out. Now envision that this ad is run on television during professional basketball games. Considered individually, the robot's physical attributes, its dress, and its stance tell us little. Taken together, they lead to the only conclusion that any sports viewer who has registered a discernible pulse in the past five years would reach: the ad is about Michael Jordan.

Viewed separately, the individual aspects of the advertisement in the present case say little. Viewed together, they leave little doubt about the celebrity the ad is meant to depict.…

Television and other media create marketable celebrity identity value. Considerable energy and ingenuity are expended by those who have achieved celebrity value to exploit it for profit. The law protects the celebrity's sole right to exploit this value whether the celebrity has achieved her fame out of rare ability, dumb luck, or a combination thereof.… Because White has alleged facts showing that Samsung and Deutsch had appropriated her identity, [she is entitled to a trial on her common law right of publicity claim.]

[In the next section, the court dismisses the defendant's claim that their parody is protected under the First Amendment:]

In defense, defendants cite a number of cases for the proposition that their robot ad constituted protected speech. The only cases they cite which are even remotely relevant to this case are *Hustler Magazine v. Falwell* and *L.L. Bean, Inc. v. Drake Publishers*.… Those cases involved parodies of advertisements run for the purpose of poking fun at Jerry Falwell and L.L. Bean, respectively. This case involves a true advertisement run for the purpose of selling Samsung VCRs. The ad's spoof of Vanna White and Wheel of Fortune is subservient and only tangentially related to the ad's primary message: "buy

Samsung VCRs." Defendants' parody arguments are better addressed to non-commercial parodies. The difference between a "parody" and a "knock-off" is the difference between fun and profit....

[After the appellate decision, and before the trial, the defendants sought a rehearing. They lost, but two justices agreed with them, expressing their views in this dissenting opinion:]

KOZINSKI, Circuit Judge, with whom Circuit Judges O'SCANNLAIN and KLEINFELD join, dissenting. ☀

Saddam Hussein wants to keep advertisers from using his picture in unflattering contexts.... Clint Eastwood doesn't want tabloids to write about him.... The Girl Scouts don't want their image soiled by association with certain activities.... George Lucas wants to keep Strategic Defense Initiative fans from calling it "Star Wars." ... And scads of copyright holders see purple when their creations are made fun of....

Something very dangerous is going on here. Private property, including intellectual property, is essential to our way of life. It provides an incentive for investment and innovation; it stimulates the flourishing of our culture; it protects the moral entitlements of people to the fruits of their labors. But reducing too much to private property can be bad medicine. Private land, for instance, is far more useful if separated from other private land by public streets, roads and highways. Public parks, utility rights-of-way and sewers reduce the amount of land in private hands, but vastly enhance the value of the property that remains.

So too it is with intellectual property. Overprotecting intellectual property is as harmful as underprotecting it. Creativity is impossible without a rich public domain. Nothing today, likely nothing since we tamed fire, is genuinely new: Culture, like science and technology, grows by accretion, each new creator building on the works of those who came before. Overprotection stifles the very creative forces it's supposed to nurture.

The Panel's opinion is a classic case of overprotection....

The ad that spawned this litigation starred a robot dressed in a wig, gown and jewelry reminiscent of Vanna White's hair and dress ... posed next to a Wheel-of-Fortune-like game board.... The gag here, I take it, was that Samsung would still be around when White had been replaced by a robot.

Perhaps failing to see the humor, White sued, alleging Samsung infringed her right of publicity by "appropriating" her "identity." Under California law, White has the exclusive right to use her name, likeness, signature and voice for commercial purposes. But Samsung didn't use her name, voice or signature, and it certainly didn't use her likeness. The ad just wouldn't have been funny had it depicted White or someone who resembled her—the whole joke was that the game show host(ess) was a robot, not a real person. No one seeing the ad could have thought this was supposed to be White in 2012. The district judge quite reasonably held that, because Samsung didn't use White's name, likeness, voice or signature, it didn't violate her right of publicity.... Not so, says the panel majority: The California right of publicity can't possibly be limited to name and likeness. If it were, the majority reasons, a "clever advertising strategist" could avoid using White's name or likeness but nevertheless remind people of her with impunity.... To prevent this ... the panel majority holds that the right of publicity must extend beyond name and likeness, to ... anything that "evoke[s]" her personality....

Intellectual property rights aren't like some constitutional rights, absolute guarantees protected against all kinds of interference, subtle as well as blatant. They cast no penumbras, emit no emanations: The very point of intellectual property laws is that they protect only against certain specific kinds of appropriation. I can't publish unauthorized copies of, say, *Presumed Innocent*; I can't make a movie out of it. But I'm perfectly free to write a book about an idealistic young prosecutor on trial for a crime he didn't commit.

So what if I got the idea from *Presumed Innocent*? So what if it reminds readers of the original? … All creators draw in part on the work of those who came before, referring to it, building on it, poking fun at it; we call this creativity, not piracy.

The majority … [is] creating a new … right…. It's replacing the existing balance between the interests of the celebrity and those of the public by a different balance, one substantially more favorable to the celebrity. Instead of having an exclusive right in her name, likeness, signature or voice, every famous person now has an exclusive right to anything that reminds the viewer of her….

Consider how sweeping this new right is. What is it about the ad that makes people think of White? It's not the robot's wig, clothes or jewelry; there must be ten million blond women (many of them quasi-famous) who wear dresses and jewelry like White's. It's that the robot is posed near the "Wheel of Fortune" game board. Remove the game board from the ad, and no one would think of Vanna White…. But once you include the game board, anybody standing beside it a brunette woman, a man wearing women's clothes, a monkey in a wig and gown would evoke White's image, precisely the way the robot did…. The panel is giving White an exclusive right not in what she looks like or who she is, but in what she does for a living.

This is entirely the wrong place to strike the balance. Intellectual property rights aren't free: They're imposed at the expense of future creators and of the public at large. Where would we be if Charles Lindbergh had an exclusive right in the concept of a heroic solo aviator? If Arthur Conan Doyle had gotten a copyright in the idea of the detective story, or Albert Einstein had patented the theory of relativity? … [I]intellectual property law is full of careful balances between what's set aside for the owner and what's left in the public domain for the rest of us: The relatively short life of patents; the longer, but finite, life of copyrights; copyright's idea-expression dichotomy; the fair use doctrine; the prohibition on copyrighting facts; the compulsory license of television broadcasts and musical compositions…. All of these diminish an intellectual property owner's rights. All let the public use something created by someone else. But all are necessary to maintain a free environment in which creative genius can flourish.

The intellectual property right created by the panel here has none of these essential limitations…. Future Vanna Whites might not get the chance to create their personae, because their employers may fear some celebrity will claim the persona is too similar to her own. The public will be robbed of parodies of celebrities, and our culture will be deprived of the valuable safety valve that parody and mockery create. Moreover, consider the moral dimension, about which the panel majority seems to have gotten so exercised. Saying Samsung "appropriated" something of White's begs the question: Should White have the exclusive right to something as broad and amorphous as her "identity"? Samsung's ad didn't simply copy White's shtick like all parody, it created something new. True, Samsung did it to make money, but White does whatever she does to make money, too; the majority talks of "the difference between fun and profit," but in the entertainment industry fun is profit. Why is Vanna White's right to exclusive for-profit use of her persona a persona that might not even be her own creation, but that of a writer, director or producer superior to Samsung's right to profit by creating its own inventions? …

The panel, however, does more than misinterpret California law: By refusing to recognize a parody exception to the right of publicity, the panel directly contradicts the federal Copyright Act. Samsung didn't merely parody Vanna White. It parodied Vanna White appearing in "Wheel of Fortune," a copyrighted television show, and parodies of copyrighted works are governed by federal copyright law….

Finally, I can't see how giving White the power to keep others from evoking her image in the public's mind can be squared with the First Amendment…. The First Amendment isn't just about religion or politics—it's also about protecting the free development of our national culture. Parody, humor, irreverence are all vital components of the marketplace of ideas. The last thing we need, the last thing the First Amendment will tolerate, is a law that lets public figures keep people from mocking them, or from "evok[ing]" their images in the mind of the public....

In our pop culture, where salesmanship must be entertaining and entertainment must sell, the line between the commercial and noncommercial has not merely blurred; it has disappeared. Is the Samsung parody any different from a parody on Saturday Night Live or in Spy Magazine? Both are equally profit-motivated. Both use a celebrity's identity to sell things—one to sell VCRs, the other to sell advertising. Both mock their subjects. Both try to make people laugh. Both add something, perhaps something worthwhile and memorable, perhaps not, to our culture.

Commercial speech is a significant, valuable part of our national discourse....

For better or worse, we are the Court of Appeals for the Hollywood Circuit. Millions of people toil in the shadow of the law we make, and much of their livelihood is made possible by the existence of intellectual property rights. But much of their livelihood and much of the vibrancy of our culture also depends on the existence of other intangible rights: The right to draw ideas from a rich and varied public domain, and the right to mock, for profit as well as fun, the cultural icons of our time.

QUESTIONS

1. Is there intellectual property at stake in this case? Explain. How might copyright law apply to the case?

2. Try to articulate the moral judgments each side uses to bolster its legal arguments. Which do you find more persuasive? Why?

Trademarks

Federal trademark law—the **Lanham Trademark Act (1946)** and the **Federal Trademark Dilution Act of 1995**—protects a company's ownership rights to the name, logo, or symbol that identifies its products. Nike's swoosh, McDonald's arches, and the Xerox name are all identifiable trademarks. The company has an economic interest in the mark it has created, and a right to prevent competitors from using it for their own benefit or in ways that would harm its rightful owner. Cases involving **infringement** require a showing that the use of a competitor's mark is substantially likely to confuse consumers about the source of a product, or suggest that the trademark's owner made an endorsement it didn't make. Anyone—even a noncompetitor—can be guilty of **dilution** if they do something to blur or tarnish a trademark, whittling away its selling power through unauthorized use on dissimilar, usually shoddy, products. But not every use is an infringement or dilution of another's trademark. For example, independent candidate for president Ralph Nader borrowed from the long-running "priceless" ad campaign known as the "Priceless Ads." Nader's ads began with a series of items showing the price of each ("grilled tenderloin for fund-raiser: $1,000 a plate; "campaign ads filled with half-truths: $10 million;" "promises to special interest groups: over $100 billion"). It ends with a phrase identifying a priceless intangible that cannot be purchased ("find out the truth: priceless. There are some things that money can't buy."). The ad was shown on television for a two-week period and appeared on Nader's Web site. When MasterCard sued the campaign for infringing and diluting its trademark, it lost. The court found that there was no infringement because viewers would not be confused into thinking MasterCard endorsed the Nader campaign, and no dilution because it was a noncommercial use that could not harm MasterCard.[12]

---

12 MasterCard International Inc. v. Nader 2000 Primary Committee, Inc., 2004 WL 434404 (D. Ct. 2004).

PATENTS AND TRADE SECRETS

United States patent law protects the rights of those who discover tools, machines, processes, and other "novel, useful and not-obvious" inventions. The range of patentable ideas is enormous—from the chemical method for making pearl ash that won the first U.S. patent, to such recent inventions as Amazon.com's one-click Internet checkout ("business method"), a new variety of hybrid corn, and receptor genes on the human genome sequence. The U.S. Office of Patents and Trademarks initially decides whether a patent should be authorized, but the courts must make a final determination if a competitor challenges its validity.

The patent, once acquired, gives the inventor a complete monopoly for a limited time (20 years), during which no one else may use or profit from the invention without permission. In the United States, most patent applications are now published 18 months after the application is filed, the rest when the patent office issues a patent. Assume, for example, that a pharmaceutical company develops and patents a new medicine that is approved by the FDA. During the patent period, the company ("inventor") has complete control over distribution of the drug, deciding whether and how to license it to other manufacturers. Once the patent has expired, however, the chemical makeup of the drug becomes public information, and generic versions can legally be sold.

One alternative to patent protection is to keep your idea to yourself, and to sue anyone who tries to use it. Under state tort laws, a lawsuit can be brought against someone who wrongfully takes ("misappropriates") or discloses a trade secret. You don't register your trade secret as you register a trademark; you don't need to go through a lengthy and costly application procedure as you do for a patent. Suppose, for example, that you create a great recipe for chocolate chip cookies. Written down, the recipe is a "fixed, tangible expression" that can be copyrighted, preventing anyone from reproducing it in other cookbooks without your permission. But the value of the recipe is in the cookies—and even if it remains unpublished, it will lose some of its allure if competitors make the same cookies. If you did not want to go through the patent process, you might still maintain a near-monopoly use of your recipe as long as (1) it has some economic value, and (2) you have taken reasonable steps to keep it secret. In most states, you could sue to stop anyone who wrongfully discovered your recipe from using or disclosing it. Under the Uniform Trade Secrets Act—adopted in some form by 44 states by 2007—includes theft, bribery, misrepresentation, breach or inducement of a breach of a duty to maintain secrecy, or espionage through electronic or other means in its definition of improper means of learning a trade secret. Figuring out the recipe by taste trials ("reverse engineering"), however, would not be considered wrongful.

INEVITABLE DISCLOSURE OF TRADE SECRETS

One of the most contentious issues in current trade secret law involves former employees. What happens when a software engineer leaves one company for another—bringing with her not only her general skills and talents, but particular knowledge acquired over years with the first company?

William Redmond, Jr., began working for PepsiCo in 1984. In 1994, a year after he began heading the Northern California Business Unit, Redmond became the General Manager of the entire California business unit, a unit with annual revenues of more than $500 million, representing twenty percent of the company's U.S. profits. Earlier that year, another PepsiCo executive, Donal Uzzi, left the company to head the Gatorade division of Quaker, a PepsiCo competitor. From May until November 1994, Uzzi tried to woo Redmond away from PepsiCo. Redmond said nothing to anyone at PepsiCo until he had a firm, written offer from Quaker. When he did, PepsiCo sued to stop him from working for Quaker. The federal appeals court ruling is the most frequently cited case dealing with what is called the "inevitable disclosure rule."

PEPSICO, INC. v. REDMOND

United States Court of Appeals, Seventh Circuit, 1995

54 F.3d 1262

Flaum , Circuit Judge. ✳

The facts of this case lay against a backdrop of fierce beverage-industry competition between Quaker and PepsiCo, especially in "sports drinks" and "new age drinks." Quaker's sports drink, "Gatorade," is the dominant brand in its market niche. PepsiCo introduced its Gatorade rival, "All Sport," in March and April of 1994, but sales of All Sport lag far behind those of Gatorade. Quaker also has the lead in the new-age-drink category [with Snapple].... PepsiCo's products have about half of Snapple's market share. Both companies see 1995 as an important year for their products: PepsiCo has developed extensive plans to increase its market presence, while Quaker is trying to solidify its lead by integrating Gatorade and Snapple distribution. Meanwhile, PepsiCo and Quaker each face strong competition from Coca Cola Co., which has its own sports drink, "PowerAde," and which introduced its own Snapple-rival, "Fruitopia," in 1994, as well as from independent beverage producers....

Redmond's relatively high-level position at PCNA gave him access to inside information and trade secrets. Redmond, like other PepsiCo management employees, had signed a confidentiality agreement with PepsiCo. That agreement stated in relevant part that he

> w[ould] not disclose at any time, to anyone other than officers or employees of [PepsiCo], or make use of, confidential information relating to the business of [PepsiCo] ... obtained while in the employ of [PepsiCo], which shall not be generally known or available to the public or recognized as standard practices.

PepsiCo filed this...suit on November 16, 1994, seeking a temporary restraining order to enjoin Redmond from assuming his duties at Quaker and to prevent him from disclosing trade secrets or confidential information to his new employer....

The Illinois Trade Secrets Act ("ITSA"), which governs the trade secret issues in this case, provides that a court may enjoin the "actual or threatened misappropriation" of a trade secret....

The question of threatened or inevitable misappropriation in this case lies at the heart of a basic tension in trade secret law. Trade secret law serves to protect "standards of commercial morality" and "encourage invention and innovation" while maintaining "the public interest in having free and open competition in the manufacture and sale of unpatented goods." Yet that same law should not prevent workers from pursuing their livelihoods when they leave their current positions. This tension is particularly exacerbated when a plaintiff sues to prevent not the actual misappropriation of trade secrets but the mere threat that it will occur....

The ITSA [and precedent cases] lead to the same conclusion: a plaintiff may prove a claim of trade secret misappropriation by demonstrating that defendant's new employment will inevitably lead him to rely on the plaintiff's trade secrets....

PepsiCo presented substantial evidence...that Redmond possessed extensive and intimate knowledge about PCNA's strategic goals for 1995 in sports drinks and new age drinks. The district court concluded on the basis of that presentation that unless Redmond possessed an uncanny ability to compartmentalize information, he would necessarily be making decisions about Gatorade and Snapple by relying on his knowledge of PCNA trade secrets. It is not the "general skills and knowledge acquired during his tenure with" PepsiCo that PepsiCo seeks to keep from falling into Quaker's hands, but rather "the particularized plans or processes developed by [PCNA] and disclosed to him while the employer-employee relationship existed, which are unknown to others in the industry and which give the employer an advantage over his competitors."…

Admittedly, PepsiCo has not brought a traditional trade secret case, in which a former employee has knowledge of a special manufacturing process or customer list and can give a competitor an unfair advantage by transferring the technology or customers to that competitor.…PepsiCo has not contended that Quaker has stolen the All Sport formula or its list of distributors. Rather PepsiCo has asserted that Redmond cannot help but rely on PCNA trade secrets as he helps plot Gatorade and Snapple's new course, and that these secrets will enable Quaker to achieve a substantial advantage by knowing exactly how PCNA will price, distribute, and market its sports drinks and new age drinks and being able to respond strategically.…

…PepsiCo finds itself in the position of a coach, one of whose players has left, playbook in hand, to join the opposing team before the big game.

For the foregoing reasons, we affirm the district court's order enjoining Redmond from assuming his responsibilities at Quaker through May 1995, and preventing him forever from disclosing PCNA trade secrets and confidential information.

QUESTIONS

1. What effect does the outcome of this case have on Redmond's ability to earn a living? Should PepsiCo have to re-hire him?

2. Suppose Redmond had been terminated by PepsiCo before he was hired by Quaker. Do you think this case would be decided differently? Should it be?

3. If you were offered a job by PepsiCo, what impact would cases like Redmond have on your decision?

4. Assume that you are starting a new company to produce computer software and need to hire engineers and computer analysts. What impact might decisions like this one have on your hiring process?

5. Does Redmond's willingness to sell his expertise to the highest bidder violate your sense of commercial morality?

Global Intellectual Property Rights (IPR)

Bioprospecting—the worldwide search for health and medicinal uses of natural substances is a lucrative business. A 2005 report concluded that 62 percent of all cancer drugs were created from bioprospecting discoveries. The key ingredient of Taxol, owned by Bristol-Myers Squibb Company, for example, comes from the bark of the yew tree. As Gelvina Rodriguez Stevenson, author of the next reading explains, it is the traditional knowledge about the use of herbs and plants to heal, shared among native peoples, that provides a map to modern pharmaceutical companies. Stevenson explores the limitations of using patent law to protect the rights of tribal peoples to their traditional knowledge.

TRADE SECRETS: PROTECTING INDIGENOUS ETHNOBIOLOGICAL (MEDICINAL) KNOWLEDGE

GELVINA RODRIGUEZ STEVENSON[13]

Today, most major drugs are plant-derived. It is currently believed that there are approximately 35,000 plants in the developing world that have medicinal value.[14]...The ethnobiological knowledge of indigenous peoples can be extremely effective in focusing the search for new medicines. It is estimated that, by consulting indigenous peoples, "bio-prospectors" can increase the success ratio in trials for useful substances from one success in 10,000 samples to one success in two samples; ... [a]pproximately three quarters of the plant-derived compounds currently used as pharmaceuticals were discovered through research based on plant use by indigenous peoples. Potential cures may be lost as rain forest area diminishes. The rainforest is considered a warehouse of valuable compounds which could aid the development of useful new medicines. It is estimated that only 1,100 of the 35,000 to 40,000 plants with possible undiscovered medicinal or nutritional value for humans have been thoroughly studied by scientists.... It has been suggested that much of the orally transmitted indigenous knowledge ... will also be lost, since it is estimated that 3,000 of the world's 6,000 languages will vanish....

In 1992, the United Nations hosted a Conference on Environment and Development (UNCED) in Brazil.... [This] resulted in the United Nations Convention on Biological Diversity [CBD] which commits signatory countries to conserve biodiversity and equitably share resulting benefits. The signatories also agreed that the benefits of utilizing biodiversity, including technology, should be shared with the source country. The CBD has been ratified by 168 of the 177 countries that are parties to it ... [but has yet to be ratified by the United States.]...

...Recent advances in microelectronics and molecular biology...enable companies to screen plants more efficiently. This has made bio-prospecting more profitable....

Recently, companies have been protecting these expanding interests by seeking patent protection for valued plant-derived drugs. This has led to an increase in biotech-related patent claims and caused a backlog at the Patent and Trademark Office.

Using U.S. Patents to Protect Indigenous Ethnobiological Knowledge

A patent is a legal certificate that gives an inventor exclusive rights to prevent others from producing, selling, using, or importing his or her invention for a limited period of time.

While patent law varies somewhat in different countries, it generally protects inventions of a particular subject matter. "Inventions" include machines and other devices, chemical compositions, manufacturing processes, and uses for such inventions that are found to be (1) new, (2) non-obvious, and (3) useful. U.S. patent law requires that an invention be new, i.e., not known or used by others in the United States or published in any country....

The non-obvious requirement establishes that... [a claimed invention must do more than add some elements to a prior invention. New elements must not be ones that are obvious "to a person having ordinary skill in the art to which said subject matter pertains."] In other words, a patent is considered obvious if a person could have easily created the invention from what was already publicly known....

---

13 Gelvina Rodriguez Stevenson, "Trade Secrets: The Secret to Protecting Indigenous Ethnobiological (Medicinal) Knowledge," 32 *N.Y.U. J. Int'l. L & Pol.* 1119, 1122–24, 1131–67 (2000).

14 The Ottawa-based Rural Advancement Foundation International (RAFI) has estimated that in the early 1990s, germplasm from developing countries was worth at least $32 billion dollars per year to the pharmaceutical industry.

In order to satisfy the usefulness requirement, commonly known as the utility requirement, the invention must be useful to society. The patent applicant must know exactly what the invention will be useful for and must explain in the application how the invention will be useful.

A naturally occurring subject matter, often called a "product of nature," such as a plant or human cell, is not patentable. However, United States courts have held that the "discoverer" may obtain a patent on the biological matter in a purified, isolated, or altered form. The Supreme Court, in fact, has held that genetically altered living organisms are patentable as "manufactures" or "compositions of matter." Patent procurement is expensive and procedurally complex. In the United States, the only way that an inventor may obtain a patent is by filing a timely application with the Patent and Trademark Office, a federal government agency.... In general, [patents] are awarded to a natural person, but can be, and frequently are, assigned to another party or corporate entity. Patents ... may be assigned or licensed in exchange for a payment of royalties.... A patent owner may file a civil suit for infringement against anyone who, without authority, makes, uses, or sells the patented invention. The infringer need not be aware that he is infringing and is held to infringe even if he achieves the same invention independently. Under U.S. law, possible remedies include injunctions and damages, with a minimum damage award included in the statute, and attorney's fees.

It is difficult for indigenous peoples to obtain a patent on their ethnobiological knowledge for a number of reasons. All of the above-mentioned prerequisites for patentability, because they are grounded in Western notions of intellectual property, make it easier for Western pharmaceutical companies to obtain a patent on a modification of indigenous ethnobiological knowledge than for indigenous communities. Perhaps the most fundamental reason for this disparity is that patent law is based primarily on the goal of providing incentives to individuals for commercial innovation rather than the goal of protecting communal knowledge....

[The] rigid requirements that the inventor be known and be the first to invent, or the first to file in jurisdictions outside the United States, in order to receive a patent, pose an immense obstacle for indigenous communities who wish to patent their ethnobiological knowledge. Another problem with awarding a patent to a "medicine man" ... or even to the indigenous community, is that the same cultural and ethnobiological knowledge is often found among several distinct indigenous societies.... It would be unfair if one community were granted a patent, because other neighboring groups which have used the same information for just as long, if not longer, would then be suddenly infringing on a patent while they continued their ancestral practices. Discovering which group was the first to discover the knowledge and first to make use of it is nearly impossible and likely to create societal disruption.

Even if [one indigenous person] were able to show that he was the inventor and were granted a patent, the individualism upon which the patent is philosophically based would still create problems for [his group.] [For example, in] 1992, a British company, The Body Shop, entered into a supply contract with Chief Paulinho Paiakan, a respected leader of the Kayapo. Chief Paiakan agreed to supply to The Body Shop 6,000 liters a year of natural oil to use in hair conditioners in exchange for a small percentage of the profits. The Body Shop gave their payment to Chief Paiakan. [According to] Stephen Corry, an indigenous rights activist and Director General of the organization Survival International ... "[t]he project has caused deep divisions amongst the Kayapo exacerbated by the way Paiakan has accumulated great personal wealth and power." ...

A great deal of indigenous ethnobiological knowledge has been published and documented by ethnobotanists and other scholars.... This will bar indigenous communities from satisfying the novelty requirement.

An illustration of the barrier that the utility requirement can pose is evident in the problems the National Institute of Health (NIH) has had with the patenting of genes. The NIH failed to receive a patent for gene fragments that are used as markers to aid in the mapping of genes. The Patent and Trademark Office rejected … the NIH claim that the gene fragments satisfied the utility requirement by their use as markers in the mapping of genes.… The NIH case suggests that although much indigenous knowledge has shown its utility by the simple fact that it has led to the development of products and processes patented by pharmaceutical companies, the PTO may not consider this utility claimable under U.S. standards.

Products of nature, also known as naturally occurring subject matter, are not patentable.… [This means that] Western pharmaceutical companies that isolate an active chemical in a plant and create a genetically engineered plant or animal can receive a patent while indigenous peoples, who use the natural form of the plant, cannot.…

Traditional knowledge presents unique problems in determining non-obviousness because it is difficult to determine what the prior art might have been. Presumably, the prior art would be knowledge that the indigenous people had prior to the invention. Since both prior art and claimed invention would be generations old, it would be difficult to determine at what point in time an indigenous group had acquired or developed a particular piece of knowledge, i.e., the invention.…

And even if patent law was able to conceive of the entire community as the inventor, neighboring communities are likely to be aware of the plant and its use. This will automatically characterize the plant and its use as obvious. Most importantly, the mere fact that indigenous people often will have possessed the knowledge for centuries may further ensure that the knowledge is considered obvious.…

Technically, patent holders have the legal right to prevent imports into the United States of products that were created using technology patented in the United States. Thus, an indigenous community in a developing country could be precluded from exporting products that were developed using existing species if that product is patented in the United States.…

Finally, once an invention is patented, the characteristics of the invention are made public, enabling others to obtain the knowledge. Some of the knowledge may be sacred to indigenous communities and they may not want this knowledge shared with other cultures. A patent is effective only for [a limited time period] … and after expiration, its subject matter is freely available for use by the public.

QUESTIONS

1. What are the required elements to obtain a patent? Why is each so difficult for indigenous peoples to demonstrate? What values within indigenous cultures make it difficult or impossible for them to secure U.S. patents for their "inventions"?

2. Elsewhere in her article, Stevenson writes that "the law's preference for pure substances makes it easier for pharmaceutical companies to satisfy the non-obvious requirement and makes it difficult for indigenous communities to do so." She uses as an example the neem plant. For centuries, farmers in India used ground neem seed as a natural pesticide. Scientists learned from the Indians how they extracted, identified, isolated, and purified the active components in the seed, and used that knowledge to synthesize the active chemical in a lab. In 1994, W.R. Grace and Agrodyne succeeded in getting a patent on the neem derivatives as an advance over the widely known prior art. Review the *Harvard Business Review* article, "Strategy and Society" in Chapter 1. How might Porter and Kramer advise W.R. Grace?

3. Stevenson proposes that trade secret is a more advantageous route than patent law for native peoples. Articulate how trade secret law might be used to protect their rights.

4. For centuries, the Quechua Indians of the Peruvian Andes have been using the frost-resistant root of the maca plant to boost stamina and sex drive.
Internet Assignment Find out what has happened in the lawsuit against New Jersey-based PureWorld Botanicals, which in 2001 was granted a patent for MacaPure, derived from the active compound in the maca plant.

Highlights in the Development of International IPR

- *The Paris Convention* (1883). The first international agreement on IPR was founded on the principle of "national treatment." Signatories agreed to provide foreigners the same IPR protection given to their own citizens, but each nation continued to have its own rules as to what was patentable and how. The World Intellectual Property Organization (WIPO), a specialized agency of the United Nations, currently administers the terms of the Paris Convention.

- *Biodiversity Convention* (1992). An outgrowth of the global Rio Conference, the aims of this agreement are to conserve biological diversity and sustain biological resources for future generations. It recognizes states' sovereign rights over biological resources and calls for protection of the rights of communities and indigenous people to the customary use of biological resources and knowledge systems. Signatories agree to facilitate environmentally sound use of their resources by other members and to assist in the transfer of technology to developing countries so that they can capitalize on their own natural resources, even if it requires sharing innovations protected by intellectual property rights. The United States has not signed this treaty.

- *Trade-Related Aspects of IPR (TRIPS) Agreement* (1994). Strongly supported by the United States and adopted within the framework of the Uruguay Round of Multilateral Trade Negotiations that created the World Trade Organization (WTO), TRIPS incorporates IPR protection into the General Agreement on Tariffs and Trades (GATT). According to TRIPS, "the protection and enforcement of intellectual property rights should contribute to the promotion of technological innovation and to the transfer and dissemination of technology, to the mutual advantage of producers and users of technological knowledge and in a manner conducive to social and economic welfare, and to a balance of rights and obligations."

- *Doha Declaration* (2001). In recognition of the epidemics of HIV/AIDS, tuberculosis, and malaria in developing nations, WTO Ministers reaffirmed TRIPS but agreed to interpret it "in a manner supportive of WTO Members' right to protect public health, and in particular, to promote access to medicines for all." One modification of TRIPS allows countries without the capacity to produce pharmaceuticals to issue compulsory licenses to import them when urgently needed. Another extended the deadline for the least developed countries to enforce TRIPS in relation to pharmaceuticals until 2016.

Human Rights and IP

Law scholar Madhavi Sunder's work is interdisciplinary, cross cutting IP, globalization studies, and human rights law. She has coined the term IP3—identity politics, Internet Protocol, and intellectual property—at the intersection of culture, technology, and economics. She writes:

> *Developing countries … ask how intellectual property laws might affect the poor differently from the rich. Women ask how the failure to protect traditional knowledge affects them differently from men. American student activists ask what has happened to our "free culture"—who is capable of exercising freedom in our culture, and who is not. An AIDS patient in India asks whether he will live.*

In the next reading, Sunder discusses what she calls the "capabilities approach to development"—an idea pioneered by fellow scholars Amartya Sen and Martha Nussbaum—in which people would increasingly experience a range of freedoms, from freedom to enjoy life/health to freedom of movement, freedom to do creative work, and freedom to participate fully in social, economic, and cultural institutions. Sunder then makes links to intellectual property law.

TOWARD A CULTURAL ANALYSIS OF INTELLECTUAL PROPERTY
MADHAVI SUNDER[15]

Development as Freedom

… Intellectual property law is, of course, essential to all of these freedoms. We can readily see intellectual property law as a means of development (and implicitly as a means of thwarting development) in the health context. Patents and copyrights determine our access to drugs and education, while trademarks and rights of publicity define the contours of freedom of speech and the ability to play with cultural icons. As Sen has written, however, when assessing development as freedom, we must begin with the question, "What is development for? Development must entail not only economic growth, but also a life that is culturally fulfilling."… Recognizing people's humanity requires acknowledging their production of knowledge of the world. This recognition, in turn, fuels remuneration to new creators.…

Intellectual Property as Social Relations

Traditionally, real property rights [rights in land] have been considered perpetual and unqualified; they do not automatically expire within a term of years and, for the most part, they were thought to advance private interests in autonomy, efficiency, and sovereignty, not public interests in community and human rights. Intellectual property rights, on the other hand, were foundationally understood as limited exclusive rights, and offered by the state not to reward private persons but to promote the public interest in art and science. Real property rights were conceptually absolute and private; intellectual property rights were qualified and public-minded.

… [Over the last century t]he scope and duration of intellectual property rights… have grown substantially, so that today many of these rights have become virtually perpetual and unqualified. Furthermore, we have moved far away from an understanding of intellectual property as serving the public interest, toward a regime that conceptualizes rights almost exclusively as the private economic rights of creators. The irony now is that, while multiple owners may carry different sticks in the bundle of rights that comprises full ownership of real property, intellectual property rights, or rights in public goods that can, in fact, be shared by many are concentrated in the hands of a few.

But increasingly, this conception of intellectual property law is being challenged. From the disaggregation of intellectual property rights through Creative Commons licenses to the Doha Declaration's assertion that intellectual property rights serve human values, intellectual property is being re-envisioned as limited by the property and personal rights of others, not just by economic incentive theory alone. Intellectual property rights are increasingly being understood as property rights that structure social relations....

The New Enlightenment

The old [original, 18th century] Enlightenment understood freedom and equality as developed in opposition to [religion-based medieval] culture.... Increasingly we now understand that we develop our autonomous selves through and within a cultural discourse, "inhabit[ing]" tradition, not just resisting it.... The New Enlightenment recognizes that liberty demands autonomy within culture, and simultaneously understands that equality requires the capability to participate equally in the social and economic processes of cultural creation. The freedom and equality battles of this new century will not only be about access to physical space, but also to discursive space. The crucial question will be: who will have power to make our cultural world?...

QUESTIONS

1. What does Sunder mean by "discursive space"? What is she saying as she distinguishes the "Old" from the "New" enlightenment? Do you agree with her argument?

2. Some reformers would re-conceptualize IP by first identifying the minimum standards—for health, welfare, education—that government ought to meet for its citizens, and then adopting (or modifying) IP law to help achieve those human rights outcomes. International lawyer Laurence Helfer cites as an example a 2001 report by the U.N. High Commissioner for Human Rights, analyzing the impact of TRIPS on the right to health:

   > [The right to health] includes an obligation for states to promote medical research and to provide access to affordable treatments, including essential drugs.
   > The High Commissioner's report analyzes how intellectual property affects these two obligations. It acknowledges that patents help governments promote medical research by providing an incentive to invent new medical technologies, including new drugs. But the report also asserts that pharmaceutical companies' "commercial motivation ... means that research is directed, first and foremost, towards 'profitable' disease. Diseases that predominantly affect people in poorer countries ... remain relatively under-researched." One way to remedy this market imperfection is to create incentives for innovation outside of the patent system.[16]

   How would you apply this human rights approach to the problem of supplying expensive but essential drugs—for malaria, tuberculosis, or HIV—to poor people in underdeveloped nations?

3. In response to indigenous peoples' concerns that an open-access public domain in their knowledge may lead to exploitation and misappropriation, iCommons, the Alexandria Archive Institute, and the Electronic Frontier Foundation are collaborating to develop a "cultural heritage license."

---

16 Laurence R. Helfer, "Toward a Human Rights Framework for Intellectual Property," 40 *U.C.Davis L. Rev.* 971 (2007); part of a Symposium: *International Rights Approaches to Intellectual Property.*

Internet Assignment Find out the current status of the World Heritage License. Who would grant such a license? What provisions would be in it?

4. A proposed DevNat would have copyright holders distribute their work for free in the developing world while allowing them to demand market prices in developed countries. Would that satisfy the concerns raised by Sunder?

CHAPTER **PROBLEMS**

1. Rebecca Charles was arguably the first NYC chef to feature New England food on the menu of the Pearl Oyster Bar in 1997. In 2007, Ed McFarland, the sous-chef at Pearl for six years, opened his own restaurant nearby—copying, according to Charles, "each and every element" of Pearl Oyster Bar, including the white marble bar, the gray paint, the chairs and bar stools, the packets of oyster crackers, and the dressing on the Caesar salad. Does Charles have any claim that her intellectual property rights were taken?

2. **Internet Assignment** Visit three Web sites: a commercial homepage, an advocacy site, and a personal Web page. Identify the elements of each site that appear to be original and those that may have been borrowed from another source. Which elements might you borrow without permission to create your own Web site? Which would seem to be protected by trademark or copyright?

3. Jeff Koons, a visual artist, is known for incorporating into his artwork objects and images taken from popular media and consumer advertising, a practice that has been referred to as "neo-Pop art" or "appropriation art." His sculptures and paintings often contain such easily recognizable objects as toys, celebrities, and popular cartoon figures. In 2000, Koons was commissioned by Deutsche Bank and the Guggenheim Museum to create an exhibition for the Deutsch Guggenheim Berlin gallery. To create his "Easyfun-Ethereal" paintings, Koons culled images from advertisements and his own photographs, scanned them into a computer, and digitally superimposed them against backgrounds of pastoral landscapes. He then printed color images of the resulting collages for his assistants to use as templates for applying paint on seven billboard-sized, 10' × 14' canvasses.

One of the "Easyfun-Ethereal" paintings, "Niagara," depicts four pairs of women's feet and lower legs dangling prominently over images of confections—a large chocolate fudge brownie topped with ice cream, a tray of donuts, and a tray of apple Danish pastries—with a grassy field and Niagara Falls in the background. By juxtaposing women's legs against a backdrop of food and landscape, he says, he intended to "comment on the ways in which some of our most basic appetites—for food, play, and sex—are mediated by popular images."

One of the pairs of legs in the painting was adapted from "Silk Stockings," a photograph taken by Andrea Blanch that first appeared in *Allure*. An author and a professional photographer for over 20 years, Blanch has published her photos in commercial magazines, photography periodicals and collections, and as ads.

Koons had scanned the image of "Silk Sandals," cropped it, deleted the background, inverted the orientation of the legs and modified the color. He never sought permission to use the photo from anyone. What claims might Blanch and/or *Allure* make? How might Koons defend himself?

4. While the recording industry continues to be aggressive in its war on piracy, having sued more than 20,000 people for copyright infringement since 2003, some of its victims have been equally aggressive in defending themselves. Catherine Lewan, a former KaZaa user, settled the lawsuit brought against her by Sony BMG, and then turned around and filed a class action lawsuit against Sharman Networks, the company that created KaZaa. Lewan claimed that users were defrauded into believing that downloads from KaZaa were not only free, but legal. And, in 2007, Tanya Anderson, plagued by a lawsuit against her by RIAA, filed suit against Atlantic Recording Company, Capitol Records, RIAA, and MediaSentry—the software used by the recording industry to fine copyright infringers—accusing them of illegally investigating thousands of private citizens.

   a. What ethical issues surface in these scenarios?

   b. **Internet Assignment** Find out what has happened in these suits.

5. Imagine yourself as a software developer who has written new generation peer-to-peer software. What can you do with it? What should you do with it?

6. A family afflicted with Canavan, a rare genetic disorder, raised money, collected DNA samples, and persuaded scientists from the Miami Children's Hospital to search for the gene mutation that caused the disease. The researchers found the gene, and, without getting the consent of the parents of the children whose DNA they used, patented it for the hospital. When the hospital began to collect royalties on a genetic-screening test, patient groups were outraged.

   a. Did the hospital act ethically?

   b. Can you articulate any legal claims against the scientists and/or hospital?

   c. **Internet Assignment** Find out what happened in the lawsuit filed against Miami Children's Hospital.

7. Misappropriation of trade secrets has been a federal crime since passage of the Economic Espionage Act (EEA) of 1996.

   Internet Assignment Find a criminal case involving wrongful taking of a trade secret in violation of this law. What kind of secret was taken? What was the outcome?

8. The HIV/AIDs pandemic continues to ravage the population of the less developed world. Nearly 80 percent of developing countries lack the capacity to produce anti–retroviral drugs and the money to pay the full costs of importing patented drugs.

   a. Is there a duty to aid the people in these nations? If so, who owes the duty and what should they do?

   b. One solution would be for an industrialized country to amend its patent laws to allow the production of generics solely for export to countries in need. These cheaper drugs would not be sold in the country where they were made. Who would be the stakeholders if the United States were to consider such a change in its laws? How would each of them respond?

9. The draft A2K Treaty would permit countries where urgently needed medicines are unaffordable at market prices to temporarily distribute these medicines at cost for "compassionate use." Both the developing nations' license and the draft A2K provision act as mechanisms for wealth distribution from the richer to the poorer parts of the world. *Draft Treaty on Access to Knowledge*, available at the Web site of the Consumer Project on Technology. http://www.cptech.org/a2k/.

a. **Internet Assignment** Find out about the Consumer Project on Technology. Who are they? Who funds them? What influence would you expect them to have?

b. What considerations would likely govern the U.S. Congress should the A2K Treaty become law?

10. **Internet Assignment** Visit the WTO (http://www.wto.org) to interact with the organization on a number of topics, or to listen in on ministerial meetings through live audiostream.

CHAPTER **PROJECT**

Ethics Roundtable: Protecting Collective Property

I. PREPARATION

Read through the "Tivas Scenario." Students will be assigned to consider it from an "ethical perspective" or a "national perspective."

Tivas Scenario[17]

Tivas is a hypothetical indigenous community in southern Mexico that predates European contact. It is home to the Tivani people, who have had little interaction with Western industrial society. Its members maintain most of their traditional way of life. While treatments for common afflictions are generally well-known to all members of the community, the methods of preparing plants to treat serious illnesses are known solely by the community's respected "medicine man," M. For example, many members of the community know that toenail and finger-nail fungi should be treated with the green, oval shaped leaves that grow abundantly near the river. They also know that the leaves with the thickest veins and a reddish tint found primarily in the fall treat the affliction best. However, they do not know how M prepares the leaves to make the cream he applies to the nails. That secret is known only to M and other medicine men in a few neighboring indigenous communities.

The United States pharmaceutical company "BioCo," like many of its peer companies, has committed research and development money to study plants to identify useful new medicines and chemicals. It has determined that it would cut costs in half by studying the plants already used by indigenous communities to treat various afflictions. Looking specifically for medicines that treat nail fungi, and having read an article in Natural Geographic about the traditional medicinal practices of the Tivani (including their treatment of nail fungi), BioCo sends "Botanist" and "Chemist" to southern Mexico.

Botanist and Chemist move to a hotel in a small city an hour's drive from Tivas. They drive into the community and attempt to establish a relationship with M. Sensing that M is wary of them, they explain that they are looking for a medicine that will treat people in the United States who are afflicted with nail fungi and that they understood that the Tivani had identified a plant that treats the fungi. They explain that if this plant proves useful, it will help many people. M emphasizes that the plants, and the way in which he prepares them to treat fungi, have been passed down for generations through the chain of medicine men and are

---

17 This Tivas Scenario was derived from the Tivas hypothetical written by Gelvina Rodriguez Stevenson as part of "Trade Secrets: The Secret to Protecting Indigenous Ethnobiological (Medicinal) Knowledge." Reprinted with permission from 32 N.Y.U.J. Int'l L. & Pol. 1119, (2000) 1122–24.

extremely sacred. He does not share with them any information about the spiritual value of the plants, but does give them general information about the plant and brings the scientists directly to the anti-fungal plant.

The scientists stay for a couple of months, testing and collecting the anti-fungal and other plants. They eventually return to the United States, thanking M for his help and promising to be in touch. Upon their return, BioCo invests considerable time and resources into their efforts to isolate "frungoid," the active chemical in the newly "discovered" plant, Frundanialosis, which is actually the plant that M showed them.

After two years, BioCo isolates the active chemical, frungoid. BioCo immediately files for a patent at the United States Patent and Trademark Office (PTO). A year later they are granted a patent for frungoid and after frungoid receives FDA approval, they begin to market it. They are assured protection for their patent in all countries that are signatories to the General Agreement on Tariffs and Trade (GATT), and in Mexico and Canada under the North American Free Trade Agreement (NAFTA).

Within a year, BioCo has made $1 million in profits. BioCo sends a one-time check to M for $10,000, 1 percent of the first year's profits. M has received more money than he has ever had, but this creates a number of problems.

2. THE ETHICAL ROUNDTABLE

The Ethical Roundtable will take place as a fishbowl exercise. Teams of two students role-play each of the following perspectives in a discussion of the scenario:

- Global free marketers
- Utilitarians
- Deontologists
- Virtue ethicists
- Tivani people
- Bio Co. shareholders
- M
  Botanist
- Chemist

3. RESPONSE

The rest of the class will be assigned to represent different nation-members of the World Trade Organization (WTO) as it considers policies governing intellectual property. After listening to the Ethical Roundtable, WTO members will discuss their responses from the perspective of the nation they represent.

How to Read and Brief a Case

Common law or case law refers to those principles and rules of law that we can glean from studying how judges have resolved the disputes before them. The common law has been developing over centuries—since medieval times—and is still changing.

While the common law is always undergoing change, it is normally gradual, incremental change because of the important principle of **stare decisis**. Under this doctrine, judges are guided by the rules of previously decided cases, or precedent. Stare decisis gives stability to the development of the common law, as judges look to what has gone before to determine the result in the case at hand. But judges sometimes break with precedent and create a new rule of law. If not overruled on appeal, that new rule becomes part of the common law and may become the basis for even more radical changes in the law.

We learn the principles of the common law by reading "judicial opinions," the written decisions of judges. A typical appellate court decision (or case) will be signed by those justices whose views prevailed—producing what is called a "majority opinion" to affirm or reverse a trial judge's rulings. Justices who disagree with the majority sometimes feel strongly enough to write a "dissenting opinion." In this book, we have edited the cases for clarity, but where there are dissenting opinions we like to include them, to give you a richer sense of the varying perspectives within a dispute.

Cases are not the only sources of law. The elected representatives in congress and state legislatures debate and pass laws, called statutes. These too can change over time, as legislators decide to amend them. Statutory law exists at both state and federal levels and as town and local ordinances.

Reading a Case

The language and logic of case law takes getting used to, and requires practice and skill. Of varying lengths (from a page to more than a hundred pages) and styles (from pompous to playful), every judicial opinion includes certain basic elements:

- Facts.
  The background story: what happened in the real world to cause the parties to go to court to resolve their dispute.
- Law.
  References to relevant legal principles, precedent, statutes, or other sources of guidance for determining the outcome of the case.
- Resolution.
  Weaving together of facts and relevant law, as the judge decides the outcome of the case and explains the reasoning.

The Case Brief

To analyze a judicial opinion, lawyers write what is called a case brief, a summary of the important elements of a case. Following we show you how to write a brief of the first case in our book, *Yania v. Bigan*. We include explanations of each step. Case brief writing is an excellent way for you to prepare for class.

Caption: *Yania v. Bigan*

The "caption" names the parties to the lawsuit. Usually the first name is that of the plaintiff (the party who brought the suit), and the second is the defendant (the party sued). However, in some jurisdictions, the names are reversed when a case is appealed by the defendant. Always read through the case itself to see who filed the lawsuit, as that will be the name of the "plaintiff."

Citation: Supreme Court of Pennsylvania, 1959

155 A.2d 343

The "citation" identifies the Court that issued the opinion you are reading and the year the case was decided, and a reference to the reporter in which the case was published. Throughout this text, you will find cases from many different courts, including state courts (like this one) and federal trial ("United States District Court") and appellate courts ("United States [Circuit] Court of Appeals" or "United States Supreme Court"). The higher the court, the more important the precedent.

Facts:

1. Coal-miner and landowner Bigan cut large trenches into his property to remove coal.
2. One cut contained 8–10 feet of water, a pump to remove the water, and side walls 16-18 feet.
3. Another coal-miner, Yania, was on Bigan's property to discuss business. Bigan stood near the pump and used words to "entice" Yania into jumping from the side wall of a trench.
4. Yania fell into the water and drowned. Bigan made no attempt to rescue him.

Think of the "facts" of the case as everything important that happened before there was a lawsuit. Sometimes, in reality, the facts are "disputed"—that is, the parties disagree about what happened. But for purposes of a case brief, the "facts" are whatever the court determines the facts to have been. In this case, we only know what the widow claims to have happened—and the judge accepts her version as true. Where a case includes not only the majority opinion but also a concurring opinion (expressing agreement with the majority but for different reasons), or a dissenting opinion, you may see additional facts and should include these in your brief as well.

Legal History/Procedure:

1. Yania's widow filed a suit ("complaint") against Bigan.
2. Bigan made a motion to dismiss.
3. The trial judge granted the motion to dismiss.
4. On appeal, the Supreme Court of Pennsylvania upheld the dismissal.

The legal history/procedure part of a case begins with the lawsuit—who sued whom for what—and ends with the ruling in the case you are briefing.

Sometimes, before there is a trial, the judge will rule on what are called "pretrial motions." In *Yania* for example, the defendant made a pretrial motion to dismiss the complaint, and the judge granted the motion (ruling, in other words, that there should be no trial). The plaintiff appealed that decision, arguing that he should have had a trial. Here, the appellate court (the Supreme Court of Pennsylvania) disagreed, and "affirmed" the decision of the trial judge to dismiss the case. Had the court instead agreed with Yania's widow, the case would have been "reversed" and "remanded"—sent back to a judge for a trial.

Civil law is law that does not involve a criminal charge.[1] In the civil context—and all of the cases in this book are civil cases—the purpose of most trials is to settle a dispute about what really happened. A trial is a fact-finding process, a resolution of the most credible way to determine what happened and of the fairest way to apply the law to those facts. If the facts are not contested, a judge applies the appropriate law and renders a judgment for one side or the other without a trial. In either case, the losing party has a right to appeal judicial "errors of law" (e.g., erroneous instructions to the jury or evidentiary rulings). Once the facts have been determined at a trial, however, they will not be revisited on appeal.

If there was a trial in the case you are briefing, the legal history should include the outcome of the trial (e.g., "The jury found for the plaintiff and awarded damages.") and any post-trial motions (e.g., "The trial judge overturned the jury and entered a judgment for the defendant."), as well as any rulings by the appellate courts (affirming or reversing the trial court).

Legal procedure can be quite complex, and some cases go on for years. In this text, we have tried to simplify the procedure wherever possible, so you will not always see all of the steps in the case's legal history. However, you should always be able to figure out—either from the case itself or surrounding text—who sued whom for what, and who won.

Issues (Holdings):

1. Did Bigan "cause" Yania's death by convincing him to jump? (No) or: Can a person legally "cause" another adult with full mental capacity to do something, by words alone? (No)

2. Did Bigan have a "duty to warn" Yania of the dangers of jumping into the cut that was violated by "failing to warn"? (No) or: Does a landowner have a "duty to warn" a person of a known danger on his property? (No)

3. Did Bigan have a "duty to rescue" Yania from drowning? (No) or: Does a landowner have a "duty to rescue" a drowning business associate on his property who voluntarily put himself in danger? (No)

Think of the "issues" in a case as the questions of law that the judge must resolve in order to determine who should win. There are many ways to frame an issue, and you will want to practice writing both a narrow issue and a broader one. The "holding" of the case is really the answer to the question, and if you write your issues as questions that require a "yes" or "no" answer, your holdings will be easy to write. It will also make it easier for you to identify the "rule of law" that grows from the case. As you read, watch for language in the case that signals an issue ("Before us today..." "At issue..." "The question to be determined...") or a holding ("Today we hold..." "The court finds...").

Reasoning:

1. (Causation) Bigan did not push or touch Yania; all he did was talk. Yania was an adult, of full mental capacity, and he freely chose to jump. The court finds "no merit" in the argument that it was Bigan's fault.

2. (Duty to warn) A landowner has no duty to warn of danger that is open ("not concealed") and obvious, especially to another coal miner.

3. (Duty to rescue) There is a moral duty to rescue, but not a legal one. Bigan did nothing to cause Yania's situation—Yania brought it on himself. It would be different if Bigan had caused Yania to be at risk, but he did not.

---

1 In the U.S. system, a criminal defendant is not obliged to confess, and is always entitled to a trial. The government prosecutor must convince a jury that the defendant committed the crime charged beyond a reasonable doubt.

The "reasoning" section spells out the rationale that explains the "holdings" of the court. Reasoning can be based on logic, as in the edited version of *Yania v. Bigan* that is in your text, or on:

- An interpretation of the U.S. Constitution or one of its Amendments
- An interpretation of a statute (act) passed by Congress or a state legislature
- The application of the precedent set by a prior, similar case (the name of the case will sometimes be omitted). A common law case precedent may be followed, distinguished (when the judge decides its facts are not similar enough to the case at hand), or overturned.
- Precedent may be overturned based on the real world consequences of prior rulings, or changes in the business and social reality.
- Where there is no applicable statute or precedent ("a case of first impression") the court will need to consider political, economic, and business implications; social policy; justice; ethical or moral concerns; and basic fairness or equity.
- References to precedents from other state courts or even international law
- Commentators (lawyers, scholars, or other authorities)
- Social science studies and literature

Reasoning of the Dissent: (none in *Yania*)

When a case is appealed, it is always heard by a panel of appellate judges (three or more, nine on the Supreme Court) who must determine by a vote whether to affirm or reverse the lower court. When your text includes a dissent, outline the reasoning of the dissent as well.

Rule of Law:

The "rule of law" refers to the precedent set by the case. If you have carefully framed broad "issues" you can create a rule of law by turning your question into a statement.

Your Response:

For your own purposes, and to prepare for class discussion, you might want to include something that would not be included in a lawyer's case brief: your own reflections on the reasoning and the implications of the decision.

Evaluating Internet Sources

Many college and university libraries have compiled guidelines for assessing the worth of online sources. One of the best, offered by librarians Jan Alexander and Marsha Ann Tate, provides an extensive checklist for identifying and evaluating different kinds of Web sites:

- Advocacy (usually ending with domain .org),
- Business/marketing (.com or .net),
- Informational (.edu or .gov),
- News (usually .com) and Personal.[1]

Alexander and Tate created the following criteria:

- **Authority/Objectivity:** Look for Web sites that give the author's name, title, organizational affiliation, and contact information. This will help you identify biases, as well as expertise. Government and educational sites, along with online scholarly journals, provide such indices of authority and objectivity. Traditionally, publications that have undergone peer review or are published in scholarly journals (such as law reviews) are given greater weight than those published by the author ("vanity publications").

- **Accuracy:** Pay attention to whether information sources are cited, to how well the page has been edited for grammar/spelling, and to whether the information on a Web site can be verified by referring to other sources.

- **Currency:** Check when the Web site was last revised. Outdated links are a sign that a Web site is not current. (Laws change when amendments, new laws, or new court interpretations have occurred since a Web site was last revised.)

Another excellent place for advice about Web site evaluation is http://www.rhetorica.net.[2] Some ideas from it include:

- **Beware persuasive writing:** Written advocacy for a particular view can be flawed by illogical reasoning. Learn some basics of logical analysis to monitor this. For example, check that the premises (underlying assumptions) of an argument are logical; if not, the rest should not be considered persuasive. And look for a logical connection between premises and conclusions.

- **Rev up your bias-detector:** If you identify bias, you might not necessarily dismiss a Web source as useless. But potential bias is another factor in helping you decide how to evaluate a particular Web source.

- **Notice the "spin":** There are many subtle ways to put a spin on information. Pay special attention, for example, to the use of labels, euphemisms, and metaphors. What impression is created by the title or headline? By the writer's tone and word choice? What details are included, and do they support the overall analysis? If the text is not clear, ask yourself: Is this a deliberate attempt to confuse?

- **"Unpack" visual and audio elements:** Suppose you read a story posted on a Web "news site." Note how it is designed, its placement (front page? buried?), and the kind of material that surrounds it—textual, visual, audio, advertising. What do all of these elements—and

---

1 Called "How to Evaluate and Create Information Quality on the Web," the online version can be found at http://www3.widener.edu/wolfgram/. Alexander and Tate include links to additional sites with Web evaluation materials.

2 Check out "Critical Questions for Detecting Dias," at http://www.rhetorica.net/bias.htm.

the way they are joined—tell you about the intended audience? The point of view of the author? Consider the message being sent by such things as color choices, relative size, and the particular juxtaposition of images and text.

Web sites—or Web news sources—are posted by a person or an organization of some kind. It makes sense to find out what you can about the individual or organization in order to best evaluate what they have created online.

Art Silverblatt, Julie Ferry, and Barbara Finan, in *Approaches to Media Literacy,* provide excellent tools for helping readers become more sensitive to the prevailing ideology in a media presentation. They make the following suggestions:

- **Identify ownership patterns** in the media, generally to assess how they affect media content.

- **Analyze an organization** (e.g., CNN, Fox News) to see how the ownership, resources, and internal structure (e.g., decision making) of a particular media organization influence the content of its products.

- **Uncover the "World View"** of a particular media presentation (such as a Web site) by thinking about the types of people who are depicted within it. Are characters presented in a stereotypical manner? Are they in control of their own destinies, or under the influence of others? Is there a supernatural presence in this world? Stories—and ads—reveal a world view by the way they portray what it means to be successful, how success is achieved, and what kinds of behaviors are rewarded.

- **Unpack an individual author** by finding out what you can about his or her expertise or educational background (is it relevant to the topic at hand?), employment or professional experience, and membership/leadership role in organizations or political/advocacy groups. Look for clues as to who funds/publishes his or her research. If he or she has been honored or recognized in a special way, by whom?

Stakeholder Ethics Role Play

A person faces a business ethics dilemma, with a tough decision to make. In this exercise, students play the roles of a decision maker and of several "stakeholder" advisors. After the stakeholders offer their points of view, the decision maker makes a choice and explains the reasons behind it.

The role play can done in a "fishbowl" format, with the decision maker and the various advisors in a circle in the middle of the room and with the rest of the class arranged in a larger circle around them, observing. Or, to involve more participants, the decision maker and the different stakeholders can be represented by small groups. (Recommended size of groups is three to six students.) In another variation for even more participation, students can replicate the same exercise in separate groups, each of which would have one decision maker being advised by several stakeholders.

1. First Plenary: Introduction

The decision maker defines the problem and explains the process of the role play to all.

2. Break-Out #1: Stakeholders Meet Separately

Students in each stakeholder group meet to identify their own interests and to articulate how they want to see the problem resolved (or, if they represent an ethical perspective, to articulate the direction their approach to ethics dictates and the reasons for it). Each group should appoint a "scribe" to take notes and another student to lead intra-group discussion. A "reporter" arranges the points into a cogent argument. Meanwhile, the decision maker can meet with the instructor to prepare questions for the stakeholder groups at the plenary session.

3. Plenary Session

The decision maker moderates a plenary session, asking each stakeholder representative to offer advice. As they present their interests and preferred outcomes, the decision maker asks questions to clarify or challenge a point of view. This phase of the exercise may evolve into a free-form discussion among the various stakeholders, with the decision maker acting as facilitator/referee, and with the stakeholders querying and challenging each other. The goal is that the class achieve a refined sense of the different perspectives.

Next, the decision maker should lead a brainstorming session on options, with anyone free to suggest a means of resolving the dilemma and with no discussion of whether any one suggestion is either wise or practical. Roles are irrelevant here—the goal is to unlock creative approaches, to bring a full range of ideas to the surface. The resulting list of options should be placed on the board/screen or printed out before the session ends.

4. Break-Out #2: Stakeholders Regroup

While the decision maker takes time to think about what has just transpired and to weigh options, the stakeholder groups reconvene to discuss solutions and decide which to recommend, given the information they now have regarding all the stakeholder concerns.

5. Final Plenary

The decision maker asks each group to report back its final recommendation and then explains to the class how he or she will deal with the dilemma, and the reasons for this choice.

6. Individual Follow-Up Memo

One way to allow each student to participate more fully is to assign a brief memo, in which each person (regardless of role) recommends and justifies a solution to the dilemma.

Mock Trial Materials

Order of Representation

1. Opening statement by plaintiff's attorney
2. Opening statement by defendant's attorney
3. Plaintiff's case: Direct examination of plaintiff's witnesses by plaintiff's attorney, followed by cross-examination by defendant's attorney
4. Defendant's case: Direct examination of defendant's witnesses by defendant's attorney, followed by cross-examination by plaintiff's attorney
5. Closing statement by plaintiff's attorney
6. Closing statement by defendant's attorney
7. Trial judge charges the jury
8. Jury deliberates and returns a verdict

Directions for Attorneys

You have the important responsibility of making sure that your team pulls together to prepare a strategy and materials for the trial and to present your case. Be sure to collaborate on all of this. Exchange telephone numbers and/or e-mail addresses and develop a schedule of regular meetings.

You control what the jury will learn about the case from your client's perspective, depending on how you deliver both the opening and closing statements and how you handle the questioning of witnesses.

Preparation

Read the witness statements in the chapter project carefully and reread the chapter.

Opening Statement

First introduce yourself and your client to the judge and jury and then briefly explain how you view the facts of the case. An opening statement is to the evidence later given at the trial as the picture on the box of a jigsaw puzzle is to the pieces inside the box; you are giving the jury a thumbnail sketch of what's to come. As you tell what happened from your client's point of view, use language and emphasis to try to build sympathy toward your client and against the other side. Be clear and speak audibly. Practice will greatly improve your delivery. Rehearse—with your teammates, with anyone who can stand to hear you, alone in front of a mirror—as much as possible.

Direct Examination of Your Own Witnesses

Let your witness tell the story. Questions should be short, simple, and understandable, and your witness should be doing most of the talking. Your job is to keep your witnesses on track, to help them remember every detail you want the jury to hear, and in the right order. If the witness rushes through or mumbles something important, be sure to go back to it. You might say, "Excuse me, Mr. Witness, but I don't believe the jury heard that last remark. Would you mind repeating what you just said?" Remember that the jury knows nothing about this case beyond what it hears at this trial. As your witnesses testify, they should tell the story in ways that put the best possible spin on the facts from your client's perspective. A witness may embellish the facts, but if he or she contradicts or changes them, your opponent is free to use the witness role description to show that the witness may be lying. Practice with your witnesses.

Cross-Examining a Hostile Witness

Again, questions should be simple and understandable. Prepare by making a list of the crucial facts you want the witnesses to admit. Then build up to each one in small steps, with questions that a person can't waffle around on. Your questions might begin with, "Isn't it true that … ?" You might tell the witness you are going to ask a few simple questions, and ask leading questions that require a simple "yes or no" answer. Then, if the witness tries to explain further, interrupt politely but firmly: "Yes or no, please."

At the trial, pay close attention to the direct questioning of the witness you are about to cross-examine. Be ready to make changes in your prepared questions at the last minute, depending on what actually happens on direct examination.

If a witness says something that contradicts an earlier statement (in the text), emphasize the discrepancy by asking the witness; "Did you make this statement earlier?" Show the witness the statement; ask him or her to read the relevant portion to the jury. This is a very effective way to challenge the credibility of a hostile witness.

Take your time. You have the upper hand psychologically because a hostile witness has no idea what you might ask. If a witness doesn't give you the answer you had hoped to hear, it is probably a good idea not to linger too long on that particular point, but to keep moving to another line of questioning. What you don't want to do in cross-examination is allow a hostile witness to offer long-winded explanations, or to repeat something you wish the jury had never heard in the first place. Try to end with something punchy, so when you say "No further questions," you will sound appropriately dismissive.

Objecting to Evidence

Listen carefully as your opponent asks questions. You may interrupt the trial with objections for any of the following reasons:

1. Irrelevant: The question strays too far from the issues of the trial.
2. Badgering the witness: The opposing lawyer is being rude or overbearing to your witness.
3. Speculation: The witness is being asked to offer an opinion but does not possess the appropriate expertise to answer.
4. Asked and answered: The witness has already been asked and has already answered the question.

Be ready to object and to justify your objections. The judge will sustain or overrule them.

Communicating with Your Teammates

During the trial, you may confer with your teammates. In fact, you should be helping each other as the trial unfolds. This means you may whisper helpful comments or pass notes. Try not to disturb the proceedings, however. You may also, as an attorney, interrupt the trial to confer with another attorney on your own team as she is questioning a witness.

Closing Statement

Make a persuasive summary of the evidence you have presented and describe the weaknesses in your opponent's case. If there were some items that you couldn't effectively deal with during the Q&A of trial testimony, now is your chance to "clean it up"—to revisit parts of the case.

The closing statement is also your opportunity to go beyond the particular facts of the case and to explain to the jury the **policy reasons** that support a win for your side. Policy reasons address what is good for society in general. Policy concerns the long-term consequences—to all of us—of a certain decision. Although policy is not the same as law, law is in part based on what is considered good for society overall. For the policy portion of your closing, ask the jurors to think of the ramifications of this case for the future. Help them imagine how a ruling in this case might affect every workplace. Talk about why a decision in your favor will be good for society and/or why a decision in favor of the other side will not. Examples will help clarify your points. The "slippery slope" argument might come in handy.

Stay away from the law in the closing statements. For purposes of the mock trial, the jury will decide what the law will be. (In an actual trial, the judge would instruct the jury as to the rules of law to be applied.)

Directions for Witnesses

Read the witness statements very carefully, especially your own. Think about your character from your team's point of view. What spin will you put on the facts? You may stretch or exaggerate to make the story sound more sympathetic to your side, but if you contradict any fact given in the witness statements you may be impeached on cross-examination. In other words, be creative, but don't lie!

Work with your team to decide what you will be asked and how you will answer during "direct examination"—the friendly questioning by your own side. You and your team need to decide exactly what questions you should be asked, so that you have the maximum opportunity to develop the story from your team's point of view. You should do most of the talking, not your lawyer. The lawyer for your team should be asking you questions that are "prompts" that allow you to explain each part of the story fully.

You and your team should also try to determine what would be the approach of the opposition to your character during cross-examination. What questions are they likely to ask you? Anticipate as fully as possible and plan how you want to answer to minimize the damage. There may be certain points that are likely to hurt your side on cross-examination. Decide with your teammates whether you want to address those issues on direct examination in order to eliminate the surprise factor and maintain more control over what the jury hears.

Directions for Jurors

In the mock trial, as in the real world, jurors should learn about the case only through the trial itself. That means that you should not read anything prior to the trial.

Listen carefully as the trial unfolds. You will be asked to reach a verdict based on your reactions to the dispute as you understand it, and on the persuasiveness of the final arguments as you understand them. Keep in mind that your decision affects not just the parties in this case, but others in similar situations in the future.

When you go into deliberations, first select a foreperson. The foreperson should facilitate an open discussion in which everyone participates. Once all opinions have been aired, try to reach consensus. If this is not possible, take a vote. The foreperson reports the verdict to the judge.

Alternative Dispute Resolution

Since the early 1970s, the time-consuming and expensive process of litigating business disputes has been increasingly replaced by alternative forms of dispute resolution. ADR has been embraced by the Supreme Court, which has ruled that courts must refuse to hear lawsuits when a commercial contract calls for arbitration,[1] and by Congress, which has authorized federal agencies and federal courts to use informal alternatives to litigation such as mediation, conciliation, and arbitration.[2] In fact, to circumvent costly litigation, more and more companies have inserted binding arbitration clauses into employment contracts, so that disputes over pay, discrimination, misconduct, and other matters must be resolved not in court but by a panel of arbitrators.

Win-Win or Principled Negotiation

When opponents in a dispute focus only on their ultimate goals and approach one another with a "winner take all" attitude, the resulting agreement is too often one-sided and short-lived. In contrast, the concept of principled negotiation is that there is a better way, a way to reach a lasting agreement, satisfying at least some of the interests on each side. The leading resource for learning about principled negotiation is Roger Fisher & William Uri, *Getting to Yes* (1991). These points summarize the process they recommend:

- Separate the people from the problem. Deal with the relationships among the parties separately from the merits of the dispute.

- Focus on interests, not positions. For example, *being comfortable* may be the interest at stake, not whether a window needs to be open or closed.

- Invent options for mutual gains; be creative.

- Where thorny disagreements remain, move to objective neutral criteria to ensure a fair resolution.

- Before negotiations begin, each side should develop its BATNA (best alternative to a negotiated agreement). In a legal dispute, this almost always means that if settlement fails, a party can file suit. It requires both sides to consider what they are likely to win—or lose—if the case goes to court.

Preparation for Arbitrators and Mediators

In preparation for your role, learn more about alternative dispute resolution from one of the following:

- The Beginner's Guide to ADR, available through the Web site of the American Arbitration Association, http://www.adr.org

- National Arbitration Forum resources at http://www.arb-forum.com

- Arbitration: the WWW Virtual Library's section on Private Dispute Resolution, http://www.interarb.com

---

1 Southland Corp. v. Keating, 465 U.S.1 (1984).

2 Administrative Dispute Resolution Act of 1990 and Alternative Dispute Resolution Act of 1998.

Negotiation Exercise

Preparation

Read through your assigned witness statements carefully to understand the "facts" and to get a feel for your character. Try to identify his or her real needs and interests so that you can be open to resolutions that will best satisfy those needs. Consider both long- and short-term interests, both economic and relational, business and family concerns. Rank your interests. Decide on your BATNA.

First Round

Meet with the opposition. Try to follow the rules of principled negotiation. Explain your side's interests. Listen to and question the other side carefully to develop as complete an understanding as possible of their interests.

Break-Out

Split apart. Meet with your team to develop an offer. Develop a back-up offer.

Second Round

Meet with the opposition. Exchange your offers and discuss them. If you have difficulty forming an agreement, try brainstorming alternatives.

Repeat Rounds

Continue the process of meeting with the other side and alone with your team until the negotiation is complete.

Debrief with the Whole Class

Compare the various negotiated agreements. Which one identified the largest area of mutual interest? Which one was the most balanced? Which is most likely to survive into the future? Vote for the best agreement, giving reasons for your vote.

Mediation/Arbitration

While a negotiated agreement is arrived at by opposing sides on their own, a mediator or an arbitrator is a neutral third party who is actively involved in the agreement-making process. A mediator listens carefully to both sides, and then helps them discover their mutual interests, close their differences, and think of creative ways to craft an agreement. An arbitrator is more like a judge. An arbitrator listens to arguments made by each side, asks questions of each side, and then acts without further input to craft an agreement that both sides must then accept. (Before an arbitration, both sides agree that they will accept the terms of the agreement that will be decided for them.)

Comparative ADR Role Play

Using a single dispute, some students role play as opponents, while other students role play mediators and arbitrators. The class is evenly divided among negotiating, mediating, and arbitrating teams.

Once all the agreements have been finalized, the whole class debriefs by studying the results and discussing the comparative strengths and weaknesses of the three processes for reaching agreement.

Legislative Hearing

In this exercise some students role play legislative committee members hearing testimony on a controversial issue or bill while other students role play public witnesses offering their views on the proposed law.

The legislative committee sits as a panel facing the public witnesses in the middle of the room. If the class is large, the rest of the class surrounds them, to listen in, fishbowl style.

A committee chair calls each public witness, one at a time. After each speaker has finished a brief opening statement of opinion, legislators can ask a few questions of that speaker. When all of the speakers have been heard, the legislative committee votes, followed by the class acting as the full legislature.

Legislators/Legislative Aides

Depending on class size, some students may be assigned to role-play legislative aides.

Before the Hearing

Prepare for your role by forming your political position on the bill (for or against it), considering your own opinion and also what your "constituents" are likely to think. If you are uncertain of either, find online news coverage from your part of the state/country. (If the class is large enough to allow for legislative aides, yours can do more extensive research into your position.)

Write a list of questions to ask the various public witnesses. Try to make them provocative and interesting. Suggestions: Hypothetical questions are often very effective, setting up examples that sharpen points of disagreement. Consider asking about the long-term consequences (on business, the nation, on particular constituents, and so on) of the proposed legislation; how new laws will impact existing state or national laws; and how proposed legislation will be implemented and enforced.

During the Hearing

Listen carefully to each speaker. Be prepared to vary or adapt a planned question to fit the situation at hand. Try not to give speeches during the hearing itself, as your goal is to elicit input from the public.

After the Hearing

You will have an opportunity to articulate your position for or against the proposed legislation, giving your reasons and referring to testimony that supports your position.

Public Witnesses

Remember that you are playing a role; stay in it. Avoid drifting into advocating your real-life position on the issue.

Before the Hearing

Think about the position a person in your role is likely to take on the proposed legislation, regardless of what your personal opinion may be. Online, find out more about the group you represent.

At the hearing, you will begin by giving a short (5 minute) statement explaining your view and the reasons for it. Practice a clear and crisp opening statement before class. Prepare for questions by thinking ahead about what you are likely to be asked and how you will answer.

During the Hearing

You will need to pay careful attention to other public witnesses as they may raise points you had not considered. Be prepared to address those points when it is your turn, as part of your opening statement, since you will not be able to directly question or engage with the other public witnesses. Your interaction will be limited to speaking to the legislative panel and responding to the questions they pose to you.

Writing Exercise

Students who do not serve as either public witnesses or legislators can be given written assignments as editorial writers covering the hearing for a newspaper or magazine or as members of the larger Assembly/Senate. In their editorials or absentee ballot reports, they will articulate their opinion on the proposal and their reasons for it, based on observing the legislative committee proceedings.

GLOSSARY

A

Abusive discharge a tort, recognized in some states, committed when an employer discharges an employee in violation of a clear expression of public policy; also referred to as "wrongful discharge."

Administrative law the rules and regulations established by government agencies, as opposed to law created by courts and legislators.

Affidavit a written declaration or statement of facts, sworn before a person who has the authority to administer such an oath.

Affirm the ruling by an appellate court that agrees with a lower court decision and allows the judgment to stand.

Alternative Dispute Resolution (ADR) the resolution of disputes in ways other than through the use of the traditional judicial process; mediation and arbitration are examples of ADR.

Amicus curiae Latin for "friend of the court"; an individual or entity that petitions the Court for permission to file a brief because of strong interest in the case.

Answer the pleading of a defendant in which he admits or denies any or all of the facts set out in the plaintiff's complaint or declaration.

Appeal the process by which a party to a lawsuit asks a higher court to review alleged errors made by a lower court or agency.

Appellant the party who appeals a case to a higher court.

Appellate court a court having jurisdiction of appeal and review.

Appellee the party in a case against which an appeal is taken; that is, the party with an interest adverse to setting aside or reversing a judgment.

Arbitration a process in which a dispute is submitted to a mutually acceptable person or board who will render a decision to which the parties are bound.

Arbitrator a disinterested party who has the power to resolve a dispute and (generally) bind the parties.

Assumption of the risk in tort law, a defense to negligence when a plaintiff has voluntarily exposed herself to a known risk.

B

Bill of Rights first ten amendments to the U.S. Constitution adopted in 1791; sets forth specific individual protections against government intrusion.

Bona fide Latin for "in good faith"; honestly, sincerely.

Brief in litigation, a formal legal document submitted by attorneys for each side of a dispute outlining the issues, statutes, and precedents that make up the legal arguments of each side.

Burden of proof proof in a civil case by a fair preponderance of the evidence; proof in a criminal case beyond a reasonable doubt.

Business Judgment rule legal doctrine that relieves directors and officers of liability for decisions that were consistent with prudent business judgment.

C

Case at bar the particular case that is before the court.

Case of first impression a lawsuit raising a novel question of law; without precedent in the particular jurisdiction.

Case law the law created when an appellate court issues a written opinion in a lawsuit. Sometimes referred to as common law. CONTRAST: statutory law.

Cause of action the facts, which evidenced a civil wrong, thereby giving rise to a right to judicial relief.

Caveat emptor Latin for "let the buyer beware"; the concept that the buyer bears the loss if there is anything defective in the goods she purchases.

Cease and desist order an order by an agency or court directing someone to stop an unlawful practice.

Certiorari a means of obtaining appellate review; a writ issued by an appellate court, such as the Supreme Court, to an inferior court commanding the record be certified to the appellate court for judicial review.

Chattel personal property; tangible property that is mobile.

Claim a cause of action.

Class action a suit brought by or against a group with common interests in resolving particular issues of law or facts. Sometimes called a "representative action." The named plaintiff in a class action is a representative of the group.

Collective bargaining the process whereby union representatives bargain with management on behalf of employees concerning wages, hours, and other terms and conditions of employment. The result of this process is a collective bargaining agreement.

Collective works under U.S. copyright law, collective works are those that originate from more than one author.

Comity respect or deference; the doctrine that allows an administrative agency or court to defer to the actions or decisions of another body.

Commerce clause the clause in Article II, Section 8 of the Constitution that gives Congress power to regulate commerce among the several states.

Commercial speech speech that proposes a commercial transaction; the Supreme Court has interpreted the First Amendment as giving more limited protection to commercial speech than to political speech.

Common law also called case law or judge-made law; as distinguished from law created by the enactments of legislatures, the common law is comprised of the principles and rules that derive solely from custom and from judgments and decisions of courts.

Communitarianism the belief that individual liberties depend on the bolstering of the foundations of civil society: families, schools, neighborhoods. It is through these institutions, according to communitarians, that we acquire a sense of our personal civic responsibilities, of our rights and the rights of others, and a commitment to the welfare of the whole of society.

Comparable worth the idea that jobs should be evaluated on the basis of the education, experience, skill, and risk involved so that different jobs of similar worth receive similar compensation; sometimes referred to as "pay equity."

Compensatory damages money that compensates an injured party for the injury sustained and nothing more; such compensation as will simply make good or replace the loss caused by a wrong or injury.

Complaint the first pleading by the plaintiff in a civil case. Its purpose is to give the defendant the information on which the plaintiff relies to support its demand. In a complaint, the plaintiff sets out a cause of action, consisting of a formal allegation or charge presented to the appropriate court.

Concurring opinion with reference to appellate court cases, a concurring opinion is one by a judge who agrees with the majority opinion's conclusions, but for different reasons, and who therefore writes a separate opinion. CONTRAST: dissenting opinion, majority opinion.

Consent decree a court decree entered by consent of the parties. It is not a judicial sentence but is an agreement of the parties made under the sanction of a court.

Consumer Product Safety Commission (CPSC) an independent federal agency created in 1972 to protect the public from death or serious harm caused by dangerous products.

Contract a legally enforceable agreement between two parties.

Copyright protects the original work of authors, painters, sculptors, musicians, photographers, and others who create original literary or artistic works.

Corporate Social Responsibility the idea that corporations have a responsibility to all major stakeholders, not only to those who own stock in the company.

Corporation a legal entity created by statute authorizing its officers, directors, and stockholders to carry on business.

Cost-benefit analysis a way to reach decisions in which the costs of a given action are compared with its benefits.

Counterclaim a claim presented by a defendant that, if successful, defeats or reduces the plaintiff's recovery.

Criminal law a set of laws, the violation of which is an offense against society. Crimes include both minor crimes (misdemeanors) and more serious felonies.

D

Damages a monetary award granted by a court to a winning party.

Declaratory judgment a judicial opinion that declares the rights of the parties or expresses the court's interpretation of a law without ordering anything to be done.

Deep ecology an ethical belief system based on ecological concerns that begins with the premise that the biotic community in which we find ourselves has intrinsic value.

Defamation the disparagement of one's reputation; a civil action (tort) involving the offense of injuring a person's character, fame, or reputation by false and malicious statements.

Default omission to perform a legal or contractual duty; the failure of a party to appear in court or defend an action after being properly served with process.

Defendant the party against whom an action is brought in a civil case; the accused in a criminal case.

Defense an assertion offered by a defendant who, if successful, relieves her of liability, reduces the plaintiff's recovery, or defeats a criminal charge.

Demand futility a court's ruling that shareholders can sue directors of the company without first demanding that an interested board of directors sue themselves.

Deontology the study of duty; as developed by Immanuel Kant, the notion that there are certain moral rights and duties that every human being possesses, that ethical choices derive from universal principles based on those rights and duties.

Deposition a pretrial discovery process of testifying under oath (but not in open court) and subject to cross examination, where the testimony is recorded and intended to be used at trial.

Design defect in product liability law, the concept that a seller should be liable for harm caused by a product that was not well designed.

Dicta/Dictum Latin; an abbreviated form of *obiter dictum* ("a remark by the way"); an observation or remark made by a judge in pronouncing an opinion in a case, concerning some rule, principle, or application of law, or the solution of a question suggested by the court, but not necessarily involved in the case or essential to its determination.

Disclaimer of warranty seller's claim that no promises (warranties) were made when goods were sold.

Discovery pre-trial processes that allow each side to obtain information about the case from the other side for use in preparing for trial or settlement. Discovery devices include pre-trial depositions, motions to produce documents or to inspect premises, written interrogatories, and pre-trial medical examinations.

Disparate impact discrimination in an employment context, discrimination that results from certain employer practices or procedures that, although neutral on their face, have a discriminatory effect. For example, height and weight requirements for all applicants are not discriminatory on their face, but will have the effect of excluding more women than men.

Disparate treatment discrimination in an employment context, any practice or decision that treats applicants or employees differently depending on their race, sex, religion, or national origin.

Dissenting opinion in appellate courts, an opinion written by a judge who disagrees with the result reached by the majority, as well as its reasoning. CONTRAST: concurring opinion.

Due process a concept embodied in the Fifth and Fourteenth Amendments to the U.S. Constitution, meaning fundamental fairness. Due process mandates that government may not take life, liberty, or property from citizens unless they are given notice and a fair opportunity to be heard.

Duty of care in tort law, all persons have a duty to exercise reasonable care in their interactions with others.

E

Economic loss doctrine a common law rule, followed in some states, that holds that a person harmed by another's breach of contract may not bring a tort action unless there was injury to a person or property other than that which was the subject of the contract.

Eminent domain the right of the government to take privately owned land for public use, paying the owner a just compensation.

Employment-at-will doctrine the common law rule that holds that whenever an employment relationship is of an indefinite duration, either party—the employer or the employee—may terminate the relationship at any time, for good cause or bad, in good faith or with malice.

En banc where most appellate cases are heard by only some of the judges, a decision en banc is one heard by the full court.

Enterprise Liability legal theory that allows a plaintiff to sue every company within a particular enterprise if plaintiff cannot identify the particular firm that caused her harm.

Environmental Protection Agency (EPA) federal agency established in 1970 to oversee national environmental policy and laws.

Equal Employment Opportunity Commission (EEOC) five-member commission created in 1964 to administer Title VII of the Civil Rights Act by issuing interpretive guidelines, investigating, holding hearings, and keeping statistics.

Equal protection a concept embodied in the Fifth and Fourteenth Amendments to the U.S. Constitution that government cannot treat persons in similar situations differently.

Equity a system of justice that developed in England separate from the common-law courts. Few states in the United States still maintain separate equity courts, although most apply equity principles and procedures when equitable relief is sought. A broader meaning denotes fairness and justice.

Exclusivity rule Under workers' compensation laws, the exclusivity rule provides that workers' compensation is the only remedy available for some injuries.

Executive branch branch of the U.S. government that includes the president and is charged with enforcing the law; the powers of the president as established in Article II of the U.S. Constitution. Also used to refer to the governor of a state.

Expert testimony trial testimony from an authority recognized by the court as having special knowledge.

F

Fair use under American copyright law, the right to use limited portions of a copyrighted work, without permission, for education or criticism.

False Claims Reform Act a federal statute that allows citizens to file a civil suit against any company known to be defrauding the government; also referred to as *qui tam*.

Federal Register a publication providing notice of rule making by federal agencies.

Federal Trade Commission (FTC) a bipartisan, independent administrative agency authorized by Congress to prevent unfair methods of competition and unfair or deceptive trade and advertising practices.

Federalism the Constitutional relationship between the states and federal government whereby responsibility and autonomy is divided between them.

Feminist ethics the notion that the right thing to do stems from a sense of responsibility for one another based on caring relationships, rather than from allegiance to abstract principles. CONTRAST: utilitarian analysis of consequences or deontological universal rights/duties.

Fiduciary a person having a legal duty, created by his or her undertaking, to act primarily for another's benefit. For example, corporate officers are fiduciaries who owe fiduciary duties of loyalty and care to their shareholders; lawyers have fiduciary duties to their clients.

Fiduciary duty the legal duty that arises whenever one person is in a special relationship of trust to another.

Food and Drug Administration (FDA) federal regulatory agency responsible for overseeing safety of food, drugs, and cosmetics sold in the United States.

Fundamental freedoms those rights given special priority and protection under the U.S. Constitution, including the right to free speech, free religion, free press, the right to vote, and the freedom to travel.

G

General Agreement on Tariffs and Trade (GATT) created in 1948 as an agreement; GATT grew to be both an agreement and an organization that negotiated international trade and tariff rules. In 1995, GATT was replaced by the World Trade Organization (WTO).

Gross negligence a conscious or reckless act or omission that is likely to result in harm to a person or property; a higher level of culpability than simple negligence.

I

Implied warranty a warranty or promise created by law under certain conditions. For example, when a merchant sells a good, the law implies a promise ("implied warranty of merchantability") that the good is fit for its ordinary purpose.

Indictment a formal accusation made by a grand jury that charges a person has committed a crime.

Infringement violating the exclusive rights of a copyright or patent holder by using the protected work without permission or license.

Injunction a court order directing someone to do or not to do something.

Instructions to the jury directions that a trial judge gives to the jury explaining the law to be applied to the facts that the jury finds.

Intellectual property laws copyright, patent, trademark, trade secret, and other laws that protect intangible property that is the work product of the human mind.

Intentional torts a category of civil wrongs giving redress to the victims of willful wrongdoing. Wrongful or abusive discharge of an employee, misappropriating a trade secret, and battery are all intentional torts.

International law law considered legally binding among otherwise sovereign, independent nations. Treaties are a form of international law.

Interrogatories a discovery device consisting of a series of written questions directed to the opposing party, to be answered in writing, under oath.

Intrusion an intentional tort, committed when one party intrudes on the solitude of another in an overly offensive way. Sometimes referred to as invasion of privacy.

J

Judgment official ruling by a court.

Judicial branch branch of the U.S. government that consists of the federal courts and its powers as set forth in Article III of the U.S. Constitution; sometimes referred to as the judiciary.

Judicial review the process whereby a court reviews legislative action to ensure that it was Constitutional or administrative agency action to ensure that it was Constitutional, legal, and in compliance with the agency's enabling legislation.

Jurisdiction the power of the court or a judicial officer to decide a case; the geographic area of a court's authority; the power of a court over a defendant in a lawsuit.

L

Learned Intermediary a person with special training and expertise, such as a doctor, who stands between the seller of a prescription drug or other product, and the patient who uses it.

Legislation the act of passing laws; the making of laws by express decree; also used as a noun to mean a statute or statutes adopted by a legislative body. CONTRAST: case law.

Legislative branch branch of the U.S. government that consists of Congress, whose powers are set forth in Article I of the U.S. Constitution. Each state also has its own legislature, the governmental body that enacts state laws.

Legislative history the background and events leading up to the enactment of a statute.

Lobbyists those who attempt to influence legislators to pass laws that favor special interests.

M

Magnuson-Moss Warranty Act federal statute designed to prevent deception in sales contracts by making warranties easier to understand.

Mediation an alternative dispute resolution process in which a neutral third person attempts to persuade disputing parties to adjust their positions to resolve their differences. Unlike judges or arbitrators, mediators do not impose solutions on the parties.

Misappropriation a wrongful taking of something belonging to another, such as illegal taking of a trade secret or benefiting economically from the use of another's name or likeness, thereby misappropriating his right of publicity.

Motion a request to a judge or court for a rule or order favorable to the petitioning party, generally made within the course of an existing lawsuit.

N

National Labor Relations Act also known as the Wagner Act; federal statute enacted in 1935 that established the rights of employees to organize unions, engage in collective bargaining and to strike.

National Labor Relations Board (NLRB) federal agency created by the Wagner Act to oversee union elections and to prevent unfair and illegal labor practices.

Negligence voluntary conduct that foreseeably exposes the interests of another to an unreasonable risk of harm; also the name of the civil (tort) action brought by a plaintiff injured by the negligence of another.

NGOs non-governmental organizations or NGOs are voluntary and charitable not-for-profit associations, such as the Red Cross and Public Citizen.

Nominal damages minimal damages awarded for a breach of contract or technical injury, but where no actual harm was suffered.

Non-delegation doctrine interpretation of the U.S. Constitution that stops Congress from delegating too much of its power to another branch of government or to an administrative agency.

Nuisance improper activity that interferes with another's use or enjoyment of his property.

O

Occupational Safety and Health Act of 1970 federal statute that requires health and safety protections for employees at their places of work.

Occupational Safety and Health Administration (OSHA) federal agency that promulgates and enforces workplace health and safety standards, conducts inspections and investigations, keeps records, and conducts research.

Order decision of an administrative law judge; final disposition of a case between the government and a private party.

P

Patent the exclusive right or privilege to make, use, or sell an invention for a limited period of time, granted by the government to the inventor.

Pay Equity the idea that jobs should be evaluated on the basis of the education, experience, skill, and risk involved so that different jobs of similar worth receive similar compensation; sometimes referred to as "comparable worth."

Per curium Latin; "by the court"; used to indicate an unsigned opinion by the entire court rather than a single judge; sometimes refers to a brief statement of the court's decision unaccompanied by a written opinion.

Petitioner a party that files a petition with the court, applying in writing for a court order; a party that asks a court to hear an appeal from a judgment; a party that initiates an equity action.

Plaintiff a person or entity that brings an action or complaint against a defendant; the party who initiated a lawsuit.

Pleadings the formal allegations of the parties of their respective claims and defense, including the plaintiff's complaint, defendant's answer, and plaintiff's reply.

Police power the legal right of state government to legislate for the public health, welfare, safety, and morals.

Precedent a previously decided court case that serves to notify future litigants how subsequent similar cases will be resolved.

Preemption in federal-state relations, the concept that where there is a direct conflict between federal and state actions, the federal law will have priority and the state action will be void.

Prima facie Latin; "at first sight"; a fact presumed to be true unless disproved by evidence to the contrary.

Privilege in tort law, the ability to act contrary to another person's right without that person having legal redress for such actions. Privilege is usually raised as a defense.

Privity of contract the relationship that exists between promisor and promisee of a contract.

Probable cause reasonable ground for supposing that an individual has committed a crime.

Procedural law that part of the law which concerns the method or process of enforcing legal rights.

Products liability the legal liability of manufacturers and sellers to buyers, users, and sometimes bystanders, for injuries suffered because of defects in goods sold. Liability arises when a product has a defective condition that makes it unreasonably dangerous to the user or consumer. Sometimes referred to as "strict liability."

Proximate cause event(s) or action that, in natural and unbroken sequence, produce(s) an injury that would not have occurred absent the event(s) or action.

Public Domain in copyright law, creative or government works that can be freely copied and used by anyone without asking permission are said to be "in the public domain."

Punitive damages awards unrelated to the victim's injuries that are designed to punish the wrongdoer; damages awarded to a plaintiff that are greater than the amount necessary to compensate her loss; generally granted where the wrong involved intent, violence, fraud, malice, or other aggravated circumstances.

Q

Qualified immunity protection from being sued that is available and is limited to certain circumstances.

Qui tam Latin, "Who as well—." A law suit brought by whistleblowers under the federal False Claims Act against those who are alleged to have defrauded the government.

Quid pro quo Latin, "this for that"; the giving of one thing for another.

R

Regulatory Takings newly enforceable restrictions on the use of one's property, such as a newly adopted restriction on building in certain areas of the wetlands.

Remand to send back; the sending of a case back to the same lower court out of which it came for the purpose of having some action taken. For example, appellate courts often reverse a finding and remand for a new trial.

Remedies the aid that a court gives to a party who wins a lawsuit.

Remedies at law court award of land, money, or items of value. CONTRAST: Remedies in equity.

Remedies in equity relief deemed to be appropriate, based on fairness, justice, and honesty to remedy a situation, such as an injunction, restraining order, specific performance, or the like. CONTRAST: remedies at law.

Respondeat Superior Latin, "Let the master answer." Doctrine which makes an employer ("master") responsible for the acts of an employee ("servant") committed within the scope of the employment.

Respondent the party that contests an appeal or answers a petition

Restatement a book published by the American Law Institute consisting of its understanding of the law created by the judiciary throughout the country; each volume of the Restatement covers a different area of law, such as agency law, contracts, and torts.

Restitution equitable remedy in which a person is restored to her original position prior to loss or injury, or is placed in the same position she would have been in absent a breach.

Reverse decision of an appellate court to overthrow, vacate, set aside, void, or repeal the judgment of a lower court.

S

Shareholder a person who owns stock in a corporation.

Shareholder derivative suit a law suit initiated by shareholders on behalf of the corporation where the board of directors fails to do so or a demand to sue is deemed futile.

Sovereign immunity doctrine preventing a litigant from asserting an otherwise meritorious claim against a sovereign (government).

Stakeholder in ethical analysis, a person or group whose interests will be impacted by actions or decisions by an organization.

Standing to sue the legal right to bring a lawsuit; in order to have standing, an individual or group must have a personal stake in the outcome of the suit.

Stare decisis Latin, "Let the decision stand." Doctrine under which courts stand by precedent and do not disturb a settled point of law. Under stare decisis, once a court has laid down a principle of law as applied to a certain set of facts, the court adheres to that principle and applies it to future cases in which the facts are substantially the same. (Stare decisis does not mean "the decision is in the stars.")

State action in Constitutional law, the term is used to designate governmental action necessary to bring a constitutional challenge to such action.

Statute an act of a legislature declaring, commanding, or prohibiting something; a particular law enacted by the legislative branch of government. Sometimes the word is used to designate codified law or legislation as opposed to case law.

Statute of limitations a statute prescribing the length of time after an event in which a suit must be brought or a criminal charge filed.

Stay a court order to stop, arrest, or forbear. To stay an order or decree means to hold it in abeyance or to refrain from enforcing it.

Strict liability liability without fault. A case is one in strict liability when neither care nor negligence, neither good nor bad faith, neither knowledge nor ignorance will exonerate the defendant.

Strict Scrutiny in Constitutional law, government actions or laws that discriminate on the basis of race or ethnicity, or that infringe on fundamental freedoms like free speech are closely scrutinized by the courts to see if there is a compelling reason to justify the discrimination or infringement.

Subpoena a writ ordering a person to appear and give testimony or to bring documents that are in his or her control.

Substantive law that part of the law which creates, defines, and regulates rights. CONTRAST: procedural law.

Summary judgment a pretrial decision reached by a trial court after considering the pleadings, affidavits, depositions, and other documents, on the ground that no trial is needed because no genuine issue of fact has been raised.

Supremacy clause a clause in Article VI of the U.S. Constitution which provides that all laws made by the federal government pursuant to the Constitution are the supreme laws of the land and are superior to any conflicting state law.

Supreme Court of the United States highest level of the federal judicial system, with nine justices appointed by the president of the United States for life.

Suspect classification in Constitutional law, differentiating between persons based on their race, national origin, or religion.

T

Takings term referring to government seizure, regulation, or intrusion on private property for which the owner is entitled to compensation under the Fifth Amendment to the U.S. Constitution.

Title ownership of property.

Tort French word meaning "wrong"; a civil wrong or injury, other than a breach of contract, committed against the person or property of another for which a civil court action is possible. Assault, battery, trespass, and negligence are all examples of tort actions.

Tortfeasor a person who commits a tort.

Trademark a distinctive mark, logo, or motto of stamp affixed to goods to identify their origin. Once established, a trademark gives its owner the right to its exclusive use.

Trade-Related Aspects of Intellectual Property Rights (TRIPS) Agreement a treaty adopted in 1994 that incorporates protection for intellectual property into GATT.

Trade secret something of economic value to its owner (e.g., an unpatented formula, a client list) that is protected by law because its owner has taken reasonable steps to keep it secret.

Treaty an agreement or contract between two or more nations that must be authorized (ratified) by the supreme power of each nation to become international law.

Trespass to land entering onto or causing anything to enter onto land of another; remaining on or permitting anything or anyone to remain on land owned by another.

Trespass to personal property sometimes called trespass to chattels; unlawful injury to (or other interference with) the personal property of another that violates the owner's right to exclusive possession and enjoyment of her property.

U

Unconscionability against public policy; unduly harsh and one-sided; shocking to the conscience.

Uniform Commercial Code (UCC) a comprehensive code, drafted by the National Conference on Commissioners on Uniform State Laws, which has been enacted in all the states. It includes articles governing the sale of goods, commercial paper, banking, and other commercial laws.

Utilitarianism an approach to ethical reasoning in which ethically correct behavior is not related to any absolute ethical or moral values but to an evaluation of the consequences of a given action to those who will be affected by it. In utilitarian reasoning, a good decision is one that results in the greatest good for the greatest number of people affected by it.

V

Verdict the answer of a jury given to the court concerning the matters of fact committed to their trial and examination; it sets no precedent, and settles nothing but the specific controversy to which it relates. It is the decision made by the jury and reported to the court, such as guilt or innocence in a criminal trial or whether the defendant is liable to the plaintiff in a civil case and the amount for which she is liable.

Virtue ethics the ethical theory, derived from Aristotle, that our moral abilities (or virtues) are a matter of good habits, developed through training and repetition, within communities.

Void null; ineffectual; having no legal force.

W

Warranty seller's assurance to the buyers that the goods sold will meet certain standards.

Warranty of merchantability seller's promise to the buyer that goods sold will be fit for their ordinary purpose.

Whistleblowing an employee's reporting an employer's illegal or unethical acts.

Workers' compensation a program under which employers are required to make payments to employees who are injured during the course of their employment, regardless of negligence or fault.

World Trade Organization (WTO) created by the Uruguay Round of GATT in 1994 to administer GATT and to resolve disputes.

Writ a commandment of a court given for the purpose of compelling a defendant to take certain action, usually directed to a sheriff or other officer to execute it; a court order directing a person to do something.

Writ of certiorari an order of a court to an inferior court to forward the record of a case for reexamination by the superior court. Cases are often brought to the attention of the U.S. Supreme Court when the losing party applies for a writ of certiorari. If the writ is granted, the Court agrees to allow an appeal.

Wrongful discharge See Abusive discharge.

Z

Zoning restrictions on land use imposed by state or local government.